EDUCATIONAL
TESTS
AND
MEASUREMENT
AN INTRODUCTION

1800
Oxford University
Written exams required. Two passing categories established: Honours and Passing. Top 12 examinees' names published.

1800-1820
Oxford and Cambridge Universities
Large increases in bachelor's examinees.

1824
Cambridge University
Competitive exams: honors and poll exams. Exams standardized.

1836
University of London
Established to give exams only.

1837
Horace Mann
Secretary of Massachusetts State Board of Education. Calls for oral and written teacher competency exams.

1845
Samuel Gridley Howe
Boston School Committee written exams to evaluate schools.

1847
Queen's Scholarship Exam
Competitive stipend exams for promising teachers.

1850
Throughout the United States
Teacher "competency" exams by local school boards. Annual teacher exams.

1853
India Civil Service Examination
Competitive civil service appointment exams to eliminate some patronage.

1856
Chicago Public Schools
Written exams for elementary promotion and admission to high school.

1861
Payment by results
Reading, writing, arithmetic tests to determine government funding of schools.

1864
Rev. George Fisher
Scale books: first criterion-referenced tests.

1865
New York Board of Regents
Sets exams for elementary pupils.

1870
Samuel King
First superintendent of Portland, Oregon schools publishes exam scores of pupils in newspapers.

1877
Samuel King
Parent/teacher outrage forces King's resignation.

1878
New York Board of Regents
Sets exams for secondary pupils.

1880-1890
Teachers and other educators
Elementary school promotion examinations under heavy criticism.

1889
F. Y. Edgeworth
Research essay test score reliability.

Key

- Ancient and Modern China
- Ancient Greece
- Medieval Universities
- England
- Jesuits
- United States 1800–1900
- Modern Testing

1890
Manchu Dynasty
Candidates can hire agency to take exam for them.

1890
James McKeen Cattell
Introduces term "mental test."

1893
James McKeen Cattell
Research on predictive validity of mental ability tests.

1897-1904
Joseph Mayer Rice
Uses tests to evaluate U. S. schools; publishes results in *The Forum*.

1899
Charles W. Eliot
College Entrance Examination Board (CEEB) founded.

c.1900
Throughout United States
Eighth grade promotion exams generally eliminated in public schools.

Continued on Inside Back Cover

EDUCATIONAL TESTS AND MEASUREMENT AN INTRODUCTION

ANTHONY J. NITKO
University of Pittsburgh

HARCOURT BRACE JOVANOVICH, INC.
New York San Diego Chicago San Francisco Atlanta
London Sydney Toronto

To Veronica

ISBN: 0-15-520910-8

Library of Congress Catalog Card Number: 83-80601

Printed in the United States of America

PREFACE

This basic textbook for an introductory educational testing and measurement course for elementary and secondary school teachers does not require the reader to have had any prior courses in measurement or statistics. The text serves equally well for undergraduate and beginning graduate level courses for teachers who have had little or no previous formal training in testing.

I have written the text from the viewpoint that testing and instruction should blend together in the teaching and learning process, and I remind the reader frequently that instructional design and decisions affect both what pupils learn and how learning is tested. The book conveys the view that educators are professionals whose experiences and judgments should be used frequently to help formulate appropriate test usage for the schools. Although I encourage using professional judgment throughout the text, I also point out erroneous judgments and test abuses.

Whenever possible, I have attempted to integrate the concepts of criterion-referencing and norm-referencing, often describing how *both* referencing schemes are necessary to interpret pupils' test results and to make sound educational decisions. I favor an approach to referencing schemes that asks educators first to identify the kinds of information needed for a particular purpose and then to select the appropriate method(s) of obtaining that information. I hope I have avoided the kind of CRT versus NRT opposition that sometimes creeps into introductory books.

The text is arranged in four parts:

Part I   Background
Part II   Principles of Classroom Test Development
Part III   Principles of Test Score Interpretation
Part IV   Principles of Standardized Test Usage

In each chapter the basic themes are listed along with the important terms and concepts the chapter covers. An overview describes the chapter's scope and sequence; the body of the chapter then follows. Each chapter concludes with a summary; where the amount of information in a chapter is extensive, the summary appears in list form to facilitate learning and recalling information. The Additional Readings suggested for each chapter are collected at the back of the book (pp. 616-622).

Part I of the text presents a background for educational testing and measurement and foreshadows much of what is to follow. Chapter 1 introduces basic terminology and describes several decision-contexts in which teachers tend to use tests. Chapter 2 discusses social and legal issues of testing. It alerts teachers to the legal and ethical considerations when they use test results in making decisions about students. Chapter 2 also helps to motivate the student to study the technical aspects of testing which come later in the book.

Part I concludes with a chapter on basic statistical concepts. Instructors have differing opinions as to whether they should teach statistical concepts as a separate unit or should introduce them gradually as needed. Chapter 3 gives the instructor the option of using either approach. Instructors preferring gradual introduction may assign only those sections relevant to the lecture at hand. Chapter 3 emphasizes statistical *concepts* rather than computation. However, Appendix A provides step-by-step guides for computing the most common statistics a classroom teacher is likely to use.

Part II of the book is a guide for constructing and using teacher-made tests. Instructors may select some chapters for optional reading or independent study. This part of the book covers basic principles of using essay and completion items (Chapter 6), matching and true-false items (Chapter 7), and multiple-choice items (Chapter 8). A separate chapter, Chapter 4, describes techniques of writing behavioral objectives for instructors who wish to use this approach to define a test's domain. Chapter 5 discusses test planning, including the usual discussion of developing a test blueprint, but goes beyond this, describing various instructional decision-contexts and the things a teacher needs to consider when planning different kinds of tests. I devote Chapter 9 to techniques for writing items to test complex cognitive processes and skills, including the use of context-dependent items. Thus I separate the very basic procedures of item-writing from the more complex procedures, since I find that this separation often facilitates students' learning the material and gives the instructor an option of omitting some complex material if desired. Part II also contains chapters on constructing observation and rating scales (Chapter 10), using pupil responses to improve items (Chapter 11), administering tests and helping students to exhibit their best performance (Chapter 12), and reporting pupil progress to parents and school administrators (Chapter 13). Ample examples illustrate all these chapters. Taken together, this set of ten chapters provides comprehensive materials on classroom test construction and use.

Part III discusses basic measurement principles applicable to both published and teacher-made tests: norm-referencing (Chapter 14), reliability (Chapter 15), validity (Chapter 16), and criterion-referencing (Chapter 17). Some instructors may prefer to cover these topics before classroom test construction (Part II). Part III permits instructors to cover the material in it before Part II. I have found that preservice teachers can make more sense out of the technical material in Part III after they have become familiar with classroom test construction, and so I have placed Part III after Part II. In-service teachers, being more experienced, may profitably cover Part III before Part II without loss of continuity, if the instructor so desires.

Part IV describes the major kinds of published achievement, aptitude, and noncognitive tests. Emphasis is on using test scores for educational decisions, especially those associated with classroom practice. Some testing and measurement instructors require their students to locate and evaluate standardized tests. Chapter 18 is a how-to-do-it guide for locating and evaluating published tests intended for specific educational purposes. Chapter 19 covers published achievement tests, integrating norm-referencing and criterion-referencing in a way consistent with the text as a whole. I urge the reader to appraise criterion-referenced tests critically against professional standards of quality in the manner consistent with the way professionals have critically appraised norm-referenced tests. Chapters 20 and 21 deal with individually and group-administered scholastic aptitude tests, respectively. Although the classroom teacher will likely administer only group aptitude tests, knowledge of the nature of individual scholastic aptitude testing is important. A teacher may have to participate with a team of professionals using such tests or may otherwise have access to a professional report that discusses the use of such tests. Chapter 22 describes the broad domain of noncognitive measures, including interest inventories and their potential use in various educational decisions.

Although no single introductory course is likely to cover all of these chapters in detail, the text permits each instructor the flexibility of choosing material to suit the needs of the students at hand, perhaps using the same text in different ways with different groups of students. The book provides ample material for both independent study and later reference while teaching.

The back matter of the book is especially important for complete student learning. I have already mentioned a statistical computation appendix (Appendix A). Appendix B illustrates how to compute several kinds of reliability coefficients as well as indices of decision consistency. Appendix C provides a table of squares and square roots. Condensed versions of cognitive, noncognitive, and psychomotor taxonomies are presented in Appendix D. An IOX Test Specification is illustrated in Appendix E. Appendix F lists major test publishers and agencies from which collections of behavioral objectives can be obtained. Appendix G lists specific achievement, aptitude, and interest inventories, along with their publishers, the grades or ages of pupils for whom they are intended, and, where applicable, references to the *Mental Measurement Yearbook* so the reader may quickly locate a review of the test. Normal curve information is provided on the inside back cover.

A student workbook, co-authored by Norman W. Mulgrave, is available to accompany the textbook. The workbook provides a comprehensive set of study questions for each chapter as well as several types of exercises to help students learn the more difficult concepts and principles.

I could not have written this book without the help of many persons. A sabbatical leave granted by the University of Pittsburgh gave me the opportunity to begin the needed research. Through the kind assistance of Frederic M. Lord and Ernest J. Anastasio, the Educational Testing Service provided office space and library privileges, permitting me to begin writing the first chapters. I am very much indebted to the reviewers whose critical reading of each chapter contributed immensely to improving both the technical accuracy and the pedagogical presentation of the final version: Peter W. Airasian, Jack I. Bardon, Ronald A. Berk, Lois E. Burrill, Philip H. DuBois, Robert A. Forsyth, Robert M. Gagné, Ronald K. Hambleton, Huynh Huynh, and Darrell L. Sabers. Megan Nitko was kind enough to compile the table of squares and square roots found in Appendix C. Tony, Bob, Megan, and Veronica Nitko helped to compile the indices. My students at the School of Education, University of Pittsburgh, and at the Malawi Certificate Examination and Testing Board, Zomba, Malawi, used drafts of text chapters and workbook exercises and provided insightful feedback that has greatly improved the usefulness of the text. Graduate student assistants, Sunee Dhanasarnsombat, Patricia Maldonado, Do Soon Park, and Emad M. J. Wajeeh, helped to locate material and to make statistical computations. Melva Hogan, Veronica Nitko, and Denise Morrin typed early drafts of chapters. Theresa Dunn worked tirelessly typing most of the final version. William J. Wisneski, Albert I. Richards, Gene Carter Lettau, Melinda Benson, Harriet Meltzer, Diane Polster, and Robin Risque, all of Harcourt Brace Jovanovich, Inc., graciously encouraged me at every stage, from acquisition through production, as well as applying their considerable editorial and artistic talents to the production of the book. To all these persons, and to others I have failed to mention, I offer my sincere thanks and appreciation.

And I never would have completed this book had it not been for the encouragement and support of my wife, Veronica, and my children, Tony, Bob, and Megan. I thank them for their tolerance during those long periods when I was writing and away from the mainstream of family activities. Most thanks, however, go to Veronica, whose encouragement sustained me through the much too long period during which I put this book together. To Veronica, then, I lovingly dedicate this book.

Anthony J. Nitko

CONTENTS

*Sections with asterisk are optional. They may be omitted without loss of continuity.

APPENDIXES

PART ONE
BACKGROUND

Themes

● Tests and measurements provide certain information to teachers, administrators, parents, pupils, and others about various human characteristics. Combined with other information and experience, this test information is useful for making decisions in the practical world.

● Distinctions can be made between testing, measuring, and evaluating, even though these are highly related concepts.

● Test information has been used regularly in connection with such classes of decisions as selection, placement, classification, career and guidance counseling, diagnosis and remediation, and program improvement and evaluation.

● Certain terms and concepts are used to describe each of the various characteristics of a test. These are used to help understand the nature of any given testing procedure.

Terms and Concepts

measurement
test
evaluation
formative evaluation
summative evaluation
selection decisions
placement decisions
classification decisions
diagnostic decisions
item sampling

item
objectivity
standardization
verbal tests
performance tests
power tests
speed tests
norm-referencing
criterion-referencing

INTRODUCTION

1

It is almost impossible for you to have attended school without having been exposed to a rather wide variety of educational and psychological testing procedures. The fact that at this moment you are reading this book for a testing and measurement course places you, not only among test takers, but among the successful test takers. Think for a few minutes: How many tests have you taken to this point in your life? When did your testing experiences begin? Consider the examples below.

For Robert, being subjected to systematic testing procedures began when his parents made application for him to be enrolled in a pre-school at age 3. The application blank itself presented a series of questions that required his parents to rate his cognitive and social-emotional development. One of the questions required them to rate his leadership ability: Was he a leader or follower? To what extent? They replied, "He's definitely a follower!" A letter from the school's director came back a few weeks later: "Congratulations! Your son has been accepted into our pre-school program. He will be the only follower among 25 leaders!"

Megan's educational testing began in kindergarten with an interview and an observation. While there was a lower age limit, below which admission to kindergarten was not possible, the state in which she lived had no mandatory kindergarten requirement. On registration day, Megan and her mother came to school and were briefly interviewed. Like Robert, Megan's cognitive and social-emotional skills were rated but this time by a teacher. Megan's development was judged normal and she attended kindergarten.

During the year she experienced difficulty in paying attention to the teacher and participating in group activities, although she was neither aggressive nor hostile. She was given a "readiness" test at the end of kindergarten and performed as an average child. Her teacher recommended that she continue on to first grade, but her parents balked: They didn't think that she was ready.

They took her to a child guidance clinic and requested further psychological testing. The clinical psychologist administered an individual intelligence test and a "projective test" in which she was asked to tell a story about what was happening in each of a set of pictures. The psychologist interviewed her, her parents, and her teacher. She was described by the psychologist as a normal girl, both in cognitive ability and in social-emotional development.

Her parents withdrew her from the school she was attending and placed her in another school to repeat kindergarten. They reported that, whereas, her first experience was difficult for her, her second kindergarten year was a great success. In their view, a teacher who was particularly sensitive to Megan's needs, helped her cognitive development to proceed rapidly; by the end of the year she had also become more confident in herself and regularly participated in group activities.

In the situations illustrated above, tests provided information. Different persons evaluated the test information and reached different conclusions. Decisions needed to be, and were, made, however. Perhaps different decisions could have been made based on the same information.

These brief anecdotes show tests being used rather early in the lives of two persons. Most of us recall more easily the testing in which we engaged later in our lives as older children and as adults. Some may not even associate the term "test" with two of the procedures—Robert's ratings and Megan's interviews. Yet, as shall be explained below, these are included in the broad definition of "tests," because the basic principles of testing and measurement apply as well to them as to other, more familiar procedures.

Also illustrated, especially by Megan's situation, is that tests can contribute to a decision, but they may not be interpreted in the same way by everyone concerned. Although it may appear that Megan's parents were right in having her repeat kindergarten, there is no way of ascertaining what would have happened if she had gone to first grade straight away, since she didn't.

Decisions involve the use of a variety of kinds of information. Sometimes test scores need to be placed on the "back burner"; at other times they play a more dominant role. This book will examine a variety of decisions for which tests are used in education. Each time, it will identify the basic principles that relate to the evaluation and use of tests and testing information. It will emphasize basic principles rather than prescriptions to follow blindly, even though you will find some of those, too. However, if you understand the basic principles, you should be able to determine when those and other prescriptions are inappropriate.

Distinctions Between Measurements, Tests, and Evaluations

Measurements

Measurement refers to the quantitative aspects of describing the characteristics or attributes of persons. A frequently cited definition is that measurement is the assignment of numerals to certain aspects of persons[1] according to rules (Stevens, 1946). This is a rather terse statement that, taken out of context, requires explanation. A broader and, perhaps, clearer definition of *measurement* is *a procedure for assigning numbers (usually called scores) to a specified attribute or characteristic of persons in such a*

---

[1]Definitions of measurement usually include the phrase "objects or events" instead of, or along with, "persons," or sometimes the term "experimental units." For ease of reading, and since this book deals mostly with measuring persons, I have omitted these more technical phrases.

manner as to maintain the real world relationships among the persons with regard to the attribute being measured (Lord and Novick, 1968).

Logically, in order to measure a characteristic of a person according to the above definition, you need to (a) identify the person you want to measure, (b) identify the characteristic of that person to be measured, and (c) specify the procedure to be used to assign numbers to the characteristic.

An important aspect of the number-assigning procedure is that the resulting scores should maintain the relationships among the people that exist in the real world. At the *minimum* this would mean, for example, that if you are a better speller than I, a spelling test designed to measure our spelling ability should result in your score (i.e., your measurement) being higher than mine. For many of the characteristics measured in education and psychology the "procedure" is to count the number of correct answers or number of points earned on a test. There has been considerable debate in the field of psychometrics as to whether this procedure is sufficient to call measurement in psychology and education anything but crude (e.g., Campbell, 1928; Johnson, 1928, 1936; McGregor, 1935; Stevens, 1951; Suppes & Zinnes, 1963; Rozeboom, 1966; Pfanzagl, 1968). Although this debate surfaces from time to time, most measurement specialists would probably agree that even if this counting procedure is crude, as a practical matter, measurements should be empirically evaluated to determine their usefulness (Rozeboom, 1966; Lord and Novick, 1968; Jones, 1971).

Tests

Say the word "test," and what most persons think of will probably be school examinations, college entrance examinations, or employment tests involving writing or marking answers. This constitutes a rather narrow view of the world of testing. The definition adopted here, to which most of the principles described in this book can be applied, is broader and more inclusive.

An educational or psychological *test* is defined as *a systematic procedure for observing and describing one or more characteristics of a person with the aid of either a numerical scale or a category system* (cf. Cronbach, 1970). Notice that certain tests may yield measurements (as defined previously), and so a person's behavior would be described quantitatively. But other procedures, such as the play interview (e.g., Murphy, 1956) which is sometimes used with preschoolers by child development specialists, also qualify as tests under the definition adopted above. Thus, a child's cognitive development could be observed by using the *Wechsler Pre-School and Primary Scale of Intelligence* (Chapter 20) and described as having a percentile rank of 50 (Chapter 3). Or, this play behavior could be observed and categorized as "ego-centered" or "drive-centered" (Murphy, 1956). The former test uses a numerical

scale describing the percent of children of the same age that this child's performance exceeded; the latter test uses a category system based on psychoanalytic constructs to describe what has been observed. The definition of tests adopted here is broad enough to include nearly all systematic procedures the school uses to describe the behavior of a child: teacher observations, questionnaires, interviews, class projects, term papers, and paper and pencil examinations.

While it is natural to assume that tests are designed to provide information about an individual, this need not be so always. Many states have testing programs designed to determine whether their school systems have attained certain set goals. Although tests are administered to individual pupils, the focus is on measuring the effectiveness of the school system or the programs operating in a school building; individual names are not associated with scores (e.g., see Seiverling, 1976b and Table 1.1). In such cases, the score for the school system or for the building at a specific grade level is usually the average score of the pupils who took the test.

Another example of a testing program designed to assess groups rather than individuals is the National Assessment of Educational Progress (Tyler, 1966; Merwin and Womer, 1969). This is an effort to assess the impact of the nation's educational efforts. Initially, test questions were assigned to pupils on a random sampling basis, so that within a school no two pupils had the same questions. Thus, comparisons of individuals were not possible. Similar random sampling plans were designed for schools and states so that they could not be identified or compared.[2] The original idea was to produce numbers—analogous to the gross national product (Stake, 1970)—that would show the progress of education in the entire country. An example of

---

[2]It is now possible to incorporate local, as well as state, assessments into the National Assessment procedures (e.g., Educational Commission of the States, 1977).

Goals of Quality Education

Communications Skills—Quality education should help every student acquire communication skills of understanding, speaking, reading and writing.

Mathematics—Quality education should help every student acquire skills in mathematics.

Self-Esteem—Quality education should help every student develop self-understanding and a feeling of self-worth.

Analytical Thinking—Quality education should help every student develop analytical thinking skills.

Understanding Others—Quality education should help every student acquire knowledge of different cultures and an appreciation of the worth of all people.

Citizenship—Quality education should help every student learn the history of the nation, understand its systems of government and economics, and acquire the values and attitudes necessary for responsible citizenship.

Arts and the Humanities—Quality education should help every student acquire knowledge, appreciation, and skills in the arts and the humanities.

Science and Technology—Quality education should help every student acquire knowledge, understanding, and appreciation of science and technology.

Work—Quality education should help every student acquire the knowledge, skills, and attitudes necessary to become a self-supporting member of society.

Family Living—Quality education should help every student acquire the knowledge, skills, and attitudes necessary for successful personal and family living.

Health—Quality education should help every student acquire knowledge and develop practices necessary to maintain physical and emotional well-being.

Environment—Quality education should help every student acquire the knowledge and attitudes necessary to maintain the quality of life in a balanced environment.

Richard F. Seiverling, *Educational Quality in Pennsylvania: A Decade of Progress* (Harrisburg, Pa.: Bureau of Research and Evaluation, Pennsylvania Department of Education, 1979), p. 23. Reprinted by permission of the author.

Table 1 • 1   An example of one state's (Pennsylvania) educational goals that form the basis for a testing program designed to assess the system instead of individual pupils.

an exercise administered during one of the National Assessments is shown in Figure 1.1.

Evaluation

During the past twenty or so years there has been an increasing call for the evaluation of educational, psychological, and other social-action programs, procedures, and products. The association of the term "evaluation" with "programs" goes back further in time than that, of course, but during the 1960s and 1970s the call for educational program evaluation became especially intense and organized. Today most agencies that fund educational programs require them to be formally evaluated. A professional career specialization, called *program evaluator*, has developed because of this increased requirement for evaluation.

A continued and somewhat related use of the term evaluation has been in connection with individual pupils or clients. For example, pupils' grades are often referred to as evaluations; a reading specialist evaluates a pupil's reading progress; a clinical psychologist gives a series of tests in order to evaluate a client's mental state. These two uses are prevalent, and often careful attention is needed in order to distinguish between "program or curriculum evaluation" and "individual pupil evaluation." Also, it is often necessary to distinguish between "measurement" and "evaluation."

Common to all uses of the term evaluation, however, is the notion that the value or worth of someone or something is to be judged. Evaluation, then, involves judgment.

Judgment may or may not be based on tests. Clearly, evaluation does occur in the

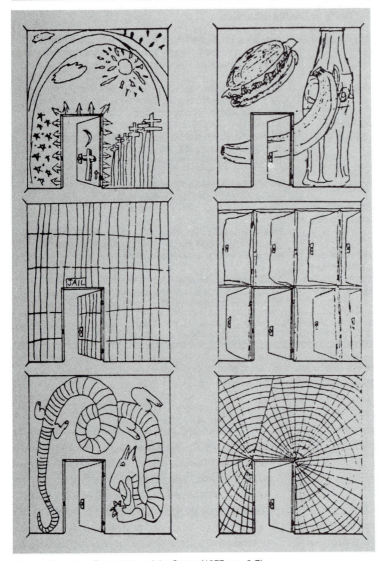

A survey of art skills by National Assessment marks the first comprehensive attempt to measure student achievement in one of the most complex and important areas of human endeavor.

17 Year Olds. The designs were given points for three major elements: fitting the shape of the wall (60% of the drawings met this criterion); coherent integration of design elements (48% met this criterion); and integration of the door into the overall design (21% met this criterion).

. . . Each drawing was also scored for imagination. One-fourth of the designs contained "unusual or surprising elements."

13 Year Olds. Fifty-five percent of the students drew designs that fit the shape of the wall. About 40% of the drawings contained integrated elements, but only 20% incorporated the door into the overall design. Seventeen percent of the designs contained unusual or surprising elements, such as objects drawn in an unusual scale or objects not normally found on a bedroom wall.

9 Year Olds. Forty percent of the children created a design that "fit artistically" within the shape of the wall. About one-third of the designs were drawn with the elements of the design related to each other in an integrated, coherent or consistent manner. Only 12% of the drawings included the door as an integral part of the overall design.

Source: Education Commission of the States (1977, pp. 6-7)

Figure 1 • 1 One kind of assessment exercise used in the *National Assessment of Educational Progress* (1974–1975): Students were asked to create a picture of a bedroom wall with an off-center door. (The above were drawn by 13- and 17-year-olds.) Other tasks included drawing in perspective and drawing a person running.

absence of tests, measurements, or other objective information. Even if these kinds of objective information are available and used, evaluators will have to integrate them into their own experiences and knowledge bases in order to come to decisions. So degrees of subjectivity and bias influence all evaluations. Testing and measurement attempt to reduce some of the subjectivity which influences evaluation. To say that the use of tests and measurements

Stages in planning and development	Evaluation activities (question to be answered)	Possible evaluation instruments, procedures
Identify basic *purposes* and values sought by entity involved (school, agency).	Identify purposes. Determine relative perceived worth (what are the basic purposes of this entity?).	Surveys, analyses of documents, judgments, ethnographic studies, historical analyses.
From among those basic purposes identified, select those which represent current *needs*.	Determine present level of attainment of each purpose (what important purposes are not being attained?).	Surveys, testing programs, analysis of records, ethnographic studies, historical analyses.
Specify *goals* of new program or activity (or goals of effort to revise existing program).	Assess clarity, quality of statements. Determine relative worth (is development directed toward clear and worthwhile goals?).	Logical analysis, surveys, judgments, Delphi technique, ratings, hierarchy analysis.
Develop *rationale* concerning promising ways of achieving goals.	Examine rationale for pertinence, completeness, empirical basis (is development based on a defensible approach?).	Logical analysis, expert judgment.
Develop *plan* of program for achieving goals.	Assess clarity, specificity of plan, its relationship to goals, basis in rationale (is the planned program an implementable procedure for achieving program goals?).	Logical analysis, expert judgment, Delphi, decision-theory, task analysis, systems analysis.
Implement planned program and study its *operation*.	(a) Assess validity and feasibility of implementation (can this program be implemented as planned?). (b) Determine any changes necessary if program is to achieve goals (how can this program be improved?).	(a) Observation, interview, study of records. (b) Tests, attitude measures, observation, simple experiments, quasi-experiments, decision theory.
Certify program as completed.	(a) Describe operating characteristics of completed program (what things actually take place when this program is in operation?). (b) Assess achievement of intended and unintended outcomes (what results does this program produce?).	(a) Observation, interview, analysis of materials, study of records. (b) Tests, attitude measures, observation, ethnographic studies.

Source: C. M. Lindvall, "A Perspective on the Development of a Specialization in Educational Evaluation within the Division of Educational Studies," Working Paper 34 (Programs in Educational Research Methodology, School of Education, University of Pittsburgh, 1977), p. 6. Reprinted by permission of the author.

Table 1 • 2   Stages in a comprehensive development effort showing related evaluation activities and procedures.

(or, in general, quantitative information) greatly improves evaluation is itself a bias toward the technological, however. It is known, too, that there is a "politics of evaluation" (see e.g., House, 1974; Popham, 1975).

One way to think about curriculum evaluation is to think of the steps or stages required in the development of a program (Lindvall, 1977). Table 1.2 represents a synthesis of what several writers have proposed as evaluation approaches to curriculum. The first column describes the stages themselves. Suggestions of possible evaluation activities and of evaluation questions that might be asked at each of these stages appear in the second column. The third column suggests a variety of procedures and tests that could be used to answer the questions posed at each stage and thus illustrates how testing and measurement relate to various kinds of evaluations. (Columns two and three are not meant to be exhaustive.) Notice, too, that this scheme implies that no single academic discipline has a monopoly on the evaluation of programs. Different points of view and different types of analysis are required by different stages of evaluation.

A set of educational materials, an instructional procedure, or an educational program can be evaluated during the course of its development as well as after it has been completely developed. The terms formative and summative evaluation have been used to distinguish the roles of evaluation during these two periods (e.g., Cronbach, 1963; Lindvall and Cox, 1970; Scriven, 1967).

Formative evaluation is concerned with judgments made during the design and/or development of a program which are directed toward modifying, "forming," or otherwise improving the program before it is completed. Such evaluations have the advantage of providing the developer with insight on how to improve the program or procedure before it is actually used in the schools. A teacher engages in formative evaluation when revising lessons or learning materials by using information obtained from their previous use.

Summative evaluation describes judgments about the merits of an already completed program, procedure, or product. Such an evaluation tends to summarize strengths and weaknesses; it describes the extent to which a properly implemented program or procedure has attained its stated goals and objectives. Summative evaluations are usually less directed toward providing the developer with suggestions for improvement than are formative evaluations. Summative evaluations are directed more toward informing the consumer whether a particular method "works" and under which conditions or under what degree of implementation.

Part of determining the degree of implementation is an analysis of whether there are sustaining mechanisms in the school environment to assure that the effects of the innovation continue to be produced (Glaser and Nitko, 1971). Teachers may, for example, bring new ideas and innovations into the classroom, but the school conditions necessary to sustain these ideas in the way they were intended to be used may be missing. The summative evaluation statement that these methods "work" would apply, then, only to situations in which the sustaining mechanisms were present in the school environment.

It can be seen from Table 1.2 that evaluation may not require testing or measurement. Judgments about different aspects of educational programs require different techniques such as logical analysis or historical analysis. Even if tests (as defined in this book) are used, they may yield qualitative descriptions and not measurements. This should be apparent from Table 1.2. Similarly, even if individual pupils are tested as part of the evaluative process, there may be no measurement: Teachers can— and often do—evaluate pupils on the basis of systematic observation and qualitative description, without measuring them.

Uses of Tests in Certain Classes of Decisions

Tests are used for a great many reasons and test scores serve as information for a variety of kinds of decisions. It is helpful to review some of the categories of decisions or situations, because the usefulness of a test will depend very much on the type of decision one wishes to make. A test will serve some decision contexts well, but not others. There is no simple answer to the question "Is this a good test?" Tests are good for some purpose(s) and not as good for others. A prerequisite you need to acquire before being able to judge the worth of a test is the ability to understand the decision context in which the test will be used.

Any classification of kinds of decisions is likely to be incomplete and somewhat arbitrary. In this section the following classes of decisions are described.[3]

1. Selection decisions
2. Placement decisions
3. Classification decisions
4. Counseling and guidance decisions
5. Educational diagnostic and remediation decisions
6. Program improvement and evaluation decisions

Selection Decisions

Most persons are familiar with *selection decisions:* An institution or organization decides that some persons are acceptable while others are not; those not acceptable are rejected and no longer are the concern of the institution or organization. This feature—rejection and the elimination of those rejected from immediate institutional concern—is central to a selection decision (Cronbach and Gleser, 1965).

Tests are often used to provide part of the information on which to base selection decisions. For example, applicants for positions as hospital admitting clerks may take a medical terminology spelling test, a typing test, a personal interview and complete an application blank containing biographical information. On the basis of the information collected through these procedures, a particular hospital hires some applicants and rejects others. The institution, from its viewpoint, is not accountable

for those persons not hired (assuming fair and legal hiring practices, of course).

Similarly, college admissions are often selection decisions: some candidates are admitted and others are not; those not admitted are no longer the college's concern. Some critics may argue, however, that while those rejected are no concern of the particular institution, they are of society generally, and thus from a broader social consideration there may not be a selection decision (e.g., Cronbach, 1957).

When tests are used for selection, it is imperative to show that the scores on these tests bear a relationship to success in the program or job for which the institution or organization has selected persons. If investigation does not show these tests can distinguish between those likely to succeed and those unlikely, then such tests should be improved or eliminated. To continue to use such tests for selection for employment may even be illegal (United States Supreme Court, 1971; EEOC, CSC, DOL, and DOD, 1978). Notice that in the hospital admitting clerks example there were four tests: spelling, typing, application, and interview. All the information obtained from these tests must bear a relationship to success on the job in order to be retained.

Selection decisions need not be perfect, however, and tests cannot be expected to have perfect validity for selection (see Chapter 16). The use of imperfect tests in selection is shown in a simplified way in Figure 1.2. Some applicants would have been successful had they been selected instead of rejected, and some, even though they were accepted, turned out to be unsuccessful. Tests can be evaluated, then, in terms of the consequences of the decisions made when using them. This subject is taken up in Chapter 16.

Keep in mind, however, that this figure illustrates "consequences" only in terms of "successful" or "unsuccessful" persons. There may be other considerations (such as the degree or level of success) and sometimes unintended consequences that need to be identi-

[3]These categories follow closely those used by Cronbach (1970) and Cronbach and Gleser (1965).

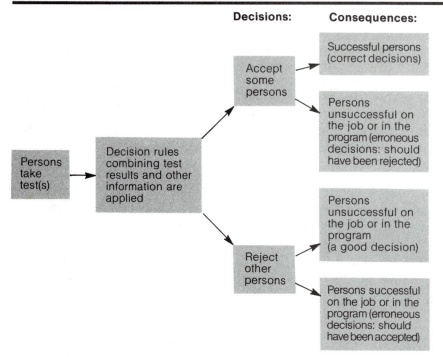

Decisions: **Consequences:**

Persons take test(s) → Decision rules combining test results and other information are applied

Accept some persons → Successful persons (correct decisions)

Persons unsuccessful on the job or in the program (erroneous decisions: should have been rejected)

Reject other persons → Persons unsuccessful on the job or in the program (a good decision)

Persons successful on the job or in the program (erroneous decisions: should have been accepted)

Figure 1 • 2 A simplified illustration of the process of using tests in a selection situation and the consequences of those decisions. The tests and the decision rules are evaluated in terms of their consequences.

fied before the test is finally evaluated (Cronbach and Gleser, 1965; Cole, 1977). (See also Chapter 16.)

Placement Decisions

Selecting someone to fill a job opening or to be admitted to a particular college is quite different than sectioning a high school class into those receiving different levels of instruction (e.g., remedial, regular, honors), forming reading groups in first grade, or dividing a group of kindergarteners into those who will or will not receive extra perceptual skills training. The difference is this: In job and college selection situations rejection is possible; the institution is not concerned about what happens to those rejected. In the school situations the institutions must make provision for all persons; unconcerned rejection is not possible. Those pupils not put into honors sections, tions, upper reading sections, or special training sections, for example, still need to be taught and to be educated to the limits of their ability. Nor can persons be legally excluded from the educational process because of their handicaps (Public Law 94-142, 1975).

Such school determinations are *placement decisions* and are characterized as follows: Persons are assigned to different levels of the same general type of instruction or work; no one is rejected, but all remain within the instruction to be assigned to some level or treatment (Cronbach and Gleser, 1965; Cronbach, 1970). Those pupils not enrolled in honors sections, for example, must be placed in other instructional programs. Those with low first grade reading readiness test scores cannot be sent home. They must be placed into appropriate programs and taught to read. In placement decisions, the institution must account for all persons; unconcerned rejection is not possible.

Many, if not most, decisions in schools are of the placement variety. Even those decision contexts that use the language of selection are, upon closer examination, more often than not placement decisions. For example, if individuals are "screened" for learning disabilities or "selected" for a gifted and talented program, the purpose is to place *all* persons into appropriate instructional programs. The schools are not free to teach some to read and to reject the rest. If one instructional method is inappropriate for a particular pupil, then an appropriate alternative method needs to be found. In the end, all pupils are taught, and most learn to read.

The criteria used to evaluate the adequacy of placement tests are different from those used to evaluate selection tests. Placement tests are useful to the extent that they improve the decision to *differentially* assign persons to instructional programs. Details concerning how to judge the validity of placement tests are given in Chapter 16.

Classification Decisions

Some decisions are concerned with assigning a person to one of several different categories, jobs, or programs. These types of decisions are called *classification decisions* (Cronbach and Gleser, 1965). For example, once persons are inducted into the military service, they need to be assigned to particular jobs. The assignment of psychiatric labels, frequently termed "diagnosis," is a classification decision, too. Legislation in the area of special education has given a legal status to many labels for handicapped children and strongly encourages the classification of pupils into one (or more) of a few designated categories.[4] An example of one such set of labels is shown in Table 1.3.

It is possible to conceptualize classification as a more general term which subsumes

selection and placement as special cases (Cronbach and Gleser, 1965). Classification is concerned with the assignment of persons to different categories, jobs, or programs. If these categories represent ordered levels of a similar kind of program or job (e.g., three levels of reading instruction); then the assignment of persons is called placement. If one of the categories to which persons are assigned is "rejection," then the process is called selection. This book, however, will consider the three types of decisions separately. Classification will refer to cases where the categories are essentially unordered, placement will refer to the case where the categories represent levels of instruction or treatment, and selection will refer to the case where persons are accepted or rejected.

Counseling and Guidance Decisions

Tests are frequently used to assist students in exploring and choosing careers and in directing them to prepare for the careers they select. A single test is not used for making guidance and counseling decisions. Rather frequently, a *series of tests* is administered, including an interest inventory, various aptitude tests, a personality questionnaire, and an achievement battery. This information, along with additional background information, is discussed with the student during a series of counseling sessions. This facilitates a student's decision-making process and is an entrée to the exploration of different careers. Exploring career options is likely to be an on-going and changing series of decisions perhaps occurring over long periods of a person's life.

Counseling and guidance decisions are considered *individual decisions* as opposed to *institutional decisions* (Cronbach and Gleser, 1959; 1965). An institution (school, industrial firm, government or social agency, etc.) can replicate its decision over many persons and under essentially the same conditions. As a result, the institution looks at the overall or average correctness of its decisions. A college,

---

[4]But the legal labeling of persons on the basis of their test scores has a history that is as old as mental testing itself (e.g., Kamin, 1974).

1. **"Deaf"** means a hearing impairment which is so severe that the child is impaired in processing linguistic information through hearing, with or without amplification, which adversely affects educational performance.

2. **"Deaf-blind"** means concomitant hearing and visual impairments, the combination of which causes such severe communication and other development and educational problems that they cannot be accommodated in special education programs solely for deaf or blind children.

3. **"Hard of hearing"** means a hearing impairment, whether permanent or fluctuating, which adversely affects a child's educational performance but which is not included under the definition of "deaf" in this section.

4. **"Mentally retarded"** means significantly subaverage general intellectual functioning existing concurrently with deficits in adaptive behavior and manifested during the developmental period, which adversely affects a child's educational performance.

5. **"Multihandicapped"** means concomitant impairments (such as mentally retarded-blind, mentally retarded-orthopedically impaired, etc.), the combination of which causes such severe educational problems that they cannot be accommodated in special education programs solely for one of the impairments. The term does not include deaf-blind children.

6. **"Orthopedically impaired"** means a severe orthopedic impairment which adversely affects a child's educational performance. The term includes impairments caused by congenital anomaly (e.g., clubfoot, absence of some member, etc.), impairments caused by disease (e.g., poliomyelitis, bone tuberculosis, etc.), and impairments from other causes (e.g., cerebral palsy, amputations, and fractures or burns which cause contractions).

7. **"Other health impaired"** means limited strength, vitality, or alertness due to chronic or acute health problems such as a heart condition, tuberculosis, rheumatic fever, nephritis, asthma, sickle cell anemia, hemophilia, epilepsy, lead poisoning, leukemia, or diabetes, which adversely affects a child's educational performance.

8. **"Seriously emotionally disturbed"** is defined as follows:
   i. The term means a condition exhibiting one or more of the following characteristics over a long period of time and to a marked degree, which adversely affects educational performance:
   A. An inability to learn which cannot be explained by intellectual, sensory, or health factors;
   B. An inability to build or maintain satisfactory interpersonal relationships with peers and teachers;
   C. Inappropriate types of behavior or feeling under normal circumstances;
   D. A general pervasive mood of unhappiness or depression; or
   E. A tendency to develop physical symptoms or fears associated with personal or school problems.
   ii. The term includes children who are schizophrenic or autistic. The term does not include children who are socially maladjusted, unless it is determined that they are seriously emotionally disturbed.

9. **"Specific learning disability"** means a disorder in one or more of the basic psychological processes involved in understanding or in using language, spoken or written, which may manifest itself in an imperfect ability to listen, think, speak, read, write, spell, or to do mathematical calculations. The term includes such conditions as perceptual handicaps, brain injury, minimal brain disfunction, dyslexia, and developmental asphasia. The term does not include children who have learning problems which are primarily the result of visual, hearing or motor handicaps, of mental retardation, or of environmental, cultural, or economic disadvantage.

10. **"Speech impaired"** means a communication disorder, such as stuttering, impaired articulation, a language impairment, or a voice impairment, which adversely affects a child's educational performance.

11. **"Visually handicapped"** means a visual impairment which, even with correction, adversely affects a child's educational performance. The term includes both partially seeing and blind children.

Source: U.S. Office of Education, Department of Health, Education, and Welfare, 1977.

Table 1 • 3   Classification decisions require the assignment of persons to categories, jobs, or programs. Labeling handicapped children is one type of classification decision. This is how one federal agency defined the labels in 1977 when implementing P.L. 94-142.

for example, may select only the students scoring highest on the admissions tests since these are likely to have the highest probability of success. Some of those selected will, however, not succeed in the college's view. Yet, on the average, the college's goal is to make more correct than incorrect decisions on those applicants admitted. Maintaining a high *average* level of success is the criterion of decision success from the institution's viewpoint. A school may judge its procedure of placing pupils into alternative instructional programs successful if it leads to higher overall *average achievement,* even though some individual pupils may be placed into inappropriate programs.

Individual decisions, on the other hand, serve the interest of the particular person. A person usually cannot replicate a decision and, therefore, cannot average the outcomes in the same way that a college or school can average its risks over many students. Because of the consequences of a decision, and because of the passage of time, a decision cannot be replicated under the same conditions. Further, the values that underlie the decision are unique to the individual and, thus, what is a correct decision for one person may be an inappropriate decision for another (Cronbach and Gleser, 1965). For example, two persons with nearly identical test results could be told that they would be under extreme academic pressure if they were to attend a highly competitive college. Yet, one person may be willing to sacrifice and risk failure in order to have the opportunity to attend. The other person might breathe a sigh of relief and opt to attend an institution with a more relaxed pace and lowered academic pressure.

Educational Diagnostic and Remediation Decisions

Sometimes the instruction a teacher or school pre-arranges is not effective for an individual student: The student may need special remedial help or a special prescription, relying on alternative methods or materials. Tests providing some of the information needed to make this type of decision are called *diagnostic tests.* Diagnostic decisions relate to the question, "What learning activities will best adapt to this student's individual requirements and thereby maximize the student's opportunities to attain the chosen goal?" Diagnosis implies prescribing the content and the nature of the instruc-

tion the student is to receive[5] (Glaser and Nitko, 1971; Nitko and Hsu, 1974).

The art of diagnostic testing is not well developed. One direction toward which diagnostic testing has turned is the fine-grain analysis of an individual's performance domain. What microscopic prerequisite skills are strong or weak? What misinformation or inappropriate processes and associations may interfere with the pupil's performance with regard to learning the skills and content? Tests can be designed to answer only some questions such as these (see Chapters 17 and 19).

General survey achievement batteries, such as the *Metropolitan Achievement Tests,* the *California Achievement Test,* the *Comprehensive Test of Basic Skills,* the *Stanford Achievement Test,* or the *Iowa Test of Basic Skills* are not well suited to this fine-grain analysis (nor do they claim to be). The reason is that there are too few questions on them that test any one of these microscopic skills. For example, such a survey battery may have about 35 test questions covering all of third grade arithmetic computation. Such a test can describe a pupil's general level of performance in arithmetic, but not the specific malfunctions and idiosyncrasies that lead to poor arithmetic performance.

To be diagnostic in the sense described here, tests need to contain a good many questions covering each of the performance domains. It would require administering more than one or two test items, for example, in order to conclude that a pupil does or doesn't know enough of the addition number facts from 0 to 5 (e.g., $0 + 1 = \_\_$, etc.) in order to proceed with new instruction. In helping students, a teacher might even find it advisable to administer all 36 of these number fact questions to an individual pupil. Thus, there

[5]The distinction used here between diagnostic testing and placement testing is not conventional. No doubt customary diagnostic tests involve both placement and diagnosis. Placement and diagnostic decisions in the instructional context can be put into the same category since they both imply differential assignment of students to levels of instruction of the same general nature. In this book, however, the use of the terms will be kept separate.

would be 36 questions on a specific performance category, rather than 36 questions covering the whole of third grade arithmetic. (For more details see Chapter 5 and Chapter 16.)

Another type of diagnosis involves assessing pupils that have been referred by the teacher for "possible mildly handicapping conditions" (Tucker, 1977). A teacher may initiate such requests to pupil services or to special education personnel because a pupil is unable to succeed in the teacher's class. Such a serious diagnostic decision should be made only after a comprehensive assessment of the pupil is conducted over a considerable period of time. The diagnostic decision may be reached after the diagnostician follows a series of sequential steps (Tucker, 1977):

Step 1. Direct classroom observation—information obtained from teachers and others with whom the pupil works directly.

Step 2. Inspection of school records—information from cumulative records is used to decide if the observations in Step 1 represent a temporary situation or could be explained in terms of the pupil's past history.

Step 3. Information on language dominance—parents and others are consulted to determine whether native English is spoken in the home and how language dominance may account for the referral.

Step 4. Individually administered educational testing—fine-grain analysis of the pupil's performance in the relevant school subjects.

Step 5. Individually administered sensory-motor testing—assessment of visual and auditory acuity, perception, and skills and motor skills.

Step 6. Observation of adaptive behavior—information obtained to determine if the pupil's playground, home, neighborhood, and community behaviors are within normal ranges

and whether the only problems are those which occur in school.

Step 7. Obtaining medical and/or developmental information—determining whether the behaviors observed in the classroom can be explained and then treated by a medical intervention.

Step 8. Personality testing—individually conducted psychological tests, pupil self-reports, and interviews to determine if there is an emotional basis for the pupil's school problem.

Step 9. Scholastic aptitude testing—individually administered tests of intellectual functioning.

According to this approach, after each step comes the question of whether further testing (i.e., the next step) is needed. Both the parent(s) and the school are involved in making these decision beginning with Step 3. Only if the parent(s) and the school *both* agree, is the next step undertaken. If they do not both agree, the approach suggests that the pupil should be retained in the regular class, and the teacher or the school be given the necessary assistance to permit the child to receive the proper educational program.

The diagnostician uses the test situation to collect information on several aspects of the pupil's performance including the style or manner of working, the content of the responses, and the pattern of scores on the tests (Cronbach, 1970). These are integrated and interpreted using the diagnostician's knowledge and experience. Note that so-called diagnostic tests do not make the decisions: Test results need to be interpreted from the viewpoint of the diagnostician.

Program Improvement and Evaluation Decisions

The nature of program evaluation, both formative and summative, has been described

How can item sampling be used in a classroom?

We usually think of administering the entire test to each examinee. This is a good procedure if we are interested in comparing one examinee to another. A program evaluator, however, is often more interested in the group average than in the individual scores since the group average summarizes the performance of everyone. But to obtain an estimate of the group's performance it isn't necessary to have everyone complete every item on the test. One could administer different samples of items to different examinees. Below, Professor W. James Popham (1975) describes how he used item sampling to help him evaluate some slide presentations he made to his classes. As you read, consider how you might use item sampling in your school to help evaluate instruction.

When wishing to evaluate the effectiveness of 30-minute tape-slide instructional programs on a pretest-post-test basis, I would devise criterion-referenced tests of 10–20 items, one test per program then have each of the items printed on a 3 by 5 inch card. Having shuffled the cards adroitly with all the flourish of a Las Vegas blackjack dealer, I would distribute them, one card at a time, to the 150–200 students enrolled. No one objected to these 30 second tests, since they took such a small bit of time. Yet, when I assembled the data collectively, they gave me a good idea of how the total class could perform before and after the instructional program. For each item, I typically had 10–20 individual responses, enough in fact to supply some evidence regarding how the entire class might perform on the item (pp. 226–227).

Source: W. James Popham, *Educational Evaluation*, © 1975, pp. 226–227. Reprinted by permission of Prentice-Hall, Inc., Englewood Cliffs, New Jersey.

Box 1 • 1

already. Tests often contribute information to these evaluative decisions. They are, however, institutional decisions, rather than individual decisions, and, consequently, the tests can be said to contribute to administrative information.

Tests used for evaluation and program improvement decisions need not be administered to every pupil, nor do all pupils need to receive the same set of test questions. What is sought is information about the instructional program; consequently, individual pupils need not be compared to one another (see the box for an example). The technique for administering different samples of test items to different pupils is known as *item sampling,* or *matrix sampling* (Lord and Novick, 1968; Sirotnik, 1970).

In program evaluation it is helpful to obtain measures of the instructional *process* as well as the *products* of instruction (i.e., of pupil achievement outcomes). Figure 1.3 suggests various kinds of instructional process constructs and variables and how they might be measured (Cooley and Lohnes, 1976; Cooley and Leinhardt, 1975). The figure also illustrates that there are many ways to measure a given variable and that several variables can be used to define a construct.

Other Uses of Tests

The six general categories of decisions outlined in the preceding pages do not exhaust all the uses of test results. Below, a few of these additional uses are discussed apart from the above scheme even though it would be possible to incorporate them into it.

One of the most obvious reasons for giving tests is to help in *assigning grades to students.* While good teaching practice and common sense indicate that scores on tests should not be the only information on which to base a student's grade, many teachers fall back on test scores to justify the grades assigned. Assigning grades involves evaluative decisions, but subjective judgments are often difficult to justify and/or articulate. Tests, especially those of the "objective" variety, give the appearance that judgmental subjectivity is

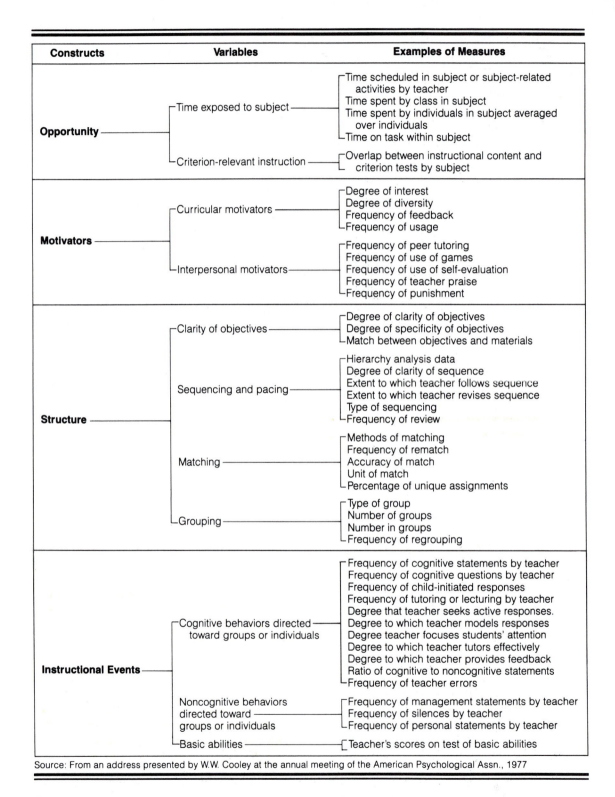

Constructs	Variables	Examples of Measures
Opportunity	Time exposed to subject	Time scheduled in subject or subject-related activities by teacher Time spent by class in subject Time spent by individuals in subject averaged over individuals Time on task within subject
	Criterion-relevant instruction	Overlap between instructional content and criterion tests by subject
Motivators	Curricular motivators	Degree of interest Degree of diversity Frequency of feedback Frequency of usage
	Interpersonal motivators	Frequency of peer tutoring Frequency of use of games Frequency of use of self-evaluation Frequency of teacher praise Frequency of punishment
Structure	Clarity of objectives	Degree of clarity of objectives Degree of specificity of objectives Match between objectives and materials
	Sequencing and pacing	Hierarchy analysis data Degree of clarity of sequence Extent to which teacher follows sequence Extent to which teacher revises sequence Type of sequencing Frequency of review
	Matching	Methods of matching Frequency of rematch Accuracy of match Unit of match Percentage of unique assignments
	Grouping	Type of group Number of groups Number in groups Frequency of regrouping
Instructional Events	Cognitive behaviors directed toward groups or individuals	Frequency of cognitive statements by teacher Frequency of cognitive questions by teacher Frequency of child-initiated responses Frequency of tutoring or lecturing by teacher Degree that teacher seeks active responses. Degree to which teacher models responses Degree teacher focuses students' attention Degree to which teacher tutors effectively Degree to which teacher provides feedback Ratio of cognitive to noncognitive statements Frequency of teacher errors
	Noncognitive behaviors directed toward groups or individuals	Frequency of management statements by teacher Frequency of silences by teacher Frequency of personal statements by teacher
	Basic abilities	Teacher's scores on test of basic abilities

Source: From an address presented by W.W. Cooley at the annual meeting of the American Psychological Assn., 1977

Figure 1 • 3 Constructs defining the instructional process, variables defining the constructs, and examples of possible ways to measure the variables.

reduced, even though this is not necessarily true. Suggestions for assigning grades are given in Chapter 13.

Tests also provide *feedback to students* about their learning. Feedback, however, is likely to improve learning only under certain conditions. Simply giving a test and reporting a score to the student is not likely to affect the student's performance, however. It is important for learners to review both correct and incorrect answers and, in addition, to be given the opportunity to correct their wrong answers.

A review of the research on feedback in programmed learning indicates that conditions both within the learner and in the instructional setting determine the effect of feedback on student learning (Kulhavy, 1977):

1. Feedback *does not facilitate learning* if the
   a. correctness of a response was known to the learner before actually responding (e.g., copying the correct answer without having mentally processed the material);
   b. material to be learned was too difficult to be comprehended by the learner so that the learner's responses were essentially guesses.
2. Feedback *does facilitate learning* when the conditions in (1) are absent if it
   a. confirms the learner's correct responses, telling him/her how well he/she understands;
   b. identifies errors and corrects them (or allows the learner to do so).

If these results can be generalized for the use of classroom tests, as they seem to be (cf. Cook, 1951), then tests can be used to provide feedback that facilitates learning, provided they are integrated into the instructional process in a way similar to the integral frames of a programmed text. The feedback the classroom test provides will not facilitate learning if the students have not had command of the prerequisite learning and/or have comprehended little or nothing of the lesson before

the test was administered. It is especially important that student errors on the test be corrected—or that students correct their own errors—before going on to new instruction for which the material tested is prerequisite. Similarly, it is important that feedback, either in the form of test results or other information, be provided frequently during the course of the lesson. Additional discussion of feedback appears in Chapter 12.

Remember that tests provide *feedback to the teacher* as well as to students—information about how well students have learned and how well the teacher has taught. Of course, if students have failed to grasp important points, material should be re-taught before proceeding to new material.

Tests also serve as *motivators* for students to study. Unfortunately, some teachers use this form of accountability as a weapon rather than a constructive force. Teachers may hope that by using a test as a possible threat, they can increase the seriousness with which their students study. Sometimes the "surprise-quiz" or "pop-quiz" is used in this manner by teachers to encourage more frequent studying and less cramming.

Employing tests this way cannot be justified on empirical grounds. Further, it would seem that tests and other forms of accountability ought to be viewed in a more positive light, for example, as roles integral to instruction and as mechanisms for feedback to students (cf. Glaser and Nitko, 1971). Also, teachers or parents stressing test performance as the sole or major criterion for school success may result in undue test anxiety for students and, consequently, poorer test performance in the long run. This point is discussed again in Chapter 12.

Tests are used frequently for purposes that have no direct or immediate application to the world of practical matters. Social scientists, generally, and psychologists, particularly, use tests to measure the variables about which they have formulated research hypotheses. Frequently, tests or test-like situations form the basis on which human behavior is observed in more or less standardized situations. Through a series of observations, hypothesis formulations, and reformulations, theories develop. Tests in this context serve as *scientific tools* that may not have a practical application to ordinary human affairs for many years.

Describing the Varieties of Tests

In the course of reading and studying about tests you will encounter many terms describing them. Table 1.4 is a partial list of such terms which appear in this section.

The Kinds of Items on Tests

The questions, exercises, and tasks appearing on a test are called *items*. A test is often described in terms of the kinds of items it con-

tains. Test items can require examinees to construct or supply their own answers, or they can offer examinees choices from among two or more pre-established alternative answers. The latter type of items are called *choice items* and include true-false items, multiple-choice items, and matching exercises. A variety of complex as well as simple behaviors can be tested with choice items. How to construct choice items is the subject of Chapters 7, 8, and 9. Sometimes choice items are referred to as *recognition items*.

A variety of items require the examinee to supply or construct a response. *Completion items* present an incomplete sentence, and the examinee is required to supply a word or short phrase that best completes the sentence. This item type is used for personality adjustment testing as well as in achievement testing (e.g., Loevinger, Wessler, and Redmore, 1970).

Sometimes the item asks a question, and the student must write a short response. In

By kind of item	By emphasis on time
Choice items (true-false, multiple choice, matching)	Power tests
Completion items	Speed tests
Short answer items	
Essay items	**By score-referencing scheme**
	Norm-referencing
	Criterion-referencing
By how observations are scored	
Objective tests	**By what attribute is measured**
Subjective tests	Achievement tests
	Survey batteries
	Specific subject tests
By degree of standardization	Aptitude tests
Standardized tests	General scholastic aptitude tests
Nonstandardized tests	Readiness tests
	Tests of specific aptitudes
	Personality and adjustment measures
By administrative conditions	Projective techniques
Individual tests	Structured tests
Group tests	Self-report questionnaires
	Interest inventories
	Vocational or career interests
By language emphasis of response	Other interest inventories
Verbal tests	Attitude and values questionnaires
Performance tests	

Table 1 • 4   A partial list of some terms used to describe and classify tests.

this type of item, the student usually is not free to give expression to creative and imaginative thoughts. With a corresponding lack of imagination, such items are called *short-answer items*. *Essay items* permit the testing of a student's ability to organize ideas and thoughts and allow for creative verbal expression. Chapter 6 gives suggestions for the construction of these varieties of constructed-response items.

Descriptions of the advantages and disadvantages of each of these types of test items come in Chapters 6 through 9. Here, however, I want to note that there is no one type of item that has marked superiority over the others. Each item type has its strengths and weaknesses which must be weighed before you select a type. Of principal importance in classroom testing is identifying the kind of performances you want to observe and then selecting the types of items that permit you to observe these performances most directly and accurately.

Objective and Subjective Tests

A test can be described in terms of its *objectivity*—the degree to which every observer of the examinee's performance will give exactly the same report on results (Cronbach, 1970). Objectivity and subjectivity thus refer to the scoring side of testing rather than to the type of test items or to the content of tests. True-false and multiple-choice tests are said to be objective because once the scoring key is set, nearly everyone who scores a student's responses arrives at the same report. But decisions concerning test content and correct answers are usually subjective. Essay tests, on the other hand, have a history of being scored differently by different persons and differently by the same persons on different occasions, thus making them even more subjective. Note, however, that objectivity is a matter of degree. Humans scoring multiple-choice tests frequently err (e.g., Phillips and Weathers, 1958), and, although less frequently, so

do scoring machines (Watkins, 1962). Too, essay tests can be made more objective by carefully controlling their scoring. (See Chapter 6.)

Degree of Standardization

Standardization can improve the objectivity of tests. *Standardization* refers to the degree to which the observational procedures, administrative procedures, equipment and materials, and scoring rules have been fixed so that exactly the same testing procedure occurs at different times and places (Cronbach, 1970).

This use of "standardized" is not followed by all testing and measurement specialists. Some tests are accompanied by norms showing how a representative sample of persons scored on them. Such tests are sometimes called standardized, and test publishers frequently refer to the process of collecting this norm-referenced information as the "standardization phase" of test development. Some educators and test specialists refer to nearly all commercially available tests as "standardized tests."

In this book, I will follow Cronbach's (1970) emphasis on the standardization of the testing procedure. A test can have norm-data, for example, and still fail to specify sufficiently its procedures, materials, and scoring. If so, then the observations and scores are not comparable from place to place, tester to tester, or from time to time. Exactly what the test results mean is open to question when this occurs. Suppose that the directions for administering and scoring an achievement test, for example, fail to tell students whether they should guess and/or whether the scores will be "adjusted" for guessing. If you tell your students they should guess when they are uncertain, your group will be at an advantage, because lucky guesses tend to raise scores. On the other hand, suppose I tell my class to avoid guessing on those questions about which they are uncertain. As a consequence, some members of my class will be at a disadvantage. Some pupils will guess regardless of instructions and, since there is no penalty, their lucky guesses will bias their scores. Others, perhaps more cautious, acquiescent, or timid, will not guess; they will not benefit from possible lucky guesses. Now, if norms are provided, what do they mean? Are higher scoring persons those (1) who know more, or (2) who know more *and* are lucky guessers, or (3) who know less *but* are exceptionally lucky guessers? Standardization is essential for tests designed to yield comparable results from time to time and from place to place.

But standardization is an ideal, and so we speak of *degree of standardization*. Even if all directions are specified and production of test materials is quality-controlled, no two situations can be identical. Examiners vary in personality and rapport; environmental and social conditions change. Many individually administered tests require the examiner to judge the quality of the examinee's responses, and no matter how well these quality-judging scoring rules are described, the examiner needs to exercise professional judgment. As a consequence, teachers and other test administrators need to keep in mind that they should use their professional judgment when interpreting the test results their pupils attain.

Individual and Group Tests

Tests may be administered to one person at a time or simultaneously to a group of persons. Some tests are especially designed to be administered to one person at a time. These *individual tests* allow the maximum amount of interaction between the examiner and the examinee and are rich in opportunities for clinical observation. The examiner can observe not only an examinee's approach to and performance on the examination tasks but sometimes also can ask questions that follow up on an examinee's response to clarify it and to understand it more completely. An individual test offers the opportunity to establish rapport with the examinee permitting the test administrator a more personalized and perhaps more optimal set of testing conditions.

Providing individual attention and personalized testing conditions requires special facilities (such as a private testing room), time, and money. It may require, for example, an hour or more to obtain an assessment of each examinee's general mental ability, a costly procedure.

Group tests sacrifice rapport, personalized testing conditions, and clinical observation for increased efficiency and reduced cost. In the same time it takes to administer and score an individual test, an entire class can be tested. Where large groups need testing, where finances are tight, and where only coarse information is required, group testing becomes a more attractive option. Frequently, tests originated as group tests can be administered individually; the converse is seldom possible.

Verbal and Performance Tests

Some tests call for observing the verbal responses of examinees: for example, how well they can define words, write answers to questions, and/or define similarities or differences between concepts. These tests are called *verbal tests*. Most school tests are verbal since schools emphasize verbal attributes.

Other tests are designed to elicit and observe nonverbal responses: assembling objects, completing puzzles, psychomotor activities, and so on. These are called *performance tests*. Mental processing sometimes may be inferred from how well a student can copy geometric designs or assemble a puzzle. Figure 1.4 shows one performance item from a test designed to assess children's motor function.

Although performance tests emphasize nonverbal responses, verbal ability or language ability are definitely not irrelevant to success on these tests. Directions to examinees are usually oral, requiring examinees to carry a large aural-verbal load. Also, verbal

Touching Thumb to Fingertips – Eyes Closed

With eyes closed, the subject touches the thumb of the preferred hand to each of the fingertips on the preferred hand, moving from the little finger to the index finger and then from the index finger to the little finger, as shown in the figure below. The subject is given 90 seconds to complete the task once. The score is recorded as a pass or a fail.

Trials: 1

1   2   3   4

Touching thumb to fingertips – eyes closed

Administering and Recording

Have the subject sit beside you at a table. Have the subject extend the preferred arm. Then say: **You are to touch your thumb to each of the fingertips on this hand. Start with your little finger and touch each fingertip in order. Then start with your first finger and touch each fingertip again as you move your thumb back to your little finger** (demonstrate). **Do this with your eyes closed until I tell you to stop. Ready, begin.**

Source: Bruininks (1978, p. 84)

Figure 1 • 4   Example of a performance item designed to assess certain fine motor movements of the hand. Notice the verbal directions. Would verbal mediation (e.g., counting to oneself) help a child to perform better on this item?

mediation may facilitate learning and performing skills (Adams, 1971; Boucher, 1974). However, it is possible to administer tests through gesturing and pantomime to reduce the amount of verbal language comprehension required by the examinee.

Speed and Power Tests

Quite frequently the main focus in testing students is to assess the amount of knowledge, comprehension, or understanding they possess. Often there is less concern about the rapidity of a student's responses to questions than about the content of those responses. Accordingly, time limits on such tests are very generous (sometimes nearly unlimited), allowing all students enough time to consider each question and attempt to answer it. These tests are called *power tests.*

In contrast, sometimes it is not the contents of students' responses that are of prime interest. Rather, it is the speed with which they perform tasks or answer questions. Such tests are called *speed tests.*

When the focus of a test is to measure speed of performance, it is important that the test be designed in such a way that score interpretation does not confound rapidity of performance with difficulty of the task. For this reason, speed tests contain questions or tasks that are relatively easy. People score differently on speed tests, not because the items are hard, but because individuals complete the tasks at different speeds.

The purpose of testing may change over

the course of instruction, even though the items on the test remain essentially the same. Early in the course of learning, emphasis is usually not on speed of performance. Speed of performance frequently becomes important after students have mastered tasks. Learning addition facts in first grade is an example. At first, students are permitted to use their fingers and toes and other "maniputables" when being quizzed. Eventually, speed of response becomes important: A student is marked on the number of addition facts correctly answered within a fixed time limit (or, alternately, the time it takes to complete a fixed number of facts). If the time limits were removed, then practically every pupil would get all the facts correct. Similar speed vs. power concerns appear in the learning of other academic skills such as reading where, initially, overt and slow phonetic blending is permitted; later, speed of response (i.e., automatic decoding of words) counts more.

For many children, tests are a mixture of speed and power, even when the test developer intends only power. Such tests are called *partially speeded tests*. When constructing tests, the teacher will have to check the time limits carefully to be sure that all students have the opportunity to consider each test question before the time is up.

Norm-Referenced and Criterion-Referenced Tests

Chapters 14 and 17 point out that the "number right" score one obtains from a test is not very meaningful in and of itself. This score needs to be referenced to something outside the test in order to interpret this score. For example, if I told you that my spelling test score was 49, what would this mean? What kinds of words could I spell? Am I a better speller than you?

Two kinds of score referencing schemes are prominent today, although these don't exhaust all of the possibilities: One is called *norm-referencing*, the other *criterion-referencing*.

Both schemes often proceed by using a new type of score *derived from* the original "number right" score on the test. The derived scores are developed to reflect additional "outside" information in a more direct way than the original number right score. If the derived score reflects the position of an examinee in a group which took the test, then it is called a norm-referenced score. Percentile ranks, grade-equivalent scores, and standard scores are examples of norm-referenced scores. Because these types of scores are used so extensively in education and psychology, Chapter 14 explains them in detail.

For some tests it is possible to develop a score that describes the performance repertoire of an examinee—the kinds of tasks an examinee with that score is able to do. Such tests are called criterion-referenced tests. It is not always possible to develop criterion-referencing schemes for tests, but it is always possible to develop norm-referencing schemes. A special kind of criterion-referencing scoring scheme is shown in Figure 1.5. This figure illustrates that sometimes it is possible to reference persons' number right scores (called "raw scores" in this figure) in both ways. The many kinds of criterion-referencing schemes are described in Chapter 17, and examples of criterion-referenced and norm-referenced achievement tests are presented in Chapter 19.

Related to criterion-referenced testing are a number of procedures such as domain-referenced tests, objectives-based tests, content-referenced tests, and mastery tests. Chapter 17 deals with the distinctions among these.

Attributes that are Measured

Tests are designed to observe and measure a variety of human attributes. Among them are academic achievement (described in Chapter 19); a variety of general scholastic and special aptitudes (Chapters 20 and 21); and personality, interests, and attitudes (Chapter 22).

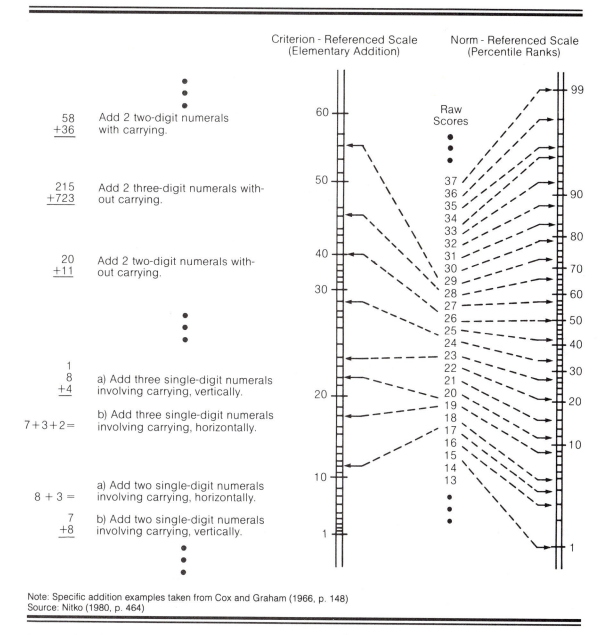

Criterion - Referenced Scale
(Elementary Addition)

Norm - Referenced Scale
(Percentile Ranks)

$\begin{array}{r} 58 \\ +36 \\ \hline \end{array}$ Add 2 two-digit numerals with carrying.

$\begin{array}{r} 215 \\ +723 \\ \hline \end{array}$ Add 2 three-digit numerals without carrying.

$\begin{array}{r} 20 \\ +11 \\ \hline \end{array}$ Add 2 two-digit numerals without carrying.

$\begin{array}{r} 1 \\ 8 \\ +4 \\ \hline \end{array}$ a) Add three single-digit numerals involving carrying, vertically.

$7+3+2=$ b) Add three single-digit numerals involving carrying, horizontally.

$8 + 3 =$ a) Add two single-digit numerals involving carrying, horizontally.

$\begin{array}{r} 7 \\ +8 \\ \hline \end{array}$ b) Add two single-digit numerals involving carrying, vertically.

Note: Specific addition examples taken from Cox and Graham (1966, p. 148)
Source: Nitko (1980, p. 464)

Figure 1 • 5   Hypothetical example of two ways to reference test scores: Criterion-referencing and norm-referencing.

Although Chapters 19 through 22 respectively will explain these more fully, I will describe a few points here.

Academic achievement tests attempt to measure the knowledge, abilities, and skills that are the focus of direct instruction in schools. *Scholastic aptitude tests* and *specific aptitude tests* reflect learned behavior also. A considerable

	Achievement Tests	Scholastic Aptitude Tests	Interest Tests	Specialized Aptitude Tests
Examples	Reading Arithmetic Language	School ability Readiness I.Q.	Vocational inventories Preference tests	Clerical Mechanical Space relations Mathematics
Contents	Typical problems from basic skill areas; measure ability to transfer or apply skills learned in schools	Variety of verbal reasoning and numerical reasoning problems; measure abilities required in most school courses	Lists of activities related to a variety of occupations; students indicate preferences—e.g., outdoor, persuasive, scientific, and so forth	Reasoning and skill problems in specific skill areas judged to be critical to success in various occupations
Kinds of Scores	Grade equivalents percentiles (based on national samples of students)	Percentiles I.Q.s (based on national samples of students)	Percentiles or other ranks (based on samples of students or samples of persons in occupations)	Percentiles (based on samples of students)

Source: Larsen (1974, p. 5)

Figure 1 • 6 Tests are used to measure a variety of human attributes. These are a few examples.

debate can be waged over the issue of whether achievement and aptitude are distinct (Chapter 20). One, but not the only, distinguishing feature of the *tests*, however, is that the adequacy of the items on many scholastic aptitude tests is judged by the tests' ability to predict the academic accomplishments of students in a particular instructional setting.

Still other human attributes tested are the nonacademic or affective. In psychological testing, the procedures for testing such attributes as emotional adjustment, interpersonal relations, motivation, interests, and attitudes are called *personality tests* (Anastasi, 1976). Examples of the kinds of variables tested by adherents to different personality theories or modes are given in Table 1.5.

Related to and subsumed under personality attributes are three overlapping categories: *interests, attitudes,* and *values.* These are often measured by questionnaires asking for the examinee's degree of agreement with various statements. It is sometimes useful to distinguish them in the following way (Nunnally, 1967, pp. 514–515):

Interests are preferences for particular activities. . . . [Example of statement on questionnaire:] *I would rather repair a clock than write a letter.*[6]

Values concern preferences for "life goals" and "ways of life," in contrast to interests, which concern preferences for particular activities. . . . [Example of statement on questionnaire:] *I consider it more important to have people respect me than to like me.*

Attitudes concern feelings about particular social objects—physical objects, types of people, particular persons, social institutions, government policies, and others. . . . [Example of statement on questionnaire:] *The United Nations is a constructive force in the world today.*

[6]Italics added.

Model	Typical Dimension	Typical Instrument
Psychoanalytic	Ego synthesis	Rorschach
Interpersonal	Docility	Interpersonal Check List
Transactionai	Need achievement	Activities Index
Cognitive	Cognitive complexity	Role-Construct Repertory Test
Multivariate	Cyclothymia	16 Personality Factor Questionnaire
Social learning	Behavioral competence	Survey of Problematic Situations

Source: From J. S. Wiggins, *Personality and Prediction*, Table 10.3, p. 460. Copyright © 1973 by Addison-Wesley Publishing Co. Reprinted with permission.

Table 1 • 5   Examples of instruments employed in assessing target dimensions under different personality models.

Summary

The following statements summarize the main points of this chapter.

1. Tests and measurements provide information to teachers, administrators, parents, pupils, and others about a number of human characteristics. Decisions in the practical world are made using tests along with other information; different decisions can be made on the basis of the same information.

2. Distinctions can be made between measurement, tests, and evaluation:

   a. *Measurement* is a procedure for assigning numbers to specified attributes or characteristics of persons in a manner that maintains the real world relationships among persons with regard to what is being measured.

   b. *Tests* are systematic procedures for observing persons and describing them with either a numerical scale or a category system. Thus, tests may give either qualitative or quantitative information.

   c. *Evaluation* involves judging the value or worth of a pupil, of an instructional method, or of an educational program. Such judgments may or may not be based on information obtained from tests.

   i. *Formative program evaluation* judges the worth of a program while it is under development, so that the program can be redesigned, refined, or improved.

   ii. *Summative evaluation* focuses on the outcomes of an already developed program and judges the value of the program in attaining its goals and objectives.

3. Tests are used regularly in relation to a number of classes of decisions:

   a. *Selection decisions* are made when it is necessary to accept some persons and reject others. Those rejected are no longer the concern of the institution or organization.

   b. *Placement decisions* involve assigning all persons to different levels of the same type of instruction or work. The institution or organization must account for all persons; unconcerned rejection is not possible.

c. *Classification decisions* involve the assignment of persons to one of several categories, jobs, or programs that are not necessarily thought of as levels of work or instruction.

d. *Career counseling and guidance decisions* are made by individuals as they explore possible careers and the world of work. These are *individual decisions* as contrasted with *institutional decisions.*

e. *Educational diagnostic and remediation decisions* relate to the question, "What learning activities will best adapt to this student's individual requirements and thereby maximize the student's opportunities to attain chosen goals?" Diagnosis implies that both the content and the nature of the instruction the student will receive are known.

f. *Program improvement and evaluation decisions* are often improved by the use of test information. It is frequently helpful to measure the instructional *process* as well as the outcomes or *products* of instruction.

g. Tests serve other purposes, such as: (a) providing information for *grading students,* (b) giving *feedback to students* to facilitate learning, (c) providing *feedback about the effectiveness of teaching,* (d) *motivating students to study,* and (e) serving as *scientific tools* in research in education and the social sciences.

4. Tests can be described in a variety of ways:

a. *Group and individual tests* differ in the number of persons to whom they are simultaneously administered as well as in the manner of their administration. Group tests sacrifice maximum examinee-examiner interaction, personalized testing conditions, and fertile clinical observations for cost and efficiency.

b. Tests differ in their objectivity—the extent to which every observer of the examinee's performance on the test will give exactly the same report of what was observed. The scoring of a test is *subjective* if the report of the observed performance varies a great deal from one observer to the next.

c. *Standardization* is the extent to which a test's observational procedures, equipment and materials, and scoring rules are pre-established so that exactly the same testing procedure can be followed at different times and in different places. This view of standardization has nothing to do with whether norm-referenced data are provided. It provides a way to improve a test's objectivity and the interpretation of the examinee's performance on the test.

d. *Verbal tests* focus on the verbal responses of examinees, while *performance tests* focus on nonverbal responses. Verbal ability may be necessary to understand the directions on performance tests and to mediate the nonverbal responses.

e. If a test is designed to measure *speed* of responding, then the items are generally not difficult under unspeeded conditions. Many tests are concerned with assessing the amount of knowledge or understanding an individual possesses, independent of speed, and testing conditions are essentially untimed. Such tests are called *power tests.* Many tests in education are *partially speeded;* often this is unknown to both the examinee and examiner.

f. *Norm-referenced tests* describe the examinee by stating where an examinee is located in a specified group of persons. *Criterion-referenced tests* describe the performance repertoire of an examinee, independent of group membership—the kinds of things an examinee with that score can do.

g. The questions on a test are called *items,* and a test can be described in terms of the types of items it contains. There are *choice items:* true-false, multiple-choice, and matching exercises. There are also *supply items:* completion, short answer, and essay. No item type has a uniformly distinct advantage under all circumstances.

h. Tests are described also in terms of the attributes they are designed to observe. Among these attributes are academic achievements; scholastic—and other—aptitudes; personality traits; and interests, attitudes, and values.

Themes

● Educators should be aware of ethical issues when they use tests for making educational decisions.

● Before deciding to use a test for a particular purpose, educators should carefully weigh both positive and negative consequences of such testing.

● Guidelines exist to help teachers and other school personnel use tests professionally and responsibly.

● Some criticisms of testing can be viewed as objections to using tests for purposes of social control.

● Almost any aspect of test development and use can be the basis for litigation. Educators should be aware of this when they plan testing programs and decisions.

● Tests can be criticized in many ways for being unfair and/or biased. Awareness of these ways can inform and improve professional test use.

Terms and Concepts

test security
truth-in-testing legislation
right to access school records
right to privacy (and confidentiality)
right to parent involvement
right to be tested fairly
consent (informed, presumed, implied, proxy)
construct interpretations
values implied in test use
evidence of practical usefulness of tests
social consequences of testing
APA *Standards*
APGA guidelines for test users

social control mechanisms (authoritarian vs. internalized)
social norms
liberal, progressive viewpoint
revisionist viewpoint
psychometric basis for litigation
nonpsychometric issues litigated
Uniform Guidelines
Aspects of test bias (mean differences, misinterpretations, invalid prediction, facial bias, experience differential, selection bias, wrong criterion, conditions of testing)

2

SOCIAL, LEGAL, AND ETHICAL ISSUES IN TESTING

This chapter summarizes much of what this book presents about the use and interpretation of test results from the perspective of social, legal, and ethical concerns. Although testing is recognized as being a useful tool, test usage may have both positive and negative consequences.

The first section discusses several facets of testing which involve ethics: secrecy and test security, violation of an individual's privacy, confidentiality of information, informed consent, and the validity of interpretations one applies to scores from particular tests. The section presents the ideal situation in which decisions to use a test for a particular purpose are made after the test user has identified (a) anticipated positive and negative consequences of use, (b) the likelihood of occurrence of these consequences, and (c) the subjective values attached to each consequence.

The second section identifies various ethical standards and guidelines for interpretation which various professional organizations have authorized. Many decisions in which persons' test scores play a part may be characterized as social control decisions. Frequently criticisms of tests can relate to the desirability of using tests as instruments of social control.

The third section discusses the role of tests in such social control decisions and illustrates how two different interpretations of history can lead to two radically different characterizations of tests and testers. Of special concern in this section is the role of testing in maintaining the superiority of one group over another.

The fourth section focuses on legal aspects of testing, especially testing programs which have the potential to limit the access of individuals to full participation in society: minimum competency tests, employment selection tests, and educational admissions tests. The various psychometric and nonpsychometric issues plaintiffs attack in legal proceedings, conflicting legal opinions of the courts, and legal guidelines for personnel selection are among the matters discussed. The final section discusses various ways in which tests can be biased toward women and minorities. Each of these constitutes different definitions of test bias.

Ethical Issues in Test Use

Secrecy and Access

Secrecy and *test security* have long been the hallmarks of the testing industry, beginning in the late 1920s and early 1930s when large-scale abuse of testing abounded. Withholding test information—either about the items on a test or the exact score(s) an examinee attained—often was justified on the grounds that release of this information would do more harm than good. For example: (a) An examinee might attempt to memorize only specific answers ("a" or "b") rather than focusing on mastery of the general skills the test was designed to measure; this behavior would distort the measurement of knowledge and ability. (b) Certain tests which measure highly sensitive and personal characteristics require a high degree of professional training in order to interpret the scores; examinees lacking this training might cause themselves harm by misinterpreting the results. (c) Releasing test items might result in their being used by unqualified examiners who would misinterpret scores causing examinees harm. (d) Releasing copies of old forms of a test might require the test developer to spend unreasonable sums of money to develop new forms, assuming that new forms of the test could, in fact, be developed.

In recent years, however, the public has become aware that some test abuses have resulted from such secrecy. For example: (a) Professionals themselves vary in qualifications and have, in fact, misinterpreted tests or abused results. (b) Decisions made about educational placement, ostensibly on the basis of valid and objective test results, have later been discovered to be biased, misinterpreted, or otherwise invalid. (c) Errors in scoring occurred which could not be detected because the tests could not be scrutinized by those having the greatest stake in their accuracy—the examinees. (d) Although some tests publicly were declared to measure learned skills and abilities, examinees were unable to check their content to decide whether their preparation had been adequate or whether they should seek special remediation or training. (e) Although professionals may have interpreted test results properly, test records were often open to other persons who used the results either unprofessionally or in a manner unauthorized by and detrimental to the examinee.

Problems such as these have spawned a renewed public interest in the ethics of secrecy and the right of examinees to know. There have been a number of state and federal legislative bills proposed as "sunshine" or *"truth-in-testing,"* especially in relation to tests used in the "gatekeeping" context of admission and certification. The first state law on truth-in-testing was passed in 1979 in New York. It required test publishers to disclose admissions test items, the answer key, and a copy of the examinee's answer sheet upon request. The law was amended subsequently to exempt some low volume tests. The immediate response of some national testing programs was to curtail some testing in New York. Federal legislation (H.R. 3564 and H.R. 4949) was proposed in 1980, but has not been enacted at this writing. An interesting outcome of the release of hitherto secure forms of the *Preliminary Scholastic Aptitude Test* (PSAT) and the *Scholastic Aptitude Test* (SAT) follows in Box 2.1 Experienced teachers know that students frequently choose non-keyed answers to test questions based on reasoning which is valid but was unanticipated when the test was constructed. But for the media, these events take on a "man bites dog" character, and stories of examinees discovering errors on tests make national newspaper headlines.

Parents' and Children's Rights in School Testing

Your state and school district are likely to have policies and procedures related to statutory matters of rights of students' and parents' access to school records (including test results) and the need for them to participate with educators in making educational decisions. Three federal laws covering these matters, which apply to school districts receiving federal education funds, are: The Family Education Rights and Privacy Act of 1974 (Public Law 93-380), The Education of All Handicapped Children Act of 1975 (Public Law 94-142), and the Handicapped Rehabilitation Act of 1973. Table 2.1 summarizes some of the pupil and parental rights under these laws. While perhaps there is no legal requirement to do so, professional ethics may suggest that some of the principles underlying the rights summarized in Table 2.1 can apply to classroom testing practices.

Privacy, Confidentiality, and the Teacher

Two important questions are whether it is unethical to obtain certain information from a pupil, and does a pupil have the right to expect that certain information be held in confidence. Privacy and confidentiality affect the teacher in several ways. In the classroom itself,

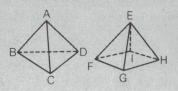

In pyramids ABCD and EFGHI shown above, all faces except base FGHI are equilateral triangles of equal size. If face ABC were placed on face EFG so that the vertices of the triangles coincide, how many exposed faces would the resulting solid have?

(A) Five (B) Six (C) Seven
(D) Eight (E) Nine

MICHAEL GALLIGAN marked (B) as the answer to this SAT question which was the correct answer as originally scored by ETS. But Galligan noted that (C) could also be counted as correct because 8 is the cube of 2 and 4 is the square of minus 2, which is by definition a different integer.

Row A	7	2	5	4	6
Row B	3	8	6	9	7
Row C	5	4	3	8	2
Row D	9	5	7	3	6
Row E	5	6	3	7	4

Which row in the list above contains both the square of an integer and the cube of a *different* integer?

(A) Row A (B) Row B (C) Row C
(D) Row D (E) Row E

DANIEL LOWEN marked (A) as the answer to this PSAT/NMSQT question. When the test was originally scored, (C) was counted as the correct answer. But depending on whether the faces considered in the question are those of the original two solids or those of the combined solid, both choices (A) and (C) can be considered correct.

Box 2 • 1

for example, teachers sometimes keep charts or post pupils' progress. Such a public display may or may not be in the form of grades. This practice raises the question of whether such evaluations should be confidential. Another example is the practice of keeping scores, grades, and anecdotal comments in a pupil's records. Ethical questions arise about who has authorized access to these files. Teachers and certain other persons have legitimate rights to obtain necessary information from them to help in teaching a given pupil. Many schools have forms or other means by which records can be kept on who has used a pupil's records and for what purposes. Usually a pupil's test scores and other records cannot be transferred to another institution without that student's

(parents') authorization. Wagging tongues in teachers' lounges are still another way violations of confidentiality can occur.

Another issue is the purging of files and other student records of outdated and/or erroneous information. Certainly, if a teacher gives an incorrect grade, the affected pupil's record should be corrected. Sometimes the teacher (or others) will score a standardized test incorrectly, discovering this fact after the information has been entered on the record. This will necessitate changing the record also. Information such as teachers' anecdotal records should be purged when they are no longer necessary (usually within a year or two). Some schools have policies relating to the systematic purging of pupil records. Others may depend

Table 2 • 1   Some pupil and parent rights in relation to testing and school records as mandated by Federal legislation.

on the pupil's parents to come in and periodically review the records for unnecessary, damaging, or erroneous information.

Still another point concerns the use of pupil records for research. Usually, obtaining test scores for research purposes is not considered a violation of privacy provided the identity of the pupil remains anonymous. The Department of Health and Human Services (HHS) issued revised regulations early in 1981 for protecting the welfare of human subjects in research projects funded by HHS. Although teachers are not expected to be researchers, they should be sensitive to ethical principles of privacy and confidentiality because they (a)

may collect data to use on their research projects for graduate courses and degrees and (b) may have to be protective of the rights of pupils under their care when requests from others (within and outside the school) are made for pupil information.

The following conditions may constitute a violation of the right to privacy (adapted from Miller, 1968; Prosser, 1960): (a) intrusion on physical solitude; (b) publication of private matters involving ordinary decencies; (c) creation of a false public image of . . . [the research subject]; and (d) appropriation of some element of individual information for . . . [purposes other than research] (e.g., commercial, judicial, or personal application of the data without respondent's permission) (Boruch, 1971, p. 413).

Consent

Privacy is not violated if persons give consent to others to obtain and use personal information. Without going into a detailed ethical analysis of the matter, we shall state that there are at least four levels of consent (McCormick, 1974; O'Donnell, 1974): informed consent, presumed consent, implied consent, and proxy consent. *Informed consent* is obtained directly from the pupil and presumes that the pupil in giving that consent has received and understands the following information (Boruch, 1971): (a) the exact nature and extent to which personal information will remain anonymous, (b) to what extent participation is voluntary rather than required, (c) who (or what agency) is requesting the information and for what purpose will it be used, and (d) what will happen to the information after it is collected (including whether and/or when it will be destroyed). Obviously, not very many young pupils will be able to understand the implications of all of this information, so their consent may not be truly informed. Often consent must come from a *proxy*, such as a parent or a school official. The extent to which school officials can grant permission for collecting and using pupil information will depend, among other things, on the degree to which such consent is *presumed* or *implied* by the fact that pupils are entrusted to their care.

Consider the Evidence for and Consequences of Test Use

The ethical use of tests places a demand on the teacher (or other users) to understand (a) what the test measures, (b) the factors affecting test performance, and (c) how to interpret test results. Table 2.2 lists some guidelines for score interpretation which professional test-ing associations have published in the *Standards for Educational and Psychological Tests* (APA, 1974).

The test users' ethical responsibility is to see that the specific uses and interpretations of the test are valid and involves not only checking to see whether evidence for that particular use and interpretation exists, but also knowing—or anticipating—the consequences. Among the questions to consider for ethical use and interpretation are these (Messick, 1979):

1. **Construct interpretations** To what extent is there empirical and logical evidence to support the interpretation of test scores as reflecting a particular degree of or status on a construct?[1] If the test scores of an examinee are interpreted as a reflection of that examinee's "understanding of scientific principles," for example, what evidence exists that alternative explanations or counter-interpretations (e.g., sex bias, speed of responding, reading comprehension skills, hearing loss, muscular fatigue, etc.) are either more appropriate interpretations or modify the intended interpretations? This matter is discussed in more detail under "construct validation" in Chapter 16.

2. **Values implied** What is the value system within which you are interpreting the test results? If you value reading skills over scientific knowledge or mathematics skills, does your bias influence the way you interpret the scores or report them to parents and pupils? Do your own value system and personal bias influence the way you interpret a school aptitude test score? Do your values for neatness, obedience, and/or conformity result in your being pedantic or vindictive and cause you to

---

[1]In a general sense, *constructs* are categories, terms, or phrases used to represent ideas, experiences, or observations within a particular logical framework. In testing, educators frequently use such constructs as verbal ability, quantitative reasoning, spelling ability, reading comprehension, and self-concept.

I. Administration and scoring

I1. A test user is expected to follow carefully the standardized procedures described in the manual for administering a test. Essential.

I2. The test administrator is responsible for establishing conditions, consistent with the principle of standardization, that enable each examinee to do his best. Essential.

I3. A test user is responsible for accuracy in scoring, checking, coding, or recording test results. Essential.

I4. If specific cutting scores are to be used as a basis for decisions, a test user should have a rationale, justification, or explanation of the cutting scores adopted. Essential.

I5. The test user shares with the test developer or distributor a responsibility for maintaining test security. Essential.

J. Interpretation of scores

J1. A test score should be interpreted as an estimate of performance under a given set of circumstances. It should not be interpreted as some absolute characteristic of the examinee or as something permanent and generalizable to all other circumstances. Essential.

J2. Test scores should ordinarily be reported only to people who are qualified to interpret them. If scores are reported, they should be accompanied by explanations sufficient for the recipient to interpret them correctly.

J3. The test user should recognize that estimates of reliability do not indicate criterion-related validity. Essential.

J4. A test user should examine carefully the rationale and validity of computer-based interpretations of test scores. Essential.

J5. In norm-referenced interpretations, a test user should interpret an obtained score with reference to sets of norms appropriate for the individual tested and for the intended use. Essential.

J6. Any content-referenced interpretation should clearly indicate the domain to which one can generalize. Essential.

J7. The test user should consider alternative interpretations of a given score. Essential.

J8. The test user should be able to interpret test performance relative to other measures. Very desirable.

J9. A test user should develop procedures for systematically eliminating from data files test-score information that has, because of the lapse of time, become obsolete. Essential.

Source: *Standards for Educational and Psychological Tests*, 1974. Courtesy of the APA.

Table 2 • 2 Standards for administration, scoring, interpretation, and reporting of test scores.

deduct points on a classroom test because students don't conform to your idiosyncracies, rather than because they lack the knowledge being tested?

3. Practical usefulness What evidence exists to support or validate the particular way you use the test to make decisions? If you use last spring's scores on a standardized spelling test, for example, to decide this fall whether a pupil should get a 15 word per week or a 50 word per week spelling assignment, what empirical evidence supports your contention that the pupils will learn to spell better by using the test this way? What evidence exists to support using a reading readiness test to group pupils for reading instruction? What evidence supports your claim that this criterion for grouping helps pupils to read better than another kind of testing for group placement?

4. Social consequences What are the intended *and* unintended consequences of using (or not using) test scores in a particular way? Although difficult to accomplish, ethical considerations would lead to attempts to enumerate the potential positive and negative consequences of using a particular test, not only in the classroom, but at each level of the educational enterprise (Cole, 1977): The intention might be, for example, for a teacher to use test scores to improve a child's skills, but the teacher may give up on a child with low scores; a school board may use scores to fund school programs; a parent may use scores to discourage or encourage a child's future aspirations; a child's self-judgment may be positively or negatively affected by the results of a test.

A complete analysis of consequences would involve such things as (a) listing intended purposes or uses of the test, (b) listing anticipated positive and negative consequences or outcomes, (c) gathering evidence supporting the likelihood of each consequence if the test is used, (d) associating with each consequence the desirability or value of that consequence occurring, and (e) combining all this information to make a decision about whether to use the test for each intended purpose (Cole, 1977). It is unlikely, to be sure, that a single examiner would be able to conduct such an elaborate evidential and consequential analysis, because (a) it would require the competence and knowledge of several persons and (b) each individual working within a particular framework of values would be unlikely to think of all the potential positive and negative consequences of using a particular test.

Guidelines for Test Uses

Throughout this book I will discuss specific professional and ethical standards along with specific testing practices and technical matters. Indeed, the point of understanding the technical side of testing is that it leads to an understanding of both the strengths and weaknesses of testing. Considerable practical social benefit can come from the appropriate use of tests in schools. Not all usage of tests is appropriate, however, and intended social benefit will not occur from inappropriate use. Teachers play a significant role in test interpretation and use, both through the assessment and evaluation procedures they develop themselves and through their use and interpretation of published tests. There is every indication that the overwhelming majority of

professional teachers can and do conduct themselves properly in these matters.

Several guidelines for test use and interpretation exist which spell out concisely what to expect of both those who develop and promulgate tests and those who use them. The *Uniform Guidelines on Employee Selection Procedures* (EEOC, 1978) set standards for avoiding bias in personnel decisions. The *Guidelines for Assessment of Sex Bias and Sex Fairness in Career Interest Inventories* (Diamond, 1975) help in the development and interpretation of career interest inventories. I have already referred to the *Standards for Educational and Psychological Tests* (APA, 1974; see also Brown, 1980) in this chapter. The American Psychological Association's (1977) *Ethical Standards of Psychologists* contain several sections providing guidelines for test interpretation, privacy, and confidentiality. Other professionally established standards related to test use and interpretation include: *Principles for the Validation and Use of Personnel Selection Procedures* (Division of Industrial and Organizational Psychology, 1975), *Standards and Ethical Considerations for Assessment Center Operations* (Task Force on Assessment Center Standards, 1978), *Ethical Behavior in Early Childhood Education* (Katz & Ward, 1978), and *Responsibilities of Users of Standardized Tests* (APGA, 1980).

Issues of Social Control

There are several ways to characterize the debate surrounding the use of tests. One views some criticisms of tests as stemming from basic concerns of social control. Society sanctions some types of social control. The accountability of the schools to the public which supports them provides an example as do limited access to certain jobs or certain levels of education. Methods of social control which obviously suppress the rights of individuals or groups generally are not sanctioned, and have become the focus of criticism.

Social Control Mechanisms

Sociologists view social control as authoritarian and/or internalized. *Authoritarian control mechanisms* are constraints which forces external to the individual openly impose. They are seen as generally less desirable means of control than those means which result in individuals *internalizing* certain social norms, voluntarily conforming to social norms out of a sense of social order and obligation to fellow human beings. The idea is for individuals to subordinate some personal needs and desires so that the "greater good" can prevail.

The objectives of social control are frequently linked to preserving the values and status quo of a dominant group. Social control procedures directed toward attaining these objectives often center on an appeal to rationality, logic, and science. Appeals to these attributes or states increase the likelihood that individuals will accept and, therefore, internalize the objectives of the agents of social control. Part of this internalization includes an acceptance by the individuals of their social role in relation to those objectives.

A particular social control mechanism is open to criticism in proportion to the extent to which those being controlled perceive it as irrational, capricious, arbitrary, or unjust. When this perception occurs, decisions are viewed as invalid and too subjective. One way to increase at least the appearance—if not the fact—of the objectivity and the validity of social control decisions is to base the decisions on reliable and valid information (i.e., "data"). Quantifiable information is more likely to be accepted as reliable and scientifically valid than qualitative information.

Tests as Social Control Mechanisms

Developers of standardized educational and psychological tests claim these standardized tests are both objective and scientifically valid in certain (often specific) decision contexts. It is not surprising, therefore, that authorities have come to use tests as mechanisms of social control. If a decision-maker can point to the results of an objective and valid test as the information on which a control decision was based, those being controlled are more likely to accept and internalize the decision and its consequences. Thus, rather than accepting teachers' judgments as to the competence of high school seniors, school boards and school authorities seek the results of a more objective, minimum competency test on which to base graduation decisions. Similarly, tests aid administrators in making decisions about which teachers in the applicant pool possess some minimum level of knowledge about the subject matter and the pupils they propose to teach, which applicants for a machinist job possess the necessary skills related to success on that job, which candidates have sufficient command of verbal and mathematical skills to succeed in college, or which career fields a youngster might explore.

Two Interpretations of Social Forces

An individual's view of the justice of using tests for social control depends on that person's perspective of past and present social forces. A *liberal, progressive view* leads to a belief that (a) authorities can adjust social institutions to approach the American ideal, (b) intelligent use of science and technology enhances this progress and ultimately makes life better, and (c) a meritocracy with the help of professional experts will guide government and corporate powers in order to improve the human condition (Karier, Violas, & Spring, 1973). This social view has tended to dominate the perspective of the testing profession in the past.

While it is true that there was a natural affinity between their ideas and a hierarchically organized, differentiated society, testers worked with the social structure, not for it. What distorted their public remarks was chiefly their conviction that they were right. It was so obviously cruel and inefficient to instruct everyone in the same things at the same pace, and so obvious that systematic measurement was providing better information for teachers, that the testers of the 1920s could conceive of no risk or error save that of failure to take the tests seriously. The spokesmen for tests, then and recently, were convinced that they were improving social efficiency, not making choices about social philosophy. Their soberly interpreted research did place test interpretation on a more substantial basis. But they did not study the consequences of testing for the social structure—a sociological problem that psychologists do not readily perceive (Cronbach, 1975, p. 13).

Other interpretations of history are possible. Testing and those engaged in it can be viewed as serving the interests of corporate capitalism rather than of grass roots democracy (Cohen & Lazarson, 1972; Bowles & Gintis, 1976):

> If one believes this society is *not* structured to enhance the dignity of man but rather fosters a dehumanizing quest for status, power, and wealth, then the liberal histories fail to explain how we got where we believe we are. . . . If one starts with the assumption that this society is in fact racist, fundamentally materialistic, and institutionally structured to protect vested interests, the past takes on vastly different meanings (Karier, Violas, & Spring, 1973, p. 5).

In this *revisionist point of view,* tests are valid representations of the socioeconomic hierarchy that the corporate state controlled.

The tests and the meritocracy as well, served to mask power so well that any real revolutionary opposition was effectively immobilized. If a man truly believes he has a marginal standard of living because he is inferior, he is less likely to take violent measures against the social system than if he believes his condition is a product of social privilege (Karier, 1973, p. 136).

Examples of Social Control through Testing

Intelligence tests, discussed in Chapters 20 and 21, have been the most prominent tests used to argue the superiority of the dominant group. Concerns about social control and its effects on minorities are not limited to aptitude tests, however. Achievement tests can serve as social control mechanisms for access decisions, either for admission (entry) to a school or job, or credential or certifying competence (exit). A case in point is the National Teachers Examinations (NTE) which the Educational Testing Service (ETS) conducts and which many states use as part of the criteria for teacher selection. During the 1976–1977 academic year about 50 percent of the graduates of teacher-training programs took the NTE (Teachers, 1978). A thumbnail sketch of the NTE appears in Box 2.2; a review of the NTE can be found in *The Eighth Mental Measurements Yearbook* (8:381).

The NTE are made up of what are called Common Examinations and Area Examinations. The Common Examinations, 3½ hours long, provide a general appraisal of a prospective teacher's professional preparation and academic achievement.

Each of the two-hour Area Examinations measure the candidate's knowledge of a specific field. There are currently 26 area examinations emphasizing reasoning and application of principles rather than mere recall of specific facts. All questions are objective and multiple-choice.

The NTE are only one measure of teacher competence and are intended for use in conjunction with other criteria in the certification and selection process. The exams are not designed to measure teacher aptitude, interests, attitudes, motivation, or maturity. They are also *not* intended to be a measure of classroom teaching performance, but rather of the academic knowledge basic to successful teaching.

ETS recommends that the NTE *not* be used in decisions about retention, hiring, or tenure of experienced teachers.

Source: From *ETS Developments, Volume XXV, Numbers 2 and 3.* Copyright © 1978 by Educational Testing Service. All rights reserved. Reprinted by permission.

Box 2 • 2

The use of the NTE for certification and promotion in South Carolina was challenged by the National Education Association, the South Carolina Education Association, and the United States Justice Department, on the grounds the test was biased against minorities. As a result of passing scores set by the South Carolina Department of Education, many more black than white applicants failed the NTE. The United States Supreme Court eventually decided the case in favor of the Department of Education. The basis for the decision is summarized below (Teachers, 1978, p. 1):

> The court said: "Since we find that the NTE create classifications only on permissible bases (presence or absence of knowledge), and that they are not used pursuant to any intent to discriminate, their use in making certification decisions by the State is proper and legal."
>
> That court also found, based on a validity study performed by ETS, that the tests and their uses in promotion at the local level met requirements under Title VII of the Civil Rights Act of 1964.

The validity study involved 456 South Carolina college and university faculty members. These persons judged the ". . . relationship between the test questions (their emphases and subjects) and the curriculum that the tests were intended to measure. Decisions were based on educators' first-hand knowledge of college curricula" (p. 2).

From the perspective of those whose access to teaching was denied, the Supreme Court decision and the content validity study are far off target because a teaching certificate should be based on a performance test (Hilliard, 1979). Among the criticisms of the NTE, Hilliard (1979, pp. 212–213) lists these.

1. There is an implicit assumption that there is a *standard curriculum* for teacher preparation nationwide. No such curriculum exists, nor is there any serious attempt to demonstrate that it does. It is ludicrous to assume that 456 or any other number of South Carolina college and university faculty have done the systematic homework to know if the test content matched South Carolina teacher education content. Who has the data to answer that question for the whole nation? That could be determined only by a systematic examination of course syllabi, tests, reference lists, assignments, and observation of instruction. This has not been done. . . .

2. There is an implicit assumption that the knowledge of what the NTE measure is related to the curricula of primary and secondary schools and to successful teaching practice. We have virtually *no* data on this.

3. There may also be an implicit assumption that there *ought* to be a common content for the teaching bachelor's degree. . . .

4. There seems also to be an implicit assumption that *if there were* a common or universal content that there would be no "bias" against African-Americans. . . . Clearly there has been a permeating European-American ethnocentrism in the curricula of American education. A review of the NTE reveals that the same bias is still present in the examination itself. . . .

The point of the critique above is not to castigate a particular test at the expense or to the neglect of other tests. Rather, it is to illustrate some of the arguments and issues surrounding tests when they are used to provide information for making social control decisions—decisions which when negative deny individuals access to social status and material goods.

The Courts Challenge Testing Characteristics

Plaintiffs seeking legal redress for real and/or perceived violations of rights frequently bring social control testing programs to the courts. Notable among legal issues are race or sex discrimination, tests' contribution toward segregation in schools, unfairness of particular tests, and the violation of certain state and/or federal statutes. Among the recent educational testing practices brought to courts are minimum competency testing programs designed to control promotion and/or graduation.

Court cases frequently involve "class action suits," in which the plaintiffs represent an entire group of persons, and the judgments handed down by the court apply to all members. This was true, for example, in the Debra P. et al. vs. Turlington (1979) case which challenged Florida's minimum competency test. The court recognized the following classes (Fisher, 1980, p. 7): "(a) . . . all present and future twelfth grade public school students in the State of Florida who have failed or who hereafter fail the SSAT-II [i.e., the State Student Assessment Test, Part II]. (b) . . . all present and future twelfth grade black public school students in the State of Florida who have failed or who hereafter fail the SSAT-II. (c) . . . all present and future twelfth grade black public school students in Hillsborough County Florida who have failed or who hereafter fail the SSAT-II."

Psychometric Issues Attacked in Court

The following aspects of testing have been raised in courts in connection with minimum competency (Fisher, 1980). They appear, however, to be more widely applicable in court cases involving tests than simply to minimum competency issues.

1. Test security Plaintiffs and special interest groups will seek to know the content of the test, sometimes before the test is used. Related to this issue are matters of test secrecy, applicable state and federal "sunshine" laws, and "truth-in-testing" legislation.

2. APA Standards The APA (1974) *Standards* have been mentioned earlier in this chapter. While not a legal document, the APA *Standards* do represent professional opinion and values as to what constitutes good test development practices. Plaintiffs sometimes use these *Standards* as a basis for arguing against the quality or use of a particular test or testing program.

3. Reliability (See Chapter 15.) Plaintiffs may challenge either the magnitude of a test's reliability data or the appropriateness of using particular techniques for ascertaining reliability.

4. Validity (See Chapter 16.) With educational tests designed to certify minimum competence, the relation of content presented on the test to content taught in the classroom is likely to be challenged. (This is called "curricular relevance" in this book.)

5. Test development procedures Every aspect of test development may be challenged in a particular case: the test plan, the qualifications of the item writers, the correspondence between items and objectives, the readability level, the correct and alternative options to multiple-choice items, the tryout and field test procedures, steps taken to reduce or minimize culture, race, and/or regional bias.

6. Passing scores Several methods for setting passing scores exist (see Chapter 17), all of which plaintiffs may attack. Fisher notes that such attacks may not succeed if a person or group legally empowered to do so set the passing score.

7. Mechanical issues Plaintiffs can criticize aspects of the test, such as the quality of instructions and directions for administering, the color of the ink, the size of the print (some states have laws on this for certain grade levels), and other surface features of the test.

Non-Psychometric Issues

Fisher (1980) also outlines some of the non-psychometric issues which are the basis for legal redress in the use of tests. Although his remarks center on minimum competency testing, they seem to be applicable to several social control uses of tests:

1. **Legal authority** Plaintiffs may challenge a test or testing program, not so much on the basis of whether the test is of high quality, but whether the program has been legally authorized or whether individuals making the decisions about the testing have the legal authority to do so.

2. **Segregation in the schools** Here the challenge can be that the tests are biased against the lower scoring group and/or that they reflect the past segregation in the schools which lowered the quality of education, and hence, the plaintiffs should not be denied access or certification based on test results.

3. **Property interests in a diploma** The theory is that "the student has the right to expect that a diploma will be forthcoming assuming that all courses were passed, and any substantive change in the graduation requirements cannot take place without due notice to the student" (p. 4).

4. **Stigmatization** The results of the test may be used to deny a diploma or certificate or to label a person. The plaintiff's challenge is that such occurrences which result from testing are illegal because they result in stigmatizing a person.

Notice that in matters of test use and abuse, the application of particular laws is seldom clear. The resultant legal decision of a court case depends on the particular circumstances surrounding a given case, the evidence brought to bear in the case, and the opinion of the judge and jury involved.

Legal Guidelines for Personnel Selection

Title VII of the Civil Rights Act of 1964 and the Equal Employment Opportunity Act of 1972 have made it illegal to discriminate on the basis of race, color, sex, religion, or national origin when hiring or promoting. Consistent with these laws and with several executive orders, several federal agencies have consolidated their regulations and issued the *Uniform Guidelines on Employee Selection Procedures* in 1978. The agencies were the Civil Service Commission, the Equal Employment Opportunity Commission, the Department of Justice, and the Department of Labor. Among the aspects of testing covered by the *Guidelines* are such factors as the impact of the testing program on minorities and the standards for validity studies such as job analysis, criterion-related validity, content validity, and documentation of validity evidence. Persons engaged in selection testing should contact their local EEOC for the most recent version of the *Guidelines*.

Definitions of Test Bias

Some of the concerns surrounding the appropriateness of tests for various decisions focus on whether a particular test is biased against particular groups. Exactly what is meant by a "biased test" is not always clear because many definitions of test bias exist in the literature. Sometimes test users have more than one type of bias in mind, although they do not distinguish between types. The following catalogue of definitions of test bias are adapted from Flaugher (1978).

Test Bias as Mean Differences

A great many persons use this approach to test bias: A test is said to be biased against a particular group because the average (mean) test scores of that group are lower than the average scores of another group. Most test specialists would not subscribe to this definition of bias because average differences in groups' performances could represent real differences in the level of their attainment, rather than an artificial difference. "Bias" carries with it the idea of "unfair" or "unjust." Thus, differences as differences may not represent bias. If one group receives an inferior education or has been socialized away from learning or developing certain skills, a test measuring these things will likely indicate that this group scores lower on the average than a group which has had the opportunity or encouragement to learn.

While differences in group means do not *necessarily* indicate that a test is biased, they should not be dismissed lightly. Such differences may indicate that the groups have been treated unfairly (not given equal opportunity to acquire the abilities measured by the tests), and thus they have developed different ability levels. However, such mean differences in groups *may* mean that the test is biased, too. In other words, several factors can cause a mean difference between groups, including a biased test. The problem is that knowing that such differences exist does not in itself explain why they exist.

Test Bias as Misinterpretation of Scores

In order for the same interpretation to be placed on each examinee's score, the test evaluator must demonstrate that the test measures the same characteristics for each examinee. That is, does a test measure "reading comprehension" or "understanding of science" or "intelligence" in the same way for all persons? Bias of this type can creep into the interpretations of test results when test users try to make inferences about examinees' performances which go beyond the content domain of the test (Cole, 1978). It is one thing to say, for example, that a female has difficulty solving two-step arithmetic word problems which involve knowledge of male suburban experiences; but another to interpret performance on the test as an indication that females have lower arithmetic reasoning skills than males. The latter interpretation goes beyond the content domain and demands more than cursory evidence that the interpretation is unbiased.

Bias as Sexist and Racist Test Content: Facial Bias

Facial bias is the offensive stereotypic use of language and pictures in the test items and materials. Ours has been a white, male-dominated, Anglo-conformity culture. Testing (and other educational) materials have tended to perpetuate this image through the use of language and pictures. One can judge the content of test items (and other material) according to whether they represent male or female, white or nonwhite, as well as whether the content depicts certain role-stereotypes. Table 2.3 shows one set of criteria for such judging. Under the definition of bias described here, a test would be biased if its items did not represent a balance of gender and race and/or if its items perpetuated undesirable role-stereotypes. This type of judgment about the offensive nature of test content can be called facial bias (Cole & Nitko, 1981). Criteria such as those in Table 2.3 have been applied to the rating of achievement tests (e.g., Donlon, Ekstron, Lockheed, & Harris, 1977; Tittle, McCarthy, & Steckler, 1974) and intelligence tests (e.g., Zoref & Williams, 1980). Special concerns for race and sex bias in vocational interest inventories are discussed in Chapter 22 and guidelines for minimizing these effects are given in the Diamond (1975) reference mentioned previously.

Test Bias as a Lack of Predictive Validity

Predictive validity refers to the extent to which a test is able to estimate a person's probable standing on a second measure called a criterion (see Chapter 16). The criterion of interest in test bias is usually some measure of job or school success. Under this definition of test bias, a test would be biased if it predicted criterion scores better for one group of persons (e.g., whites) than for another (e.g., Chicanos). A "fair" or unbiased test would, according to this definition, predict criterion scores with equal accuracy for all groups tested. Although there have been a number

Gender representation: the extent to which an item can be characterized as representing a male or female.	
1. Pictorial items. Which gender does the item picture? Features checked include attire, length of hair, facial characteristics, and make-up (e.g., barrettes in a baby's hair mean the illustration presents a female).	**2. Verbal items.** Nouns and pronouns indicate gender: he/she, him/her, John/Jane (e.g., "Marion bought a bell for his bike," describes a male).
Gender role-stereotype: the extent to which an item can be characterized as depicting a male or female stereotyped role. Male role-stereotyped items depict males as intelligent, strong, vigorous, rugged, contributing to history, mechanically apt, professional, famous, etc. Female role-stereotyped items depict females as domestic, passive, generally inactive, crying, physically attractive, and non-intellectual.	
1. Pictorial items. Does the picture illustrate a gender role-stereotype? (e.g., woman fixing a meal, little girl playing with dolls, man carrying a picnic basket while escorting woman to park, man watching contact sports, or boy being mischievous.)	**2. Verbal items.** Does the item contain statements which are gender role-stereotyped? (e.g., question: "Who invented the electric light bulb?" [male role-stereotype] or story theme: brother and sister get a horse, boy rides horse while sister watches and laughs when brother falls in mud [female role-stereotype]).
Race representation: the extent to which an item can be characterized as representing a white or nonwhite person.	
1. Pictorial items. Are physical features such as skin color, eye shape and color, hair color and texture varied?	**2. Verbal items.** Do famous persons to be identified come from various races (e.g., George Washington, Martin Luther King, Jr.)?
Race role-stereotype: the extent to which an item can be characterized as depicting a white or nonwhite role-stereotype. White role-stereotyped items depict whites as wealthy, technically or academically trained, professional, intelligent, and inclined toward academic or intellectual pursuits. Pictures or verbal themes show whites operating instruments such as stethoscopes or surveying transoms. Nonwhite role-stereotyped items depict nonwhites as poor, unskilled, athletic (e.g., boxer, football lineman), culturally primitive, and religiously pagan.	
1. Pictorial items. Are role-stereotypes depicted (e.g., white male executive, oriental coolies, native American warriors, and black bellboys)?	**2. Verbal items.** Does the verbal content or story theme represent a role-stereotype (e.g., "Who wrote Hamlet?")?

Source: Zoref, L. and Williams, P. "A Look at Content Bias in IQ Tests." *Journal of Educational Measurement*, 1980, Volume 17, pp. 313–322. Copyright 1980, National Council on Measurement in Education, Washington, D.C.

Table 2 • 3   Criteria for judging test items for racial and sexist content.

of empirical studies on bias and predictive validity, a recent review of them concludes that, if such biases exist, ". . . they are so elusive, difficult to detect, and debatable . . . [that] they are not very potent phenomena relative to all the other possible sources of problems in the interaction of minorities and testing. Rather than continue this debate, it seems more appropriate to turn our energies to aspects that have greater impact on real-life decisions" (Flaugher, 1978, p. 674).

Test Bias as Test Content vs. Experience Differential

This definition classifies a test as biased if the items use questions or set tasks that are in some way judged "unfair" to a particular subgroup. For example, consider two high school vocabulary tests, one consisting of word meanings likely to be learned in a white, middle-class suburban high school, and the other comprised of slang word meanings likely to be learned only by urban, street-wise, black youth. Would either or both tests be biased? The answer depends on the use and interpretation of the results. Clearly, one would expect black youth to perform better than white youth on the latter test (Williams, 1975a). However, if the latter test is interpreted as a test of knowledge of this culture-specific domain of vocabulary, then it would not be biased against white youth who have not had the experience needed to acquire this learning. On the other hand, if the latter test were interpreted as a broad measure of verbal ability, it might well be biased against white youths, just as the former middle-class suburban vocabulary test might be biased against black youths. But it is very possible that the suburban vocabulary test might validly measure the verbal ability of white suburban youth as developed by their experience and that the black urban vocabulary test might validly measure the verbal ability of black urban youth as developed by their experience.

When experiences and test content are radically different, it is probably not possible to offer the same construct interpretation (e.g., general verbal ability) for one subgroup's performance as that offered for another subgroup whose experience and test content more nearly match. If test interpretations are restricted to the limited domain from which the items are sampled (e.g., white middle class vocabulary knowledge or knowledge of urban black slang), the issue of content bias is less likely to be raised. Seldom, however, does a teacher, counselor, or other test interpreter limit interpretation to the content domain: Most often, even for achievement tests, construct interpretations such as math concepts, listening comprehension, and spelling ability abound (Cole, 1978).

Test Bias as the Statistical Model Used for Selection Decisions

When there are a limited number of openings and a great many applicants, some procedure will have to be used to select those few applicants who will fill the openings. Most persons in this culture would reject the lottery (random drawing) as a means of selection because a random process is uncorrelated with the ability to succeed on the job or in school. It is felt that selection should occur based on "merits." Combinations of various types of tests provide information serving to rank applicants in order of merit. Among the information-gathering tools are interviews and the application blank itself as well as a variety of performance and paper-and-pencil tests. All such tests must show some positive relationship to job or school success. The problem arises when certain subgroups score consistently lower on one or more of the tests used in the selection process. The question is whether the statistical model or procedure used for selection is fair to all persons, regardless of group membership.

At least 10 actuarial or statistical models for reducing selection bias have appeared in the literature (Cleary, 1968; Thorndike, 1971; Cole, 1973; Einhorn and Bass, 1971; Darlington, 1971, 1976; Linn, 1973; Gross & Su, 1975; Novick and Peterson, 1976). A description of the details of each of these statistical selection models is beyond the scope of this book. Overviews of the meaning and implication of each can be found in Jensen (1980), Peterson and Novick (1976), Cronbach (1976), and Darling (1976).

Test Bias as the Wrong Criterion Measure

Selection tests are used to predict success on a second measure called a criterion. But the criterion measure itself may be biased, making the selection *process* biased, even if the selection *test* is unbiased. For example, suppose a job did not require reading skills and that on-the-job performance is the relevant criterion. Suppose further that an employer used a paper-and-pencil test of job knowledge as a substitute criterion measure instead of using a measure of actual job performance. Since in this case the paper-and-pencil test would be interpreted erroneously as the "ability to do the job," it would be a biased test against those who could not read or who were poor paper-and-pencil test takers, but who might well be able to perform the job. Some criteria represent traditional cultural values (e.g., supervisors' ratings, grade point average, etc.) and may be used as proxies to the ultimate criterion measures (Flaugher, 1978). Persons able to perform well on the ultimate criterion may not necessarily perform well on these proxy measures.

Bias Stemming from the Atmosphere and Conditions of Testing

Basic stresses of test-taking, such as test anxiety, feeling unwelcomed, or being tested by a member of the opposite sex or another race (see Chapter 12 for a more complete discussion of many of these factors), can affect the performance of some groups adversely. Others have argued that it is unfair to students and teachers in schools serving the impoverished to use an officially mandated test which serves ". . . to inflict on them periodic, detailed documentation of just how very far away from anything approaching the norm they are" (Flaugher, 1978, p. 677).

Summary

1. This chapter presented a number of ethical issues including: secrecy and access to test results, privacy and confidentiality of test results, informed consent, and the need for an analysis of evidence for and consequences of test use. Several guidelines for test interpretation and ethical use were mentioned.

2. Social control mechanisms can be overt and external to the person being controlled and/or internalized and part of the person's belief system.

3. Social control mechanisms are subject to criticism if they are irrational, capricious, arbitrary, or unjust. Decisions based on such mechanisms are invalid and too subjective.

4. Certain standardized educational and psychological tests, claiming to being both objective and scientifically valid, have come to be used as social control mechanisms. If the controlled individuals accept the objectivity and validity of the tests, then they are likely to accept and internalize the consequences of decisions made using the tests.

5. The acceptance of the justice of test use for certain social control activities depends on an individual's perspective on past and present social forces. I presented two such perspectives, a liberal, progressive view and a revisionist view. A teacher's academic competence test illustrated the use of tests for social control decisions.

6. In the courts, tests have received attacks for their perceived racial or sex discrimination, their contribution to school segregation, their unfairness, and their violation of individuals' rights under state and federal statutes and constitutions.

7. Among the technical aspects of testing attacked in court are: test security, adherence to APA *Standards*, reliability, validity, test development procedures, passing scores used, and mechanical issues such as quality of printing and administrative procedures.

8. Other issues of testing attacked include: the legal authority of examiners to use tests or impose testing requirements, the potential of the testing program to segregate the schools, the legal rights of examinees to possess the credential in question (e.g., high school diploma), and the stigmatization resulting from labeling persons.

9. Legal opinions and court decisions will vary depending on the circumstances and merits of the case, the quality of the suit or defense, and the disposition of the judge or jury.

10. *The Uniform Guidelines on Employee Selection Procedures* (EEOC, 1978) provide standards for the validation necessary to establish that a selection testing program is nondiscriminatory.

11. Test bias has many definitions including whether (a) average differences in the performance of tested groups exist, (b) test scores are properly interpreted, (c) test items contain racist or sexist content, (d) a test has the same predictive validity in tested groups, (e) test content matches the experience of tested groups, (f) the statistical model used to select applicants for a job or for entrance to school is fair to both groups, (g) the criterion against which the test is validated is the correct one, and (h) the atmosphere and conditions of testing bias the test results.

Themes

● Quantitative concepts can be useful for describing and understanding the results of classroom testing, interpreting norm-referenced test scores, and understanding the basic data provided in test manuals and reports.

● One way to enhance the interpretation of test results is to summarize by tabulating and, perhaps, graphing a frequency distribution how a group has performed on a test. The form or shape of a distribution often gives insight into test score interpretation.

● Statistics are summary indices which attempt to capture concisely a specific attribute of the entire collection of scores for a group. One class of such summary indices—*measures of central tendency*—focuses on what is an average or typical score for a group.

● Another important class of statistics—*measures of score variability*—focuses on summarizing the extent to which people in a group differ from one another.

● One aspect of score interpretation concerns ascertaining a person's relative standing in a group. By transforming a test score, a new, norm-referenced score that more or less directly reflects a person's relative standing will result.

● An understanding of human attributes and the interpretation of test results often hinge on the extent to which test scores are correlated with other test scores and measures of other variables. Quantitative indices of the degree of relationship among pairs of scores are helpful in understanding such correlations.

Terms and Concepts

statistic

frequency distribution

histogram, frequency polygon

skewed distribution (positive, negative)

unimodal, bimodal

symmetrical distribution

continuous vs. discrete attribute

measure of central tendency (mean, median, mode)

measure of variability (range, variance, standard deviation)

deviation (deviation score)

raw score

transformed score

rank

percentile rank

percentile

percentage score

quartile

linear transformation

linear standard score (z-score)

correlation vs. causation

correlation coefficient (Pearson product-moment correlation coefficient)

linear relation vs. curvilinear relation

scatter diagram

ceiling effect, floor effect

3
BASIC
STATISTICAL
CONCEPTS*

*Your instructor may postpone this chapter or may assign different sections of it at different junctures of the course. The chapter is written to accommodate individual differences in the preferences of instructors.

$\mathbf{T}$his chapter discusses statistical concepts and methods used to describe the results of classroom testing, to interpret certain norm-referenced test scores, and to understand the basic data provided in published test manuals and reports. The focus is on concepts rather than computations, although the computations of some statistical indices are illustrated so that you will understand the origin of their numerical values. If you are interested in applying statistical methods to your own test data, you will find step-by-step computation procedures and examples in Appendix A.

Five categories of data summary techniques provide the beginning student with a repertoire of quantitative concepts useful to understanding testing and measurement. These categories are

1. the distribution of scores,
2. the typical or average score,
3. the variability of scores,
4. a score's position in a group,
5. the degree of relationship among scores.

Many of these statistical concepts will be new, and you should not expect to understand them completely after only one exposure. The concepts are used and elaborated throughout the text, however, so things should become clearer as you proceed in the course.

Describing Distributions of Test Scores

It is difficult to come to a full understanding of a person's test score by considering it in isolation: A comparison of that score with other scores often enhances the interpretation. For example, we might ask such questions as

1. Do other pupils in the class have similar scores?
2. What scores do most pupils tend to obtain?
3. Are scores widely scattered along the score scale or do they tend to bunch together?
4. Does the pattern of scores in the class appear unusual in some way? Or are the scores as expected?

Frequency Distributions

Consider the scores shown in Table 3.1. Suppose that they represented the scores of a class

25	24	26	26	27
28	28	28	32	29
26	27	20	28	29
27	26	25	36	26
31	26	14	27	27

Table 3 • 1 Scores of 25 pupils on a test of simple addition facts.

on a test of all 36 single-digit additional facts up to $5 + 5 =$ _____ . The arrangement of the scores in the table does not make it easy to answer these four questions.

A simple way to remedy this problem is to organize the scores into a *frequency distribution,* a table showing the number of persons obtaining each score (see Table 3.2). The *frequency* associated with each score represents the number of persons who obtained that score.

From Table 3.2 we can obtain additional information that broadens our interpretation

Score	Tally	Frequency
36	/	1
35		
34		
33		
32	/	1
31	/	1
30		
29	//	2
28	////	4
27	↗↗↗	5
26	↗↗↗ /	6
25	//	2
24	/	1
23		
22		
21		
20	/	1
19		
18		
17		
16		
15		
14	/	1
13		
		25

Table 3 • 2 Frequency distribution of the test scores of Table 3.1.

of the pupils' scores. The bulk of the pupils (80%) obtained scores between 24 and 29. There are two pupils (scores of 14 and 36) whose scores are atypical compared to the rest of the class. These "outliers" signal the teacher to try to find out why these two scored as they did. Perhaps a high or a low score is due to scoring error. Or, perhaps, the score represents a real accomplishment (the score of 36) or a real problem (the score of 14). The teacher, having the most information about the pupils, can check the reason(s) behind the pupils' performance and plan appropriate instruction. We cannot tell whether the pattern of scores is unusual for this class. To do that, more information is needed such as the distribution of scores in other classes and the time of year the test was administered. Nevertheless, organizing scores into a frequency dis-

tribution has helped to provide initial information so that the teacher can begin to interpret the test scores and plan for further arithmetic instruction.

Histograms and Polygons

Frequency distributions are often graphed because graphs permit an increased understanding of the distribution of scores. The shapes of distributions of test scores take on special meanings for certain interpretations of test scores.

Two common types of graphs of frequency distributions are the histogram and frequency polygon. For both, a scale of score values is marked off on a horizontal axis. The *histogram* (sometimes called a bar graph) represents the frequency of each score by a rectangle. The height of each rectangle is made equal to (or proportional to) the frequency of the corresponding score. Figure 3.1 (A) shows a histogram for the scores of Table 3.2. A *frequency polygon* for these same scores is shown in Figure 3.1(B). A dot is made directly above the score-value to indicate the frequency. (If no one has obtained a particular score-value, the dot is made at 0.) The dots are then connected with straight lines to make the polygon.

Shapes of Score Distributions

A graph communicates in an easy manner the shape or form of a frequency distribution. Using the names of these shapes is a compact way of describing how the scores are distributed.

Figure 3.2 shows a variety of distributional forms, their corresponding names, and examples of measurement situations that might give rise to them.

Using Frequency Distributions and Their Graphs

The illustrations of Figure 3.2 are idealized and do not represent actual distributions. Never-

A. Example of a histogram for a class.

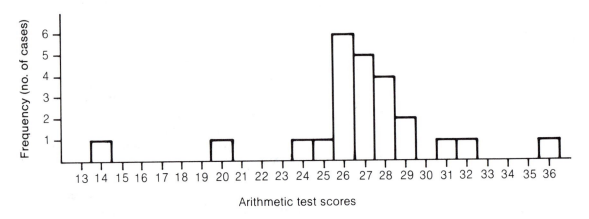

B. Example of a frequency polygon for a class.

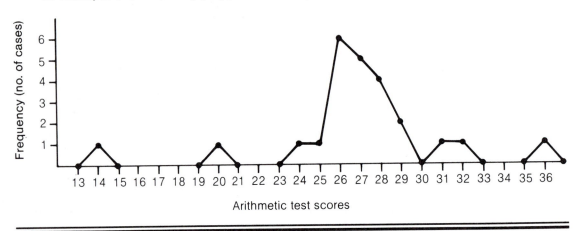

Figure 3 • 1 Two ways of graphing the same data: Histogram and frequency polygon for the scores in Table 3.2.

theless, it is helpful to have a mental picture of these distributional forms because in practice, actual test score distributions resemble the ideal forms at least roughly and can be described by using the terms.

Score distribution shape depends on both the test-takers and the test The shape a score distribution has reflects the characteristics of the test as well as the ability of the group being tested. There is no single "natural" shape toward which the test scores of a given group of students tends. A test composed of items that are not too difficult and not too easy for a particular group is likely to result in distributions of scores similar to those illustrated by A, B, or C of Figure 3.2. (See Chapter 14, for this explanation.) This same group,

Histogram	Description of distribution form	Examples of when such shapes might occur

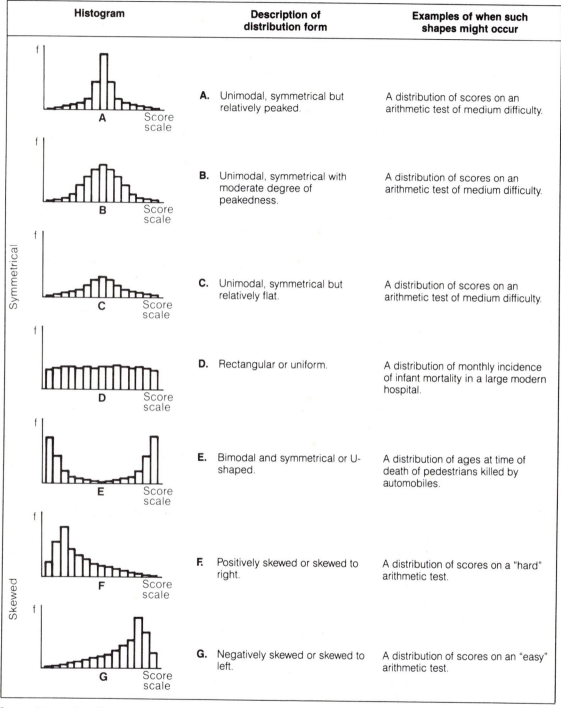

A. Unimodal, symmetrical but relatively peaked.

A distribution of scores on an arithmetic test of medium difficulty.

B. Unimodal, symmetrical with moderate degree of peakedness.

A distribution of scores on an arithmetic test of medium difficulty.

C. Unimodal, symmetrical but relatively flat.

A distribution of scores on an arithmetic test of medium difficulty.

D. Rectangular or uniform.

A distribution of monthly incidence of infant mortality in a large modern hospital.

E. Bimodal and symmetrical or U-shaped.

A distribution of ages at time of death of pedestrians killed by automobiles.

F. Positively skewed or skewed to right.

A distribution of scores on a "hard" arithmetic test.

G. Negatively skewed or skewed to left.

A distribution of scores on an "easy" arithmetic test.

Source: Adapted from Blommers and Forsyth (1977, pp. 30–31)

Figure 3 • 2   Histograms showing various forms of frequency distributions.

with the same ability, could take a test in the same subject made up of items that few persons could answer correctly or a test made up of "easy" items. In these latter cases, skewed distributions (F or G) might result. It is not accurate, therefore, to come to a conclusion about the *underlying ability* distribution of a group of students by examining only the shape of the distribution of observed test scores. The characteristics of the test the group took also needs to be made a part of the decision.

Choice between histogram or polygon   For many classroom purposes, you could use either a polygon or a histogram since the choice between them is rather arbitrary. The polygon emphasizes the continuous nature of the attribute that underlies the scores you see on the test while the histogram emphasizes the discrete nature. Although observed test *scores* usually are discrete whole numbers (0, 1, 2, . . .) the underlying characteristic a test is designed to measure is often thought of as continuous rather than discrete.

Continuous vs. discrete attributes   An attribute or characteristic is said to be *continuous* if we conceptualize that the true measure a person possesses can correspond to any conceivable point on (at least a part of) an unbroken number line (Blommers and Forsyth, 1977). Thus, a person's spelling ability—as compared to the number of words spelled correctly on a particular spelling test—can be thought of as being located at any point along some part of an unbroken number line. Two persons could have spelling abilities that differ by such small amounts that it would be impossible for a particular test to detect this difference so these persons obtain the same score. Thus, the test scores are only approximations of the true measure of the attribute a person possesses. To emphasize this continuous underlying quality, a polygon could be used because, as a picture, it conveys the idea that every possible point on the score scale has a frequency.

An attribute is discrete if true amounts of it are conceived as corresponding to only some points of a scale. This means that the scale is broken; gaps occur in the scale. Like the term continuous, the term discrete refers to the true nature of the underlying attribute rather than the numbers obtained from the measurement process. For example, we might read that the average size of a class at a particular school is 27.4 pupils. The attribute in question, class size, is discrete since it is not possible for the true size of a class to include a fraction of a pupil. To decide whether an attribute is continuous or discrete, we have to think about the way the attribute that underlies the measurements or test score is conceptualized.

Comparing two distributions   It is sometimes useful to compare two or more frequency distributions by graphing more than one frequency distribution on the same axes using polygons, rather than histograms. A graph could compare, for example, a class of students before and after instruction, or it could compare two different classes of students. Such a graph would display the forms of the distributions, the variability or disbursement of scores, and the place(s) along the score scale where the scores tend to cluster. Box 3.1 illustrates this with scores taken from an actual study.

Summary of Distributions of Scores

The interpretation of test scores can often be enhanced if the scores are summarized into frequency distributions.

Frequency distributions

1. tell how many persons obtained each score value.
2. can be graphed as either histograms or frequency polygons; the choice depends on the characteristic being measured and the purpose for constructing the graph.
3. help to answer questions, such as,

Was the special curriculum helpful?

Graphs can assist in studying how a group improves or how a specially instructed group compares to a group not receiving special instruction. In the following illustration, the question was whether certain visual-motor spatial relations skills would improve without special instruction and to what extent, if any, special instruction accelerated the acquisition of these skills. The names of 50 first graders were put into a hat and one-half of them were drawn at random and assigned to a group that received special instruction in visual analysis of spatial relationships during a free period. The other half continued with their free period without special instruction. The special instruction consisted of individualized lesson plans and practice on visual-motor tasks designed to teach pupils how to analyze and copy geometric patterns and designs. The pupils in the instructed group received from 16 to 22 hours of instruction over a 3 month period. Both groups received the same design copying test before the instructional phase began and again after the instructional phase ended.

Graphs A, B, and C show the frequency distributions of scores on a design copying test that was used as part of the study. As an exercise, for each graph you should (a) describe the forms of the distributions, (b) compare the disbursement or spread of the scores along the score scale before and after the instructional period, and (c) describe for each polygon where the bulk of the scores tend to be clustered or to be located on the score scale. Do you think that the special instruction improved the students' ability to copy geometric designs? Explain.

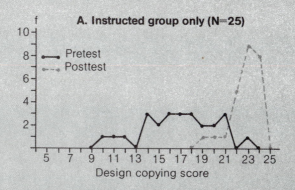

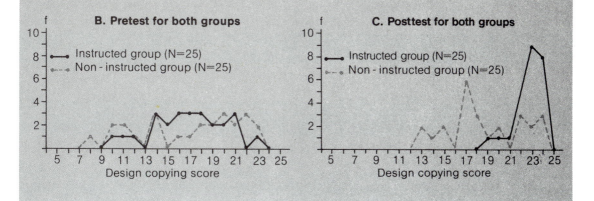

Box 3 • 1

a. Which scores in a class are similar?

b. What scores do most pupils tend to obtain?

c. Does the pattern of scores for a group appear unusual?

The form or shape of the graph of a frequency distribution

4. may be described as unimodal vs. bimodal or as symmetrical vs. skewed; distributions may be skewed positively or negatively.

5. is often described by a combination of these terms.

6. is dependent on the characteristics of the test administered and the group that is tested; there is no "natural" shape toward which educational and psychological test score distributions tend.

An attribute to be measured may be thought of as

7. continuous if one can think of the true amount of it that a person possesses as corresponding to any conceivable point on an unbroken numerical scale.

8. discrete if the true amounts of it that a person possesses can be conceived of as corresponding to only some parts of a scale.

Measures of Central Tendency

It is quite common when interpreting test scores to speak of the "average test score." In this connection, we speak of the "average child" "being above average in spelling" or "of average intelligence."

There are many ways to define averages, but I shall discuss only three of them: the *mean*, the *median*, and the *mode*. As will become clear, these averages are more precisely thought of as *indices of location* of the distribution on the

score scale. They are summary numbers or *statistics* that quantitatively capture certain characteristics of a distribution of scores—in this case, characteristics that relate to the position of the group on the score scale.

The Mode (Mo)[1]

The modalities of distributions of test scores appear in Figure 3.2. The terms used were "unimodal" and "bimodal." More formally, the *mode* is defined as *the score-value that has a frequency which is large in relation to other frequencies near it in the distribution* (Blommers and Forsyth, 1977). For example, in Figure 3.1, the score 26 is the mode of the distribution since this score occurs most frequently in this distribution. Looking at Figure 3.2, Distribution E, we see that there are two modes; such distributions are called bimodal. The two modes of a distribution do not *have* to have exactly the same (equal) frequency for the distribution to be called bimodal.

Notice that the *mode is a score-value* and not the number corresponding to the frequency. Many persons erroneously report the number corresponding to the frequency instead of the score-value when asked to name the mode. The illustration below should make this clear.

It is possible to compare the modes of two distributions. Suppose the following illustra-

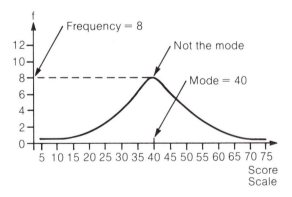

[1]Karl Pearson (1894) was the first to call this already known index the "mode" (Dudycha & Dudycha, 1972).

tion represented the score distributions of two schools, A and B. Which distribution has a larger mode? Notice that although the frequencies of the modes of the two distributions are different (18 and 9, respectively), the values of their modes (20 and 25, respectively) do not depend on a comparison of the heights of the two graphs. Distribution B has the larger mode (=25) because the modal *score-value* is located at a higher point on the score scale.

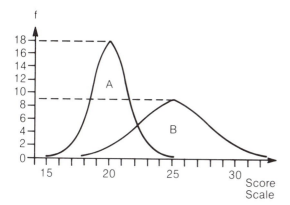

Usefulness of the mode   The mode is a useful summary number that communicates information about the location of a large number of scores in a distribution. Distributions may have more than one mode, indicating concentrations of scores at more than one score level. You should note also that a distribution sometimes does not have a mode. For example, the uniform distribution pictured in Figure 3.2(D) does not have a mode.

Another point about the mode can be mentioned. Since the mode is the score that occurs most often in a distribution, it is the score that is most likely to be observed if we picked someone from the group at random. In this sense the mode acts as a kind of average. Sometimes when we ask, "What was the average score on the test?," we mean, "What score occurred most often?" or "If I put everyone's score into a hat and drew out a score at random, what score would I most likely have drawn?" Use the mode when you want to report this kind of information.

The Median (Mdn)[2]

Defining the median   The *median* is *the point on the score-scale which is so located that the same number of scores are above it as are below it*. To find the median of a distribution we have to find the point on the score scale below which one-half of the scores occur. For example, consider these five scores which have been arranged in order of magnitude: 3, 5, 7, 8, 9. The median is 7, since two scores are above it and two below.

Now, consider the set of six scores 3, 5, 6, 8, 9, and 10 on the score scale below with little dots. What is the median?

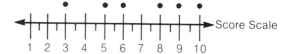

It should be clear that any point on the score scale larger than 6.0 and smaller than 8.0 would split the set of scores so that three scores (8, 9, and 10) are above that point and the other three scores (3, 5, and 7) are below it. Thus, any number, such as, 6.01, 6.02, . . . , 7.99 would satisfy the definition of the median. By convention, the value chosen for the median, however, is the number that is halfway between the two middle scores. In this example the median is 7.0.[3]

The "middle score procedure" described above works fine when no two persons have the same score. Very often, however, several persons do have the same score. As an example of how the counting or "middle score" procedure fails us, consider the ten scores shown here and try to compute the median.

[2]Details of how to compute this widely known index were published by Gustav Fechner (1874); it was dubbed the "median" by Sir Francis Galton (1883) (Dudycha & Dudycha, 1972).

[3]Using this convention implies that the number 7.0 is meaningful. To use the score scale in this way usually means that some continuous characteristic underlies the measurements obtained from the test.

Student	Score	Student	Score
Sara	2	Tony	4
Mike	3	Megan	5
Bill	3	Marya	5
Nancy	4	Andrea	5
Bob	4	Kevin	6

Here there is no single middle score below which half the persons lie (Nancy, Bob and Tony all have scores of 4). In such cases, a procedure to estimate the median is used, resulting in the above example in estimating the median as 4.17, rather than 4.0. The procedure for doing this appears in Appendix A. The procedure uses a convention which assumes that (a) the characteristic being measured is continuous and (b) the persons' true measurements are evenly spread over an interval around their whole number score obtained from the test. This permits the apportionment of the tied scores over the continuous number line to estimate the median.

One thing to note from the last two paragraphs is that the number used for the median need not be an actual score someone obtained. This emphasizes the fact that the median is a point on the number line. The mode, however, must be a score persons obtained.

Usefulness of the median   One use of the median stems directly from its definition. Since one-half of the scores in a distribution are smaller (and one-half are larger) than the median, the median has a straightforward, rather "natural" interpretation. Table 3.3 shows this with the distribution of responses and the median response of a class of pupils to part of a questionnaire asking them to rate one teacher's examinations, assignments, and grading practices. The medians are computed using the procedure described in Appendix A. If the teacher wanted to summarize the class's ratings for each question, the median for each question could be reported. Those numbers would communicate that on each characteristic half the class rated the teacher

higher than the reported median and half lower.[4]

Certainly being above (or below) the median on any characteristic cannot be defended as an educationally sound goal. But persons believe that being above the median (i.e., in the upper half of the group) is more desirable than being in the lower half. A parent once called a school principal on the telephone about his son's test scores. He had just received the score report the school sent home and was furious. "I know that my son isn't in the top half of his class," he shouted, "but I sure as heck didn't think that he deserves to be in the *bottom* half!"

The median is useful when we want a summary number that is not affected by a few atypical extremely large or small scores. Consider, for example, Item 3 in Table 3.3, where 19 out of 20 pupils rated the teacher above average or outstanding and only one pupil rated the teacher poor. The median more accurately describes the bulk of the rating than would some other summary number which might be "pulled down" because of this single, very low rating. As long as the scores do not shift past the median, altering scores does not change its numerical value. Again, in Item 3, for example, the rating of 1 could be changed to 2, 3, or 4 without changing the numerical value of the median. Once a rating shifts past the median, however (e.g., changing the 1 to a 5), then the numerical value of the median will change.

The median is useful when you want a single summary number as being representative of the typical score of a group. This is because the median is the one point on the score scale that is closest, on the whole, to all of the scores. Another way of saying this is that the median is the one point on the number line such that the sum of the distances of all the scores to that point is the least. So typ-

---

[4]Because 50 percent of the scores lie below the median, the median is also called the *50th percentile*. Percentiles are discussed later.

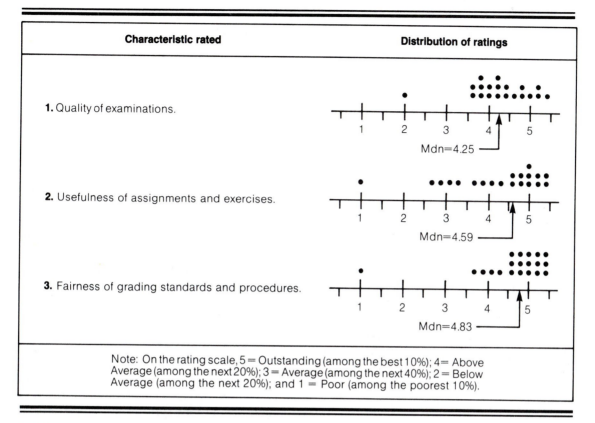

Characteristic rated	Distribution of ratings
1. Quality of examinations.	Mdn=4.25
2. Usefulness of assignments and exercises.	Mdn=4.59
3. Fairness of grading standards and procedures.	Mdn=4.83

Note: On the rating scale, 5 = Outstanding (among the best 10%); 4 = Above Average (among the next 20%); 3 = Average (among the next 40%); 2 = Below Average (among the next 20%); and 1 = Poor (among the poorest 10%).

Table 3 • 3   Student ratings of one instructor's examinations, assignments, and grading practices.

icalness can be defined here as *aggregate proximity* (Blommers & Forsyth, 1977).

The Mean(M)[5]

Defining the mean   Most persons are familiar with the average known as the *arithmetic mean* or simply the "mean." The *mean is the point on the score scale obtained by finding the sum of all of the scores and dividing by their number*. A variety of symbols have been used to represent the mean, such as, M, $\overline{X}$, and the Greek letter μ. The symbol M is used in this chapter.

[5]The mean was known to Pythagoras in the sixth century B.C.

We can compute the mean of the 25 arithmetic test scores previously presented in Table 3.1. To do so we sum all of the scores and then divide by 25.

$$M = \frac{25 + 28 + 26 + \ldots + 27}{25}$$

$$= \frac{668}{25}$$

$$= 26.72$$

We can represent the definition of the mean by the formula:

$$M = \frac{\Sigma X}{N}$$

$$= \frac{\text{Sum of all the scores}}{\text{Total number of scores}} \quad \text{[Eq. 3.1]}$$

where M represents the mean, N represents the total number of scores involved, and Σ (Greek capital sigma) represents "sum of" or "summation of," meaning that whatever separate values are symbolized by what follows it are to be added together—in this case, the different values of X, which stands for the individual score values.

Although Equation 3.1 can be used to compute the mean, when the number of scores is large and when computations in addition to the mean are to be made also, it is easier to organize the scores into a frequency distribution first. Procedures for and an example of computing the mean from a frequency distribution are given in Appendix A. Some hand-held calculators and microcomputers have programs for computing the mean and other statistics.

Usefulness of the mean An important property of the mean is that its value is affected by every one of the scores of the group since the sum on which the mean is based includes every score. This is not true of the median and the mode. This property makes the mean a useful summary number in situations in which interest focuses on the total rather than the typical (e.g., Blommers & Forsyth, 1977). When evaluating the effectiveness of an instructional innovation—for example, a new method of teaching beginning reading—it would be useful to include a measure of reading achievement in the data collection procedures. The concern of the evaluator may be the impact of the innovation on every student. The mean reflects this impact since both high achievers and low achievers (or both gains and losses) would enter into its computed value.

This same property of the mean makes it less useful as a summary number when inter-est focuses on the typical. The distribution of individual incomes, for example, is positively skewed in the United States. The mean income is larger than the median income because the mean reflects all incomes, high and low (see Figure 3.3).

Relationship Among the Indices of Central Tendency

The relationship among numerical values of the indices depends on the shape of score distribution. Figure 3.4 shows three distributions and the locations in each of the mean, median, and mode. When the distribution is unimodal and symmetrical, mean, median, and mode have the same numerical value. If the distribution is unimodal and negatively skewed, the mean is less than the median; the median in turn is less than the mode. The mean has been "lowered" by the extremely low scores in the distribution. If the distribution is unimodal and positively skewed, the reverse situation exists: The mean is greater than the median; the median in turn is greater than the mode. The value of the mean has been "raised" by the extremely high scores in the distribution. If you had no information about a distribution of scores, other than the numerical values of the mean and median, you could use them to guess the type of skewness of the distribution by comparing these two numbers.

Which index to compute and use depends on the purpose for which you want to use the information. Since much is lost when a single number represents an entire distribution of scores, it is advisable to report all three indices when summarizing score distributions.

Summary of Measures of Central Tendency

The mode is

1. a score-value that has a frequency which is large in relation to the frequencies of other score-values near it.

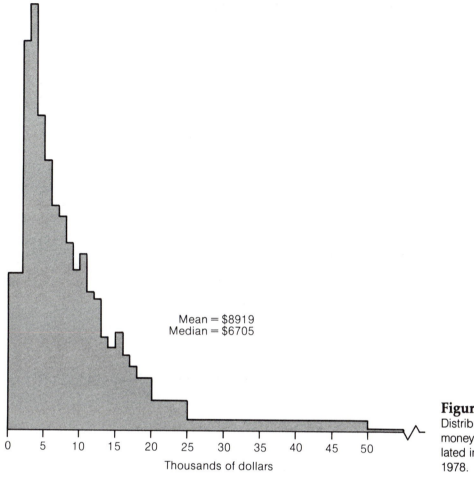

Mean = $8919
Median = $6705

Figure 3 • 3
Distribution of total money income for unrelated individuals in 1978.

Thousands of dollars

Source: Data from U.S. Bureau of Census (1979).

2. not necessarily a unique value; there may be more than one mode for a distribution.
3. information about the location of the bulk of scores in the distribution.
4. the score most likely to be observed if someone is selected at random from the group.

The median is

1. the point on the score scale located in such a way that the same number of scores are above it as are below it.

2. called the 50th percentile, since half of the scores are below it.
3. not affected by the numerical values of extremely high or low scores.
4. unaffected by changes in the numerical values of scores as long as these changes do not cause a score to shift past the median point.
5. the one number that is closest to all of the scores in the sense of aggregate proximity so that the median can be called the "typical score" in the distribution.

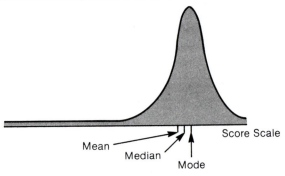

A. A unimodal and negatively skewed distribution

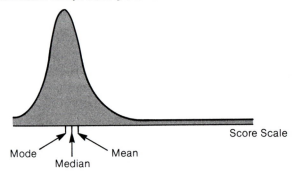

B. A unimodal and positively skewed distribution

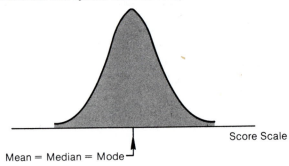

C. A unimodal and symmetrical distribution

Figure 3 • 4   Relationship among mean, median, and mode in distributions of different shapes.

The mean is

1. the point on the score scale found by summing the scores and dividing by their number.
2. affected by every score in the distribution which makes it a useful summary number when the total amount of the quality possessed by the group is of concern.

The mean, median, and mode are often used together because

1. if the distribution is unimodal and symmetrical, all three values will be identical.
2. if unimodal distributions are skewed negatively, they will have their means less than their medians.
3. if unimodal distributions are skewed positively, they will have their means greater than their medians.
4. in any symmetrical distribution the mean and median will be equal.

Score Variability

Suppose you were assigned to teach two sections of a course and you knew only that the two groups had the same average ability. Could you assume that, within limits, you would need to accommodate pupils' individual differences to the same extent in both groups? The figure below, showing the graphs of two distributions on the same axis, can illustrate that individual differences (variability) play impor-

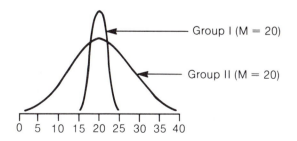

Group I (M = 20)

Group II (M = 20)

tant roles in interpreting scores, even when the groups have the same average. Although the means of the two groups are identical, it is obvious that the two groups differ in at least one way. Most pupils cluster near the mean in Group I and the mean is a good describer of most individuals in that group. The situation is quite different in Group II, however, since most pupils' scores are some distance away from the mean. If you were teaching these two groups, it is likely that your instruction would have to be much more adaptive to individual differences for Group II than for Group I.

Groups may differ both in their mean and in their variability as is illustrated in the figure below. Here Group IV has a higher average and a smaller variance. The pupils in Group III vary widely from their mean and some of them score at levels that are above the mean of Group IV. This figure is somewhat (though not exactly) like the situation illustrated in Box 3.1 in that pupils scored higher and more like each other after instruction than before instruction.

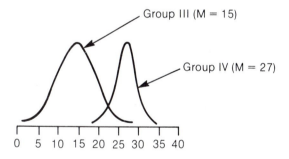

Group III (M = 15)

Group IV (M = 27)

While possible, presenting graphs of distributions and discussing their variability ultimately becomes cumbersome and statistically nonproductive. Consequently, indices are used to quantify the degree of variability present in a distribution.

The Range (R)

One way in which individual differences are reflected within a classroom is in the distance between the highest and lowest scores. A quantitative index that reflects this distance is the ==*range,* **defined** as *the difference between the highest score in the group and the lowest score in the group*==. This definition is summarized by the formula:[6]

$$R = H - L \qquad \text{[Eq. 3.2]}$$

$$= \text{highest score} - \text{lowest score}$$

Figure A in Box 3.1 shows the score distributions of a group before and after receiving instruction. Compute the ranges.

Pretest	Posttest
$R = 24 - 9$	$R = 25 - 18$
$= 15$	$= 7$

These numbers imply that on the posttest the group is more alike, being distributed along a distance of 7 points on the score scale. The distance on the score scale over which they were distributed on the pretest was approximately twice that of the posttest.

==A weakness in range as a quantitative index of variability is that it is based on only two scores==—the highest score and the lowest score—and ==ignores the variability of the scores between these two points==.

Another problem with using range is that a change in one of the extreme scores can radically alter the value of the range and perhaps distort the impression of the variability of the group. For example, suppose the majority of the children in a class have nearly the same level of achievement in spelling scores, between 70 and 80 (i.e., $R = 10$) points on a 100 word review test. The addition of one student with an exceptionally high score (e.g., 100) would increase the range drastically, making it 30 points. Although 30 would describe the range of scores, it would not describe accurately the variability of the group as a whole.

Thus, while range describes some aspects of the variability of scores in a group, and even though it is easy to compute, it doesn't convey

[6]Some books define the range as $R = H - L + 1$.

enough information about variability to make it very useful in interpreting test scores. It is used frequently, however, to describe the distance on the score scale over which the scores are distributed.

The Mean Deviation (MD)[7]

In distributions with little variability—in which scores are very similar—the distance from an individual score to the mean will be small on the average. On the other hand, in distributions with a great deal of variability—in which scores do differ from each other a great deal—the distance between the mean and each individual score will be large on the average. These observations suggest that the average of the distances between the mean and individual scores serve as a quantitative index of the variability of a distribution. As an example, consider these two groups of scores.

Group I (mean = 14)	
Score	*Distance from mean*[8]
10	$\lvert 10\text{-}14 \rvert = 4$
10	$\lvert 10\text{-}14 \rvert = 4$
12	$\lvert 12\text{-}14 \rvert = 2$
12	$\lvert 12\text{-}14 \rvert = 2$
14	$\lvert 14\text{-}14 \rvert = 0$
14	$\lvert 14\text{-}14 \rvert = 0$
16	$\lvert 16\text{-}14 \rvert = 2$
16	$\lvert 16\text{-}14 \rvert = 2$
18	$\lvert 18\text{-}14 \rvert = 4$
18	$\lvert 18\text{-}14 \rvert = 4$
	sum of distances = 24
	average distance $= \dfrac{24}{10}$
	$= 2.4$

[7]This section may be omitted without loss of continuity.

[8]Notice that we are concerned here only with the distance from the mean to each score, not the direction of that distance. Thus, only *absolute values* are used: the algebraic sign of the difference (+ or −) is not reported. The vertical bars on each subtraction designate that an absolute value is being used.

Group II
(mean = 14)

Score	Distance from mean
12	$\lvert 12\text{-}14 \rvert = 2$
12	$\lvert 12\text{-}14 \rvert = 2$
14	$\lvert 14\text{-}14 \rvert = 0$
14	$\lvert 14\text{-}14 \rvert = 0$
14	$\lvert 14\text{-}14 \rvert = 0$
14	$\lvert 14\text{-}14 \rvert = 0$
14	$\lvert 14\text{-}14 \rvert = 0$
14	$\lvert 14\text{-}14 \rvert = 0$
16	$\lvert 16\text{-}14 \rvert = 2$
16	$\lvert 16\text{-}14 \rvert = 2$

$$\text{sum of distances} = 8$$
$$\text{average distance} = \frac{8}{10}$$
$$= 0.8$$

Although both groups have the same mean (=14) they differ in their variability. Thus, the average distance from the mean is 2.4 in Group I but only 0.8 in Group II.

The example above illustrates another quantitative index of variability called the *mean deviation*. The difference between a group's mean and a person's deviation score is called a *deviation*. (It may be referred to as the person's *deviation score*, also.) The mean deviation is the average of the absolute values of these deviations for the group. In the above example, the mean deviation is 2.4 for Group I and 0.8 for Group II. The definition is summarized by the formula below.

$$MD = \frac{\Sigma \lvert X - M \rvert}{N} \qquad \text{[Eq. 3.3]}$$
$$= \frac{\text{sum of the absolute deviations}}{\text{total number}}$$

In the formula, *MD* stands for mean deviation, *X* for score, *M* for mean, *N* for the total number, Σ for "sum of," and the vertical bars for "the absolute value of" the quantity within them.

The mean deviation has an intuitive appeal. The arithmetic mean is the average score. You and I know intuitively that everyone's score is not equal to the average and could ask, "To what extent do people differ from the mean?" One answer to this question is to report the mean deviation which tells the extent to which people differ on the average from the mean.

The mean deviation would serve well as a measure of the variability, if it were unnecessary to have an index of variability that would be used for other purposes in statistical analysis. However, because the mean deviation uses absolute values, it is unsuited for use in more complex statistical development. Consequently, we need to describe another index of variability of a distribution. This other index of variability is also based on deviations and, thus, is somewhat similar to the mean deviation in both definition and interpretation.

The Standard Deviation (SD)[9]

Definition of the standard deviation The most frequently used index of variability is the *standard deviation*, defined as *the square root of the average squared deviation*. This may be a little clearer if we consider first the average squared deviation and then consider the standard deviation.

The average squared deviation is known as the *variance*, symbolized as SD^2, s^2, or σ^2. This is shown below.

$$SD^2 = \text{the variance}$$
$$= \text{the average squared deviation}$$
$$= \frac{\text{sum of the squared deviation}}{\text{total number of scores}}$$
$$= \frac{\Sigma(X - M)^2}{N} \qquad \text{[Eq. 3.4]}$$

[9]The standard deviation is sometimes symbolized by s or by the lowercase Greek sigma, σ. The formula for the standard deviation was published in 1832 by J. F. Enke, a student of Karl Friedrich Gauss. The term "standard deviation" was first used by Karl Pearson; the term "variance" by R. A. Fisher (1918) (Dudycha & Dudycha, 1972).

The standard deviation is simply the square root of the variance as is shown below.

SD = the standard deviation

$= \sqrt{\text{the variance}}$

$= \sqrt{\text{the average squared deviation}}$

$= \sqrt{\dfrac{\text{sum of squared deviations}}{\text{total number of scores}}}$

$= \sqrt{\dfrac{\Sigma(X - M)^2}{N}}$ [Eq. 3.5]

As an illustration of the standard deviation, assume that these were the test scores of five pupils:

9, 12, 20, 16, 18.

The scores can be arranged as follows and the standard deviation obtained.

X	$X - M$	$(X - M)^2$
9	-6	36
12	-3	9
16	1	1
18	3	9
20	5	25
$\Sigma X = 75$		$\Sigma(X - M)^2 = 80$

$\dfrac{\Sigma X}{N} = M = 15$

$SD = \sqrt{\dfrac{\Sigma(X - M)^2}{N}}$

$SD = \sqrt{\dfrac{80}{5}} = \sqrt{16}$

$SD = 4$

The scores are placed in the first column. The sum of the scores and their mean (M), are at the bottom of this column. The second column shows the deviation, $(X - M)$, of each score from the mean. The third column shows the square of each of these deviations, $(X - M)^2$; the sum of these squares, $\Sigma(X - M)^2$, is shown at the bottom. Equation 3.5 says first find the sum of the squared deviations, divide this sum by N—the total number of scores—and then take the square root of the resulting quotient. In this example, the sum of the squared deviations is 80 and the total number of scores is 5. When 80 is divided by 5, the resulting quotient is 16. (Recall that 16 is the value of the variance.) The square root[10] of 16 is 4. Thus, the standard deviation of this group of scores is 4. Appendix A gives a step-by-step procedure for calculating the standard deviation.

Usefulness of the standard deviation The standard deviation describes the variability of distribution. Large numerical values mean that the scores spread out away from the mean; smaller values indicate that the scores tend to be closer to the mean. Although it is not strictly correct to do so, as a practical matter, little interpretive harm is done if the standard deviation is thought of as the average amount by which scores differ from the mean.[11]

Another way to think about the standard deviation is to note that its magnitude is related to how much the scores vary from each other.[12] The more persons' scores on a test are similar to each other, the smaller will be the value of standard deviation. This interpretation recognizes that the standard deviation describes how scores differ from each other as well as differing from the mean.

[10] The square root of a number can be found very simply with modern pocket calculators. However, a table for finding square roots is presented in Appendix C in case you don't have access to a calculator. The table will be sufficiently accurate for most practical work.

[11] Strictly speaking, this average is equal to the mean deviation (MD) described in the previous section. The mean deviation will generally be slightly smaller than the standard deviation.

[12] The variance of the group is equal to one-half of the mean of the squares of the pairwise differences between persons. See an introductory statistics book, e.g., Anderson and Sclove (1974, p. 121), for further details and examples.

A large value for the standard deviation of a group on a particular test is not necessarily good or bad. Persons will need to reach into their own experience to interpret a particular value. For example, if in one school system the standard deviation of *Otis-Lennon School Ability Test* scores was 5 points, we would be surprised because, in the general school population the standard deviation is about 16. A value of 5 would indicate an unusual degree of homogeneity of scores and would make us look for an explanation.

The mean and standard deviation do not tell anything about the shape of a distribution of scores. A distribution with a given standard deviation may have nearly any shape. This is shown by Figure 3.5. The mean and standard deviation of each of those distributions has the same numerical value, yet each is a different shape.

The standard deviation can be used to compare the variability of two or more groups only when the groups were measured by instruments having the same units of measurement. For example, compare these two sets of scores, representing persons' weights.

$$
\begin{array}{cc}
& \begin{array}{cc} \textit{Set A} & \textit{Set B} \end{array} \\
\begin{array}{c} M = 52.5 \\ SD = 2.96 \end{array} &
\left\{\begin{array}{c} 48 \\ 52 \\ 54 \\ 56 \end{array}\right\}
\left\{\begin{array}{c} 105.6 \\ 114.4 \\ 118.8 \\ 123.2 \end{array}\right\}
\begin{array}{c} M = 115.5 \\ SD = 6.51 \end{array}
\end{array}
$$

The standard deviation of Set A is 2.96, while for Set B it is 6.51. Before you conclude that the persons in Set B are about twice as variable in their weight as those in Set A, you should know that the unit of measurement of the scores in Set B is pounds while the unit of measurement of the scores in Set A is kilograms (1 kilogram = 2.2 pounds). Each measurement in Set B is 2.2 times that of Set A. The persons have the same variability in weight; the unit of measurement is different so the standard deviations are different.

While you would not say that persons' weights are twice as variable in Set B, it is not uncommon for persons to conclude (erro-

neously) that a group of pupils is more variable in reading than in spelling, or in scholastic aptitude than in achievement, etc. simply because the standard deviation of one measure is larger than another. To make this kind of comparison, one would have to be assured that one ability was measured by the same scale with the same units as another ability (e.g., one unit of spelling ability would have to be equal to one unit of reading ability). It is highly unlikely that this would be the case. For these reasons, it is recommended that comparisons of standard deviations be limited to groups that have taken the identical test.

Another use of the standard deviation is in the development of another kind of score—a score telling the location of one person relative to other persons. Such a score—called a linear standard score—will be a topic of the next section.

There are considerably more uses for the standard deviation than those mentioned here. You will encounter many of them as you study the material in this book. Below is a summary of material presented concerning measures of variability.

Summary of Score Variability

Distributions of test scores

1. are described incompletely by measures of central tendency.
2. may differ in both central tendency and variability of scores.
3. can have their degrees of variability described by one or more numerical indices.

The range is an index that

1. tells the distance between the highest and lowest scoring persons.
2. is based on only two scores (highest and lowest) and is easy to compute.

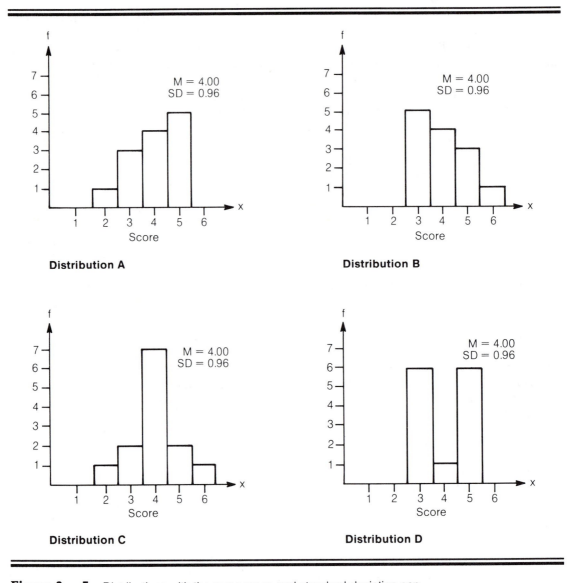

Figure 3 • 5 Distributions with the same mean and standard deviation can have different shapes.

3. ignores the other scores that contribute to the variability of a distribution.
4. can increase its value drastically by the addition of a single score to the group and thereby can be misleading about the variability of the majority of the scores.
5. is not recommended to compare the variability of groups of different sizes.

The mean deviation is an index that

1. is based on the deviation of each of the scores from the mean of the distribution.
2. is equal to the mean of the absolute values of the deviations from the mean.
3. tells the average distance between the mean and persons' scores.

4. is not used in complex statistical analysis because it involves the use of absolute values.

The standard deviation

1. is equal to the square root of the average squared deviation from the mean. (The average squared deviation is called the variance.)
2. can be thought of as the average distance between the mean and persons' scores (even though this is not strictly true).
3. is also based on the deviation of each of the scores from the mean of the distribution.
4. is related to the differences among persons on the characteristic measured by the test: The more persons differ from each other the larger the standard deviation.
5. yields a numerical value that takes on meaning when it can be related to experience with the group and the characteristic being measured.
6. cannot be used to infer the shape of a distribution because distributions with various shapes can have the same mean and standard deviation.
7. can be used to compare the variability of two groups when they have taken the same test; when the tests differ, differences in the units of measurement interfere with comparisons of variability.
8. forms the basis for a norm-referenced score called a linear standard score.

Describing a Pupil's Relative Location in a Distribution

So far we have discussed statistical indices which summarize the scores of an entire group. This section discusses a few different ways to describe an individual's performance relative to or compared to other individuals'. These kinds of descriptions are part of what is known as *norm-referencing*. More complete discussions of both norm-referencing and criterion-referencing are found in Chapters 14 and 17.

A reason for studying norm-referencing techniques lies in their usefulness in answering some rather limited but frequently asked questions. Pupils (and/or their parents) often want to know their class rank or where they stand relative to the class average. Similarly, teachers and school administrators often want information concerning how the pupils in one classroom compare with those in another, or how pupils in their building compare with those in other buildings.

There are many kinds of norm-referencing schemes or scores. This section, however, describes only three: ranks, percentile ranks, and linear standard scores. The latter two types form the basis for developing the many other norm-referenced scores used with educational and psychological tests and discussed in Chapter 14.

Before proceeding, please note that in the discussion below we will speak of raw scores and transformed scores. *Raw scores* are simply the scores obtained by counting the number of right answers or the number of points a person got on a test. *Transformed scores* are scores obtained *from* the raw scores: Various procedures are applied to the raw scores, transforming them into new numbers (i.e., into another kind of score).

Ranks

Perhaps the easiest to learn of the norm-referenced scores is ranking; most people have learned it already. To rank raw scores, they *are ordered from largest to smallest*. The largest score is assigned a rank of 1; the next largest, a rank of 2; and so on, down to the smallest score. In this way, all of the raw scores are transformed into ranks.

The procedure for ranking a set of scores is demonstrated in Table 3.4. Note what is done when persons have the same score. In this case they are tied for the ranks. The tie is resolved by awarding each of the tied persons the average of the ranks for which they are tied. For example, two persons have a score of 34 and thus are tied for ranks of 6 and 7. Rather than arbitrarily awarding one person the rank of 6 and the other a rank of 7, each person is awarded the average of 6 and 7, viz.,

$$\frac{6+7}{2} = 6.5$$

Interpretations of simple ranks of this sort depend on the number of persons being ranked in the group. For example, suppose I told you that of all the classes in testing and measurement I have taught, your class's average midterm exam score ranked second. You might be proud as a group until I also told you I have taught only one other class. Adding another thirteen classes might cause this class's rank to drop, say, from second to fifteenth! Although the class rank has changed from second to fifteenth, the relative location of the group— dead last—has not changed. The problem of interpreting ranks dependent on numbers of persons or objects being ranked is largely overcome when you use percentile ranks.

Score	Rank	
40	1	
36	3 ⎫	Three scores tied
36	3 ⎬	for ranks 2, 3, and 4.
36	3 ⎭	
35	5	
34	6.5 ⎫	Two scores tied
34	6.5 ⎭	for ranks 6 and 7.
33	8	
31	9	
30	10	
26	11	
25	12.5 ⎫	Two scores tied
25	12.5 ⎭	for ranks 12 and 13.
24	14	
23	15	

Table 3 • 4 Ranking 15 scores on an educational psychology test.

Percentile Ranks (PR)[13]

Test publishers and schools use percentile ranks extensively for norm-referenced interpretations of test scores. The *percentile rank* is a *number that tells what percentage of the persons in a defined group have scored lower than the raw score in question.* For example, if 84 percent of the pupils in your class scored lower than Jamie's raw score of 46, then 84 is the percentile rank corresponding to the raw score 46. The symbol for percentile rank is *PR*.

To change a person's raw score into a percentile rank, you need to first conceptualize the raw score as a point on a number line. Then you compute the percentage of scores in the whole distribution below that particular point. The following formula summarizes percentile rank:

$$PR = \frac{\begin{bmatrix} \text{no. of} \\ \text{persons} \\ \text{below} \\ \text{score} \end{bmatrix} + \frac{1}{2} \begin{bmatrix} \text{no. of} \\ \text{persons} \\ \text{having} \\ \text{score} \end{bmatrix}}{\text{total number of persons}} \times 100$$

[Eq. 3.6]

Suppose these numbers represent the raw scores of 25 students on an arithmetic test:

14	26	26	27	29
20	26	27	28	29
24	26	27	28	31
25	26	27	28	32
25	26	27	28	36

To find the percentile rank of the raw score 26, we note that there are five students with scores lower than 26 and six students with scores equal to 26. Substituting this information, along with the total number of students, into Equation 3.6 gives us:

---

[13] Percentiles or "scales of merit" were developed by Sir Francis Galton (1889) (Walker, 1929). The relationship between simple ranks and percentile ranks is given by the equation $PR = (1 - \text{Rank} - 0.5 \div N)$.

$$PR = \frac{5 + \frac{1}{2}(6)}{25} \times 100 = 32$$

Thus, the percentile rank of the raw score 26 is equal to 32. Or, alternately, 32 percent of the class scored below the point 26.

The number of persons having a raw score is multiplied by one-half before being added to the "number below" because a percentile rank is computed for a *point* on a number line that represents the score scale. Even though you report a raw score as a whole number, it is conceptualized as being located somewhere in an interval that extends one-half unit above and one-half unit below the exact point in question. Procedures for computing percentile ranks for a group of scores are described in Appendix A.

Interpreting percentile ranks Although I discuss percentile ranks again in Chapter 14, here are a few suggestions for using and interpreting them:

1. A student's percentile rank depends on the group in which the comparison is made. The same raw score can be the highest in a slow group and the lowest in a bright group.
2. Percentile ranks are relatively easy to compute and can be explained to and understood by most parents and pupils who have acquired the concept of percentage.
3. When published tests are administered, the school often reports a pupil's percentile ranks for both local and national norm groups. The percentile rank in a local group indicates more about a pupil's likely performance day-to-day in the classroom. The national percentile rank may be meaningful if a pupil has to compete with a broader group outside of the local community.
4. The term percentile rank refers to the fraction of the group scoring below a given point. The point itself is called a *percentile*. A percentile and a percentile rank are

inverses. Thus, in the example above, the percentile rank of the point 26 is 32; and the *32nd percentile* is 26.
5. Avoid confusing percentile and percentile rank with *percentage score*. A percentage score is the percentage of the questions a pupil answered correctly. If a pupil answered 26 out of 36 questions correctly, then the pupil got 72 percent of the questions. Thus, the pupil's percentage score is 72.
6. Don't give a percentile rank a more precise interpretation than is warranted because all scores contain a certain degree of error or unreliability.
7. Equal numerical differences between percentile ranks do not mean equal differences in raw scores. The difference, for example, between the percentile ranks of 32 and 38 is four, but the difference between the corresponding raw scores may be 10 points or one point. (We cannot tell from looking at the percentile ranks.)

Special percentiles Certain percentiles are frequently reported in testing and measurement literature. Among the most frequently reported are *quartiles,* listed below with symbols that are often used with them.

Name	Symbol	Explanation
First quartile	Q_1	The score point below which twenty-five percent of the scores fall. This score is the twenty-fifth percentile.
Second quartile or median	Q_2 or *Mdn.*	The score point below which fifty percent of the scores fall. This score is the fiftieth percentile.
Third quartile	Q_3	The score point below which seventy-five percent of the scores fall. This score is the seventy-fifth percentile.

Notice that these are points of the score scale and not intervals. Technically, then, it is incorrect to say that someone's score is "in" the third quartile. Rather, that a person's score is "at" a particular point on the score scale such as the third quartile.

Formulas for computing these quartiles (indeed for computing any percentile) are found in introductory statistics books and will not appear here. These formulas are simply variations of Equation A.1 for the median. For the distribution of test scores in Table 3.2[14], the quartiles are:

$$Q_1 = 25.7$$

$$Q_2 = 26.8$$

$$Q_3 = 28.2$$

Linear Standard Scores: z-Scores

Definition of z-scores[15] Simple ranks of percentile ranks are scores which describe persons' location in a distribution. These norm-referenced scores do not, however, describe the level of a score relative to the average of a group. A *z-score*, on the other hand, is a norm-referenced score that describe a person's location in terms of distance from the mean relative to the standard deviation. The z-score expresses location in terms of the number of units a person is located above or below the mean—the size of the unit being equal to the numerical value of the standard deviation. A compact way of saying this would be that a person's test score is located below the mean a distance, for example, equal to one and one-half times the standard deviation of the group. The person's z-score in this example would be equal to −1.50.

A linear z-score as described above is defined by the formula:

[14]See also Appendix A, Table A.1.
[15]The z-score scale was first used by James McKeen Cattell (1890).

$$z = \frac{X - M}{SD} = \frac{\text{raw score} - \text{mean}}{\text{standard deviation}} \qquad [\text{Eq. 3.7}]$$

The example below will illustrate this definition and how to obtain z-scores:

Pupil	Raw score	Deviation score $(X - M)$	z-score
Jimmy	9	−6	−1.50
Bill	12	−3	−0.75
Sally	16	1	0.25
Arthur	18	3	0.75
Bertha	20	5	1.25

Mean = 15, Standard deviation = 4

To transform a person's raw score to a z-score, first the mean is subtracted, and then this deviation is divided by the standard deviation. Thus, Jimmy's z-score is found by Equation 3.7 to be:

$$z = \frac{9 - 15}{4} = \frac{-6}{4} = -1.50$$

When persons such as Jimmy have raw scores *below* the mean, their z-scores will have *negative* algebraic signs. Persons such as Sally, Arthur, and Bertha, whose raw scores are *above* the mean will have *positive* z-scores. If a person has a raw score exactly *equal* to the mean, the z-score will be *zero*.

Usefulness of z-scores A z-score is one way to express a person's relative achievement or relative ability. The standard deviation is a number that expresses how people, on the average, differ from the mean. The numerator of Equation 3.7 is an individual's deviation from the mean, while the denominator is the average deviation. Thus, if a person's z-score was between +1 and −1, it would indicate that that person differed from the mean by less than average. Persons whose z-scores are greater than +1 or smaller than −1 deviate from the mean distances more than the average. Since in some distributions very few persons have z-scores less than −1.5 or greater than +1.5, someone with a z-score lower than −1.5 is viewed as having atypically low attainment (relative to the rest of the group) and someone with z = +1.50 or higher is viewed as having atypically high attainment. Note that this is a relative interpretation of ability rather than an absolute interpretation.

If the same characteristic is measured in the same group but with, say, two different metrics, the two sets of measures will yield two different means and standard deviations. However, converting each set of measures to z-scores will reference both to the same type of scale making them equivalent. Consider the weight measurements example presented earlier in which the same persons were measured in both pounds and kilograms. Notice what happens below when each person's measurements are converted to z-scores.

Person	Weight in kilograms		Weight in pounds	
	X	z	X	z
A	48	−1.52	105.6	−1.52
B	52	−0.17	114.4	−0.17
C	54	0.51	118.8	0.51
D	56	1.18	123.2	1.18

Even though the "pounds" mean and standard deviation are different than the "kilograms" mean and standard deviation, the persons' relative positions in the distributions are the same. Thus, each person's z-score in the pounds distribution is identical to that person's z-score in the kilogram distribution.

A z-score is a linear transformation of a raw score. This means that if you graphed the raw scores against their corresponding z-scores, the resulting plot would be a straight line. A result of this linear property is that the shape of the raw score distribution and the z-score distribution will be the same. Only the numerical scale on which persons' abilities are measured will change. Note that for any group, the mean of the z-scores will always be zero

and the standard deviation of the z-scores will always be one, regardless of the numerical values of the mean and standard deviation of the raw scores.

As a norm-referencing score, the z-score has several practical disadvantages. One disadvantage is that a z-score is difficult to explain to students and parents: Understanding it requires an understanding of the mean and standard deviation. Another practical disadvantage is that "plus" and "minus" signs are used. Transcription errors, resulting in omitted or interchanged algebraic signs, are frequent. Further, it is difficult to explain to students why their test performances are reported as negative (and/or fractional) scores (e.g., "I got 15 of the 45 questions right. How could my score be −1.34?"). Likewise, the decimal point is subject to frequent transcription error.

These practical problems are easily overcome, however, by transforming the z-score to yet another kind of score. I shall describe how to do this in Chapter 14. These additional transformations are easy to accomplish, and they maintain the conceptual norm-referenced advantage[16] of z-scores while overcoming their practical limitations.

Summary of Relative Location in a Distribution

Scores

1. obtained by counting the number of right answers are called raw scores.
2. that tell the examinees' relative location in a given group are called norm-referenced.

Ranks

1. are obtained by ordering raw scores from largest to smallest and assigning numbers telling the order.

---

[16]This is not to say that norm-referenced scores are without conceptual *disadvantage*. Such disadvantages are discussed in Chapter 17.

2. for which there are ties are resolved by assigning each of the tied persons the average of the ranks for which they are tied.
3. can be interpreted only if the number of persons in the group is known.
4. usually change as more persons are added to a group.

Percentile ranks

1. tell the percentage of persons in a defined group that have scored lower than the raw score in question.
2. are computed for points on the number line that represents the score scale rather than for raw score integers.
3. are widely reported, norm-referenced scores because they are easy to compute and are easy for pupils, parents, teachers, and other test consumers to understand.
4. are generally more useful if the reference group is a local one rather than a nationally defined group.
5. are distinguished from percentiles, which are points on the score scale for which a given percentage of the group scored lower.
6. are also distinguished from percentage scores, which tell the percent of the items on the test a person answered correctly.
7. should not be given more precise interpretations than are warranted. They are usually reported to the nearest whole number.
8. do not have a linear relationship to raw scores. A difference of a fixed amount between successive percentile ranks may represent a larger or smaller difference between the corresponding raw scores depending on their location on the score scale.
9. of special points, called quartiles, should be noted: the first quartile, the second quartile and the third quartile.

z-scores

1. are linear standard scores: linear transformations of the raw scores.
2. tell a person's distance and direction from the mean by stating how many standard deviation units a person is above or below the mean.
3. express persons' deviation from the mean in terms of the standard deviation of their group. The same deviation may, therefore, result in larger or smaller z-scores depending on the standard deviation.
4. can be used to make scores in two distributions relatively equivalent even though the original distributions may have different standard deviations.
5. have the same shape distributions as the original distribution of raw scores.
6. have a distribution with a mean equal to zero and a standard deviation equal to one regardless of the numerical values of the mean and standard deviation of the raw score distribution.
7. have the disadvantage of being (algebraically) signed decimal fractions. Their understanding depends on knowledge of the concepts of the mean and the standard deviation. These disadvantages are largely overcome by further transforming them.

The Correlation Coefficient

Correlation refers to the relationships between two or more sets of scores. A correlational line of inquiry asks: How do persons' relative standings on one measure relate to their relative standings on other measures? We may ask, for example, how persons' scores on college entrance examinations relate to their grade point averages computed at the end of their first year of college. The answer to such a question depends on such factors as the nature of the entrance examination taken, the college attended, the courses taken, and the manner in which grades are assigned. A *correlation coefficient is a statistic that quantifies the degree of relationship observed between two or more measures of attributes*. Correlation coefficients are bits of information which help to answer such questions as: Which items should be included in a norm-referenced test so that its reliability will be high? Do two (or more) given tests measure the same attribute? How stable are individuals' test scores over given periods of time? Is this test a useful predictor of future success in this school or job? Does the test really measure the attribute it claims to measure? Since the answers to these and many other kinds of questions are founded, at least in part, on data consisting of the numerical values of correlation coefficients, some understanding of the correlation coefficient is prerequisite to subsequent study of measurement principles.

Defining the Correlation Coefficient (r)[17]

We will begin the discussion of the correlation coefficient by calling to mind the z-score:

$$z = \frac{X - M}{SD}$$

This score represents the number of standard deviation units a raw score falls above (or below) the mean.

When we speak of the relationship between two sets of scores, we assume there are scores available on at least two tests for each person. Consider a person's z-score on each test—Test

X and Test Y. The question the correlation coefficient answers is: "How do persons' z-scores on Test X relate to their z-scores on Test Y?"

The symbol for the correlation coefficient is r_{xy} (sometimes ρ_{xy} is used), and the formula that defines it is

$$r_{xy} = \frac{\Sigma z_x z_y}{N} \qquad \text{[Eq. 3.8]}$$

The sum that is placed in the numerator is found by first obtaining each person's z-scores on Test X (i.e., z_x) and on Test Y (i.e., z_y), then multiplying, for each person, z_x by z_y. The sum of all such z-score products (i.e., $\Sigma z_x z_y$) is placed in the numerator. To obtain the numerical value of the correlation coefficient, divide this sum by N, the total number of pairs of z-scores. From this formula, you can see that the *correlation coefficient is the average product of persons' z-score pairs on two measures.*

It will be helpful in understanding the correlation coefficient if you see a couple of numerical examples of its computation. These examples are shown in Table 3.5.

This table shows the scores of eleven pupils on each of three tests. The pupils have been arranged in descending order according to their verbal (V) aptitude scores. Look at the first two columns of tests scores and notice that the two tests order the pupils in about the same way. However, the relationship between the V-scores and the arithmetic (A) scores is not as strong.

This correspondence is more apparent if the z-scores are examined. The correspondence between the verbal z-scores and the reading z-scores is quite close. This means that the pupils' verbal aptitude and reading test scores have a high degree of relationship (or correlation). However, since the correspondence between the verbal z-scores and the arithmetic z-scores is not as close, the comparison indicates a somewhat lower relationship between verbal aptitude test scores and arithmetic test scores for these eleven people.

[17]This chapter discusses only the coefficient known as the *Pearson product moment correlation coefficient,* named after Karl Pearson (1857–1936) who, through the synthesis of the earlier work of Galton, Adrian, Plana, Gauss, and Bravais, derived the formula (Walker, 1958). Other types of correlation coefficients are used in testing and measurement also. These types will be mentioned as they occur in other chapters. Appendix A discusses the computation of the *rank difference correlation.*

A correlation coefficient quantifies the degree of relationship that is present in the scores. For each pupil listed in Table 3.5, the products of the z-scores for the verbal and the reading tests and for the verbal and the arithmetic z-scores were computed. These are shown in the last two columns. The sums of these products are shown at the bottoms of the columns. When these sums are divided by the number of pupils, the *correlation coefficient* results. The correlation between the verbal and reading test scores is .967 and is .710 between the verbal and the arithmetic test scores. You can see that the numerical values of the correlation coefficients reflect the impression you had when you compared the scores in the table. The number .967 reflects a high degree of relationship, while the number .710 shows a somewhat lesser degree of relationship.

Graphing Relationships via Scatter Diagrams

The relationship between the *paired scores* is also apparent if they are plotted on a graph as in Figure 3.6. In these graphs the verbal score scale is the horizontal axis and the reading and arithmetic score scales are the vertical axes. For example, look at the mark for Pupil B in Figure 3.6(A). This pupil's verbal and reading scores were 77 and 54, respectively. This mark, located in the upper right hand corner of the graph, occurs at the intersection of one line running vertically from the verbal score of 77 and the other line running horizontally from the reading score of 54. The intersection of these lines marks a point that represents the paired scores for this pupil. The paired scores for all the other pupils are marked in the same way. This kind of graph, showing the relationship between the paired scores on two tests is called a *scatter diagram* (sometimes a scattergram).

A teacher can obtain considerable insight into the relationship between sets of test scores without actually computing a correlation coefficient by making a scatter diagram.

In Figure 3.6(A) the marks lie along an almost straight line from the lower left of the graph to the upper right. In Figure 3.6(B), however, the marks do not come as close to lying along a straight line, although there *is a trend* in the graph from the lower left to the upper right. The tendency for the points of a scatter diagram to lie along a straight line is central to the concept of correlation[18]: The higher the degree of correlation between two sets of measure, the closer the points come to lying along a straight line. As the degree of correlation between two sets of measures becomes less, the points tend to scatter away from this straight line, and not lie close to it. The pattern of the scattering of these points around the straight line is elliptical. The more narrow the elliptical pattern is, the higher the degree of correlation. The less the degree of correlation, the wider these elliptical patterns of scatter diagrams become. When there is no relationship between the scores on the two measures, the pattern will widen until it is circular, rather than elliptical (see Figure 3.7).

Interpreting Correlation Coefficients: Degrees of Relationship

The degree of relationship between two sets of measures is reflected in the numerical value of the correlation coefficient. A perfect *positive* correlation would have a correlation coefficient of +1.00 ($r = +1.00$). The plotted points on the scatter diagram would all fall exactly on a straight line extending upward from left to right. In this kind of situation, a person's z-

---

[18] Actually, the interpretations of the correlation coefficient in this chapter assume that in a large population of persons the relationship between the two sets of scores follows a linear trend. What this means is that the average (mean) scores on the second test for all persons having the *same* score on the first test, all fall along a straight line.

Pupil	Verbal Score (V)	Reading Score (R)	Arith-metic (A)	z-scores			Product of z-scores	
				z_V	z_R	z_A	$z_V z_R$	$z_V z_A$
A	82	59	48	1.56	1.32	0.25	2.06	0.39
B	77	54	65	1.30	0.88	1.83	1.14	2.38
C	70	55	43	0.92	0.97	−0.21	0.89	−0.19
D	65	58	58	0.66	1.23	1.18	0.81	0.78
E	59	51	40	0.34	0.61	−0.49	0.21	−0.17
F	53	44	47	0.02	0.00	0.16	0.00	0.003
G	45	38	55	−0.41	−0.53	0.90	0.22	−0.37
H	41	34	44	−0.62	−0.88	−0.12	0.55	0.74
I	34	35	25	−0.99	−0.79	−1.88	0.78	1.86
J	30	30	40	−1.20	−1.23	−0.49	1.48	.59
K	23	26	33	−1.58	−1.58	−1.14	2.50	1.80
Sums							10.64	7.81

$$\Sigma z_V z_R = 10.64 \qquad \Sigma z_V z_A = 7.81$$

$$r_{VR} = \frac{10.64}{11} = 0.967 \qquad r_{VA} = \frac{7.81}{11} = 0.710$$

Adapted from *Measuring Pupil Achievement and Aptitude*, Second Edition, by C.M. Lindvall and A.J. Nitko, © 1975 by Harcourt Brace Jovanovich, Inc. Reprinted by permission of the publisher.

Table 3 • 5 Hypothetical scores for 11 pupils on a verbal aptitude test, a reading test, and an arithmetic test.

score on one measure would be exactly equal to the person's z-score on the second measure.[19]

An absolute lack of relationship between two measures will result in a correlation coefficient of 0.00 ($r = 0.00$). In such a relationship, the person's score on one measure can in no way be predicted from their score on the other measure. Persons' z-scores on one measure are completely unrelated to their z-scores on the second measure.

Also, measures may be perfectly related in a negative manner. A perfect *negative* correlation ($r = -1.00$) is reflected in a scatter diagram in which the plotted points all fall exactly on a straight line extending downward from left to right. Persons would have z-scores on the two measures that are identical in absolute numerical value, but are of opposite alge-

braic signs. For example, a person having $z_x = +1.65$ would have $z_y = -1.65$.

Figure 3.7 shows the scatter diagrams and corresponding correlation coefficients for different degrees of relationships between two sets of scores. Each dot represents a pair of scores for a person. Compare scatter diagrams (A) and (E). Both show perfect correlation, but (A) shows a perfect positive correlation, while (E) shows a perfect negative correlation. The *strength* of the relationship is identical in both cases, but the *direction* of the relationship differs. Since the correlation is perfect in both cases, knowing a person's score on one test would allow us to predict exactly the score the person would obtain on the second test: Perfect correlation means perfect prediction.

Perfect correlations, however, are seldom found in practical work with educational and psychological test scores. The reasons for this are many and include such things as the tests

[19] A person's raw scores may not be identical on the two measures, but the person's z-scores would be identical.

A. Scatter diagram for verbal vs. reading

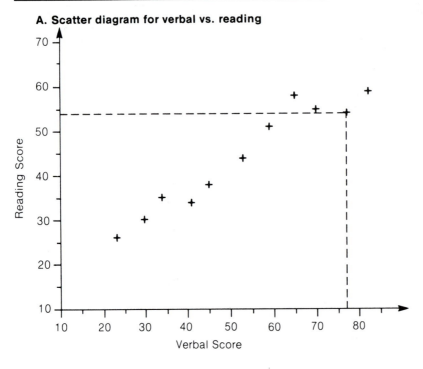

B. Scatter diagram for verbal vs. arithmetic

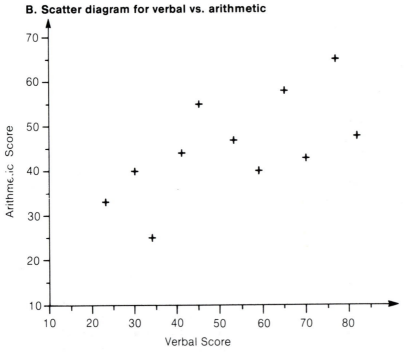

Figure 3 • 6
Scatter diagrams of the (A) verbal aptitude vs. reading tests and (B) verbal aptitude vs. arithmetic tests for the 11 pupils' scores shown in Table 3.5.

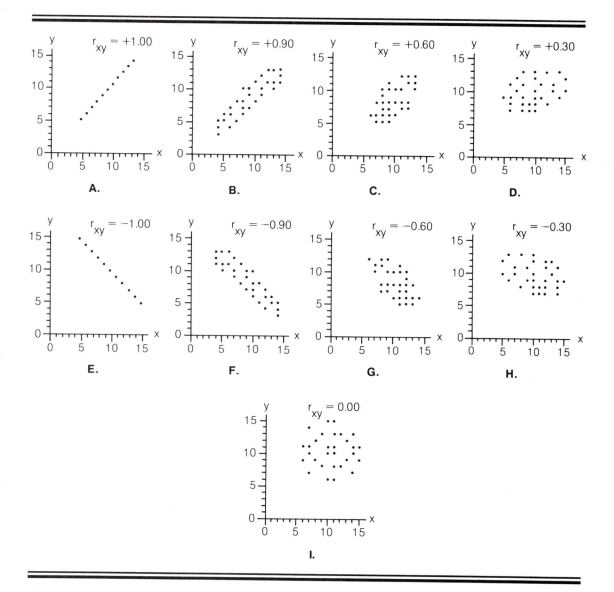

Figure 3 • 7   Scatter diagrams showing different degrees of correlation.

containing random error of measurement, the units of measurement being unequal, the distributions of the test scores not having identical shapes and skewness, and the two variables possibly not being related in a simple, linear manner (Carroll, 1961).

Other degrees of relationship are shown in Figure 3.7. In (B) and (F) the correlation is +0.90 and −0.90, respectively. Tests correlating to this extent would be said to be highly related. Again, notice that the degree of relationship is the same except the direction of the relationship is different. In both cases, the plotted points in the scatter diagram tend to fall along straight lines, even though they do not fall exactly along lines as in (A) and (E). Although perfect prediction of scores on one test from scores on another is not possible here, reasonably accurate prediction would be possible, even though not perfect.

Comparing (C) and (G), we see that as the relationship between the test scores becomes lower, a greater scatter occurs away from a straight line. There is still a tendency in (C) for high scores on one test to be associated with high scores on the other, and for low scores on one to be associated with low scores on the other. Similarly, in (G), a negative relationship holds: high scores on one test are associated with low scores on the other, while lower scores on one test are associated with high scores on the other. It would still be possible to predict a person's scores on Test Y from knowledge of the person's score on Test X, but such predictions would have to be made with a broader margin of error than in the case for a correlation of $+0.90$ or -0.90.

In (D) and (H) the correlation is $+0.40$ and -0.40, respectively. The elliptical pattern is broader here because the degree of relationship is lower. Predictions of persons' Test Y scores from their Test X scores are made with lessened confidence and a wider margin of error.

Finally, (I) shows the case where there is a complete lack of relationship between the scores on the two tests. There is no tendency for scores to be associated in the way illustrated by the other figures. A person with a high score on Test X could have either a high, middle, or low score on Test Y. Thus, the scores are said to be unrelated or uncorrelated, and $r = 0.00$. Note the circular pattern of the points in the scatter diagrams.

In practical work with tests, correlations of exactly zero are as rare as correlations of exactly $+1.00$ and -1.00. These particular numerical values, however, serve as benchmarks: Actual correlation coefficients take on meaning in the context of these limiting values.

Interpreting Correlation Coefficients: Further Considerations

In spite of its exceptionally frequent use in testing and measurement and in educational and psychological research, the correlation coefficient is often misused and misinterpreted. Many of the reasons for confusion are technical and cannot be explored in depth in this chapter. However, the student should be aware that some experience in using and interpreting (and perhaps, misinterpreting) this statistical index is necessary for complete mastery. Some of this experience can be gained through studying the material in subsequent chapters of this book.

"Good correlations" Frequent questions are "What is a 'good' numerical value for the correlation coefficient? Is $r = 0.70$ high enough? Or, is $r = 0.90$ better?" As you study the uses of correlation in education, you will come to realize that such questions cannot be answered in the abstract. There is no magic point on the number line above which lie good correlation coefficients and below which lie poor ones. Before particular values of correlation coefficients can be evaluated, evaluators need to identify particular interpretive contexts. First, persons interpreting correlations must have an understanding of the tests being used and the variables these tests are supposed to measure, as well as an understanding of the host of circumstances and factors affecting status on these variables.

As an example, think of a group of first grade pupils in a particular school and the correlation between their scores on a verbal aptitude test administered at the beginning of the school year and their scores on a reading achievement test administered at the end of the school year. Suppose that $r = 0.96$ (recall Figure 3.7). With a relatively small margin of error, you could predict pupils' end-of-year reading achievement from their beginning-of-year aptitude test scores. Is this a "good" correlation? Does this degree of correlation imply that "them that has, gets"? Suppose in another school with similar first graders, the correlation between the same two test scores is zero. Is this "bad"? One could argue that 0.96 is bad because the instruction in first grade did not suit all the children. As a consequence, the children's relative achievement at the end of first grade pretty much reflected their relative ordering at the beginning of the year. From that same viewpoint it may be argued that the correlation of zero is good, because the second school, perhaps, adapted instruction to the pupils allowing both "low" and "high" entry skill pupils to achieve equally and thus "upsetting" the relationship between entry skills and final performance. What is good or bad for a correlation coefficient depends on the context, then, and not on the particular number per se. The number expresses the degree of relationship and not how that relationship should be interpreted. Incidentally, in this hypothetical example, the arguments for or against a particular value of r being "good" or "bad" cannot be supported by considering the numerical value of the correlation coefficient alone. Several factors, including, among others, pupils' general level of performance (i.e., the means) and their variability (i.e., the standard deviations), need to be considered.

Even when the correlation coefficient may be used legitimately as an indicator of the possible accuracy with which scores may be predicted (for example, in selection situations), experience is needed in order to interpret particular values. It is unusual, for example, for tests to correlate with measures of success on the job higher than .60 (Cronbach, 1970). Yet correlations smaller than this can make substantial improvement over simple random selection in the quality of those selected for particular jobs.

Correlation and causation   Correlation does not imply causality: If two measures correlate,

the underlying attributes are not necessarily causally related. For example, of several subtests in a readiness battery, a measure of the ability to recognize names of alphabet letters when they are said aloud has the highest correlation with reading achievement measured at the end of the first grade (Bond & Dykstra, 1967; DeHirsch, Jansky & Langford, 1966; Durell, 1958; Hildreth, Griffiths, & McGauvran, 1969). This does not imply, however, that knowing letter names is prerequisite to reading or that knowledge of letter names causes good reading, as several training experiments have shown (Beck, 1981; Jenkins, Bausell, & Jenkins, 1972; Samuels, 1972; Ohnmacht, 1969). Perhaps a third variable, the home environment, plays a part: Those pupils who learn to read best under traditional instruction come from homes that stress early learning of a number of intellectual skills including learning the names of the alphabet. The third variable—learning general intellectual skills—may thus be the cause of the relationship between the scores on the alphabet test and the reading test. If so, then teaching pupils the alphabet in school may not significantly improve reading scores.

Similarly, there would be a correlation between the dollar amount of damage done by a fire and the total cost of the equipment brought to the scene of the fire by the fire department. The more costly the equipment brought to the fire, the more damage is done by the fire. This doesn't, of course, mean that if fire fighting equipment is abandoned and replaced by the bucket brigade, the dollar damage of fires will decrease. The magnitude of the fire is the third variable—the fire, not the equipment, causes the damage. Larger fires are only *contained* by the use of more costly equipment.

There would be a positive correlation between shoe size and reading comprehension grade-equivalent scores for a population of elementary school children (cf. Blommers & Forsyth, 1977). Children with larger feet read better: They are older and have more reading instruction. The larger feet are in eighth grade and so are the better readers. Of course, we wouldn't recommend a reading readiness program in which we stretched each child's feet. Yet educators *have* recommended instructional procedures primarily on the basis of correlations rather than on demonstrations of the effectiveness of these procedures (Cronbach & Snow, 1977).

Extraneous factors can raise or lower the correlation Correlation coefficients appear in test manuals and research reports. When we encounter them, our first tendency is to interpret them as reflecting the degree of relationship between the attributes underlying the observed test scores. A number of extraneous factors can be identified, however, which raise (or lower) the correlation coefficient reported, masking the true nature of the relationship between the variables being measured.

Suppose, for example, that two human characteristics have a certain degree of relationship when no extraneous factors are operating. The calculated value of the correlation coefficient, r, will be lower than it should be whenever one or more of the following factors are operating (Carroll, 1961; McNemar, 1969):

1. Error of measurement Random errors of measurement in one or both tests will lower the obtained correlation.

2. Restricting the range Shortening the range of scores on one or more of the measures (e.g., by considering only pupils placed into a homogeneous ability group) will lower the obtained correlation.

3. Shapes of the distributions Unless the distributions of scores on the two tests have identical shapes and degrees of skewness, the correlation cannot reach 1.00.[20] In general,

differently shaped and skewed distributions for the two tests will lower the obtained correlation.[21]

4. Lack of linear relationship The Pearson product moment correlation discussed in this chapter measures the degree of linear relationship between two tests. If the test scores have a systematic *curvilinear* relationship, the correlation expressed as Equation 3.8 will not detect this relationship, and if r is used, it may lead to a belief the variables are essentially unrelated.

The calculated value of the correlation coefficient will be spuriously higher than it should be when one or more of the following factors are operating (Carroll, 1961; McNemar, 1969):

1. Special selection of persons Special selection or elimination of persons for or from a group can increase the correlation over what it would be in the complete population. The correlation would be higher, for example, when the scatter diagram of the scores of those remaining in the group has a more elliptical shape.

2. Heterogeneity on a third variable If the correlation between two variables is due in part (or whole) to a third variable, the correlation will become larger when the measures of the persons on the third variable become more heterogeneous (i.e., spread-out) on the third variable. Consider again the example of shoe size vs. reading comprehension. The third variable, number of years of reading instruction, is correlated with both shoe size and

---

[20] Carroll (1961) outlines a method for determining the maximum value a correlation coefficient can have.

[21] Among the things which cause two tests to result in differently shaped distributions in a group are scaling problems and floor and ceiling effects. Scaling problems occur when the tests have unequal units of measurement. A "floor" effect means that the test is too hard and, hence, doesn't measure the low ability pupils very well. The distribution is positively skewed. A "ceiling" effect is just the reverse: The test is too easy, doesn't measure the high ability pupils well, and hence, the distribution is negatively skewed.

reading comprehension. If we look only at pupils with the *same* number of years of reading instruction, shoe size and reading comprehension correlate zero. But if we look at pupils with a wide range of years of reading instruction, the correlation between shoe size and reading comprehension becomes positive.[22]

3. Part with whole correlation If Total Score = Part A + Part B + Part C, for example, then the correlation between Total Score and one of the parts will be increased because the part is included in the Total Score.

Correlation coefficients and sample size A correlation coefficient is computed on the test scores obtained from the *sample of persons*, not on the scores of all the persons in a population. This means that the correlation computed from the sample only *estimates* the numerical value of the correlation in the population. Such estimates of correlation coefficients will vary from sample to sample because of the persons who happen by chance to be in any particular sample. If, for example, the correlation between two tests was .50 in the entire population, it would not be unusual for

---

[22]The statistical procedure for eliminating the extraneous influence of a third variable on a correlation is called *partial correlation* (see, e.g., McNemar, 1969).

10 different samples of 30 persons each to show correlations such as: 0.35, 0.25, 0.22, 0.69, 0.30, 0.55, 0.47, 0.49, 0.62, 0.53.

In small samples, one person's score can often affect the numerical value of the correlation coefficient substantially. Figure 3.8 demonstrates the effect on the numerical value. The correlation of 0.70 (Panel A) drops to 0.60 (Panel B) when the person with $X = 12$, $Y = 12$ is replaced by a person with $X = 13$, $Y = 7$, even though all the other persons' scores remain the same.

Fluctuations in the size of the correlation coefficient will be larger if samples, instead of being randomly drawn from the same, common population, come from different colleges, communities, or companies (Cronbach, 1970). Figure 3.9 shows an example of these fluctuations for the correlation of the scores on the *American College Test* (ACT) with first semester college grade point averages.

Examples of typical correlations The student unfamiliar with correlation coefficients frequently must learn through experience what numerical values of correlation coefficients to expect to see in the literature or in test manuals. I have already implied that the size correlation considered "good" or "high" is relative. For example, if existing tests seldom attain a correlation of .60 with success criteria then a correlation of .65 by a new test would indi-

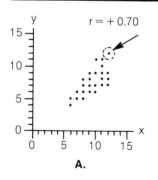

A.

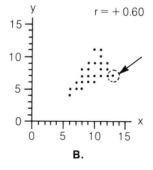

B.

Figure 3 • 8 An example of how one person's test scores can alter the value of the correlation coefficient. In this example, $N = 25$.

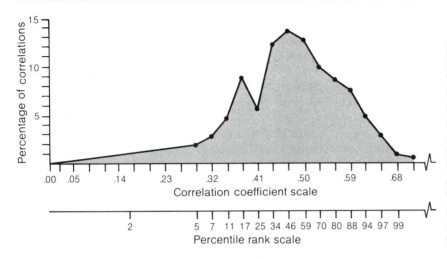

Figure 3 • 9
Distribution of correlations of weighted ACT scores with overall first semester freshman GPA for 437 colleges (1965–1967). It is unusual for tests to correlate above 0.60 with a criterion measure. In this example, approximately 91% of the correlations are less than 0.60.

Source: Multiple correlation data from Cole & Hanson (1973, p. 137)

cate an improvement. Table 3.6 presents several correlations so that you can begin to get a "feel" of the size of correlations to expect when studying about educational and psychological tests.

Summary of Correlation

The correlation coefficient

1. is a statistical index that quantifies the degree of relationship observed between two or more measures.
2. describes the extent to which persons' relative standing in the distribution of measures of one attribute corresponds to their relative standing in the distribution of measures of another attribute.
3. may reflect a positive, negative, or no relationship between variables.
4. is defined as the average product of persons' z-score pairs on two measures.
5. is positive when persons' z-scores on one measure tend to have the same algebraic sign as their z-scores on a second measure; negative when z-scores on one mea-

sure tend to correspond to opposite signed z-scores on a second measure; zero when no systematic relationship exists between persons' z-scores on the two measures.

6. is interpreted based on the assumption that in a large population, there is a linear relationship between the two sets of scores.

The scatter diagram

1. is a graph of the pairs of scores for persons in a group.
2. will appear as an elliptical pattern when scores are related: the narrower the elliptical pattern the higher the degree of relationship.
3. can be used to gain insight into the relationships among persons' test scores without computing the correlation coefficient.

Degrees of relationship

1. A perfect positive relationship would result in $r = +1.00$, and all points of the scatter diagram would fall on a straight line extending upward from left to right.

Variables	Subjects	r	References
1. Salary of high school teachers vs. infant death rate	Averages of teachers' salaries and infant mortality rates in 280 U.S. cities with population over 30,000	− .69	Thorndike (1939)
2. Score on *Measurement Competency Test* vs. gain score on same test	National sample of 341 teacher-training school graduates tested two years apart	− .51	Mayo (1967)
3. Attitudes toward school activities and teachers vs. anxiety about school	3206 sixth through twelfth graders in one Maryland county school district	− .43	Epstein & McPartland (1976)
4. Attitudes toward school activities and teachers vs. number of unexcused school absences	Same group as (3) above	− .29	Epstein & McPartland (1976)
5. Number of statistics courses taken vs. gain score on *Measurement Competency Test*	Same group as (2) above	− .09	Mayo (1967)
6. Percent increase in body weight vs. gain score on arithmetic test	522 twelve-year-old boys over a two-year period (Harvard Growth Study)	+ .01	Dearborn & Rothney (1941)
7. Popularity in classroom vs. reputation for disturbing class	349 sixth-graders in Nashville City Schools	+ .01	Brozovich (1970)
8. Popularity in classroom vs. *Lorge-Thorndike Intelligence Test* scores	349 sixth-graders in Nashville City Schools	+ .26	Brozovich (1970)
9. Illicit drug use vs. stated church attendance	803 men and women ages 18 to 85 in New York City ghetto	+ .28	Kleinman & Lukoff (1978)
10. Illicit drug use vs. friends' use of drugs	803 men and women ages 18 to 85 in New York City ghetto	+ .48	Kleinman & Lukoff (1978)
11. High school grade point average vs. college grade point average	Undergraduate Chicanos at a western multi-campus university Campus 1 ($N = 261$) Campus 2 ($N = 84$) Campus 3 ($N = 180$) Campus 4 ($N = 131$)	 + .37 + .42 + .21 + .30	Goldman & Hewitt (1975)
12. High school grade point average vs. college grade point average	Undergraduate Anglos at the above university Campus 1 ($N = 5,635$) Campus 2 ($N = 5,500$) Campus 3 ($N = 2,926$) Campus 4 ($N = 3,127$)	 + .37 + .40 + .43 + .30	Goldman & Hewitt (1975)
13. College student course achievement vs. student rating of instructor's rapport with class	Average correlation from studies representing students in 28 different courses	+ .31	Cohen (1981)
14. College student course achievement vs. student rating of instructor's skill in teaching	Average correlation from studies representing students in 40 different courses	+ .50	Cohen (1981)
15. Popularity in classroom vs. reputation as good looking	349 sixth-graders in Nashville City Schools	+ .80	Brozovich (1970)

Table 3 • 6 Examples of correlation coefficients reported in various research articles and reports.

2. A perfect negative relationship would be reflected in $r = -1.00$, and all points of the scatter diagram would fall on a straight line extending downward from left to right.
3. No relationship is reflected in $r = 0.00$.
4. r-values of $+1.00$, 0.00, and -1.00 are benchmarks against which real world correlations are compared. Do not expect them in actual practice.
5. The numerical values of r always fall between -1.00 and $+1.00$.
6. The *degree* (or strength) *of relationship* between two measures is reflected in the numerical value of r, irrespective of its algebraic sign; the *direction* of the relationship is shown by the algebraic sign of r.

Interpreting correlation coefficients

1. Interpreting correlation coefficients requires experience, knowledge of the variables being correlated, and knowledge of the group to whom the measures are applied.
2. There are no magic numbers that distinguish "good" from "bad" correlation coefficients; numerical values of r are meaningful in a relative manner and within a particular interpretative context.

3. Correlation does not imply causation.
4. A particular numerical value of the correlation between variable X and variable Y can arise because X influences Y, or because Y influences X, or because variable Z influences both X and Y, or for neither of these reasons (i.e., by chance selection of the persons in the group).
5. Factors reducing the magnitude of the correlation coefficient include
   a. errors of measurement.
   b. restricting the range of the scores.
   c. differences in the shapes and degrees of skewness of the score distributions.
   d. lack of a linear relationship between the two characteristics being correlated.
6. Factors increasing the magnitude of the correlation include
   a. a special selection (or elimination of certain types) of persons.
   b. heterogeneity on a third variable.
   c. correlation of a subscore with a total score that includes the subscore.
7. Correlations computed on small samples of persons drawn from larger populations of persons will show relatively large fluctuations in value from sample to sample. These fluctuations become smaller as the sample becomes larger.

Summary

This chapter has presented some of the basic statistical concepts used to interpret test results. After each section, a listing of the main ideas appeared. A more concise summary of the chapter follows.

  1. *Distribution of scores:* Scores of groups can be summarized and interpreted by tabulating a *frequency distribution* and/or plotting a *histogram or polygon*. Special terms describe the shapes of distributions including their *symmetry*, *modality*, *peakedness*, and *skewness*. These graphs can also be used to compare two or more distributions of scores.

  2. *Measures of central tendency:* Among the summary numbers or *statistics* used with test scores are those that reflect the average or typical score of the group. Among these are the *mode*, *median*, and *mean*. These indices may be used jointly as well as singly to describe a distribution of scores.

3. *Score variability:* Statistics describing the variability or spread of scores are important in understanding a group's score distribution. Of these, the *standard deviation* has been the most frequently used with educational and psychological tests. This index, a type of average of the deviations from the mean, measures the extent to which persons' scores differ from each other.

4. *Relative location in a distribution of scores:* Individuals' scores can be interpreted in terms of their relative location in a distribution. Scores which express this relative standing directly are called *norm-referenced* scores. Among those described are simple *rank* in the group; *percentile rank,* or percent of the group that person's score exceeded; and a *linear standard score* called the *z-score.*

5. *The correlation coefficient:* The degree of relationship between two sets of scores is quantitatively described by the *correlation coefficient.* The correlation quantifies the relationship between the *z*-scores on two tests. This relationship can be displayed in a *scatter* diagram, also.

PART TWO

DEVELOPING AND USING CLASSROOM TESTS

Themes

● Before instructional procedures and testing schemes can be designed, it is necessary to clearly define changes in educational behaviors students should attain through instruction. Such statements of behavior are called specific instructional objectives.

● Statements of the specific behaviors pupils are expected to learn help teachers to plan tests, to clarify which test exercises are most appropriate, and to evaluate and judge the validity of existing tests.

● Broader developmental instructional objectives are frequently as useful to teachers as narrower, specific instructional objectives are, if teachers can further clarify the former by identifying specific objectives for each.

● Instructional objectives tend to be classified into three broad domains of human performance: cognitive, affective, and psychomotor. Taxonomies defining the various facets of each domain have been developed. These taxonomies provide the teacher with a means of checking to assure that the teacher has identified, taught, and assessed all important learning goals.

● Techniques which can help teachers to clearly state specific instructional objectives and to verify whether test items match the instructional intent of such objectives are available. Verifying the match between instructional intent and corresponding test items increases the likelihood that a teacher's test will be a valid assessment of pupils.

Terms and Concepts

instruction

specific objectives (instructional objectives, behavioral objectives, "can do" objectives)

educational goals

developmental objectives

taxonomies of instructional objectives (affective, cognitive, psychomotor domains)

knowledge, comprehension, application, analysis, synthesis, evaluation

discrimination, concrete concept, defined concept, rule, higher-order rule,

cognitive strategy

test plan, blueprint

characteristics of objectives (pupil orientation, behavior orientation, content orientation)

overt vs. covert behavior

indicator behavior

main intent

action verb

abstractions vs. specific performances

matching test items to objectives

4

WRITING INSTRUCTIONAL OBJECTIVES

In Chapter 1 I defined a test as a systematic procedure for observing a person's behavior and describing it with the help of either a category system or a numerical scale. In this chapter, I focus on the behavior to be observed— why it is important, how to specify the behavior, and how to check whether a test exercise will elicit the intended behavior. This is a prelude to subsequent chapters which describe the details of developing particular kinds of test items and testing devices.

The opening section of the chapter discusses the importance of specifying objectives both for designing classroom instruction and for designing classroom tests. However, before moving on to how to write objectives, I discuss several important issues about instructional objectives such as the important relation between educational goals and objectives and the importance of identifying both specific, "can do" objectives and somewhat broader developmental objectives. The next section describes various available resources, so that you can be sure that the full range of potential pupil performance is considered when you design instructional lessons and develop tests. Among the resources discussed are taxonomies for cognitive, affective, and psychomotor behavior domains. The third section describes how clear, useful statements of instructionally important behavior can be phrased. Such clarity is important if you are to develop the right kind of lesson and the right kind of test. The final section describes a way in which you can review both the instructional intent of an objective and the corresponding test exercise to be sure they are closely matched. Such matching is important to assure the validity of the test.

Importance of Specifying Objectives

Instructional Objectives Help Direct the Instructional Process

Instruction is a process that provides conditions which facilitate the production of certain planned changes in the behavior of students. A teacher instructing pupils to solve quadratic equations, such as, $3x^2 + 4x + 1 = 0$, is interested in changing pupils' behavior so when presented such equations they will be able to determine the value(s) of the unknown quantity x. Instruction can be thought of as involving three fundamental steps (Lindvall and Nitko, 1975):

1. deciding what the student is to learn.
2. conducting the actual instruction.
3. evaluating the learned behavior.

Step 1 provides information to both teacher and pupil about the behavior they are to look for. This information guides the teaching effort and provides a criterion for deciding whether pupils have learned the desired change. Step 2 is the heart of the teaching process itself. Step 3, evaluating whether learning has occurred, is central to teaching because through such evaluation teacher and pupil come to know whether the desired change has occurred. While teaching always begins with the learner in a particular behavioral state, ascertains the characteristics of this state, and deploys particular instructional procedures, assessing the changing state of the learner provides information for further allocation of instructional methods and resources (Glaser and Nitko, 1971).

The process can be viewed cyclically: Information from Step 3 is used to decide what remains to be learned (Step 1), and then remedial teaching can proceed (Step 2).

Additional Reasons for Using Specific Objectives

The three steps described above represent a rather simplified description[1] of the instructional process, but they do illustrate that instruction can be greatly facilitated when a teacher uses carefully specified statements of the particular behaviors which each pupil is to acquire. Additional reasons why specific rather than broad or vague statements of pupil behavior should be used in the classroom follow (Gow, 1976):

1. They help teachers and/or curriculum designers make their own educational goals explicit.
2. They communicate the intent of instruction to pupils, parents, other teachers, school administrators, and the public.
3. They provide the basis for analyzing what is to be taught and for constructing learning behaviors.
4. They describe the specific performances against which the teacher can evaluate the success of instruction.
5. They can be used to focus and to clarify discussions of educational goals with parents (and others).
6. They communicate to students the behaviors they are expected to learn and perform.
7. They make it easier to individualize instruction.
8. They help teachers evaluate and revise both instructional procedures and instructional objectives.

[1]Compare, for example, Figure 1.3.

Importance of Objectives for Classroom Testing

By definition, a test is a systematic procedure for observing behavior. Obviously, before you can design a procedure for observing behavior, you need to know what behavior you want to observe. Regardless of the position you may take on the issue of whether specific pupil behaviors need to be described in order for instruction to be effective, you do have to describe the behaviors you want to test, otherwise you may elicit unwanted responses. In this chapter, specific statements about pupil behaviors are viewed as having at least heuristic values, such as those that follow, for classroom test construction and use:

1. **The general planning of test procedures** is made easier by knowledge of the specific behaviors one wishes to observe.

2. **The selection, design, and development of particular testing procedures** depend on knowledge of which specific behaviors should be elicited from pupils and observed by the teachers.

3. **Evaluation of an existing test** is facilitated by knowledge of the specific behaviors it is designed to elicit or which the educator hopes it will elicit.

4. **For a proper judgment of the content validity of a test,** knowledge of the specific behaviors which constitute the domain to be tested is essential (see Chapter 16).

Educational Goals vs. Specific Behaviors

Schooling and other organized instruction should help students attain educational goals. One of the many ways to define educational goals is that they ". . . are those human activities which contribute to the functioning of a society (including the functioning of an individual *in* society), and which can be acquired through learning" (Gagné and Briggs, 1979, p. 45).

Educational goals are frequently stated in broad terms which give direction and purpose to overall planning and educational activities. Examples of statements of broad educational goals appear in such reports as: *Cardinal Principles of Secondary Education* (Commission on the Reorganization of Secondary Education, 1918); *The Purpose of Education in American Democracy* (Educational Policies Commission, 1938); *Behavioral Goals of General Education in High School* (French et al., 1957); *General Education in a Free Society* (Harvard Committee on the Objectives of Education in a Free Society, 1945). Documents prepared by state departments of education (see Table 1.1) and by local school systems also often reflect broad statements of educational goals.

Such broad statements of desirable human activities which comprise educational goals are useful for guiding the educational enterprise. The statements need to be made more specific, however, before particular instructional procedures and particular testing techniques can be employed in the classroom. The statement, for example, "Every student should acquire communication skills of understanding, speaking, reading, and writing," is so broad that a classroom teacher could not develop a lesson plan and an assessment procedure. The process of deriving, from the broad statements of goals, those specific pupil performances toward which to direct instruction, is difficult and seldom attempted, however. What happens, rather, is that educators use various means of simplifying educational goals, such as organizing them into "subject-matter" areas (e.g., mathematics or English) (Gagné and Briggs, 1979). The subject area becomes the framework within which educators can define specific objectives. The National Assessment of Educational Progress (Chapter 1) is an example of a national effort to derive specific learning objectives for each of the subject-matter areas. The number of objectives and subobjectives derived for each NAEP subject area varies, but the example below shows how a general educational goal can be subdivided into general objectives and these, in turn, into specific objectives. It is the latter which teachers can use to develop test exercises.

General goal: Pupil is able to read literature of excellence.[2]

A. *General objective:* To be acquainted with a wide variety of literary works.
   1. *Specific objectives:*
      a. to recognize children's "classics" such as *Mother Goose, Winnie-the-Pooh, Child's Garden of Verses,* and *Mary Poppins* [age 9].
      b. to recognize authors and works of certain children's books such as Aesop or LaFontaine, Anderson or the Brothers' Grimm, *The Jungle Book, Tom Sawyer,* and *Charlotte's Web* [age 13].
      c. to recognize typical passages of English literature such as Shakespeare and English and American nineteenth-century novelists [age 17].

B. *General objective:* Pupil able to understand the basic metaphors and themes through which the values and tensions in Western culture have been expressed.
   1. *Specific objectives:*
      a. to know some of the common Biblical figures [age 9].
      b. to know about the Arthurian legends, a few Greek myths, and American folk figures [age 9].
      c. to recognize the use of the above figures in a modern context such as a work of literature, a sentence, a slogan, or a trade name [ages 9, 13, 17].

[2]Adapted from Greenbaum, Garet, and Solomon (1977, pp. 72–73). The example is meant to be illustrative rather than comprehensive. Ages in brackets indicate the earliest age at which that objective ought to be attained.

Specific Objectives as "Can Do" Statements

Tests are procedures for systematically observing and describing behavior. Since *behavior* is to be observed, the types of statements of objectives that have the most value for developing classroom tests are those which describe in specific terms *what a pupil can do* as a result of studying a particular lesson or unit of study. For example, a high school biology unit on living cells may have as a general objective that students should "learn the organizations and functions of cells." But what *can* the student *do* to demonstrate learning of this general objective. There may be several answers to this question, each phrased as a specific instructional objective and each describing what a student "can do." For example:

1. The student can draw models of various types of cells and label their parts.
2. The student can list the parts of a cell and describe the structures included in each.
3. The student can explain the functions which cells perform and how these functions are related to one another.

The answers to questions of what a pupil can do as a result of instruction become statements that suggest ways of testing or observing pupils. Robert Forsyth (1976) has referred to these as "can do" statements. They have also been termed "specific instructional objectives," "behavioral objectives," or "instructional objectives."

"Can Do" vs. Developmental Objectives

Some of the skills and abilities an educator teaches are more aptly stated at a somewhat higher level of abstraction than specific instructional objectives of the "can do" variety can express. Consider these:[3]

[3]The first seven of these statements are from Gronlund (1973, p. 17); the eighth is from Forsyth (1976, p. 11).

The student should, for example, be able to

1. apply concepts and principles to new situations.
2. demonstrate mathematical reasoning ability.
3. write a creative short story.
4. demonstrate critical thinking skills.
5. use a scientific approach in solving problems.
6. perform skillfully on a musical instrument.
7. evaluate the adequacy of a given experiment.
8. make valid inferences and draw logical conclusions concerning materials read.

Each of these statements implies a set of skills and/or abilities that are continuously developed throughout life, and, hence, these objectives can be called "developmental objectives" (Gronlund, 1973).

At first glance, it might seem that all one needs to do is to insert a "can do" phrase in front of each of the above statements to transform them to specific instructional objectives. As Forsyth points out, however, it is not that simple: First, each statement represents a broad domain of rather loosely related (i.e., not highly correlated) performances, and second, each statement represents skills or abilities typically thought of as continuous or developmental in nature, rather than the all or none dichotomy implied by the "can do"/"can't do" statement.

The problem of a broad, heterogeneous domain To illustrate why it is difficult to make "can do" statements out of broad, developmental objectives, consider the inferences objective above. These three questions are taken from the social studies reading subtest of the *Iowa Tests of Educational Development*. Each question requires the student to make an inference about the implications of a passage based on the information read in a particular passage (Forsyth, 1976, p. 12):

1. From his manner and formal training, what opinion might people have formed of John Marshall?   [28%]

2. What do the last two sentences suggest about Patasonian's acceptance of U.S. aid?   [44%]
3. Suppose an uninsured and unemployed motorist damaged someone's car. Which speaker offers a plan that would allow the injured party to collect benefits?   [64%]

The numbers indicate the percentage of a statewide sample of Iowa 10th graders answering the item correctly. These (and other data that are not shown) indicate that persons who get one question right are not necessarily the same persons as those who get another question right (Forsyth, 1976). Thus, whether a person "can do" this inference objective depends very much on the particular passage and question asked. In effect, this makes a "can do" statement relatively meaningless because the answer to "can do what?" depends on the specific question and passage.

Broad, developmental objectives such as the one we are discussing can be made more narrow and thus transformed into "can do" statements. To do so, however, may destroy the usefulness of the statement as an instructional goal. The following revision of the inference objective achieves this narrowing by specifying the number, type, and length of words and sentences in the passage; the content of the passage; and the type of test question asked (Forsyth, 1976, p. 14):

> Johnny can make inferences and draw logical conclusions when given reading material that has no more than 200 words (at least 85% of the words are from the EDL list), that has between 10 and 20 sentences (with a maximum sentence length of 20 words), that is based on the life of John Marshall, and that requires him to answer multiple choice questions using four alternatives.

Clearly such narrow objectives have little usefulness to teachers in planning and assessing the effects of instruction.

The problem of continuous development of skill   The second concern, the continuous or developmental nature of these objectives, stems from the fact that ". . . students cannot be expected to fully achieve such objectives. Even the simplest of these . . . is a matter of degree and can be continuously developed throughout life. All we can reasonably expect to do for a particular course or unit of instruction is to identify a sample of specific learning outcomes that represent degrees of progress toward the objectives" (Gronlund, 1973, p. 17). The essential concern here is that the skill(s) represented by these objectives are complex, the number of tasks that can be used to demonstrate learning is vast, and that each represents goals to continuously work toward rather than to master completely (Gronlund, 1973).

Designing instruction for and measuring attainment of developmental objectives   One way to begin designing instruction and to measure progress toward these important developmental objectives is to specify for each broad objective, several specific behavioral objectives that represent the key performances expected of a pupil at a particular grade or age level. This is illustrated below for a broad objective in science:

Understands Boyle's Law[4]:

1. States a definition of Boyle's Law.
2. States the domain to which Boyle's Law applies.
3. Describes the relation between Boyle's Law and Charles' Law.
4. Uses Boyle's Law to explain an observation in a lab experiment.
5. Appropriately analyzes a new (to the student) situation in terms of Boyle's Law.
6. Solves a new problem or makes an appropriate choice for a course of action taking into account the implications of Boyle's Law.

[4]Based on Klopfer (1969).

Although this list of six specific objectives might be made longer, the given list would likely be considered adequate for describing what is meant by "understanding Boyle's Law." Specific test exercises could then be prepared for testing achievement of each of the six specific objectives. A student's overall score on such a test could be interpreted as indicating the *degree* to which a student has acquired such an understanding, rather than as a "mastery/nonmastery" or "can do/can't do" description.

Locating Objectives That Cover the Range of Pupil Performance

Simply writing objectives "off the top of your head" is likely to be a frustrating experience because there is a seemingly endless number of objectives. Further, persons unaccustomed to writing objectives are likely to write first those objectives that have a narrow focus and represent lower-level cognitive skills. This situation may be improved by following a systematic procedure which helps to bring to mind the wide range of important learning objectives toward which to direct teaching (and testing).

Taxonomies of Instructional Objectives: Cognitive Domain

A taxonomy is a hierarchical scheme for classifying behaviors. Generally, educational objectives fall into one (or more[5]) of three domains: cognitive, affective, and psychomotor (including perceptual). Behaviors within each domain are classified by a taxonomy. Since there is more than one way to conceptualize a classification scheme, several different taxonomies have been developed for sorting behaviors in a given domain. A number of these taxonomies are described here and

[5]A single complex performance will likely involve components of more than one domain.

summarized in Appendix D. Chapter 5 will examine how such taxonomies can be used to develop a plan for a test covering a unit of instruction. You may want to look ahead to skim that section at this time.

Bloom's Taxonomy   When developing a list of objectives, a teacher will find the *Taxonomy of Educational Objectives, Handbook I: Cognitive Domain* (Bloom, Engelhart, Furst, Hill, and Krathwhol, 1956) to be of considerable value. This taxonomy, developed by a group of college and university examiners, describes a comprehensive outline of a range of cognitive abilities that might be taught in a course of instruction. The taxonomy classifies cognitive performances into six major headings arranged from simple to complex (Bloom et al., 1956):

1. *Knowledge* . . . as defined here, involves the recall of specifics and universals, the recall of methods and processes, or the recall of a pattern, structure, or setting. For measurement purposes, the recall situation involves little more than bringing to mind the appropriate material . . . (p. 201).

2. *Comprehension* . . . represents the lowest level of understanding. It refers to a type of understanding or apprehension such that the individual knows what is being communicated and can make use of the material or idea being communicated without necessarily relating it to other material or seeing its fullest implications . . . (p. 204).

3. *Application.* The use of abstractions in particular and concrete situations [to solve new or novel problems]. The abstractions may be in the form of general ideas, rules of procedures, or generalized methods. The abstractions may also be technical principles, ideas, and theories which must be remembered and applied . . . (p. 205).

4. *Analysis.* The breakdown of a communication into its constituent elements or parts

such that the relative hierarchy of ideas is made clear and/or the relations between the ideas expressed are made explicit. Such analyses are intended to clarify the communication, to indicate how the communication is organized, and the way in which it manages to convey its effects, as well as its basis and arrangements . . . (p. 205).

5. *Synthesis.* The putting together of elements and parts so as to form a whole. This involves the process of working with pieces, parts, elements, etc., and arranging and combining them in such a way as to constitute a pattern or structure not clearly there before . . . (p. 206).

6. *Evaluation.* Judgements about the value of material and methods for given purposes. Quantitative and qualitative judgements about the extent to which materials and methods satisfy criteria. Use of a standard of appraisal. The criteria may be those determined by the student or those which are given to him . . . (p. 207).

Examples of objectives and items from each level of this taxonomy are described in detail in Bloom's book. A more complete explanation along with examples of how the categories of the taxonomy can be adapted and applied to different curricular areas[6] appears in the *Handbook on Formative and Summative Evaluation of Student Learning* (Bloom, Hastings, and Madaus, 1971). Appendix D will give you a further idea of the scope of this taxonomy and may help you identify into which taxonomic categories the various objectives can be classified. The value of such a taxonomy to teachers is that it calls attention to the variety or spectrum of abilities and skills toward which they can direct instruction and testing.

Note that behaviors in the first three categories listed are more easily tested with short

---

[6]The areas are: pre-school development, language arts, social studies, art, science, mathematics, literature, writing, second language, and industrial education.

answer, true-false, multiple-choice, or matching test items. Behaviors from the last three categories might be partially tested by such item formats, but their assessment usually requires a variety of other procedures such as essay questions, homework, class projects, observing performance in labs, and so on. These tasks require a pupil to actually produce or create something, rather than simply to answer questions. Examining the various subcategories of the taxonomy in Appendix D should make this more apparent.

Gagné's levels of complexity   Another way to bring to mind the various levels of behaviors that need to be taught and learned is provided by Gagné (1964, 1977). He states that (a) students learn capacities (called abilities here) for certain kinds of performances, (b) these capacities can be arranged in an hierarchy of complexity, and (c) capacities lower in the hierarchy are prerequisite to learning those higher in it. This concept has direct implication for both the nature and manner of learning and for instructional methods, which Gagné describes in considerable detail in two very readable books: *The Conditions of Learning* (Gagné, 1977) and *Principles of Instructional Design* (Gagné and Briggs, 1979). Table 4.1 defines each of these capacity levels, describes what performance characteristics learners must exhibit when responding to test items, and gives an example of a specific objective classified under each type of ability.

Traditionally, test developers have pointed to the Bloom taxonomy as the basis for forming a content-by-category test blueprint (see Chapter 5). The Gagné taxonomy, however, seems to provide a way to organize objectives to be learned and tested into categories distinguished by the fact that behaviors within a category can be learned by similar learning experiences or taught by similar instructional tactics, rather than being distinguished only by the specific content they contain (Gagné, 1964). Bloom's *Taxonomy* subcategories (see Appendix D) such as "knowledge of termi-

Type of ability or capacity	Characteristics of responses to test items	Example of a specific objective
1. **Discrimination:** ability to respond appropriately to stimuli that differ. The stimuli can differ in one or more physical attributes such as size, shape, or tone. *(capacity verb: discriminates)*	The learner's response must indicate that the learner has distinguished between the different stimuli. The learner may do this by indicating "same" or "different."	Given two cardboard cutouts, one a triangle shape and the other a square shape, the learner can point to the one that is a "square."
2. **Concrete concept:** ability to identify a stimulus as belonging to a particular class or category. The members of the class have one or more physical properties in common. (capacity verb: *identifies*)	The learner's response must indicate that two or more members of the class have been identified.	Given several differently shaped figures of various colors and shapes, half of which have triangular shapes, the learner can point to all the "triangles."
3. **Defined concept:** ability to demonstrate what is meant by a defined class of objects, events, or relations—that is, demonstrate an understanding of a concept. (capacity verb: *classifies*)	The learner's response must go beyond memorization to identify specific instances of the defined concept and to show how these instances are related to each other (and are thereby members of the same concept or category).	Given descriptions and brief biographies of each of several different persons not born in this country, the learner is able to identify all the persons who are immigrants and state their relationship to each other.
4. **Rule:** ability to make responses that indicate a rule is being applied in a variety of different situations. (capacity verb: *demonstrates*)	The learner's response must indicate that a particular rule is being applied in one or more concrete instances, but the learner need not be able to state the rule.	Given a "story" problem of the type presented in class involving two single-digit addends, the pupil is able to add the digits correctly.
5. **Higher-order rule** (problem solving): ability to form a new (for the learner) rule to solve a problem, by combining two or more previously learned rules. (capacity verb: *generates*)	The learner's response must indicate that a new complex rule has been "invented" and applied to solve a problem that is new or novel for the learner. Once the rule is invented, the learner should be able to apply it to other situations (transfer of learning).	Given an announcement about a specific job opening for which the learner is qualified, the learner is able to generate and write an appropriate letter of application for that job.
6. **Cognitive strategies:** ability to use internal processes to choose and change ways to focus attention, learn, remember, and/or think. (capacity verb: *originates*)	The learner's response must indicate that an original solution has been found which solves a problem novel or new to the learner. The conditions of the task are such that neither type nor manner of solution is pre-specified. "Original" means "not previously taught to this learner."	Given a description of a city's air pollution problem and access to pertinent data, the pupil is able to originate a solution to the problem by applying an appropriate scientific model.

Source: Adapted from *The Conditions of Learning*, 3rd Edition, by Robert M. Gagné. Copyright © 1977, 1970, 1965 by Holt, Rinehart and Winston. Also adapted from *Principles of Instructional Design*, 2nd Edition, by Robert M. Gagné and Leslie J. Briggs. Copyright © 1974, 1979 by Holt, Rinehart and Winston. Reprinted by permission of Holt, Rinehart and Winston, CBS College Publishing, a division of CBS, Inc.

Table 4 • 1   Gagné's levels of complexity in human skills, characteristics of responses to item testing these capacities, and examples of specific objectives written for each capacity.

nology" and "knowledge of classifications and categories," for example, would seem to require the same conditions of learning; similarly "knowledge of generalizations," "comprehension," and "comprehending the interrelationship of ideas" appear difficult to distinguish from each other on the basis of required conditions for learning (Gagné, 1964).

An advantage of the Gagné approach, then, is its usefulness, not only for calling to mind various types of performances that might be put on a test, but also for designing instructional strategies. Chapter 9 will describe ways of developing test items for several of the categories in the Gagné scheme.

Other taxonomies of cognitive objectives   The teacher is likely to encounter several varieties of taxonomies of cognitive performances in other teacher preparation courses and will no doubt become familiar and comfortable using one. Some of these will be specific to certain subject areas, such as, reading comprehension (e.g., Barrett, 1967; Clymer, 1968; Smith and Barrett, 1974) while others attempt to be broad and comprehensive (e.g., Ebel, 1979; Hannah and Michaelis, 1977; Pierce and Gray, 1979). Use them as tools for planning tests and instruction, but don't be a slave to them.

Taxonomy of Instructional Objectives: Affective Domain[7]

Although this book focuses on measuring cognitive objectives, it should be recognized that important learning occurs in schools which relates to feelings, interests and attitudes, and emotional sets. Goals and objectives of this type belong to what has come to be called the *affective domain*. Schools and teachers frequently espouse affective outcomes for students, such as (Krathwohl, Bloom, and Masia, 1964, p. 167):

[7]This section may be omitted without loss of continuity.

Readiness to revise judgments and to change behavior in the light of evidence.

Changes his mind when new facts or insights demonstrate the need for revision of opinions formerly held.

Views problems in objective, realistic, and tolerant terms.

If affective goals and objectives for students are considered important, they should be articulated and assessed in order to decide the degree to which students have attained them. An outline of one taxonomy of affective objectives follows below. Other parts of this book will describe ways in which such goals may be measured (see Chapter 22).

"Krathwohl's" taxonomy   A subcommittee of the group of college and university examiners who developed the taxonomy of cognitive objectives has developed a second volume which classifies affective objectives in a comparable fashion: *Taxonomy of Educational Objectives, Handbook II: Affective Domain* (Krathwohl, Bloom, & Masia, 1964). The book describes each category of the taxonomy and presents specimen items and other examples of ways of assessing pupils in each category.

An outline of the categories of this taxonomy is given in Figure 4.1. An organizing theme of the taxonomy is the degree to which affective behavior states are organized and internalized within individuals. Higher levels of the taxonomy reflect a greater intensity of these properties whereas the lower levels reflect very little. For the educator, this taxonomy ". . . provides the panorama of objectives. Comparing the range of the present curriculum with the range of possible outcomes may suggest additional goals that might be included. Further, the illustrated objectives may suggest wordings that might be adapted to the area you are exploring" (Krathwohl, 1964, p. 33). A more detailed outline of the taxonomy along with illustrative objectives is shown in Appendix D.

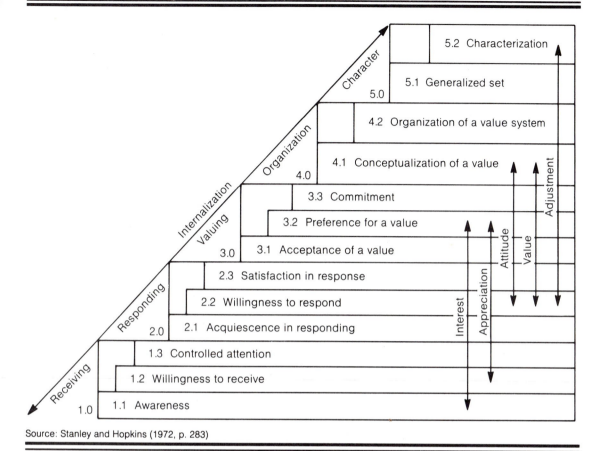

Figure 4 • 1 A characterization of the meaning of the affective terms defined by the Krathwohl et al. (1964) taxonomy.

Taxonomies of Instructional Objectives: Psychomotor (and Perceptual) Domains[8]

The role of psychomotor and perceptual learning has become increasingly important, not only for physical education curricula, but for school programs generally. Psychomotor and perceptual skills become of special concern for early childhood and preschool education and the early years of elementary school. A detailed study of the psychomotor domain is beyond the scope of this chapter. However, an example of a taxonomy is presented in Appendix D. For suggestions on using tax-

[8]This section may be omitted without loss of continuity.

onomies in the psychomotor domain, you might read Anita J. Harrow's *A Taxonomy of the Psychomotor Domain* (1972) or *A Comprehensive Framework for Instructional Objectives* (Hannah and Michaelis, 1977). Other psychomotor and perceptual taxonomies include Simpson's (1966–67), Dave's (1971; Hannah and Michaelis, 1977), Moore's (1967), Hannah and Michaelis' (1977), and Goldberger's (1980).

Other Sources for Locating Objectives

Specific instructional objectives may be obtained from a variety of sources including the following:

1. Instructional materials and teachers' manuals often list the objectives they are designed to teach. These may not cover the full range of performance a teacher wishes to teach and test, however.

2. Curriculum guides for some district and/or state (and/or county) departments of education have developed specific objectives in recent years. It may be possible to borrow such guides from other districts if your curriculum guide does not have them.

3. Books on teaching methods sometimes contain specific objectives.

4. Manuals accompanying criterion-referenced achievement tests list objectives the tests are designed to measure.

5. Large collections of objectives are maintained by various agencies and are available for a nominal cost. Some of these agencies are listed in Appendix F.

More than likely you will have to adapt the objectives found in these sources to your own situation. Objectives are usually developed for specific purposes, and frequently you will find no consistent form and quality from one developer to another. Nevertheless, these sources and the taxonomies do provide a starting place: It is much easier to adapt and revise objectives than to write them without any assistance.

Another point to keep in mind is that frequently an objective will cut across several lessons or subject areas. The ability to use library and print resources to obtain information for a report, for example, is likely to be common to both social studies and language arts curricula. The above sources may list objectives that are specific to the content of a particular lesson, and thus the important learning skills objective you are looking for may not appear. But you should be aware of such broader, encompassing objectives and include them in your list for teaching and testing.

Source: Vimcet Associates', Catalog, n.d.

Reviewing the List of Objectives Written for a Course or Unit

It is important to develop a complete or comprehensive list of objectives. I quote Gronlund (1976, pp. 54–55) who gives the following questions that should be used as criteria when reviewing the final list of objectives developed for a course or unit of instruction:

1. Do the objectives include all important outcomes of the course?
2. Are the objectives in harmony with the general goals of the school?
3. Are the objectives in harmony with sound principles of learning?
4. Are the objectives realistic in terms of the pupils and the time and facilities available?
5. Are the objectives defined in terms of changes in pupil behavior?

The next section of this chapter discusses ways to phrase or write objectives so they can communicate your instructional intent and help you develop a test plan or "blueprint." This plan, discussed in the next chapter, will go a long way toward assuring you develop the kind of test you want.

Writing Specific Objectives

Characteristics of Specific Objectives

Objectives meeting the following minimum criteria can be used as a basis for classroom instruction and test construction (Lindvall, 1964; 1967):

1. Objectives should be oriented toward the pupil.
2. Objectives should be worded in terms of observable behavior describing what a pupil can do after required learning experiences.
3. Objectives should state the specific content to which the behavior should apply.

Pupil-orientation It seems obvious that, since the focus of instruction is on changes in pupil behavior, instructional objectives should describe pupil performances. Yet it is not unusual for some curriculum guides and other materials available to teachers to contain such statements as "to provide for student participation in classroom discussion." The problem is that this goal is for the teacher rather than the pupil. Objectives need to be pupil-oriented if they are to be the basis for designing testing procedures which allow you to come to a decision about whether the pupils actually have learned what you intended from the lesson.

Behavior orientation Not only should an instructional objective refer to a pupil, it should state a behavior—that is, an observable activity. This can be accomplished by being sure that the statement includes an "action verb" that specifies a pupil behavior. A balance is necessary between verbs that are too broad (and thus imply too many nonequivalent behaviors) and those that are too specific (and which are often just ways of marking answers). Consider this objective which is too specific:

> *Poor:* The pupil is able to put an "X" on the picture of the correct geometric shape (circle, triangle, rectangle, square, or ellipse) when the name of the shape is given.

The main intent of such an objective is to *select* or *identify* the correct shape, not just to make Xs. Any response which indicates the pupil has correctly identified the required shape can no doubt be acceptable. Thus, the objective could be written as:

> *Better:* The pupil is able to identify a picture of a geometric shape (circle, triangle, rectangle, square, or ellipse) when the name of the shape is given.

Table 4.2 suggests some verbs which maintain this balance and illustrates verbs that are too specific or too broad to make useful instructional objectives.

A useful distinction to make is between overt and covert behaviors: *Covert behaviors* ==are activities that are internal or "cognitive," so that they are observed only by the person engaged in them== (e.g., when someone is mentally adding or computing). *Overt behaviors* ==are activities which are manifest==, so that they can be observed by persons in addition to (or other than) the person engaged in them (e.g., writing an answer to an addition or subtraction problem). Both kinds of behaviors are frequently incorporated into instructional objectives (Mager, 1973).

Source: Mager (1973, p. 31)

When an instructional objective has as its main intent or principal purpose a pupil performance that is covert, then it is necessary to include a further clarification concerning how one would know that the covert behavior was performed. For example, suppose the objective is that

> the pupil is able to recall the names of the eight colors in his or her crayon box. (The colors are red, blue, yellow, green, orange, brown, purple, and black.)

The main purpose here would be for the learner to *recall* names. But the teacher wouldn't be able to tell if the pupil could do this unless there is an *indicator* of the behavior. "*Indicator behavior* is an activity through which the existence of the main intent will be inferred" (Mager, 1973, p. 25).

In the above example of a "recall" objective, an indicator behavior could be any one of a number of activities such as speaking or writing or printing. One caution though: The indicator behavior should be simple, direct, and within the capability of the pupil (Mager, 1973), otherwise the indicator clouds the inference you wish to make about the main intent. The objective above is mainly about recalling color names, not about being able to read or to write the names. If this objective is intended for youngsters who are not yet able to write, then using writing as an indicator behavior is certainly not appropriate. Thus, a test which requires the child to write the names of the crayon colors is *invalid*. An alternate test such as asking the child to *say* the color name of each crayon as you present it, would be within the child's repertoire and, hence, would be a more valid test of the objective. Usually, adding a sample test item to an objective which states a covert main intent will clarify the intended pupil performance. Table 4.3 summarizes this discussion on overt, covert, main intent, and indicator behaviors.

As an aid in helping beginners to write objectives that describe behaviors, Table 4.4 lists further examples of various "action" verbs. These verbs are organized according to certain categories of cognitive and affective taxonomies which were discussed earlier in this chapter. When verbs such as these are used in statements of objectives, the objectives will usually satisfy the second criterion of expressing pupil performance in terms of observable behavior.

Content orientation   A stated instructional objective should indicate the content to which the performance is to apply. An objective which

Specific but acceptable verbs			
count	multiply	draw	name
select	divide	construct, make	explain
choose	delete	list	describe
pick out	order, arrange	rename	match
identify	sort, classify	alphabetize	convert
add, total	label	complete, supply	regroup
subtract, take away	measure	rephrase	
	weigh	state	

Too broad, unacceptable verbs			
respond	use	infer	test
do	generate	examine	apply
perform	deduce	observe	interpret

Too specific, essentially indicator verbs			
check	shade	put a mark on	write the letter of
circle	put an X on	color the same as	draw a line between
underline	draw a ring around	write the number of	put a box around

Toss-up verbs, requiring further clarification			
demonstrate	distinguish	answer	predict
discriminate	collect, synthesize	compare	locate
differentiate	determine	contrast	give

Source: Reprinted from C. M. Lindvall, "Criteria for Stating IPI Objectives," in *Design and Development of Curricular Materials: Instructional Design Articles* (Volume 2), pp. 214–215, Doris T. Gow, Editor. Published in 1976 by the University Center for International Studies, University of Pittsburgh. Used by permission.

Table 4 • 2 Examples of action verbs sometimes used in instructional objectives.

Type of performance stated in the objective	Example of an objective exhibiting that type	Action to be taken before test development can proceed	Example of the modification
An overt main intent	". . . to write a specific instructional objective that satisfies the three criteria stated in the text."	None. Proceed straight away to test development.	No modification needed.
A covert main intent	". . . to recognize the objectives in a given list which are worded in terms of the pupil."	Add an appropriate indicator.	". . . to recognize (by pointing to or marking) the objectives. . . ."
An overt indicator	". . . to place a check mark (√) next to the objectives in the given list which are worded in terms of the pupil."	State or clarify the main intent.	The main intent is to recognize or identify certain types of objectives. "Checking" is the indicator. Rewrite as per above.

Note: (a) *main intent*—the principal purpose of the objective; (b) *indicator*—how the occurrence of a covert behavior will be ascertained; (c) *overt*—manifest, visible, audible, observable; (d) *covert*—internal, cognitive, mental; (e) covert indicators are not considered possible.
Source: Adapted from *Measuring Instructional Intent: Or Got a Match?* by Robert F. Mager (Belmont, Ca.: Pitman Learning, Inc., 1973).

Table 4 • 3 Summary of the types of pupil performances that are typically encountered in statements of instructional objectives and how these are related to classroom test development.

Table 4 • 4
Examples of action verbs to use when writing instructional objectives.

Source: From *Measuring Educational Outcomes: Fundamentals of Testing*, pp. 26–27, Fig. 2.2, by Bruce W. Tuckman, © 1975 by Harcourt Brace Jovanovich, Inc. Reprinted by permission of the publisher.

states, for example, that "the pupil is able to write definitions of the important terms used in the text," needs to be modified to include either a list of "important words" or some description of ways in which such important words can be delineated. Without this specificity of content, it would not be possible to know with certainty whether the content of a given test item was adequate for evaluating pupil performance on this objective. Perhaps more importantly, without the specification of content it would be difficult for both teacher and pupil to determine what was to be learned.

Mager's criteria[9] The criteria for statements of objectives in the previous section have been found useful for most purposes of classroom instruction and test development. There are, however, other schemes and criteria that have been used. One of the most prominent schemes

in education has been Robert F. Mager's (1962, p. 12):

First, identify the terminal behavior[10] by name; you can specify the kind of behavior that will be accepted as evidence that the learner has achieved the objective.

Second, try to define the desired behavior further by describing the important conditions under which the behavior will be expected to occur.

Third, specify the criteria of acceptable performance by describing how well the learner must perform to be considered acceptable.

Objectives meeting these criteria will be quite specific and will quite clearly describe the intended pupil performance. Communi-

[9]This section may be omitted without loss of continuity.

[10]"*Terminal behavior* refers to the behavior you would like your learner to be able to demonstrate at the time your influence over him ends" (Mager, 1962, p. 2).

cation, however, is the primary focus of the Mager scheme and, therefore, it is not necessary to compulsively apply all three criteria to each objective as long as the intended pupil performances are clearly communicated (Mager, 1962, p. 12). Figure 4.2 shows an objective and illustrates each of the three components listed above.

The Mager scheme is similar to the Lindvall scheme presented previously in that both call for statements describing specific pupil behavior with respect to particular instructional content. Mager's scheme, however, clarifies the context in which the behavior occurs by including in the statement of the objective the (a) specific conditions under which the performance is to be done and (b) criteria or standards by which the quality of the performance is to be judged acceptable. If you are interested in learning more about this scheme for stating objectives, you should consult the book *Preparing Instructional Objectives* (2nd ed.) (Mager, 1976).

Abstractions vs. Performances

In order to design instruction or build a test, you need to identify the behavior or performance to be taught and observed. Statements such as ". . . to demonstrate an understanding of the . . ." do not represent single performance but rather abstractions or hypothetical states of the learner (Mager, 1973). An *abstraction*, in this context, represents a state of the learner which is inferred after observing several examples of behavior. We cannot see a student "understand" or "think critically," for example, but we infer the student has attained such states after observing the student perform several different kinds of behaviors. "Demonstrating an understanding" or "knowing" or "appreciating" implies that the pupil is able to perform a number of specific behaviors before the observer is willing to conclude that the pupil has attained that state. For example, " 'Understand' may be translated into such behavioral terms as being able 'to explain,' 'to give examples,' or 'to put into one's own words.' 'Knowing' implies being able 'to list,' 'to supply terms,' or 'to associate events with persons' " (Lindvall and Nitko, 1975, p. 13).

Using an abstraction to describe a performance to be tested is fine as long as one is able to communicate what the abstraction signifies. This means, ultimately, being able to specify the particular behaviors one needs to observe before concluding that the pupil has attained the abstract state. The box illustrates one man's attempt to specify what is meant by the phrase "The student is able to understand. . . ." The example of objectives given previously related to understanding Boyle's Law is an application of the ideas in the box.

Conditions of performance	When given five different quadratic equations with one unknown and without the aid of books, notes, calculators, or other reference materials, the pupil
Pupil performance	is able to use the standard quadratic formula to solve for the unknown correctly
Criteria for successful performance	in at least four of them within a period of twenty-five minutes.

Figure 4 • 2 An instructional objective in algebra illustrating the three components suggested by Mager.

Making Sure Test Items Match Instructional Objectives

Chapters 6 through 10 will discuss the details of writing unambiguous test questions and procedures for developing non-paper-and-pencil tests. Here we wish to point out that the basic purpose of any achievement test is to determine the extent to which each pupil has attained the specific objectives delineated

The Dallas Monster: When Specificity Gets Out of Hand

Statements of specific objectives should help teacher, parent, and pupil clarify learned performances. Sometimes, however, things get out of hand. When this occurs, it is time to rethink what level of specificity is really needed. This magazine article illustrates this point.

The Dallas Monster

"When a student comes home with a B, it doesn't really communicate anything to the parent," says Dallas School Superintendent Nolan Estes. That could be true, but the "report cards" that the younger pupils in the Dallas Independent School District are coming home with this winter may well have completely eliminated any communication between home and school. The latest educational innovation, imposed upon Dallas parents and children for the first time this fall, is an 8½ in. by 14 in. number-filled sheet that looks more like a page from a company audit than a report card. To assist them in deciphering the report, which is used for kindergarten through third grade, pupils' parents are supplied with a 32 page booklet called *Your Child Starts School* and a 28 page manual with the remarkable title *Terminal Behavioral Objectives for Continuous Progression Modules in Early Childhood Education*. Says School Board Member James Jennings, who labeled the whole package a "monster": "Seventy percent of the parents will never raise the lid on a cover with a title like that."

Those brave or curious enough to look inside will find lists of anywhere from seven to 23 specific skills in 39 "modules" under seven basic "curriculum areas" (e.g., mathematics, social sciences, art). The wording may well represent a new low in educators' jargon. Skill No. 5 in the basic concepts module in the communications curriculum area, for example, is "oral response on a concrete level using objects." That means, the manual explains helpfully, that a child can "identify a toy car by saying a word, phrase or sentence about it."

In the wake of the criticism that descended on school officials, minor revisions have been made in the report card; for example, the phrase "goals and accomplishments" has been substituted for "terminal objectives." Superintendent Estes also hired a freelance writer last November to write yet another supplementary pamphlet, which in effect will explain the explanation. At last report the writer was only halfway through the job. Reason for the delay: he is having difficulty understanding the manual.

Source: From "The Dallas Monster," an article in *Time*, February 18, 1974, p. 59. Reprinted by permission from *Time*.

Box 4 • 1

by the teacher and/or school. While this purpose sounds very straightforward, it is not always an easy criterion to meet.

Matching Test Items to "Can Do" Objectives

The specific items or procedures used on a test should permit the pupil to display the skill or knowledge stated in the objectives. An objective that calls for the pupil to actually build an apparatus, write a poem, or perform a physical skill would need to be assessed by a procedure that gave the pupil the opportunity to perform. Procedures requiring the pupil *only* to list the parts of an apparatus, to analyze an existing poem, or to describe the sequence of steps needed for performing a physical skill are not valid since they do not match the objectives. A very basic requirement for the validity[11] of a classroom test is that the testing procedures used should match the intentions of the specific objectives in the test plan. The methods of developing a test plan are the subject of the next chapter.

Figure 4.3 is a checklist that, if applied to each test item or procedure you develop, will help maintain a good match between the original intention of the instructional objectives and the actual test items. The objective and the three test items here illustrate how to use this checklist.

Objective: Students will explain in their own words the meaning of the concept of culture. (9th grade)

[11] A more complete discussion of validity is found in Chapter 16.

In stating terminal behaviors (or other large objectives), we sometimes have occasion to use *the shorthand expression:*

"The student understands X."

X may be an idea, principle, process, or institution. The problem is: "What do we want to include in the shorthand expression, 'understand' "?

"The student understands X" suggests that the student possesses two kinds of competencies, *viz.*:

A. The student has knowledge about X.
B. The student can apply his knowledge about X.

Both of these competencies are inside the student, and, hence, their presence or absence at any time can only be inferred. A challenge to testing for these competencies is to devise situations that will allow us to make reasonable inferences about the presence or absence of the competency. However, situations that test for knowledge and for application are not beyond the bounds of present testing technology, especially if there are operational definitions of "knowledge" and "application."

To operationally define the knowledge competency, we shall use selected categories from the Bloom taxonomy for the cognitive domain (numbers of categories in parentheses).*

A. "The student has knowledge about X" means that he can [formulate or recognize a statement that correctly]:

1. ... describes or defines X.
2. ... delimits the area, domain, or field to which X applies or/and in which X functions.

3. ... expresses the relationship of X to Y (Y is another idea ... [principle, process, or institution]).

Defining the application competency is a somewhat more difficult problem, since applications extend in several directions and can require a high degree of sophistication. We shall confine ourselves to just three categories to operationally define the application competency.

B. "The student can apply his knowledge about X" means that he uses his knowledge about X to:

1. formulate an explanation of an observed or reported event.
2. analyze a situation or an argument that he has not encountered previously.
3. choose a course of action in confronting a real problem or a hypothesized situation.

While it is clearly possible to add more categories of behavior to both the above lists, we propose that when we use the shorthand expression "understand" our intention is to include only the six categories listed. At the same time, we should agree that the student's demonstration of full mastery of "understanding X" must include an acceptable performance in *all three* categories of behavior under the knowledge competency *and* in *all three* categories under the application competency. In actually testing for mastery in "understanding X," however, it may not be feasible (due to lack of time, materials, or ingenuity) to test for all six behaviors, and we may have to be content with making inferences about the student's mastery on the basis of sampling his behavior in one or two categories under the knowledge competency *and* in one or two categories under the application competency.

*See Appendix D.

Source: From "An Operational Definition of 'Understand,'" by L. E. Klopfer, Learning Research and Development Center, University of Pittsburgh, 1969, pp. 1–3. Reprinted by permission of the author.

Box 4 • 2

Item 1. Name three things which are important to the culture of native Americans.

Item 2. Write several paragraphs comparing three different cultures. In your essay, make sure you describe the similarities and differences among the cultures you have chosen.

Item 3. Write a paragraph telling in your own words what is meant by the term *culture.*

Let's apply the checklist in Figure 4.3 to the objective and items listed:

Step 1 The stated performance in the objective is "using your own words to explain the meaning of. . . ."

Step 2 This seems to be an overt performance and appears to be the main intent of the objective.

1. What performance is stated in the objective?
2. What is the performance?

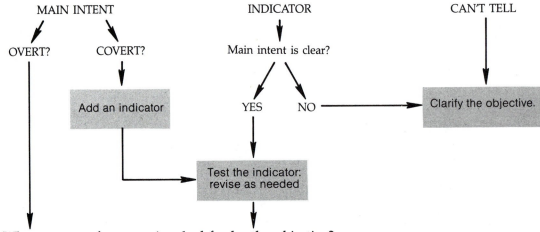

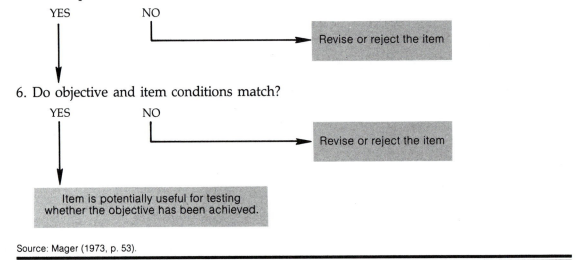

3. What overt performance is asked for by the objective?
4. What performance is asked for by the item?
5. Do the performances match?

6. Do objective and item conditions match?

Source: Mager (1973, p. 53).

Figure 4 • 3   A checklist to help analyze an objective and a proposed test
item to determine if the item tests for achievement of the objective.

Step 3   Thus, the objective asks us to observe pupils explaining the meaning of culture in their own words.

Steps 4a, 5a   Now consider Item 1: The performance in this item is "naming," not "explaining" and the naming applies to a specific cultural situation rather than to the general concept of culture. Thus, the item does not match the main intent of the objective and should be revised or rejected.

Steps 4b, 5b Consider Item 2: The performances in the item are to "compare" and "describe" ("write" is an indicator behavior). Although these are worthwhile activities, they seem to go beyond the main intent of the objective which calls for explaining the concept in a general way. Thus, the item doesn't match this specific objective.

Steps 4c, 5c In Item 3, the student is to "tell the meaning of" the concept ("write," again, is an indicator behavior). This seems to match the more limited scope of the stated objective. Thus, this item is potentially useful for testing this objective.

If you would like a more detailed explanation of how to use the procedure in Figure 4.3, you should consult Mager's (1973) easy-to-read book: *Measuring Instructional Intent: Or Got a Match?*

Matching Test Items to Developmental Objectives

As I previously indicated, a developmental objective can be measured by taking a sample of appropriate behavior from the large, perhaps nearly limitless, behavior domain implied by it. Usually, a developmental objective can be broken down into several more specific objectives, each of which describes one facet of the developmental objective that is appropriate at a particular level of educational growth. Once the specific objectives have been identified and test items written to measure each, the matching procedures described by Figure 4.3 can be applied.

Sometimes, to assure the validity of a classroom test, several different assessment procedures may be necessary. This is especially the case with developmental objectives because they imply a broad domain of performance application, but the use of several assessment procedures to measure a specific objective should not be discredited. For example, assessing spelling achievement might be done both by scoring several samples of pupils' written assignments as well as by using a dictated spelling test. The test provides the opportunity to observe a pupil's spelling of word patterns which might not appear in the natural course of the student's writing, but which may well fall within the purview of the objective. Observing a pupil's natural writing habits permits an inference about how well the student is likely to spell in other than testing circumstances. Using both procedures increases the comprehensiveness of the assessment of the development of spelling ability. Another reason for using more than one testing procedure is to obtain more reliable measures. A teacher's subjective evaluation of a pupil's written essay on a topic might be supplemented by a test made up of more objectively scored items. This would serve as a supplement to the less reliable evaluation of the pupil's written work.

Summary

The following statements summarize the major points of this chapter.

1. Instructional objectives derive their major importance from the fact that specifying them helps to direct the instructional process toward the important learning outcomes a teacher and school have in mind.

2. This direction is accomplished by specifying what it is the student is expected to learn and developing tests and other procedures which will evaluate the intended learning outcomes.

3. Beside these direct lesson-oriented benefits of specific objectives, a number of other benefits for their use can be identified: (a) making educational goals explicit, (b) communicating instructional intent to others, (c) analyzing and sequencing what is to be taught, (d) evaluating instructional procedures, (e) providing focus in discussions with parents, (f) clarifying to students what is expected of them, (g) facilitating individualized instruction, and (h) facilitating the revision of instructional procedures.

4. Specifying objectives has heuristic value for classroom testing through (a) facilitating the general planning of test development, (b) clarifying the specific behaviors for which test exercises should be designed or selected, (c) facilitating the evaluation of an existing test, and (d) facilitating a judgment of the content validity of a test.

5. Statements of general educational goals are useful to guide the overall educational enterprise but must be more specific to be implemented in the classroom.

6. Specificity is accomplished by organizing goals into subject-matter areas and then developing several general objectives for each goal. Each general objective is subsequently defined by more specific behaviors which can be taught and measured in order to infer the degree to which students have obtained general objectives and goals.

7. At least two kinds or levels of objectives useful for classroom instruction can be identified: (a) specific, "can do" objectives and (b) broader, developmental objectives.

8. Developmental objectives are never fully attainable, but they can be optimized at a particular educational level by writing several important, specific behaviors defining educational development at that level. Performance on this sample of objectives can be used to estimate the degree students have attained the developmental objective at the defined level.

9. Developmental objectives cannot be considered "can do" objectives because (a) they imply several behaviors which are not highly related to each other, (b) narrowing their meaning to a single, specific objective destroys the intent of the developmental objective, and (c) it is reasonable to expect degrees of development or growth in certain developmental areas.

10. When writing the objectives for a lesson or unit and for a classroom test, it is important to positively identify the full range of pupil behavior to be learned. This is done by: (a) referring to taxonomies of cognitive, affective, and/or psychomotor objectives; (b) reviewing instructional materials and teachers' manuals; (c) consulting curriculum guides from various sources; (d) reviewing books on methods of teaching the subject; (e) reviewing criterion-referenced tests of a subject; (f) and/or reviewing banks or pools of objectives developed by various agencies.

11. The Bloom et al. taxonomy orders levels of cognitive objectives. From simplest to most complex these are: knowledge, comprehension, application, analysis, synthesis, and evaluation. (See Appendix D for details.)

12. Gagné's scheme for describing learned behavior orders behaviors in these categories (simplest first): discrimination learning, concrete concept learning, defined concept learning, rule learning, higher-order rule learning, and cognitive strategy learning.

13. Other cognitive behavior taxonomies are listed in the text.

14. The Krathwohl et al. taxonomy orders affective objectives in these categories: reception, response, value, organization, and character. (See Appendix D for details.)

15. Harrow's taxonomy orders psychomotor objectives in these categories: reflex movements, basis-fundamental movements, perceptual abilities, physical abilities, skilled movements, and non-discussive communications. (See Appendix D for details.) Other psychomotor taxonomies were listed.

16. Criteria for reviewing the quality and importance of the objectives selected for a unit or a course were listed.

17. The minimum criteria for a written statement of a specific objective are: (a) worded in terms of the pupil rather than the teacher or school, (b) worded in terms of observable behavior, and (c) worded so the specific content to which behavior is applied is clear.

18. Specific examples for action verbs which describe behavior are given in Tables 4.2 and 4.4.

19. A distinction can be made between two types of behaviors found in instructional objectives: (a) overt behaviors and (b) covert behaviors. Covert behaviors need to be accompanied by indicator behaviors if teachers are to know whether they have been learned.

20. Abstractions, such as "understanding" or "evaluation," are ideas which represent a learner's state. They are inferred from observing several different kinds of learner behaviors. Thus, if abstractions are used, they must be further defined by specific objectives before being taught and tested.

21. It is important to the validity of a test that its exercises closely match the instructional intent of the objectives. A procedure for doing this is given in Figure 4.3.

22. Sometimes several different methods of observing pupil performance need to be used before the teacher can feel confident that the pupil has met the instructional intent.

Themes

● The assessment of student performance should be used to guide the instructional process. This means that different kinds of tests are likely to be needed for different instructional decisions.

● The kinds of tests a teacher develops will depend on factors such as a teacher's values and beliefs, the kinds of decisions required in a particular instructional approach, the curriculum organization, the availability of various instructional resources, and the educational and maturational level of the pupils in the class.

● Whether tests such as course and unit pretests, placement tests, posttests for instructional units, and formative evaluation tests should be developed and used depends on the extent to which an instructional system can adapt instruction to individual pupil differences.

● Complete test plans should contain certain elements and the adequacy of a proposed test can be judged by several criteria.

Terms and Concepts

instructional approach
personal belief system
placement decisions
diagnostic decisions
monitoring decisions
attainment decisions
curriculum organization
test blueprint (test specifications, test plan, table of specifications)
unit of instruction

course pretest vs. unit pretest
course placement test
equivalence of pretest and posttest
formative evaluation tests
elements contained in a complete test plan
item difficulty level
relative achievement level
criteria for judging a planned test (validity, reliability, comprehensiveness, objectivity, economy)

5
PLANNING
CLASSROOM
TESTS

A teacher is familiar with the need to develop plans for teaching particular lessons. There is a similar need to develop a plan for a test before actually constructing it. Testing and instruction are intertwined, so it is important to develop good assessment procedures that provide appropriate information needed for instructional decisions. This chapter has five sections. The first describes reasons why it is important for a teacher to acquire test development skills as part of teaching competence. The second gives an overview of the process of classroom test development, describing the instructional decisions for which assessment information is needed and the component activities which are involved in the test development process. The third section considers in some detail the relationship between the test planning process and the instructional planning process. Among the relationships considered are those between: a teacher's beliefs, instructional methods, and tests; the various instructional decisions for which information will be needed; the pupils' levels of development and test procedures; a curriculum's organization and the testing procedure adopted; and the availability of instructional resources and testing procedures. The fourth section describes how to develop a plan or "blueprint" for a test covering one unit of instruction. A fifth section describes the things to take into account when planning for such tests as course and unit pretests, placement tests, posttests, and diagnostic and formative tests. The final section discusses some overall considerations when planning tests, including criteria for judging a planned test.

Importance of Acquiring Test Development Skills

Knowledge and skill in test development are important for the following reasons:

1. *Developing a test helps you clarify the behaviors you feel are important for students to learn.* The behaviors you require your students to perform and on which you base your evaluations of them serve as the "operational definitions" of your teaching objectives.
2. *Skills acquired in the process of learning to develop tests can be applied to other aspects of lesson or to curriculum planning and development.* Teaching involves changing pupil behaviors and requires that you be able to recognize the behaviors you wish pupils to perform at the end of the lesson. When

developing a test, you begin with a clear description of this performance and continue to define, in a rather precise fashion, the conditions of that performance and how you will elicit and observe it. The skills employed when defining and eliciting behaviors are useful also for both teaching and lesson development, since these behavior changes are the focus of teaching.

3. *Skills and knowledge you acquire concerning test development will help you evaluate the quality of commercial testing materials.* Poor testing materials may lead to inappropriate decisions about pupil progress and mastery and thus may render ineffective an otherwise useful instructional program. Commercial curricular testing materials which frequently accompany teachers' editions are often not prepared by skilled

item writers and, therefore, vary greatly in their quality. If you acquire test development skills, you will be able not only to recognize poor quality testing materials, but also will be able to revise them and to improve their quality. (It is usually much faster to revise test items than to create them from "scratch.")

4. *Well-constructed classroom tests can lead to more objective and fairer procedures for judging and evaluating pupils.* Pupils are more likely to be evaluated on the basis of their knowledge and performance than might otherwise occur if a teacher's assessment techniques are technically sound. Of course, objectivity and fairness are not guaranteed since, unfortunately, sometimes tests are used unprofessionally.

5. *Knowledge of the current state of the art of test development leads to an appreciation of the limits of testing and to an understanding of how testing abuses occur.*

Overview of the Test Development Process

Classroom testing should be part of the teaching/learning process. This means that testing should be integrated into the particular instructional procedures you use in order to provide information to both you and the pupil to decide such matters as: "(1) What a pupil is prepared to study next, (2) How a pupil's study of a given objective, topic, or unit might best be carried out, (3) When a pupil has mastered a specific instructional objective (or some limited specific skill), (4) When a pupil has mastered a limited amount of instruction (or some larger body of skills such as those found in one textbook chapter), (5) When a pupil has achieved a major composite goal (such as the ability to prepare a certain kind of report, conduct a particular kind of study, achieve a given level in some physical performance), [and] (6) When a review of past learning or an integra-

tion of such learnings is needed" (Lindvall and Nitko, 1975, p. 19).

One way to understand the classroom test construction process is to analyze the component activities that are involved in it. One such analysis is shown in Figure 5.1. This figure does not represent a step-by-step guide for learning how to construct classroom tests, but it does represent a characterization of the various activities that would be involved when a teacher develops a test following all of the recommendations found in Part II of this textbook. As you study the material in these chapters, you may find it useful to occasionally turn back here to Figure 5.1 to see how the techniques you are learning "fit into" the overall test construction process.

Preliminary Considerations: Relating Instructional Approaches to Testing Procedures

As is indicated in Figure 5.1, teachers bring to the actual test construction process some degree of understanding of (a) their own values and beliefs, (b) the cognitive, affective, and psychomotor characteristics of the pupils they are teaching, (c) the behaviors they would like their pupils to acquire, and (d) the goals and structure of the curriculum they follow. These understandings are seldom verbalized or otherwise made explicit. Rather they are internalized and integrated into the individual's gestalt of the teaching-learning process. A teacher's unique integration of these four areas affects the identification of the particular behaviors ultimately taught and tested in the classroom.

The purpose of this section is to help the reader bring these understandings to conscious awareness so that the reader can begin to think about how particular instructional approaches are related to the testing procedures ultimately adopted. This kind of forethought provides the backdrop against which

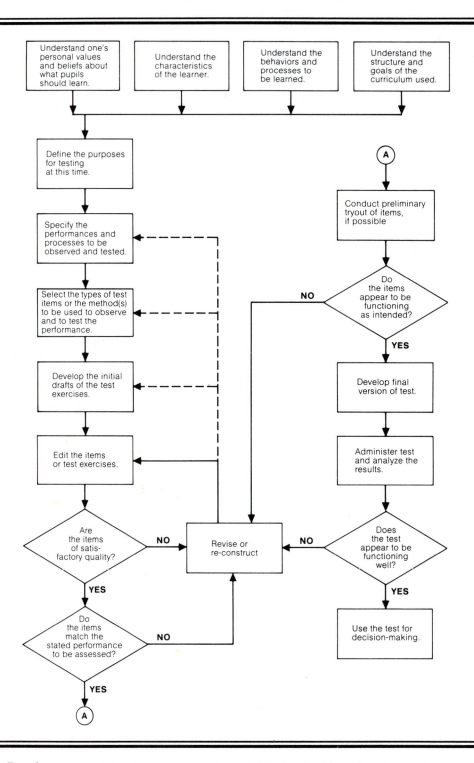

Figure 5 • 1 Flowchart showing the component activities involved in a classroom test.

the basic issues of planning for a particular test are played. Among the important points to consider are the following five:

1. *The basis of what and how you test lies in your instructional approach and your belief system.* The behaviors which you value and believe to be important will eventually become part of the pupil evaluation procedures you use. Even the types of test items you use will reflect these values. The items on the test become the operational definition of the educational goals and pupil outcomes which you value. As your values and instructional approach change, so will your tests and evaluation procedures.

2. *Within any belief system and instructional approach, there will be different decisions for which you will need information about pupils.* The form and content of tests, as well as other types of information-gathering procedures, will differ depending on the nature of these decisions. For example, some instructional approaches attempt to adapt to the rate and style of a pupil's learning by developing an individualized plan of study for each learner. In such cases, these are four of the basic decisions that need to be made about each individual (Nitko, 1969; Glaser and Nitko, 1971; Nitko and Hsu, 1974):

   a. *Placement decisions:* deciding where in the instructional sequence the learner should begin to avoid repeating unnecessarily what the learner already knows and to attain new goals.

   b. *Diagnostic decisions:* deciding the learning activities the learner should engage in to increase the chances of learning the objectives the teacher has set for the individual. Making such a decision may require integrating information gathered about a particular pupil from a variety of sources.

   c. *Monitoring decisions:* deciding whether the pupil appears to be attending to instruction as it is occurring, if the

assigned learning activity is working, and/or whether a new (different) learning activity should be assigned.

   d. *Attainment decisions:* deciding, at the end of a particular segment of instruction, whether the pupil has acquired the instructional goals.

To plan for classroom testing you will need to understand the instructional system well enough to identify the appropriate decision points and the kinds of information you will need in order to make those decisions. In some cases it may not be necessary to develop a paper-and-pencil test to evaluate what learning pupils have attained:

It may be possible, even essential, to obtain the needed information by observing the students, by examining their daily work, by talking with them, or by using some other informal procedure. Also, in decisions dealing with how a pupil's study can best be carried out, a teacher's general knowledge of the pupil's attitudes, interests, typical style of study, and need for personal attention may represent the critical data. The important thing is to use every means available for getting information pertinent to making a specific instructional decision (Lindvall and Nitko, 1975, p. 20).

3. *A pupil's educational and physical development and maturity will place boundaries on both the instructional approach and the testing procedures used.* Older, more able students might be able to participate in developing their own tests and/or in evaluating their own test performance. With some students, particularly young ones, written examinations requiring independent reading are out of the question. Spoken test directions or oral examinations may be inappropriate for pupils exhibiting hearing impairments. Those with physical impairments involving the arms or hands may find written examinations fatiguing.

4. *The way a curriculum is organized will place a restraint on the nature of the testing program.* Some curricula are organized in a hierarchy of prerequisite learning objectives (see Figure 5.3). In such curricula, a high level of mastery of prerequisite skills is assumed before more complex skills in the hierarchy are taught. This means that testing procedures, often called "pretests," are designed to provide information about the attainment of such prerequisites and pupils are permitted few errors on them. Other curricula are organized in a "spiral" fashion so that a student reviews previously taught material quite frequently with an eye toward gradual correction of errors (see Chapter 17, Figure 17.2). Tests in these latter curricula check, not so much for initially high levels of mastery, but more for the seriousness of the errors committed and whether the general process being taught has been acquired sufficiently well to proceed.

5. *The available instructional resources frequently determine the nature of the tests developed.* Some schools use pre-packaged instructional materials that have short tests for each objective (sometimes called "curriculum-embedded tests") built into them. Others may have various types of diagnostic tests, placement tests, or pretests and posttests designed into the instructional package. Workbooks in mathematics, reading, social studies, and science frequently have tests (or test-like exercises) included. A teacher is more or less committed to using these tests if the school system requires them. Some of these tests are not built by professional test developers, and they may be of poorer quality than if a teacher had developed them. The teacher may attempt to rewrite the tests to make them more usable if this occurs. Box 5.1 illustrates one particular instructional approach and the types of testing and decision situations found therein. You may want to analyze this case study to identify how each of the five points above is applied to an actual instructional situation.

Developing a Blueprint for a Test Covering an Instructional Unit

Rather than simply making up test questions immediately, a teacher should formulate a test plan first. This is done by making a "blueprint" or "table of test specifications" describing both the content which the test should cover and the behaviors expected of the student for that content. In addition to describing the content the test will cover, the "blueprint" serves as a basis for setting the number of test items and for assuring that the test will have the desired emphasis and balance.[1] Figure 5.2 illustrates such a blueprint for a science unit on forces.

The row headings along the left margin are the major topics the test will cover. You can use a more detailed outline if you wish. The column headings across the top are the major classifications of the Bloom et al. taxonomy of cognitive educational objectives. These categories appear in more detail in the last chapter and Appendix D. Notice that there is an increasing complexity from left to right in the types of behavior implied by the column headings. Behaviors which demonstrate knowledge or comprehension, for example, are lower-level cognitive performances, while those behaviors reflecting the ability to synthesize or evaluate are higher level cognitive performances.

The body of the blueprint lists the specific objectives to test (observe). The objectives are thus doubly classified by both a content topic and a level of complexity of the taxonomic category. In this example, most of the objectives are at the lower and middle levels of the tax-

[1]See Appendix E for an alternate procedure for specifying the items to be on a test.

onomy. If a different emphasis is desired, a teacher would be able to use the blueprint to identify where to write other objectives to be tested.

Note that it is difficult to classify objectives and items into the categories of the Bloom et al. taxonomy. This does not render this approach to test planning useless, however. The purpose of formally laying out this two-way grid is not to promote exact or rigorous classification. Rather it is to aid the teacher in recalling that there are higher-order cognitive skills which need to be systematically taught and evaluated in the classroom.

The numbers in the blueprint describe the emphasis of the test, both in terms of percentage of the total number of items and in terms of the percentage of items within each row or content category. The decision of how many questions to include on a test is based on the importance of the objectives, the type of questions, the subject matter, and the amount of time available for testing. Suppose that a teacher planned to use 40 test items for this unit. The blueprint shows that of these forty, the teacher has decided that 20% or 8 items should be used to test instructional objectives which deal with "Two-Dimensional Forces." Notice there are only two objectives for this topic—one at the "knowledge level" and one at the "application level." Of the 8 items, the teacher decided that 2 items ($= 25\%$ of 8) should deal with the knowledge level objective and the remaining 6 items (or 75%) with the application level objective. Thus, with regard to the topic of two-dimensional forces, this unit test emphasizes the application objective. Notice, too, that 63% ($= 25 \div 40$) of the *test questions* deal with the higher taxonomic levels of application and synthesis even

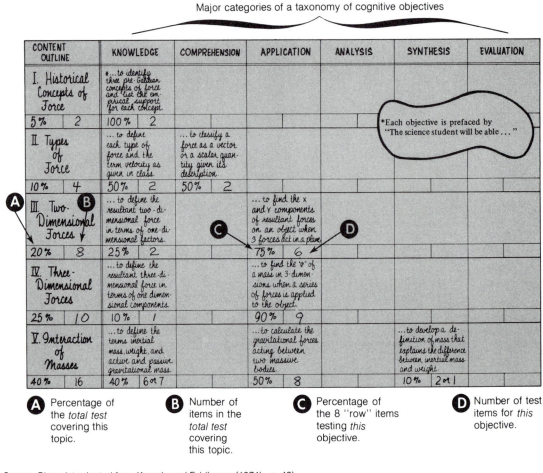

A — Percentage of the *total test* covering this topic.

B — Number of items in the *total test* covering this topic.

C — Percentage of the 8 "row" items testing *this* objective.

D — Number of test items for *this* objective.

Source: Blueprint adapted from Kryspin and Feldhusen (1974b, p. 42).

Figure 5 • 2   Example of a blueprint for a test on a science unit.

though there are many *objectives* at the lower levels of the taxonomy. This example illustrates that the weighting or emphasis of a test is based on the number of items in a particular category, not the number of objectives, reflecting the fact that some objectives are more important for a pupil evaluation than others.

Pupils will expect the various numbers of questions on a test to correspond to the amount of time devoted to the objectives in class and to the emphasis which they perceived the teacher has placed on the objectives. If the test you are planning does not meet this expectation, it seems fair to notify the students of this fact well in advance of the test (Sax, 1974).

This advanced planning for developing a classroom test allows a teacher to view the test as a whole. In this way, a teacher can maintain whatever balance or emphasis of content coverage and whatever complexity of performance necessary and the test need not be too easy nor too hard for the pupils.

; described n the many ompeting mpletely eed not for each teacher ach year, vill have bjectives ated with n entailed. hers could in a subject eague's blue- our particular le time saving

Planning for Tests Having Different Instructional Purposes

Before beginning to write objectives and test items you will need to know the purpose for which your test will be used. In this section we review briefly several types of classroom tests and state some suggestions to keep in mind when planning for them.

Table 5.1 is an outline of various phases of instruction showing the instructional decisions for each phase and, at the bottom, possible sources of information needed to make those decisions. Notice that not all of the information would be obtained from teacher-made tests and that various sources of information beside paper-and-pencil tests should be used.

Pretests and Placement Tests for an Entire Course

Nature of course pretests For some courses, such as upper elementary school and high school mathematics, it may be desirable to develop a pretest specifically for what you plan to cover for the semester or year to learn (a) if pupils have learned and retained prerequisite knowledge skills and (b) if pupils have already mastered part of the content of the course.

The extent to which a group of pupils has attained the necessary prerequisites is likely to vary greatly from class to class and from year to year. Thus, a test covering specific prerequisite skills will help the teacher adapt or adjust instruction to the particular pupils at hand, perhaps by forming smaller instructional groups or by individualizing instruction. When testing prerequisite skills at the beginning of the year or semester, the teacher will have to be able to analyze the planned, upcoming instructional objectives to identify the prerequisites which pupils should have learned previously. Unlearned prerequisites will have to be remediated before proceeding. Only salient or crucial prerequisites should be tested, since the length of the test must be kept in mind. Frequently, too, more than one question per prerequisite objective will be necessary to assure that pupils have attained sufficient mastery. In a few schools, curricula with learning hierarchies are available. These provide an excellent basis on which to begin to identify prerequisites.

But pretesting isn't always necessary If you are teaching a subject for which nearly all pupils have about the same level of entry skills, a teacher-designed pretest is not likely to be needed. Also, if your instructional approach does not permit pupils who have learned already half of the content of the course, to progress immediately to more advanced topics, then course placement testing will not be useful. Formal course placement and pretesting are most useful when the teacher (a) knows little about the competence of the individual pupils and (b) is working within an instructional system that can adapt instruction to individual differences in competence.

	Phase I: Planning Instruction	Phase II: Guiding Instruction	Phase III: Evaluating results of Instruction
Major questions or decisions	What is to be studied? (What are the needs of these pupils with respect to this content?) Where should instruction start?	How should instruction be carried out? When is the class (or a student) ready to move on?	Have pupils mastered and retained important learning outcomes?
Basis for planning	Course outline. Specification of units and objectives. The textbook outline. Specification of prerequisite sequences.	Diagnostic outline of units or major topics. Identification of possible instructional alternatives. Specification of mastery criteria for objectives, units, topics.	Specification of essential content and skills (especially those needed as basis for subsequent courses).
Specific types of information needed	Do students already have mastery of any of course content? What have students studied before? Do students have prerequisites for course? What is present student status in mastery within sequence? Do certain topics have special interest and meaningfulness for students?	Do students have mastery or partial mastery of some topics within units? What type of instruction is most effective for this class (or for this student)? Have students mastered what they have been studying (objective, topic, unit)?	Have students retained the essential content and skills?
Possible sources of information	Course pretest. Standardized achievement tests. Student records. Placement test. Readiness tests. Aptitude tests.	Unit pretest. Interview with student. Student records. Personal knowledge of student. Aptitude tests. Quiz covering a given objective or topic (CET).* Unit posttest. Student work. Interview. Observation.	End-of-course exam. Standardized achievement test. Projects. Observation.

*Curriculum embedded test.
Source: From *Measuring Pupil Achievement and Aptitude,* Second Edition, p. 208, Tab. 10.1, by C. M. Lindvall and A. J. Nitko, © 1975 by Harcourt Brace Jovanovich, Inc. Reprinted by permission of the publisher.

Table 5 • 1 Outline for obtaining information needed in an evaluation program designed to aid in decision-making in all phases of instruction.

Pretesting for a Single Unit of Instruction

Nature of unit pretests Courses are usually divided into a series of smaller instructional sequences called units. Sometimes the entire curriculum is organized into instructional units that are then arranged in at least a roughly prerequisite order. Figure 5.3 shows this arrangement for an elementary school mathematics curriculum. The content topics are in a rough prerequisite order (from top to bottom in the figure). Each topic is developing

Content (Topic)	Level of Complexity						
	A	B	C	D	E	F	G
Numeration/Place Value	*	*	*	*	*	*	*
Addition/Subtraction	*	*	*	*	*	*	*
Multiplication		*	*	*	*	*	*
Division		*	*	*	*	*	*
Fractions	*	*	*	*	*	*	*
Money	*	*	*	*			
Time	*	*	*	*	*		
Systems of Management		*	*	*	*	*	*
Geometry		*	*	*	*	*	*
Applications		*	*	*	*	*	*

ADDITION / SUBTRACTION UNIT

4. Given a word problem that requires both addition and subtraction, the student solves the problem and writes the answer with the appropriate label. LIMIT: four four-digit addends; six-digit sums

3. Given an addition or subtraction word problem, the student solves the problem and writes the answer with the appropriate label. LIMIT: five six-digit addends; six-digit sums

2. Given an addition example or a list of addends, the student adds using the standard algorithm. LIMIT: five four-digit addends

1. Given an addition or subtraction example, the student solves using the standard algorithm. LIMIT: two six-digit addends

* Indicates a unit of instruction consisting of one or more instructional objectives.

Source: Adapted from Nitko (1974, p. 69, Figure 1); objectives from Learning Research and Development Center and Research for Better Schools (1972).

Figure 5 • 3 Example of a curriculum layout for Individually Prescribed Instruction in Elementary Mathematics. The inset represents a unit of instruction and the shaded boxes mean a pupil has sufficient mastery of these objectives to proceed with a new instructional objective. (See text.)

over a range of complex behaviors that are also in a rough prerequisite order (from A to G). Each cell represents an instructional unit consisting of several instructional objectives which perhaps can be arranged in a learning hierarchy. The objectives for one unit appear in the inset.

A unit pretest, as I have said, seeks to ascertain the extent to which a pupil has already acquired (a) the prerequisites and (b) the upcoming objectives. The results of a unit pretest are used to place a pupil at a particular objective within the unit so that the pupil will not need to be taught objectives already known. This "unit profile" is illustrated for a hypothetical student by the shaded boxes of the inset in Figure 5.3. Since the objectives of that unit are arranged in a prerequisite sequence, and since the hypothetical student has already learned the objectives represented by the shaded boxes, this pupil would skip instruction on Objectives 1 through 3 and begin with Objective 4. After learning Objective 4, the pupil would proceed to another unit.

Deciding if a pretest is necessary Before deciding to pretest a student at each unit, the teacher must weigh this practice against its ultimate usefulness. First, if the instructional system cannot adapt instruction to pupils who already have mastered various degrees of the upcoming unit, then, as in course placement and pretesting, knowing unit pretest information is not very helpful. Second, even if the instructional system within which the teacher works can accommodate such pupils, pretesting still may not be beneficial.

To see why not, consider Figure 5.3 again. Although the unit represented by the inset contains only 4 objectives, other units contain many more objectives. The Level D Applications unit, for example, contains 9 objectives (which are not shown here). Suppose that each objective was tested by 8 test items, not an unlikely number of items in order to attain a modestly reliable measurement. The pretest

then would contain $8 \times 9 = 72$ items! This is a lot of items and such a test would likely take a long time for a child to complete, especially an elementary school youngster who doesn't have command of very many of the objectives. The total time to both test and teach may be, perhaps, five to seven class periods: say, two or three periods for pretesting plus three or four periods instruction for those objectives not yet learned. It might be entirely more efficient to have all children take instruction for each unit of the curriculum instead of pretesting to see if some few children could test out of a unit. Eliminating such pretesting would reduce the amount of time a child would have to spend in a unit from say five to seven periods to perhaps three or four periods. Instead, the teacher might use informal methods and observational procedures to help identify those pupils experiencing difficulty or needing enrichment.

Unlike a *course* pretest where passing the test permits the students to "opt-out" of large segments of the course, a unit pretest may take longer to administer and score than the instruction itself. A "unit" is rather arbitrary, of course, and at the secondary school level a unit may represent 4 to 6 weeks (or longer). The rule is, know your curriculum sequence, instructional plans, and pupils and then decide whether the pretest is necessary; examine the consequences of both pretesting and of not pretesting.

Posttesting for a Single Unit

Importance of unit posttests Unit posttests are likely to be more necessary for an instructional decision-making process than their pretest counterparts. This is because pupils who have not learned the objectives of the unit are likely to have difficulty learning more advanced material. It is desirable to design unit posttests so they give information, not only about what pupils have learned, but about errors they are making. In this way, the teacher can remedy serious pupil errors. You may want to review some of the types of criterion-referenced diagnostic tests described in Chapter 17 for some ideas on this point.

Designing Equivalent Pre- and Posttests

The discussion of pre- and posttests thus far has not assumed that these two tests are equivalent or interchangeable. Pretests could be different from posttests. You may want, for example, to test for mastery of previously learned prerequisites at pretest time, whereas, at posttest time you may just wish to emphasize the few important terminal objectives of the unit or course. Some instructional systems in which you will be teaching may take a different view.

Some instructional systems will use a pretest and posttest that are considered identical or interchangeable in terms of what they measure. Not that the identical questions or items appear on each, but rather that the scores are to be interpreted as equivalent or interchangeable. Chapter 15 discusses ways to check on the equivalence of two tests. If you develop two tests that you will interpret as equivalent, then the burden of proof of providing evidence of their equivalence rests with you. The nature of such evidence is discussed in Chapter 15.

One way to begin developing such equivalent tests is to be faithful to the test blueprint. If both tests are built to the same specifications they are more likely to yield equivalent results. Equivalent forms should be built by carefully matching items on the two forms of the test. If specific objectives have been written, this would mean developing at least two items per objective: one item would be placed on each test form. The items of each pair thus created should be checked for their equivalence of content, difficulty, and psychological process they are designed to measure. It is helpful to use the Mager procedure outlined in Figure 4.3 to check whether both items match their common objective.

Formative Evaluation of Pupil Performance

Nature of formative evaluation tests We introduced the idea of tests designed for formative instead of summative evaluation in Chapter 1. *Summative evaluation of pupil performance* refers to the process of judging the extent of a pupil's mastery of material for the purpose of certifying competence, assigning grades, or reporting grades to parents or administrators (Bloom et al., 1971). *Formative evaluation of pupil performance* focuses on identifying particular learning difficulties and identifying learning activities in which a pupil may engage in order to overcome these difficulties. Such tests are closely linked to the process many educators call educational diagnosis and prescription although Bloom and his associates separate formative evaluation from diagnosis. The results of a pupil's performance on formative evaluation tests are not used to assign grades, but to provide feedback and further guidance in learning for both learner and teacher.

Example of a plan for a formative evaluation test Figure 5.4 shows the structure of a formative evaluation test for a chemistry unit. Panel A shows a version of the test blueprint. The columns represent the categories of the taxonomy. The circles with numbers represent items on the test. If successful performance on items from the higher levels of the taxonomy require the pupil to be able to perform successfully on certain lower-level items, then these items are connected with lines. A pupil's error pattern could be marked on this blueprint by putting "X's" on those circles representing items a student missed.

Panel B shows the answer sheet for this test. Notice first that the directions tell the students that the test does not count as part of the course grade but rather is designed to inform the student about learning difficulties. Second, each test item is keyed to one or more alternate learning resources. These may be

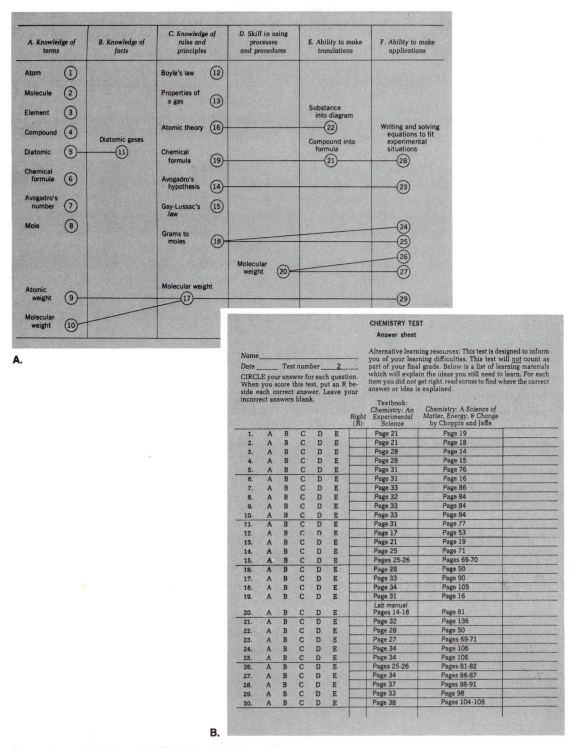

A.

B.

Source: Bloom et al. (1971, p. 212, Table 6-1; p. 132, Figure 6-1)

Figure 5 • 4 Example of how a formative evaluation test is planned and interpreted.

pages in textbooks, as in the figure, or may be other resources such as film strips, cassette tapes, manipulatives, games, group study sessions, and so on.

It should be apparent that considerable planning is required to design and implement such a system of formative evaluation tests. Frequently, this will require several teachers working together and a considerable amount of moral support and encouragement from the school administration. You should read carefully the appropriate chapters in the Bloom et al. (1971) book before undertaking the design of formative evaluation tests.

Overall Considerations When Planning Classroom Tests

By now you have an idea of the general process of developing a test plan by writing specific objectives and by classifying these objectives in a test blueprint. Figure 5.1 depicted the first few steps of test development as:

> Define the purpose for testing at this time.
> ↓
> Specify the performance and processes to be observed and tested.
> ↓
> Select the types of test items or the methods to be used to observe and to test the performance.
> ↓
> Develop the initial drafts of the test exercises.

So far, the first two of these have been discussed. The last step, developing test exercises, is the subject of the next few chapters. In this section attention is directed toward some of the general considerations when selecting the testing procedures to be used to implement the test blueprint.

The discussion in this section will be general necessarily because I assume that you are not yet familiar with the technical aspects of test construction and test evaluation. This sec-

tion, however, will give you some idea how the knowledge you will acquire through studying this book is integrated into the initial planning stages of test construction.[2]

What Should be Specified Ahead of Time?

The overall planning for a test should take the following into consideration (e.g., Ebel, 1979; Gronlund, 1976):

1. **Formats of test items to be used** Many varieties of items and test exercises have been invented including:

a. Choice formats ("objective" items)
   i. true-false
   ii. multiple-choice
   iii. matching exercises
b. Short answer/completion format
c. Essay format
d. Performance observation formats
   i. checklists
   ii. rating scales
   iii. sign and category systems
e. Interviews, in-depth observation
f. Long-term activity formats
   i. projects
   ii. extended written assignments
   iii. laboratory exercises

An evaluation of the advantages and disadvantages of various paper-and-pencil test formats is presented in Table 5.2. The points listed in the table are discussed in more detail in subsequent chapters.

2. **Number of items of each format** Both the amount of time available for testing and the desired accuracy of the scores will determine the extent of testing. Tests with more items (i.e., more observations) are more reliable than shorter tests. However, most achievement tests

---

[2]It may be helpful to review this section again after completing your study of the chapters in Parts II and III of this book.

Factor	Essay	Short Answer, Completion	Objective
Can measure ability to solve novel problems	+ +	+	+ +
Can measure ability to organize, integrate, or synthesize	+ +	+	- -
Can measure originality or innovative approaches to problems	+ +	+	- -
Can isolate specific abilities in subject area from general skills of writing, spelling, and language usage	- -	-	+ +
Has potential value for diagnosis	- -	+	+ +
Can sample adequately the objectives of instruction	-		+ +
Can sample adequately the content of instruction	- -	-	+ +
Is free from opportunities for guessing answer	+ +	+ +	- -
Gives consistent scores from scorer to scorer	- -	-	+ +
Is accurate in differentiating levels of competency among examinees	- -	-	+ +
Can be scored by unskilled clerk or machine	- -	-	+ +
Can be scored quickly	- -	-	+ +
Takes little time for writing items	+	+	-

Note: + + = great advantage, + = slight advantage, -- = great disadvantage.
Source: From *Measurement and Evaluation in Psychology and Education*, Fourth Edition, by R. L. Thorndike and E. P. Hagen. (New York: John Wiley & Sons, Inc., 1977), p. 257, Table 7.3. Reprinted by permission of the publisher.

Table 5 • 2 Summary of the advantages and disadvantages of various formats of paper-and-pencil test items.

should be considered power tests, so everyone should have enough time to answer each item if they know it. Practical experience with the subject matter and pupils you are teaching will help you decide on the length of the test.

3. Types of performances to be observed You should develop a test blueprint or some variation of it to specify the various levels of performance to be observed.

4. Number of performances within each type As Figure 5.2 illustrates, the number of objectives within each taxonomic category is delineated. You may simply write the objectives (performance statements) under each category.

5. Content to be covered by the test Again, the test blueprint can be the vehicle for delin-

eating the content or topics the test will cover (see Figure 5.2).

6. Number of items to test each content topic/ taxonomy category combination The number of items testing each objective (performance) is specified. This, also, is shown in the example blueprint in Figure 5.2.

7. Complexity level and item difficulty Items on a test should match the conditions stated in the objectives. The complexity of an item is increased by altering the "givens" or conditions under which the pupil is expected to perform. Such conditions frequently change the performance from one at the knowledge level to a higher level of a cognitive level of a taxonomy, such as, "application." Figure 4.3 suggested a systematic procedure to use to match test items with objectives.

The difficulty level of test items has a technical meaning: the percentage of pupils answering the item correctly is called the *item difficulty level*. An item's difficulty level is not a property of the item alone but a function of three things: the complexity of the item, the ability of the pupils responding to it, and the nature (or quality) of instruction preceding the item's use. The combination of these three results in the percentage of pupils who correctly answer an item being higher or lower.

A teacher can manipulate the complexity of an item or the nature of the preceding instruction in order to make the items (and, hence, the test) harder or easier. Alternately, one can make a preliminary tryout of the items and then *select* certain items because of their difficulty level. When the purpose of a test is to make discriminations among the *relative achievement*[3] of pupils, then somewhat easier items are preferred, because difficult items tend to result in guesses and random responses on the part of pupils. When choice format items are used for tests designed to measure relative achievement, the following are recommended difficulty levels:

Type of Item	Recommended Difficulty Level[4]
True-False	Between 75% and 85% passing
Three-option multiple-choice	Between 67% and 77% passing
Four-option multiple-choice	Between 63% and 74% passing
Five-option multiple-choice	Between 60% and 69% passing

[3]This means distinguishing who is the best, next best, etc. student, rather than deciding how much a given pupil has learned in an absolute sense (see Chapter 11).

[4]Combines the traditional standards (e.g., see Ebel, 1979) with Lord's (1952) recommendation. Perhaps the first to suggest that the difficulty level of an item should be above 50% and dependent on the number of choices allowed in an item was Lindquist (1936).

These estimates are based on the idea that choice items should not be so difficult that they elicit random responses. (See Chapter 11 for a more detailed discussion of this matter.)

If items match the objectives and the conditions of performance specified therein, and if each objective has been taught and studied conscientiously, then the test should be of appropriate difficulty. Some items may be very easy, so that nearly all pupils pass them. While such items are not very efficient in discriminating the levels of relative achievement, they might be appropriate to use in the classroom for absolute achievement interpretations.

Criteria for Judging the Proposed Testing Procedures

There are certain criteria that can be used to judge any testing procedure being planned. Below, these criteria are described in general terms so you have an idea of what to keep in mind. Later chapters of this book will discuss them in more technical detail. The basic criteria by which the most appropriate procedures to use are judged are summarized in Table 5.3 and discussed below.

Validity   Chapter 16 discusses validity in some detail. Here, I wish to point out that the basic purpose for any test is to determine the extent to which each pupil has attained the important objectives delineated in the test plan. While this sounds very straightforward, it is not always an easy criterion to meet because there are a considerable number of factors which influence a pupil's test score. A number of these are described in Chapters 12 and 16.

Reliability   This refers to the consistency with which a given testing procedure reports a pupil's performance (see Chapter 15). A single test item, sampled from a pool of a thousand items, would be an unreliable basis on which to infer a pupil's mastery of the subject. In general, longer tests (with more items per

Table 5 • 3 Criteria by which classroom testing procedures (e.g., items) are judged appropriate.

objective) are more reliable than shorter tests (with fewer items per objective).

Two possible sources of unreliability for classroom assessment procedures, for example, are the fluctuations in judgments of the quality of a pupil's work caused by (a) fluctuations in judgement from one teacher to the next and (b) fluctuations in one teacher's judgement from one day to the next. In general, oral quizzes, ratings of performances, and essay questions are less reliable than more objective procedures such as multiple-choice, true-false, and matching questions.

The foregoing does not mean that more subjective procedures should be eliminated. Rather, the teacher should be aware of their limitations when measuring specific objectives. As the forthcoming chapters will indicate, there are ways to improve the reliability of these subjective methods. After considering the effects of inconsistency when assessing pupil achievement, you will realize that an unreliable test procedure cannot be very valid.

Objectivity A test procedure is said to be objective if two or more observers of a pupils' performance can agree on the report of the performance, that is, on what rating or score to give it. Objectivity is obviously related to reliability (and thereby, to validity) because

inconsistency in the reported scores means they are unreliable.

Subjectivity is not bad in and of itself. Surely, as a professional and an expert in the field, a teacher's judgement is of value and importance to the student. What students seek, however, is consistent application of that judgement so that it does not reflect idiosyncratic, erratic assessment.

As with reliability and validity, objectivity is not an all or nothing characteristic. These are matters of degree: A test is more or less objective. Even when the scoring of a test is objective, one should not conclude that the entire process of test development is objective. The questions appearing on a test and the particular answers designated as "correct" are frequently results of subjective decisions which reflect differences of opinion from one test developer to the next.

Comprehensiveness The extent to which a test includes a representative sample of behaviors from all the important objectives of instruction contributes much to the success of a test. One reason I stressed the importance of using various taxonomies of objectives was because of the importance of comprehensiveness. Such taxonomies help a teacher call to mind the various important abilities toward which instruction is directed. Coupling the taxonomy with a content outline and writing a test blueprint help to ensure that many important behaviors are tested, rather than just those easiest to test or those that first come to mind. The comprehensiveness of a test can only be ensured by consciously planning for it.

Ease of construction and scoring   Two practical concerns to keep in mind are how easy it will be to devise the test tasks and to score them. It is easier to develop essay items, for example, than to develop items for rating scales or multiple-choice items. But once developed, the latter are easier and faster to score and have the added advantage that you can use them again.

Economy of pupil time   The proposed testing procedure is balanced against a judgement about what is the best way to use a pupil's time in class. Some procedures such as interviews and individual observations of pupil performances require a rather long time to complete. Also, while one pupil is being interviewed or observed, the teacher must plan for ways to keep the remainder of the class occupied. Group administered objective-tests can test all pupils at the same time. Teachers must

judge what the appropriate balance is between occupying a pupil's time with testing procedures vs. occupying it with other activities according to individual circumstances.

Economy of teacher time   Essay tests, term papers, projects, and written work generally require much pupil time to complete and much teacher time to grade and evaluate. When planning to use these procedures, you must decide whether this is a wise investment of your time. But teacher grading time and pupil learning time need not be entirely independent. For example, a term paper or a project can be evaluated with the pupil present. If this is done in a non-threatening way, the pupil can see what the teacher is judging and taking into account when grading the assignment. This opportunity may also permit the pupil to ask questions and otherwise clarify what is to be learned. When this occurs, the teacher's time which is spent grading is identical with the pupil's instructional time. Testing and learning blend together. Learners can look forward to testing as feedback about their accomplishments and as opportunities for guidance toward their chosen goals.

Summary

This chapter has reviewed procedures used in planning a classroom test. Emphasis was placed on the fit of a test to particular instructional programs and to particular belief patterns a teacher uses. To design a test requires that the purposes for decision-making and testing be specified. Among the instructional decisions are placement decisions, diagnostic decisions, monitoring decisions, and attainment decisions. The kinds of tests a teacher uses will be a function also of the curriculum organization, available instructional resources, and the educational and maturational level of the pupils.

To plan a test, I recommend that you prepare a two-way table, called a test blueprint. The names of the major categories of a taxonomy head the table columns while the row heading indicates the major topics of the subject matter to be tested. In the body of the table, the "cells," formed by a combination of a particular taxonomy category and a particular subject-matter topic, contain specific instructional objectives. Thus, the blueprint serves as a double-entry classifying scheme for specific objectives. After objectives are classified, the number of test items that will be used to test each objective is recorded in the table. Thus, the test blueprint serves as a plan which assures that all important objectives are included and that they receive the proper emphasis on the test.

The chapter describes several particular kinds of classroom tests: course and unit pretests, placement tests, posttests for units of instruction, and tests for formative evaluation of pupil performance. Discussed are some factors to keep in mind when planning for these tests and when deciding whether to use them at all. When pretests and posttests are considered equivalent or interchangeable, special planning is needed.

Among the elements which a complete test plan should consider are (a) the formats of the items used, (b) the total number of items, (c) the types of performances to be observed, (d) the content and complexity of the performance, and (e) the number and difficulty level of the items planned for each performance category. The planned testing procedures can be judged by several criteria of test quality: validity, reliability, objectivity, comprehensiveness, and the practical criteria of ease of construction and scoring and economy of pupil and teacher time.

Once a test plan has been formulated, the teacher proceeds to the actual development of test items or text exercises. How to develop these testing materials is the subject of the next few chapters.

Themes

● A teacher should be certain that each test item developed (a) measures educationally important objectives, (b) elicits only desired behaviors, and (c) does not inhibit desired behaviors from being performed.

● Essay test items may be of the restricted response type or of the extended response type. The former limits the substantive content of the answer and the form of the written response. The latter requires an elaborated written response in which a pupil is free to choose the way to organize and express ideas and relationships.

● Essays should go beyond testing for simple recall and comprehension of material. They should be designed so pupils can apply their knowledge and skills to new problems or novel situations.

● Many skills and abilities can be measured equally well by either essay, short-answer, completion, or response-choice items. When this occurs, response-choice items are preferable because their greater objectivity results in greater test validity.

● Practical suggestions for constructing and scoring essays, short-answer, and completion items have evolved from the experience of test developers over the past 60 years. The reliability and validity of classroom tests can be greatly improved by applying these principles.

Terms and Concepts

three fundamental principles of test
  construction
restricted response essay items
extended response essay items
interpretive exercises (context-
  dependent items)
testing knowledge of the subject matter
  vs. testing general ability
halo effect in scoring
carry-over effect in scoring
analytic scoring method
holistic scoring method

*extrinsic vs. intrinsic evaluation of
  compositions
*attributes of a writing sample
  (correctness, communicative
  effectiveness, rhetorical
  effectiveness, intellectual and/or
  aesthetic quality)
short-answer items (question,
  completion, association)
*Cloze reading exercises
*interlinear exercises

*These concepts are covered in optional sections.

6
DEVELOPING ESSAY AND COMPLETION ITEMS

Classroom paper-and-pencil tests usually include one or more of the following item formats: essay questions, completion (or fill-in) items, or response-choice items (multiple-choice, true-false, etc.). This chapter discusses only the first two of these formats. Response-choice formats are discussed in the next three chapters. A subsequent chapter discusses non-paper-and-pencil techniques for pupil assessment such as the use of systematic classroom observation.

This chapter opens with a general discussion of some basic considerations that are common to all classroom testing procedures, including essay questions and other formats. These few basic concerns are the key points to keep in mind when developing nearly every type of classroom test. A second section describes the different varieties of essay questions. A third section discusses the purposes, uses, and misuses of essays in general. Suggestions for constructing essays are presented in a fourth section. A fifth section gives suggestions for overcoming one of the serious limitations of essay tests, namely, the subjectivity with which they tend to be scored. A sixth section describes the usefulness and limitations of another type of test item format, the completion item, and provides suggestions for constructing this type of item. The chapter ends with optional sections which discuss cloze exercises and the interlinear exercises. Both are methods of assessing certain limited aspects of language arts achievement.

Three Basic Principles of Classroom Test Construction

When you decide to construct a classroom test you will want it to accomplish a few very basic things. First, you will want the test to focus on the important objectives of the course. It is a waste of both your time and students' time to test whether they have learned trivial behaviors or minor points of content. The testing procedures you decide to use, therefore, should be limited to test items which measure only educationally important objectives and content.

A second fundamental principle which applies regardless of the item format used is that test exercises should be written so they elicit from pupils (examinees) only those behaviors you want to observe. If a pupil in fact has the desired degree of learning, the pupil should make the correct response to an item designed to elicit that learning. If, on the other hand, a pupil does not have the desired degree of learning, the deficiency should also be apparent in test results. Sometimes items are so poorly written they elicit unwanted behaviors from pupils such as bluffing, test fear and/or anxiety, wild guessing, or craftiness (test-wise skills). These extra, unwanted behaviors may lead the teacher to evaluate a pupil incorrectly. For example, the teacher may conclude that a truly knowledgeable student does not have the requisite knowledge, or, conversely, that a poorly prepared student does have the requisite knowledge. Many of the specific suggestions in this and the next several chapters are designed to help you apply the second principle to each type of item format.

A third companion principle is that the items which appear on a test should not prevent or inhibit a pupil from performing the behavior you want to observe. Sometimes imprecise wording in a question, for example, makes an item so ambiguous that a pupil answers it incorrectly when, in fact, the pupil knows the correct answer. Similarly, simple matters such as inappropriate vocabulary, poorly worded directions, or poorly drawn diagrams may lead an otherwise knowledgeable pupil to respond incorrectly. Even the format or arrangement of an item on a test page can inhibit some students from responding correctly. The third principle is amplified and applied to each item variety discussed in this and the subsequent chapters.

Although not all measurement experts would agree that there are only three basic principles, most are likely to agree that these three are the important and fundamental principles for constructing classroom tests. I could present a long list of principles common to the development of many types of tests, but I feel that a short list is easier to remember and apply to classroom test construction. These three encompass most of the specific suggestions made over the years for writing test items except, perhaps, those suggestions directed specifically toward practical tips for efficient scoring. The three principles are summarized below for future reference, so that you can use them as a checklist or rephrase them as questions to review each test item you develop.

Three Fundamental Principles of Test Construction

1. Test items should measure only educationally important objectives (content and behavior).

2. Test items should elicit only the behaviors which the test developer desires to observe.

3. Test items should not prevent or inhibit the performance of desired behavior.

Varieties of Essay Test Items

Restricted Response Varieties

What are restricted response items? These essay questions restrict or limit what the pupil is permitted to answer. The way a question is phrased limits both the substantive content of the answer and the form of the written response. Here are two examples:

Example 1.
Write a brief essay comparing and contrasting the terms "measurement" and "testing" as they relate to (a) the degree of quantification of observation, (b) the process of observation, and (c) the way in which the observations are recorded.

Example 2.
List five of the suggestions for constructing essay questions that were presented in the text. For each suggestion you list, write a short statement explaining why that suggestion is useful to the essay test developer.

The restricted response item format need not be limited to testing for recall and comprehension. The item can be designed to require pupils to apply their skills to solve new problems or to use their skills to analyze a novel situation. One way to do this is to write questions which require the students to apply their knowledge to specific material which is included with the test (e.g., a description of a particular problem or social situation, an extract from a literary work, or a description of a scientific experiment or finding). Essay and response-choice items based on this kind of material are called *interpretive exercises* or *context-dependent* items. The student is expected to read, listen to, analyze, or otherwise interpret the accompanying material and then to answer one or more test items based on it.[1] Box 6.1 illustrates restricted response items

[1]Suggestions for constructing interpretive exercises are given in Chapter 9.

Box 6 • 1

and an extended response item which require students to analyze a particular poem in various ways. The items are intended for a literature course at the secondary school level.

What are the advantages of restricted response questions? Their format has the advantage of narrowing the focus of a test question to specific and well-defined behaviors. The nature of these items makes it more likely that pupils will interpret each question the way the teacher intended. As a consequence of this specificity and likely uniform pupil interpretation of the intent of a question, a teacher is in a better position to have a clear idea about the correctness of the answers to a question. The teacher's clarity about correct answers can lead to improved reliability of scoring.

Do not assume, however, that many skills tested by restricted response essays cannot be tested by more objective, response-choice items. A poor use of the restricted response essay format is to test for factual information. Often this factual information is better tested through response-choice items. As illustrated in Table 6.1, multiple-choice interpretive exercises rather than restricted response essays test many abilities more accurately. Frequently, the major difference between essays and response-choice items is that the essays require recalling and supplying answers rather than recognizing already supplied answers. If recognition behavior is the main intent of certain instructional objectives, then response-choice items are preferable because they allow for more objective (and therefore more reliable) scoring.

Extended Response Varieties

What are extended response essay questions? They elicit elaborated written responses from the pupil which require expressing ideas and their interrelationship in a literate and organized manner. Usually no single answer is considered correct, a student is free to choose the way to respond, and degrees of correctness or merit of a student's response can be judged only by a person skilled or informed on the subject (Stalnaker, 1951).

The two broad categories of extended response essays are questions dealing with students' ability to write in various ways *about the subject matter* and questions designed to measure students' *general writing ability*. Most of this chapter concerns essays directed toward assessing command of a subject rather than the assessment of general writing ability. (But see Table 6.5.) Examples 3 and 4 below contrast these two purposes.

The following test item, originally used with 9-year-olds in the National Assessment of Educational Progress, assesses pupils' expressive writing skills using a role elaboration situation. In particular, it taps pupils' skills in expressing their "sensitivity to audience"— a basic communications skill (Klaus, Lloyd-Jones, Brown, Littlefair, Mullis, and Verity, 1979, p. 14):

Example 3.
Sometimes people write just for the fun of it. This is a chance for you to have some fun writing.

Pretend that you are a pair of tennis shoes. You've done all kinds of things with your owner in all kinds of weather. Now you are being picked up again by your owner. Tell what you, as the tennis shoes, think about what's going to happen to you. Tell how you feel about your owner. Space is provided below and on the next two pages.

The pupils' responses to the preceding item are evaluated in terms of the degree to which their writing skills exhibit role elaboration, expressing the "feelings" and "thoughts" of tennis shoes in an imaginative and unified manner. Since evaluating imagination and creative expression is the purpose of this particular exercise, English mechanics and handwriting are not supposed to enter into the evaluations (Klaus et al., 1979).

The essay here, however, *is* designed to assess the students' competence in reasoning and applying knowledge in a subject-matter area. Developed as a college-level examination, the exam provides the student with both music and lyrics; the question calls for the student to relate the two in the essay. The essay is designed to represent the synthesis level of the *Taxonomy*, but it does somewhat restrict the students' options for responding.

Example 4
Essay (40 minutes)
Write an essay in which you consider the relationship between words and music in the song "Orpheus with His Lute" by Sir Arthur Sullivan. The text and the vocal line of the song are printed on Music Plate XIX. The text is taken from Act III, Scene 1, of *King Henry the Eighth.*

The song will be played once as you begin work on this essay, and twice more thereafter, at ten-minute intervals. It is recommended that you first spend about ten minutes of the time allotted to this essay in planning your remarks. Although the text is printed on the music plate, it may be useful for you to see how it appears when printed as verse.

Orpheus with his lute made trees,
And the mountain tops that freeze
  Bow themselves when he did sing.
To his music plants and flowers
Ever sprung, as sun and showers
  There had made a lasting spring.
Every thing that heard him play.
Even the billows of the sea,
  Hung their heads, and then lay by.
In sweet music is such art.
Killing care and grief of heart
  Fall asleep, or hearing die.

Source: Bloom, Hastings, & Madaus (1971, p. 199)

Extended response essays require a pupil to integrate subject-matter knowledge by using complex verbal reasoning skills. The wording

Box 6 • 2

of such items need not be "complicated," however. The ultimate in expanded directions for writing an essay may be those in the box.

What are the advantages of extended response essay questions? Some instructional objectives relate to a student's ability to organize ideas, develop a logical argument, present evaluations of certain thoughts, communicate thoughts and feelings, or demonstrate other abilities requiring rather original written expression. The restricted response essay format does not lend itself to testing these objectives because a more extended response is required in order for pupils to demonstrate such skills and abilities. The extended response essay is thus suited to measuring objectives requiring students to use a combination of skills

Type of test item	Examples of complex learning outcomes that can be measured
Objective interpretive exercises	Ability to— identify cause-effect relationship identify the application of principles identify the relevance of arguments identify tenable hypotheses identify valid conclusions identify unstated assumptions identify the limitations of data identify the adequacy of procedures (and similar outcomes based on the pupil's ability to *select* the answer)
Restricted response essay questions	Ability to— explain cause-effect relationships describe applications of principles present relevant arguments formulate tenable hypotheses formulate valid conclusions state necessary assumptions describe the limitations of data explain methods and procedures (and similar outcomes based on the pupil's ability to *supply* the answer)
Extended response essay questions	Ability to— produce, organize, and express ideas integrate learnings in different areas create original forms (e.g., designing an experiment) evaluate the worth of ideas

Adapted with permission of Macmillan Publishing Co., Inc. from *Measurement and Evaluation in Teaching*, Third Edition, p. 236, Table 10.1, by Norman E. Gronlund. Copyright © 1976 by Norman E. Gronlund.

Table 6 • 1   Examples of varieties of learning outcomes that can be observed using objective interpretative exercises and essay items.

such as interpreting material, solving a problem, and explaining the problem and its solution in a coherent manner.

A disadvantage of the extended response essay is that scoring the response in an objective manner is difficult and often time-consuming. And when the grades or scores for a test are very subjective, the validity of the test is lowered. If a teacher attends mainly to the quality of ideas in Johnny's paper, to the neatness and grammatical elegance of Sally's, and to the poor spelling in Harry's, then each person is graded on a different basis. The results of this inconsistency are that the test no longer represents a valid assessment of the same aspects of each pupil's work. Suggestions for improving the reliability, and hence the validity, of scoring essays appear later in this chapter.

Usefulness of Essay Items

Abilities and Skills Measured

The preceding paragraphs have described some of the abilities and skills which essays, particularly extended response essays, afford the student the opportunity to demonstrate. Table 6.1 provides a concise summary of these skills and abilities.

Note that the outcomes listed in the table are suggestive, rather than exhaustive (Gronlund, 1976) and that it is frequently possible to use multiple-choice items to measure some of these same abilities. Suggestions for developing multiple-choice and essay items to measure higher-level abilities are given in Chapter 9. What is perhaps unique about the essay format is its capacity for offering pupils the opportunity to exhibit their abilities for written production, organization, expression, and interrelationships among ideas.

Sometimes teachers use the essay format to test for abilities such as recall of information or comprehension. Although the essay can be used in this way, to do so does not capitalize on the unique features of this item format. Memory, recall, and comprehension are more reliably tested with completion and response-choice items. An important point: *Use the test item format that elicits the behavior stated in the instructional objective you are testing.*

Influence on Pupils' Studying Strategies

One use of tests is to motivate pupils to study. It seems reasonable to conclude that the type of response pupils are expected to produce will influence their method of study. Some research indicates that when students know that essay questions will be asked, they tend to focus on learning broad concepts and to articulate interrelationships, contrasts, comparisons, and so on; those preparing for response-choice questions focus on facts, details, and specific ideas (e.g., Douglas and Tallmadge, 1934; Terry, 1933). But because students report that they prepare differently for different types of test questions doesn't mean that they will in fact perform differently on different forms of tests. Some studies have found little if any difference in performance on essay or response-choice questions even though pupils reported different study strategies (Hakstain, 1971; Vallance, 1947).

Since both essay and choice formats can call for knowledge of specific facts, and both can call for application of complex reasoning skills, the format of the questions may not be the key issue in how students plan their study strategies (Ebel, 1979). The kinds of study strategies students use in preparing for examinations are likely to be more a function of the nature of the cognitive performance the test will require of them rather than the format (essay or not essay) of the question. If two different question formats require the same kind of cognitive abilities, the formats ought to elicit the same types of study strategies and pupil performance.

If it is important for pupils to learn and demonstrate writing skills in a particular subject-matter area, perhaps the best advice is to be sure (a) to specify those skills in course (or unit) objectives and (b) to provide opportunities to observe pupils performing them. This may mean including both essay and response-choice items on a test. Various written assignments such as compositions and term papers can achieve the same purposes, however.

Content Sampling

Answering essay questions takes a pupil a long time and limits the breadth of content a given essay can cover. If students can answer one or two response-choice items in one minute, then they can answer 30 to 60 items in a half hour test which can cover a broad area of content and many objectives. In the same time they can probably answer only one or two essay questions. Although in-depth coverage of a narrower topic can be accomplished using essays, broad general coverage can be obtained using more objective items. One way to overcome the shortcoming of limited content sampling with essays is to plan to accumulate evidence from a series of essays or take-home compositions written over a longer period of time (Coffman, 1971). Several out-of-class essays written over a marking period may provide a better assessment of a particular objective than a single essay written during a brief examination period.

Reliability of Essay Scoring

A serious problem is the tendency for essay test scores to be strongly influenced by factors which lower their reliability. The lack of essay test reliability was a major justification for turning to true-false and multiple-choice tests in education. Grades assigned to a pupil's response may vary widely from one reader to the next, both because of reader inconsistency and because of differences in grading standards. Further, the same reader may mark the same essay differently from one day to the next. Another factor is the topic (subject) of the essay. A pupil's scores may vary widely, even when marked by the same reader, depending on the questions. Other factors besides the student's ability which affect scores on essay tests include halo effects, carry-over effects, bluffing ability, spelling, penmanship, and grammar. *Halo effect* refers to the idea that our judgments on one characteristic of a person are influenced by our judgments on other characteristics or by our general impression of that person. Thus, we may tend to grade a student we admire more leniently on a particular essay because we "know in our hearts" that the student has command of the objective or topic. The halo effect works the other way, too: An unadmired student may be marked down on a particular essay. One way to correct this flaw is to score the essays only after concealing the names of the pupils. A *carry-over effect* occurs when our judgment of a pupil's response to question 1 affects our judgment of that pupil's response to question 2. Unless certain precautionary scoring procedures are followed, there is a tendency for scores on adjacent questions to be more related than non-adjacent questions. One way to avoid this problem is to score question 1 for all pupils first, then go back and score question 2 for all, and so on.

Many of the suggestions in the next sections are directed toward improving the reliability and validity of scoring essays. Reviews of research studies on these aspects of essay scoring can be found in Coffman (1971), Stalnaker (1951), and Stanley and Hopkins (1972).

Efficient Use of Teacher Time

Essays and compositions take a long time to score and mark. This time is well worth it if the essay is the best way to assess an important objective, and if the pupils benefit from the teacher's review of their responses. Sometimes, because teachers must score large numbers of essays or because they are under the pressures of the day, they score essays carelessly, a breach of professional ethics and an abuse of responsibility. Assessing and grading students is serious business. Careful planning, including deciding whether the essay format is the only appropriate method of assessment, can greatly alleviate inappropriate scoring of essay tests.

Suggestions for Constructing Essay Items

Suggestions for constructing essay questions follow the three general principles stated at the beginning of this chapter. These specific suggestions, culled from several sources, are summarized in Table 6.2. Figure 6.1 gives an example of an essay item which applies the principles listed in Table 6.2. Rules 1, 2, 3, and 5 are discussed here.

Defining the Behavior

As with all test construction, you must know what behavior you wish to observe before creating a way to elicit it. Chapter 4 described ways to specify performance. Objectives requiring essay items may be the most difficult to articulate because the behaviors required are often complex, and a teacher is frequently concerned with assessing a pupil characteristic phrased as a construct or as an abstract state. For example, you may want a pupil to demonstrate the ability to analyze critically and evaluate a particular literary work or a partic-

1. Define the behavior the examinee is expected to exhibit or describe the process to be exhibited before beginning to write the essay question.
2. Ask questions that require the examinee to demonstrate the ability to use essential knowledge and to do so in situations that are new or novel for the examinee, rather than simply recalling information from a textbook or a classroom.
3. Ask questions that are relatively specific or focused, and which require relatively brief responses.
4. If a test includes several essay questions, be sure that they cover the appropriate range of topics and complexity of behavior called for in the test blueprint, but be sure that the complexity of the questions are within the educational maturity level of the examinees.
5. Require all examinees to answer the same questions; don't give optional questions.
6. Word questions so that all examinees will interpret the task the way you intend.
7. Word questions so that all examinees know the limits of the tasks, their purposes, and can answer them in the time allotted.
8. Word questions so that experts can agree on the correctness of an examinee's response.
9. Word questions calling for examinee opinion on controversial matters so that they ask the examinee to give evidence to support the opinion and evaluate the examinee's response in terms of the evidence presented rather than the opinion or position taken.
10. Word questions so the examinee can judge the approximate length of the answer desired and knows the point-value or weight each will be given.

Source: Coffman (1971), Ebel (1979), Greene, Jorgensen, and Gerberich (1942), Gronlund (1976), Lindvall and Nitko (1975), Mehrens and Lehmann (1973), Sax (1974), Stalnaker (1951), Stanley and Hopkins (1972), Thorndike and Hagen (1977).

Table 6 • 2 Ten general principles for constructing essay items for subject-matter testing.

ular point of view. This may require observing several specific behaviors before one is able to conclude that the pupil has the ability to evaluate (see Chapter 4).

A practical suggestion here is to focus on the type of response you wish the student to make, rather than worrying about how the objective is stated. You may, for example, write a specimen answer or an outline of the major points to be made and the way(s) you expect the student to approach the problem presented in the essay. Then, you can refine the essay question so that it will direct the student to make the kind of response required—if it is in the student's repertoire.

Essential Knowledge Applied to New Situations

The unique format of essay questions permits the teacher to test a student's command of higher cognitive processes and skills. This is done best by requiring the student to apply these processes and skills to new or novel problems and situations rather than simply recalling information from the textbook or classroom. A pupil's ability to recall information is an important educational goal and reflects general competence, but recall of information is frequently assessed better by test items other than essays.

It is helpful to study different ways of phrasing questions so they elicit higher level cognitive processes and skills. Various catalogues or classifications of such "thought" questions have been attempted from time to time. A useful listing is presented in Table 6.3. Phrasing questions in a manner similar to that given in the table will frequently improve the quality of the question. Monroe and Carter (1923), Odell (1928), Curtis (1943), Wesley and Wronski (1958), and Bloom et al. (1971) have provided similar classifications.

Focus Questions; Clarify Limits and Purposes

Unless a question is phrased in a way that focuses attention to the issues or points on which you want the pupils to write, you are likely to find so many different interpretations of the question that it will be impossible to evaluate the responses. Consider the extended response item in Box 6.1. An unfocused version of this item might be: "Write an essay analyzing the poem." It is unlikely that such an unfocused item would lead students to the particular analysis of mood which the developer of the item had in mind. If an item is not

Time limit specified; essay length implied — *(Principle 10).*	**Essay** (Suggested time: 2½ hours) **Directions:** Read the following Comment on Selections I and II of the Reading materials and answer the question based on them.	College level essay. Materials given to examinees beforehand *(Principle 4).*
	Comment: "Each of the three statements—of a leading American policy planner, of Britain's (1951) Foreign Secretary, and of one of the Soviet Union's official newspapers—claims to prescribe indispensable conditions for the achievement of peace. But no one of the statements really deals with the crucial factors which underlie the conflict between East and West. No one of them indicates the fundamental policies, both domestic and foreign, which are necessary to achieve peace."	Situation new to the examinees *(Principle 2).*
Question is focused on certain issues *(Principle 3).* Question not limited to simple recall *(Principle 2).*	**Question:** Do you agree or disagree with this Comment? In defending your answer, make clear your own view of the indispensable conditions, both within and between nations, of lasting peace, and describe and defend a major line of policy which the United States might now employ.	
Examinee's position does not affect grading *(Principle 9).* Experts judge essay's internal consistency and evidential arguments *(Principle 8).*	Your essay will be judged *not* in terms of the particular view which you accept but in terms of the thoughtfulness and consistency of your essay as a whole, and the adequacy of the information which you bring to bear upon the issues with which you deal. Refer, when appropriate, to authors read in the Social Sciences 3 Course, but do not use such references as a substitute for presenting your own consistent, coherent point of view.]	Elaboration intended to help: — all interpret the task in the same way *(Principle 6).* — examinees know the limits, grading criteria, etc. *(Principle 7).*

Source: Question from *Handbook on Formative and Summative Evaluation of Student Learning*, Bloom et al. (Eds.), p. 198. Copyright © 1971 by McGraw-Hill Book Company. Used with permission of McGraw-Hill Book Company.

Figure 6 • 1   Example of a college-level essay item that illustrates the application of the item construction principles of Table 6.2.

1. **Comparing**	8. **Creating**

1. **Comparing**
   Describe the similarities and differences between. . . .
   Compare the following two methods for. . . .
2. **Relating cause and effect**
   What are major causes of. . . ?
   What would be the most likely effects of. . . ?
3. **Justifying**
   Which of the following alternatives would you favor and why?
   Explain why you agree or disagree with the following statement.
4. **Summarizing**
   State the main points included in. . . .
   Briefly summarize the contents of. . . .
5. **Generalizing**
   Formulate several valid generalizations from the following data.
   State a set of principles that can explain the following events.
6. **Inferring**
   In light of the facts presented, what is most likely to happen, when. . . ?
   How would (Senator X) be likely to react to the following issue?
7. **Classifying**
   Group the following items according to. . . .
   What do the following items have in common?

8. **Creating**
   List as many ways as you can think of for. . . .
   Make up a story describing what would happen if. . . .
   Write a list of questions that should be answered before. . . .
9. **Applying**
   Using the principle of . . . as a guide, describe how you would solve the following problem situation.
   Describe a situation that illustrates the principle of. . . .
10. **Analyzing**
    Describe the reasoning errors in the following paragraph.
    List and describe the main characteristics of. . . .
    Describe the relationship between the following parts of. . . .
11. **Synthesizing**
    Describe a plan for proving that. . . .
    Write a well-organized report that shows. . . .
    Write a set of specifications for building a. . . .
12. **Evaluating**
    Criticize or defend each of the following statements.
    Describe the strengths and weaknesses of the following. . . .
    Using the criteria developed in class, write a critical evaluation of. . . .

Source: Adapted with permission of Macmillan Publishing Co., Inc. from *Measurement and Evaluation in Teaching*, Third Edition, p. 241, by Norman E. Gronlund. Copyright © 1976 by Norman E. Gronlund.

Table 6 • 3   Types and examples of essay question phrasing.

focused, it will not be possible to distinguish those pupils who know the answer—but misinterpreted your question—from those who don't know the answer.

Sometimes, if the nature of the task itself is not clear, specifying the manner and criteria by which pupils' responses will be evaluated may increase clarity. Had the writer of the essay item shown in Figure 6.1, for example, stopped with the phrase "Do you agree or disagree with this comment?" there's no telling what kind of responses would have been made; they would likely range from simple "yes" or "no" through long-winded polemic entanglements.

Focusing the question and specifying limits of the intended response to it do not mean that you need to provide the pupils with information that "interferes with" or "gives away" the intended answer. If you intend for the essay to test the examinee's ability to organize a written argument, for example, you do not provide organization in the question. But you could tell the examinee that organization is important or that you will evaluate the paper on the basis of how well it is organized.

An important practical suggestion here is to have a colleague or friend review the questions and, if possible, to pretest them on a few students. The questions can then be revised if necessary. Following such steps greatly improves essay questions.

Avoid Optional Questions

For subject-matter essay testing, all examinees should answer the same questions especially when essays are graded in a relative manner: when grading depends on an ordering of essay questions after a comparison of one with another.

Some feel that offering students options is fairer, permitting the students the opportunity to "put their best foot forward." Research doesn't bear this out, however (Stalnaker, 1951; Coffman, 1971; Wilson, 1976). Some students will choose to answer questions on which they do least well (Meyer, 1939; Stalnaker, 1936; Cowan, 1972; Taylor & Nuttall, 1974). Further, topics on which questions are based vary in difficulty, and persons grading essays frequently change their evaluations based on the perceived nature and difficulty of topics. If the questions asked on a test represent important learning outcomes, then it seems logical and fair to hold all students accountable for them (Ebel, 1979). Perhaps the story would be different if general writing ability is being assessed, rather than subject-matter competence (Coffman, 1951). You could argue that general writing ability may be manifest by writing on any one of a number of topics. If this occurs, it is advisable to score papers on each topic separately, rather than mixing topics together to reduce the topic-to-topic differences that tend to raise or lower the reader's rating of an essay.

Scoring Essay Tests

Rules for scoring essay tests focus on increasing the objectivity (and, consequently, the reliability) of the scoring. There are two general methods for scoring subject-matter essays: the *analytic* (also called scoring key, point method, or atomistic) method and the *holistic* (also called global, sorting, or rating) method.

Analytic Scoring Method

This method entails developing an outline and/or a list of major elements to be included in the ideal answer and deciding on the number of points to be awarded to pupils for including each element. The analytic scoring method works best on a focused, restricted response question. An example of an analytic scoring key for a restricted response essay based on material covered in Chapter 1 of this book follows. The question asks students to describe why distinguishing various decision contexts is important when testing and to define and compare selection, placement, and classification decisions.

Analytic scoring key for essay on selection, placement, and classification decisions

1. Reasons for distinguishing
   decision contexts   4 points

2. Selection decisions
   a. Description   2 points
   b. Example of selection
      decision   2 points

3. Placement decisions
   a. Description   2 points
   b. Example of placement
      decision   2 points

4. Classification decisions
   a. Description
   b. Example of
      classification decision   2 points

5. Comparison of the three
   decision types
   a. Similarities   4 points
   b. Differences   4 points

In this example the decision to award 2 points or 4 points for certain elements of the answer is arbitrary. You will have to decide which elements are more important to the objectives of the course and, therefore, should be given more points. The number of points assigned to each element reflects its value in relation to the total number of points on the test.

Usually pupils' responses will match the intended answer to various degrees: a response which is essentially correct receives the full point credit; a completely incorrect answer or an omission receives no points; and a partially correct response receives a partial credit award. This assignment of partial credit increases the subjectivity of the scoring process. You retain more objectivity if you can specify the number of partial credit points each type of partially correct answer will receive. This may be difficult for the beginning teacher because the types of errors and partial knowledge pupils display to a particular question are unknown. After reading a few papers, however, patterns of errors and misconceptions will emerge and can be formulated into a partial credit scoring scheme.

Holistic Scoring Method

This method entails making a judgement about the overall quality of the response. The reader does not analyze the specific content elements that a student included in the answer. Holistic scoring is probably more appropriate for extended response essays involving a student's abilities to synthesize and create and when no definite correct answer can be prespecified. Judging the overall quality of an answer is often less objective than the analytic method because scoring criteria usually have not been specified.

One way to implement the holistic method is to decide beforehand on the number of quality categories into which answers will be sorted. Usually, between three and five categories are employed, such as: A, B, C, D, and E; excellent, satisfactory, unsatisfactory; or 4, 3, 2, 1. To use this method, you read an essay and make a judgment as to which category it will be assigned. After reading and categorizing all of the essays, you should reexamine all the papers within a category to be sure they are enough alike in quality to receive the same grade or rating. Those papers that are dissimilar are assigned to a higher or lower category depending on the results of this second judgment. You might also compare the papers in one category with those of another to decide whether the distributions between categories

are meaningful or whether further reassignments are necessary.

One refinement of the holistic method is to determine beforehand the overall quality characteristics of the papers which will fall in each category. Essentially, this means defining what an "A" paper is, a "B" paper, and so on. Another refinement is to select "specimen" answers from previous administrations of the test to serve as examples for each category. You can then compare unrated pupil answers to the quality of the specimens and decide into which category to place them. A third way of implementing is to read through the essays and compare one with another to decide which are "the best," "the next best," and so on. Then you assign the essays to these various categories. The first two of these three methods are consistent with a grading philosophy based on absolute standards, while the third is consistent with a group-referenced philosophy. These grading issues are discussed in Chapter 13.

Specific Scoring Suggestions

The above paragraphs describe two methods of scoring essays. There are, however, some general principles which apply regardless of which method is used. These principles are summarized in Table 6.4.

Scoring guide Scoring guides and model answers have been mentioned in connection with analytic and holistic methods. The point of using these devices is to improve the reliability of scoring so that the same standards are applied from paper to paper and from reader to reader.

Grade one question at a time If there is more than one essay question on an exam, score all answers to the first question before moving on. Then grade all answers to the next question. This method not only improves the uniformity of scoring standards for each pupil

1. Prepare some type of scoring guide (e.g., an outline, an "ideal" answer, or "specimen" responses from past administrations).
2. Grade all responses to one question before moving on to the next question.
3. Periodically rescore previously scored papers.
4. Score penmanship, general neatness, spelling, use of prescribed format, and English mechanics separately from subject-matter correctness.
5. Score papers without knowing the name of the pupil writing the response.
6. Provide pupils with feedback on the strengths and weaknesses of their responses.
7. When the grading decision is crucial, have two or more readers score the essays independently.

Source: Coffman (1971), Ebel (1979), Greene, Jorgenson, and Gerberich (1942), Gronlund (1976), Lindvall and Nitko (1975), Mehrens and Lehmann (1973), Sax (1974), Stalnaker (1951), Stanley and Hopkins (1972), Thorndike and Hagen (1977).

Table 6 • 4   Summary of principles for scoring responses to subject-matter essay items.

but also allows the reader to become more familiar with the scoring guide for a given question and the reader is less likely to be distracted by responses to other questions (Mehrens and Lehmann, 1973). Finally, using this method helps to reduce the "carryover effect" discussed in Chapter 5. Additional reduction in carryover effects is accomplished by reshuffling the papers after scoring each question.

Score subject-matter correctness separately from other factors   Factors other than answer content affect reader evaluation. Among such factors are spelling, penmanship, neatness, and English mechanics. In order not to confound a judgment of the quality of the substantive content of a pupil's answer with these other factors, score the latter factors separately— perhaps by using a rating scale (see Chapter 10). Scoring separately for correctness of content and other factors also permits the teacher freedom to weight each factor appropriately. A teacher, for example, can weigh spelling "zero" or more heavily depending on the school policy or classroom practices. But if these fac-

tors are to receive a weight of zero, why bother rating them separately? The answer is that teachers (and essay readers, generally) are influenced unknowingly by factors such as penmanship and neatness even when they have explicit instructions to grade on the basis of content alone (Marshall, 1967; Scannell and Marshall, 1966; Marshall and Powers, 1969). The ancient Chinese examiners also recognize this influence when they created the Bureau of Examination Copyists. By scoring such factors separately, their influence on essay grades can reflect the teacher's intentions more nearly.

Score essays anonymously   This prevents the "halo effect" mentioned previously. Further, if students know that this is a teacher's policy, they are likely to perceive the grading process as fair (Mehrens and Lehmann, 1973). One suggestion for maintaining anonymity is to have pupils write their names on the back of the answer sheet or exam booklet. Other more elaborate methods such as using student numbers or other codes are also effective.

Provide pupil feedback   An important part of grading essays is the opportunity it gives teachers to examine the expressive abilities and thought processes pupils use. Teachers should note strengths and weaknesses in these areas for each pupil and explain the assigned grade so that comments on the essay will provide an opportunity for further pupil learning. The following maxims for commenting on student compositions, when the focus of such compositions is the teaching of general writing skills, were suggested by Hirsch (1977). They do, however, seem to be useful for commenting on pupil responses to essay questions, too.

1. Comment on just two or three points in any paper. . . .
2. Select those matters for comment which are most important for an individual student at a particular time. . . .
3. Summarize the commentary in usable form.
4. Begin writing comments only after a rapid analysis of the paper as a whole. . . .

In 1978 a committee of the National Council of Teachers of English surveyed a national sample of fourth grade teachers concerning their programs and practices for teaching written composition. The following was among the 17 items in the questionnaire which was returned by 31.9% of 1000 teachers sampled.

The extent to which these practices are used in evaluating children's writing:

	never	seldom	frequently	almost always
assign a single letter or numerical grade	27.1	22.0	33.1	17.8
assign separate grades for content and mechanics	26.4	28.3	32.8	12.5
comment on mechanical items needing improvement	1.6	8.3	52.7	36.9
comment on compositional items needing improvement (organization, sentence structure, etc.)	2.5	10.1	51.6	35.8
comment on mechanical aspects that are especially good or show improvement	0.3	0.6	48.9	44.8
comment on compositional aspects that are well done or show improvement	0.0	6.6	46.4	47.0
have individual conferences with children	1.3	22.0	45.6	31.1
have group evaluation by students	30.8	47.2	19.8	2.2
have each child evaluate own writing	12.3	39.9	38.7	8.9
have another teacher evaluate writing	65.3	27.8	6.3	0.6
evaluate by a teacher team	79.7	16.5	3.8	0.0
evaluate according to previously established standards	24.5	30.3	36.9	8.3
use a scale or checklist	38.3	36.3	21.2	4.2
give objective tests on punctuation and capitalization	3.2	17.4	54.4	25.0
give objective tests on grammar	4.4	16.7	53.3	25.6
evaluate only selected pieces of writing	22.9	33.1	36.6	7.3
assign grade depending on student's ability	13.5	10.6	40.8	35.0
assign grade according to individual improvement	11.0	10.6	50.0	28.4

Adapted from "Classroom Teacher's Reports on Teaching Written Composition," by W. T. Petty and P. J. Finn. In *Perspectives on Writing in Grades 1–8*, edited by S. M. Haley-James (Urbana, Ill.: NCTE, 1981), p. 31, Fig. 1. Used by permission of NCTE.

Box 6 • 3

5. Choose those comments which will be likely to induce the greatest improvement in the intrinsic effectiveness of the student's next paper. . . .
6. State the comments in an encouraging manner. (p. 160)
7. Do not hesitate to repeat a comment over several papers. . . .
8. Keep track of the comments, so that nothing of great importance for a particular student is omitted during the course. . . .
9. Make clear from the tone of the comments that they deal with a craft to be learned and not with the teacher's personal taste. (p. 161)

Another suggestion for giving feedback is to individually review answers and comments with students. A brief conference of 10 to 20 minutes with each pupil will be more personal and can provide more information than cryptic comments in the margin. A short conference may also save the teacher hours of writing copious notes and commentary to clarify a point for the student.

Independent scoring The idiosyncrasies of individual readers do affect essay scores. The suggestions in Table 6.4 help reduce imprecision but do not entirely eliminate it. The ancient Chinese realized that when important decisions rest on the scores of essays, more than one reader is necessary. Realistically, however, even though everyday grading decisions are important, it is unlikely that the classroom teacher will find time or consistent cooperation of colleagues to carry out independent scoring of essays. Nevertheless, such a practice would improve the consistency of scoring.

Scoring Essays Which Assess General Writing Ability[2]

The scoring procedures described so far refer primarily to essays used to assess subject-mat-

[2]This section may be omitted without loss of continuity.

ter competence, although some suggestions can apply to the assessment of general writing ability. In this section, however, the focus is exclusively on scoring essays designed to assess a pupil's general writing ability.

A major problem encountered when grading a pupil's writing ability is the extent to which a teacher judges the extrinsic and/or intrinsic quality of a pupil's paper (Hirsch, 1977). *Extrinsic evaluation* of an essay occurs when the reader of a paper judges the quality of its ideas and intentions, quite apart from the intentions which the writer had in mind. This model of judgment is exemplified by Plato who ". . . banished Homer's poetry from his ideal state [because Homer's] . . . ideas were wrong, misleading, and harmful" (Hirsch, 1977, p. 182). *Intrinsic evaluation* of an essay occurs when the reader of a paper judges its quality in terms of the degree to which it attained its own implicit intentions. This is called an Aristotelian model (Hirsch, 1977).

In composition, the main objection to purely intrinsic judgments of writing is a pedagogical one. If a composition teacher gives a student a high mark whenever he expresses well what he aimed to express, the student will quickly learn to limit his aims. He will write trivial and simple A papers, instead of writing ambitious, difficult C papers which would tax him and develop his skill in writing and thinking. . . . it is palpably unfair for the teacher to give a high grade to a successful simple paper and a lower grade to a paper that succeeds slightly less well in accomplishing a more difficult aim.

The pedagogical reasons, then, for adding extrinsic judgments are compelling, but equally compelling are the pedagogical reasons for *isolating* them [i.e., scoring them separately] from intrinsic judgments. To the extent that one is teaching and nurturing skill in writing, one needs to diagnose the student's strengths and weaknesses in that skill, quite apart from his other skills (Hirsch, 1977, p. 185).

Space does not permit a complete cataloguing here of the many methods educators have proposed to assess writing ability. A few methods are listed in Table 6.5, however, along with references where further information may be obtained. Overviews of methods of assessing writing skills may be obtained by consulting Cooper (1977), Lloyd-Jones (1977), Hirsch (1977), and Brown (1979).

The methods mentioned in Table 6.5 assess different aspects of written work and do so with varying degrees of reliability and validity. Two of the ways the methods differ from each other are in the (a) *attributes of the writing* they attempt to assess and (b) *size of the unit of discourse* on which they base their evalua-

Method	Description	Reference
1. CEEB: Advanced Placement English Examination (essay section); English Composition Test	Holistic method. Readers are socialized (trained) to agree to quality levels of the essays. A "table leader" supervises trained readers to assure these socialized quality levels are used when assigning ratings to individual essays.	Smith (1976); "Fine art of essay testing" (1977); ETS (1978).
2. ETS Composition Scale	Generally holistic. After some socialization to the rubrics, readers rate each paper on ideas, organization, wording, flavor, usage conventions, punctuation conventions, spelling, and neatness.	Diederich (1974; n.d.).
3. Primary Traits Scoring	A discourse mode (expressive, persuasive, explanatory) is selected and an essay item devised for it. Primary rhetorical traits (abilities) needed to write the essay are identified and formalized into rating scales (scoring guides). Readers are socialized and score each paper on each of the primary traits.	Lloyd-Jones (1977); Klaus et al. (1979); Brown (1979).
4. Relative readability or intrinsic communicative effectiveness	An "optimal" synonymous version of a student's written piece is created. Then the student's original version is judged in relation to the optimal version for communication effectiveness (relative readability).	Hirsch (1977, 1978).
5. T-unit	Number of words per T-unit are measured as ways of assessing syntactic maturity of a written discourse. "A T-unit is a single main clause plus whatever else goes with it" (Hunt, 1977).	Hunt (1977); Hunt and O'Donnell (1970).
6. Various types of English usage tests	Usually multiple-choice items dealing with grammar, punctuation, lexical features, and so on. References are only examples.	Godshalk, Swineford, and Coffman (1966); Cole and Hanson (1973).

Table 6 • 5   Summary of some methods used to assess writing ability.

tions. The size of the discourse unit to be evaluated ranges from "atomistic" (words, sentences, etc.) to "holistic" (the entire composition is judged as a single unit). Hirsch (1978) has logically ordered the attributes of the writing that are assessed according to their degree of objectivity.[3] Attributes of a composition such as lexical, grammatical, orthographic, or "mechanical" *correctness* are evaluated with rather high degrees of objectivity. The least objectively evaluated attributes of a composition are its *intellectual and/or aesthetic quality*. Intermediate degrees of objectivity can be obtained by evaluating such attributes as communicative effectiveness and rhetorical effectiveness. *Communicative effectiveness* refers to the ease with which the writer communicates ideas to the reader; it is similar to Hirsch's "relative readability" in Table 6.5. *Rhetorical effectiveness* refers to the extent the composition has attained its intended rhetorical purpose (e.g., persuading the reader that a particular point of view is reasonable or expressing the "feelings" of a pair of old tennis shoes). Figure 6.2 shows how each of the assessment methods in Table 6.5 relate to both the attributes measured and the size of the unit assessed. Note that some methods require making judgments about several attributes of the composition while others are primarily concerned with judging a single attribute.

Short-Answer and Completion Items

Varieties of Short-Answer Items

Short-answer items require the examinee to respond to the item with a word, short phrase, number, or symbol. Three generic types are usually distinguished: question, completion, and association (Odell, 1928; Wesman, 1971). Here are some examples.

1. Question variety

Example 5
1. What is the capital city of Pennsylvania?
(Harrisburg)
2. What is the Greek letter commonly used as a symbol for the standard deviation? ____ (σ)
3. How many microns make up one millimeter?
(1,000)

2. Completion variety

Example 6
1. The capital city of Pennsylvania is (Harrisburg).
2. $4 + 6 \div 2 =$ ____ (7). ____

3. Identification or association variety

Example 7.
On the blank next to the name of each chemical element, write the symbol used for it.

Element	Symbol
Barium	(Ba)
Calcium	(Ca)
Chlorine	(Cl)
Potassium	(K)
Zinc	(Zn)

Usefulness of Short-Answer Items

Abilities elicited by short-answer items It seems obvious that short-answer items observe performance from the lowest level of the cog-

---

Teachers read 82,000 essays Some 164 high school and college teachers gathered in Princeton, New Jersey in December 1982 to read 82,000 College Board *English Composition Test* essays. Each essay was read by two different readers. This was the fifth reading of such essays since 1978. The December *English Composition Achievement Test* was a 60-minute test requiring 20 minutes for essay writing and 40 minutes for answering multiple-choice items.

Source: Based on information from the Educational Testing Service.

Box 6 • 4

[3]Hirsch calls this "normalization" rather than objectivity.

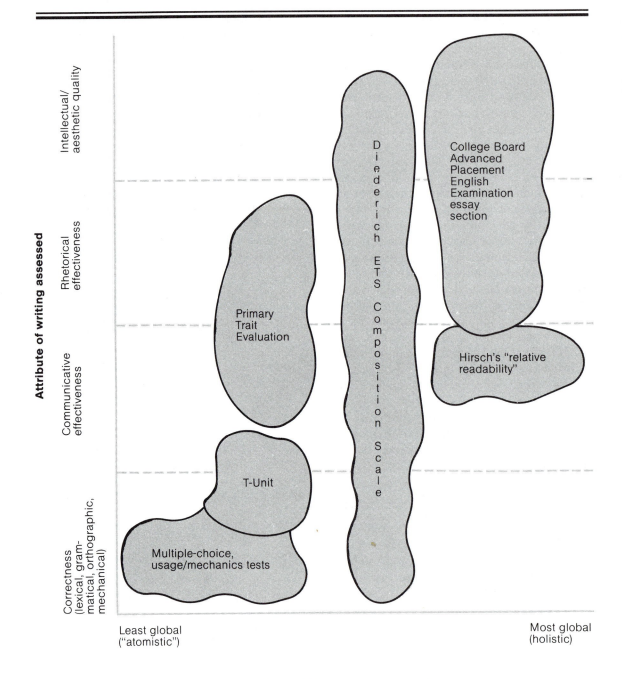

Attribute of writing assessed

Intellectual/
aesthetic quality

Rhetorical
effectiveness

Communicative
effectiveness

Correctness
(lexical, gram-
matical, orthographic,
mechanical)

College Board
Advanced
Placement
English
Examination
essay
section

Diederich ETS Composition Scale

Primary
Trait
Evaluation

Hirsch's "relative
readability"

T-Unit

Multiple-choice,
usage/mechanics tests

Least global
("atomistic")

Most global
(holistic)

Size of discourse unit scored

Figure 6 • 2   Relationship between several methods of scoring written discourse in terms of the attribute and size of the discourse unit assessed. Attributes
are ordered in terms of their degree of objectivity with the least objective at the top.

nitive *Taxonomy*: knowledge of terminology, facts, classifications, etc. It is less obvious, perhaps, that the short-answer format can be used to observe higher level abilities such as the following (Gronlund, 1976):

1. Ability to make simple interpretations of data and applications of rules (e.g., counting the number of syllables in a given word; demonstrating knowledge of place value in a number system; identifying the parts of an organism or apparatus when given a picture; applying the definition of an isosceles or equilateral triangle).
2. Ability to solve numerical problems in science and mathematics.
3. Ability to manipulate mathematical symbols and balance mathematical and chemical equations.

As you will see in other chapters, multiple-choice and other objective items can also assess these abilities.

Strengths and shortcomings The short-answer and completion item formats are popular because they are relatively easy to construct and score. But short-answer items, while frequently scored more objectively than essay items, are not free of subjectivity. Teachers cannot anticipate all possible responses and synonyms for the responses they expect and, therefore, often have to make subjective judgments as to the correctness of pupils' responses. Spelling errors, grammatical errors, and legibility tend to complicate the scoring process further. For example, to the question, "What is the name of the author of *Alice in Wonderland?*," students may respond: Carroll Lewis, Louis Carrol, Charles Dodgson, Lutwidge Dodgson, or Lewis Carroll Dodgson. Which, if any, should be considered correct? While subjective judgment is not in and of itself improper, it does slow down the scoring process and tends to lower the reliability of the obtained scores.

Another advantage of the short-answer format is that students have a low probability of getting the answer correct by blind guessing. A student who guesses blindly on a true-false item has a 50-50 chance of guessing correctly; on a four-option multiple-choice item, the student has one chance in four of blindly guessing the correct answer. For most short-answer items, however, the probability of blindly guessing the correct answer is zero. Short-answer items will not prevent students from *attempting* to guess the answer—such items only lower the probability of guessing correctly.

In principle, guessing can be distinguished from partial knowledge. Partial knowledge can lead a pupil to select the correct answer to a multiple-choice item. Partial knowledge is less likely to result in the (exact) correct answer in short-answer items. Teachers, however, often give some credit for responses judged to be partially correct. Such "adjustments" to the score must be recognized as arbitrary decisions which can lead to less reliable scores because teachers tend not to apply the adjustment consistently from pupil to pupil. If partial credit is to be given, then some type of scoring key should indicate the kinds of responses to receive each level of partial credit. Using such a scoring key helps to make the assignment of partial credit more consistent from pupil to pupil.

Suggestions for Constructing Short-Answer and Completion Items

Short-answer and completion items are not as easy to construct as you might assume. Table 6.6 summarizes some of the principles for constructing them which, if followed, will help you avoid creating flawed items. Again, these principles are applications of the Three Fundamental Principles of test construction mentioned at the beginning of the chapter.

Source © 1981 United Feature Syndicate

Use the Question Form

Essentially, a completion item asks a question: The examinee must read the incomplete sentence and mentally convert it to a question before answering. Therefore, the most straightforward thing to do is ask a direct question in the first place. Scrutinizing most completion items will indicate that they could be phrased as questions. Further, the meaning of the item is often clearer if phrased as a question instead of an incomplete sentence.

Example 8.
The author of *Alice in Wonderland* was _____ .

is more ambiguous[4] than example 9:

[4]Some possible answers to the item include: "a story-writer," "a mathematician," "an Englishman," and "buried in 1898."

Example 9.
What is the pen name of the author of *Alice in Wonderland*? (Lewis Carroll).

Occasionally, however, the question form of the item implies a longer or more complex response than intended, so the incomplete sentence serves better. Examples 10 and 11 show this exception:

Example 10.
Why are scoring guides recommended for use with essay tests?

vs.

Example 11.
The main reason for using a scoring guide with an essay test is to increase the (objectivity) of the scoring.

1. Use the question form of the short-answer variety if possible.
2. Word each item in specific terms with clear meanings so that the intended answer is the only one possible, and so that the answer is a single word, brief phrase, or number.
3. Word each item so that the blank or answer space is toward the end of the sentence.
4. Avoid copying statements verbatim from texts or classroom materials.
5. Omit important rather than trivial words.
6. Avoid "butchered" or "mutilated" sentences; use only one or two blanks in a completion sentence.
7. Keep the blanks of equal length and arrange the items so the answers are placed in a column at the right or left of the sentences.
8. State the precision, numerical units, or degree of specificity expected of the answer.
9. Word the items to avoid irrelevant clues or specific determiners.

Source: Ebel (1951, 1979). Greene, Jorgensen, and Gerberich (1942), Gronlund (1976), Lindvall and Nitko (1975), Mehrens and Lehmann (1973), Odell (1928), Sax (1974), Stalnaker (1951), Stanley and Hopkins (1977), Thorndike and Hagen (1977).

Table 6 • 6   General principles for writing short-answer (completion) items.

Word Item Specifically and Clearly

Usually, short-answer items should elicit a single, correct answer. The question or incomplete sentence should be worded so that this intended purpose is clear to the pupil. Consider example 12:

Example 12.
Where is Pittsburgh, Pennsylvania located? _____

Several answers are possible depending on the degree of specificity desired: "Western Pennsylvania," "southwestern corner of Pennsylvania," "Ohio River," "Monongahela and Allegheny Rivers," etc. If a specific answer is desired then the question must be phrased in a specific way as in examples 13 and 14.

Example 13.
Pittsburgh, Pennsylvania is located at the confluence of what two rivers?

(Allegheny and Monongahela)

or

Example 14.
What city is located at the confluence of the Monongahela and Allegheny Rivers?

(Pittsburgh, Pennsylvania)

Specificity of phrasing is important because you want to elicit a certain answer. Some pupils who know the desired answer will not give it because they misinterpreted the question. This is especially likely for learners at the elementary levels who interpret questions rather literally. For example, in one classroom, fourth graders were given a bar graph to interpret. The following poorly phrased question was asked:

Example 15.
Was the population greater in 1941 or 1951? _____

One hapless pupil examined the graph and responded "Yes."

Put the Blank Toward the End of the Sentence

A completion item needs to be mentally phrased as a question before it is answered. Blanks placed at the beginning or in the middle of the sentence have to be mentally rearranged before a pupil can respond to the item. Even a knowledgeable examinee will have to read the item twice to answer it. Consider examples 16 and 17.

Example 16.
_____ is the name of the capital city of Illinois.

vs.

Example 17.
The name of the capital city of Illinois is (Springfield) .

Teachers of elementary level arithmetic recognize that skill in solving missing addend problems (e.g., "5 + __ = 12" or "__ + 5 = 12") is quite difficult to learn. When blanks are not placed at the end of a sentence, the verbal item functions much the same as these arithmetic problems. Unlike missing addend problems, however, putting blanks at the beginning of a sentence places an unintended barrier in the path of a youngster who in fact has command of the relevant knowledge. Youngsters are sometimes observed stopping and puzzling at a blank without reading the entire item because they realize that they should write an answer there, but they lack the experience to read ahead and mentally rearrange the item as a question. If the teacher rephrases the item as a direct question, or places the blank at the end, these youngsters are able to display the knowledge they have acquired.

Avoid Copying Statements Verbatim

Using directly quoted material encourages rote memorization rather than comprehension and understanding. Further, textbook statements used as test items are usually quoted out of context and may lead to item ambiguity or to more than one correct answer. One suggestion for teachers is first to think of the answer and then to make up a question to which that answer is the only correct response (Ebel, 1979).

Omit Important Words

A completion item should require the examinee to respond to important aspects of knowledge and not to trivial words. The blank functions to test for an important fact or concept. Verbs should be retained in the statement unless the correct verb form is the focus of the item (Thorndike and Hagen, 1977).

One or two blanks   When more than one or two blanks occur, a sentence usually becomes unintelligible or ambiguous so that several unintended answers could be considered correct. For example:

Example 18.
_____ and _____ are two methods of scoring _____ tests.

A better item would be the following:

Example 19.
Two different methods of scoring essay tests are the (analytic) and (holistic) methods.

Attend to Length and Arrangement of Blanks

The length of the blank is sometimes taken as a clue to the answer. To avoid such unintended clues, keep all the blanks the same length. When testing older pupils, considerable scoring time may be saved by using short blanks in the item and placing spaces to record answers in the right or left margin of the paper or on a separate answer sheet. A "strip key" containing the correct answers can then be laid along the edge of a pupil's paper, and scoring can proceed very quickly. Typing the items in a way that results in all blanks occurring in a "column," accomplishes the same purpose. For example, instead of spreading the items across the page, they can be arranged as follows:

Example 20.
Personnel decisions in which rejection of some persons is permitted are called
_____(selection decisions)_____

Example 21.
Personnel decisions in which all persons must be assigned to one of several jobs are called
_____(classification decisions)_____

Specify the Precision Expected in the Answer

The items should specify the kind of the numerical units for the pupil to use or how precise or accurate the answer should be. This will clarify the task for the pupil and save time for those pupils who continue to work to achieve a degree of precision that is beyond the teacher's intentions. The following examples include such specificity.

Example 22.
If each item to be mailed weighs 1¾ oz., how much will ten items weigh?   (17½)   oz.

Example 23.
Three cars sped past a check point at speeds of 60.1 mph, 55.3 mph, and 48.7 mph, respectively. What (to the nearest whole mph) is the average speed of the cars?   (55)   mph.

Example 24.
A kilogram is equal to   (2.2)   pounds. (Express your answer to one decimal place.)

Avoid Irrelevant Clues

A test item is designed to elicit a specific behavior, but sometimes the wording of an item provides an irrelevant clue, so that an examinee gets the answer correct without performing that behavior. The verb in a sentence, for example, may unintentionally clue the examinee that the intended answer is plural or singular, or an indefinite article may be a clue that the desired response begins with a vowel. Compare the following:

Example 25.
A specialist in urban planning is called an (urbanist) .

vs.

Example 26.
A specialist in city planning is called a(n) (urbanist) .

Other Methods Related to the Completion Format[5]

Cloze Reading Exercises

Cloze[6] reading exercises are popular with reading specialists for measuring both the

[5]This section may be omitted without loss of continuity.
[6]"Cloze" signifies that the reader is presumed to use a Gestalt process of "closure" when guessing the deleted word from the surrounding context.

reading comprehension of an individual pupil and the "readability" level of a passage. The method is usually applied as follows. A representative reading passage is selected. Every fifth word is deleted and replaced by a blank, except for the first and last paragraphs which remain intact. The pupil's task is to read the passage and to write in each blank the word believed most likely to have been there. The score is the number of pupil-supplied words that exactly match the original deleted words. (Other scoring variations are possible.) An example of a cloze reading exercise is shown in Figure 6.3.

The cloze technique dates back to Ebbinghaus in 1897 (Buros, 1978), but Taylor (1953) is credited with applying it to reading. Many variations of the technique exist and a great deal has been written about it (e.g., Buros' (1978) lists 400 references). Reviews of the literature (e.g., Alderson, 1978; Elley, 1978) indicate that several problems exist both in identifying whether the procedure really measures reading comprehension and in reconciling such practical matters as comparability of scores when different passages and/or when different methods of deleting words are used. The teacher is cautioned against using this procedure until consulting at least the following references: Alderson (1978); Bormuth (1964, 1967); Elley (1978); Koslin, Koslin, Zeno, and Wainer (1977); Rankin (1965); Smith (1978); and Taylor (1953, 1956). Special procedures for constructing a multiple-choice version of cloze (sometimes called MAZE) are described by Koslin et al. (1977), in the *User's Manual for Degrees of Reading Power* (CEEB, 1980) and in Chapter 9 of this book. These procedures have much to recommend for them over procedures previously described in the literature for MAZE.

Interlinear Exercises

The interlinear exercise consists of several lines of running text into which some spelling, grammatical, or punctuation errors have been introduced deliberately. The pupil's task is to

WRITE THE WORD ON THE BLANK LINE THAT BELONGS WITHIN THE STORY.

Thinking About Foods

When the Bentons had their Sunday dinner, there was so much good food that no one was hungry or disappointed. Everyone ate and ate. The grownups ate mostly chicken and salad. But the children liked the ice cream best. Each of them had two helpings for dessert.

Did you ever ask <u>1. other</u> people what food they <u>2. like</u> best? Most children will <u>3. say</u> ice cream, cake, and <u>4. candy</u>. These things taste good, <u>5. but</u> doctors say that we <u>6. need</u> other food to make <u>7. us</u> strong and to keep <u>8. us</u> well.

A good breakfast <u>9. is</u> very important. It gives <u>10. us</u> the energy to work <u>11. all</u> morning without getting tired. <u>12. An</u> orange and hot or <u>13. cold</u> cereal with milk make <u>14. a</u> good break- fast. So do <u>15. an</u> egg, buttered toast, milk, <u>16. and</u> an

If <u>41. some</u> members of your family <u>42. don't</u> get home at noon, <u>43. you</u> probably have your biggest <u>44. meal</u> at night. A meal <u>45. at</u> night is sometimes called <u>46. dinner</u> and sometimes called supper. <u>47. Most</u> people have meat or <u>48. fish</u> and several vegetables. Many <u>49. people</u> make a point of <u>50. broiling</u> or baking the meat instead of frying it. A fresh salad is good with it.

The dessert may be cake or some other sweet treat. Such things taste good but are not the best things for us. So you're really lucky if your family is large -- then no one gets too much dessert!

Story from "Thinking About Foods," in *Break Through*, © 1975 by Charles E. Merrill Publishing Company. Cloze exercise from a Master's Thesis by Nancy Brown. Used by permission of Charles E. Merrill Publishing Company and Nancy Brown.

Figure 6 • 3   Example of a cloze reading exercise.

find and correct these errors. Below is an example along with the changes that a pupil might make.

Example 27.

Bobby like some subjects a lot and other very little. Him favorites are reading, english and science. In english, him teacher let him right story about base ball and soccer the subjects he like least is mathematics social studies and spelling.

The interlinear exercise tests one component of writing skill: the ability to edit. It is not a direct measure of writing ability. It is a useful measure of the student's ability to apply the rules of convention and usage when directed to do so.

Some subjectivity may enter into the scoring of these exercises because there may be unanticipated pupil responses and grammatical and punctuation conventions are sometimes debatable. It is best to score only those errors deliberately introduced into the material. Other changes a pupil introduces are not scored. In this way, all pupils are scored on the same basis: their ability to correct errors presented to them. For long passages scoring can be made quicker if a template is made from a clear acetate sheet. On the template is marked the location of the introduced errors, and when it is placed over the pupil's responses, it provides a means of quickly locating relevant parts of the pupil's answers. Rather than extracting material, the teacher should write an original passage so that the teacher can control the type and frequency of errors. Multiple-choice versions of interlinear exercises can be created also.

Summary

The following statements summarize the main points of this chapter.

   1. *Three fundamental principles* guide most recommendations for constructing test items. Test items should:

      a. measure only educationally important objectives.

      b. elicit only the behaviors which the test developer desires to observe.

      c. not prevent or inhibit the desired behaviors from being performed.

   2. *Essay items* require the examinee to write a somewhat lengthy response to a question or problem.

      a. *Restricted response essays* restrict or limit both the substantive content and the form of the written response.

      b. *Extended response essays* permit the student to make fuller use of written verbal reasoning and writing skills, including a full elaboration of the answer to a substantive question.

   3. *The restricted response format:*

      a. can be used to measure a variety of complex learning outcomes (see Table 6.1).

      b. narrows the focus of the item to more specific content and to well-defined behaviors.

c. can be used as "context-dependent" or "interpretive" exercises.

d. is likely to result in nearly all pupils interpreting the intent of the item in basically the same way.

e. is likely to be more reliably scored than the extended response format.

4. *The extended response format:*

a. can be used to measure a more complex variety of learning outcomes (see Table 6.1).

b. can be used to assess either the ability to write about the subject matter or the student's general writing ability.

c. has the unique feature of permitting the student to display the abilities needed for written production, organization, and expressing ideas and the inter-relationships among the above.

d. should not be used to elicit lower-level abilities such as simple recall of information.

5. *Students may study differently* when preparing for essay tests than when preparing for more objective tests. Study habits are more likely influenced by the substantive nature of the questions and the abilities required to answer them than by their surface characteristics.

6. *Essay questions sample a more narrow range of content* than briefer, objective questions but generally require that a more in-depth understanding of that specific part of the content be displayed. This is a disadvantage if the instructional objectives require broad-band content coverage.

7. *The subjectivity involved in grading essays* presents a serious threat to the reliability and validity of the scores:

a. a given reader may be inconsistent.

b. there are often larger reader-to-reader differences.

c. the type and topic of the question influences a reader's scoring.

d. halo effects, carry-over effects, bluffing, penmanship, spelling, and grammar all influence the scoring.

8. *In order to be graded fairly* and for pupils to benefit from the reading, the teacher should carefully plan for essay testing.

9. *Table 6.2 summarizes ten maxims for constructing essay tests with which most test construction textbooks tend to agree.*

10. Suggestions for phrasing essay questions are summarized in Table 6.3.

11. *Subject-matter essay questions can be scored analytically or holistically.* The method used often depends on the nature of the essay question posed.

12. *Suggestions for scoring essay questions,* which apply to either analytical or holistic scoring, are summarized in Table 6.4.

13. Suggestions for commenting on pupils' essays and compositions are presented.

14. *Several of the methods* used for the *assessment of general writing skills and abilities* are described in Table 6.5 and further classified in Figure 6.2 according to the attributes assessed and size of discourse unit scored.

15. *Short-answer items* require the examinee to respond with a word, short phrase, number, or symbol.

16. *Three types of short-answer items* were identified: the *question variety, the completion variety,* and the *association variety.*

17. *Short-answer items elicit various abilities* including:

a. simply recalling terminology, facts, symbols, and classifications.

b. applying rules and making simple interpretations of data and other information.

c. solving science and mathematics problems.

d. manipulating symbols and balancing mathematical and chemical equations.

18. *Short-answer items are more objective* than essay items but are not free of subjectivity in scoring.

19. *The chances of a student blindly guessing* the correct answer on a short-answer item is much less than on a response choice item.

20. *Nine maxims for constructing short-answer items* are summarized in Table 6.6.

*21. *A cloze reading exercise* consists of a "stand-alone" passage in which every fifth word has been deleted. The examinee's task is to supply the exact words that have been deleted.

*22. *Cloze exercises* have been used to test both (a) an individual's reading ability and (b) the "readability" of the passage itself.

*23. *Precisely what the cloze procedure measures* is not clear.

*24. An *interlinear exercise* consists of several lines of running text into which spelling, grammatical, or punctuation errors have been introduced by the test developer. The examinee's task is to find these errors and write in the corrections.

*25. *Interlinear exercises measure one aspect of general writing ability:* the ability to locate and edit errors in a completed text. It is not a direct measure of writing ability.

*26. *Ways of creating and scoring interlinear exercises* are suggested.

*Optional section.

Themes

● Writing test items involves learning the specific function of each part of an item and becoming skillful in formulating items so these functions are fulfilled.

● When the parts of an item do not function properly, it is less likely that the item will measure the instructional intent of a teacher.

● Suggestions for formulating better test items represent the clinical lore of item writing. This lore represents an admixture of wisdom gained through years of common sense, experience, and empirical research.

● Although true-false and matching items are criticized because teachers often use them to test for lower-level cognitive behaviors, these item types need not be limited to testing such behaviors. Experienced item writers have learned to use these forms to measure more complex cognitive skills and abilities.

Terms and Concepts

clinical lore

response-choice item

true-false item

propositions

blind guessing

verbal clues (specific determiners, grammatical clues, etc.)

double negatives

test-wiseness

matching exercise

premises and responses

classification variety of matching exercise

homogeneous premises and responses

perfect matching

plausible options (or responses)

7
DEVELOPING
TRUE-FALSE AND
MATCHING ITEMS

This is the first of three chapters on how to write response-choice items. The suggestions in these chapters represent a distillation of item writing maxims that have become part of the achievement testing tradition in this country. To borrow a term from Wiggins (1973), these chapters represent a summary of the "clinical lore" of response-choice test item construction. " 'Lore' is *not* here used in a pejorative sense but rather in the general sense connoting 'knowledge or wisdom gained through study or experience' " (Wiggins, 1973, p. 200).

If you are not an experienced teacher and/or have not constructed classroom tests before, it may be hard for you to relate to some of these suggestions. A rather typical assignment in a course in testing and measurement is to have persons construct, review, and revise items for the course. Sometimes I ask my students to write response-choice items early in the course before they come to this chapter. Reviewing their items before they read and study this body of clinical lore helps to sensitize them to the need for observing these maxims.

Approximately the first half of this chapter discusses the use and development of true-false items, while the second discusses matching exercises. In turn, each half is divided into two sections. The first section describes the item, telling its "anatomy" or parts and its usefulness in measuring learning outcomes. Each part of an item has a certain function to perform if an item is to measure the intended objective. The second section of each half provides examples and suggestions for constructing your own items of that type. The suggestions, which represent the clinical lore of item writing, are generally directed to the functions the parts of the items should fulfill, namely to measure the intended instructional objective.

Description of the True-False Item

Anatomy of the True-False Item

A true-false item consists of a statement or proposition which the examinee must judge and mark as either true or false. Figure 7.1 illustrates several varieties of this type of item: Some require an examinee to choose "yes" or "no" or "right" or "wrong" instead of true or false, others require an examinee to respond true or false to a cluster of statements, and still others require that each false statement be made true by substituting correct words (or phrases) for the incorrect ones in the item.

Usefulness of True-False Items

Advantages and criticisms Teachers often use true-false items because (a) certain aspects of the subject matter readily lend themselves to verbal propositions that can be judged true or false, (b) such items are relatively easy to write, (c) they can be scored easily and objectively, and (d) they can cover a wide range of content with a relatively short period of testing. But some educators have severely criticized true-false items—especially poorly constructed true-false items. Among the more frequent criticisms are that true-false items (a) are often used only to test specific, frequently trivial,

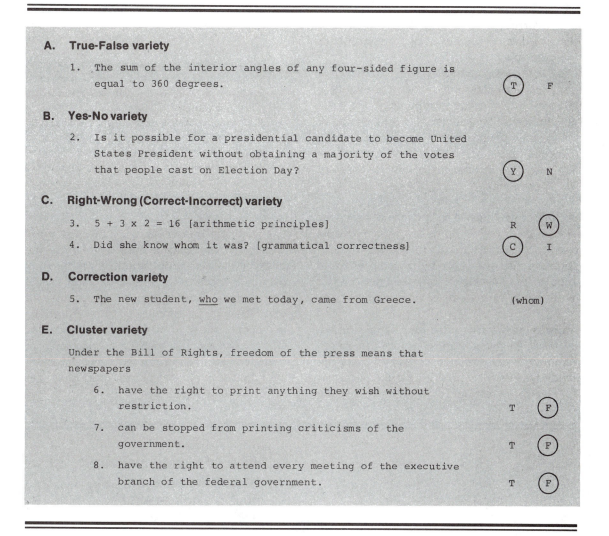

A. True-False variety

   1. The sum of the interior angles of any four-sided figure is equal to 360 degrees.   (T) F

B. Yes-No variety

   2. Is it possible for a presidential candidate to become United States President without obtaining a majority of the votes that people cast on Election Day?   (Y) N

C. Right-Wrong (Correct-Incorrect) variety

   3. 5 + 3 x 2 = 16 [arithmetic principles]   R (W)

   4. Did she know whom it was? [grammatical correctness]   (C) I

D. Correction variety

   5. The new student, <u>who</u> we met today, came from Greece.   (whom)

E. Cluster variety

Under the Bill of Rights, freedom of the press means that newspapers

   6. have the right to print anything they wish without restriction.   T (F)

   7. can be stopped from printing criticisms of the government.   T (F)

   8. have the right to attend every meeting of the executive branch of the federal government.   T (F)

Figure 7 • 1   Examples of five varieties of true-false items.

facts; (b) can be ambiguously worded; (c) can be answered correctly by blind guessing, and (d) may encourage students to study and accept only oversimplified statements of truth and factual details. Much of this chapter is devoted to offering suggestions for improving true-false items so they are not constrained by the limitations these criticisms imply.

Reaching beyond factual details   Although writing true-false items based on trivial, factual details is easy, well-written true-false items can test a student's ability to identify the correctness or appropriateness of a variety of meaningful propositions including the following (Ebel, 1972):

1. *generalizations* in a subject area.
2. *comparisons* among concepts.
3. *causal or conditional* propositions.
4. statements about the *relationship* between two events, concepts, facts, or principles.

5. *explanations* for why events or phenomena occurred.
6. *instances or examples* of a concept or principle.
7. *evidential* **statements**.
8. *predictions* about phenomena or events.
9. *steps* in a procedure or process.
10. numerical *computations* (or other kinds of results obtained from applying a procedure).
11. *evaluative statements* about events or phenomena.

Examples of items of each of these types are shown in Table 7.1. Some of the key phrases used to construct items in each category appear, too. You may want to refer to Table 7.1 from time to time to glean some suggestions for writing true-false items in your subject areas.

Validity of the true-false item type   Professor Ebel, perhaps more than any other contemporary measurement specialist, has defended the use of well-written true-false items for classroom testing. He offers the following argument for the validity of this type (Ebel, 1979, pp. 111–112):

1. The essence of educational achievement is the command of useful verbal knowledge.
2. All verbal knowledge can be expressed in propositions.
3. A proposition is any sentence that can be said to be true or false.
4. The extent of a student's command of a particular area of knowledge is indicated by his success in judging the truth or falsity of propositions related to it.

Note in connection with the last point above that requiring a pupil to identify the truth or falsity of propositions is not the only means of ascertaining a pupil's command of knowledge. Chapter 4 gives an example of other means in connection with Klopfer's operationalization of "to understand" (see Box 4.2). I discuss this idea of a command of knowledge further in connection with assessing knowledge of concepts and principles later in this book (Chapter 9).

"All right, Jones, for your final Ph.D. oral exam we have a single question: TRUE or FALSE...."

© Vimcet Associates, Inc.

Type of statement	Examples of introductory words or phrases	Examples of true-false items
Generalization	All . . . Most . . . Many . . .	Most good true-false items are tests of ability to apply information. (T)
Comparative	The difference between . . . is . . . Both . . . and . . . require . . .	The difference between the raw scores corresponding to the 45th and 55th percentiles is likely to be smaller than the difference between the raw scores corresponding to the 5th and 15th percentiles. (T)
Conditional	If . . . (then) . . . When . . .	When one has a normal distribution the standard deviation and standard error are considered equivalent. (F)
Relational	The larger . . . The higher . . . The lower . . . Making . . . is likely to . . . Increasing . . . tends to . . . How much . . . depends on . . .	Making a test more reliable is likely to make it less valid. (F)
Explanatory	The main reason for . . . The purpose of . . . One of the factors that adversely affect . . . Since . . . Although . . .	One of the factors that adversely affect the reliability of an objective test is the amount of guessing the students do in answering it. (T)
Exemplary	An example of . . . One instance of . . .	An example of a "factual information" question is to ask how horsepower of an engine is calculated. (F)
Evidential	Studies of . . . reveal . . .	Studies of the marking standards and practices of different faculty members reveal that they tend more toward uniformity than toward diversity. (F)
Predictive	One could expect . . . Increasing . . . would result in . . .	One could expect to increase the reliability coefficient of a test from .30 to .60 by doubling its number of items. (F)
Procedural	To find . . . one must . . . In order to . . . one must . . . One method of . . . is to . . . One essential step . . . is to . . . Use . . . of . . . The first step toward . . .	One method of ensuring that scores from a 100-item test and scores from a 25-item test will carry equal weight is to multiply the latter scores by 4. (F)
Computational	(Item includes numerical data and requires computation or estimation.)	The range of the scores 2, 3, 4, and 6 is 5. (T)
Evaluative	A good . . . It is better to . . . than . . . The best . . . is . . . The maximum . . . is . . . The easiest method of . . . is to . . . It is easy to demonstrate that . . . It is difficult to . . . It is possible to . . . It is reasonable to . . . It is necessary to . . . in order to . . . The major drawback to . . . is . . .	It is difficult to obtain reliable scores from a group in which the range of abilities is very wide. (F)

Source: Robert L. Ebel, *Essentials of Educational Measurement,* © 1972, pp. 183–185. Adapted by permission of Prentice-Hall, Inc., Englewood Cliffs, N. J.

Table 7 • 1   Types of statements that might be used to write true-false test items.

Guessing on true-false items: An ill wind? Charles Schultz's Peanuts character Linus once observed, "Taking a true-false test is like having the wind at your back." A common criticism of true-false tests is that they are subject to error because students can answer them by using blind guessing. It is well-known that on a single true-false item, there is a fifty-fifty chance of answering the item correctly if true or false is selected at random. This means that persons guessing randomly can expect to get on the average one-half of the true-false items correct.[1] Several points can be made, however, which blunt this criticism (Ebel, 1972):

1. Blind (or completely random) guessing is quite unlike informed guessing (or guessing based on partial knowledge).
2. Well-motivated students (at least at the college level) tend to guess blindly on only a small percentage of the questions on a test.
3. It is very difficult to obtain a "good score" on a test by blind guessing alone.
4. The fact that a given true-false test has a high reliability coefficient[2] would be evidence that scores on that test are not seriously affected by blind guessing.

Blind guessing, of the type which is assumed by the "fifty-fifty chance" statement, is by definition random responding. But most everyone's experience is that seldom do examinee's respond in this fashion to very many test questions. Rather, persons tend to use whatever partial knowledge they have about the subject of the questions and/or about the context in which the questions are embedded, to make an *informed guess.* Such informed guessers have a higher than fifty-fifty chance of success on true-false items (but how much higher we are unable to say for sure). This means that scores from true-false items (as with other item types) are measures of partial knowledge when informed guessing occurs.

Ebel (1968) asked college students to report the items on the midterm and final exams on which they responded by blind guessing. While 60–70% said they had guessed blindly on 1 or more items, overall, blind guessing was minimal: only about 5% of the students' responses were blind guesses. Outside of this study little research has been done to identify the extent to which pupils engage in blind guessing.

Although a person who is guessing blindly on a single true-false item will have a fifty-fifty chance of being correct, the laws of chance indicate that the probability of getting a *good* score on a test made up of many true-false items is quite small, especially for longer tests. This is illustrated in Table 7.2. Chances are only 2 in 100, for example, that a person who has guessed blindly on a 15-item test will get 80% or more of the item correct. If the test has 20 true-false questions, and someone guesses blindly on *all* items, that person has only two

---

[1]For example, the average "guessing score" (called the *expected chance score*) for a true-false test of 50 items is 25; for 10 T-F items it is 5; etc.

[2]See Chapter 15 for an explanation of reliability coefficients.

© 1968 United Feature Syndicate, Inc.

Number of T-F items on the test	Chances of getting the following percentage of T-F questions right:		
	60% or better	80% or better	100%
5	50 in 100	19 in 100	3 in 100
10	38 in 100	6 in 100	1 in 1,000
15	30 in 100	2 in 100	3 in 100,000
20	25 in 100	6 in 1,000	1 in 1,000,000
25	21 in 100	2 in 1,000	3 in 100,000,000

Note: Computations are based on binomial probability theory.

Table 7 • 2   Chances of obtaining various "good" scores by blind guessing on various true-false tests.

chances in 1,000 of getting 80% or more items correct. Chances of getting perfect (100% correct) papers are even smaller.

Suggestions for Constructing True-False Items

Getting started   In order to write good true-false items a teacher must be able to identify propositions that (a) represent important ideas, (b) can be defended by competent critics as true or false, and (c) are not obviously correct to persons with general knowledge or good common sense (Ebel, 1972). These propositions are then used as a *basis* to derive true-false items.

In this regard, Ebel suggests that it is helpful to think of a segment of knowledge as being represented by a paragraph and of propositions as the main idea(s) of that paragraph. These main ideas can then be used as a basis for writing true-false items. As an example, consider the following paragraph in Chapter 6 of this book as a segment of knowledge:

> Answering essay questions takes a pupil a long time and limits the breadth of content a given essay can cover. If students can answer one or two response-choice items in one minute, then they can answer 30 to 60 items in a half hour test which can cover a broad area of content and many objectives. In the same time they

can probably answer only one or two essay questions. Although in-depth coverage of a narrower topic can be accomplished using essays, broad general coverage can be obtained using more objective items. One way to overcome the shortcoming of limited content sampling with essays is to plan to accumulate evidence from a series of essays or take-home compositions written over a longer period of time (Coffman, 1971). Several out-of-class essays written over a marking period may provide a better assessment of a particular objective than a single essay written during a brief examination period.

Among the main ideas or propositions in this paragraph are these:

a. For the same amount of testing time, an objective test can cover a much broader range of content than can an essay test.

b. Essays written outside of class and over a longer period of time are likely to provide better assessments than giving an in-class essay test.

These ideas or propositions can then be rephrased in various ways to form true-false questions. These are some examples (only one or two of these items would actually appear on a test):

Example 28.
Essay items should be used when a teacher wants to assess a student's in-depth knowledge of a limited topic. (T)

Example 29.
If the time allotted for testing an extensive content area is short, then it follows that a single, in-depth essay question would make the best kind of test. (F)

Example 30.
If a teacher wants to cover a broad subject matter in a limited testing period, it is better to use several restricted response essays rather than a single extended response essay. (T)

Example 31.
Assigning several out-of-class essays during a semester increases content validity. (T)

Improving true-false items Initial drafts of all items should be subjected to editorial scrutiny. You will recall from Figure 5.1 that editing items is an important step in the test development process. Various suggestions for improving the quality of true-false items can serve as guidelines when you review the first drafts of test items. These are summarized in Table 7.3 and discussed below.

1. Make sure the item is either definitely true or definitely false A proposition should not be so general that a knowledgeable examinee can find exceptions which change the intended

---

1. Make sure the item is either definitely true or definitely false.
2. Avoid verbal clues (specific determiners) that give away the answer.
3. Test important ideas, knowledge, or understanding (rather than trivia, general knowledge, or common sense).
4. Keep the word-length of true statements about the same as that of false statements.
5. Avoid copying sentences directly from textbook and other written materials.
6. Avoid presenting items in a repetitive or easily learned pattern.

Sources: Ebel (1951, 1979); Greene, Jorgensen, and Gerberich (1942, 1943); Gronlund (1976); Lindquist (1936); Lindvall (1967); Stanley and Hopkins (1972); Thorndike and Hagen (1977); Weidemann (1926); Wesman (1971).

Table 7 • 3 Suggestions for writing true-false items.

truth or falsity of the statement. In other words, make sure the item is phrased in a way that makes it unambiguous to the *knowledgeable examinee*. (Items should, of course, appear ambiguous to the unprepared or unknowledgeable student.) A few suggestions for reducing item ambiguity include the following (Lindvall and Nitko, 1975):

a. Use short statements where possible. This permits the examinee to identify more easily the idea you want judged true or false. Complex, cumbersome statements make identifying the essential element in the item difficult for even the knowledgeable examinee (Ebel, 1951). If the information you want to describe in the statement is complex, use different sentences to separate the description from the statement to be judged true or false. Frequently, editing can shorten a long complex statement which contains extraneous material irrelevant to the main idea of the item.[3]

Example 32.
Poor: Although a single item is generally an unreliable measure, and although it is frequently difficult to write additional items, a test's reliability usually can be improved by making the test longer and thereby increasing the number of times the pupils' behaviors are observed. (T)

Example 33
Better: Tests containing more items are usually less reliable than shorter tests. (F)

b. Use exact language. Frequently, quantitative terms can clarify an otherwise ambiguous statement. For example, instead of saying, "equal to approximately $5.00 . . ." or "approximately one-half of . . . ," say "between $4.00 and $6.00 . . ." or "between 45 and 55 percent. . . ."

[3]This suggestion applies to the development of all item types, of course.

---

c. Have only one idea per statement, unless the statement is designed to test knowledge of the relationship between two ideas.

Example 34.
Poor: The Monongahela River flows north to join the Allegheny River at Columbus where they form the Ohio River. (F)

In the above item, a student may respond "F" for an inappropriate reason: The student may think (erroneously) that the Monongahela River does not flow north, may be unaware that the confluence of the rivers is at Pittsburgh, and/or may not know anything about the three rivers. Thus, the student would get the item right without having the knowledge the right answer implies. A separate statement for each idea may be necessary in order to identify precisely which information the student knows.

d. If the item content expresses an opinion, value, or attitude, you should attribute the statement to an appropriate source. The attribution may be in the form of an introductory clause, such as, "According to the text . . ." or "In the opinion of most specialists in this area . . ." or "In Jones' view. . . ." This referencing reduces ambiguity in two ways: (1) it makes clear that the statement is not to be judged in general, but rather in terms of the specific source, and (2) it makes clear that you are not asking for a student's personal opinion.

e. Use positive statements and avoid double negatives which many pupils find especially confusing. Consider the following:

Example 35.
Poor: It is not undesirable to use double negatives inadvertently in a true-false item.

Source: Sax (1974a, p. 84).

Example 36.
Poor: The Monongahela River does not flow north. (F)

Example 37.
Better: The Monongahela River flows southward. (F)

If you must use a negative function word, be sure to underline it or to use all capital letters so that it is NOT overlooked.

2. Avoid verbal clues (specific determiners) that give away the answer A *specific determiner*[4] is a word or phrase in a true-false (or multiple-choice) item that gives the examinee an unintended clue to the correct answer. Words such as "always," "never," and "every" tend to make propositions false.

Example 38.
Poor: It is always better to use a longer test than a shorter one. (F)

Words such as "often," "usually," "frequently," tend to make propositions true.

Example 39.
Poor: Frequently, it is better to use a longer test instead of a short test. (T)

Test-wise examinees[5] will use these clues to respond correctly even though they do not have command of the requisite knowledge. Essentially, specific determiners are function words that "over-qualify" a given statement and make it incorrect (Sarnachi, 1979).

It should be noted that *some* propositions *are* "always" true or "never" true or "often" false or "usually" false. For this reason some test constructors may find that using such propositions, which utilize specific determiners "in reverse," helps to discriminate the knowledgeable student from the merely test-wise one (Ebel, 1979). Personally, however, I wouldn't recommend using such tactics with elementary school pupils. Some evidence exists (Slakater, Koehler, and Hampton, 1970) indicating that youngsters do not attend to spe-

---

[4]This term was probably used first in connection with true-false items by C. C. Weidemann (1926).
[5]Test-wiseness is discussed in Chapter 12.

cific determiner clues in multiple-choice items until the ninth grade, even though they do use other types of test-wiseness skills as early as fifth grade. The same seems likely to be valid for true-false items.

3. Test important ideas, rather than trivia, general knowledge, or common sense This suggestion is really a restatement of the first fundamental rule of test construction (see Chapter 6). You need to be especially sensitive to this point when writing true-false items, however, because it is easy to write items such as those below which test for trivial knowledge.

Poor:

Example 40.
George Washington had wooden teeth. (T)

Example 41.
The author of this text provides six suggestions for writing true-false items. (F)

Example 42.
Validity varies from test to test. (T)

Example 43.
During their school experiences, pupils take both teacher-developed and professionally developed tests. (T)

Example 44.
A true-false item should be neither definitely true nor definitely false. (F)

Item 40 reflects trivia rather than important information about Washington's role in the early days of the nation. The following item tests for knowledge of a more significant fact about Washington.

Example 45.
Better: The work of the Constitutional Convention received more rapid public acceptance because of George Washington's active involvement at the Convention. (T)

Item 41 is a textbook related statement that doesn't test an important understanding. It

would be better to test an examinee's understanding of principles of item writing rather than to test a questionable idiosyncratic fact.

Example 46.
Better: A good procedure for developing true-false items is to insert the word "not" into a true proposition taken from a textbook. (F)

Items 42 and 43 test rather common knowledge or what good common sense can figure out. Items should reflect the specialized knowledge and understanding a pupil obtains from serious study of the subject.

Item 44 takes a textbook statement (Table 7.3) and makes it false by inserting negative function words (neither . . . nor). Such a practice of taking an otherwise true statement and inserting a little noticed "not" (or other negative) makes the item tricky, and even well-prepared students can overlook the negative (Ebel, 1979). If the suggestions in this chapter for *developing* true-false items are followed, such a flawed item is unlikely to occur.

4. True statements and false statements should have approximately the same number of words There is a tendency for inexperienced item writers to make true statements more qualified and wordy than false statements. Test-wise students can pick-up on this irrelevant clue and get the item right without knowledge or understanding of the desired concept. Keeping a watchful editorial eye by rewriting inappropriate statements is the easiest way to correct this type of flaw.

5. Avoid copying sentences directly from textbooks and other written material Sentences copied from a text are frequently uninterpretable because they have been taken out of context. In addition, the practice of using such statements is likely to communicate to pupils that what is important is the text's exact (and often idiosyncratic) phrasing rather than their own comprehension. This encourages students to engage in rote learning of text-book sentences.

Copying items from a text is more likely when a teacher wants to test for knowledge of verbal concepts (including definitions) and statements of principles (rules). But testing for comprehension demands *paraphrasing* at the minimum (see Chapter 9), and enhancing a pupil's comprehension of concepts and principles seems to be a more important educational goal than encouraging a student to memorize textbook statements word-for-word. Again, if you follow the earlier stated suggestions for initially deriving items in this chapter it is unlikely that you will copy statements from a textbook.

6. **Don't present items in a repetitive or easily learned pattern (e.g., TFTF . . . , TTFFTT . . . , TFFTFF . . . , etc.)** The reason why some teachers develop such patterns is, of course, to make scoring easier. But if it's easy for the teacher to remember, it will be easy for test-wise students to learn also. Test results will then be invalid. Also you should avoid a consistent practice of having more true answers than false or more false answers than true. Students, especially in the upper grades, soon discover such practices. Not all educators agree on proportions of true and false answers, however. Some test specialists (e.g., Ebel, 1972) recommend having more false items than true ones, because false items tend to discriminate[6] better. That is, false items tend

---

[6]"Discrimination" is a technical term used in connection with empirical analysis of item response data. See Chapter 11 for an explanation.

---

to differentiate the most knowledgeable students from the least knowledgeable better than true items. Box 7.1 gives some examples of poor true-false items.

Description of the Matching Exercise

Anatomy of the Matching Exercise

Figure 7.2 shows an example of a matching exercise with its various parts labeled. A matching exercise presents the pupil with a list of *premises*, a list of *responses*, and a set of *directions for matching* the elements of these two lists. The matching exercise shown in Figure 7.2 requires simple matching based on remembered associations. Matching exercises can be devised, however, to test for comprehension of concepts and principles. Examples of these latter types appear in Chapter 9.

Each of the premises are numbered; therefore, each premise constitutes a separately scorable item. You can construct matching exercises with more responses than premises, more premises than responses, or an equal number of each. The latter case, as we shall observe, is generally considered to be undesirable because it results in "perfect matching." Premises are usually listed in the left-hand column and responses in the right-hand column, but sometimes responses and premises may be placed above or below one another.

Matching exercises are much like multiple-choice items. Each premise functions as a

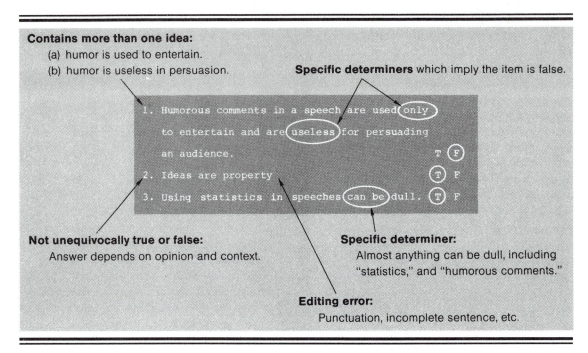

Contains more than one idea:
(a) humor is used to entertain.
(b) humor is useless in persuasion.

Specific determiners which imply the item is false.

> 1. Humorous comments in a speech are used (only) to entertain and are (useless) for persuading an audience. T (F)
>
> 2. Ideas are property (T) F
>
> 3. Using statistics in speeches (can be) dull. (T) F

Not unequivocally true or false:
Answer depends on opinion and context.

Specific determiner:
Almost anything can be dull, including "statistics," and "humorous comments."

Editing error:
Punctuation, incomplete sentence, etc.

Box 7 • 1

separate item, and the items in the list of responses function as "foils" or alternatives. Matching exercises, then, can be rewritten as a series of multiple-choice items in which the same alternatives are repeated for each premise. This leads to an important principle for constructing matching exercises: *Use matching exercises only when you have several multiple-choice items which require repeating the identical set of alternatives (foils).*

Advantages and Criticisms

A matching exercise provides a space-saving, compact, and objectively measurable way to test a number of important learning outcomes such as a student's ability to identify associations or relationships between two things. Among the relationships that you could use as a basis for developing matching exercises are these (Gronlund, 1976):

Possible Premise Sets	*Associated Response Sets*
Accomplishments	Persons
Noted events	Dates
Definitions	Terms and phrases
Examples, applications	Rules, principles, and classifications
Concepts (ideas, operations, quantities, and qualities)	Symbols, signs
Titles of works	Authors, artists
Foreign words and phrases	English correspondence
Uses and functions	Parts, machines
Names of objects	Pictures of objects.

You can also develop matching exercises using pictorial materials to test the pupil's ability to match words and phrases with pictures

In the left-hand column below are descriptions of some late-nineteenth century American painters. For each description, choose the name of the person being described from the right-hand column and place the letter identifying it on the line preceding the number of the description. Each name in the right-hand column may be used once, more than once, or not at all.

Instructions for matching

Item numbers

Description of Painter	Name of Painter
(e) 1. A society portraitist, who emphasized depicting a subject's social position rather than a clear-cut characterization of the subject.	a. Mary Cassatt
(d) 2. A realistic painter of nature, especially known for paintings of the sea.	b. Thomas Eakins
(b) 3. A realistic painter of people, who depicted strong characterizations and powerful, unposed forms of the subject.	c. John LaFarge
(a) 4. An impressionist in the style of Degas, who often painted mother and child themes.	d. Winslow Homer
	e. John Singer Sargent
	f. James A.M. Whistler

Premises

Responses

Figure 7 • 2 Anatomy of a matching exercise.

of objects or with locations on maps and diagrams.

Because rote memorization can be used to learn the associations between the pairs of elements in two lists, *and* because teachers frequently use matching exercises to test such rote associations as names and dates, the matching exercise has been criticized: It is often seen as an item format which can only be used to test for memorized factual information. But matching exercises can also be used to assess aspects of a pupil's comprehension of concepts, principles, or schemes for classifying objects, ideas, or events (see, however, Chapter 9). If you want to test pupils on these higher-level abilities, design items which present new examples or instances of the concept or principle to the pupil and which require the pupil to match these examples with the appropriate concepts or principle names. In this context "new examples" mean instances of concepts that have not been previously taught to or encountered by the *student*. Similarly, test items can describe a novel situation to the student, and the student can decide which of several rules, principles, or classifications is likely to apply. An example of this type of matching exercise is given below in an exercise based on material presented in Chapter 1 of this text. Sometimes this type is called a *classification variety* of matching exercise.

Example 47.
Classification variety of matching exercise
Each of the numbered statements below describes a testing situation in which *ONE* decision is represented. On the blank next to each statement write the letter:
A—if the decision is primarily concerned with *placement*.
B—if the decision is primarily concerned with *selection*.
C—if the decision is primarily concerned with *program improvement*.
D—if the decision is primarily concerned with *theory development*.
E—if the decision is primarily concerned with *motivating students*.

(A) 9. After children are admitted to kindergarten, they are given a perceptual skills screening test to determine which children should be given special training in perceptual skills.

(A) 10. At the end of third grade all pupils are given an extensive battery of reading tests and reading profiles are developed for each child. On the basis of the results, some children are given a special reading program while the others continue with the regular program.

(B) 11. High school seniors take a national scholastic aptitude test and send their scores to colleges they wish to attend. On the basis of these scores, colleges admit some students and do not admit others.

(E) 12. Students are informed about the objectives their examination will cover and about how many points each examination question will be worth.

A serious practical limitation of matching exercises is the difficulty encountered when attempting to find *homogeneous* premises and responses. The premises and responses that together form a matching exercise should refer to the same thing. In the above illustration, for example, all premises and responses refer to some type of decision. In the example in Figure 7.2, all premises and responses refer to late nineteenth-century painters. The reason why a matching exercise should be comprised of homogeneous premises and responses derives from its relation to multiple-choice items: the entire list of responses has to function as a plausible set of responses for *each* premise, otherwise, the pupils' matching task may be trivial. Consider the following non-homogeneous poor matching exercise:

Example 48.
Poor matching exercise on social studies

(d) 5. Pennsylvania's official state flower   a. Ruffed grouse

(a) 6. Pennsylvania's official state bird   b. Pittsburgh

(b) 7. Major steel producing city   c. 1,950,098

(c) 8. 1970 population of Philadelphia   d. Mountain laurel

     e. Allegheny River

Since all responses are not plausible distractors for each premise, pupils can answer the items on the basis of general knowledge and common sense, rather than on any specialized knowledge acquired in the classroom.

Attempts to make the above matching exercise more homogeneous may result in creating items that do not correspond to the teacher's intended objectives. For example, one could alter the exercise above by making all the premises refer to *different states* and all the responses to *different official state birds:* The task would be to match the birds with the states. The local curriculum, however, may only require students to identify *their own state* bird (or other symbols). Creating a homogeneous matching exercise, as in this example, may result in creating a test that does not match the curriculum and, therefore, cannot be used.

Applying the rule mentioned earlier in this chapter would help the situation: The teacher should reserve the matching exercise technique for use in those situations when several multiple-choice items require the same set of options. Returning to the above example, note that each premise could be turned into a separate multiple-choice item, each with a different set of (homogeneous) plausible responses. The homogeneous options for an item on Pennsylvania's official state flower, for example, could all be flowers native to the Pennsylvania region.

Suggestions for Constructing Matching Exercises

Many of the suggestions for constructing other varieties of response-choice items apply to matching exercises as well, especially suggestions for writing multiple-choice items.[7] A few maxims, however, which apply particularly to matching exercises and which, when followed, result in improved item quality, are summarized in Table 7.4 and are discussed below.

1. Make a matching exercise homogeneous Although this point has been discussed previously, I would like to add that often the degree pupils perceive the exercise as homogeneous varies with the maturity and educational development of the group being tested (Lindquist, 1936; Gronlund, 1976). What may be a homogeneous exercise for primary school children may be less so for middle school youngsters and even less so for high schoolers. Consider, for example, the matching exercise below in which the task is to match American historical events with their dates. For younger, less experienced students such a matching task would likely be difficult, but would appear homogeneous in the sense that

[7]Multiple-choice item construction is discussed in the next chapter.

---

1. Within a single matching exercise, make the premises and responses homogeneous.
2. Write directions that explain completely the intended basis for matching.
3. Check to see that all the responses function as plausible options to each premise.
4. Keep the list of premises and responses within a single matching exercise relatively short.
5. Avoid creating "perfect matching" in which each response matches only one premise.
6. Place the longer phrases (sentences) in the premise list and the shorter phrases, words, or symbols in the response list.
7. If at all possible, arrange the responses in a logical, meaningful order.
8. Use numbers to identify the premises and letters to identify the responses.
9. Avoid using incomplete sentences for premises.
10. Keep all the premises and responses belonging to a single matching exercise on the same page.

Sources: Ebel (1951, 1979); Greene, Jorgensen, and Gerberich (1942, 1943); Gronlund (1976); Lindquist (1936); Lindvall (1967); Stanley and Hopkins (1972); Thorndike and Hagen (1977); Wesman (1971).

Table 7 • 4   Summary of principles for constructing matching exercises.

all responses would be plausible options for each premise. High school students would find the task easier—even though they didn't know the exact dates—because they could use partial knowledge to organize the dates into "early," "middle," and "recent" history. For them only "f" and "g" would be plausible options for item 1, for example.

Example 49.
Column A below lists important events which happened in American history. For each event find the date it happened from *Column B*. Write the letter you see near the date on the blank to the left of each event. Each date in *Column B* may be used once, more than once, or not at all.

Column A (events)	Column B (dates)
(f) 13. United States entered World War I	a. 1492
	b. 1607
(d) 14. Lincoln became president	c. 1776
	d. 1861
(g) 15. Truman became president	e. 1880
	f. 1917
(b) 16. Pilgrims landed at Cape Cod	g. 1945

2. Explain completely the intended basis for matching It is important to make the directions to a matching exercise clear. Ambiguity is not a problem if the examinees clearly understand the nature of the task they should perform. Elementary students may need oral explanations and, perhaps, some practice with this format before the test. The classification variety of matching exercise (Example 47) usually requires more elaborate directions and may require special oral explanations even for high school students. Avoid long, involved written directions, which place an unnecessary premium on reading skill. Remember the Third Fundamental Principle in Chapter 6: The item shouldn't get in the way of a student's performance of the behavior you want to observe.

3. All responses should function as plausible options for each premise Earlier sugges-

tions on homogeneous premises and responses apply here. Also, avoid using specific determiners and grammatical clues such as beginning some premises or responses with *an* and others with *a*, or having some plural while others are singular, or stating some in the past tense while others are stated in the present or future tense, etc. And avoid using incomplete sentences as premises (see Suggestion 9 below).

4. Use short lists of responses and premises Usually, no more than 5 to 10 responses are recommended for a single matching exercise. The reasons are: (a) longer lists make maintaining homogeneity difficult, (b) longer matching exercises overload a test with one kind of behavior, and (c) longer lists require too much examinee "searching time" (Ebel, 1951). Additionally, it is easier to develop several shorter homogeneous exercises than a single long one. Finally, some evidence exists suggesting that longer matching exercises result in a lower percentage of correct answers (Shannon, 1973).

If an exercise is too long, it may be separated into two or more shorter exercises. Another way to keep the list of responses short is by permitting each response to be used as a correct answer more than once. When you do this, examinees should be alerted by either oral or written directions. One standard phrase that is used to do this is: "Each of the [names, dates, etc.] may be used once, more than once, or not at all" (see Figure 7.2).

5. Avoid "perfect matching" If the examinee knows all the answers but one, then the final choice will be automatically correct because it is the only one left. "Giving away the final answer" reduces the validity of the test. The ways to avoid perfect matching are to include one or more responses that do not match any of the premises and to use the same responses for more than one premise. Remember, even an "unmatchable" response must be plausible to the less knowledgeable pupil.

6. Longer phrases appear in the premise list; shorter phrases in the response list A pupil proceeds with a matching exercise by reading a premise and then searching through the response list for the correct answer. The response list is re-read for each premise. It is, therefore, more efficient and less time-consuming for pupils if they can read the longer phrases only once, while they can re-read or scan the shorter phrases (words, symbols) as often as necessary.

7. Arrange the responses in a logical order A pupil saves time if the list is arranged in some meaningful order. Dates arranged chronologically, numbers in order of magnitude, words and names alphabetically, and qualitative phrases in a logical sequence. Besides saving time, such arrangements may contribute to the clarity of the task, reduce pupil confusion, and lower incidences of pupil carelessness and oversight.

8. Identify premises with numbers and responses with letters Each premise is a separate item; therefore, premises should carry numbers which indicate their position in the test sequence. Thus, if ten multiple-choice items are followed by a five-premise matching exercise, the five premises should be consecutively numbered 11 through 15.

9. Avoid using incomplete sentences for premises When incomplete sentences are used for premises it is (a) difficult to make all responses homogeneous and (b) easier for examinees to respond correctly on the basis

of superficial features such as grammatical clues or sentence structure (Lindquist, 1936). You can see the consequences of not following this maxim by examining the poorly written matching exercise below. It is both non-homogeneous and contains grammatical clues.

Example 50.
Poor matching exercise in biology[8]

(c)	17. Most normally green plants lose their color when	a.	through their stomata
(e)	18. The common characteristic of flowering plants is	b.	contracts into a rounded mass
(d)	19. Almost all plants which form coal	c.	grown in the dark
(b)	20. When an expanded amoeba is strongly stimulated it	d.	are now extinct
		e.	the formation of a reproductive body

10. Keep everything belonging to a single matching exercise on the same page Having the complete exercise on one page rather than flipping back and forth between two pages is easier and less annoying for the examinee. For some examinees, having to turn the page back and forth may interfere with the response a teacher intends by increasing their likelihood of carelessness, confusion, and short-term memory lapses. In short, being able to answer a test item while flipping pages is a skill irrelevant to the behavior being tested.

[8]From *The Construction and Use of Achievement Examinations*, edited by H. E. Hawkes, E. F. Lindquist, and C. R. Mann, p. 69. Copyright 1936 by American Council on Education. Used by permission. Adapted from an illustration in *Traditional Examinations and New Type Tests*, by C. W. Odell (New York: Century Co., 1928), p. 380.

Summary

The following statements summarize the main points of this chapter.

1. The suggestions for writing true-false and matching items represent the "clinical lore" of experienced item writers and nearly all maxims can be subsumed under the Three Fundamental Principles.

2. True-false, multiple-choice, and matching exercises are called *response-choice* items.

3. A *true-false item* consists of a statement or proposition that the examinee must judge as true or false. Variations include yes-no, right-wrong, cluster, and correction varieties (Figure 7.1).

4. True-false items are frequently criticized because they can:

    a. be used to test specific, trivial facts.

    b. be ambiguously worded.

    c. be answered correctly by blind guessing.

    d. encourage students to study factual details and to accept oversimplified statements of truth.

5. Carefully constructed true-false questions frequently reach beyond factual details, however. Examples are described in Table 7.1.

6. Advantages of true-false items that are frequently cited include:

    a. ease of construction,

    b. objectivity and ease of scoring, and

    c. increased coverage of content per unit of testing time.

7. One logical argument for the validity of true-false items concludes that a pupil's judgments of the truth of propositions in an area of knowledge reflect the pupil's command or mastery of that area.

8. While it is possible to guess blindly on true-false items, it is difficult to get good scores by this process when the test has many items (Table 7.2).

9. A *blind guess* is a completely random response, much like flipping a coin; an *informed guess* is a response based on partial knowledge and test-wiseness.

10. Most well-prepared and well-motivated pupils are unlikely to use blind guessing, but they may use informed guessing.

11. The ability to write good quality true-false items begins with the ability to identify propositions in a subject area that:

    a. reflect important concepts.

    b. competent authorities can defend as true.

    c. are not obvious or common knowledge.

12. How to get started in writing true-false items is described earlier in this chapter.

13. As with all written items (Figure 5.1), true-false items should be subjected to editorial scrutiny.

14. The six maxims in Table 7.3 summarize suggestions for reviewing and improving true-false items.

15. A *matching exercise* consists of a list of premises, a list of responses, and a set of directions for matching the elements of the two lists.

16. Matching exercises are like multiple-choice items in that each premise functions as a separate item. Unlike most multiple-choice items, however, each premise has the same list of options (or responses).

17. Matching exercises should be used only when several multiple-choice stems would require repetition of the same set of options.

18. An advantage of the matching exercise is that it provides a space-saving, compact, and objectively scorable way to test pupil learning outcomes, such as:

    a. the ability to identify relationships, and

    b. the ability to classify things.

19. A criticism of the matching exercise is that teachers frequently use it to test for rote associations rather than comprehension of concepts, principles, or schemes of classification.

20. The "giving away" of answers to matching exercises can be avoided by constructing *homogeneous* premises and responses so that each response functions as a plausible option to each premise. The homogeneity of premises and responses is often a function of the group being tested as well as the content of the exercise itself.

21. Suggestions for constructing matching exercises are summarized in Table 7.4.

Themes

● The skillful writer of multiple-choice items must recognize the function of each part of the item and design the item so the parts function as intended.

● Although multiple-choice items are highly valued objective measurement tools, a teacher must recognize both their strengths and their limitations in order to use them wisely in the classroom.

● Studying suggestions for writing multiple-choice items will help the teacher avoid constructing flawed items and increase the likelihood that the intent of the instructional objectives are met.

Terms and Concepts

alternatives, responses, options
distractors, foils
stem
continuum of knowledge acquisition
varieties of multiple-choice items
direct vs. indirect measurement
relative vs. absolute interpretation
nonfunctioning words
textbookish phraseology
cluing items, linking items
incomplete stem
negatively worded stems
plausible distractors

functional alternatives
correct answer variety
best answer variety
homogeneous vs. heterogeneous
   alternatives
verbal clues, grammatical correctness
tandem arrangement of options
overlapping alternatives
"none of the above"
"all of the above"
filler alternatives
specific determiner
effect of insufficient and wrong learning

8
DEVELOPING MULTIPLE-CHOICE ITEMS: BASIC PRINCIPLES

This chapter extends the clinical lore of item writing to multiple-choice items. By studying and applying the maxims contained here, you will have a grasp of the basic principles of multiple-choice item writing.

The chapter begins by discussing the usefulness of multiple-choice items: structure and function, varieties which tend to be used, advantages and criticisms, and when not to use them. Next, suggestions for constructing multiple-choice items are presented and illustrated with both positive and negative examples. After describing how to get started writing items, the remainder of the chapter offers suggestions in three areas: improving the item stem, improving the alternatives, and wording the correct answer. These suggestions are essentially corollaries of the Three Fundamental Principles of Test Construction in Chapter 6.

On the whole, this chapter concerns the basic principles of writing multiple-choice items which measure rather simple instructional objectives. The next chapter expands these principles and describes ways to write items that test more complex cognitive processes such as comprehension, interpretation of pictorial materials, and application.

Usefulness of Multiple-Choice Items

Anatomy and Function of a Multiple-Choice Item

A multiple-choice item consists of one or more introductory sentences followed by a list of two or more suggested responses from which the examinee chooses one as the correct answer. The introductory part of an item is called the *stem*, and its functions are to ask a question, set the task to be performed, or state the problem to be solved. As a general rule, after the examinee has read the stem, he or she should understand the task at hand and know what task is required by the stem.

The suggested responses are called *alternatives, responses,* or *options*. Usually, only one of the alternatives is the correct or best answer to the question or problem posed. The remaining incorrect alternatives are called distractors or "foils." Their function is to appear as plausible answers or solutions to the problem for those examinees who do not possess sufficient knowledge. Conversely, they should not appear to be plausible to those who in fact

have the desired degree of knowledge. Figure 8.1 illustrates these points.

In its entirety, the multiple-choice item functions as a stimulus to elicit a pupil response that will be one of several bases for a teacher to infer the extent to which the pupil has attained a particular instructional objective.[1] To make this inference accurately may, of course, require that several test items be administered and that other information be obtained.

Pupils acquire knowledge and successful performance in various degrees. Further, perfect knowledge or perfect performance, even if it is possible to attain, is seldom a desired educational goal. Given this, it is sometimes useful to conceptualize a student as being located at some point along a *continuum of knowledge or performance acquisition* for a given instructional objective.[2] A test item can be constructed in such a way that persons with

---

[1] Of course, this is the function of all test items that are used in the classroom.

[2] This is not an entirely satisfactory conceptualization from a strict scientific viewpoint, but it does have pedagogical value.

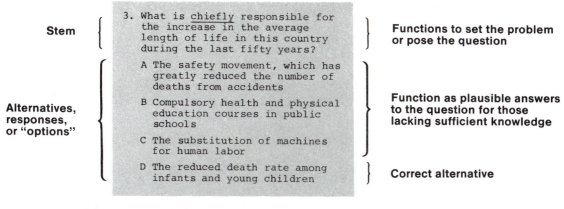

Stem $\left\{ \begin{array}{c} \\ \\ \\ \\ \end{array} \right.$	3. What is <u>chiefly</u> responsible for the increase in the average length of life in this country during the last fifty years? $\left. \begin{array}{c} \\ \\ \\ \end{array} \right\}$ **Functions to set the problem or pose the question**
Alternatives, responses, or "options" $\left\{ \begin{array}{c} \\ \\ \\ \\ \\ \\ \\ \end{array} \right.$	A The safety movement, which has greatly reduced the number of deaths from accidents B Compulsory health and physical education courses in public schools C The substitution of machines for human labor $\left. \begin{array}{c} \\ \\ \\ \\ \\ \\ \end{array} \right\}$ **Function as plausible answers to the question for those lacking sufficient knowledge** D The reduced death rate among infants and young children $\left. \begin{array}{c} \\ \end{array} \right\}$ **Correct alternative**

Source: Lindquist, Feldt, Forsyth, and Neckere (1970, p. 23)

Figure 8 • 1   The parts of a multiple-choice item and their functions.

a certain level of knowledge will be able to answer it correctly, while others, lower on the continuum of knowledge acquisition, will not. Consider this simple illustration:

1. In what year did the United States enter World War I?	2. In what year did the United States enter World War I?	3. In what year did the United States enter World War I?
a. 1776	a. 1901	a. 1913
b. 1812	*b. 1917	b. 1915
*c. 1917	c. 1941	c. 1916
d. 1981	d. 1950	*d. 1917

All three items ask the same question, but the degree of knowledge required to answer that question increases from Item 1 to Item 3. You can easily see how this is done in this example: The examinee is required to make finer distinctions between the dates comprising the alternatives. (Of course, manipulating the alternatives is not the only way to create items testing higher levels of ability.)

For which degree of knowledge should an item be written? That would depend on several factors including the type of pupil, the level of instruction, the purpose for which the test will be used, and the degree of knowledge your experience has indicated pupils need to attain. In effect, you would decide which degree of knowledge about a given subject is sufficient for the purposes at hand and then construct test items that distinguish those who lack sufficient knowledge from those who have acquired it.

The above statement represents an idealized situation. Seldom will real test items separate persons this neatly; it is likely that some less knowledgeable pupils will answer items correctly that other more knowledgeable pupils will not. In general, though, it is important when constructing tests to keep in mind the principle that *the function of a test item is to identify or distinguish those who have attained the particular level of knowledge* (skill, ability, or performance) *you have identified as sufficient* (or necessary) *for the classroom purpose or decision at hand.*

Varieties of Multiple-choice Items

A number of variations of multiple-choice items have been used by both teachers and professional test developers. These are illustrated in Box 8.1. Space does not permit a description

Examples of different varieties of multiple-choice items

A. The correct-answer variety
Who invented the sewing machine?
- a. Fulton
- *b. Howe
- c. Singer
- d. White
- e. Whitney

B. The best-answer variety
What was the basic purpose of the Marshall Plan?
- a. militarily defend Western Europe
- *b. reestablish business and industry in Western Europe
- c. settle United States differences with Russia
- d. directly help the hungry and homeless in Europe

C. The multiple-response variety
What factors are principally responsible for the clotting of blood?
- a. contact of blood with a foreign substance
- *b. contact of blood with injured tissue
- c. oxidation of hemoglobin
- *d. presence of unchanged prothrombin

D. The incomplete statement variety
Millions of dollars worth of corn, oats, wheat, and rye are destroyed annually in the United States by
- a. mildews.
- b. molds.
- c. rusts.
- *d. smuts.

E. The negative variety
Which of these is *NOT* true of viruses?
- a. Viruses live only in plants and animals.
- b. Viruses reproduce themselves.
- *c. Viruses are composed of very large living cells.
- d. Viruses can cause diseases.

F. The substitution variety

Passages to be read
Surely the forces of education should be fully utilized

to acquaint youth with the real nature of the dangers

to democracy, for no other place offers as good or
$\overline{1}$

better opportunities than the school for a rational
$\overline{2}$ $\overline{3}$
consideration of the problems involved.

Items to be answered
1.
- *a. , for
- b. . For
- c. —for
- d. no punctuation needed
2.
- a. As good or better opportunities than
- b. as good opportunities or better than
- c. as good opportunities as or better than
- *d. better opportunities than
3.
- *a. rational
- b. radical
- c. reasonable
- d. realistic

G. The incomplete-alternatives variety[a]
An apple that has a sharp, pungent, but not disagreeably sour or bitter, taste is said to be (4).
a. p   b. q   *c. t   d. v   e. w

H. The combined response variety
In what order should these sentences be written in order to make a coherent paragraph?
- A. A sharp distinction must be drawn between table manners and sporting manners.
- B. This kind of handling of a spoon at the table, however, is likely to produce nothing more than an angry protest against squirting grapefruit juice about.
- C. Thus, for example, a fly ball caught by an outfielder in baseball or a completed pass in football is a subject for applause.
- D. Similarly, the dexterous handling of a spoon in golf to release a ball from a sand trap may win a championship match.
- E. But a biscuit or a muffin tossed and caught at the table produces scorn and reproach.
  - a. A, B, C, D, E
  - *b. A, C, E, D, B
  - c. A, E, C, D, B
  - d. B, E, D, C, A

[a]The numeral in parentheses indicates the number of letters in the correct answers (which in this case is "tart"). Using this convention serves to rule out borderline correct answers.

Adapted from "Writing the Test Item," by R. L. Ebel (1951) and A. G. Wesman (1971). In *Educational Measurement*, First and Second Editions. Reprinted with permission of the American Council on Education.

Box 8 • 1

of each one of these in this textbook. Most of the suggestions concerning item writing that are made in this chapter will be applicable to all varieties, however. If you would like more detail about a particular variety, you should read the *Educational Measurement* reference by Ebel (1951) or Wesman (1971) listed in the section of Additional Readings.

Advantages and Criticisms

Direct vs. indirect measurement Among measurement specialists, the multiple-choice item has been consistently regarded as a highly valuable, applicable, and versatile objective item type (e.g., Ebel, 1951, 1979; Gronlund, 1976; Lindquist, 1936b; Lindvall, 1967; Noll, Scannell, and Craig, 1979; Thorndike and Hagen, 1977). We can distinguish, however, between direct and indirect measures of educational outcomes (Lindvall, 1961). A multiple-choice test can be *a direct measure* of certain abilities. Well-written multiple-choice items can help to assess a pupil's ability to discriminate and make correct choices; to comprehend concepts, principles, and generalizations; to make judgments about and choices among various courses of action; to infer and reason; to compute; to interpret new data or new information; and to apply information and knowledge. The multiple-choice test cannot serve as a direct measure of certain important educational outcomes such as the ability for recollection (as opposed to recognition) of information under minimal prompting conditions, the ability to articulate explanations and give examples, the ability to produce and express unique or original ideas, the ability to organize personal thoughts, or the ability to display thought processes or patterns of reasoning. The preceding are important educational outcomes, and while many of them can be determined with various types of paper-and-pencil tests, other outcomes may require alternate testing techniques such as observing a pupil working alone or in a group, interviewing a pupil, or rating a pupil's production or creation. These latter techniques are discussed in Chapter 10.

In many cases, nevertheless, the multiple-choice format can serve as an *indirect* means of testing abilities (Lindvall, 1961) which can be directly observed only by rather complex, subjective, or time-consuming methods such as extended written assignments, construction of products, or systematic observation of pupils over extended periods of time. One way to judge the technical quality of indirect measures is by collecting data on the extent to which the direct and indirect procedures order or rank pupils in the same way. For instance, you could ask whether the scores on a multiple-choice test of English mechanics would provide the same relative ordering of a group of pupils as you would obtain from administering an extended response essay test. Although good writers usually have command of writing mechanics, and although you would expect the relative ordering on the multiple-choice and essay tests to be fairly close, the essay test measures writing ability more directly. Thus, in order to find out *how good a writer* a pupil is, you would need to examine actual samples of a pupil's writing rather than depend on a test of English mechanics.[3]

Advantages of multiple-choice items The following advantages of multiple-choice items are frequently listed.

1. Among the various types of response-choice items, the multiple-choice item can be used to test a greater variety of instructional objectives. The various types of capacities have been discussed above; it is useful to keep in mind the distinction between direct and indirect testing of certain objectives.
2. Multiple-choice tests[4] do not require the examinee to write out and elaborate their answers, minimizing the opportunity for less knowledgeable examinees to "bluff" or "dress-up" their answers (Wood, 1977). This lack of opportunity to write is considered a disadvantage to some (see below).

[3]The point being made concerns the distinction between *relative interpretation* and *absolute interpretation* of test scores. Further explanation in a somewhat different context is given in Chapter 11.
[4]These advantages apply to other response-choice items as well.

3. Multiple-choice tests focus on reading and thinking and thus do not require the writing process to occur under examination conditions. ". . . examination writing is far from being the highest form of the art; how could it be when nervous individuals have to write against the clock without a real opportunity to draft and work over their ideas. . . ?" (Wood, 1977, p. 196).

4. There is less of a chance for an examinee to guess the correct answer to a multiple-choice item than to a true-false item or to a poorly constructed matching exercise. The probability of blindly guessing the correct answer to a 3-choice item is 1/3; to a 4-choice item it is 1/4; etc.

5. If the distractors on multiple-choice items are based on common pupil errors or misconceptions, then the items may give "diagnostic insight" into difficulties an individual pupil may be experiencing. Note, however, that a single item is not a reliable basis on which to formulate a diagnosis.

Criticisms of multiple-choice items Wood (1977) has made a summary of the several criticisms of multiple-choice tests.

1. They require pupils to choose from among a fixed list of options, rather than to create or express their own ideas or solutions, a point discussed above. Exclusive reliance on multiple-choice testing may lead to students having little or no opportunity to write.

2. Poorly written multiple-choice items can be superficial, trivial, and limited to factual knowledge. (Of course, so can poorly constructed testing techniques of any type.)

3. Brighter pupils may detect flaws in multiple-choice items due to ambiguities of wording, divergent viewpoints, or additional knowledge of the subject, but since usually only one option on an item is keyed as correct, they may be penalized.

4. Multiple-choice items tend to be based on "standardized," "vulgarized," or "approved" knowledge and give students the impression that there is a single, correct answer to every problem. This may foster acceptance of correctness by fiat and misrepresent a body of knowledge as fixed and limited. (This could also be true of any type of testing procedure, but may show up in other forms in the criteria a teacher uses for scoring the pupils' response rather than in the formulation of the question or in the task setting aspects of the test.)

5. The type of examination used can shape the content and nature of instruction. Those objecting to multiple-choice testing frequently express concern that this format will shape education in undesirable ways.

If you would like to pursue these criticisms in more detail you may want to read the book and articles by Banesh Hoffman (1962, 1967a, 1967b) and the book by Jacques Barzun (1959). Robert Wood (1977) has summarized these and other arguments against multiple-choice testing and offers a defense of the technique, as does Ebel (1972, pp. 187–190).

When not to use multiple-choice items in classroom testing As I indicate in previous chapters (especially Chapter 4) *items must correspond to or match the instructional objectives you want them to test.* You would not, for example, substitute multiple-choice questions on English mechanics and grammar for actual samples of writing when an instructional objective calls for a pupil to write. Nor would you use multiple-choice items when the main intent is to have pupils organize their own ideas, develop their own logical arguments, express their own thoughts and feelings, or otherwise demonstrate their abilities of self-expression.

There are times, however, when the teacher might feel there is a choice between writing a completion or short-answer items or writing multiple-choice items; perhaps on the surface either format would seem appropriate. One of these instances is when the teacher is testing for simple recall of information. However, multiple-choice items should *not* be used in classroom testing when (Lindquist, 1936b):

1. there is only *one* correct answer and when that answer is a single word or number, or
2. the item calls for a numerical answer, as in computational problems, or
3. it is obvious that there are only two possible plausible options (e.g., yes vs. no, male vs. female, positive vs. negative, etc.), or
4. writing the answer doesn't take any longer than using an answer sheet or marking the answer to the multiple-choice question.

The reasons for these suggestions are that when the above conditions exist, it is difficult to write good items requiring the pupil to demonstrate the required degree of recollection and that (in the case of situations 2 and 4) there is no advantage to the multiple-choice format over the more direct, short-answer format, especially when recall is desired. There are exceptions to these suggestions, of course, as when a large number of pupils are to be tested, and machine-scoring will be used, or when there are many multiple-choice items but only one or two that fit the above circumstances. But it is often desirable in classroom testing to use a mixture of item formats with each item specifically designed to test the instructional objectives in the most appropriate manner.

Some writers recommend that multiple-choice items not be used when (a) the test will be used only once, and (b) there are few pupils. The reasons for this recommendation are (a) it is easier to formulate short answer questions than to write good multiple-choice items, and (b) with few students scoring will not be time-consuming. Even if the number of pupils

is small, if a teacher plans to teach the same subject at the same level in subsequent years, it is usually worthwhile to develop a "pool" of multiple-choice items over time which the teacher can then select for future tests.

Suggestions for Constructing Multiple-Choice Items

Getting Started

I follow Ebel's suggestion that you begin the task of writing multiple-choice items in much the same way you begin writing true-false items: Think of a segment of knowledge as expressed in the instructional materials and then write one or more statements that summarize the main idea(s) of this segment. These summaries of ideas become the basis on which you formulate items.

The task of formulating multiple-choice items from statements of main ideas involves three steps (Ebel, 1979):

1. Create the stem of the item by forming a question or an incomplete sentence that implies a question.
2. Write the correct answer to the question in the stem in as few words as possible.
3. Write distractors that are plausible to pupils lacking the degree of knowledge you want the item to assess.

The following illustrates this process. Recall from Chapter 7 that a paragraph was presented, and two main idea statements were written to summarize it. This was one of the idea statements:

> For the same amount of testing time, an objective test can cover a much broader range of content than an essay test.

The following are two multiple-choice items that can be written on the basis of this statement. As an exercise, you might want to write others based on this statement or on the second statement listed in Chapter 7.

Example 51.
When the amount of time to be used for testing is limited and the amount of content to be tested is extensive, objective items are preferred to essay items because objective items
   a. are easier to score.
   b. are less subject to bluffing.
*c. can cover more content.[5]

Example 52.
Suppose it has been decided that only 50 minutes can be devoted to testing a broad area of the curriculum and that the essay format is most appropriate. Which of the following best describes the type of essay(s) that should be on the test?
*a. Several focused questions of the restricted response variety.
   b. Two or three extended response essays, each having clearly specified time limits.
   c. A single essay question requiring an in-depth explanation of a carefully chosen and important subtopic.

Suggestions for Writing Multiple-Choice Items[6]

You should edit first drafts of all items carefully (see Figure 5.1). Several item-writing maxims can serve as guidelines for improving items in this editorial stage, and these maxims are the subject of this section.

The beginner should not be discouraged by the difficulty involved in writing good multiple-choice items. Writing items, as is true with other forms of functional writing, requires practice, frequent rewriting, and editing. This task is unlike free-wheeling, expressive writing in which few extrinsic standards apply. It will be most helpful as you write items if you have them "critiqued" by your instructor or classmates. Critics should keep in mind, however, that there is a lot of "ego" invested in

the creation of an item and that, to the uninitiated, critiquing someone's item is frequently perceived by that person as a personal affront. Nevertheless, criticizing items is a valuable aid to learning skills in item writing.

Writing the Stem of the Item

The stem of a multiple-choice item should ask (or imply) a direct question or should clearly formulate a problem. Incomplete sentences sometimes can be used to good advantage as stems (see Example 75), but experience indicates that beginners usually produce better items when the stem contains a direct question. A question is implied, of course, when an incomplete sentence is used, but frequently, incomplete sentences require the examinee to *mentally rephrase* the stem to make it a question. While older and brighter pupils are usually able to do this without difficulty, the younger, more average pupils and, perhaps, those with some learning difficulties may find that this "extra" process places an additional hurdle for them to overcome in expressing their acquired knowledge.

Direct question asked or implied   After having read the stem, a pupil should understand the nature and purpose of the item: in other words, what response the teacher expects. Consider these examples:

Poor: Incomplete stem

Example 53.
W. E. B. DuBois
*a. actively pressed for complete political participation and full rights for blacks.
   b. taught that the immediate need was for blacks to raise their economic status by learning trades and crafts.
   c. emphasized helping blacks through the National Urban League.
   d. founded the Association for the Study of Negro Life and History.

---

[5]Correct answers to multiple-choice items will appear with a bold face asterisk* throughout this book.
[6]See Appendix E for an alternative procedure for writing multiple-choice items.

To do	To avoid

1. If possible, write as a direct question.
2. If an incomplete sentence is used, be sure
   a. it implies a direct question.
   b. the alternatives come at the end (rather than in the middle) of the sentence.
3. Control the wording so that vocabulary and sentence structure are at a relatively low and non-technical level.
4. In items testing definitions, place the word or term in the stem and use definitions or descriptions as alternatives.
	1. Avoid extraneous, superfluous, and non-functioning words and phrases that are mere "window dressing."
	2. Avoid (or use sparingly) negatively worded items.
	3. Avoid phrasing the item so that the personal opinion of the examinee is an option.
	4. Avoid textbook wording and "textbookish" or stereotyped phraseology.
	5. Avoid "cluing" and "linking" items (i.e., having the correct answer to one item be clued or linked to the correctness of the answer to a previous item).

Sources: Ebel (1951, 1979); Greene, Jorgensen, & Gerberich (1942, 1943); Gronlund (1976); Lindquist (1936b); Lindvall (1967); Millman (1961); Sax (1974a); Stanley & Hopkins (1972); Thorndike & Hagen (1977); Wesman (1971).

Table 8 • 1 Suggestions for constructing multiple-choice items (with emphasis on how to formulate the stem of the item).

Better: Asks a question

Example 54.
Which of the following comes closest to expressing W. E. B. DuBois' ideas about priorities of the activities of blacks during the early 20th century?
a. Blacks should first improve their economic condition before becoming fully involved in politics.
b. Blacks should postpone the fight for equal access to higher education until their majority acquire saleable trade skills.
c. Blacks should withdraw from white society to form a separate state in which they have complete political and economic control.
*d. Blacks should become active, seeking out complete citizenship and full political participation immediately.

Example 53 is poor because the stem does not set a task or ask a question. The student must read the entire item and *infer* that the teacher must be trying to find out something about W. E. B. DuBois' ideas. Example 54 is better because the intent of the item is clear after the stem has been read.

A simple procedure can ascertain whether a stem is functioning appropriately: cover the options and read the stem. After reading the stem, can you tell what is expected? If not, the stem is incomplete and needs to be revised. An examinee should not be required to men-tally reconstruct the item and infer what you had in mind when you wrote it.

Put the alternatives at the end Failure to follow this rule can lead to problems similar to those encountered with completion items when the blank is not placed at the end of the incomplete sentence (Chapter 6). Consider these examples:

Poor: Options in middle of stem

Example 55.
Before the Civil War, the South's
*a. emphasis on staple-crop production
b. lack of a suitable supply of raw materials
c. short supply of personnel capable of operating the necessary machinery
was one of the major reasons manufacturing developed more slowly than it did in the North.

Better: Options at the end

Example 56.
Before the Civil War, manufacturing developed more slowly in the South than in the North. One of the major causes of this was the South's
*a. emphasis on staple-crop production.
b. lack of a suitable supply of raw materials.
c. short supply of personnel capable of operating the necessary machinery.

Failure to write an item so the alternatives come at the end of the sentence frequently leads to unnecessary re-reading on the part of the pupil. Younger children and those with learning problems are likely to become confused when this maxim is violated.

Control vocabulary and sentence structure When testing for subject-matter learning, you should make sure to word an item at a level suitable for the students being tested. You don't want unnecessarily complex sentence structure to interfere with students being able to display the learning they have acquired. The sentence length and the difficulty of vocabulary of an item can make it unreasonably hard or easy, quite independent of the content being tested: for example, tests taken by deaf and hard-of-hearing pupils who frequently have relatively large language and vocabulary deficits. These pupils may well have acquired the specific knowledge, concept, or principle being tested, but the phrasing of the item may interfere with their being able to demonstrate this knowledge (cf. Suppes, 1974).

The following examples illustrate how a simple information item can be complicated by uncontrolled language.

Poor: Unnecessary wordiness

Example 57.
Given the present day utilization of the automobile in urban settings, which of the following represents an important contribution of Garrett A. Morgan's genius?
  a. automobile safety belts
  b. crosswalk markers
*c. traffic lights
  d. vulcanized rubber tires

Better: More concise

Example 58.
Which of the following did Garrett A. Morgan invent?
  a. automobile safety belts
  b. crosswalk markers
*c. traffic lights
  d. vulcanized rubber tires

Avoid extraneous words and "window dressing" The poor item above demonstrates how extraneous wording can complicate an item unnecessarily. Less obvious is the use of words that tend to "dress-up" a stem to make it sound as though it is testing something of practical importance (Ebel, 1965). Often such window dressing creeps into an item when an item writer is struggling to measure higher-level cognitive abilities (e.g., applications).

Poor: Window dressing

Example 59.
There are ten pre-service teachers in the Department of Education who recently registered for the college-sponsored weight loss program. At the beginning of the program each was weighed, and the ten had a mean weight of 139.4 pounds. Suppose there were but three men in this group, and their mean weight was 180 pounds. What was the mean weight of the women at the beginning of the program?
  a. 115.0 pounds
*b. 122.0 pounds
  c. 140.0 pounds
  d. 159.7 pounds

Better: More concise

Example 60.
Ten persons have a mean weight of 139.4 pounds. The mean weight of three of them is 180 pounds. What is the mean weight of the remaining seven persons?
  a. 115.0 pounds
*b. 122.0 pounds
  c. 140.0 pounds
  d. 159.7 pounds

The words used in an item should be functional. Sometimes names, places, and other "facts" about a situation are necessary pieces of information: *including them in an item provides the pupil with the basis on which to determine which alternative is correct.* This is illustrated by Example 61.

Acceptable: Important facts included

Example 61.
A company owns a fleet of cars for which it paid all expenses including fuel. Three readily available types of gasoline were tested to see which was giving better mileage. The results are shown below in miles per gallon.

	Mean	Median
Type A	19.1	18.5
Type B	18.5	19.1
Type C	18.8	18.9

Assuming they all cost the same, which type of gasoline should the company use?
*a. Type A
 b. Type B
 c. Type C

Avoid negatively worded stems Items should be stated positively if possible. Negatively worded stems, such as, "which of the following is not . . ." tend to confuse examinees, especially younger or less careful pupils. Even well-prepared pupils may overlook the "not" in a question when it appears on an examination.

Poor: Negatively phrased stem

Example 62.
Sometimes a teacher finds it necessary to use a mild form of punishment. When this occurs, which of the following should not happen?
 a. Children should not believe all of their behavior is bad.
 b. Children should understand the reason(s) why they are being punished.
*c. Children should understand that the teacher, not the children, controls when the punishment will end.

Better: Positively phrased stem

Example 63.
Sometimes a teacher finds it necessary to use a mild form of punishment. When this occurs, it is important that the children understand

 a. that it may be a long time before happy times return to the classroom.
*b. the reason(s) why they are being punished.
 c. that the teacher, not the children, controls when the punishment will end.
 d. All of the above correctly complete the sentence.

If negatively worded items *are* used with older learners (a) use the negative in only the stem or the options (not both) and (b) either underline the negative or place it in CAPITAL LETTERS.

Avoid requiring personal opinion You may want to ask a pupil's personal opinion but do not do it in the context of a multiple-choice test where the examinee needs to select one option as best or correct. Since everyone is entitled to an opinion, every option would be correct in an opinion item. Use essays to evaluate the manner in which a pupil uses evidence to support an opinion, but don't score the opinion or the position taken (see Chapter 6).

Poor: Answer a matter of personal opinion

Example 64.
Which of the following men contributed most toward the improvement of the self-confidence of black people?
 a. W. E. B. DuBois
 b. Eugene K. Jones
 c. Booker T. Washington
 d. Carter G. Woodson

There is no single correct answer to the above question since each man's contributions can be judged and evaluated in different ways. It could form the basis for an extended response essay or a term paper in which the pupil supports the opinion with evidence and logical argument.

Avoid textbook wording As with true-false items, copying sentences verbatim from the text results in a poor item because: (a) Frequently, a sentence loses its meaning when taken out of context, (b) such a practice encourages rote memory of textbook material instead of comprehension, (c) awkwardly worded items with implausible distractors are likely to result, and (d) learners who do not have an understanding of the underlying concept or principle may obtain clues to the correct answer. New, perhaps unfamiliar, wording of the stem and correct option may be used to test a deeper comprehension of a concept or principle (Lindquist, 1936b). The procedure suggested earlier in this chapter of stating main ideas of textbook passages in your own work and rephrasing these as questions is a practical one for avoiding "textbookish" items.

The poor item below is weak because most introductory statistics books associate the term "typical" with "median" and often use "income examples" to illustrate the application of the median. Knowing these superficial facts, the examinee can mark "b" without demonstrating an in-depth understanding of this statistical index. Item 66 tests a different objective but is better because it presents a novel situation and thus is more directed toward application of the concept.

Poor: Uses textbookish wording

Example 65.
The annual incomes of five employees are: $8,000; $8,000; $10,000; $11,000; and $25,000, respectively. Which index should be used to summarize the typical employee's income?
 a. mean
*b. median
 c. mode

Better: Novel situation for students

Example 66.
Over several years, a teacher keeps a record of how long it takes students to complete the 50-question final exam. The mean time was 56 minutes and the median time was 20 minutes. The teacher used this information to set the time limits for future administrations of the exam.

The teacher set the time limits for the test as 20 minutes, reasoning that the typical student could complete the test in that time. In all likelihood, these time limits are:
 a. just about right
*b. too short
 c. too long

When testing older students, it may be helpful to use stereotyped phraseology, certain "pat phrases" or verbal associations *to make distractors plausible* to those pupils lacking the required degree of knowledge. These phrases may be put into the stem or into the distractors. The better item above, although it is a bit wordy and places a premium on reading, does just this. The examinee who interprets the correctness of using a particular statistical index only on the basis of the verbal association of "typical" with "median" will fail to notice that the teacher who sets the time limit for the test at 20 minutes will be assuring that only half of the class will have enough time to complete it; surely this is inappropriate for a classroom test.[7]

Create independent items: avoid "linking" and "cluing" With the possible exception of interpretative exercises,[8] each item should test a distinct performance and the correct answer to an item should not be clued by another item.

Two flaws to avoid are linking and cluing. *Linking* means that the answer to one (or more) item(s) is dependent on obtaining the correct answer to a previous item such as occurs when a computational result from one item is needed to answer a subsequent item. *Cluing* means that the correct answer to one item is found in (or strongly suggested by) the contents of another item. Linked items frequently result in doubly penalizing a student for an incorrect answer, as illustrated here:

---

[7]The median and its properties are discussed in Chapter 3.
[8]Interpretative exercises are discussed in Chapter 9.

State of pupil's knowledge:	Score on two independent items	Score on two "linked" items:
Knows neither item	0	0
Knows first only	1	1
Knows second only	1	0
Knows both items	2	2

Both linking and cluing result in errors of measurement that are not independent.

Preceding item

Example 67.
The perimeter of a rectangle is 350 centimeters. The length of the rectangle is 3 centimeters longer than the width. What is the width?
  a. 18.7
*b. 86.0
  c. 89.0
  d. 116.7

Poor subsequent item: linked to Item 67

Example 68.
What is the area of the rectangle described in Example 67?
  a. 1050 sq. cm.
  b. 7396 sq. cm.
*c. 7654 sq. cm.
  d. 8188 sq. cm.

Better subsequent item: independent of Item 67

Example 69.
The width of a rectangle is 4 centimeters and the length is 3 centimeters. What is the area?
  a. 9 sq. cm.
*b. 12 sq. cm.
  c. 16 sq. cm.
  d. 17 sq. cm.

    Examples 67 and 68 illustrate linked items. The "preceding item" (Item 67) is primarily computational. The poor "subsequent item" (Item 68) is linked to it. A pupil could make an incorrect computation in Item 67, obtaining 89.0, for example. Having already made a mistake in Item 67, the pupil would get Item 68 wrong also because $89 \times (89 + 3) = 8188$ is keyed as the wrong answer. One solution to the problem is shown in the better subsequent item: A new numerical value is presented for the pupil's interpretation and the item as a whole is independent of the preceding item.

    It should be noted that items need not be linked to provide clues to other items. It is helpful to review all the items in a test to see if any item suggests an answer to other items.

Definitions go in the alternatives A common tactic for the novice item writer to use in attempting to test a pupil's knowledge of special terms or other vocabulary is to place a paraphrase of the definition in the stem and to have the pupil select the correct term, phrase, or word from among a list presented as alternatives. The problem with this approach is that it increases the likelihood that pupils will get the answer correct by only superficial knowledge of the term in question. Pupils can obtain the correct answer through knowing that the words in the definition "look like" (seem similar to) a term in the set of alternatives (Lindquist, 1936b). If displaying a more in-depth knowledge of a term is desirable, it is better to put the term in the *stem* and suggest various definitions in the alternatives. The item can be made easier or harder depending on how similar the alternatives are. This is illustrated below:

Poor: definition stem

Example 70.
The increase in length per unit of length of a metal rod for each degree rise in temperature (Centigrade) is known as the
*a. coefficient of linear expansion of the metal.
  b. elasticity of the metal.
  c. specific heat of the metal.
  d. surface tension of the metal.

Better: definition options

Example 71.
The coefficient of linear expansion of a metal rod is the

a. increase in length of the rod when its temperature is raised 1°C.
*b. increase in length when the temperature is raised 1°C divided by the total length of the rod at the original temperature.
c. ratio of its length at 100°C to its length at 0°C.
d. rise in temperature (degree Centigrade) which is necessary to cause a 1 per cent expansion in length of the rod.

Source: Adapted from Lindquist (1936b), pp. 145–146.

Improving the Set of Alternatives

The alternatives of a multiple-choice item present response choices to the examinee. In order to avoid ambiguity to the knowledgeable pupil and in order for distractors to appear plausible to less knowledgeable pupils, the alternatives should be appropriate to the stem. In this way, the item functions better as a complete unit. Suggestions for improving the quality of the alternatives are summarized in Table 8.2. They are discussed in more detail below.

Functional alternatives The point of plausibility has been mentioned previously. Notice that this maxim calls for using from three to five *functional alternatives.* By this it is meant that each alternative attracts at least one of the pupils who do not have the requisite degree of knowledge. The item may have five alternatives, but if two of them are easily eliminated by even the most superficial learner, and if only the remaining three are seriously considered plausible, then in reality the item has only three functional alternatives. For practical purposes you may as well eliminate the two non-functional alternatives.

Teachers sometimes ask if each multiple-choice item should have the same number of alternatives and, if so, how many should there be. It has long been recognized that for classroom testing there is no virtue in having the same number of alternatives for each item (Lindquist, 1936b; Ebel, 1965). If you can write five functional alternatives, then the item is more likely to distinguish those who have the desired degree of knowledge from those who do not. But the problem is that the more alternatives you try to write, the harder it will be to make them functional. Two functional alternatives are permissible, but with only two

To do	To avoid
1. In general strive for creating three to five functional alternatives. 2. All alternatives should be homogeneous and appropriate to the stem. 3. Put repeated words and phrases the stem. 4. Use consistent and correct punctuation in relation to the stem. 5. Arrange alternatives in a list format rather than in tandem. 6. Arrange alternatives in a logical or meaningful order. 7. All distractors should be grammatically correct with respect to the stem.	1. Avoid overlapping alternatives. 2. Avoid making the alternatives a collection of true-false items. 3. Avoid using "not given," "none of the above," etc. as an alternative in *best-answer* type of items (use only with *correct-answer* variety). 4. Avoid using "all of the above"; limit its use to the *correct-answer* variety. 5. Avoid using verbal clues in the alternatives. 6. Avoid using technical terms, unknown words or names, and "silly" terms or names as distractors. 7. Avoid making it harder to eliminate a distractor than to choose the keyed alternative.

Sources: Ebel (1951, 1979); Greene, Jorgensen, & Gerberich (1942, 1943); Gronlund (1976); Lindquist (1936b); Lindvall (1967); Millman (1961); Sax (1974a); Stanley & Hopkins (1972); Thorndike & Hagen (1977); Wesman (1971).

Table 8 • 2 Suggestions for improving the quality of the alternatives in multiple-choice items.

alternatives, guessing is likely to play a major role. As a rule of thumb, strive to write between three and five functional alternatives. This means that each item will have between two and four distractors. Don't waste your time trying to create the same number of alternatives for each item if by so doing you are creating "fillers" or non-functional distractors. Give yourself and your students a break! (Incidentally, if a separate answer sheet is used for machine scoring, check to see how many spaces are allowed per item and adjust the number of alternatives accordingly.)

Homogeneous alternatives This is essentially the same maxim as for matching exercises. The alternatives should be homogeneous in the sense that each should be a member of the same set of "things." Further, each alternative should be appropriate to the stem. For example, if the stem is intended to require pupils to identify someone's name, then all alternatives should be names and all names should be appropriate to the question. This point should be clear if you compare the alternatives to Items 72 and 73.

Poor: heterogeneous options

Example 72.
What is the official state bird of Pennsylvania?
 a. mountain laurel
 b. Philadelphia
*c. ruffed grouse
 d. Susquehanna

Better: options belong to same category

Example 73.
What is the official state bird of Pennsylvania?
 a. goldfinch
 b. robin
*c. ruffed grouse
 d. wild turkey

Although lack of homogeneity is one of the primary reasons why distractors do not function, adjusting the degree of homogeneity is one way to control the difficulty level of an item. This latter point is illustrated in the first section of this chapter. In general, the more homogeneous the alternatives, the more difficult the item. As indicated in connection with matching items, homogeneity in the sense described above is also a function of the perceptions of the group being tested. Item 73 here could be made more homogeneous (and more difficult) by specifying the scientific names of several species of grouse. The items in the first section illustrate this point, too: Item 1 may appear homogeneous to younger pupils, but will likely appear quite heterogeneous to older pupils.

Put repeated words in the stem In general, it is helpful to put into the stem certain words or phrases which would need repeating in each alternative. This helps to make the stem more complete and to reduce the amount of reading required of the examinee. To accomplish this suggestion it is sometimes helpful to use an incomplete sentence as a stem as shown below in the elementary school science item numbered 75. But as Item 76 shows, the same purpose is accomplished by rephrasing the question.

Poor: words repeated in options

Example 74.
Which of the following is the best definition of a *seismograph*?
 a. An apparatus for measuring sound waves.
 b. An apparatus for measuring heat waves.
*c. An apparatus for measuring earthquake waves.
 d. An apparatus for measuring ocean waves.

Better: Alternative I

Example 75.
A *seismograph* is an apparatus for measuring
*a. earthquake waves.
 b. heat waves.
 c. ocean waves.
 d. sound waves.

Better: Alternative II

Example 76.
What type of waves does a *seismograph* measure?
*a. earthquake   c. ocean
 b. heat   d. sound

Consistent, correct punctuation   If the stem asks a question directly (and, therefore, ends in a question mark), the options can be either (a) complete sentences, (b) single words, terms, names, phrases, or (c) other incomplete sentences. The complete sentences should begin with a capital letter and end with an appropriate punctuation mark (period, question mark, exclamation point) as in Item 54. Don't use a semicolon or other inappropriate terminal punctuation. If the options to a direct question stem are of the second or third kinds, no terminal punctuation is used, but you should use a consistent rule for capitalizing the initial word in each option: Throughout the test, either capitalize all initial words or capitalize no initial word (except a proper noun, of course). This principle is illustrated by Item 61 and Item 76.

If the stem is an incomplete sentence, then each option needs to be a plausible word or phrase that completes the sentence. Each option, therefore, should begin with a lower case letter (except if the initial word is a proper noun) and should end with the appropriate terminal punctuation (period, exclamation point, question mark). An example is Item 75. There are exceptions to these rules, of course, as in Item 77 which is part of a test on using punctuation correctly.

Exception to above rule on using the same punctuation for each option

Example 77.
Julia became very frightened and shouted,
 a. "Please save me."
 b. "Please save me?"
*c. "Please save me!"

Arrangement of alternatives   Unless the alternatives are very short, they are less con-

fusing and easier to read if they are arranged one below the other in list form rather than in tandem or beside one another.

Poor: Tandem arrangement of options

Example 78.
A test-retest reliability coefficient is calculated from test scores separated by a one-week time interval. Which of the following would likely *lower* the numerical value of this coefficient? (a) Differences in the extent to which examinees have learned the information required to answer the particular items on the test. (b) The fact that some examinees have better command of general test-taking skills than do others. (c) The fact that a few examinees do better on the particular types of items used. *(d) Some examinees became upset during the second test administration. (e) All of the above would likely lower the test-retest reliablility coefficient for a particular test.

If possible, alternatives should be arranged in a logical or meaningful order, such as: order of magnitude or size, degree to which they reflect a given quality, chronologically, and/or alphabetically. This arrangement makes locating the correct answer easier for the knowledgeable examinee, reduces reading and search time, and lessens the chance that careless errors will be made. Remember, you don't want to have the format of the item "get in the way" of a pupil who knows the answer.

Acceptable: options in a discernable order

Example 79.
Which of the following is made from the shells of tiny animals?
*a. chalk
 b. clay
 c. shale

Example 80.
A pupil's percentile rank is 4. What is the corresponding *stanine*?
*a. 1   c. 3
 b. 2   d. 4

Plausible distractors   This has been discussed previously. Many of the suggestions which follow are directed toward this goal.

Grammatically correct relationship to the stem Don't clue the correct answer or permit distractors to be eliminated on superficial bases such as lack of subject-verb agreement, inappropriate indefinite article, singular/plural confusion, etc. The indefinite article *a* in Item 81 below, for example, gives the pupil the clue that alternative (c) is correct since the other two alternatives begin with vowels and thus require *an* as the indefinite article. In Item 83, the conjunction *when* is appropriate only to the phrasing of option (b). In Item 85, a plural verb form in the stem clues the pupil that more than one definition is to be chosen.

Poor: grammatical incorrectness clues the answer

Example 81.
An angle of 90° is called a
  a. acute angle.
  b. obtuse angle.
*c. right angle.

Example 83.
Green plants may lose their color when
  a. are forming flowers.
*b. grown in the dark.
  c. are placed in strong light.
  d. temperature drops.

Example 85.
Which of the following are called scarfs?
  a. band of cloth worn around the neck
  b. type of wood joint
*c. both (a) and (b) are scarfs.

Better: all options have grammatically correct relation to stem

Example 82.
Angles of 90° are called
  a. acute angles.
  b. obtuse angles.
*c. right angles.

Example 84.
Green plants may lose their color when
  a. flowers are formed.
*b. grown in the dark.
  c. placed in strong light.
  d. surrounding temperatures drop.

Example 86.
What is a *scarf*?
  a. band of cloth worn around the neck
  b. type of wood joint
*c. Both (a) and (b) are scarfs.

Poor: overlapping options

Example 87.
What is the population of Modesto, CA?
  a. over 60,000
  b. over 40,000
*c. over 30,000

Example 89.
Why is there a shortage of water in the Lower Basin of the Colorado River?
  a. The hot sun shines almost always.
  b. There is a wide, hot desert.
  c. The temperatures are very high.
*d. All of the above are reasons why.

Example 91.
How long does a *perennial* plant live?
*a. It continues to live year after year.
  b. It lives for only one growing season.
  c. It needs to be replanted each year.
  d. It dies after the first year.

Better: options are distinct

Example 88.
The population of Modesto, CA, is approximately
*a. 60,000.
  b. 40,000.
  c. 30,000.

Example 90.
Why is there a shortage of water in the Lower Basin of the Colorado River?
*a. There is low rainfall, and there are only a few tributaries to the Colorado River.
  b. Water is soaked up quickly by the desert.
  c. A dam in the Upper Colorado River made the lower part dry up.

Example 92.
How long does a *perennial* plant live?
*a. It continues to live for several years.
  b. It lives for only two years.
  c. It lives for only one year.

Overlapping alternatives Each alternative should be distinct and not a subset of another alternative. When alternatives include one another, the less knowledgeable, but testwise examinee will be provided with clues to the correct answer. Several examples of this flaw are on p. 205. Option (c) in Item 87 includes (a) and (b): even if you don't know the correct answer you would choose it. In Item 89, options (a), (b), and (c) essentially say the same thing so that option (d) can be chosen even if one doesn't know anything about the need for water in the Lower Colorado River Basin. Similarly, for Item 91, (b), (c), and (d) all say essentially the same thing, but here "all of the above" is not one of the choices. The testwise pupil will know that option (a) must be correct.

Avoid a collection of true-false alternatives A frequent cause of this type of flaw is that the item writer has not had a clear problem or question in mind. Item 93, below, illustrates this.

Poor: options a collection of T–F statements

Example 93.
Reliability is
*a. increased by making the test longer.
b. decreased by making the test longer.
c. unrelated to the test's standard deviation.
d. the same as the test's standard error of measurement.

Better: stem poses a problem

Example 94.
Which of the following situations will likely result in an increase in a test's reliability coefficient?
*a. A 40 question test is *lengthened* to 50 questions.
b. A 50 question test is *shortened* to 40 questions.
c. The coefficient is recomputed using *only the highest scoring* 27% of the examinees.

In Item 93, it is difficult to identify any single question to which an examinee must respond. All options are related only by the fact that they could begin with the phrase, "Reliability is . . . ." Options (b), (c), and (d), when used with that phrase, become false statements. This item really embeds three ideas: how test length affects reliability, how group variability (standard deviation) affects reliability, and the relationship between a reliability coefficient and the standard error of measurement.[9] Only one of these ideas should be selected and used as a basis for a revised item as is done with Item 94.

None of the above This option should be used only sparingly and never with the "best answer" variety of multiple-choice item. The very nature of a best-answer question leads the pupil to believe that, although all of the options are to some degree incorrect, one of them is "best." It seems unreasonable to require the pupil to choose "none of the above" under these conditions.

It does make sense, however, to use "none of the above" with some "correct answer" questions. Since the pupil is to choose only a completely correct answer, it may be reasonable that none of the choices presented to the pupil are completely correct. Most of the time this option would be likely used in subject areas such as arithmetic, certain English mechanics, spelling, and the like where a single, completely correct answer can be definitely established and defended. Some professionals recommend using it only when persons are more likely to solve a problem first before looking at the options (as opposed to searching through the distractors before being able to proceed with the solution to the problem) (Wood, 1977).

[9]Understanding these concepts of reliability is not necessary at this point. They are explained, however, in Chapter 15.

Two problems associated with using "none of these" are (1) pupils may not believe that this answer can be correct and not take it seriously and (2) pupils may be given credit for an item when in fact they arrived at the wrong answer (Ebel, 1951). To avoid the first problem, use "none of these" as the correct answer to a few easy items near the beginning of the test. It may then be used as either a correct or incorrect answer later in the test. The second problem is handled by using "none of these" as a *correct answer* in an item when the distractors encompass most of the wrong answers that can be expected (see Item 95 below) or using it as a *distractor* for those items in which most of the probable wrong answers cannot be incorporated into the distractors (Ebel, 1951) (see Item 96).

Acceptable uses of "none of the above":

as a correct answer

Example 95.
What is the sum?

106
+ 21
—
?

a. 27
b. 106
c. 327
*d. None of the above

as a plausible distractor

Example 96.
What is the sum?

46
47
+ 48
—
?

a. 161
b. 171
*c. 141
d. None of the above

More than likely, items such as 95 and 96 would be better as completion (open-ended) items than as multiple-choice items. Testing for this

information with completion items would permit a teacher to check the pupil's wrong answers to determine *why* the pupil responded incorrectly; then the teacher can design effective instructional remediation.

Two final comments on this point. Do not use "none of these" as a "filler" in an attempt to increase the number of distractors. Remember, distractors must be plausible. Second, as an option "none of the above" is probably less confusing to older pupils than to younger ones.

All of the above This option, if used at all, should be limited to "correct answer" varieties. It cannot be used with "best answer" varieties because "all of the options" cannot be simultaneously "best." Two further difficulties arise: (1) pupils who know that the first option is correct may simply choose it and inadvertently go on to the next item; (2) pupils who know that 2 out of 4 options are correct can choose "all of the above" without having knowledge of the correctness of the third option. This option can also be confusing to elementary and junior high students. Generally, the recommendation is to avoid using it. An item with multiple answers may be rewritten as two or more items.

Verbal clues Verbal clues in the alternative frequently lead the less knowledgeable but verbally able student to the correct answer. Verbal clues include using: overlapping alternatives, silly or absurd distractors, "clang" or other associations between words in the stem and in the correct alternatives, repetition or resemblance between the correct alternative and the stem, and specific determiners. Item 97, for example, uses the word "agriculture" in both stem and alternative and creates a "Who is buried in Grant's tomb?" type of question. Similarly, in Item 98, one can easily associate the terms "educational testing" and "educational measurement" to come up with the correct answer without knowing the contents of any of the journals listed.

Poor: association of stem and answer

Example 97.
Which government agency is most concerned with our nation's agricultural policies?
*a. Department of Agriculture
 b. Department of Education
 c. Department of the Interior
 d. Department of Labor

Poor: resemblance of answers and stem

Example 98.
In which journal can you find recent research articles on educational testing practices?
 a. *American Psychologist*
*b. *Journal of Educational Measurement*
 c. *Journal of Abnormal Child Psychology*
 d. *Memory and Cognition*

Poor: specific-determiners

Example 99.
Which of the following was one of E. L. Thorndike's contributions to educational measurement?
 a. He invented all of the types of multiple-choice items now in use.
 b. He constructed every educational test published between 1900 and 1920.
*c. He helped educational testing to gain scientific respectability.

Specific-determiners are words that over qualify a statement in a manner to make it always true or always false. We saw how these operated with true-false items in Chapter 7, but they can occur in multiple-choice items as well. An example is shown as Item 99. Alternatives (a) and (b) can be easily eliminated: no one "invented all" of anything nor would anyone "construct every . . . test published." After these are eliminated only option (c) remains.

Technical and unfamiliar words Persons writing multiple-choice items sometimes use highly technical or unfamiliar words as distractors. Such words are usually beyond the knowledge-base of the pupils; thus these words may require more ability to reject the wrong answer than needed to choose the correct

answer (Ebel, 1951). Some studies indicate, however, that examinees view options containing unfamiliar technical words as less plausible, thereby making such alternatives non-functional. In one study, when college students were instructed to mark answers to items for which (unknown to them) no real answer existed, students chose options containing familiar, nontechnical words more frequently than options containing either (a) familiar technical words, (b) vaguely familiar technical words, or (c) unfamiliar technical words (Strang, 1977).

Don't make a distractor too plausible Incorrect alternatives sometimes may be made so plausible that generally good students get the item wrong, while less able students respond correctly. (Such items are said to be negatively discriminating—see Chapter 11.) The good student's knowledge, while perhaps normally sufficient for selection of the correct answer when embedded in another context, may be insufficient for rejection of all the distractors in a particular item (Lindquist, 1936a). The American history item in Box 8.2 illustrates this. Thus, while an item should be considered a test of a student's ability to eliminate the distractors as well as the ability to select the correct answer, the ability required to *eliminate* the incorrect answer should not be greater than the ability needed to make a *direct choice* of the correct answer (Lindquist, 1936b).

Wording the Correct Alternative

The correct alternative should be worded so that (a) those pupils without the requisite knowledge are not clued as to the correct answer and (b) those pupils who have the requisite knowledge are able to select the correct answer.

1. In general, there should be only one correct or best answer to a multiple-choice item While it is possible to write items that have more than one correct alternative (see Box 8.1), such items may not function as

The Effect of Insufficient Learning or Understanding

The failure of an item to function because of insufficient or wrong learning is something beyond the control of the test constructor. . . .

What was one of the important immediate results of the War of 1812?
1. The introduction of a period of intense sectionalism (39%)
2. The destruction of the United States Bank (7%)
3. The defeat of the Jeffersonian Party (7%)
4. The final collapse of the Federalist Party (43%)
(4 per cent omitted the item)

The correct response to this item is number 4. Nevertheless, the pupils who selected the first and incorrect response were, on the average, superior in general achievement to those who selected the correct response (number 4). Again, the pupils selecting the first and incorrect response apparently did so because of positive but insufficient learning. They knew that a period of intense sectionalism did set in before the middle of the century, and therefore chose the first response. Apparently they did not know, or failed to recall, that a short period of intense nationalism was an immediate result of the Second War with Great Britain, and that this war, therefore, could not be considered as "introducing" an era of sectional strife. Other pupils, with less knowledge in general, were able to select the correct response since they were not attracted to the first response by a certain knowledge that intense sectionalism did develop in the nineteenth century. (It should be noted, however, that for an abler group of pupils, capable of making the judgment called for, this same item might have shown a high positive index of discrimination). . . .

The Effect of Wrong Learning

Wrong learning, as well as insufficient learning, on the part of the pupils for whom the test is intended may cause an item in that test to show a negative index of discrimination. . . .

In the second half of the fifteenth century the Portuguese were searching for an all-water route to India because
1. They wished to rediscover the route traveled by Marco Polo (4%)
2. The Turks had closed the old routes (59%)
3. The Spanish had proved that it was possible to reach the east by sailing westward (10%)
4. An all-water route would make possible greater profits (26%)
(1 per cent omitted the item)

It will be noted that more than half of the pupils selected response number 2. The negative index of discrimination indicates furthermore that the average achievement of the pupils who selected this response was superior to that of the 25 per cent of the pupils who chose the correct response (number 4). Authoritative historians no longer would accept the second response as a sufficient explanation of Portuguese attempts to round Africa, nor would they deny that response number 4 is the best of those given. An analysis of current textbooks in American history, however, will reveal that these lag behind research and that many of them still present the now disproved explanation: "The Turks closed the old routes." It is not surprising, therefore, that the superior pupils are more likely to select this response than those who have made little or no effective attempt to learn the facts contained in their textbooks. This being the case, the inclusion of this item in the test not only contributed nothing to its effectiveness but even detracted from it. There can be little question, however, that the item is free from technical imperfections or ambiguities, and that it does hold the pupil responsible for an established fact of considerable significance in history.

Adapted from *The Construction and Use of Achievement Examinations*, edited by H. E. Hawkes, E. F. Lindquist, and C. R. Mann, pp. 56–63. Copyright © 1936 by American Council on Education. Used by permission of Houghton Mifflin Company.

Box 8 • 2

intended, especially for elementary and junior high school students. Students may, for example, mark the first correct alternative they encounter and skip to the next item without considering all of the alternatives. Some beginning item writers attempt to compensate for this behavior by using the combined-response variety of multiple-choice items (Box 8.1), or by using "all of the above." This usually results in poorer quality items.

2. Be sure that competent authorities can agree that the answer keyed as correct (or best) is in fact correct (or best) Violating this rule is likely to result in teacher conflict with the more able student (or student's parent). Further, for the teacher to insist there is only one correct answer when pupils also see a logical and equally correct alternative is likely to lead pupils to view the teacher as arbitrary and capricious. To avoid such embarassment have a knowledgeable colleague review the correctness of your items before you use them.

3. The correct alternative should be a grammatically correct response to the stem The knowledgeable student is faced with a conflict if the content of the keyed response is correct, but the grammar is incorrect.

4. Check over the entire test to ensure that the correct alternative appears with approximately equal frequency in each possible response position Use the answer key you develop to tabulate the number of a's, b's, c's, etc. that are keyed as correct. Sometimes teachers favor one or two positions (e.g., "b" and "c") for the correct answers. Students will quickly catch on and this reduces the validity of the test. Also, avoid repetitive, easily learned patterns, such as, aabbccdd . . . , abcdabcd . . . , etc. By using a scoring stencil,

you can score exams just as quickly without such patterns.

5. Avoid phrasing the correct alternative in a "textbookish" or stereotyped manner To test for comprehension and understanding requires at least a paraphrasing of textbook statements. Students quickly learn the idiosyncratic or stereotyped manner in which the textbook or the teacher's classroom presentation phrases certain propositions. Items that reflect such idiosyncracies encourage students to select answers that "sound right" to them, but which they do not understand. If you follow the suggestions for getting started at the beginning of the chapter, you are less likely to write stereotypic items. For more mature students, however, stereotyped phrases in the *distractors* that have a "ring of truth" may serve to distinguish those students who have grasped the concept from those with only superficial

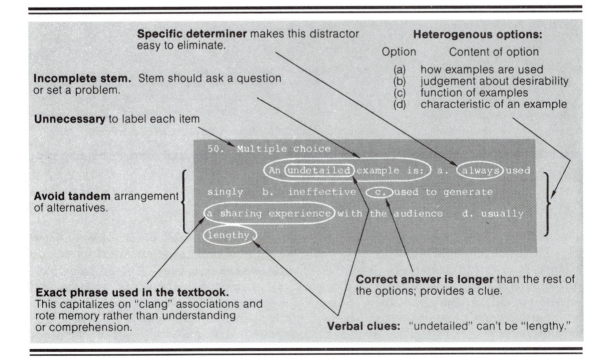

Specific determiner makes this distractor easy to eliminate.

Incomplete stem. Stem should ask a question or set a problem.

Unnecessary to label each item

Avoid tandem arrangement of alternatives.

Heterogenous options:

Option	Content of option
(a)	how examples are used
(b)	judgement about desirability
(c)	function of examples
(d)	characteristic of an example

50. Multiple choice

An (undetailed) example is: a. (always) used singly   b. ineffective   (c.) used to generate (a sharing experience) with the audience   d. usually (lengthy.)

Exact phrase used in the textbook. This capitalizes on "clang" associations and rote memory rather than understanding or comprehension.

Correct answer is longer than the rest of the options; provides a clue.

Verbal clues: "undetailed" can't be "lengthy."

Box 8 • 3

knowledge (Ebel, 1979). I would recommend using this tactic with senior high school and college students, but not with elementary school pupils.

6. The correct alternative should be of the same overall length as the distractors Item writers sometimes make the correct option longer by phrasing it in a more completely explained or more qualified manner than the incorrect options. The testwise student can pick up on this and mark the longest or most complete answer without having the requisite knowledge.

7. An advantage of a multiple-choice test is that it reduces the amount of time required for writing answers and uses this time to **increase the content coverage of the test** *Don't defeat this purpose by requiring students to write out their answers.* Have the students either mark (circle, check, etc.) the letter of the alternative chosen, write the letter on a "blank" next to the stem created for that purpose, or use a separate answer sheet. Separate answer sheets are not recommended for children below fourth or fifth grade (cf. Aleyideino, 1968; Beck, 1974; Cashen & Ramseyer, 1969; Davis & Trimble, 1978; Gaffney & Maguire, 1971; Moss, Cole, Trent, 1979; Muller, Calhoun, & Orling, 1972; Ramseyer & Cashen, 1971). However, should your state have a testing program that uses separate answer sheets with tests in the primary grades, it might be helpful to use answer sheets with some classroom tests in order to give the children practice.

Summary

The following statements summarize the main points of this chapter.

1. The suggestions for writing multiple-choice items represent the "clinical lore" of experienced item writers and nearly all of them can be subsumed under the Three Fundamental Principles in Chapter 6.

2. A *multiple-choice item* consists of one or more introductory sentences followed by two more suggested responses from which the examinee chooses the correct answer. Varieties are illustrated in Box 8.1.

3. All the parts of a multiple-choice item (see Figure 8.1) must fulfill their functions before the item as a whole will work:

   a. The *stem's* function is to ask a question, set the task to be performed, or state the problem to be solved.

   b. The *alternatives* (responses or options) suggest to the examinee responses to the question or problem specified by the stem. One alternative is usually the correct or best response.

   c. The *distractors* (foils) have the function of appearing plausible to the examinees who do not possess sufficient knowledge to select the correct alternative.

4. The basic function of a test item is to identify or distinguish those students who have attained the particular level of knowledge (skill, ability, or performance) which the teacher has identified as sufficient (or necessary) for the classroom decision(s) at hand.

5. Among measurement specialists, the multiple-choice item is considered to be the most highly valued, applicable, and versatile type of *objective* item.

6. Multiple-choice items are only an *indirect* procedure for observing such important learning outcomes as the ability

    a. to recall with minimal prompts.

    b. to produce and express unique ideas.

    c. to articulate explanations and give examples.

    d. to organize personal thoughts.

    e. to display thought processes or patterns of reasoning.

7. Multiple-choice items can provide opportunities to observe *directly* such important learning outcomes as the ability

    a. to discriminate and make correct choices.

    b. to comprehend concepts, principles, and generalizations.

    c. to make judgements about and choices among various courses of action.

    d. to infer and to reason.

    e. to compute.

    f. to interpret new information.

    g. to apply information and knowledge.

8. Indirect observational procedures can be substituted for direct observation procedures only when *relative interpretations* (as opposed to *absolute interpretations)* need to be made. This is because the indirect procedures tend to preserve the relative ordering of the persons with respect to the achievement being tested.

9. The advantages of multiple-choice items include their:

    a. versatility in assessing a variety of instructional objectives.

    b. reduction of opportunities for the examinee to "bluff" or "dress-up" an answer.

    c. focus on reading and thinking and thereby not on writing under examination conditions.

    d. reduced chances for an examinee to obtain the correct answer by blind guessing.

    e. usefulness in obtaining "diagnostic insight" when distractors are based on common pupil errors or misconceptions.

10. Among the criticisms of multiple-choice items are these:

    a. Such items require pupils to choose from among fixed options and do not offer the opportunity for pupils to express their own ideas.

    b. Poorly written items can focus on trivial facts.

    c. Brighter pupils who are forced to choose a single option may be penalized if they have detected ambiguities, recognize divergent viewpoints, or have additional knowledge of the topic.

    d. The possibility of getting the item right through blind guessing cannot be eliminated entirely.

    e. Multiple-choice items tend to be based on "standardized" conceptions of knowledge which may lead pupils to believe that a single, correct answer will be found for every problem in life.

    f. They may shape the content and nature of instruction in undesirable ways (e.g., limiting instruction to only those skills measured by the test).

11. All test item formats must match the instructional objectives of the learning segment.

12. Among instances in the classroom for which multiple-choice items are *not* recommended even though they would be appropriate are

    a. for problems or questions requiring a single-word or single-number answer.

    b. for computational problems in general.

    c. for questions with only two plausible answers (e.g., Yes—No).

d. for items for which writing the answer doesn't take any longer than marking an answer to the multiple-choice item.

13. The process of getting started in writing multiple-choice items is described.

14. As with all types of test items, multiple-choice items should be carefully edited before administering them.

15. Suggestions for improving the stems of multiple-choice items are summarized by the maxims in Table 8.1. Illustrative examples follow the table.

16. Suggestions for improving the quality of the alternatives in multiple-choice items are summarized by the maxims in Table 8.2. Illustrative examples follow the table.

17. Special care should be taken to word the correct alternative in a way that

a. permits those who have the minimum desired degree of knowledge to select the correct alternative, and

b. does not permit those who lack the requisite knowledge to select the correct alternative on the basis of test-wiseness or superficial clues.

18. Suggestions for wording the correct alternative are discussed in the last section.

Themes

● An important educational goal is to facilitate students' learning of higher level cognitive skills and abilities such as the ability to comprehend and to apply knowledge in new situations.

● Teaching pupils higher level cognitive abilities is important, as is assessing their progress toward attainment of such abilities.

● Teachers can become competent in the development of tests to assess pupil's ability to comprehend and apply concepts and principles and their ability to use reference materials, ability to read paragraphs, graphs, maps, and tables.

● Specific techniques for developing assessment procedures in these higher levels of the cognitive domain are provided.

● A basic tenet of these techniques is that materials presented in test items should not be identical to materials presented during instruction, so that pupils have the opportunity to display their ability to comprehend and apply knowledge.

Terms and Concepts

higher level skills/abilities
basic item construction rule
context-dependent items (interpretive
    exercise)
concept acquisition
defined vs. concrete concepts
techniques for assessing concept
    acquisition
indicator behavior
acquisition of principles
rule-governed behavior

techniques for assessing: rule
    acquisition; ability to use reference
    materials; ability to read maps,
    tables, and graphs
functions of pictures (diagrams) in test
    items
use of pictures to assess: oral language
    fluency, listening comprehension,
    reading comprehension
testing reading skills with passages
MAZE techniques

WRITING ITEMS TO TEST HIGHER LEVEL COGNITIVE ABILITIES

Quite often test items are designed to assess a pupil's ability for simple recollection or recognition of important information such as: (a) specific facts (e.g., names, dates, events, places, and things); (b) statements of rules or principles, generalizations, and theories; and (c) descriptions of procedures to use in dealing with materials. The usefulness of a pupil's fount of knowledge or "information store" should not be minimized. A base of knowledge in a subject is important (a) when learning complex intellectual skills, (b) in communicating with others in the context of everyday living, and (c) as a "medium" or "carrier" of thought for more reflective and creative thinking and problem solving (Gagné and Briggs, 1979). In terms of what is needed to profit from day-to-day instruction, the amount of information a pupil possesses appears to enhance the learning of intellectual skills by (a) facilitating an understanding of the instruction (for example, by providing labels for concepts which can be combined to form principles or rules) and (b) providing the context for cues that permit intellectual skills to be retrieved from memory (Gagné and Briggs, 1979).

Instructional objectives which deal mainly with the recall of facts, concepts, generalizations, or principles, however, are classified in the lowest category of the Bloom et al. *Taxonomy* of the cognitive domain (see Appendix D). This chapter, on the other hand, focuses on the development of test items to assess more than simple recall of information. The chapter is concerned with writing items for testing complex achievement—instructional objectives that would be classified in the higher levels of the *Taxonomy*. You may recall that some methods for assessing certain types of higher level abilities are described in Chapter 6 in connection with essay testing. Examples of the abilities which restricted and extended response essays can appropriately assess appear in Table 6.1. You should review this table now. In this chapter we shall look at techniques for assessing such higher level skills and abilities as the following, which are often a major intention of classroom instruction (The numbers in brackets are the identification numbers of the items presented later in this chapter as examples.):

Ability to identify new examples of a particular concept or idea [100]
Ability to distinguish positive and negative examples of a concept [101, 110]
Ability to provide new examples of a particular concept [102]
Ability to state a definition of a concept in one's own words [103, 104]
Ability to identify whether a particular concept has been applied to a new situation [105–109]
Ability to demonstrate or identify the relationship(s) between two or more concepts or ideas [111]
Ability to use a principle in a new situation [112]
Ability to predict or infer what will happen in a new situation when a principle has been applied [113, 114]
Ability to produce a new example of an application of a principle [115]
Ability to analyze a new or novel situation and state the principle which it illustrates [116]

Skill in using reference materials such as a dictionary or encyclopedia [117–121]

Skill and ability to read graphs, tables, and maps [122–129]

Ability to translate concepts and principles from a verbal form into a pictorial or symbolic form [130–135]

Ability to make inferences and interpretations after reading a passage [136–140]

Ability to comprehend what is read [141]

This chapter is organized in the following way. The first section discusses the general nature of items which test higher level abilities. The next section is concerned exclusively with the development of items to test whether learners have acquired concrete and defined concepts. I describe four procedures for developing such items along with their advantages and disadvantages. The third section describes methods for testing a pupil's comprehension and application (rather than memorization) of rules or principles that form the basis for much of what is learned in schools. Three techniques are discussed, along with their advantages and disadvantages. A fourth section presents items used to test the abilities to use reference material; to read graphs, tables, and maps; to identify objects or parts of objects and a variety of comprehension abilities such as listening comprehension, reading comprehension, and fluency of spoken language.

General Characteristics of Items Assessing Higher Level Abilities

A Basic Rule of Item Construction

A basic rule for testing behaviors which are classified in the higher levels of a taxonomy of cognitive objectives is that the test materials must be new or novel to the student. The wording (language) of the item should not be identical to that actually used in a lesson but should paraphrase it. Similarly, the specific examples used to illustrate a point or process during a lesson should not be the same ones appearing on the test. If this rule is not followed, the teacher will have no assurance that a pupil has comprehended or can apply knowledge. When test item language and example are identical with that used during instruction, the student's response to the test item may be only to the particular phrasing or the superficial appearance of the item, rather than a reflection of the student's comprehension or application of knowledge.

As an example, consider teaching the concept *triangle*. Suppose that during the lesson you had used three particular pictures of triangles. If these same three pictures were used to test whether the student had acquired the concept, there would be no assurance that the student could identify all varieties and sizes of triangles; the student might have acquired only the specific knowledge that the particular three figures shown during instruction were triangles. "New" triangles need to be part of testing for the acquisition of this concept.

Use of Interpretive Introductory Materials

Testing higher level behaviors and intellectual skills of the type described in the sections below often requires using introductory material followed by several test items with answers which are dependent on the content of the introductory materials. These are called *context-dependent* items or interpretive exercises. The introductory material may be of various types, including: pictures, graphs, drawings, paragraphs, poems, formulas, tables of numbers, lists of words or symbols, specimens (of rocks, plants, animals, etc.) maps, films, and sound recordings.

Context-dependent items have these *advantages*: (1) they provide an opportunity to test examinees on materials that are relatively close to the contexts toward which learning is directed, (2) they provide, through the introductory materials, the same context for all persons, (3) the introductory materials tend to lessen the burden of memorizing and sometimes moderate the effects of prior experience with content; and (4) they are frequently the only means to test certain intellectual abilities.

Some *disadvantages* of context-dependent items are that (1) they may be difficult to construct, (2) the teacher must be sure that the introductory material serves its function, (3) responding to the questions may require examinees to use additional abilities such as reading comprehension that go beyond the major focus toward which the questions are directed; and (4) special facilities (such as copying machines and/or drawing skill and equipment), not normally accessible to teachers, may be required.

Although many of the examples in this chapter use short answer, completion, and multiple-choice item formats, context-dependent essay tests can be developed as well. Examples of such essay items are illustrated in Chapter 6. Beside essay questions, two other context-dependent items types are discussed in Chapter 6: cloze reading exercises and interlinear exercises.

Layout of Context-Dependent Test Material

The way in which context-dependent material is arranged on the pages of a test booklet is frequently important, not just for the sake of an attractive appearance, but because a poor arrangement may lead a pupil to misread or misinterpret the test items. A poor arrangement can jeopardize the validity of the test.

Figure 9.1 shows one kind of arrangement. Note that a side-heading, underlined or in capital letters, directs the attention of pupils to the introductory material and to the particular items based on it. Some students will skip over introductory material or become confused concerning the particular test items to which it refers. A side-heading helps to avoid this. The introductory material to be read or interpreted is placed in the center of the page. A drawing should be neat and clear and be labeled if necessary. Photographs and magazine pictures may not be legible when photocopied, so check the reproduction equip-

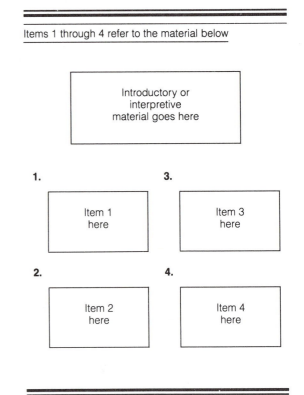

Figure 9 • 1 Arrangement of context-dependent test material is frequently important.

ment to be used with your test beforehand. If the introductory material is a passage or poem, centering and single spacing are usually all right, but young children and those with certain handicaps and disabilities may have difficulty with this arrangement. The items may be placed one under another or as shown in the figure.

It is important to keep all the items that refer to the same piece of introductory material on the same page as the introductory material if possible. Otherwise, pupils will be distracted by the turning of pages back and forth while taking the test, and some pupils whose short-term attention and memory are not good may lose their place or make careless errors. To keep the entire exercise on one page you may have to type the exercise on a separate page and leave white space on the preceding page. If so, type "GO ON TO THE NEXT PAGE" in that white space to avoid having pupils think they have reached the end of the test.

Assessing the Acquisition of Concepts

The acquisition of concepts is an important category of learning because acquired concepts form the bases for still higher-order learnings. A *concept* is an idea that represents a class of things (objects, events, or relations). The individual members of the "class of things" are distinct, yet all class members have one or more attributes in common. Examples of concepts include *red, friendly, mother, ball, round, beside,* and so on. A pupil is said to have acquired the concept *red,* for example, if that pupil can point to or identify various examples or instances of things as "red" (red tricycle, red book, red lipstick, etc.), and when that pupil does not refer to non-red things (green tricycle, puple book, pink lipstick) as "red." The individual members of the class of

things represented by a concept are referred to as "instances," "examples," or "exemplars."

A distinction can be made between *concrete concepts* and *defined concepts* (Gagné, 1970). A concrete concept refers to a class, the members of which have in common one or more physical, tangible qualities that can be heard, seen, tasted, felt, and/or smelled. Examples of concrete concepts include large, triangle, green, house, and dog. A defined concept refers to a class of objects, events, relations, etc., the members of which can be defined in the same way. Defined concepts are sometimes called abstract or relational concepts (Gagné, 1970). The essential attributes of defined concepts are not tangible and frequently involve relationships among other concepts. Defined concepts are usually learned by definitions. Gagné gives an example of the defined concept *diagonal*—a line connecting the opposite corners of a quadrilateral figure. The relationship is "connecting" and the two concepts that are related are "opposite corners of a quadrilateral figure" and "line." Examples of defined concepts include *beside, friendliness, uncle,* and *mother.* Some concepts are learned initially as concrete concepts and later as defined concepts. Students initially learn *rectangle* as a concrete concept and later in school learn that it is a defined concept (i.e., a parallelogram all of the angles of which are right angles). Helpful suggestions for developing lessons to teach concepts are found in *Principles of Instructional Design* by Robert M. Gagné and Leslie J. Briggs (1979).

Testing the Acquisition of Concrete Concepts

In items testing concept attainment the pupil is required to either: (a) *give the name of the class* to which different examples of the concept belong, (b) to *identify different examples* of the concept when given the name of the concept, or (c) to *produce new examples* when given the concept name. The three items here illustrate these varieties.

Possible Items for Testing Concept Learning

Pupil required to name the concept

Example 100.
What are figures in this group called?
(*Ans.:* Simple, open curves)

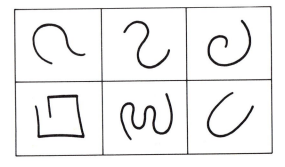

Pupil required to discriminate exemplars from nonexemplars

Example 101.
Show me the simple, open curves.
(*Ans.:* A, D)

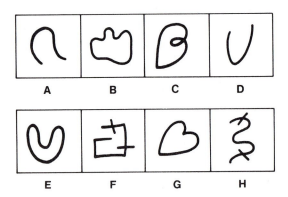

Pupil required to produce new examplars

Example 102.
Here is a pencil and paper. Draw three simple, closed curves. Be sure that each is different from the others you draw. Don't draw any that were shown in class.

Source: Examples 100-102 prompted by Hively et al. (1973).

Critique of item types Item 100 is usually unsatisfactory because it requires the pupil to recall the name of the concept and does not require the student to discriminate the concept *simple, open curve* from nonexemplars. The pupil may have acquired the concept, but may not have acquired the appropriate verbal label for it. Item 101 requires the student to discriminate *simple, open curve* from examples of other concepts, such as: *simple, closed curves* (B, E, G); *non-simple, open curves* (F, H); and *non-simple, closed curves* (C). Item 102 requires (a) the student to think up examples, (b) the teacher to judge the correctness of the examples, and (c) the teacher to judge whether those examples produced have been explicitly taught (cf. Jenkins and Deno, 1971). The ability to think up or recall untaught examples may not be necessary for the acquisition of concepts.

Items such as Item 101 are preferable because they (a) do not require the pupil to produce the concept name[1] in order to be correct and (b) allow the teacher to control (i) the familiarity of the stimulus materials, (ii) the number of discriminations required, and (iii) the number of exemplars presented to the student for classification (cf. Jenkins and Deno, 1971). An essential point is that the pupil's response must indicate that two or more instances of the concept can be identified.

Indicators The particular indicator behavior (Chapter 4) which an item testing concept acquisition requires must be well within the repertoire of the pupils being tested. Thus, it *may not* matter whether the pupil (a) spoke the concept name aloud; (b) pointed to, circled, or marked the exemplars; (c) placed printed labels bearing the concept name onto exemplars; or (d) saw pictures or drawings instead of actual specimens. I say may not because *for some types of pupils it will matter* and, thus, for these pupils the Third Fundamental Principle of Test Construction (see Chapter 6) will be

---

[1]The ability to name the concept can be tested separately if desired.

---

violated. Some pupils may experience difficulty in learning the verbal label or name of the concept even though they may have learned the concept itself. Such pupils will not be able to say or write the concept name when given an example or vice versa. Being able to isolate the fact that the "what" a pupil needs to learn is the concept name, rather than the concept itself, has important implications for teaching. Pupils who are deaf, for example, frequently acquire concepts but do not have appropriate verbal labels for them. (See Suppes, (1974) for a review of research on concept formation in handicapped children.) Similarly, a pre-printed label bearing a concept name requires the ability to read, an ability which may not be part of the concept to be learned. Young, inexperienced children may have difficulty associating a drawing or picture of an exemplar with actual, real-life specimens, especially if the drawings lack realism, are poorly reproduced, or try to represent three dimensional objects. Such children may not be able to demonstrate their acquired knowledge because of the poor quality of testing materials unless the teacher takes special care when developing the items.

Testing the Acquisition of Defined Concepts

One of three strategies is often used to test for the acquisition of abstract or defined concepts: (1) requiring a pupil to *produce a correct definition* of a concept, (2) requiring a pupil to *classify events as instances* (or non-instances) of a concept, and (3) requiring a pupil to *produce a "new" or "novel" example* of a concept (Jenkins and Deno, 1971). A less frequently used strategy is (4) to design a series of test items in which the pupil is required to do two things: (a) *identify examples of the component concepts* that make up the defined concept and (b) *give an example of the relationship* among these component concepts (Gagné and Briggs, 1979).

An essential characteristic of any item designed to test whether a student has learned a defined concept is that the item must require a pupil's response to go beyond simply memorizing the concept definition. The response must indicate that the pupil can both identify "new" specific instances of the concept and show how these instances are members of the same class or concept.

Items that require producing a definition This type of item, illustrated by Items 103 and 104 below, is not very satisfactory for testing whether a pupil has learned a concept, because the pupil could respond correctly by simply repeating a string of words learned in class or in the text without comprehending the meaning of the concept.

Example 103.
Define a *prejudice act* in your own words.

Example 104.
Tell what is meant by *lonesome*.

Items that require identifying instances A second type of item requires a pupil to identify (classify) the concept exemplars, as below.

Directions. Read each numbered statement. In front of the statement mark:

P — if it is most likely an example of a *prejudice* action.

NP — if it is most likely *not* an example of a prejudice action.

Example 105.
(NP) Sam, a white man, was overcharged by a black cashier at the company cafeteria. He became upset and refused to speak with the cashier for two weeks afterward.

Example 106.
(P) Ron, a white man, made it a personal rule never to socialize with his fellow workers who were black, unless he was forced to do so.

Example 107.
(P) John, a black manager of a local drug store, was convinced that women are incompetent pharmacists.

Example 108.
(NP) Bill, a professional golfer, stated that in his entire career, no woman against whom he competed ever beat him.

Example 109.
Which statement most nearly describes the concept of *lonesome*?
  a. Ten year old Megan decides to play alone today with her dollhouse, even though her friends asked her to play with them.
  b. Each morning Professor Cory closes her office door to be by herself while writing up her research reports.
*c. Each lunch period 15 year old Marya stands by herself not speaking to anyone in the crowded school cafeteria.
  d. Clarese, a cloister nun, speaks to no one each day and spends many hours alone while praying.

The advantages of such items are first, that the teacher can create the examples so that they are clearly instances or non-instances of the defined concept, making scoring more objective. Second, the teacher, in creating the examples and non-examples, can decide how many to include and can control their familiarity (novelty) to the pupils in the class (Jenkins and Deno, 1971). Items requiring identifying instances provide some assurance that a student has not responded simply by learning a verbal chain of words that comprise a definition.

A disadvantage of items requiring identifying instances is that they do not allow the student to express a personal perception or enriched nuance of the concept. Also, pupils' misunderstandings are less likely to surface in objective items. Finally, these items do not require the pupil either to display the ability to state the components of the concept or to relate the instances to one another.

These items frequently are difficult to write because often defined concepts are not completely applicable to a particular situation unless a lot of assumptions or qualifications are specified in the stem. (Items 105 through 109 might be subject to such criticism. The instances and non-instances a teacher makes

up need to be carefully chosen to avoid ambiguity, unnecessary wordiness, and misinterpretation.

Limitations of verbal items   Some definitional concepts cannot be tested in the manner illustrated by Items 105–109. Two of these are (1) relational concepts (e.g., uncle, aunt) and (2) concepts whose exemplars can be described verbally only by repeating the concept name for each examplar (Anderson, 1972). An aunt is a sister of a mother or father. If you tried to write an "instance" of *aunt* you would need to mention this relationship in the options. Thus, with this type of verbal item, a pupil's comprehension of the concept is not completely ascertainable. The concept *wings* is an example of the second type of concept (Anderson, 1972). Each instance you wrote would have to include the word "wings" (airplane wings, bird wings, angel wings, etc.), and so the item would be answerable on the basis of matching a word in the stem with a word in the options. However, a concept such as *tools* can be assessed by the types of items described in this section because instances of tools can be written without repeating the term tool (e.g., screwdriver, wrench, and saw are all examples of tools).

Items that require producing examples   A third type of item for testing attainment of defined concepts requires students to produce examples or instances of the concept that are new or different from those presented by the teacher or text. An example is given below.

Example 110.
Describe two examples of *prejudice actions* that were not discussed in class or in the text, but which you witnessed or experienced during the past few weeks.

Items that require producing examples force students to apply an understanding of the concept in question to their personal experiences and to recall and articulate those instances. This is quite different than (a) recalling the definition of a concept or (b) recognizing given instances of it. Perhaps for younger learners recognizing instances is more suitable than either recalling definitions or producing examples. Requiring production of examples can become very subjective, however, and can be influenced by extraneous factors such as a pupil's ability to write (as contrasted with knowledge of the concept alone). Another disadvantage of this third type of item is that it requires the teacher to judge both the novelty of a student's production (Is it "new" for the student?) and the correctness of the production (Is it really an example of the concept?) (Jenkins and Deno, 1971).

Items that require identifying components and demonstrating relationships   A fourth variety of testing for concept attainment requires the pupil to identify examples of the components of the concept and also to show an example of the relationship of the components to another (Gagné and Briggs, 1979). Item 111 tests acquisition of the concept *zenith*, defined as "the point of the celestial sphere ("sky") that is vertically above the observer." The item (Panel A) shows a labeled diagram of the component concepts: earth, sky, and observer. The task of the examinee is to show the relationship between these components and how this relationship defines the concept *zenith*. Panel B illustrates a correct response.

Example 111.
A. Sample item for testing the attainment of the defined concept zenith.

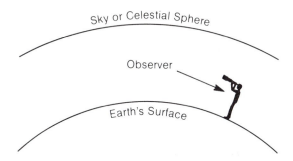

In the picture above, draw an angular diagram to show the location of the *zenith*. Label the zenith.

B. Correct response marked on the sample

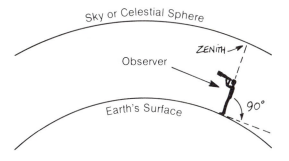

In the picture above, draw an angular diagram to show the location of the *zenith*.

Source: Prompted by Gagné and Briggs (1979, p. 227).

An advantage of this type of item is that it does not depend on highly developed verbal skills while at the same time does permit the pupil to demonstrate the relational aspects of the concept. You could simply ask for a definition of the term "zenith," but unless you could assume the pupil knew the component concepts of sky, observer, and 90° or vertical, you couldn't be sure that a pupil who gave the correct definition understood the concept *zenith*, or whether the definition simply had been memorized without understanding (Gagné and Briggs, 1979).

Assessing the Acquisition of Principles

Another important area is the learning of rule-governed or principle-governed behavior. A person's behavior is said to be *rule-governed* when the person demonstrates the capability of responding with regularity to a class of stimulus situations with a class of relational performance (Gagné, 1970; Gagné and Briggs, 1979). In other words, the pupils demonstrate that they are able to apply a rule appropriately in a variety of "new" situations.

As with the testing of concept learning, items designed to assess whether a pupil has learned a rule need to be carefully designed in order to test whether a pupil's responses are rule-governed. ==The ability to verbalize a rule (often called a stating principle) is not the same thing as the ability to use rule-governed behavior.== A pupil can memorize a rule or principle, but not be able to use or apply it. Similarly, a pupil could use a rule without necessarily being able to articulate it. An example of the application of a decoding rule learned in beginning reading is shown in Table 9.1.

Type of Item Used to Test Acquisition of Principles

Items that test for the acquisition of principles require a demonstration that the pupil is able to apply the rule to a new situation. You would test whether a pupil comprehended the *a – e* rule shown in Table 9.1, for example, by presenting a list of new words (even nonsense syllables) containing instances of the *a – e* and *a* relationships and asking the pupil to pronounce them. The words would not be the same ones used as examples during instruction. Similarly, to test whether a pupil could apply an addition rule to "story problems,"

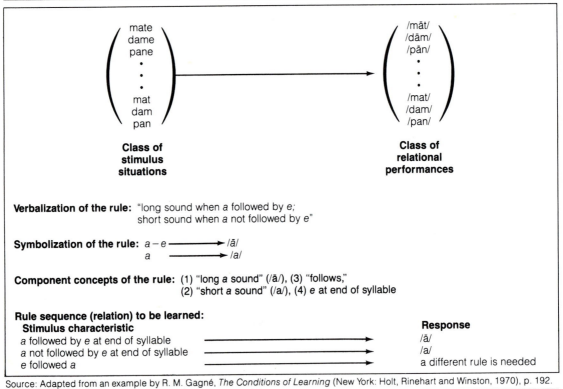

Source: Adapted from an example by R. M. Gagné, *The Conditions of Learning* (New York: Holt, Rinehart and Winston, 1970), p. 192.

Table 9 • 1 Example of the application of a rule or principle.

© 1981 United Features Syndicate, Inc.

you would need a set of story problems not specifically taught during the lesson.

Principles learned in later elementary and high school tend to be abstract and can be tested by either multiple-choice or supply items. Examples of such principles include (Jenkins and Deno, 1971, p. 96):

When performance is followed by a reinforcing event the probability of that performance increases.

Experimental studies allow conclusions regarding functional relations while correlational studies allow only statements of co-occurrence.

People tend to immigrate to, and find success in, physical environments closely resembling those from which they came.

The status of a group in a society is positively related to the priorities of that society.

The rate of increase in law enforcement officials is negatively related to the stability of the society.

The record of the past is irremediably fragmentary, selective and biased.

Basic Item Writing Techniques

Essential design requirements Asking pupils to state a principle in their own words or to recognize paraphrased statements of the principle is generally an unsatisfactory procedure because, even if pupils answer correctly, there is no assurance that they understand the principle or have the ability to produce behavior that is rule-governed. Two types of items that do seem to test comprehension of a principle have the following properties (Anderson, 1972):

Type A. The item presents an example of preceding events or causal conditions that are specified by the principle, and the pupil is required either to produce or to select an example of the consequences that would follow if the principle were in operation.

Type B. The item presents an example of a consequence specified by the principle, and the pupil is required either to supply or to select an example of the preceding events or causal conditions that, according to the principle, could have led to the given consequence.

An example of a Type A question is given below.

Example 112.
In a laboratory chamber a thirsty hamster occasionally gets a drink of water when it presses a lever with its paw. When water is no longer provided, the hampster will
  a. chirp and show its teeth
  b. soon stop pressing the lever.
*c. still press the lever frequently.
  d. begin to press the lever more frequently.
  e. begin to run around the chamber.

Source: Anderson (1972, pp. 156–157).

The principle which Example 112 is testing can be described by the following passage (Anderson, 1972, p. 156):

When reinforcement is *intermittent*, some but not all responses are reinforced. Intermittent reinforcement causes high resistance to extinction. In other words, when some but not all responses are reinforced the person or animal will continue to respond many times after the reinforcement is no longer provided. For instance, suppose a hungry pigeon in an experiment is given a pellet of food for *some* but not all pecks on an illuminated disc. When food is no longer given, the pigeon will maintain pecking the disc. If previously given food *all* the time, the pigeon would stop pecking soon after food stopped.

As I state in the last two chapters, it is frequently necessary to restate the main idea of a textbook passage before a test item can be formulated. A careful restatement of the principle in the passage above can form the basis for deriving several items, of which Item 112 is but one. Table 9.2 gives an example of this restatement. Once the general "rule" is stated, specific instances of it can be formed by substituting the appropriate terms. Item 112 is formed by substituting: (1) *hamster* for *organism,* (2) *thirsty in a laboratory chamber* for *environment* (3) *drink of water* for *reinforcer;* and (4) *pressing a lever with its paw* for *response.* The item, then, incorporates these substitutions.

Notice that the "intermittent principle" states that the organism's response will continue. Thus, the correct answer must be a paraphrasing of this part of the principle. A new item could be written by making the following substitutions in the rule in Table 9.2: (1) *principal* for *organism,* (2) *first PTA meeting* for *environment,* (3) *laughter of the audience* for *reinforcer;* and (4) *telling his favorite joke* for *response.* Try to write this item.

When creating Type A items be sure that the examples or instances are (1) different instances than the ones used during instruction and (2) phrased in different language (i.e., paraphrased) than that used in instruction. This will assure that a pupil will not respond correctly solely on the basis of memorization or verbal association.

Because these items are highly verbal, they are likely to require a good level of reading comprehension. Pupils with poor reading skills who actually comprehend the principle may miss the item.

Items requiring inference identification A variation of the above mentioned item types consists of presenting (describing) a situation containing instances of the components of the principle which are unfamiliar to the student and require the student to supply or select (a) an inference of prediction consistent with the principle or (b) an instance or conclusion con-

Table 9 • 2   Example of formulating a general statement of a principle in a way that can be used to produce many items containing specific instances of the principle.

sistent with the principle (Jenkins and Deno, 1971). Examples of such items follow.

Principle Tested

In a society the production of tools increases the probability of survival.

Sample Test Item

When Thompson explored the South American continent in 1730 he happened upon two small Indian tribes, the Zooloo and the Maylay, who were living in the wilderness. He noted that the Zooloo displayed great physical strength and endurance. They worshipped the sun and seemed very religious. Although the Maylay were not nearly as large or strong as the Zooloo, some compensated by making stone axes and spades. The Maylay appeared less religious than the Zooloo.

Example 113.
Which of the following would you predict, based on what we have studied?
*a. If one tribe is alive it is probably the Maylay.
 b. The Zooloo were probably a better organized society.
 c. The Maylay lived closer to the Amazon than the Zooloo.
 d. The Zooloo were the better gardeners.

Source: Jenkins and Deno (1971, p. 99).

Principle Tested

Correlational studies do not allow conclusions of cause and effect but only of co-occurrence.

Sample Test Item

A researcher drew random samples of children from three socioeconomic levels (SES): upper, middle and lower. He determined through interviews and observations how frequently children from each level engaged in aggressive behavior (fighting). He found that low SES children were significantly more aggressive than middle and upper SES children, and that middle SES children exhibited significantly more aggressive behavior than upper SES children.

Example 114.
On the basis of the results of this study, which of the following conclusions is most valid?
a. SES influences aggressiveness.
b. Placing children from a low SES environment into a high SES environment will decrease their aggressive behavior.
*c. SES is related to aggressiveness.

Source: Adapted from Jenkins and Deno (1971, p. 99).

Item 113 includes a passage to be read and interpreted before the item can be answered. The function of this passage is to provide an instance of one of the concepts comprising the principle, namely, the production of tools. The correct option, "a," is an instance of another component concept, survival. The prediction represented by option "a" is correct because it represents an example of the relationship between "production of tools" and "survival" which is the essential point of the principle. The passage associated with Item 114 describes an instance of the concept "correlational study" (see Chapter 3), while option "c" is an instance of "co-occurrence." To choose option "c" the examinee has to understand the relationship between these two concepts and, therefore, to "understand and apply" the rule. In both Items 113 and 114, pupils are (a) given instances of the component concepts making up the principle and (b) required to identify other components concepts that are related to the given concept in the way the principle states (Jenkins and Deno, 1971).

Items requiring pupil to produce an example This type of item is similar to the type described above, except that pupils are required to produce or think up a new example rather than simply to recognize a given example. Item 115 is an illustration of this type.

Principle Tested

People tend to immigrate to and find success in physical environments most closely resembling those from which they came.

Sample Test Item

Example 115.
Suppose President Smith forced all the grain farmers from the flatlands of the midwest to leave the country. Name two or more geographical locations in the world to which you would expect most of them to move.

Source: Adapted from Jenkins and Deno (1971, p. 100).

The item stem functions to provide the context in which (a) the pupil is required to recognize or deduce which principle is applicable; and (b) apply that principle to the given context to come up with an appropriate answer. Notice that the item requires knowledge beyond recalling the principle and recognizing its applicability to the context provided. In order to answer the item correctly, the pupil would have to know geography well enough to state two or more "geographical locations" that resemble the "flatlands of the midwest." Further, the usual criterion requires that the example be "new": The example produced should not have been given in the textbook, in other routinely assigned instructional materials, or by the teacher. These requirements make this type of item difficult, especially for younger, inexperienced learners who are not well read. Further, the pupil's performance on such items is difficult to interpret: Are the pupil's examples "new" or were they presented in the class or in the assigned materials? Does the pupil "know" the principle but cannot state examples because of a weak knowledge of geography? Are the incorrectly stated examples an indication of a lack of comprehension of the principle in question, or, instead, does the pupil misunderstand the geography?

Items requiring the pupil to produce a statement of the principle An item can be formed that is the reverse of Item 115: Instead of thinking up examples, a pupil is given one or more examples and has to supply or select the principle (or other statement) that explains the phenomena described (Jenkins and Deno, 1971). An example of this type is given below.

Principle Tested

The rate at which a behavior occurs is influenced by the consequences of that behavior.

Sample Test Item

During a recent visit to a classroom, Principal Larson noticed that Mrs. Hewmenist was having difficulty working with one of the children, Dizzy Ordur. Dizzy would work as long as Mrs. Hewmenist remained with him, but as soon as she would leave Dizzy he would "talk out" or leave his seat and she would have to return to him to get him back to work. Mr. Larson observed that this happened once in the first ten minutes, three times in the second ten minutes, and four times in the third ten minutes.

Example 116.
Why do you think Mrs. Hewmenist was having so much trouble with Dizzy Ordur?

Source: Jenkins and Deno (1971, p. 101).

The above item could be rewritten as a multiple-choice item in which the alternatives are either (a) different explanations of the phenomenon, or (b) different principles. Such a multiple-choice item should avoid stating the correct answer in textbook phraseology or in the exact phraseology used in class; otherwise, the pupil might respond to "pat verbalizations." Another problem is that if only one principle was learned in the unit, the correct alternative may be obvious, even though the pupil doesn't comprehend it. You will want to be sure that the correct response a pupil gives reflects comprehension of the principle.

The open-ended (short-answer) version in Example 116 avoids the above mentioned problems, but requires the pupil to recall without prompting and to articulate a princi-

ple. Pupils unable to do these two things will not answer correctly. Further, there may be more than one correct explanation for the phenomena stated in the item. (This occurs often where the "truth" of the principle or its unqualified application to various phenomena are open to question—a problem, incidentally, which may exist in any of the item types presented in this chapter.) Since items of these types require using a passage which explains the context in which the principle is to be applied, there is also the problem that reading ability may too highly influence a pupil's score.

The basic function of items described in this section is to test a pupil's ability to apply a principle, whether the principle is actually true or not (Anderson, 1972). An item can be written to include virtually all of the necessary qualifications, but unless you are careful, such an item may no longer evaluate the behavior you want to test.

Assessing Specific Higher-Order Skills and Abilities

Items Testing the Ability to Use Reference Materials

Undoubtedly an important ability to develop in school is the ability to use reference materials, both general reference materials and special materials for a particular subject area. Among the reference using skills to be taught and tested would be alphabetizing; using tables of contents and indexes; using encyclopedias; using dictionaries; using general reference materials, such as calendars, maps and globes, textbooks, periodical indexes, atlases, *Who's Who in America,* and magazines; and using a library and catalogue (Lindquist and Hieronymus, 1964). The items here are designed to test a few skills in obtaining information from a dictionary entry, namely, using the guide to pronunciation, locating the meaning in particular usage, and identifying the part of speech of a word.

Following is a section from a dictionary. Use it to answer questions [117–119].

---

syn chro nize (sin ′krə nīz′), v. **–nized, –niz-ing, –nizes. 1.** to happen at the same time. **2.** to operate in unison **3.** to cause to operate with exact coincidence in time or rate. **4.** to cause (sound effects or dialogue) to coincide with an action. [from *synchronous.*] **–syn′ chro ni za′ tion,** n. **–syn′ chro niz′ er,** n.

syn chro nous (sin′ krə nas), *adj.* **1.** occurring at the same time. **2.** moving or operating at the same rate. **3.** having identical periods. [Latin *synchronos,* from Greek *sunkhronos: sun-,* same + *khronos,* time.] **–syn′ chro nous ly,** *adv.* **—syn′ chro nous ness,** n.

Example 117.
The *y* in *synchronize* is pronounced like the
a. *y* in fly.
*b. *i* in tin.
c. *y* in juicy.
d. *i* in price.

Example 118.
Which meaning of *synchronize* is used in this sentence? *"Let's synchronize our watches,"* said one secret agent to another.
a. 1
b. 2
*c. 3
d. 4

Example 119.
What part of speech is *synchronousness?*
a. Adjective
b. Adverb
*c. Noun
d. Verb

Source: Wick et al. (1980, p. 34, Items 6, 8, and 9).

In the above items, the introductory material provides a "simulated" dictionary page and, thus, presents a concrete example which the student, in turn, has to analyze (or "process") in order to answer the questions. The introductory material for Examples 120 and 121, however, functions primarily to simplify or to communicate the intent of the items. Conceivably, one could write items that use neither a picture nor an introductory passage to test a student's comprehension of how information in an encyclopedia is organized, but to do so would likely result in very wordy and, perhaps, cumbersome items. The picture and the introductory materials simplify the task, focusing it on the knowledge issue at hand and, thus, make it less of a reading comprehension task.

Below is a picture of a set of volumes of an encyclopedia. Each volume contains information about topics which begin with the letters shown on the back. Use the picture to answer the exercises below.

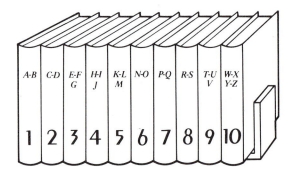

Example 120.
The playing court and equipment used in the game of badminton would be written about in which volume?
*1. Volume 1   3. Volume 3
2. Volume 2   4. Volume 7

Example 121.
If you wanted to read about the organization and New York headquarters of the United Nations, which volume would you choose *first?*
1. Volume 4   *3. Volume 9
2. Volume 6   4. Volume 10

Source: Hieronymus and Lindquist (1971, p 72, Items 61 and 65).

You can use many types of introductory materials to test abilities related to using reference materials. Examples of introductory materials include: section of an index, section of a table of contents, part of an atlas, list of words to alphabetize, reproduction of a library and catalogue entry card, section of the Dewey or Library of Congress classification system, and section of a periodical guide (index). Many times, however, you will have to rewrite or modify these materials in some manner before they are suitable for use in testing because they contain (a) matter irrelevant or extraneous to testing the objective at hand, (b) are too long, or (c) the extract is out of context and is, therefore, incomprehensible. Note that you may need to obtain written permission to reproduce copyrighted materials.

Items Testing the Ability to Read Graphs and Tables

Much information is condensed in tables and graphs. Having the skills to obtain this information is important to further learning in many areas, both in and out of school. Table 9.3 summarizes some of the skills related to effective use of tables and graphs that can be taught and tested in the classroom. Suggestions for teaching skills in reading graphs and tables as well as a bibliography of teaching materials appears in Hieronymus and Lindquist (1971b, pp. 46; 56–57).

Examples 122 and 123 illustrate the use of multiple-choice items to test skills in reading tables. Item 122 requires a pupil read the table and locate the information in a cell (Capability 3c of Table 9.3) and to compare several values read from the table to determine which is smallest (Capability 4a of Table 9.3). Item 123 requires a pupil to make an inference concerning the likelihood of an event based on understanding the trends and facts presented (Capabilities 6 and 7).

Examples 124 and 125 illustrate how a graph and multiple-choice items might be used

---

Study the chart. Then do Items 122–123.

Average Temperature (T) and Rainfall (R) Measured at Murkee Pond

	First year		Second year		Third year		Fourth year	
	T	R	T	R	T	R	T	R
January	33°	3.3 in.	20°	1.3 in.	30°	3.2 in.	35°	3.1 in.
February	33°	2.8 in.	23°	1.1 in.	34°	3.0 in.	48°	2.6 in.
March	41°	4.0 in.	34°	2.1 in.	43°	3.7 in.	46°	3.9 in.
April	51°	3.4 in.	49°	2.5 in.	52°	6.0 in.	54°	3.1 in.

Example 122.
The lowest average rainfall occurred in
E January of the third year
F January of the second year
G February of the first year
*H February of the second year

Example 123.
Which one of the following events most likely occurred in April of the third year?
*A The pond overflowed its banks.
B All water in the pond evaporated.
C The water in the pond froze solid.
D The temperature of the pond water decreased twenty degrees.

Source: CTB/McGraw Hill (1973, p. 51, Items 16 and 17)

---

1. To comprehend from the title, the topic on which a graph or table gives information.
2. To recognize from subtitles and row or column headings what is shown by each part of a graph or table
3. To read amounts
    a. by using the scale (or scales) on bar, line, and picture graphs
    b. by interpreting the sectors of a circle on circle graphs
    c. by locating a cell in a table
    d. by using special symbols and a key
4. To compare two or more values read from a graph or table
    a. by determining rank
    b. by determining differences between amounts
    c. by determining how many times greater one amount is than another.
5. To determine relative rates or trends
6. To determine underlying relationships through correct interpretation of a graph
7. To grasp the outstanding facts portrayed by a graph or table

Source: From Hieronymus, A. N. and Lindquist, E. F. *Iowa Tests of Basic Skills: Teacher's Guide to Administration, Interpretation, and Use*, p. 46. © 1971, University of Iowa. Reprinted by permission of Riverside Publishing Co.

Table 9 • 3   A simplified list of capabilities needed to read graphs and tables.

1. Ability to orient map and determine direction
    a. To determine direction from orientation
    b. To determine direction from parallels or meridians
    c. To determine direction of river flow or slope of land
2. Ability to locate and/or describe places on maps and globes
    a. Through the use of standard map symbols
    b. Through the use of a key
    c. Through the use of distance and/or direction
    d. Through the use of latitude or longitude
3. Ability to determine distances
    a. Determining distance on a road map
    b. Determining distance by using a scale of miles
    c. Determining distance on a globe
    d. Comparing distances
4. Ability to determine or trace routes of travel
5. Ability to understand seasonal variations, sun patterns, and time differences.
6. Ability to read and compare facts from one or more pattern maps
7. Ability to visualize landscape features
8. Ability to infer man's activities or way of living
    From outline maps
    From pattern maps

Source: From Hieronymus, A. N. and Lindquist, E. F. *Iowa Tests of Basic Skills: Teacher's Guide to Administration, Interpretation, and Use*, p. 44, © 1971, University of Iowa. Reprinted by permission of Riverside Publishing Co.

Table 9 • 4   A simplified list of abilities employed in map reading.

to test pupils' capabilities to draw inferences based on the displayed rates or trends (Capability 5), underlying relationships (Capability 6), and facts.

Use this graph to answer questions [124–125].

The pupils in a class took their pulses before and right after gym class. The graph shows the average pulse rates of boys and girls.

Example 124.
During this gym period—
    a. the average pulse rate of the girls increased one beat per minute
    b. everyone must have played the same game
    c. the average pulse rates of both girls and boys slowed down
    *d. the boys were probably more active than the girls

Example 125.
The pulse rates of the girls and boys one hour after gym class were probably—
    e. 80 for girls but 100 for boys
    *f. about the same as before gym class
    g. about the same as right after gym class
    h. both below 75 beats per minute

Source: Prescott, Balow, Hogan and Farr (1978, p. 19, Items 32, 33

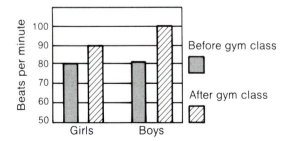

Items Testing the Ability to Read Maps

The ability to read and to learn from maps has long been recognized as important. General map reading ability involves a number of specific abilities, some of which Table 9.4 lists. Suggestions for teaching these skills and a bibliography of teaching materials are given in Hieronymus and Lindquist (1971b, pp. 44, 46; 56–57).

Examples 126 through 129 illustrate test items requiring some of the map reading skills in Table 9.4. Item 126 requires the ability to determine the direction of places on maps from a given orientation (Capability 1a). Item 127 tests the ability to visualize landscape features (Capability 7). Item 128 requires the pupil to determine distance using a scale of miles (Capability 3b). Item 129 tests the ability to

The map below shows five states. The cities are in alphabetical order beginning at the top. The key at the right tells what the signs on the map mean.

Example 126.
Which of these cities is farthest south?
1. Eton   3. Gull
2. Follet   *4. Hart

Example 127.
On which train trip could one see the mountains on one side and the ocean on the other?
1. Avis to Gull   3. Bison to Darwin
*2. Bison to Cruz   4. Darwin to Eton

Example 128.
About how far is it from Hart to the mainland at the closest point?
1. 5 miles   *3. 50 miles
2. 15 miles   4. 85 miles

Example 129.
Which way does the Ames River flow?
*1. North   3. East
2. South   4. West

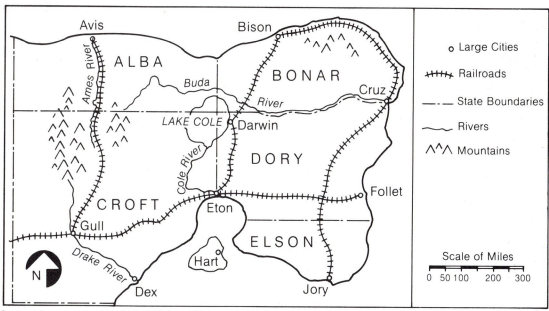

Source: Hieronymus and Lindquist (1971a, p. 54, Items 21, 22, 24 and 27)

determine the direction a river flows (Capability 1c).

Using Pictures and Diagrams to Test Other Abilities

Drawings, cartoons, pictures, diagrams, etc., can be used to good advantage to develop items that test a variety of abilities. Magazines, newspapers, and books can provide pictorial material (but be aware of situations in which copyright laws might be violated). Good quality photocopying equipment (with, perhaps, a size-reduction capacity) is usually necessary for satisfactory reproduction, however. A teacher skilled in drawing (or who has a friend, student, or colleague who is so skilled), can use these skills to develop pictorial items.

Pictures serve several functions We already have seen in Examples 120 and 121 that *a drawing can communicate the task to be performed* in a way that reduces the verbal complexity of the introductory material and the amount of reading comprehension required. Sometimes, as with maps, cartoons, or graphs, *the picture can be the main feature for the student to comprehend, analyze,* and/or *interpret.* Still another use of pictures in test items is to determine whether *a pupil can translate a concept or principle from one form to another.* An example of the latter would be to present a pupil with a particular quadratic equation of the form, $ax^2 + bx + c = d$, and ask the pupil to select the drawing that represented the graph of the equation. Pictures also serve as *substitutes for real objects or specimens.* For example, a drawing of an insect is used instead of a real insect to test a pupil's ability to identify the component parts of its body.

Examples 130 through 135 illustrate the use of pictures to serve some of these functions. In Items 130 and 131 the ideas expressed via the cartoon are the main thoughts the stu-

dent should comprehend. Item 132 illustrates how pictures can test a student's ability to translate the ideas expressed in the introductory verbal statement into graph form. (This is a type of comprehension.) The picture in Item 133 facilitates communicating the intent of the item: A good reader who is knowledgeable in science is likely to be able to answer the question without reference to the picture, but the less able reader may use the picture to clarify the situation described. The picture associated with Items 134 and 135 is a substitute for a real "body" in the identification tasks which the items require.

Example 130.
The cartoon illustrates which of the following characteristics of the party system in the United States?
*a. Strong party discipline is often lacking
 b. The parties are responsive to the will of the voters.
 c. The parties are often more concerned with politics than with the national welfare.
 d. Bipartisanship often exists in name only.

Example 131.
The situation shown in the cartoon is *least* likely to occur at which of the following times?
 a. During the first session of a new Congress
 b. During a political party convention
 c. During a primary election campaign
*d. During a presidential election campaign

Source: Stodola (1961, pp. 18–19, Items 3, 4). Cartoon courtesy of Army Times Publishing Company.

Example 132.

A scientist placed some bacteria in a dish of sterile bacteria food. He counted the number of live bacteria when he put them in and at regular intervals afterward. He observed that at first there were the same number of bacteria. Then there was a period when the bacteria increased very rapidly in number. Finally, the count leveled off and then declined rapidly as the food supply was used up.

Which of the following graphs shows the bacteria population changes described above?

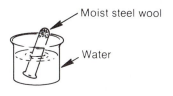

Source: Madden et al. (1972, p. 32, Item 56).

Use the drawing below to answer questions [134–135].

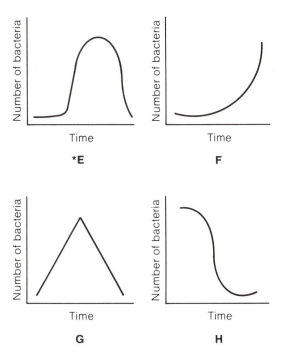

Source: CTB/McGraw-Hill (1975, p. 57, Item 32).

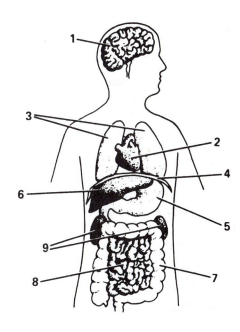

Example 133

The water rises in the test tube as the steel rusts. No matter how much steel wool is used, the water will not rise to more than about 20% above the level in the jar. This suggests that—

  5. steel wool has nothing to do with the rising
  6. nothing could make the water rise any higher
*7. only a certain portion of the air is used in rusting
  8. the steel wool was not moist enough

Example 134.
The organ numbered 7 is the—
  a. liver
  b. stomach
  c. small intestine
*d. large intestine

Example 135.
Which organ is responsible for circulation of blood?
  e. 4   f. 6   g. 3   *h. 2

Source: Prescott et al. (1978, p. 18, Items 20 and 21).

Using Pictures to Test Language Attainment

Pictures can be useful for testing some aspects of language attainment such as: listening comprehension, reading comprehension, and oral language fluency. Although lack of space prohibits a complete discussion and illustrations. I can give a few examples. [An introduction to testing second language acquisition, including the use of pictorial materials with test items, can be found in Oller's (1979), *Language Tests at School: A Pragmatic Approach* and in Heaton's (1975), *Writing English Language Tests: A Practical Guide for Teachers of English as a Second or Foreign Language*.]

Listening comprehension   You can test some aspects of listening comprehension by having a pupil listen as you read words, phrases, sentences, or paragraphs and then having the pupil perform some task which indicates comprehension. Since comprehension is a covert mental activity, if the material read to a pupil is related to one or more pictures, figures, or maps, the pupil's accurate response to these pictorial materials indicates comprehension. Heaton (1975) gives several examples. In one type of item, the student looks at a single picture, and the teacher reads a number of sentences related to the picture aloud. The pupil indicates whether the sentences are true or false in relation to the picture. In another type of item, the pupil receives a set of three or four pictures, which function as alternatives in a multiple-choice item. The teacher reads one or more sentences while the pupil listens. The pupil's task is to select the one picture described by the sentence(s) the teacher has read. A third variety of testing listening comprehension presents a map to the pupil. The teacher reads either (a) a set of directions or (b) descriptions of events which take place in one or more locations on the map. The pupil's task is to locate the place(s) referred to in the teacher's reading. In a fourth type the student looks at an incomplete line drawing or

figure while the teacher reads directions to the pupil for completing the drawing or figure (e.g., "Draw eyeglasses on Sally.").

Reading comprehension   Reading comprehension can be tested in other ways, but pictures may be helpful especially with beginning readers or beginning second language learners. Reading comprehension items using pictorial materials are much like the listening comprehension items described above except that instead of the teacher reading to the pupils, the pupils read the material themselves and mark their responses on the pictorial material or on separate answer sheets.

Oral language fluency   In this application, pictures motivate a pupil to speak. In one type of item the teacher presents a line drawing of an event or a scene and engages the pupil in either a structured or unstructured dialogue over the content or theme of the picture. The quality of the pupil's oral production is tested here. A teacher may judge the structural or functional aspects of the language the pupil uses when engaging in a dialogue centered on or around the content of the picture. To use this type of item, the teacher may have to prepare questions ahead of time, prompt the pupil frequently to get the conversation going, and select the pictures carefully to be sure that they elicit the kind of oral production necessary for an assessment.

Another variety of oral production item contains four or five very similar pictures. Both the pupil and the teacher have a set of the same pictures, but arranged in a different order. The pupil picks a picture at random but may not tell the teacher which one and must describe the picture to the teacher. The teacher must determine from the pupil's description only about which picture the pupil is talking. The pictures should be very similar in order for the item format to work. If, for example, only one of the set of four pictures contained a dog, just uttering the single word "dog" would be enough for the teacher to know to which picture the pupil is referring. Thus, the purpose of the item—an opportunity to observe the pupil's fluency in using language to describe the details of a stimulus—would not be served well. Complete discussions of these and other varieties of items for measuring language acquisition are in Heaton (1975) and Oller (1979).

Using Print Materials to Test Reading Skills

Traditional procedure of passages with questions Having pupils read material in a subject area and answer questions based on that material is a desirable way to test reading skills. While developing passages followed by questions is not easy, the teacher may find a need to do so, especially when teaching subjects for which there are not adequate tests or study booklets covering these skills. To develop such tests (a) the introductory materials need to be carefully selected to represent the kind of material pupils should be able to read; (b) the introductory material may need to be rewritten so that the interpretive questions can be answered primarily on the basis of the material presented; and (c) questions need to be phrased in a way that does not require a student to have more background (or special) information than the teacher deems appropriate for the level of pupils and subject matter at hand (Ebel, 1951; Wesman, 1971).

The steps for building a set of test items requiring reading and interpreting of a printed passage are described below (Ebel, 1951; Wesman, 1971):

1. Locate a promising passage Examine several sources (texts, periodicals, reference works, specialized books, and collections and anthologies), until you find a passage for which you can write several interpretive test items.

2. Write initial test items Write as many test items for the passage as you can. Try to exploit all of the possibilities for interpretation of the passage that fit the original test plan.

3. Rewrite the passage After you have a tentative set of items, rewrite the passage to eliminate unessential material that doesn't contribute to the items you have written.

4. Consider rewriting the test items Changes in the passage may require revising or eliminating some of the items already written. The goal of steps 3 and 4 is to produce a condensed and efficient passage and item set. [If you are most interested in reading comprehension, rather than the pupils' ability to interpret subject matter materials, this type of condensation may be undesirable, especially if part of what you want to observe is the capacity to distinguish between relevant and extraneous material (Wesman, 1971).]

5. Repeat steps 3 and 4 as often as necessary until you are satisfied that you have an efficient set of items.

Part of an interpretive exercise in social studies is shown on page 238. The original exercise contained eight items, the first five of which are in the example. Most commercial survey achievement tests contain reading comprehension subtests; these should be consulted for examples of using passages to test reading comprehension.

The MAZE Item Type

Reading comprehension can be assessed through a multiple-choice variety of the cloze exercise known as MAZE. The basic idea is to find an appropriate passage and embed a multiple-choice question in the passage which pupils can answer only if they comprehend the meaning of the surrounding passage. To better understand this procedure, consider first multiple-choice item 141 on page 239 which requires pupils to select the word that best completes the sentence (CEEB, 1980a, p. 3):

Read the two letters. Then do Items 136–140.

Dear Barbara,

Why did they ever send me to this village? The people here are very primitive, with a low level of intelligence. How can I ever help them? In the six weeks I've been here, no one has ever come to visit me. I am always alone unless I go out to talk to people.

When I ask people important questions, or try to explain important things, they just smile at me. When they talk to each other it is only about the weather and the parties they have every week. I went to one. Really—what a drunken brawl! It was such a waste of time and energy.

During the day it is so boring I could cry. The lazy men just sit around while the women work in the fields. I am trying to teach them personal cleanliness by example. I take a bath every day. No one else around here bathes more often than once a week. But I am getting a terrible rash on my skin. Every time I bathe in the river it gets worse. Maybe there is a good reason not to bathe so often here. Oh well, let's hope I learn more as I stay here longer.

Love,

Nada

Dear Mobutu,

There is a very strange woman who has come to live in our village. They say that she has come to help us, but she does not know very much. She has bathed so often in the river that she has already caught the crocodile-skin disease.

She must come from a very primitive society. She knows nothing about traditional social ritual. She came only once to the weekly social harmony gathering. She never came again, so she is not really a part of the village.

And—can you imagine?—she knows nothing about the weather! She has no idea when it will rain, when it will be hot and dry. How can she expect to live if she does not know when to plant and harvest? Surely her life, like ours, depends on the crops!

She is so strange that no man will visit her. Since she is unmarried, to visit her would be to court her, and so far no one wants her for a wife.

She does ask a lot of questions, but she does not speak our language very well. We cannot understand her, but no one will tell her. The shame would be too heavy for her and us to bear.

It is almost time for the big hunt. All the men have rested for six weeks. Now we are ready to go. When we return, we can start working in the fields again. I shall write to you then.

Your friend,

Shaaban

Example 136.
According to Nada's letter, which one of the following is she beginning to understand from the villagers' point of view?
*1. bathing
2. visiting
3. the weather
4. weekly gatherings

Example 137.
Nada thinks the men are lazy because they
5. go hunting.
6. take few baths.

*7. sit around all day.
8. talk only about the weather.

Example 138.
Why is the weather important to Shaaban's people?
1. Rain is a god.
2. They only like sunny weather.
3. Good weather brings harmony to the village.
*4. Food production is dependent on the weather.

Example 139.
For Shaaban, the weekly gatherings are not "drunken brawls," but
*5. social rituals.
 6. political events.
 7. religious services.
 8. opportunities to trade goods.

Source: CTB/McGraw-Hill (1975, pp. 63–64, Items 7–11).

Example 140.
These letters are an example of misunderstandings between people caused by differences in their
*1. cultures.
 2. religions.
 3. social classes.
 4. economic activities.

Example 141.
Then the ____ changed.
    a. price   b. road
    c. job   d. weather
    e. size

Notice that *all* options would correctly complete this sentence when seen outside the context of a reading passage. Now, consider the same item embedded in the brief passage below.

Example 141a.
It was sunny and hot for days. Then the ____ changed. It turned cloudy and cool.
    a. price   b. road
    c. job   d. weather
    e. size

Source: CEEB (1980a, p. 3)

Option d is correct because of the context in which the item is embedded. Such MAZE items appear to have a considerable advantage over the usual cloze exercises described in Chapter 6.

The following suggestions for formulating MAZE test items are based on those used for the *Degree of Reading Power* (CEEB, 1980b) test.

1. Items should be designed so that the student needs to read and understand the passage in order to answer correctly. As in the preceding example, when an item is considered in isolation, each option should make the sentence grammatically and semantically correct. However, once the item is embedded in the text, only one option should be correct.

2. The passage should contain all of the information a student needs to answer the item correctly. In order for the item to test reading ability, the student should have no need to depend on recall or past experience. This usually means the passages must be especially written for the test.

3. All options should be common (high frequency) words. All students should recognize and understand the meaning of each option. This is done to assure that when a student misses an item, the fault lies with comprehension of the reading passage rather than knowledge of the meaning of the words in the item.

Summary

The following statements summarize the main points of this chapter.

1. A *basic rule* for developing test items to test higher level abilities is that the test materials should be new or novel to the student: They should not contain any of the specific examples used during instruction and should be phrased in language that is different from that used in instruction.

2. To test for higher level abilities, it is often necessary to develop items in which the answers depend on a particular piece of introductory material presented along with them. These are called *context-dependent items* or *interpretive exercises*.

3. A *concept* is an idea that represents a class of things such as objects, events, or relationships.

4. A concept is said to have been acquired if a pupil can identify various new examples or instances of it and does not refer to non-instances as examples. Tests designed to assess concept acquisition need to preserve this criterion.

5. Distinctions between concrete concepts and defined concepts can be made:

    a. A *concrete concept* refers to a class, the members of which have in common one or more physical, tangible qualities that can be heard, seen, tasted, felt, and/or smelled.

    b. A *defined concept* or relational concept refers to a class, the members of which have in common some abstract quality or some relational quality.

6. Concrete concepts have been tested by three procedures:

    a. presenting examples to the pupil and requiring the pupil to give the concept name or label.

    b. presenting a mixture of examples and non-examples of the concept along with the concept name and requiring the pupil to identify the examples of the concept.

    c. giving the name of the concept and requiring the pupil to produce new examples of the concept.

7. Testing concept acquisition often requires that the test item call for an indicator performance on the part of the pupil. Care should be taken to (a) assure that the indicator behavior is within the repertoire of the pupil and (b) avoid confusing the inability to make an indicator response (e.g., stating the concept *label*) with lack of knowledge of the concept.

8. Considering the appropriateness of an indicator response is very important when testing young children, bilingual learners, pupils with special learning difficulties, and physically handicapped pupils.

9. Defined concepts have been tested by:

    a. requiring a pupil to produce a correct definition of a concept.

    b. presenting instances and non-instances of the concept and requiring pupils to identify the instances of the concept.

    c. giving the name of the concept and requiring a pupil to produce new instances of the concept.

    d. requiring pupils to identify the components of a defined concept and to give an example of the relationship among the components.

10. A person's behavior is *rule-governed* or principle-governed if the person regularly responds to a class of stimuli with a class of appropriate relational responses.

11. To ascertain whether a pupil has comprehended a rule requires that the items test more than the pupil's ability to verbalize or state the rule—it requires that the test items permit the pupil to apply the rule to a new or novel situation.

12. As with test items designed to assess concept acquisition, items directed toward testing the acquisition of principle-governed behavior need to present the pupil with situations that are (a) different from those used as examples during instruction; and (b) phrased in language that is not identical with that used during instruction.

13. Care must be taken so that items do not become so dependent on reading comprehension that they interfere with identifying pupils who, although they have acquired the rule-governed behavior, cannot read well.

14. Two basic types of verbal items for testing rule-governed behavior are:

    a. presenting the pupil with the antecedent conditions that are specified in the principle and requiring the pupil to state or select an example of the consequences that would follow if the rule were to be applied.

    b. presenting the pupil with the consequences and requiring the pupil to state or select the antecedent conditions that would have to exist according to the rule to produce the consequences.

15. Varieties of items similar to the above two basic types include:

    a. requiring the pupil to identify inferences or predictions consistent with the application of a principle in a given situation.

    b. requiring the pupil to produce a new example of an inference or the consequence of applying a principle in a given situation.

    c. requiring the pupil to produce a statement of the principle which explains a particular situation or set of events.

16. Using a variety of introductory material such as pictures, maps, graphs, drawings, and paragraphs helps in testing some objectives. The examples illustrate the use of items and introductory materials to test the:

    a. ability to use reference materials

    b. ability to read graphs and tables

    c. ability to read maps.

17. Pictorial material provides a means for testing comprehension of a principle, clarifying the meaning of an item, and testing the ability to identify the parts of a specimen.

18. Pictorial material can also test aspects of listening comprehension, language fluency, and reading comprehension.

19. To develop test exercises requiring a pupil to read and interpret a passage of one or more paragraphs the teacher should follow a five-step process.

20. MAZE reading comprehension items seem more effective than the usual cloze items.

Themes

● Among the types of learning outcomes which require methods of recording and organizing direct observations of pupils rather than paper-and-pencil techniques are those which assess (a) a performance of a complex skill, (b) the procedure used to accomplish a task, (c) the final product produced, and (d) social relations and learning style.

● Among the alternate techniques for recording these learning outcomes are: anecdotal records, behavior tallies, checklists, rating scales, and participation charts.

● Social relations and the social structure of classrooms can be depicted and studied using sociograms.

● A teacher needs to adopt a cognitive framework of types of pupils and types of alternative instructional methods to organize and integrate information about pupils obtained from paper-and-pencil tests and from observational procedures in order to develop effective, individualized instructional plans for pupils.

Terms and Concepts

participant (vs. nonparticipant) observer
obtrusive (vs. unobtrusive) observation
rating scales (numerical, graphical)
participation charts
leniency vs. severity error
central tendency error
guinea pig effect
role-selection effect
control effect
biased viewpoint effect
settings for observation (naturalistic, controlled, contrived)
assessment of product vs. assessment of process
anecdotal records
behavior tallies
checklists

halo error
logical error
contrast error
proximity error
anchors (numerical, agreement, objectival, behavior, specimen)
semantic differential
*preferential sociometry
*sociogram (mutual choices, chains, stars, isolates, rejectees, neglectees, cliques)
*sociometric matrix
student stereotypes (success, social, dependent, alienated, phantom)
methods of adapting instruction

*This section is optional.

10
TECHNIQUES FOR OBSERVING AND RATING PUPILS' PROCESSES, PRODUCTS, AND BEHAVIORS

In this chapter we move away from paper-and-pencil techniques to discuss ways that teachers can directly observe, describe, and evaluate a pupil's (a) performance (e.g., giving an oral report, engaging in various psychomotor activities), (b) use of a procedure or process (e.g., setting up a microscope, tying a shoe), (c) product (e.g., shop, art, or science project, essay or report), and (d) social relations and learning style (e.g., interaction with peers, manner of solving a problem, work habits, style of participation in classroom activities). Learning outcomes in these areas cannot be directly assessed by the paper-and-pencil techniques described previously. Further, the objectives in these areas of learning are quite different from the objectives for which paper and pencil typically are suitable. Frequently, however, both techniques need to be applied to obtain a comprehensive picture of a pupil a teacher can use to make better instructional decisions because of both the nature of different learning outcomes and the sociopsychological context in which learning occurs. An illustration of this is in the following box.

Observing the context of academic behaviors can help in interpreting them.

Sarah is a nine-year old fourth-grade girl with learning problems. An educational diagnostician conducted a series of interviews, observations, and tests to obtain information about Sarah on which a prescriptive instructional program could be based. One conclusion drawn from the comprehensive assessment of both cognitive and social-emotional categories of behavior was that Sarah could learn to read when given individual rather than group instruction. This conclusion led to designing a more individualized program for her. Below are the diagnostician's observations about Sarah's reading problems organized in two lists.

A. Cognitive performance

1. Given a series of fifty flashcards of vocabulary words at the second grade level, Sarah pronounces only 10 percent of the words correctly.
2. Given pictures of single objects and several objects and associated vocabulary words (ball, balls), Sarah cannot state the generalization about plurals.
3. Sarah cannot orally read simple sentences from a basal reader for the first grade.
4. When listening to pairs of words, some of which are the same and some of which are different, Sarah cannot state which pairs are the same and which are different.
5. After listening to a sentence read orally by the teacher, Sarah cannot find a picture to match the sentence from a collection of pictures.

B. Social-emotional performance

1. When sitting with a group of children during story time, Sarah "bothers" other children by touching, poking, talking, kicking, and so on.
2. When her desk is moved away from others, Sarah draws a picture; she attends to this task for five minutes.
3. When a member of a small reading group, Sarah's reaction when another child reads orally is to turn around in her chair and look out the window.
4. When asked to collect some papers from other children, Sarah refuses by stamping her foot and saying, "No!"
5. When an adult sits with her and immediately rewards her appropriate behaviors with raisins, Sarah attends to reading tasks for at least ten minutes.

Source: From *Developing Observational Skills*, pp. 19–20, by C. A. Cartwright and G. P. Cartwright. Copyright © 1974 by McGraw-Hill Book Company. Used with permission of McGraw-Hill Book Company.

Box 10 • 1

The first section of this chapter describes the general nature of observational procedures: the different types, those most useful in classroom practice, and the degree of specificity needed for an objective and valid observation. The second section offers suggestions for developing several procedures for recording observations of pupils: anecdotal records, behavior tallies, checklists, rating scales, and participation charts. A third section describes a technique, the sociogram, for identifying the social patterns underlying relationships among pupils in a classroom. The final section discusses the need to integrate information from paper-and-pencil tests and direct observation in order to adapt teaching to pupil needs. Schemes for identifying pupil "types" and adaptive education "models" are described.

General Nature of Observational Procedures

Different Types of Observational Procedures

Table 10.1 shows various ways to observe persons. The major distinction in the table is between the activity of an *observer* and the *setting* of an observation. An observer can be characterized along a participant-nonparticipant continuum. *Participant observers* become members of the group they are observing, engaging in the very activities they observe. *Nonparticipant observers* remain outside the group, not participating in the activities which they are observing. In relation to settings, persons are observed in (a) naturalistic settings, (b) settings that are established and controlled by the observer, or (c) situations contrived especially by the observer to elicit a specific type of behavior. Each of these combinations has advantages and disadvantages as a method of collecting information about pupils.

Settings	Observers	
	Participant	**Nonparticipant**
Naturalistic: immediate	Anthropologist living with Indian tribe One child observed for 24 hours	Children observed in classroom through one-way mirror
Naturalistic: retrospective	Peer ratings Peer nominations Parent interview	Unobtrusive (nonreactive) measures Analysis of personal documents
Controlled	Structured interview Typical psychological experiment	Child's reactions to teaching machine observed through one-way mirror
Contrived	Observer posing as peer	"Candid Camera" incident Hidden observer watching reactions to "rigged" situation

Source: From *Personality and Prediction*, p. 303, by J. S. Wiggins. Copyright © 1973 by Addison-Wesley Publishing Company. Reprinted with permission.

Table 10 • 1   Classification of various observational procedures.

Participant vs. nonparticipant observers A teacher concerned about Mary's behavior in junior high school might stand unobtrusively aside in the lunch room, studying subgroups and cliques and systematically observing how Mary and her friends interact with one another. This teacher is a *nonparticipant observer*. A *participant observer*, on the other hand, might try to join in a group's activities (e.g., playing baseball or eating lunch with the students) in order to observe how particular members of a group interact with one another. Another distinction is sometimes made: Participant observers are often visible to those they are observing, while nonparticipant observers usually remain out of sight.

Visible observers are frequently *obtrusive:* The persons being observed may change their typical behavior patterns because they know they are being observed. Two kinds of obser-

vation errors that can result when this occurs are known as: (a) the "guinea pig effect" and (b) the "role selection effect" (Webb, Campbell, Schwartz, and Sechrest, 1966). If students, for example, know that their behavior is being observed and recorded, they may become self-conscious (i.e., "feel like guinea pigs in a research project") and act rather unnaturally. A role selection effect occurs, for example, when the students being observed try to act as they believe the observer wants them to.

Participant observation has distinct advantages if the observer can remain unobtrusive because it offers opportunities to observe pupils in contexts in which they "open-up" and accept the teacher—contexts which would be normally closed to outside observers. Thus, by participating with a youngster in an activity such as a game, the youngster

Teacher Evaluation Team – 9:00

"Just pretend we're not here, Ms. Robinson..."

Source: Education Today Company (1979). Courtesy of David Sipress.

may be willing to discuss matters that were previously "not discussable."

But not all situations will permit participant observation. In some settings, the teacher's age, race, gender, and/or status will work against group acceptance. In circumstances where there are no role patterns for nonmembers, the would-be participant observer becomes a conspicuous, inactive, nonparticipant observer (Wiggins, 1973).

Some disadvantages of the participant observer method, especially in naturalistic settings, are that (a) it is time-consuming; (b) you have little control over what behavior occurs, and so the particular type of behavior which interests you may not occur or occur only rarely; (c) it may be very demanding, physically, mentally, and/or morally, since you will have to "move" with the group; and (d) you may become a less objective observer as you become assimilated or co-opted by the group (Wiseman and Aron, 1970). As a result of reduced objectivity, the participant observer may introduce errors into recorded observations such as: (a) "control effects" or (b) "biased-viewpoint effects" (Riley cited in Webb et al., 1966). A *control effect* occurs when, for example, a participant observer tries to alter or change the group in a way it would normally not change. A *biased viewpoint* effect occurs when the observer's report of an event does not represent the entire performance and its context as, for example, when a teacher is selective in recording or interpreting pupil behavior because it contrasts with the teacher's own values.

Varieties of observational settings Observed behavior can occur in a variety of settings, and observers can order these settings according to the control they can exercise over the events occurring in them (Wiggins, 1973). Specifying the setting in which behaviors occur is important because an individual's behavior is frequently specific to a particular setting. Behavior can be observed in its *natural setting,* a classroom, playground, or at home, and it can be recorded immediately, or the observer can recollect previously observed behavior. The latter is called retrospective observation. Persons can observe their own behavior, as when they remember and describe the activities in which they participated as youngsters. Alternately, we can ask others to recall how particular individuals acted at earlier points in time, as when a kindergarten teacher asks a pupil's mother about early development. *Controlled settings* are those in which the observer creates a special set of circumstances that attempts to elicit certain kinds of behavior. A clinical psychologist, for example, might present a preschool child with a variety of toys related to the home (e.g., male and female dolls or household articles such as tables and chairs) and encourage a child to pretend these are "Mommy," "Daddy," and dining room furniture in order to study the child's perceptions of his or her place in the family. While controlled situations have the advantage of limiting the responses likely to be elicited to those which are of principal interest to the observer, they present both an artificial and atypical setting for observation (Wiggins, 1973). A *contrived setting* is one that is apparently natural to the person who is observed, but is actually under the control of the observer (Wiggins, 1973). In a contrived setting there is an attempt to preserve the qualities of the naturalistic setting while simultaneously attempting to control the situation. Consider this example (Wiggins, 1973, p. 299): "After a particularly grueling interview, a job candidate strikes up a conversation with a fellow candidate in the waiting room. However, the 'fellow candidate' is actually a stooge who is observing his postinterview reactions."

Among the disadvantages of observations when the person is unaware of them, especially in contrived observational settings, is the ethical problem they sometimes present: Is it ethical to deceive a person as to who is observing, and why and how that observation is occurring?

© 1980 United Features Syndicate, Inc.

Should the Process or the Product be Evaluated?

A consideration when thinking about developing an observational procedure is whether to focus attention on the *product* a pupil produces or the *process or procedure* a pupil uses to produce the product. Frequently, the explicit statement of an instructional objective will be of assistance, as when the intent of instruction is to teach the process itself: For example, an elementary arithmetic teacher may be interested in teaching the "long division" algorithm, or a chemistry teacher may be interested in teaching the correct safety procedure for handling laboratory chemicals. At other times, although a specific process is taught, the teacher recognizes that it is only one of several procedures that a pupil may use. In such cases, interest focuses on the quality of the product instead. Writing a poem or term paper falls into this latter category as do algebraic derivations and geometric proofs. Sometimes both the process and the product are of equal importance such as obtaining the correct answer with the correct procedure or performing certain physical skills. The following is a useful summary of the things to take into account when deciding on whether to focus on product assessment or process assessment. Focus your assessment on the *process a pupil uses* if (Highland, 1955, p. 34):

1. The steps in a procedure can be specified and have been explicitly taught.
2. The extent to which an individual deviates from accepted procedure can be accurately and objectively measured.

3. Much or all of the evidence needed to evaluate performance is to be found in the way that performance is carried out and/or little or none of the evidence needed to evaluate performance is present at the end of performance.
4. An ample number of persons are available to observe, record, and score the procedures used during performance.

Focus your assessment on the *product a pupil has produced* if (Highland, 1955, p. 34):

1. The product of performance can be measured accurately and objectively.
2. Much or all of the evidence needed to evaluate performance is to be found in the product available at the end of performance and/or little or none of the evidence needed to evaluate performance is to be found in the way that performance is carried out.
3. The proper sequence of steps to be followed in attaining the goal is indeterminate, or has not been taught during training or when, though everyone knows the steps, they are hard to perform and skill is ascertainable only in the product.
4. The evaluation of the procedures used during performance is not practicable because persons are not available to observe, record, and score these procedures. (Examples of various characteristics to assess when evaluating pupil products and/or processes are given in Table 10.2.)

Focus of evaluation is on:	Characteristics to be evaluated:		
	Quality	**Quantity**	**Waste**
Finished product that pupil produces	1. Conformity to overall specifications 2. Dimensions, spacing, and/or strength 3. Suitability for intended use 4. General appearance	1. Number of products produced	1. Number of unacceptable products produced
		Improvement	**Safety**
		1. Improvement in one or more qualitative characteristics 2. Improvement in one or more quantitative characteristics	1. Degree to which completed product is safe for intended use
	Quality	**Quantity**	**Waste**
Process pupil uses to produce product	1. Error rate during performance 2. Efficiency of steps 3. Choice of tools, equipment, and/or materials during performance	1. Time needed to complete product or to perform process	1. Amount of excess material used during performance
		Improvement	**Safety**
		1. Reduction in number of steps for which assistance is required	1. Safe handling of tools, materials, and/or equipment 2. Accident rate during performance

Source: Adapted from *A Short Guide to the Development of Performance Tests* by L. B. Plumlee (Washington, D.C.: Test Services Section, Personnel Research and Development Center, United States Civil Service Commission, January 1975), p. 24.

Table 10 • 2   Examples of characteristics that can be evaluated for products students produce or processes students use.

Observational Procedures Useful in the Classroom

A variety of devices and procedures exist to facilitate systematic observation and recording of the results including such mechanical devices as counters, audio recorders, video recorders; preplanned schedules of observation such as checklists, rating scales, tally sheets, class participation charts; and forms for keeping anecdotal records. A teacher, however, will find only a few of these procedures practical for use in the classroom. The most useful ones are summarized in Table 10.3 and are discussed in a later section.

Be Clear About the Purpose for Observing

As can be seen from scanning Table 10.3, each variety of recording device is useful in some situations and not in others. If, for example, you are interested in noting only the presence or absence of certain behaviors—rather than in judging their quality—you would develop a checklist of behaviors, instead of a rating scale. Moreover, each type of recording device is selective in what it permits the teacher to observe and to record. Thus, it is important to know ahead of time the nature and purpose of your observation. Among the things to be decide are the "W's"—who, what, when, where, why, and how.

Who? An "observer" can be a pupil's teachers, a pupil's parent, another pupil, or even the pupil himself. For example, if the purpose of an observation is to collect information on a pupil's area(s) of interest so that high-interest reading assignments can follow, perhaps the pupil is the best person to report on the activities which are interesting. But a pupil's maturity and educational development will limit the kind of rating scale or checklist that can be used.

What? Will you be observing a pupil's manner of performance (process) or the product a pupil produces? If the product is most important, will you judge it "all" or "none" (correct or incorrect), or will you identify certain characteristics of it and then rate or comment on each characteristic? If you are assessing a process, will you identify whether certain specific behaviors in the process occurred, will you rate the extent or degree to which each step was correctly performed, or will you rate the process holistically? Answers to these questions will often depend on the reason you are making the observations in the first place.

Why? The specific reason(s) for observing pupils determine(s) the method of observing and the manner in which the observations will be recorded. Examples of specific reasons for observing along with types of observation-recording devices are summarized in Table 10.3.

Where and when? Identifying when the observations will be taken as well as the kinds of situations or places in which behaviors are likely to occur is important. A teacher should limit the conclusions drawn about the person to those settings in which the behaviors have been observed. "Hitting" behavior in preschoolers, for example, may occur only at certain times of the day, only when certain circumstances are present, or only with certain children. The "acting out" behavior of a pupil observed in one teacher's class may not occur in other classes. As a rule, a person's behavior should be observed in a variety of settings or circumstances and over a relatively long period of time before an observer draws general conclusions about the behavior pattern.

How? Knowing beforehand the form which the observational record will take is important for smooth and efficient observing and recording. Frequently, special forms have to be prepared ahead of time on which to record the behavior. If you think through the structural form before the observational period begins, you won't wonder where and how to record what you have observed. Study the

Type	Description	Recommended use	Example of situation
Anecdotal records	An observer writes a factual description of a behavior, incident, or event that occurred at a particular time and place.	These are primarily useful for keeping records of unanticipated occurrences or incidents that happen in the classroom and usually can be applied only to observations about one pupil at a time.	A student shows unusual insights into social phenomena and the teacher wants to keep a record of these so the pupil may be considered for a gifted and talented program. Two students "act-out" in class. The teacher wishes to record what occurred during the incident for future reference.
Behavior tallies	An observer counts or tallies the number of times and/or the duration of a single, specific behavior over a specified period of time.	These are primarily useful for keeping track of the occurrence of a well-defined, specific behavior which has been identified beforehand and can be anticipated to recur several times in a period of time: usually applied to observations about one pupil at a time.	A preschool teacher wants to keep track of a pupil's violent behavior toward others over several weeks to see if efforts to reduce it have been effective. A communications arts teacher tallies the number of "uh-h-h-h's" a pupil makes when giving speeches during the marking period.
Checklists	Lists of several specific behaviors or characteristics which provide space for an observer to tally or check whether each behavior occurred during a particular observation period.	These are primarily useful when specific behaviors can be listed beforehand and can be anticipated to occur during the observation period; specifically concerned with the presence or absence of several particular behaviors in a single pupil.	A science teacher wants to determine if a pupil goes through all the correct steps in using a microscope. A preschool teacher wants to identify the specific toys, games, and materials with which a particular youngster plays during the week.
Rating scales	Lists of several specific behaviors or characteristics which include space for an observer to record judgments or ratings of the quality, degree, or extent of each behavior.	These are useful when the specific behaviors can be listed beforehand and anticipated to occur in the observation period: specifically concerned with judgments of quality, degree, or extent rather than presence or absence of a behavior; usually applied to one pupil at a time.	An art teacher rates a pupil's painting as to composition, theme, texture, and/or technique. A communications teacher rates various aspects of the quality of a pupil's speaking voice.
Participation charts	Diagrams or charts which tally the number of times individuals participate in a group activity and (sometimes) the quality of their participation.	These are useful when several persons are observed at one time and when the primary interest of the observer is in recording the amount and/or quality of participation in a group activity.	A social studies teacher wants to describe the nature and extent of various pupils' contributions to group discussion of topics in a unit. A teacher wants to document a pupil's leadership skills in group activities so the pupil might be considered for a gifted and talented program.

Source: Based on information in *Developing Observational Skills* by C. A. Cartwright and G. P. Cartwright. Copyright © 1973 by McGraw-Hill Book Company. Used with the permission of McGraw-Hill Book Company.

Table 10 • 3 A few useful procedures for recording your systematic observations of pupils.

examples presented in this chapter to get some ideas.

No matter what type of procedure and form is used, each should have a place on it to record the five W's and the H. Here's an example of the information that should be contained on an observation:

Who? *Cathy Jones, 5th grade teacher.*
What? *Events leading up to and occurring during Billy Smith's acting-out in class.*
Why? *To keep a record of the behaviors and circumstances for future use and discussion with the student's parents, principal, and/or school psychologist.*
Where? *Incident occurred in Room 105.*
When? *During math class, October 9, at 10:00 a.m. when the children were doing seatwork.*

Developing Ways to Record Observations

Anecdotal Records

Usefulness of anecdotal records An anecdotal record is a written description of the facts pertaining to a behavioral episode, incident, or event that happened at a particular time and place. Anecdotal records are especially useful when the teacher does not know ahead of time exactly what behaviors to expect or in those situations when the teacher is not attempting to tally or rate a limited set of pre-specified behaviors. This is not to say, however, that anecdotal records are unsystematic nor that they should be kept only sporadically. Quite the contrary: The teacher should plan for their use and prepare a systematic way of keeping anecdotal records over time. In fact, it is primarily through systematic record keeping over time that anecdotes come to be interpretable and meaningful.

Preparing and using anecdotal records A number of suggestions for developing and using anecdotal records are summarized in Table 10.4. I shall discuss only a few of these suggestions. The rest—though perhaps equally important—seem self-explanatory.

An important means of keeping personal biases from creeping into anecdotal reports is to limit what you write to descriptions of the facts of the incident observed. In effect, the written record serves as a "picture" of the event which can be interpreted separately. Evalua-

---

1. Make observations and keep records only if there is a clear and important educational purpose for them.
2. Anecdotal records should be kept only for behaviors, events, or incidents that relate to significant aspects of pupils' educational development.
3. Do not limit record keeping to negative behavior; record positive behavior also.
4. In advance prepare some type of form that includes a place for all relevant information about a single incident for a particular pupil.
5. Be systematic. Have a plan for regularly and systematically keeping anecdotal records and have a definite way to summarize several incidents.
6. Each record should be a factual description of the incident or event, written in specific terms, and should include a description of the context or setting of the occurrence observed.
7. Keep interpretive and evaluative comments separate from the factual description of the incident; make interpretations about the typicalness of behavior only after a number of distinct observations have been made.
8. Write-up the anecdote immediately following the observation.
9. If more than one pupil is involved in an incident, keep a separate, cross-referenced record for each.
10. Maintain the confidentiality of the records.
11. Destroy the records after they have served their educational purpose.

Source: Cartwright (1974), Greene, Jorgensen, and Gerberich (1943), Gronlund (1976), Lindvall (1961, 1967); Mehrens and Lehmann (1973); Sax (1974a); Thorndike and Hagen (1977).

Table 10 • 4 Suggestions for writing anecdotal records in the classroom.

Learner: _Jay Samuels_   Date: _May 24, 1973_
Observer: _L. Martin_   Time: _9:15 a.m._

Incident: Jay was (happily) playing with blocks. Hank came skipping (merrily) over and picked up a truck which was near Jay's block construction. Jay (clobbered) Hank and (screamed) "No, no, no!" Hank (reluctantly) put down the truck and walked away.

Figure 10 • 1 An anecdotal record should describe only the facts: interpretations and evaluations of the incident (i.e., the circled words) should be put in a separate, clearly marked part of the record.

Source: Cartwright and Cartwright (1974, p. 132)

tive and interpretative language can creep into written descriptions in subtle ways, especially if the teacher is facile with language. The figure above in which the interpretive and evaluative words have been circled illustrates biased language. A more objective report results if substitutes are used for these words. (The evaluative ideas they express can be included, of course, as a separate statement, clearly marked as the teacher's interpretation of the way the pupil was feeling or the reason(s) behind the behavior.)

Be prepared to make systematic observations and to maintain this information in a systematic way. One way to prepare is to develop some type of recording form that contains space for relevant information. Figure 10.2 illustrates one such form; the teacher can easily adapt the form to suit local circumstances. A hypothetical example of an anecdote is written on the form to give you an idea of how it might be used. Multiple copies of blank forms can be made before observations are taken. As each form is completed it can be placed in a student's folder. (Such records should not be kept in a student's permanent record file in a central office, but rather with the teacher's personal folders on the pupils in the classroom. This prevents unauthorized and inappropriate use of the information.) It is helpful to have a form on which several observations about a particular pupil can be summarized. One such form is shown in Figure 10.3.

It is important that the teacher honor the confidentiality of all a student's records. A student's records should be shared only with parents, the student, and others who have legitimate needs for them and then only under certain authorized conditions. The teacher should check the Family Education Rights and Privacy Act of 1974, Public Law 93-380 (and other applicable state or federal legislation), and school policy for details of the legal requirements of pupil records.[1] This infor-

---

[1]This act gives pupils and their families the right to inspect all records kept by the school which deal with them personally, to challenge the accuracy and content of those records through appropriately established procedures, and to have certain protections concerning privacy of records. Table 2.1 describes certain rights under this and other applicable federal legislation.

Anecdotal Record

Student's Name _Andrew Potts_ Date _2-13-80_ Time _10:45am_

Teacher's Name _Darlene Patterson_

Setting: _Right after morning recess, near the water fountain in the corridor._

Description of what occurred: _Several class members were standing in line at the drinking fountain after our morning recess. When Andrew came in he pushed his way into the line right behind Dick who was waiting to be next to use the fountain. Several pupils shouted to him to go to the end of the line. By the time I spoke to him he had already taken his drink. I reminded him to always take his turn._

Interpretive comments by teacher: _Andrew seemed to react defiantly when I reminded him to take his turn. His inability to wait his turn to use various school facilities appears to be disturbing the other children in class._

Other relevant information: _Andrew's arithmetic and spelling homework assignments were incomplete when he turned them in today._

Cross-referenced? _no_ Explain: _____

Figure 10 • 2 An anecdotal record form completed for a hypothetical student.

Source: Hypothetical incident adapted from Lindvall (1961, p. 207)

mation is usually available from the school administration.

Confidentiality becomes especially important with anecdotal records because they tend to be the most subjective and biased form of record keeping and can be more easily mis-interpreted than most other forms of pupil observation and testing. Destroy all anecdotal records after they have served the educational purpose for which they were initiated. Don't use anecdotal records at all unless there is a clear educational need for so doing.

Name: *Andrew Potts*

Observer(s): *Darlene Patterson*

_____

This summary is based on ____3____ records taken from
(no. of records)

____2/10/80____ to ____2/18/80____
(date)   (date)

Is there supporting information on file?   Yes _____ No __✓__

If Yes, where is information located? _____

Summary Statement: *Repeatedly over the last week Andrew has been unable to wait his turn to use the pencil sharpener, water fountain, and the dismissal line. He pushes other children out of the way and has not responded to my requests to wait his turn. Other children seem to be upset by his actions.*

Recommendations: *Call his parents and discuss the matter with them and work out with them a plan for next steps.*

Figure 10 • 3
Example of a simple form for summarizing several anecdotal records.

Source: Form from Cartwright and Cartwright (1974, p. 155); "incidents" adapted from Lindvall (1961, p. 207).

Behavior Tallies

Sometimes the frequency or duration of a single behavior is of interest. If only this single behavior is of concern and if this behavior can be specified in advance, the teacher can keep a tally of it. Andrew Potts of our previous example continuously did things such as pushing his way to the front of the line. Once particular behaviors are isolated and a plan for their correction developed, the teacher can then tally just the number of times they occurred during a given time period in order to monitor the plan. Sometimes the *duration* of a behavior

Student's Actions		Sequence of actions
a.	Takes slide	1
b.	Wipes slide with lens paper	2
c.	Wipes slide with cloth	
d.	Wipes slide with finger	
e.	Moves bottle of culture along the table	
f.	Places drop or two of culture on slide	3
g.	Adds more culture	
h.	Adds few drops of water	
i.	Hunts for cover glasses	4
j.	Wipes cover glass with lens paper	5
k.	Wipes cover glass with cloth	
l.	Wipes cover with finger	
m.	Adjusts cover with finger	
n.	Wipes off surplus fluid	
o.	Places slide on stage	6
p.	Looks through eyepiece with right eye	
q.	Looks through eyepiece with left eye	7
r.	Turns to objective of lowest power	9
s.	Turns to low-power objective	21
t.	Turns to high-power objective	8
u.	Holds one eye closed	
v.	Looks for light	
w.	Adjusts concave mirror	
x.	Adjusts plane mirror	
y.	Adjusts diaphragm	
z.	Does not touch diaphragm	10
aa.	With eye at eyepiece turns down coarse adjustment	11
ab.	Breaks cover glass	12
ac.	Breaks slide	
ad.	With eye away from eyepiece turns down coarse adjustment	
ae.	Turns up coarse adjustment a great distance	13,22
af.	With eye at eyepiece turns down fine adjustment a great distance	14,23
ag.	With eye away from eyepiece turns down fine adjustment a great distance	15
ah.	Turns up fine adjustment screw a great distance	
ai.	Turns fine adjustment screw a few turns	16
aj.	Removes slide from stage	
ak.	Wipes objective with lens paper	
al.	Wipes objective with cloth	17
am.	Wipes objective with finger	
an.	Wipes eyepiece with lens paper	
ao.	Wipes eyepiece with cloth	18
ap.	Wipes eyepiece with finger	
aq.	Makes another mount	
ar.	Takes another microscope	
as.	Finds object	
at.	Pauses for an interval	

		Sequence of actions
au.	Asks, "What do you want me to do?"	
av.	Asks whether to use high power	
aw.	Says, "I'm satisfied"	
ax.	Says that the mount is all right for his eye	
ay.	Says he cannot do it	19,24
az.	Told to start to new mount	
aaa.	Directed to find object under low power	20
aab.	Directed to find object under high power	

Skills in which student needs further training		Sequence of actions
a.	In cleaning objective	✓
b.	In cleaning eyepiece	✓
c.	In focusing low power	✓
d.	In focusing high power	✓
e.	In adjusting mirror	✓
f.	In using diaphragm	✓
g.	In keeping both eyes open	
h.	In protecting slide and objective from breaking by careless focusing	✓

Noticeable characteristics of student's behavior		Sequence of actions
a.	Awkward in movements	
b.	Obviously dexterious in movements	
c.	Slow and deliberate	✓
d.	Very rapid	
e.	Fingers tremble	
f.	Obviously perturbed	
g.	Obviously angry	
h.	Does not take work seriously	
i.	Unable to work without specific directions	✓
j.	Obviously satisfied with his unsuccessful efforts	✓

Characterization of the student's mount		Sequence of actions
a.	Poor light	✓
b.	Poor focus	
c.	Excellent mount	
d.	Good mount	
e.	Fair mount	
f.	Poor mount	
g.	Very poor mount	
h.	Nothing in view but a thread in his eyepiece	
i.	Something on objective	
j.	Smeared lens	✓
k.	Unable to find object	✓

Source: Tyler (1930, p. 494)

Figure 10 • 4   A checklist for assessing a pupil's skill in using a microscope.

is of interest: for example, the amount of time a youngster spends in "down time" (that is, not actively engaged in an appropriate learning activity). You need some type of stop watch to measure the duration of each occurrence of such a behavior.

The teacher can devise a simple form on which to keep tally records. Remember to have a place for the who, what, when, where, why, and how on the form. It is sometimes helpful to write a concise verbal statement of the behavior you are tallying on the form as well

(Cartwright & Cartwright, 1974). Chapter 4 describes ways to phrase behavioral statements clearly.

Checklists

Usefulness of checklists A checklist consists of a list of specific behaviors, characteristics, or activities along with a place for checking whether each is present or absent. Checklists can be used to assess certain cog-

PROJECT ABLE
INSTRUCTOR REACTION FORM
(PERFORMANCE EVALUATION SET & LEARNER ACTIVITY GUIDE)

INSTRUCTIONS

This checklist is designed to assist in identifying problems in learning units and performance evaluation units. Most items will require only a check mark (√) to give your answer. Please answer all items ACCURATELY. Your comments will be most valuable.

Thanks for your help.

Name_____ School_____ City_____

Job Family Area and Level _____

Group or Grade _____ Date _____

Learning Unit No. _____

Unit Number

Performance Evaluation No. _____

NOTE: YOU MAY CHECK MORE THAN ONE ANSWER.

UNIT OVERALL EVALUATION

☐ The objectives and units are not sequenced correctly (specify).
☐ Requires extensive teacher help.
☐ Needs a greater variety of learning activities.
  Reading level within unit too difficult for my students. (Select appropriate one.)
    ☐ Better   ☐ Average   ☐ Poor
☐ Please revise as indicated on the attached copy of the unit.
☐ This unit should be deleted from the program. (Why)
☐ There is not enough difference in the units. (How should they be modified?)
☐ The typical student requires too long to complete the unit.
☐ Acceptable as is.
☐ Acceptable with minor revision.

OBJECTIVE

☐ Acceptable.
   ...s to be written in simpler language for the student.
      ...t sequence. (Where sho...

Figure 10 • 5 A checklist used by instructors to provide the developers of vocational-technical training materials with evaluative information.

Source: Ullery (1970, Appendix I, p. 3)

nitive performances such as those that involve performing a series of discrete steps in a procedure. Figure 10.4 shows a checklist for evaluating whether a pupil is able to use a microscope properly. This checklist contains descriptions of *inappropriate steps* (errors) in the sequence as well as *appropriate* (correct) ones, so that errors can be recorded for future remediation. The numbers represent the sequence that a particular student used to perform the task.

Checklists can be prepared to evaluate a student's product such as a drawing, a constructed model, an essay, or a term paper. A list of desired characteristics of the finished product is required for such applications so the teacher can then check the ones that are present. The example in Figure 10.5 shows a checklist which a vocational education teacher was asked to complete in order to evaluate part of an instructional module prepared by an outside contracting agency and tried out in the teacher's school.

Another kind of checklist consists of a list of discrete behaviors related to a specific area of a child's performance. Figure 10.6 shows, for example, a part of a long checklist concerned with identifying the particular diffi-

---

Name _____	Key
Age (CA) _____	A Yes, or very good
Original enrollment date _____	B Better than average
Recorder _____	C Average
	D Below average
	E No, or poor
	✓ Inconsistent
	O No opportunity to observe

Date of Record

Has two-word sentences (A or E)						
Has more than two-word sentences (A or E)						
Imitates phrase sequences without distortion (A or E)						
Repeats sentences of 12-13 syllables (A or E)						
Uses only simple sentence structure (A or E)						
Uses complex sentence structure (A or E)						
Responds without lag to questions (A or E)						

Figure 10 • 6
Part of a checklist to make an inventory of a child's phonological, semantic, and syntactic use of spoken language.

Source: Berry (1969, p. 248)

culties a child might be encountering in the phonological, semantic, and syntactic aspects of spoken language. Most of the items require checking present ("A" = Yes or very well) or essentially absent ("E" = No or poorly).

Sometimes pupils are the best observers of activities which concern them. Figure 10.7 shows an example of a checklist that is used as part of a career awareness and vocational guidance program. Pupils indicate what and

---

CHECK LIST OF WORK-RELATED ACTIVITIES

Thinking about your past activities can help you find out whether you might like different types of work. A number of activities are grouped below by four general types of job duties—working with PEOPLE, DATA, THINGS, and IDEAS.

DIRECTIONS: Mark the line in front of each activity to show how often you have done it.

Mark XX if you have done the activity *several times*.
Mark X   if you have done the activity *only once or twice*.
Mark O   if you *haven't done* the activity OR if the time you spent on it is *not worth mentioning*.

PEOPLE Activities

_____ Worked actively in a service group or as a volunteer aide.
_____ Helped supervise summer playground activities for children.
_____ Helped settle an argument between two friends.
_____ Instructed others in a sport such as bowling, swimming, tumbling, pool, hockey, basketball.
_____ Took care of sick or elderly people.
_____ Helped teach games or sports to young children.
_____ Helped a new boy or girl in the neighborhood to get to know others.
_____ Was selected by a group to buy a gift for someone like a friend, teacher, or club leader.
_____ Worked on a neighborhood improvement project or charity drive.
_____ Helped friends with their problems.
_____ Gave first aid to an injured person.
_____ Planned a school or church social event.
_____ Worked for a "cause" like fire prevention, ecology, or safety.
_____ Helped in a puppet show or play for children.
_____ Visited older persons to cheer them up.

[ ]

DATA Activities

_____ Operated office machines such as adding or duplicating machines.
_____ Filed letters, bills, or papers.
_____ Typed letters or reports, not assigned in class.
_____ Sorted mail.
_____ Worked out my own budget.
_____ Kept accurate records of my own expenses.
_____ Checked for spelling errors in a theme or report.
_____ Kept records of temperature, barometric pressure or rainfall.
_____ Did lettering or drafting other than a class assignment.
_____ Developed a system for sorting or storing things.

14

_____ Planned a trip using a bus, train, or airplane schedule.
_____ Figured postage costs for a catalogue order.
_____ Worked in a school with lunch tickets, filing, or sorting books.
_____ Made charts to explain things like costs, rate of growth, population changes.
_____ Took attendance or kept records for a teacher.

[ ]

THINGS Activities

_____ Used a voltmeter, micrometer, or pressure gauge.
_____ Repaired furniture.
_____ Repaired a toy that wouldn't work.
_____ Fixed mechanical things around home.
_____ Replaced burned out electrical fuses.
_____ Spliced an electrical cord.
_____ Read magazines such as *Outdoor Life, Mechanics Illustrated, Popular Science,* or *Popular Mechanics.*
_____ Helped change a part on a car engine.
_____ Refinished, painted, or stained furniture.
_____ Changed a car or bike tire.
_____ Took apart a machine to see how it operates.
_____ Developed pictures on my own.
_____ Operated a movie projector, tape recorder, or loudspeaker system.
_____ Made drawings to scale.
_____ Raised animals to be sold.

[ ]

IDEAS Activities

_____ Studied different groups of stars on my own.
_____ Studied the theory of evolution on my own.
_____ Used a microscope outside of a class assignment.
_____ Visited a science, natural history, or historical museum.
_____ Prepared a project for a science fair.
_____ Read books on art or music that were not assigned in class.
_____ Did a science experiment that was not assigned in class.
_____ Read books or magazines on science and technology.
_____ Listened to "Meet the Press" on radio or TV.
_____ Studied different cloud formations.
_____ Read the editorial page of a Sunday newspaper.
_____ Did a chemistry experiment outside of class.
_____ Collected and studied things like rocks, shells, insects.
_____ Wrote stories or news articles for a school newspaper or magazine.
_____ Wrote a short story or poetry outside of a class assignment.

[ ]

GO TO PAGE 15.

Figure 10 • 7
This checklist helps students begin thinking about the kinds of work-related activities they like and, as part of a more comprehensive program, to think about future career possibilities.

Source: The American College Testing Program (1976, p. 14)

how frequently they have engaged in work-related activities. They can then compare the activities they checked with those which others in a norm group checked and can begin to think about the kinds of work-related activities which they like to do. The guidebook accompanying this checklist recommends that, in addition to reviewing checked activities, the pupils also attempt to do some of the activities which they have not done previously. This may help them to learn more about their own preferences.

Constructing checklists Developing checklists to assess the presence of components in a process or procedure requires a thorough knowledge of the subject matter as well as the procedure in order to identify critical behaviors and steps and to list potential errors. Thus, constructing checklists requires a rather detailed analysis of the procedure and a rather careful specification of the precise characteristics of a desirable student product. But first, the teacher may need to do some observational study of pupils. If developing a procedural checklist such as that in Figure 10.4 seems appropriate, the teacher may find the following steps helpful (Gronlund, 1976):

1. List, describing clearly, each specific behavior or step in the procedure to be followed.
2. Add specific errors that are commonly made to the list (avoid unwieldy lists, however).
3. Order the correct steps and the errors in the approximate sequence in which they are likely to occur.
4. Make sure to include a way either to check the behaviors that occur or to number the sequence in which they occur.

If several equally correct procedures for accomplishing the goal are available, or if the end result, rather than the procedure, is most important, developing a checklist this way will not be useful.

Rating Scales

A teacher is sometimes concerned with more than checking whether a given behavior or particular quality is simply present or absent. When assessing the quality of a student's oral presentation to the class, for example, the teacher would probably identify several characteristics of a "good oral presentation" and then judge the *degree to which* a pupil demonstrates each of them. A very simple analysis of what constitutes a good oral presentation might include such characteristics as the extent to which the student (a) presents material relevant to the topic, (b) speaks in a smooth, unhesitating manner, (c) uses correct grammar and language patterns, and (d) makes visual contact with the audience (Lindvall, 1961). A student exhibits each of these characteristics in varying degrees rather than on an all-or-none, present-or-absent basis. Assessment of the pupil, then, requires a method of recording judgments about the extent to which each characteristic is accomplished. A simple rating scale for doing this is shown in Figure 10.8.

As this rating scale shows, such a procedure provides a means of giving specific feedback to a student concerning the strengths and weaknesses of the presentation. Also, records for oral presentations kept over several occasions can provide a means of measuring a pupil's progress.

Types of rating scales Although there are many varieties of rating scales, two varieties—numerical rating scales and graphic rating scales—when used to their full advantage serve the teacher well for most purposes. Sources such as Guilford (1954, Chapter 11) and Remmers (1963) present relatively complete cataloguings of varieties of rating scales. Examples of many types of rating scales, checklists, and other observational procedures can also be found in sources such as Borich and Madden (1977), *Evaluating Classroom Instruction: A Sourcebook of Instruments* or

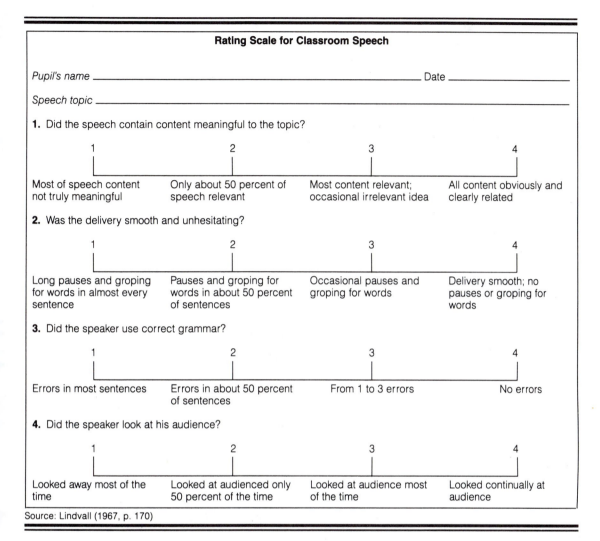

Rating Scale for Classroom Speech

Pupil's name _____ Date _____

Speech topic _____

1. Did the speech contain content meaningful to the topic?

1	2	3	4
Most of speech content not truly meaningful	Only about 50 percent of speech relevant	Most content relevant; occasional irrelevant idea	All content obviously and clearly related

2. Was the delivery smooth and unhesitating?

1	2	3	4
Long pauses and groping for words in almost every sentence	Pauses and groping for words in about 50 percent of sentences	Occasional pauses and groping for words	Delivery smooth; no pauses or groping for words

3. Did the speaker use correct grammar?

1	2	3	4
Errors in most sentences	Errors in about 50 percent of sentences	From 1 to 3 errors	No errors

4. Did the speaker look at his audience?

1	2	3	4
Looked away most of the time	Looked at audienced only 50 percent of the time	Looked at audience most of the time	Looked continually at audience

Source: Lindvall (1967, p. 170)

Figure 10 • 8   Example of a simple rating scale for assessing the quality of a pupil's oral presentation.

Simon and Boyer (1970), *Mirrors for Behavior: An Anthology of Observation Instruments.*

When using a *numerical rating scale,* the teacher must translate judgments of quality or degree into numbers. One numerical rating scale which a teacher has used in a technical drawing course is shown in Panel A of Figure 10.9. The teacher lists ten characteristics (criteria) against which each drawing is evaluated by rating each characteristic on a scale of 0 to 10 and then adding up the ratings. If a particular characteristic—e.g., quality of arcs, circles, and tangents—does not apply to a particular kind of drawing then it is omitted (a dash(–) appears in the example). The figure shows the results of using the rating scale to evaluate a ninth grader's drawing (shown in Panel B).

Notice from the example that simply providing a pupil with "numbers" is not suffi-

A. Numerical rating scale

CRITERIA OF DRAWING EVALUATION

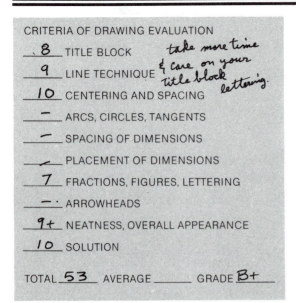

8 TITLE BLOCK

9 LINE TECHNIQUE

take more time & care on your title block lettering.

10 CENTERING AND SPACING

— ARCS, CIRCLES, TANGENTS

— SPACING OF DIMENSIONS

✓ PLACEMENT OF DIMENSIONS

7 FRACTIONS, FIGURES, LETTERING

—· ARROWHEADS

9+ NEATNESS, OVERALL APPEARANCE

10 SOLUTION

TOTAL **53** AVERAGE _____ GRADE **B+**

B. Student's technical drawing exercise

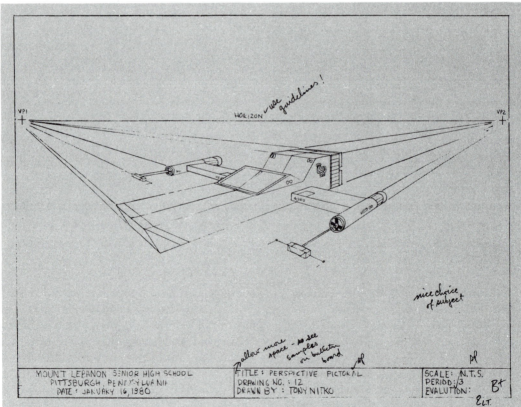

Figure 10 • 9 Example of a numerical rating scale (A) used to assess a student's technical drawing (B).

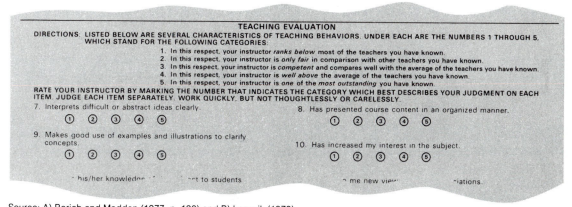

A. Rating a pupil

	Always	Very often	Often	Sometimes	Hardly	Hardly ever	Never
1. The child strikes the teacher.	1	2	3	4	5	6	7
2. The child is willing to try new things.	1	2	3	4	5	6	7
3. The child follows instructions and requests.	1	2	3	4	5	6	7
The child is ⸺ ⸺ted	1	2	3	4	⸺		7

B. Rating a college instructor

TEACHING EVALUATION

DIRECTIONS: LISTED BELOW ARE SEVERAL CHARACTERISTICS OF TEACHING BEHAVIORS. UNDER EACH ARE THE NUMBERS 1 THROUGH 5, WHICH STAND FOR THE FOLLOWING CATEGORIES:

1. In this respect, your instructor *ranks below* most of the teachers you have known.
2. In this respect, your instructor is *only fair* in comparison with other teachers you have known.
3. In this respect, your instructor is *competent* and compares well with the average of the teachers you have known.
4. In this respect, your instructor is *well above* the average of the teachers you have known.
5. In this respect, your instructor is *one* of the *most outstanding* you have known.

RATE YOUR INSTRUCTOR BY MARKING THE NUMBER THAT INDICATES THE CATEGORY WHICH BEST DESCRIBES YOUR JUDGMENT ON EACH ITEM. JUDGE EACH ITEM SEPARATELY. WORK QUICKLY, BUT NOT THOUGHTLESSLY OR CARELESSLY.

7. Interprets difficult or abstract ideas clearly.
① ② ③ ④ ⑤

8. Has presented course content in an organized manner.
① ② ③ ④ ⑤

9. Makes good use of examples and illustrations to clarify concepts.
① ② ③ ④ ⑤

10. Has increased my interest in the subject.
① ② ③ ④ ⑤

his/her knowledge ⸺ ⸺t to students   ⸺ me new view⸺   ⸺iations.

Source: A) Borich and Madden (1977, p. 190) and B) Lazovik (1978)

Figure 10 • 10 Examples of parts of numerical rating scales that use verbal descriptions to define each value.

cient. Verbal comments on the drawing—both positive and negative—are needed to give the student the feedback necessary to make improvements. In addition, students can be given the list of criteria, for example, and asked to edit their own work before turning in their assignments.

Increased objectivity and consistency in the scores from numerical rating scales can result from providing a definition of each number. The definition can be either a short verbal description or a specimen of the prod-

uct rated. The teacher can then compare a pupil's performance to the description or specimen which most nearly matches before assigning the corresponding number. The Thorndike Handwriting Scale illustrated in Figure 17.1 is an example of defining each number by a specimen. A variety of ways of defining various points on a scale are discussed in that chapter.

Figure 10.10 shows items from two numerical rating scales which have verbal descriptions for each possible rating. Instead of rating pupil products, however, these scales rate general behavior. Panel A shows items of a type that might be part of a scale to rate certain aspects of a preschooler's social-emotional function. Panel B shows items that are part of a longer questionnaire used by college students to rate their instructors.

A graphic rating scale is one in which an unbroken line is drawn to represent the particular underlying quality or dimension on which a pupil (or pupil-product) is rated. Figure 10.11 shows a simple graphic rating scale that might be used to rate a child's participation in a group project. Usually, different parts of the line are defined by specific behaviors or by verbal labels. This helps guide the observer in expressing the ratings. In Figure 10.11, the end-points of the line are "anchored" by *Never* and *Always; Usually* defines the midpoint.

The rater is permitted to check any point along the line. Thus, the graphic rating scale does not force an observer's rating into a discrete category or into being a whole number (as does the numerical rating method). In principle, this permits the rater to make and express finer distinctions among the persons being rated (Freyd, 1923), but, in practice, this advantage is lost if a rater is incapable of making such distinctions or if in the end the scale is scored by using coarse or whole number categories (Guilford, 1936).

Scoring a large number of graphic ratings is tedious and this is its chief disadvantage. A score for a graphic rating scale is obtained by measuring the distance between the endpoint and the check mark. This can be done with a ruler. Also, one can prepare a stencil or transparent plastic sheet on which are pre-printed calibrations for each item's line. The key is placed over the rating form and the number corresponding to the check mark is recorded. Sometimes the numbers are printed right on the rating form with the line, combining the features of both the numerical and the graphic rating scales. An example is the speech rating

scale shown in Figure 10.8. Note, however, that to use that scale in the manner intended by the graphic technique, it must be clear to the rater that any point on the line can express ratings, not just the numbered points.

Rating scale errors   Guilford (1954) has identified a number of "constant errors" that affect most types of ratings of people. *Leniency error* is the tendency to rate friends, close acquaintances, those we like, and sometimes pupils in general, higher on all qualities. (A *severity error* is considered to be a "negative leniency error.") A *central tendency error* occurs because very often raters hesitate to use extremes and check the middle of the scale instead. This occurs frequently when the rater knows very little about the person being rated. *Halo error* is the tendency for raters to rate a person on specific qualities in the same direction as the general, overall impression the rater has of the person (instead of judging a person's standing on each quality separately). A *logical error* happens when the rater gives similar ratings to two or more qualities that appear to be logically related in the rater's mind, even though the qualities being rated may, in fact, be independent. A *contrast error* occurs if observers rate others in the opposite direction from their own perceived position on the scale. *Proximity error* refers to the tendency for ratings on items which are adjacent to one another to correlate (correspond) more closely than items which are located further apart on the form—regardless of whether the characteristics in adjacent items are actually related to each other. Guilford (1954) provides suggestions for reducing the effects of these errors on ratings.

While the above mentioned errors tend to occur when *persons* rate each other, not all such errors occur when persons express their attitudes by means of ratings scales (Nunnally, 1978). Such errors also occur when teachers rate *products of students*—essays, term papers, and projects. Sometimes teachers have difficulty in separating the person (pupil) from the

Project Activities Rating Scale

Name: _____

Observer: _____

Description of Project Activity: _____

_____

Directions: Place a [vertical line] at any point along the line to indicate your judgment of the child's performance on that item. If you have had insufficient opportunities to observe the child, circle N/O.

1. Is the child prepared for the meetings of the group?

N/O

Never   Usually   Always

2. Does the child show an interest in the project?

N/O

Never   Usually   Always

3. Does the child participate in making plans for the next steps?

N/O

Never   Usually   Always

4. Does the child cause other children to become interested in the project?

N/O

Never   Usually   Always

5. Does the child engage in behaviors which disrupt the group activities?

N/O

Never   Usually   Always

6. Does the child contribute ideas during group meetings?

N/O

Never   Usually   Always

7. Does the child contribute materials during group meetings?

N/O

Never   Usually   Always

8. Does the child exhibit any commitment to the project above and beyond the scheduled group activities?

N/O

Never   Usually   Always

Comments:

Source: Cartwright and Cartwright (1974, pp. 122–123)

Figure 10 • 11 A simple graphic rating scale.

product, because of their knowledge of the pupil's work; errors such as those Guilford lists may be operating. I discuss some suggestions for reducing the effects of these errors when scoring essay tests in Chapter 6, although the terminology is different in this chapter. You may want to review the suggestions in Chapter 6 at this point, perhaps classifying them according to Guilford's error types.

Defining the steps on the scale One technique which improves the reliability and validity of rating scales is establishing definitions or *anchors* of the various steps on the scale. A number of different types of anchoring definitions can be listed (Nunnally, 1978). These anchoring schemes—which, incidentally, may be used alone or in combination depending on purpose and circumstance—are described below (Figures showing examples are in parentheses):

a. *numerical anchors*—numbers placed along the graphic scale or used as ratings; frequently accompanied by verbal cues (Example: Figure 10.10).
b. *degrees of agreement anchors*—phrases ranging from "completely disagree" to "completely agree" define various points on the scale. When the item is phrased as a question instead of a declarative sentence, then phrases ranging from "never" to "always" are often used (Examples: Figures 10.10, 10.11).
c. *adjectival anchors*—bipolar adjectives define the endpoints of the scale, and the person, object, or concept is rated by indicating its nearness to one of the endpoints. Examples of bipolar adjective pairs include: fair-unfair, valuable-worthless, rugged-delicate, masculine-feminine, active-passive, busy-lazy, and so on. A specific use of this technique for measuring attitudes, perceived meanings, and feelings is called the *semantic differential technique*. For more details, see the works of its foremost

developer Charles E. Osgood and his colleagues (e.g., Osgood, Suci, & Tannenbaum, 1957; Snider & Osgood, 1969).

d. *behavior anchors*—each step on the scale is described by some behavior (or set of behaviors). The rater checks the category that most nearly describes the person being rated. If a product or object is being rated, then the anchors describe characteristics of the product or object (Example: Figure 10.8).
e. *specimen anchors*—each step is associated with an actual example of a product or object that should be located at that point. The new product to be rated is compared to the given specimens and a judgment is made concerning which specimen the new product most nearly matches. The Thorndike Handwriting Scale is an example (Example: Figure 17.1).

Associated with defining the steps is the question of *how many steps* to have. The general consensus is that using more steps leads to greater reliability in the ratings of attitudes (Guilford, 1954; Nunnally, 1978). Exceptions do occur, however. For example, when opinions in members of a group are widely divided, then a moderately long questionnaire, each item having only two steps (e.g., agree-disagree), may be as reliable as a questionnaire having the same number of items, but each item having several steps (Masters, 1972; 1974). Another exception is when a large number of categories used with a rating scale becomes too confusing or too frustrating for a rater, resulting in carelessness or random responses. Such ratings will be less reliable than those based on fewer or less confusing categories (Nunnally, 1978). Too many categories are likely when teachers make holistic judgments of essays, term papers, or other pupil products. Another example is that primary pupils may not be able to make judgments along a five point scale. In such cases, fewer categories (say, four or five) may result in more consistent ratings than many categories (nine or ten).

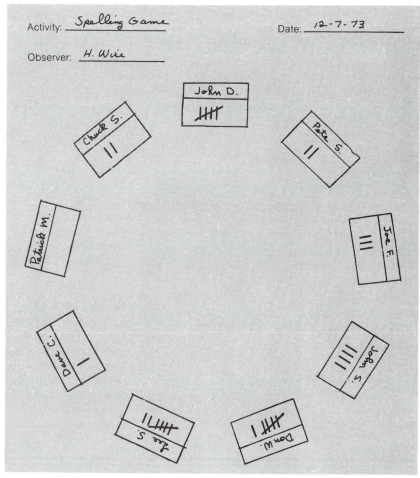

Activity: *Spelling Game*

Date: *12-7-73*

Observer: *H. Weir*

John D.
卌

Chuck S.
||

Pete S.
||

Patrick M.

Joe F.
|||

Dave C.
|

John S.
||||

Dawn.
| 卌 |

Joe S.
|| 卌

Figure 10 • 12
Example of a participation chart for tallying the number of times each pupil participated in a hypothetical spelling game.

Source: Cartwright and Cartwright (1974, p. 112)

Participation Charts

A participation chart is a simple device for tallying the behavior of several students. It consists essentially of either a chart or a diagram listing pupils' names and recording their behavior.

One example is shown in Figure 10.12. A chart such as this may be used to tally the number of times each pupil participates in a group discussion or game. Sometimes teachers evaluate pupils on the extent to which they participate in classroom discussions and use such a chart to keep a record of participation. Another reason for identifying nonparticipants is in preparation for special work with them and, perhaps, their parents to *increase* participation. Records and tallies of this sort can be used as a basis for individual discussions (a) with pupils and/or parents or (b) with

Date: 4/23/73

Activity: Social Studies Group Discussion

Observer: C. Becker

Name	Tally											Total Contributions	Total Relevant Contributions
Abel, Sam	I	I	I	–								4	3
Corning, Ellen												0	0
Cotl, Charles	–	–	I	–								4	1
Davidson, Mary	I	I	I	I	I	0	I	–				8	6
Feathers, Mary	0	I										2	1
Horn, Peter	I	I	I	I								4	4
Jacob, Jane	–	I	I	–								4	2
Moore, Susan	I	I	I	I	I	I						6	6
Motter, James	0	0	0									3	0
Smith, John	–	–	I	–								4	1
Tate, Deborah												0	0
Walker, James	I											1	1

Code: I = relevant contribution   – = neutral contribution

0 = irrelevant contribution   No mark indicates no contribution

Figure 10 • 13
Example of a participation chart for a hypothetical social studies group discussion in which both the number and nature of pupil comments are recorded.

Source: Cartwright and Cartwright (1974, p. 114)

other teachers and (c) as measures of progress or success in attaining this increased participation.

Sometimes more than the frequency of participation is of interest. One can combine the participation chart with a checklist or rating scale technique to record not only the frequency but the nature and quality of each pupil's participation. An example is shown in Figure 10.13. In such a chart some type of code is used that indicates, not only whether a pupil participated, but the quality (or kind) of participatory contribution the pupil made. The purpose of the observation will determine the kinds of behaviors recorded.

Another example is employing participation charts to tally the frequency with which certain school or classroom facilities are used. If a classroom, for example, has a variety of enrichment materials and games that pupils are free to choose to use, then it might be of interest as part of an evaluation of these materials to know which the pupils use more frequently. A librarian or resource center supervisor may have similar needs. Figure 10.14

A. Participation Chart

Week of: _5/14/73_

Observer: _____K. Wise_____

Directions: Each time a child comes to the center and spends at least five minutes there, enter a tally mark in the appropriate space.

Learning Center	Day					Total
	Mon.	Tues.	Wed.	Thurs.	Fri.	
Sound	丗 丗 丗 l	丗 丗 丗 llll	丗 丗 丗 丗 ll	丗 丗 丗 丗 lll	丗 丗 丗 丗 ll	107
Electricity	lll	l	ll	lll	lll	12
Simple Machines	丗 lll	丗 ll	丗	丗 ll	丗 llll	36

B. Graph of participation chart results

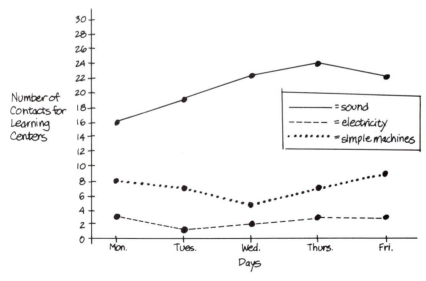

Number of Contacts for Learning Centers

—— = sound
- - - = electricity
· · · · · = simple machines

Days

Figure 10 • 14
Participation chart and graph of pupil usage of a learning resource center.

Source: Cartwright and Cartwright (1974, p. 166)

shows an example of a chart and graph kept for purposes of evaluating the usage of a learning resource center.

Sociometry: The Sociogram[2]

A variety of sociometric techniques exists which permits studying the social structure of a group. One technique, the *sociogram*, was originated by Jacob L. Moreno in 1931 and is used to identify the social relations among members of a group (Moreno, 1949). A sociogram might be used by a teacher to (Gronlund, 1976): (a) form classroom groups, (b) identify pupils whose social adjustment needs improvement, (c) design procedures for improving a group's social structure, and (d) evaluate the impact of school-based practices on a group's social structure. The methods discussed in this section are limited to what is known as *preferential sociometry* (Bjerstedy, 1956).

The Sociogram

The sociogram presents the relationship among class members as a picture or graph. Suppose we asked each of five boys to nominate three boys with whom he would like to work. The results can be represented by a sociogram such as the one in Figure 10.15.

The boxes represent the individual boys and the letters their initials. Lines connecting the boxes indicate mutual choices; arrowheads indicate the direction of the first choice of each person.

Only mutual choices are shown; therefore, the fact that no lines connect E to the other members of the group indicates that no one chose E, even though E chose others. The

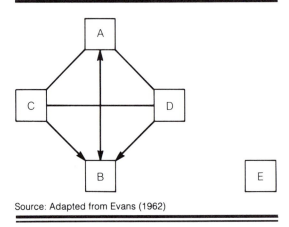

Source: Adapted from Evans (1962)

Figure 10 • 15   Example of a classroom sociogram.

sociogram shows that B is the most popular person since he was the first choice by A, B, and C. This is a tight knit group with A, B, C, and D making mutual choices. The fact that E was not among the three choices of the other four boys, means that he is an isolate (but not necessarily that he is actively rejected by them). Figure 10.16 shows how a few social structures could be depicted by a sociogram.

How to Make a Sociogram

A sociogram is developed in stages. First, pupils' choices of companions for classroom activities are collected. These choices are then tabulated and summarized in a sociometric matrix. Finally, the social structure identified in the sociometric matrix is graphed on a sociogram.

Collecting pupil's choices   The first step in making a sociogram is to obtain from pupils their choices of companions for some group activity. An example set of directions to students along with a form for pupils to write their choices is shown in Figure 10.17. A less elaborate form using only orally given directions may be used as well.

[2]This section may be omitted without loss of continuity.

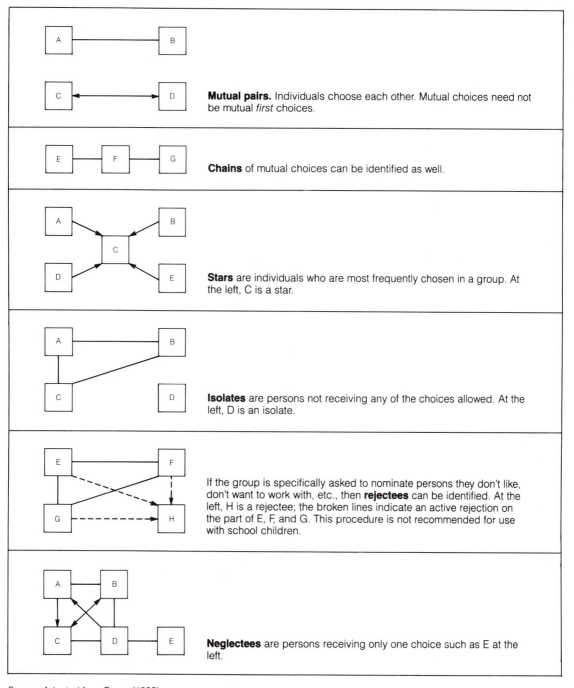

Mutual pairs. Individuals choose each other. Mutual choices need not be mutual *first* choices.

Chains of mutual choices can be identified as well.

Stars are individuals who are most frequently chosen in a group. At the left, C is a star.

Isolates are persons not receiving any of the choices allowed. At the left, D is an isolate.

If the group is specifically asked to nominate persons they don't like, don't want to work with, etc., then **rejectees** can be identified. At the left, H is a rejectee; the broken lines indicate an active rejection on the part of E, F, and G. This procedure is not recommended for use with school children.

Neglectees are persons receiving only one choice such as E at the left.

Source: Adapted from Evans (1962)

Figure 10 • 16   Example of various patterns of interactions found in sociograms.

Name_____ Date_____

During the next few weeks we will be changing our seats around, working in small groups and playing some group games. Now that we all know each other by name, you can help me arrange groups that work and play best together. You can do this by writing the names of the children you would like to have sit near you, to have work with you, and to have play with you. You may choose anyone in this room you wish, including those pupils who are absent. Your choices will not be seen by anyone else. Give first name and initial of last name.

Make your choices carefully so the groups will be the way you really want them. I will try to arrange the groups so that each pupil gets at least two of his choices. Sometimes it is hard to give everyone his first few choices so be sure to make five choices for each question.

Remember!
1. Your choices must be from pupils in this room, including those who are absent.
2. You should give the first name and the initial of the last name.
3. You should make all five choices for each question.
4. You may choose a pupil for more than one group if you wish.
5. Your choices will not be seen by anyone else.

I would choose to sit near these children:

1. _____ 3. _____
2. _____ 4. _____
            5. _____

I would choose to work with these children:

1. _____ 3. _____
2. _____ 4. _____
            5. _____

I would choose to play with these children:

1. _____ 3. _____
2. _____ 4. _____
            5. _____

Figure 10 • 17
Example of a form to use to collect pupils' nominations for companions for specific classroom activities or events.

Source: Gronlund (1959, p. 50)

Important principles for wording directions and for collecting pupil choices are (Gronlund, 1976):

1. Be sure the activities for which the pupils are making choices are real ones that are part of classroom events.
2. The basis for choosing companions for the sociometric form should be clear to the pupils.
3. Everyone should be equally free to participate in the classroom activity for which they are choosing companions.
4. Each pupil's choices should be strictly confidential.
5. The choices should actually be used to organize groups for the classroom events specified.
6. Avoid using negative choices—i.e., asking pupils to list those they would rather not have in the group—unless it is absolutely essential to the purpose of forming the sociogram.
7. Generally, restrict the number of choices: two or three for primary grades, four or five for upper grades and high schools.

Tabulating the sociometric matrix After collecting the nomination forms, you should organize them in a way that will allow you to summarize the results in a manner permitting the social structure of the group to be deduced. A *sociometric matrix* is a table for recording each pupil's choice. An example is shown in Figure 10.18. Individual pupils' names are listed both across the top and along the side margins. The names across the top represent those chosen, while the names along the side represent the persons choosing.

Figure 10.18 represents hypothetical results for a fifth grade class that was asked to name four persons with whom they would like to work. Before tabulating the choices, a diagonal line is drawn through the intersection of the rows and columns. If a choice is recorded on this diagonal line it is in error since pupils cannot choose themselves. In the figure the

boys and girls are listed separately and vertical and horizontal lines are drawn to separate them. In elementary school there is often a girls versus boys *cleavage* and drawing such lines helps to identify choices that cross-over from one group to the next. Grouping on some basis other than sex could be done if you so desire.

Once the table is set up, it is completed by taking each chooser in turn and recording the choices in the body of the table. Alan's first choice, for example, was Charles; his second was Douglas; his third was Henry; and his fourth was Fred. These ordinal numbers are placed in Alan's row.

At the bottom of the table the number of times each person was chosen is summarized, regardless of the level or order of the choice. The number of times a person was chosen is an indicator of that person's social status in the group (with respect to the requested basis for choosing) and is used to locate the person in a sociogram. Among the boys, for example, Fred is a "star" with 10 choices and among the girls it is Anne with 8 choices. Isolates (with zero choices) are Alan, Peter, and Dorcas. Neglectees (with 1 choice each) are Bruce and Charles. Some authors recommend tabulating the number of first, second, and third choices each person receives and to more heavily weigh first choices than the others. We will not do so here because (a) any weighting system a teacher is likely to use is arbitrary, (b) weighting complicates the task and computation can be a source of error, and (c) there is no indication that school children discriminate sharply between first and second choices (cf. Gronlund, 1976).

Finally, to facilitate the construction of the sociogram, circles are drawn around the *mutual choices*, regardless of the order of the choices.

Drawing the sociogram Figure 10.19 shows the completed sociogram developed from the data in the sociometric matrix. This consists of a series of concentric circles. The rings represent the total number of choices (taken from

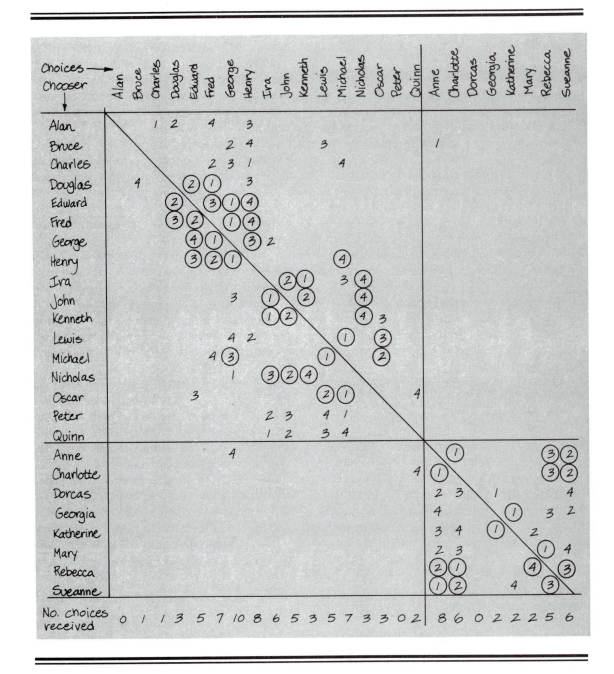

Figure 10 • 18 Hypothetical example of a sociometric matrix summarizing the choices of 25 fifth graders on the question of preferred work partners.

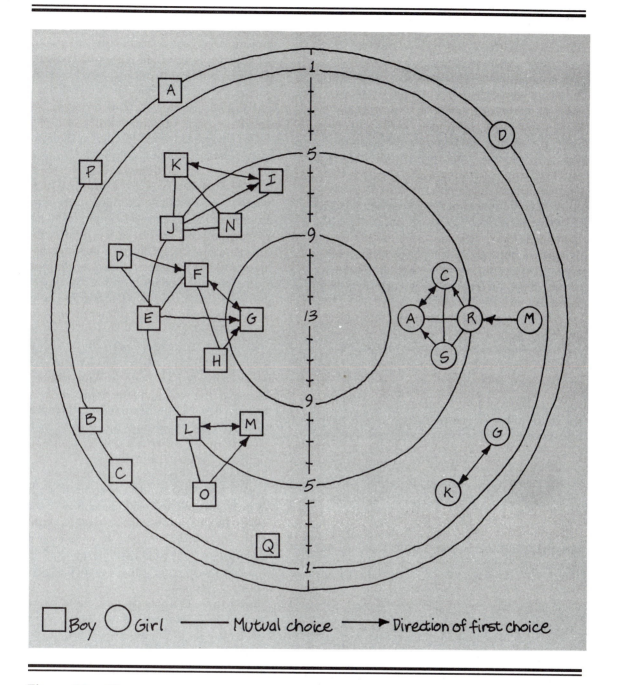

Figure 10 • 19 A completed sociogram based on the information in the sociometric matrix of Figure 10.18.

the bottom of the sociometric matrix) so the stars such as George (total = 10) and Anne (total = 8) are located toward the center of the sociogram, isolates and neglectees on the outer circles, and the others between these extremes. A "clean" appearance is obtained by following some arbitrary conventions: using squares for boys and circles for girls; restricting the lines connecting persons to only mutual choices; using the initials of the pupils to identify them; and re-arranging the layout several times until the social structure is clear. If choices other than mutual choices are included, the picture gets very complicated and the social structure is less discernible. Boys and girls are plotted on separate sides of the sociogram, especially in the lower elementary grades because there is a frequent cleavage of the class along sex lines. Few, if any, cross-overs can be expected for most questions posed to the class in these grades.

Some cliques are immediately discernible. A *clique* consists of a group of persons who tend to choose each other while avoiding others. Among the girls the clique is made up of Anne, Charlotte, Rebecca, and Sueanne. Mary is essentially a neglectee, having Rebecca as a link to the clique, but not being chosen by the other girls. Georgia and Katherine form a mutual pair. Dorcas is an isolate. Three cliques exist among the boys; the remaining boys are isolates or neglectees.

Interpreting Sociometric Data

The sociogram has obvious advantages: it is easy to understand, and several social patterns in a group can be displayed simultaneously. There are, however, several factors which you should take into account when interpreting them.

1. While a sociogram indicates relationships and mutual choices, it does not reveal the causes of the depicted social structures nor the intensity of feelings. Thus, a socio-gram is useful for bringing certain relationships to light, but it does not explain how or why those relationships come about or why pupils list their particular choices.

2. It is frequently difficult for individuals to report their choices honestly, even though the teacher assures them of confidentiality. Thus, much of the validity of classroom sociometric data hinges on the rapport between teacher and pupils.

3. The choices made depend on the specific questions asked and activities for which pupils are making nominations. For example, pupils can make nominations for (a) companions for physical activities, (b) companions for specific academic activities, and (c) the most understanding or empathetic person in class. You can expect different patterns of relationships and social structure among pupils to emerge in each instance.

4. The social pattern revealed by a sociogram is not necessarily a fixed one. As pupils come to know one another over the course of the year(s), patterns are likely to change. Thus, because social structures are not permanent among the pupils in a classroom, a teacher can initiate efforts to improve the social climate.

5. The request to nominate companions for certain activities is an over-simplification of human relationships (Wiseman & Aron, 1970). In an actual choice situation a pupil may, for example, yield to peer social pressure in selecting a companion rather than choose the person nominated on the sociometric form.

6. Terms such as *neglectee, isolate* and *clique* tend to have pejorative connotations, while the terms *star* and *mutual choice* tend to be less disparaging. It should not be assumed, however, that these stereotypic terms represent the social and emotional adjustment of the individuals involved. The star for a particular activity may in fact be quite poorly adjusted, while neglectees may be

reasonably well-adjusted. A teacher needs more information than a sociogram before making socio-emotional and academic adjustment statements about a student.

Integrating Information from Observations and Tests

As with other forms of testing, observational records and sociograms cannot be interpreted in isolation from other pieces of information. A teacher's frame of reference, professional experiences, and skills are necessary in order to blend these pieces of information into decision-making judgments and evaluations that will benefit individual pupils.

Identifying Types of Students and Their Needs

Teachers can improve their instructional planning if they observe and classify students according to the way they relate to instructional activities in the classroom. One such classification scheme was developed by Good and Power (1976) on the basis of results from several observation studies (Jackson, Silberman, & Wolfson, 1969; Silberman, 1969; Power, 1974). The classification consists of five student stereotypes which a teacher may use as a framework for thinking about combinations of several kinds of student characteristics and how these combinations might be used to better instruct pupils. The Good and Power scheme is organized according to combinations of cognitive-academic and social-adjustment behaviors as follows:

1. Success students These are task-oriented, academically successful students. They cooperate, are willing to attempt all questions, and are not discipline problems. Teachers often direct the more difficult questions to success students. These students like school and are liked by teachers and peers.

2. Social students These person-oriented students have the ability to achieve but value friendship more than schoolwork. Teachers call on them to answer the easier questions, but their answers are often incorrect or irrelevant. They are usually popular and have many friends, but some teachers don't like them.

3. Dependent students These students always seek teacher help, direction, and support, thus making great demands for teacher time. Although they are frequent hand raisers, their answers are often incorrect. They are low-level achievers. Teachers express concern for them. Peers generally reject them.

4. Alienated students These students are often disadvantaged and reluctant learners who may reject everything for which schooling stands by being either openly hostile or completely withdrawn. If hostile, they create behavior problems; if withdrawn, teachers ignore them. Teachers often either reject them or are indifferent toward them.

5. Phantom students These seldom heard or seen students are about average performers in the class. Some are shy while others are average independent workers. Seldom do they volunteer or participate in group activities. Teachers may not remember who they are. Teachers and peers may be indifferent to them.

Both observational techniques and paper-and-pencil tests may be needed to identify these stereotypes. Once teachers have identified stereotypic students in their classes however, teachers can work on ways to adapt instruction for them, such as, controlling the source and flow of information to them or controlling the degree of structure and level of abstraction of their instruction. Good and Powers (1977; 1978) list ways of adapting instruction for these stereotypes which illustrate how instruction and measurement can be integrated for the benefit of students. Regardless of whether you use the Good and

Powers scheme, it is necessary to have *some* framework into which you can integrate knowledge of pupils and teaching methods in order to improve instructional decisions.

Identifying Different Needs of Instructional Approaches

The learning environment created by a teacher provides the conditions under which learning takes place. The kinds of testing procedure used depends on knowing certain elements of this learning environment such as: (a) the kind of information required for a given decision, (b) the context in which that information is needed, and (c) how the information will be used to arrive at a decision. It is wasteful to think about the best type of test to use outside of a particular decision context.

Consider, for example, the kinds of decisions to be made, information needed, and testing procedures to be used in each of the five patterns of adapting to individual pupil differences described by Glaser (1976, 1977). One approach is to begin with a relatively fixed set of educational goals and a fixed, standard set of instructional methods. Pupils new to such a system are given tests to assess their initial competencies and a decision is made either to place a pupil in the *fixed, standard instructional procedure* or to label the pupil as a poor risk or poor learner. Poor learners enter a special educational program, away from the mainstream program, since the standard one is not appropriate for them. Those placed in the standard program continue through it, if they demonstrate satisfactory learning. Otherwise, they repeat the same instruction or drop out.

A second approach modifies the first: Those designated poor learners are provided with *supplementary, remedial instruction* in an attempt to bring their initial competencies "up to the required level." Those for whom this remedial instruction is successful are then re-entered into the fixed, mainstream program characteristic of the first approach. A third approach adapts to individual differences by providing several *alternative instructional methods,* rather than the single, fixed method which characterizes the first two approaches. Thus, a pupil's initial abilities and competencies are used to place that pupil in one of several available instructional procedures; if the correct match is made, this pupil has as good an opportunity to learn as a second pupil matched to a second method most suitable for that second pupil.

The fourth possible approach is to continue the second and third approaches. Pupils lacking the initial competencies are placed in a *supplementary remedial program* to develop these competencies *and,* after that, are differentially placed into the one *alternative instructional method* that is best suited to each pupil's needs.

A fifth approach is most idealistic and is, perhaps, least suited to elementary schools. It consists of a modification of approach four. Approach five offers not only remediation of initial deficits and placement into *alternative methods of instruction;* it offers, in addition, *equally-valued alternative outcomes* or goals. A student's particular constellation of strengths and abilities is equally valued; each has many ways to succeed in the educational system, and each is given credentials equally recognized by society. In the fifth approach, information about the student from interviews, observation, and paper-and-pencil tests is used for guidance through the course of instruction uniquely tailored to that student's goals; different students learn in different ways.

Each of these instructional approaches requires different types of information and decision-making patterns. Thus, the measurement requirements are different for each. It is impossible, then, to speak of whether it is better to use paper and pencil or systematic observational procedures or some combination of both, unless the instructional decision context is taken into account. The merits of any testing program lie in the extent to which the program provides useful information to a decision-maker—an instructional designer, a teacher, a pupil, an administrator, a parent, or a member of the public at large. Further, whatever combination of procedures are employed, they must be *designed into* the instructional process so that the information they provide is easy to obtain and is available in a usable form at the time a decision is made.

When viewed in this way, there is less of a distinction between testing and instruction. The learner can look forward to testing as an opportunity for feedback about accomplishments and progress and for guidance toward chosen goals.

Summary

The following are the main points of this chapter.

1. Direct observation permits teachers to evaluate learning objectives related to (a) pupils' performance of complex activities, (b) the procedures pupils follow to accomplish a task, (c) the quality of the products pupils create, and (d) pupils' social relations and styles of learning.

2. An observer's degree of active involvement in the activities of those being observed can be expressed on a participant/nonparticipant continuum.

    a. The *participant observer* is visible to those being observed, becomes involved in their activities, frequently takes on a definite role as a group member, and has the advantage of observing in situations that are normally closed to outsiders.

    b. The *nonparticipant* observer is less visible and more passive, observes activities from outside the group, and has less of an obtrusive effect on the group.

3. Disadvantages of participant observation include (a) it is time-consuming; (b) the specific behavior of interest to the observer may occur rarely; (c) it can be physically, mentally, and/or morally demanding; and (d) less objective observations can result.

4. Pupils may be observed in *naturalistic* settings, *controlled* settings, and/or *contrived* settings.

5. The decision to focus observation on the *process a pupil uses,* rather than the product produced, is based on whether:

    a. the specific procedural steps have been taught.

    b. it is possible to accurately describe deviations from the acceptable procedure.

    c. nearly all the information required to evaluate a pupil with respect to an instructional objective is contained in the execution of the procedure rather than in the product.

    d. it is possible to objectively record observations of the process or procedure.

6. The decision to observe and judge a *product* is more important when:

    a. it can be measured accurately and objectively.

    b. specific procedural steps are not clearly observable, have not been taught, or when skills can be determined only from a judgment of the final product.

    c. nearly all the information required to evaluate a pupil with respect to an instructional objective is contained in the final product rather than in the process for producing the product.

d. it is not possible to objectively record observations of the process or procedure.

7. The most useful methods for teachers to use in recording classroom observations of their pupils' products and procedures seem to be (a) anecdotal records, (b) behavior tallies, (c) checklists, (d) rating scales, and (e) participation charts. A summary of the definition of these methods and examples of situations in which they can be used is contained in Table 10.3.

8. Every record of pupil behavior should contain statements explicitly describing (a) who the observer was, (b) what specific performances or products were observed, (c) why those performances and pupils were observed, (d) when and where the observations took place, and (e) how the observations were made. A form on which there are places to record this information in a systematic fashion should be devised in advance.

9. Suggestions for writing anecdotal records are summarized in Table 10.3.

10. Confidentiality and objectivity are especially important for anecdotal records. A teacher should check the requirements of applicable school policy and state and federal legislation regarding pupil record keeping.

11. Suggestions for developing checklists to observe a procedure or process being performed are given. Examples of checklists have been given for: (a) observing performance of a procedure (Figure 10.4), (b) evaluating a product (Figure 10.5), (c) making an inventory of a pupil's typical behaviors (Figure 10.6), and (d) surveying past participation in activities (Figure 10.7).

12. The most useful rating scale procedures for classroom use are numerical rating scales and graphic rating scales.

    a. *Numerical rating scales* require the teacher to translate judgments of quality into a number. Examples are shown in Figures 10.9 and 10.10.

    b. *Graphic rating scales* present unbroken lines which are used to represent the dimension on which the quality of pupils' performances are rated. Examples are shown in Figures 10.8 and 10.11.

13. Among the various kinds of errors made when persons are rated are: (a) leniency errors, (b) central tendency errors, (c) halo errors, (d) logical errors, (e) contrast errors, and (f) proximity errors. Errors occur when pupil products are rated, especially when it is difficult for a teacher to mentally separate the pupil from the product.

14. Reduction in error and improvement in the reliability and validity of a rating scale may be accomplished by using "anchors" to define the various steps on the scale. Among the types of anchors are: (a) numbers, (b) degrees of agreement, (c) bipolar adjectives, (d) behavioral statements, and (e) selected specimens.

15. *Participation charts* permit the recording and/or classification of pupils' involvement in group discussions and other activities. This information is useful both for evaluating pupils and for designing an instructional plan to improve pupil involvement in classroom activities. Examples are shown in Figures 10.12, 10.13, and 10.14.

16. A *sociogram* permits the teacher to graphically display pupils' preferred companions for certain specific activities and to infer the social structure of the group from these expressed preferences.

*17. Examples of typical patterns of pupil choices are defined and illustrated in Figure 10.16; an example of a completed sociogram for a class is shown in Figure 10.19. Suggestions for developing and interpreting a sociogram are given in this chapter.

*This section is optional. It may be omitted without loss of continuity.

18. It is helpful to have some framework into which patterns of complex pupil behavior (inferred from paper-and-pencil tests, observational records, and sociograms) can be integrated, so that instructional planning can proceed for each pupil. One scheme defines five pupil "types": (a) success students, (b) social students, (c) dependent students, (d) alienated students, and phantom students. Each type can be linked to special means of teaching these pupils.

19. A teacher needs, however, to do more than simply classifying pupils into various types. Before using information about a pupil, a teacher needs to identify the type of adaptive instructional procedure that can be implemented and which interacts with the type of pupil. Since a relatively unique blend of information is needed in each situation, considerable professional judgment and skill is required of the teacher.

20. Among the ways in which instruction can be adapted are: (a) selecting certain pupils into a standard program with limited options, (b) implementing selectivity after initially low competence has been overcome by a remedial program, (c) assigning pupils to alternative instructional methods according to their different learning styles, (d) accommodating pupils' different styles of learning after initial competence deficits have been overcome, and (e) using some combination of "d" along with a procedure for permitting pupils to pursue different learning outcomes. Each type of adaptation requires specific information which a teacher needs to obtain in order to make decisions. Thus, the testing and measurement requirements differ in each case.

21. A desirable ultimate goal for classroom testing (including observational procedures) is to have very little distinction between testing and instruction so that learners can look forward to testing as an opportunity for feedback and guidance about their chosen goals.

Themes

● Analyzing the responses of pupils to items the teacher has developed identifies flawed items and provides a basis for improved item writing.

● Pupil data on items helps to identify possible learning difficulties and areas of remediation.

● The statistical characteristics of test items determine the shape, mean, and standard deviation of the total test score distribution.

● Knowledge of the statistical properties of items can help test constructors design tests for special purposes, especially tests used to rank or order pupils.

Terms and Concepts

item analysis
content analysis of item responses
final form of the test
item file
upper, middle, and lower groups
item difficulty index (p)
item discrimination index (D) (Net D)
dichotomous item scoring
graded responses, continuous scoring
item bias
relative vs. absolute achievement

negatively discriminating item
poorly functioning distractor
ambiguous alternatives
miskeyed items
blind guessing
complete vs. partial ordering of pupils
homogeneous vs. heterogeneous test
optimum difficulty level of an item
posttest-pretest difference in item
    difficulty

11
ITEM ANALYSIS: USING INFORMATION FROM PUPILS TO IMPROVE THE QUALITY OF ITEMS

A pupil's responses to the *ensemble* of items comprising a test provide the reliable and necessary information which you then integrate in making instructional decisions. A single test item is important, nevertheless, because if the individual items do not function properly, then the ensemble of items comprising the whole test will not function properly. The purpose of this chapter is to describe techniques you can use (a) to study whether individual items are fulfilling their functions and (b) to improve them.

The first section of the chapter discusses the major purposes of item analysis for classroom tests in a general way. The second and third sections discuss two rather commonly used indices of the quantitative characteristics of items, an *item difficulty index* and an *item discrimination index* and the information provided by them. I then turn to response-choice items and to using the pupils' responses to each alternative of an item to study whether (a) the distractors are functioning; (b) evidence is present for suspecting that an item is ambiguous, encouraged guessing, or is miskeyed; and (c) pupil misconceptions necessitate further instruction. A fifth section discusses how and whether to use item analysis data to select items to build a test that has the properties you desire, that is, a test that will serve the purpose you had in mind when constructing it. I suggest that when you read the fifth section, you return your thoughts to the planning phase discussed in Chapter 5 to be sure the test you are using is actually fulfilling the purpose you had in mind when planning it.

Item Analysis for Classroom Tests

As used here, *item analysis* refers to the process of collecting, summarizing, and using information about individual test items, especially information about pupils' responses to items. Standardized test developers, especially developers of norm-referenced tests, try out many more items than will appear on the final version of a test. Item analysis data from this tryout are used to select items for the final form, discarding those which fail to display certain statistical properties. (Chapter 18 discusses the process used by reputable publishers.) Classroom tests, being more closely linked to the daily teaching-learning process, serve purposes that are somewhat different from published standardized tests. Thus, the teacher

will use item analysis data in ways different than a test publisher. For teacher-made tests, the following are among the important uses of item analysis.

1. **Determining whether an item functions as the teacher intends** You can't expect to write perfect items. Professional item writers know that items which appear slick in draft form often do not function as intended.

To decide whether an item for a classroom test is functioning properly, a teacher needs to consider: (a) whether it seems to be testing the intended instructional objective, (b) whether it is of the appropriate level of difficulty, (c) whether it is able to distinguish those who have command of the learning objectives from those who do not, (d) whether the keyed answer is correct; and **(e)** (for response-choice items) whether the distractors are functioning. A procedure to help you decide whether an item seems to be testing the intended instructional objective appears in Chapter 4, in connection with Figure 4.4. The other four elements are discussed in this chapter.

2. Feedback to students about their performance and as a basis for class discussion In my view, students are entitled to know how their performance on each item is marked and what the correct answer to each item is. Further, reviewing the test makes instructional common sense: Pupils' errors can be corrected, the teacher can clarify the level of specificity and discrimination expected of the pupils, good (and/or correct) responses can be reinforced, students lacking test-wiseness skills may learn from the discussion how a correct answer is formulated or why (in response-choice items) foils are incorrect, and some test-anxiety can be alleviated if the test is viewed rationally in the context of instruction.

3. Feedback to the teacher about pupil difficulties A simple procedure such as tabulating the percent of students answering an item correctly may provide the teacher with information about the points needing additional instruction and remediation.[1] Thus, item analysis can help the teacher be more efficient in focusing the efforts of instruction on both the group and the individual. Note that a subscore based on a cluster of several items measuring the same objective or skill provides more reliable information than a single item. When a test must cover a broad area of content, however, it is often impractical to have more than one or two items per objective.

Identifying the nature of erroneous responses to items can be most helpful for a teacher. With essay, short-answer, and completion items a *content analysis of the responses* is necessary to determine the major types of pupil errors and to tabulate the frequency of their occurrence. A content analysis need not be done for every test every time; a teacher can do one unit each marking period, or colleagues can analyze different units. Teachers can exchange and save the information to use with the next group of students. Over a period of time, enough information will be available to develop a checklist (see Chapter 10) of pupil difficulties.

Some school systems have electronic test scoring equipment and the capability to tabulate the percent answering each response-choice item correctly. As schools acquire microcomputers, and as the software for item analysis becomes available, these and other tabulations recommended in this chapter will become much easier for the teacher to do on a routine basis.

4. Areas for curriculum improvement If particular kinds of items are repeatedly difficult for pupils, or if certain kinds of errors occur often, perhaps the problem extends beyond the individual teacher. A more extensive curriculum revision may be needed. Item analysis data are helpful in identifying specific problems. But any test is likely to be an incomplete representation of a school's curriculum objectives, so you should use caution when attempting to generalize item analysis data for the whole of student learning.

5. Revising the items Information about pupils' responses to and perceptions of an item can be used to revise it. Items can be reused for future testing and, if a few are revised each time, the overall quality of the test will eventually improve. It is usually less time-consuming to revise an item than to write a new one. Some teachers, especially in the junior and senior high schools (and in colleges), develop

[1]Some authorities recommend that the number of pupils answering an item correctly be obtained by a show of hands. I do not recommend this practice because it may be emotionally injurious and may violate the privacy of some students.

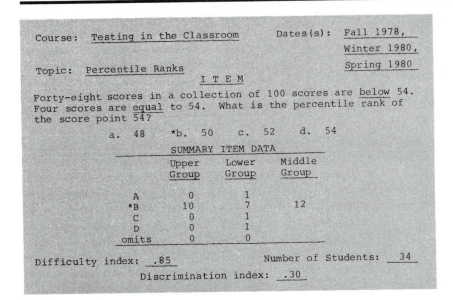

```
Course:  Testing in the Classroom        Dates(s):  Fall 1978,
                                                     Winter 1980,
Topic:  Percentile Ranks                             Spring 1980
                             I T E M
Forty-eight scores in a collection of 100 scores are below 54.
Four scores are equal to 54.  What is the percentile rank of
the score point 54?
         a.  48     *b.  50    c.  52     d.  54

                   SUMMARY ITEM DATA
                 ─────────────────────────────────────
                   Upper      Lower      Middle
                   Group      Group      Group

          A          0          1
         *B         10          7          12
          C          0          1
          D          0          1
        omits        0          0
                 ─────────────────────────────────────
Difficulty index:  .85              Number of Students:   34
                   Discrimination index:  .30
```

Figure 11 • 1 An item file card with item analysis data for one item. Tabulations were made for Item 3 on the summary record form shown in Table 11.2.

an *item file*. They write and try new items and through item analysis, they keep the best items each time, revise some, and discard the rest. Figure 11.1 shows one arrangement of a card in such a file. After several years, a file of good items accumulates, and a teacher is able to select test items from the file. Once a file of items is established, equivalent versions of a test, for example, can be constructed relatively easily. Equivalent versions of tests can be used for "make-up" tests when persons are absent during the regularly scheduled administration, when a teacher has multiple sections of the same course, or when tests are used in an alternating pattern from year to year.

6. Improving item-writing skills Logically, knowledge of how items function with a group of pupils should facilitate the acquisition of item-writing skills. Probably the most effective way to improve item-writing skills is to analyze the items and the way pupils respond to them, using this information to revise items and to try them again with pupils. Simply reading theory generally is not enough.

First Steps in Preparing for Item Analysis of Response-Choice Tests

The basic bits of data needed to begin an analysis of response-choice items (true-false, matching, or multiple-choice) are the choices made by each pupil to each item. Although this information is easier to use if pupils have marked their answers on separate answer sheets, such sheets are not necessary. An outline of the steps necessary to organize the information is shown in Table 11.1.

Before you proceed with this section, note that, although it is written primarily for conducting analyses of response-choice items, you can use several of the techniques described with any items that are scored dichotomously (i.e., simply as correct or incorrect). Item analysis techniques do exist for analyzing items scored in ways other than dichotomously. The complexity of many such procedures render them impractical for teachers without access to computers and/or sophisticated scoring equipment, however. Thus, these latter procedures lie beyond the scope of this book.

Step 1. Score each test by marking the correct answers and putting the total number correct on the test (or answer sheet).	the middle group which has chosen the correct alternative.
Step 2. Sort the papers in numerical order according to the total score.	**Step 5.** Calculate the difficulty index for each item (see text).
Step 3. Determine the upper, middle, and lower groups (see text).	**Step 6.** Calculate the discrimination index for each item (see text).
Step 4. Summarize the responses to each alternative in the upper and lower groups, and tabulate the number of	**Step 7.** Check each item to search for poor distractors, ambiguous alternatives, miskeying, and indications of blind guessing.

Table 11 • 1   Summary of the steps for doing an item analysis.

Forming Upper and Lower Scoring Groups

After you have scored the tests, arrange them in numerical order according to the total score. Next, form three groups: upper, middle, and lower scoring groups. You then contrast the responses of the upper and lower scoring groups in various ways (which I describe later) to determine whether each item is functioning as intended.

The formation of these groups is of some consequence. When the total number of pupils taking the test is between 20 and 40, select the ten highest and the ten lowest scoring papers (Whitney and Sabers, 1970), but keep the middle-scoring group intact.[2] If there are fewer than 20 pupils, the responses of only one or two pupils taking the test greatly influence the results obtained from the procedure described here. As a result, the item analysis may very well provide an erroneous indication of how a particular item would function if it were to be used again. Nevertheless, if you want to go ahead with the analysis for groups with few persons in them, separate the tests into two sets (upper and lower halves) and interpret the results cautiously. For groups larger than 40, the upper and lower scoring 27% of the group is frequently recommended

on technical grounds.[3] For purposes of classroom testing, however, when the group is larger than 40, any percentage between 25 and 33 would seem to be appropriate.

Summarize the Responses to Each Item

For each item tabulate and record the number of pupils in the (a) upper group choosing each alternative (and, separately, the number not responding (omitting)), (b) lower group choosing each alternative (and the number omitting the item); and (c) middle-scoring group choosing the *correct* alternative. Figure 11.1 shows the results of such a tabulation for one item. You also can make a form to record the necessary numbers for several items on a single page, or you may want to write in the margin of the teacher's copy of the test. Without a doubt, the most tedious part of an item analysis is tabulating the responses to items. Using an upper and lower group, instead of the entire class makes the task easier. One simplifying procedure is to make a form such as Table 11.2.

[2]Note that when there are twenty pupils, there will be no middle group.

[3]This percentage has been demonstrated optimal when a normal distribution is assumed to underlie the test scores and the item scores and when the items are of 50% difficulty (Kelly, 1939). A smaller percentage than 27 results in too few examinees and thus less stable results. A larger percentage makes the upper and lower scoring groups too alike which masks how the item distinguishes the better from the less able examinees.

Once you obtain the basic information in Table 11.2, you can make various summaries. I describe these summaries below and how to interpret them in subsequent sections of this chapter.

Computing the Item Difficulty Index (p)

The fraction of the total group answering the item correctly is called the *item difficulty index* (*p*). To compute it for each item, add together the number of pupils choosing the *correct* alternative in the upper, middle, and lower groups. Then divide this sum by the total number of persons taking the test.[4] This is illustrated below for the example item shown in Figure 11.1:

$$p = \frac{\text{no. pupils choosing correct alternative}}{\text{total no. pupils taking test}}$$

$$= \frac{\left(\begin{array}{c}\text{no. pupils choosing correct alternative} \\ \text{in upper + middle + lower group}\end{array}\right)}{\text{total no. pupils taking test}}$$

[Eq. 11.1]

$$= \frac{10 + 7 + 12}{34} = \frac{29}{34} = 0.85$$

As will be discussed later, this fraction can range from 0.00 to 1.00.

<hr>

[4]A shortcut is sometimes used:

$$\text{est. } p = \frac{\left(\begin{array}{c}\text{no. answering} \\ \text{correctly in} \\ \text{upper group}\end{array}\right) + \left(\begin{array}{c}\text{no. answering} \\ \text{correctly in} \\ \text{lower group}\end{array}\right)}{\begin{array}{c}\text{total no. pupils in upper} \\ \text{+ total number pupils in lower}\end{array}}$$

[Eq. 11.1a]

For the example in Figure 11.1, estimated $p = (10 + 7) \div (10 + 10) = 17 \div 20 = 0.85$. The fact that the shortcut is exactly equal to the actual value of *p* computed with the full group is coincidental in this example. The shortcut method is systematically erroneous (Guilford, 1954; Michael, Hertzka, & Perry, 1953). For classroom tests with relatively easy items, using the shortcut method will likely underestimate the percentage of the total class passing an item by roughly 2 to 10 percent.

Computing the Item Discrimination Index (D)

The *item discrimination index* (*D*) is the difference between the fraction of the upper group answering the item correctly and the fraction of the lower group answering it correctly. The discrimination index describes the extent to which a particular test item is able to differentiate the higher scoring pupils from the lower scoring pupils. The following equation is used to compute this index:

$$D = \left(\begin{array}{c}\text{fraction of} \\ \text{upper group} \\ \text{answering item} \\ \text{correctly}\end{array}\right) - \left(\begin{array}{c}\text{fraction of} \\ \text{lower group} \\ \text{answering item} \\ \text{correctly}\end{array}\right)$$

[Eq. 11.2]

The discrimination index for the item in Figure 11.1 is:

$$D = \frac{10}{10} - \frac{7}{10}$$

$$= 1.00 - 0.70$$

$$= 0.30$$

As we will discuss later, this index can range from −1.00 to +1.00. A hand-held calculator will facilitate computing the difficulty and discrimination indices.

Item Difficulty Index[5]

When Items are Scored Dichotomously

When items are scored dichotomously (0 or 1), the *item difficulty* (*p*) is the fraction of the persons taking an item who answer it correctly. An "easy item" is one in which the fraction *p* is relatively large. The maximum value of *p* = +1.00. An item is difficult when few

<hr>

[5]There have been a great many indices proposed in the literature. Here we discuss only those easiest for the teacher to compute. For more information see Guilford (1936, 1954), Gulliksen (1950), Davis (1951), and Lord and Novick (1968).

		Item number:									
		1	**2**	**3**	**4**	**5**	**6**	**7**	**8**	**9**	**10**
Upper group	Doris	A	C	B	B	C	C	B	A	B	D
	Jerry	A	C	B	B	C	C	B	A	B	D
	Robert	A	C	B	B	C	C	E	A	B	D
	Elazar	A	B	B	B	C	C	B	A	B	D
	Marya	A	C	B	B	C	C	B	A	B	D
	Anna	A	C	B	B	C	C	B	A	B	D
	Diana	A	C	B	B	C	C	B	A	B	D
	Harry	A	C	B	B	C	C	B	A	B	D
	Anthony	A	C	B	B	C	C	B	A	B	D
	Carolyn	A	C	B	B	B	C	B	A	B	D
										B	D
	Key	A	C	B	B	C	C	B	A	B	D
	Number choosing each option — A	10	0	0	10	0	0	0	10	0	0
	B	0	1	10	0	1	0	9	0	10	0
	C	0	9	0	–	9	10	0	0	0	0
	D	0	–	0	–	0	0	0	0	0	10
	E	–	–	–	–	–	–	1	–	–	–
	Omits	0	0	0	0	0	0	0	0	0	0
Middle group	No. right	14	12	12	13	12	13	11	11	12	12
	No. omits	0	0	0	0	0	0	0	0	0	0
Lower group	Anita	A	C	B	B	D	C	E	A	A	D
	Larry	A	C	B	B	D	C	D	A	B	D
	Charles	C	B	B	B	C	C	B	A	B	C
	Joel	A	C	B	B	C	C	E	A	B	D
	Leslie	A	C	B	B	C	C	E	A	B	B
	Alida	A	C	B	B	C	C	A	B	B	B
	Marilyn	A	C	D	B	C	C	D	C	D	A
	Wayne	A	B	A	A	C	C	B	B	C	A
	Ina	D	C	C	A	B	B	C	B	A	D
	Donald	C	B	B	B	D	C	E	C	D	D
	Key	A	C	B	B	C	C	B	A	B	D
	Number choosing each option — A	7	0	1	2	0	0	1	5	2	2
	B	0	3	7	8	1	1	2	3	5	2
	C	2	7	1	–	6	9	1	2	1	1
	D	1	–	1	–	3	0	2	0	2	5
	E	–	–	–	–	–	–	4	–	–	–
	Omits	0	0	0	0	0	0	0	0	0	0

Table 11 • 2 Item responses to the first 10 items of a 59-item test taken by a group of 34 college students. This is an example of the basic data needed to do an item analysis.

Note: The dash (–) means that that option was not available for that item.

persons respond correctly, thus p is relatively small. The minimum value of $p = 0.00$. For Item 3 of Table 11.2, $p = 0.85$ since 29 out of 34 students answer it correctly. The item difficulties for all ten items in Table 11.2 are shown below. (Verify the other nine values as an exercise.)

	Item number									
	1	2	3	4	5	6	7	8	9	10
p-value	.91	.82	.85	.91	.79	.94	.65	.76	.79	.79

Remember, item difficulty simply reflects the proportion responding correctly to an item and not the complexity of the mental processes used in responding. Essay items and some types of short answer and completion items usually are not scored simply 0 or 1, but in a more graduated or continuous scale, such as 0, 1, 2, or 4. The above index does not apply to them. One index that would quantify the difficulty level of such items is described in Whitney and Sabers (1970).

How the Difficulty Level of the Items Affects the Test Score Distribution

The shape of the distribution   The difficulty of the test items affect the shape of the distribution of total test scores. Difficult tests, containing items with $ps \le 0.25$, will tend to be positively skewed, whereas easy tests, containing items with $ps \ge 0.80$, will tend to be negatively skewed.

The shapes of total score distributions for other kinds of tests are not so intuitively deduced. Test C of Figure 11.2 shows the distribution of scores when all the items of a test are concentrated around the middle (0.50) of the difficulty scale. Test D is made up of items having difficulty values evenly spread out all along the difficulty scale (roughly from 0.10 to 0.90). Compared to Test C, Test D's *total* scores are less spread out along the score scale, and Test D is less able to reliably distinguish

among individuals. Test E is made up of items of extreme values. Two clusters of items make up the test: One cluster of very easy items (difficulty values around .80) and one cluster of very difficult items (around $0.10 - 0.30$). Intuitively, you might think that the total scores would reflect the bimodality of the item difficulties comprising the test, but this is not the case. For Test E, the total scores are more clustered in the middle than either Tests C or D, less variable than C or D, and, therefore, less able to reliably distinguish among individuals than C or D.

Average or mean test score   The difficulty of the items affects the average or mean test score: The average test score is directly related to the difficulty and number of the items comprising the test. The relationship is given below.

$$M = \Sigma p \qquad \text{[Eq. 11.3]}$$

The mean test score (M) is equal to the sum of the difficulty values (p-values) of the items comprising the test. Another way of saying this is:

$$M = k\bar{p} \qquad \text{[Eq. 11.3a]}$$

The mean test score is equal to the number of items on the test (k) times the average of p-values ($\bar{p}$). As an illustration, consider the ten items in Table 11.2. For the 34 persons who took this test, the mean score on these ten items was 7.21. As an exercise, verify this result by summing the p-values of the 10 items in Table 11.2.

Spread of scores   Figure 11.2 shows that the spread of item difficulties and the spread of test scores are related. Text C, with all p-values around 0.50, has the largest spread of test scores ($\sigma = 2.67$), while Test D ($\sigma = 2.29$) and Test E ($\sigma = 1.60$) have smaller score spreads.

Item difficulties (p-values) are not the sole factor contributing to the spread of test scores. Another factor is the correlation (Chapter 3)

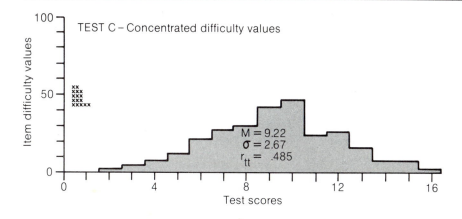

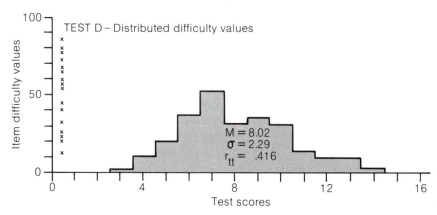

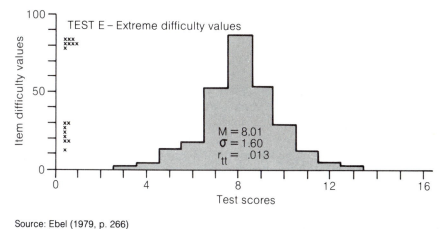

Figure 11 • 2
Distribution of test scores for three distributions of item difficulty values. The Xs on the verticle axes represent items. (In the figure M = mean score, σ = standard deviation, and r_{tt} = reliability coefficient.)

Source: Ebel (1979, p. 266)

among the items: The higher the intercorrelation, the larger the standard deviation. However, the intercorrelations among items may be affected by these *p*-values: Items for which $p = 0.00$ or 1.00 have intercorrelations of 0.00.

How to Use Information on Item Difficulty

Table 11.3 summarizes some of the ways in which *p*-values can be used in testing and instruction. For the teacher, perhaps identifying concepts to be retaught and giving students feedback about their learning are the more important uses of item difficulty data. Uses such as obtaining information about curriculum strengths or about suspected item bias require district-wide cooperation and tend to be employed only with published standardized tests. Teachers may find themselves involved in these activities as part of their service on school committees, or if they have been promoted to administrative positions. Procedures for using *p*-values to build special purpose tests are described later in this chapter.

Item Discrimination Index

Step 6 in Table 11.1 states that a discrimination index should be computed for each item; an example of how to compute it was given on page 288. This computation can be summarized by the following formula:

$$D = p_U - p_L \qquad \text{[Eq. 11.2a]}$$

where *D* stands for the numerical value of the discrimination index, p_U stands for the fraction of the upper scoring group answering the item correctly, and p_L stands for the fraction of the lower scoring group answering the item correctly. This index is sometimes referred to as the *net D* index of discrimination. Net *D* is seldom used today by commercial test developers who now use a correlation coefficient

as a discrimination index.[6] Net *D* is probably the most useful discrimination index available for use with teacher-made tests, however. The index was first presented by A. Pemberton Johnson (1951), who had used it to develop Army Air Force bombardier knowledge tests during World War II.

Importance of Item Discrimination when Testing Relative Achievement

Absolute achievement measurement focuses mainly on accurately determining the content or behavior each pupil has learned. Relative achievement measurement, on the other hand, focuses mainly on accurately determining the relative ordering among pupils with respect to the content or behavior learned. When measuring relative achievement, items which do not contribute information about ordering pupils or which provide inconsistent, confusing information about this ordering should be either revised or removed from the test.

Consider the case in which a class of pupils is ordered from high to low on the basis of a 30-item unit test. Suppose, further, that when doing an item analysis, the teacher divides the class in half based on the total test score (as usual, higher scorers in the upper group, lower scorers in the lower group). Finally, suppose that for one of the items the teacher discovers that all of the lower group pupils answered the item correctly while all of the upper group answered it incorrectly. In this case, the item difficulty index is $p = 0.50$, but the item discrimination index is $D = 0 - 1.00 = -1.00$. This negative discriminating item is poor because getting the item right is associated with a lower test score. If put on a test, negatively discriminating items would arrange pupils in an order that is quite different than the arrangement made by the positively discriminating items on the test.

[6]Usually the biserial or point biserial correlation coefficient are used; see Henryson (1971). In the future, many tests may be using a more sophisticated procedure based on latent trait theory to analyse and select test items.

Purpose	Procedure	Comments
Identifying concepts which need to be retaught	Find items with small p-values. These items may point to objectives needing to be retaught.	a. Poor test performance may not reflect poor teaching: Poor performance may reflect poorly written items, incorrect prior learning, or poor motivation on tests. b. A score based on several similar items is more reliable than performance on a single item.
Clues to possible strengths and weaknesses in school curricula	Calculate p-values for clusters of similar items for a school building or district. Compare these to p-values of the same items from the publisher's national norm-group. Note areas of strength and weakness.	a. See a and b above. b. This procedure applies to standardized tests only. c. Items must correspond to local curriculum objectives and instruction. d. No published test will cover all the objectives of a school district.
Giving feedback to students	Report p-value of each item to student along with ID number of the items missed.	a. Such reporting is more useful for high school and college students. b. See Figure 11.3.
Clues to possible item bias	Separate test papers into groups to be contrasted (e.g., males vs. females, blacks vs. whites). Compute p-values for each item separately for each group. Items for which p-value differences are unusually large are studied further to see if they may be biased.	a. This is only a crude method and not a scientifically satisfactory method (Lord, 1977). b. This procedure is not very useful in small samples of examinees because of sampling fluctuations.
Building tests that have certain statistical properties	See Table 11.4.	

Table 11 • 3   Examples of ways in which item difficulty indices can be used in testing and instruction.

In the preceding case, only the discrimination index was able to detect this malfunctioning item. The difficulty index indicated that half the class answered the item correctly but did not indicate *which half* answered correctly. For this reason, an item's discrimination index is given more weight than its difficulty index when the teacher is deciding whether the item should appear on the final version of a test. The discrimination index takes into account both the number of pupils answering an item correctly, and whether these pupils are in the upper or lower scoring group.

The numerical limits of D   If all the discriminations made by an item were *correct* discrim-

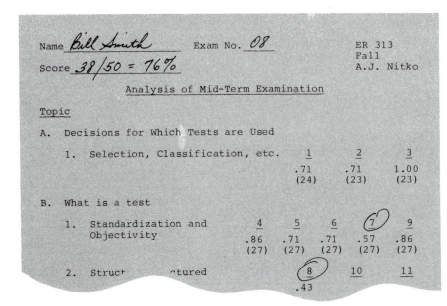

Figure 11 • 3
Item difficulty (p)
values can be used to
give feedback to stu-
dents. A page such as
this one is prepared
for each student sum-
marizing class perfor-
mance. The teacher
circles the identification
number of the items a
student misses. Deci-
mal numbers are p-
values for the class,
underlined numbers
are the identifications
of the questions, and
the number in paren-
theses is the page in
the text where more
information can
be found.

inations—everyone in the upper group answering the item right, everyone in the lower group answering it wrong—net D would equal $+1$ and the item is said to be a perfect discriminator. If the number of correct discriminations equaled the number of incorrect discriminations—an equal number of upper and lower group pupils answering the item right—then $D = 0$, since the net correct would equal 0. Such an item is said to be a non-discriminating item. Finally, if all discriminations were *incorrect* ones—everyone in the upper group answering the item wrong and everyone in the lower group answering it right—then D would equal -1 and the item is said to be a perfect negative discriminator.

The values $+1$ and -1 are seldom obtained in practice; $D = 0$ is obtained most often for very easy or very hard items. The

values -1, 0, $+1$ serve as benchmarks when interpreting D.

D can signal items needing revision A value of D less than zero is a flag indicating that the item should be carefully studied and either revised or eliminated. If a technical flaw cannot be found in the item, it might be that pupils in the upper scoring group learned the material either incompletely or entirely incorrectly (Lindquist, 1936a). (See Box 8.2 for examples of these.) Barring any rational explanation to the contrary, all items should be positively discriminating; otherwise the total score on the test won't provide usable information.

Spread of scores Intuitively, you know that if none of the items discriminated (i.e., $D = 0$ for all items), everyone would be bunched together: If individual items can't distinguish persons, then the ensemble of items won't be able to do so either. The larger the test's average level of item discrimination, the more spread out will be the test scores.[7]

***p* and *D* are related**   Figure 11.4 shows the relationship between item difficulty (*p*) and net *D* item discrimination. The boundaries of the "diamond" represent the maximum and minimum *D*-values possible (but not necessarily attained) for each value of item difficulty. For example, if $p = 0.8$, then *D* will be between -0.4 and $+0.4$. Note that it is possible for *D* to reach $+1$ only when $p = 0.5$. Some test developers recommend retaining as many items as possible which have high, positive *D*-values. Selecting items on the basis of such *D*-values will result in retaining items of only middle difficulty in Figure 11.4. The items on a test, however, must match the test blueprint. Thus, statistical considerations are not the sole determiners of whether particular items should be placed on a test. (See **But don't let the "tail wag the dog,"** [p. 296]).

Test reliability and item discrimination power   As used in this chapter, reliability refers to the extent to which the differences we observe among the examinees' test scores can be attributed to differences in the true abilities of the examinees, instead of attributing observed differences among examinees to random errors of measurement. (A more complete discussion of reliability is presented in Chapter 15.) A more reliable test will be made up of items with high, positive discrimination indices. Thus, if the primary purpose of using a test is to interpret differences in relative achievement between individuals, it is essential that the test be comprised of items with high discriminating power.

[7]For a normal distribution (see Chapter 14), the relationship between the average *D*-value $\overline{D}$, and the standard deviation, σ (see Chapter 3), is (Ebel 1967):

$$\overline{D} = \frac{2.45\sigma}{\text{number of items}}.$$

Using Item Analysis Data to Improve the Quality of Multiple-Choice Items

Identifying Poorly Functioning Distractors

The function of the distractors or foils in a multiple-choice item is to appear plausible to those lacking sufficient knowledge to choose the correct answer. Item analysis data of the type summarized in Table 11.2 can signal items in which this function may not be fulfilled.

The general rule is this: *Every incorrect alternative should have at least one lower group person choosing it, and more lower group persons than upper group persons should choose a particular incorrect alternative.* The following data from

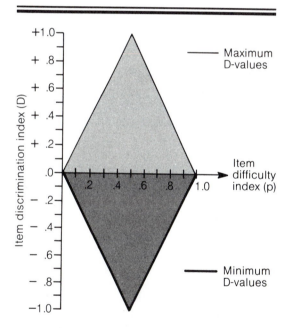

Source: Prompted by Ebel (1965, p. 353), and Kryspin & Feldhusen (1974, p. 144).

Figure 11 • 4   Relationship between item difficulty (*p*) and item discrimination (*D*). Only items with middle difficulty levels can have high, positive discriminations.

the item presented in Figure 11.1 illustrates these points:

Alternative	Upper Group	Lower Group
A	0	1
*B	10	7
C	0	1
D	0	1

Each incorrect alternative (A, C, and D) has been chosen by at least one lower group person; no pupil in the upper group chose an incorrect alternative.[8]

The rationale for this rule is as follows. Those scoring lowest on the test are, on the whole, least knowledgeable (in a relative, not absolute, sense) about the subject being tested. If they are not, then the test on which they scored lowest must lack validity. For a particular item, it is among these lower scoring pupils that one should expect to find an item answered incorrectly. Thus, if an item is functioning properly, one or more lower scoring pupils should choose each incorrect alternative, and more lower scoring than upper scoring pupils should choose incorrect alternatives.

Notice that it is not the case that every lower scoring person lacks knowledge about every item: In this example, seven out of ten lower scoring persons knew the answer. Neither is it the case that all higher scoring persons always chose the correct answer (see, for example, Items 2, 5, and 7 in Table 11.2).

If no one in the lower group chooses a particular incorrect alternative, it *may* be functioning poorly, and the teacher should review the item. Perhaps the particular alternative contains one of the technical flaws described in Chapter 8. If everyone recognizes a particular option as obviously incorrect, then the

teacher will want to either (a) eliminate it entirely (thus, reducing the number of options in the item), (b) substitute an entirely new alternative, or (c) revise the existing alternative.

But don't let the "tail wag the dog" It isn't always true that an alternative is flawed if no one in the lower group chooses it. Here's where your knowledge of the students, the instruction they received prior to taking the test, and the subject matter come into play: Perhaps in this year's group, even the lowest scoring pupils have enough knowledge to eliminate a particular distractor, yet do not have enough knowledge to select the correct answer. Perhaps in other groups a concept will not be learned as well, and this particular distractor will be plausible. Eliminating the alternative would make identifying those few individuals who lack this learning impossible.

Finally, note that even though it seems reasonable to *expect* a larger number of lower scoring pupils than higher scoring pupils to choose a particular incorrect alternative, this may not always happen. Technical flaws may cause higher scoring pupils to be deceived, such as when they know a great deal about the subject and thus are able to give a plausible reason why an unkeyed alternative is at least as correct as the keyed one. In such cases, the alternative should be revised. But sometimes there is neither a technical flaw nor a subject matter deficiency in an incorrect alternative, yet higher scoring pupils choose it in greater numbers than lower scoring ones. In these cases, the problem may be that pupils have incomplete learning or wrong learning.

Searching for Ambiguous Alternatives

Pupil responses can provide leads to possible ambiguously worded alternatives. In this context, alternatives are ambiguous if *upper group pupils are unable to distinguish between the correct answer and one or more of the supposed distractors* (Sax, 1974). When this hap-

---

[8]Note that because of fluctuations in responses from one small group of students to another, you must use the rules of thumb in this section cautiously.

pens, the upper group tends to choose a distractor with about the same frequency as the keyed response. The result is a response pattern similar to that illustrated by the item below:

Example 142.

The city of Pittsburgh, Pennsylvania is located on which river?	Upper group	Lower group
a. Monongahela River	4	3
b. Ohio River	5	3
c. Delaware River	0	1
d. Susquehanna River	1	3

The confluence of the Allegheny and Monongahela Rivers forms the Ohio River at Pittsburgh. Looking at the *upper group* reveals that they chose "a" and "b" with approximately equal frequency, thus reflecting the ambiguity in the correctness of these two alternatives. This item should be revised so that only one answer is correct or best (in some clear sense).

You might notice that very often the *lower group* is equally divided among two or more alternatives. This is usually not an indication that item revision is needed but that those with less knowledge will find many alternatives equally plausible, and so the situation becomes an ambiguous one for them. The cause of their ambiguity is likely to be insufficient knowledge.

Before concluding that the item needs revision, however, you need to study the item in relation to the pupils taking it and to judge whether the ambiguity stems from lack of knowledge rather than a poorly written item (Sax, 1974). Consider the following item:

Example 143.

3 + 5 × 2 = ?	Upper group	Lower group
a. 10	0	2
*b. 13	5	3
c. 16	5	3
d. 30	0	2

Here the student is required to apply arithmetic operations in a certain order: multiplication first, then addition. Option "b" reflects this order, while option "c" is the answer obtained by adding first and then multiplying. Apparently half the upper group followed this erroneous procedure and chose "c." The item is not technically flawed, but from the pupils' responses the teacher should realize that a number of them need to learn this principle. (The responses of the entire group to this item should be checked.)

Identifying Miskeyed Items

If a larger number of *upper* group pupils select a particular "wrong" response, check the test question and answer key to be sure the appropriate alternative has been scored as the correct answer. In the example below "c" is the correct answer, but the teacher inadvertently used "d" in the answer key.

Example 144.

Who was the fourth president of the United States?	Upper group	Lower group
a. John Quincy Adams	0	3
b. Thomas Jefferson	1	4
c. James Madison	9	3
*d. James Monroe	0	3

Again, be sure to check the item—the numbers from the item analysis only signal possible miskeying—perhaps there is no miskeying and the upper group simply lacks the required knowledge.

Identifying Items on Which Blind Guessing May Be Occurring

If all the alternatives are equally plausible to the *upper* scoring group, either the item is flawed, or the information it is testing has not been acquired. In such situations students tend to either omit the item or to guess blindly: Each option tends to be chosen an approximately equal number of times in the upper group as illustrated by this item:

Example 145.

In what year did the United States enter World War I?	Upper group	Lower group
a. 1913	2	3
b. 1915	2	2
c. 1916	3	3
*d. 1917	3	2

Look at the responses of the upper group not those of the lower group to find items on which many pupils may be guessing. The most knowledge is likely to be found in the upper scoring group. Lower scoring pupils may in fact be guessing on the more difficult items. Blind guessing adds errors of measurement to the scores.

Using Item Analysis Data to Select Items to Put on a Test

Another Purpose for Doing Item Analysis

Most teachers using item analysis procedures will do so for one or more of the following reasons: (a) to check on whether the items are functioning as intended, (b) to provide feedback to students on their test performance, (c) to provide feedback to themselves about pupils' difficulties, (d) to study areas of the curriculum that may need improvement, and (e) to provide objective data which signal the need for revising items. There is another use for item analysis: selecting some items and culling others from a pool of items. Although such item selection procedures have been used mostly by professional test developers, they can be adapted to the development of classroom tests.

Knowing the purpose of testing is prerequisite to selecting items No statistical item selection rule is helpful if it is inconsistent with the reason for giving the test. Further, any procedure for selecting some items over others changes the definition of the domain of performance. Pupil behaviors represented by eliminated items are never observed on the test.

Relative vs. absolute pupil attainment The judicious selection of items results in shorter, more efficient, and more accurate tests. In the classroom, statistically based item *selection* seems to be most applicable when a teacher is concerned with the relative achievement of pupils rather than their absolute achievement. The assessment of *relative achievement* focuses mainly on accurately determining the relative ordering of pupils with respect to what they have learned. The assessment of *absolute achievement* focuses mainly on accurately determining the precise content (or performance) each pupil has learned. As an example, consider the 100 simple addition facts typically taught in first and second grades. If a teacher wants to know only the relative attainment of the pupils (who knows the most, next most, and so on), a relatively short test, made up of only those facts which best discriminated among the learners, covering, perhaps, mostly the middle and upper parts of the addition table, would work. Addition facts which almost everyone knows (e.g., $1 + 1 = 2$) would not be included on such a test because these items would not discriminate ($D = 0$) and, therefore, would not provide information about ordering of persons. On the other hand, if the test purpose is to identify the particular combinations with which a pupil has difficulty, in order to individualize a drill program for that pupil, then finding out the absolute level of attainment would be the main reason for testing. A longer, less efficient test method, perhaps testing all 100 facts over a period of several days, would be necessary. Excluding items from the test because they do not discriminate well means being unable to observe a pupil's performance on all 100 addition facts.

Absolute, rather than relative, achievement is more important for so-called "diagnostic" tests which are intended to identify such things as whether a pupil has acquired particular reading skills, learned a certain percentage of facts in some specified domain, and/or has the ability to solve certain types of problems. Relative achievement is more important when one is ascertaining a pupil's general educational development in a subject area.

Complete vs. partial ordering For some educational decisions, you may need to distinguish the relative achievement of each pupil from every other pupil. For example, you may want to accurately rank all pupils for their overall reading comprehension. Such an ordering of all pupils is called a *complete ordering*. On the other hand, you may want to separate pupils, for example, into five ordered groups so that grades can be assigned, but you may not wish to make distinctions among the pupils within each group. Similarly, you may wish to divide the class into two groups: pass/fail or faster/slower readers. When the classifications are ordered, but there is no ordering of individuals within a classification, this is called a *partial ordering*.

When the focus of the test is on either partial or complete ordering, including items which do not contribute to ordering and distinguishing individuals is inefficient; such items are, therefore, culled from the pool. To cull, items are tried-out with pupils before the final test is developed, and item statistics (p and D) are calculated. Items with high, positive discrimination indices, generally, of middle difficulty are selected and assembled into the final test form which is used with a subsequent group of students.

Realities, content coverage, and compromises In practice, it is necessary to include test items with less than ideal statistical properties in order for a test to match its blueprint (see Chapter 5). Actual test construction tends to be a compromise between considerations of subject-matter coverage and psychometric properties (Henrysson, 1971). The general principle is: *Select the best available items which cover the important areas of content as defined by the blueprint, even though the discrimination and difficulty indices of these items have values that are less than ideal.*

Rules of Thumb for Selecting Test Items

Table 11.4 summarizes certain guidelines for selecting items for classroom tests, keeping in mind the above discussion about the differences between building a test to measure relative achievement and building one to measure absolute achievement. Note that coverage of content and objectives takes primacy over statistical indices when selecting test items by the procedures recommended here. The guidelines shown in the table necessitate an understanding of whether the prospective test should measure only one ability or characteristic of a pupil or a combination of several abilities. A *homogeneous test* will measure one ability, while a *heterogeneous test* will measure a combination.

If a test contains items for which examinees have a greater than zero chance of getting the right answer by blind guessing—such as is the case with multiple-choice, true-false, and matching items—then the recommendations for item difficulty found in Table 11.4 tend to be modified somewhat. The items selected under guessing conditions should be approximately 5 percent easier than shown in the table. Traditionally, the optimum p-value has been thought to be halfway between the probability of guessing the correct answer and 1.00.[9] More recent developments suggest, however, that for a homogeneous test, items should be easier (Lord, 1980), as the following show.

---

[9] Optimum $p = 0.5 + 0.5 (1/A)$, where A is equal to the number of alternatives the item contains.

Number of options in the item	Probability of guessing correctly	Traditional recommendation for p [10]	Lord's recommendation for p [10]
0	0	0.50	0.50
2	0.50	0.75	0.81
3	0.33	0.67	0.73
4	0.25	0.63	0.68
5	0.20	0.60	0.65

When designing a test of relative achievement, you should remember that good item discrimination takes precedence over obtaining the ideal item difficulty level if two items measure the same objective. That is, if two items measure the same objective and are of approximately the same level of difficulty (even though that level is not ideal), put the one on the test which discriminates better.

Criterion-referenced testing Item statistics play a lesser role when designing a test of absolute achievement, although they should be calculated in order to obtain data on how the items are functioning. Items exhibiting zero or negative discrimination frequently contain technical flaws which may not be noticed if item statistics are not computed. Similarly, you should do a distractor analysis.

Some experts recommend that criterion-referenced tests used for assessing mastery contain only items that are easier after instruction than before (Cox & Vargas, 1966; Carver, 1974). This recommendation is implemented by (a) administering the same items before and after instruction, (b) computing p-values for both the pretest and posttest, and (c) computing the posttest-pretest difference between these p-values. For each item compute:

$$\text{Difference} = p_{POST} - p_{PRE} \qquad \text{[Eq. 11.4]}$$

The ideal item, according to this view, has a difference of $+1.00$—i.e., $p_{POST} = +1.00$, while $p_{PRE} = 0.00$. Items which most nearly approximate this ideal are selected for the final form of the test.

However, I take the view that you should not use this index to select items when designing tests for absolute achievement interpretations. Since the content of the items in the domain is important, culling distorts and makes the test unrepresentative of the domain. Also, selecting only items with positive differences means that you use only those items for which instruction has been effective: You have no way of identifying content pupils have not learned (Difference $= 0$), or for which instruction has somehow lowered the chances of pupils responding correctly (Difference <0). Finally, in most classroom testing situations the number of pupils on whom p_{PRE} and p_{POST} is computed is relatively small which results in the difference index being highly susceptible to chance fluctuations, and you may receive erroneous information about how an item is functioning. For other comments on this technique of item selection see Cronbach (1975), Gladstone (1975), Haladyna (1975), and King (1975). A rather complete review of item statistics for criterion-referenced tests is found in Berk (1980).

[10]These recommendations apply to large populations; fluctuations in small samples are to be expected. Therefore, these recommendations provide only rough guidelines for use with classroom tests.

	Relative achievement is the focus		Absolute achievement is the focus
	Complete ordering	Partial ordering (two groups)	
General concerns	Ranking all the pupils in terms of their relative attainment in a subject area.	Dividing pupils into two groups on the basis of their relative attainment. Pupils within each group will be treated alike.	Assess the absolute status (achievement) of the pupil with respect to a well-defined domain of instructionally relevant tasks.
Specific focus of test	Seek to accurately describe differences in relative achievement between individual pupils.	Seek to accurately classify persons into two categories.	Seek to accurately estimate the percentage of the domain each pupil can perform successfully.
Attention to the test's blueprint	Be sure that items cover all important topics and objectives within the blueprint.	Be sure that items cover all important topics and objectives within the blueprint.	Be sure items are a representative, random sample from the defined domain which the blueprint operationalizes.
How the difficulty index (p) is used	Within each topical area of the blueprint, select those items with: (1) p between 0.16 and 0.84, if performance on the test represents a single ability. (2) p between 0.40 and 0.60, if performance on the test represents several different abilities. Note: Items should be easier than described above if guessing is a factor.	Within each topical area of the blueprint, select those items with p-values slightly larger than the percentage of persons to be classified in the upper group [e.g., if the class is to be divided in half (0.50) then items with p-values of about 0.60 should be selected; if the division is lower 75% vs. upper 25%, items should have $p = 0.35$ (approximately)]. Note: The above suggestion assumes the test measures a single ability.	Don't select items on the basis of their p-values, but study each p to see if it is signaling a poorly written item.
How the discrimination index (D) is used	Within each topical area of the blueprint, select items with D greater than or equal to $+0.30$.	Within each topical area of the blueprint, select items with D greater than or equal to $+0.30$.	All items should have D greater than or equal to 0.00. Unless there is a rational explanation to the contrary, revise those items not possessing this property.

Table 11 • 4   Rules of thumb for using item analysis data to build classroom tests.

Summary

The following are the major points of this chapter.

1. Item analysis refers to the process of collecting, summarizing, and using information about pupils' responses to each test item.

2. Important uses of item analyses of classroom tests are in (a) determining whether the items function as the teacher intends, (b) providing feedback to students on their performance and providing a basis for class discussion, (c) providing feedback to the teacher about the pupils' difficulties, (d) suggesting areas for curriculum improvement, (e) revising the items on the test, and (f) facilitating the improvement of item-writing skills.

3. Poorly functioning distractors on multiple-choice items can be identified by tabulating the number of persons choosing each alternative. The tabulation is done separately for an upper scoring and a lower scoring group. As a general rule, every incorrect alternative should have at least one lower group person choosing it, and more lower group persons than upper group persons should choose a particular incorrect alternative.

4. Alternatives are ambiguous if higher scoring pupils are unable to distinguish between the correct answer and one or more of the alternatives the teacher judges to be incorrect. Either a poorly written item or a lack of knowledge on the part of students may create ambiguity.

5. An item should be checked for inadvertent miskeying if a large number of higher scoring pupils choose a particular wrong response.

6. Teachers should suspect that pupils are engaging in considerable blind guessing if approximately an equal number of higher scoring pupils are choosing each alternative.

7. A measure of an item's difficulty is p, the fraction of the total group correctly responding to the item. The most difficult item has $p = 0.00$, while the easiest items have $p = 1.00$.

8. A measure of an item's discrimination power is D, the difference between the fraction of the upper extreme group answering the item correctly and the fraction of the lower extreme group answering it correctly. The index ranges from -1.00 to $+1.00$. Items which do not discriminate have D-values near zero. Many test developers strive to have items with $D \geqslant +0.30$.

9. The shape of the score distribution, its mean, and the spread of scores are affected by the p-values of the items on the test.

10. Factors affecting an item's difficulty (p-value) include (a) the effectiveness of instruction, (b) the item's technical quality, (c) the pupils' background and previous education, and (d) the pupils' motivation when taking the test.

11. Item difficulty can provide information (a) on instructional effectiveness, (b) for feedback to pupils, (c) on areas of curriculum strength and weakness, and (d) for suspecting possible item bias.

12. The item discrimination index, D, can be interpreted as the fraction of net correct discriminations the item makes out of the total possible discriminations.

13. The magnitude of the item discrimination indices in a test (a) affects the spread of total scores in the group, (b) is limited by the difficulty of the items, and (c) affects the tests ability to distinguish differences among persons in a reliable manner.

14. The assessment of relative achievement focuses mainly on the relative ordering of pupils with respect to what they have learned (e.g., who has learned most, next most, and so on). Assessment of absolute achievement focuses mainly on accurately describing the content or performance each pupil has learned. Absolute achievement is of more concern when attempting to "diagnose" pupil difficulties; relative achievement is of more concern in ascertaining a pupil's general educational development in an area.

15. The p and D indices can be used together with the test blueprint to select from a larger pool of items those which will best measure relative achievement. Rules of thumb for such suggestions are summarized in Table 11.4.

16. The p and D indices generally are not used to select items when the focus of the test is on assessment of absolute achievement.

Themes

● Classroom testing is usually considered an occasion for pupils to demonstrate their maximum or best performance rather than their typical performance.

● Teachers have control over certain information and conditions which may facilitate pupils showing their best performance on classroom tests. These include (a) designing test materials appropriately, (b) giving pupils essential information about an upcoming test, (c) recognizing and teaching test-taking skills, and (d) attempting to alleviate test anxiety.

● Students need to be informed of and perhaps taught the best strategy to use to mark and/or change answers, particularly when their scores are to be corrected for guessing.

Terms and Concepts

maximum performance test
minimum performance test
minimum test-taking skills
test-wiseness
response sets
guessing (risk-taking)
test anxiety
task-relevant vs. task-irrelevant
    responses

worry vs. emotionality
treatments for test anxiety
    (desensitization, implosion,
    relaxation, cognitive procedures,
    observational learning, study skills)
correction for guessing formulas
expected chance score

12
HELPING STUDENTS DO THEIR BEST ON CLASSROOM TESTS

As a teacher there are few things more rewarding than to see pupils doing the things you have helped them learn. Classroom testing provides one occasion on which pupils can demonstrate this learning. My view expressed in this chapter is that pupils should demonstrate their maximum capabilities on classroom tests and that teachers can do certain things to facilitate pupils showing their best performances on examinations.

This chapter has six major sections. The first section discusses how the test booklet itself can facilitate good pupil performance. The second section discusses the information a pupil needs in order to prepare for an upcoming test. Included in this section is a discussion of the minimum test-taking skills a pupil should learn. A third section deals specifically with test wiseness which includes not only general test-taking skills, but knowledge of how to take advantage of poorly constructed items. A fourth section discusses test anxiety: what it is and ways in which it has been treated. Factors to consider when deciding whether to use a correction or penalty for guessing is the theme of the fifth section. Included in that section are suggestions for telling students about their best strategy for both marking answers and changing answers already marked. The final section reviews several things a pupil might learn to do to prepare for a test and points out that pupils will differ widely in their learning of these test preparation skills.

The Test Itself

The final appearance and arrangement of a test is of importance to the students. An illegible, poorly typed, and illogically arranged test annoys the well-prepared student, can cause unnecessary errors, and gives students the impression that the teacher has not taken the evaluation task seriously.

Each Pupil Should Receive a Copy of the Test Items

As a rule, tests requiring pupils to write answers should be typed (or written neatly) and duplicated so that each student can have a copy. (Obvious exceptions are dictated spelling tests and tests of similar aural abilities.) Sometimes a teacher will write the items on the chalkboard or dictate them to the class. Although this procedure saves the teacher time, it may cause problems for pupils especially those with visual, listening comprehension, or hearing problems, and is, therefore, counterproductive. Further, dictating the questions uses time that pupils could otherwise spend in responding to the items. Reading a question and requiring students to write their responses places a demand on short-term memory which many students cannot meet (see Box 12.1).

Layout and Design of the Test Booklet

Organization of the booklet If there are many objective items, arranging them into a test booklet is useful. (The few questions that comprise an essay test may conveniently be presented on a single sheet of paper.) When an objective test is to be given to a large class, you can arrange the test booklet with a cover page that identifies the course and specifies the directions, followed by groups of items of

Box 12 • 1

one type (e.g., all the true-false items, all the multiple-choice items, all the matching items, and all the short-answer items).

A cover page has the advantage of keeping those who receive the booklet first from beginning the test before the rest of the class and before the teacher has answered all clarifying questions. Grouping the items by type of format (true-false, multiple-choice, and matching) is advantageous. When items are arranged in this manner, the examinee doesn't have to change "mental sets." Good exam form or order can reduce inadvertent errors caused by switching back and forth from one format to another.

Experts usually recommend that items appear in the order of difficulty levels with the easiest items placed first. Most pupils can go through the easiest items quickly and reserve the remaining test time for the most difficult items. Another way to arrange items is according to the sequence the content was taught or appeared in the textbook. Pupils can then use the subject-matter organization as a kind of "cognitive map" through which they can retrieve stored information to use with test items. If you use this sequential arrangement, you should encourage students to skip over items with which they experience difficulty and go on to subsequent items which

may be easier. (You should encourage students, of course, to return to the omitted items if they have time.)

Directions to pupils Test directions should contain certain minimum information: (a) How many items are on the test, and what format are they? (b) How much time will be allowed to complete the test? (c) Where and how should answers be written? (d) Will there be a penalty for incorrect guesses? (e) Is there a general strategy the examinee should follow when answering questions? For example, should examinees "guess" if they think they know the answer but are unsure? Should they answer all items or should they omit some? Which ones? Should they do each item in turn or should they skip those of which they are uncertain, returning to them later if they have time? If the examinee perceives that the answer to an item requires opinion, whose opinion is being asked (teacher, textbook author, others)? For the example of a cover page in Figure 12.1, the teacher would have to supplement the directions to cover the above points. However most written directions need not be elaborate.

Use side headings to signal a change in the general directions which may occur within the test booklet. Some items may require specific directions: for example, "Read the paragraph below before answering Items 12, 13, 14, and 15"; or "Items 9, 10, 11, and 12 are based on the data found in the table below." To draw students' attention to these changes, underline the side headings.

Duplicating the test Most schools have spirit dittos and mimeographs. Some schools have photocopying equipment usually considered too expensive for ordinary classroom use. Whatever equipment you use, be sure the master (or original) is prepared well and the equipment is in good working order. Poor quality copies may affect pupil performance.

Use the particular duplicating process that best reproduces your items. Drawing on ordinary mimeographed masters is often difficult.

No. *15*
FM. A67SPS

University of Pittsburgh

Educational Research Methodology   Testing & Meas. In the Classroom

Final Examination

DIRECTIONS TO STUDENTS

(1) This is a closed book test. Do not refer to your text or notes.

(2) Be sure your answer sheet is numbered the same as your test booklet.

(3) You must use a Number Two graphite pencil.

(4) Print your NAME on your answer sheet.

(5) All of the questions in this booklet are in the true-false, matching, or multiple-choice format. You are to choose the best answer or the correct answer to each question and then blacken the corresponding space on your separate answer sheet.

(6) Attempt to answer each question. Do not spend too much time on any one question. If a given question puzzles you, go on to the next one, which may be easier. You may guess at the right answer. Since there is no penalty for guessing, you should ANSWER EVERY QUESTION.

(7) As you work on the test, keep your place on the answer sheet. Make certain that the answer you are marking is numbered the same as the item you are answering.

(8) Do not write in the test booklet except where directed to do so.

Figure 12 • 1
An example of a test booklet cover page with directions to the students.

Spirit masters permit easier drawing, but fine detail is often not possible. Photocopying is the most versatile technique, permitting not only drawings to be reproduced, but often photographs as well. It may be possible to use several processes within one test. Whatever process you use, be sure the chemicals do not produce objectionable odors. (A pupil will have enough problems just trying to figure out the answers!)

Test security may be a problem if the tests are sent to a central location for duplication and assembly. Be sure to check the security procedures if this is a problem for you.

Preparations for Scoring the Test

Prepare for scoring a test before you administer the test. Prepare and verify an answer key in advance so that you can score students' tests efficiently and report results quickly. Advance preparation of an answer key will help you identify errors in the test items, too.

Although separate answer sheets are not recommended for use in the first three grades, with older elementary and high school pupils, it may be advisable to use a separate answer sheet for objective items. This greatly facilitates scoring and permits the test booklet to be reused. The answer sheet for completion items might consist of columns with numbered blanks, each number corresponding to an item number. The pupil writes the answer to an item on the correspondingly numbered blank.

Machine scoreable answer sheets are available in some schools. These may be used for hand scoring as well as machine scoring. If you are planning to use machine scoring, check with the office in your school that does the scoring to be sure you use the proper answer sheets, and students follow the correct answer marking procedures.

A tag board scoring key can be made: Staple an answer sheet having all the correct answers marked to half of an old manila folder. Then punch out the correct answers. (A special punch just for this purpose is available. Check with your scoring service or testing director.) To minimize scoring errors, connect the holes within a column of the answer sheet with lines. The key is then placed over a pupil's answer sheet and the items missed are marked with a colored pencil. Chapter 6 describes the scoring process for essay tests. Review those suggestions at this point.

Informing Pupils about an Upcoming Test

Test users are becoming increasingly aware that examinees ought to receive much more information about a forthcoming test than has been the usual practice in the past. A test of achievement is considered to be a test of maximum performance rather than of typical performance (Cronbach, 1970). *Maximum performance tests* attempt to assess an examinee at his or her best; *typical performance tests* attempt to assess what an examinee would do under ordinary or typical conditions. To be tested under the best conditions, a pupil needs to know at least the following information about an upcoming test:

1. When it will be given.
2. Under what conditions it will be given.
3. The general content areas it will cover.
4. The emphasis or weighting of content areas to be included on the test.
5. The types of performance on content the pupil will have to demonstrate (e.g., the kinds of items on the test, the degree to which memory will be required, etc.).
6. How the test will be scored and graded.
7. The importance of the particular test in relation to decisions about the pupil.

Minimum Information a Pupil Needs

When a test will be given   In order to do well on a test a student needs to prepare in advance. Students, particularly those taking courses taught by more than one teacher, need to organize their study efforts and set their priorities. They can learn to do this planning when they know in advance the date on which they will be held accountable.[1]

Some teachers advocate "surprise" or "pop" quizzes. The reasoning behind such tests is often some vague notion that a "good" student should always "be prepared" to perform on command. This seems hardly to be the way most aspects of one's life are conducted. Teachers, for example, make lesson plans and

---

[1] Teachers can coordinate their schedule of testing so tests are spread out. The end of a marking period is often problematic in this regard.

prepare to teach these lessons in advance. They are often resentful (and rightfully so) if asked to teach a class for which they have not had sufficient time to prepare. Some union contracts require teachers to be notified ahead of time if a supervisor, principal, or parent will come to the classroom to observe and/or evaluate them. Good planning requires knowing in advance what a person needs to accomplish. I recommend that pupils receive at least 48 hours notice before a quiz.

Some teachers believe that surprise quizzes motivate pupils. There is no evidence to support this point, but there is some evidence that students will do better if they know in advance that a test is coming (Tyler and Chalmers, 1943). An anecdote will reinforce this point: When asked to avoid giving surprise quizzes to a particular youngster, a teacher became incensed, saying "Why, if I did *that*, he would get an 'A' on all his quizzes!"

Students with special problems are likely to benefit from knowing about a test well in advance. Test anxiety and fear are likely to be reduced when a pupil can rationally plan a program of study for a forthcoming test. Handicapped children mainstreamed in the class often have regular instruction supplemented by an itinerant teacher or tutor who sees the student only once or twice a week. Suppose a hearing handicapped youngster has not understood Wednesday's lesson, and the itinerant teacher regularly comes on Monday. Further, suppose the quiz is "popped" on Friday. How can this youngster be expected to effectively plan and use the resources provided when the actions of the regular teacher are unpredictable?

Some teachers use surprise quizzes to threaten or to punish a disobedient class. I would consider this an unethical use of a test.

The conditions of testing A student should be told the conditions under which he is expected to perform: How many items will be on the test? What length of time will the student have for the testing period? Will the test be speeded? Will it be open or closed book? Will there be a penalty for guessing? And at what time of day will it be given (if not during a regular period)?

Content to be covered To say that the test will cover the first three chapters of the book doesn't help a student much. To plan and study effectively, a student needs to determine what the important areas are for which the student will be held accountable. Some teachers prepare lists of study questions to help pupils focus their efforts. This may be especially helpful for elementary pupils for whom almost everything in a book seems to be equally important. Such study questions also help older students especially when a large amount of material has been covered during the term.

For high school and college students, an alternative to developing a set of study questions is to give them either a copy of the test blueprint (see Chapter 5), a list of instructional objectives, and/or a detailed content outline indicating the number of items covering each element of the outline.

Content emphasis of the test The teacher should communicate the weighting of the content in a test by telling the students how many items (and how many points) will be devoted to each objective, content element, or blueprint cell. Students can waste hours studying a topic if it will be of little or no importance on the test. It is essential that tests cover the important topics, and that the students' study efforts and the learning objectives set for students are in agreement.

The type of performance expected Obviously, students should have the opportunity to practice the kind of behavior for which they will be held accountable. Yet, frequently students have to guess at the nature or type of question which will appear on a test. A sixth grader I know, for example, was given practice exercises on which he was to identify prepositional phrases from a given list of words and phrases. The next day, his test consisted of finding the subject, predicate, and prepositional phrase in the context of several paragraphs. He never had the opportunity to practice the task for which he was held accountable.

The best way to familiarize students with tasks which will appear on the test is to give them sample items, perhaps an old form of the test on which they can practice particularly when the types of items to appear on the test are complex and/or unfamiliar to the student. Several commercial test publishers are now providing practice tests for their examinees before they take the actual version of the test.

How the test will be scored Knowing how the test will be scored helps students prepare for tests and formulate responses, especially free-response items. If points will be deducted for misspelling important terms and proper names, then to prepare for the test students have to practice these spellings in addition to learning the main ideas and rehearsing how to organize an answer. Other facts students will need to know include whether and how partial credit is to be awarded for less than perfect answers, and how much weight will be given for the question.

The effect of the test results on decisions To effectively plan and organize study efforts, students need to know the importance of the score on the upcoming test in relation to any decisions about them. Among the decisions for which the teacher may lead a classroom test are: putting students into groups, placing them in another section of the course, assigning them to remedial instruction, giving them enrichment or advanced work, and assigning grades. Many teachers tell students at the beginning of the course or marking period the weight to be assigned in the overall evaluation of each assignment, quiz, test, and classroom activity. Students can then organize their efforts in terms of their priorities.

Minimum Test-Taking Skills a Pupil Needs

Pupils need information about the test subject and about the kind of test to be administered before they can demonstrate their best performances. Here is a list of test taking skills pupils should acquire, perhaps through explicit instruction in the classroom (Ebel, 1980):

1. skill in reading test directions and paying attention to a teacher's oral directions.
2. skill in deciding how much of the test time should be devoted to answering the different questions or parts of the test.
3. skill in reading a question carefully so that they understand what it requires for a correct response before they attempt to respond.
4. skill in detecting and responding to the most obvious or reasonable interpretation of a question, rather than to an interpretation that, while possible, was probably unintended.
5. skill in being able to select a reasonable answer to every multiple-choice or true-false item even when they know very little about the content of the item, and even though a correction for guessing will be applied. (Correction for guessing is discussed later in this chapter). For essay and short-answer tests, skill in writing "something, no matter how flimsy it may seem to be, as an answer" (Ebel, 1979, p. 181).
6. skill in deciding that they should mark and temporarily skip over a particularly difficult question and return to it later if time remains.
7. skill in keeping their place when a separate answer sheet is used and in identifying and correcting responses that have not been properly recorded on the answer sheet.
8. skill in thinking through and organizing answers before actually writing a response to an essay question.
9. skill in writing legibly when responding to an essay test.

Test-Wiseness

Before reading further, take the short test given below. Be sure to mark an answer for *every* item, even if you are unsure of the answer. There is a correct or best answer for every item.[2]

1. The Augustine National Party has its headquarters in
   a. Camden, New Jersey.
   b. St. Augustine, Florida.
   c. Palo Alto, California.
   d. Dallas, Texas.
2. Hermann Klavemann is best known for
   a. developing *all* musical scales used in the western world.
   b. composing *every* sonata during the Romantic Era.
   c. translating *all* Russian classics into English.
   d. inventing the safety pin.
3. The Davis Act of the 20th century
   a. provides more money for schools.
   b. struck down an earlier law.
   c. prohibited the manufacture, sale, transportation, or use of several specific drugs that were being used for illegal purposes.
   d. gave a raise to government employees.
4. Harold Stone's book, *The Last Friendship*, is an example of an
   a. political satire.
   b. autobiography.
   c. science fiction.
   d. biography.
5. The population of Franktown is more than
   a. 50 thousand.
   b. 60 thousand.
   c. 70 thousand.
   d. 80 thousand.

The content of the above items is fictitious, but the "right" answer to each item can

[2]Items are extracted with slight modification from Diamond and Evans (1972, p. 147).

be determined by using certain clues in the item:

Item 1. Association between a word or phrase in the stem ("Augustine National Party") and in an alternative ("St. Augustine").
Item 2. Specific determiners in the alternatives ("all," "every") result in these being eliminated from consideration.
Item 3. A longer, more qualified answer is keyed as the correct response.
Item 4. A grammatical clue ("an") is contained in the stem.
Item 5. An alternative overlaps or includes the others.

These items illustrate what is often called test-wiseness. *Test-wiseness* can be defined as "a subject's capacity to utilize the characteristics and formats of the test and/or the test-taking situation to receive a higher score" (Millman, Bishop, & Ebel, 1965, p. 707). Millman et al., outlined two major aspects of test wiseness: (1) components that can be used with nearly any test almost without regard to its purpose or by whom it was constructed and (2) components for which the use depends on the purpose of testing or on who constructed the test. This outline or taxonomy of test-wiseness principles is shown in Table 12.1.

Test-wiseness can be distinguished from two other concepts: (a) guessing or risk-taking and (b) response sets (Sarnacki, 1979; Nilsson & Wedman, 1974; Woodley, 1973). Part of test-wiseness is the ability to use an appropriate strategy for guessing on a test, that is, knowing when and how to guess; but guessing can be foolish, too, if more appropriate bases for responding are available.

As used here, the term *response sets* refers to a propensity or "set" on the part of the examinee to respond to certain kinds of items with an idiosyncratic bias or style. Among the response sets that examinees sometimes dis-

I. Elements independent of test constructor or test purpose.	II. Elements dependent upon the test constructor or purpose.

A. Time-using strategy.
1. Begin to work as rapidly as possible with reasonable assurance of accuracy.
2. Set up a schedule for progress through the test.
3. Omit or guess at items (see I.C. and II.B.) which resist a quick response.
4. Mark omitted items, or items which could use further consideration, to assure easy relocation.
5. Use time remaining after completion of the test to reconsider answers.
B. Error-avoidance strategy.
1. Pay careful attention to directions, determining clearly the nature of the task and the intended basis for response.
2. Pay careful attention to the items, determining clearly the nature of the question.
3. Ask examiner for clarification when necessary, if it is permitted.
4. Check all answers.
C. Guessing strategy.
1. Always guess if right answers only are scored.
2. Always guess if the correction for guessing is less severe than a "correction for guessing" formula that gives an expected score of zero for random responding.
3. Always guess even if the usual correction or a more severe penalty for guessing is employed, whenever elimination of options provides sufficient chance of profiting.
D. Deductive reasoning strategy.
1. Eliminate options which are known to be incorrect and choose from among the remaining options.
2. Choose neither or both of two options which imply the correctness of each other.
3. Choose neither or one (but not both) of two statements, one of which, if correct, would imply the incorrectness of the other.
4. Restrict choice to those options which encompass all of two or more given statements known to be correct.
5. Utilize relevant content information in other test items and options.
	A. Intent consideration strategy.
	1. Interpret and answer questions in view of previous idiosyncratic emphases of the test constructor or in view of the test purpose.
	2. Answer items as the test constructor intended.
	3. Adopt the level of sophistication that is expected.
	4. Consider the relevance of specific detail.
	B. Cue-using strategy.
	1. Recognize and make use of any consistent idiosyncrasies of the test constructor which distinguish the correct answer from incorrect options.
	  a. He makes it longer (shorter) than the incorrect options.
	  b. He qualifies it more carefully, or makes it represent a higher degree of generalization.
	  c. He includes more false (true) statements.
	  d. He places it in certain physical positions among the options (such as in the middle).
	  e. He places it in a certain logical position among an ordered set of options (such as the middle of the sequence).
	  f. He includes (does not include) it among similar statements, or makes (does not make) it one of a pair of diametrically opposite statements.
	  g. He composes (does not compose) it of familiar or stereotyped phraseology.
	  h. He does not make it grammatically inconsistent with the stem.
	2. Consider the relevancy of specific detail when answering a given item.
	3. Recognize and make use of specific determiners.
	4. Recognize and make use of resemblances between the options and an aspect of the stem.
	5. Consider the subject matter and difficulty of neighboring items when interpreting and answering a given item.

Millman, J., Bishop, C. H., and Ebel, R. L. "An Analyses of Test-Wiseness." *Educational and Psychological Measurement,* 1965, 25, pp. 711–713. Reprinted by permission of the publisher.

Table 12 • 1 A taxonomy of test-wiseness principles.

play are acquiescing on true-false items (Cronbach, 1946) and favoring a certain response-choice position on multiple-choice items (Rapaport & Berg, 1955). Some persons may have a tendency to choose "true" on true-false items when they are unsure of the answer which raises their score *if* there are more true than false items. Others may have a propensity for choosing the "C" option on a multiple-choice test when in doubt. (Although individual examinees may employ a positional response set, there appears to be little evidence that such a response bias is universal [Wilbur, 1970]. Some experts feel that the multiple-choice item type is essentially free of positional response biases [Cronbach, 1950].) Such response sets can be part of test-wiseness—for example, if the student knows a teacher favors true items or favors the "c" position—but response sets can lower scores if they are used unwisely. The relationship among these three concepts can be described by the diagram below.

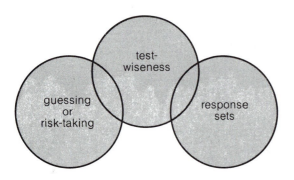

Individuals Differ in their Ability to Take Advantage of Flawed Items

The fact that individuals differ in their ability to take advantage of clues in flawed items to improve their scores has been demonstrated in a number of research studies (e.g., Bajtelsmit, 1975; Diamond & Evans, 1972; Gibb, 1964; Millman, 1966; Slakter, Koehler, & Hampton, 1970a; Woodley, 1973). The 5-item test which you took above can be used to demonstrate this. Figure 12.2 shows two distributions of scores: Panel A shows the distribution that would be expected if everyone in a group responded randomly to the 5 items; Panel B shows the distribution of scores actually obtained when the five items were administered to graduate students in education. The distributions are almost mirror images of each other: Whereas blind guessing would lead us to expect very few high scores and many low

scores,[3] the actual distribution shows very few low scores and many high scores. Whatever the five items measure, they do not reflect random responding.

Whether some individuals can raise their test scores using clues from flawed items will depend, naturally, not only on the persons' test-wiseness, but also on the extent to which such clues are actually present in the items. Flawed items can be found in some professionally developed tests (Metfessel & Sax, 1958) as well as in some homemade tests.

Test-Wiseness Is Learned

Research on test-wiseness indicates that it is only moderately related to measures of general scholastic ability, but more highly related to measures of verbal skills (Sarnacki, 1979). Test-wiseness improves as students progress through the grades (Slakter, Koehler, & Hampton, 1970a). Increases in measured test-wiseness ability seem to be greater for elementary students; on the average high school students improve little (Crehan, Koehler, & Slakter, 1974). However, just because the group average does not change, does not mean that individuals low in this ability cannot improve their skills—quite the contrary.

A number of studies indicate that both children and adults can improve their test-wiseness (Bajtelsmit, 1975; Gibb, 1964; Langer, Wark, & Johnson, 1973; Moore, Schutz, & Baker, 1966; Pryczak, 1973; Slakter, Koehler, & Hampton, 1970a, 1970b; Woodley, 1973, 1975) and that this knowledge is related to improved performance on both classroom tests and professionally-developed standardized tests (Callenbach, 1973; Gaines & Jongsma, 1974; Gross, 1976; Moore, 1971; Oakland, 1972; Omvig, 1971; Slaughter, 1977; Wahlstrom and Boersma, 1968). The teacher can teach some of the clue-utilizing strategies listed in Table 12.1 in addition to the specific test-taking skills listed at the end of the last section.

[3]Based on binomial probability theory.

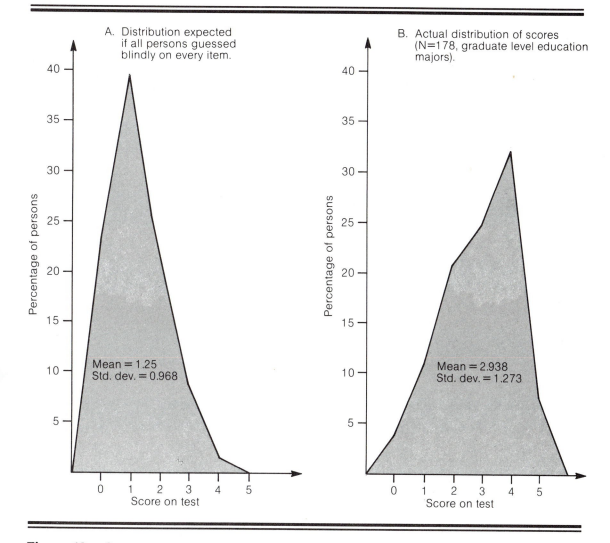

Figure 12 • 2 Comparison of what would be expected by blind guessing with what actually occurred on a 5-item test of test-wiseness.

Much of the improvement in test-wiseness ability seems to be related to increased experience with tests, maturation, and motivation to do well on tests (Slakter, Koehler, & Hampton, 1970a; Sarnacki, 1979). Some materials designed to help examinees learn test-taking skills are available. A partial list of such materials is given here. These may need to be modified by the teacher to suit local circum-

stances and different age groups. An example is shown in Figure 12.3.

1. *EAS Test-taking skills kit* (Primary, Intermediate, and Advanced Levels). Herndon, Va.: Evaluation and Assessment Services, 1980.
2. Ford, V. A. *Everything you wanted to know about test-wiseness.* Princeton, N.J.: Edu-

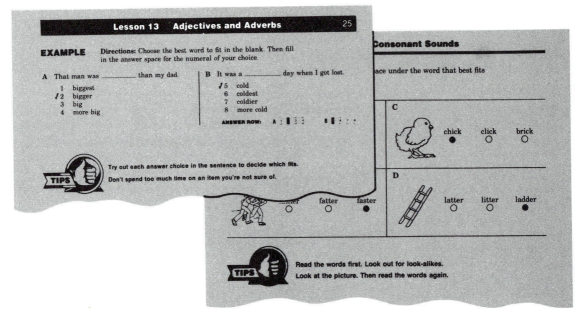

Source: Foreman and Mitchell (1980, p. 47) and Random House School Division (p. 12)

Figure 12 • 3 Examples of pages from instructional materials designed to improve test performance of elementary school pupils in vocabulary and in reading tests.

cational Testing Service, 1973. (ERIC Document Reproduction Service No. ED093 912)

3. Heston, J. C. *How to take a test.* Chicago: Science Research Associates, 1953.

4. Hook, J. N. *How to take examinations in college.* New York: Barnes and Noble, Inc., 1958.

5. Manuel, H. T. *Taking a test.* New York: World Book Co., 1969.

6. Millman, J. & Pauk, W. *How to take tests.* New York: McGraw-Hill Book Co., 1969.

7. Pettit, L. *How to study and take exams.* New York: John F. Rider Publishers, Inc., 1960.

8. Random House School Division. *Scoring high in. . . .* New York: Random House, Inc. (Separate elementary school series for reading, language, writing, and mathematics test-taking skills.) See Cohen &

Foreman (1978), Denmark (1979), Foreman & Kaplan (1978), Foreman & Mitchell (1980), Goodman (1979), and Kravitz & Dramer (1977).

9. Woodley, K. K. *Test wiseness: Test-taking skills for adults* (2nd ed). (The American College) New York: McGraw-Hill Book Co., 1978.

10. A number of "How to pass . . ." publications exist which provide practice on particular kinds of item types and questions that appear on specific examinations such as the SAT, GRE, MAT, and various professional examinations. A book store is the most likely place to locate such titles.

If you are interested in developing or using a *test* of test-wiseness skills, you should consult the following references: Bajtelsmit (1975);

Diamond & Evans (1972); Gibb (1964); Gross (1976); Millman (1966); Slakter, Koehler, & Hampton (1970a); Woodley (1973). Diamond and Evans, Gross, and Slakter, et al. have used their tests with intermediate and upper elementary children. The others have developed their tests for use mainly with high school, college, and adult populations. A general review of the area of test-wiseness is provided by Sarnacki (1979).

Test Anxiety

General Nature of Test Anxiety

Original formulation Work on the theory of test anxiety began with Mandler and Sarason (1952). In their view, a testing situation elicits two kinds of learned drives: task drives and anxiety drives. The task drives are thought to be reduced when a person engages in behaviors leading to the completion of the test tasks. The anxiety drives, on the other hand, are viewed as eliciting two kinds of response patterns: task-relevant and task-irrelevant. Task-relevant responses to test anxiety are specific to the test, facilitate completing the test, and, in turn, reduce anxiety. However, for some persons, test anxiety evokes task-irrelevant responses which interfere with task-relevant responses and which can be described as ". . . feelings of inadequacy, helplessness, heightened somatic reaction, anticipations of punishment or loss of status and esteem, and implicit attempts at leaving the test situation. It might be said that these responses are self- rather than task-centered" (Mandler & Sarason, 1952, p. 166).

Persons who report they experience heightened anxiety when faced with a testing situation tend to be both more preoccupied with themselves and more self-deprecating than persons who report little or no heightened test-anxiety (Wine, 1971), and these self-evaluating tendencies seem to be aroused by the testing situation itself (Ganzer, 1968; Mandler & Watson, 1966; Marlett & Watson, 1968; Neale & Katahn, 1968).

Worry and emotionality One view of test anxiety is that it has two components: worry and emotionality (Liebert & Morris, 1967). Worry is a cognitive aspect of anxiety: a person's cognitive concern over failure and its consequences and about how a person's own performance compared with others. Emotionality refers to somatic or autonomic arousal responses to anxiety. The worry component seems to be more salient: In general, the more a person worries, the worse the person is likely to do on a test; emotionality seems to play a role only among those who worry little (Doctor & Altman, 1969; Morris & Liebert, 1969, 1970).

Test anxiety and the focus of attention The debilitating effects of test anxiety can be interpreted in terms of the attentional focus of low- and high-test-anxious persons (Wine, 1971):

> The low-test-anxious person is focused on task-relevant variables while performing tasks. The highly text-anxious subject is internally focused on self-evaluative, self-deprecatory thinking, and perceptions of his autonomic responses. Since the difficult tasks on which the test-anxious person does poorly require full attention for adequate performance, he cannot perform adequately while dividing his attention between internal cues and task cues (p. 92).

Measuring Test Anxiety

A number of instruments have been developed over the years to measure various aspects of test-related anxiety. Several of these are listed in Table 12.2. No endorsement of these instruments is implied, and teachers contemplating using one or more of them to identify students who are text-anxious should study the references listed in the table. I recommend that if an inventory is to be used to identify high-test-anxious students for possible treatment,

Title and description	References for more information
1. *Anxiety Differential* by Alexander & Husek (1962) A semantic differential technique used to measure temporary (state) anxiety.	Alexander & Husek (1962), Allen (1970), Husek & Alexander (1963).
2. *Achievement Anxiety Test* by Alpert (1957) Reports two scales: debilitating anxiety and facilitating anxiety.	Allen (1970), Alpert (1959), Alpert & Haber (1960), Carrier (1966), Dember (1962), Gaudry (1971), Harper (1974), Huck (1974), Jacko (1974), Milholland (1964), Stanford (1963).
3. *School Anxiety Questionnaire* by Dunn (1968) Reports five scales measuring anxiety toward evaluation failure and achievement tests.	Bergan (1968), Dunn (1968, 1969, 1970a,b).
4. *Test Anxiety Scale* by Emery (1966) Subjects rate the degree to which each of several different test-taking experiences apply to them.	Emery (1966, 1967), Jones, Trimber, & Altman (1970).
5. *Pre-Examination Questionnaire* by Liebert and Morris (1967) Reports two scales: emotionality and worry. Used Mandler and Sarason Scale (see below) as a basis for development.	Liebert & Morris (1967), Morris & Liebert (1970), Spiegler, Morris & Liebert (1968).
6. *Test Anxiety Questionnaire* by Mandler and S. B. Sarason (1952) One of the original test anxiety measures. Centers on anxiety associated with group and individual intelligence tests and with course examinations. High school version developed by Mandler and Cowen (1958).	Harper (1971, 1974), Lavit (1971), Mandler & Cowen (1958), Mandler & S. B. Sarason (1952), S. B. Sarason (1960). For additional references, see Wildemuth (1977).
7. *Inventory of Test Anxiety* by Osterhouse (1969) Developed using the Liebert & Morris (1967) Scales as bases.	Osipow & Kreinbring (1971), Osterhouse (1969, 1972).
8. *Final Exam Anxiety Index* by Prochaska Subjects rate their anxiety on a scale from −50 to +50.	Prochaska (1969, 1971).

Table 12 • 2   Measures of test anxiety.

one be selected which separately measures worry, emotionality, debilitating anxiety, and facilitating anxiety.

How Test Anxiety has been Treated

Several of the techniques used to treat anxieties and phobias have been applied to treating persons with high test anxiety (Tryon, 1980):

1. **Systematic desensitization and implo-sion** Progressively more stressful stimuli are presented, and a person is taught to relax in their presence. Implosion is similar but does not emphasize relaxation. The theory postulates that repeated exposure to high anxiety stimuli will lead to the extinction of the anxiety response.

Note: These types of treatments seem to be effective in reducing the emotionality component of test anxiety, rather than the worry (cognitive) component.

Title and description	References for more information
9. *Autobiographical Survey* by I. G. Sarason (1958) The *Test Anxiety Scale* is one of six scales (Test Anxiety, General Anxiety, Lack of Protection, Defensiveness, Hostility, and Need for Achievement). In true-false format, the *Test Anxiety Scale* can be used without the others.	Allen (1970), I. G. Sarason (1958, 1959, 1961), Suinn (1969), Walter, et al. (1964).
10. *Test Anxiety Scale* by I. G. Sarason (1968) Subjects respond true or false to a series of statements describing various feelings about tests and testing situations. Designed for high school and college students.	Chambers & Hopkins (1966), I. A. Sarason & Ganzer (1962), I. G. Sarason, et al. (1968).
11. *Test Anxiety Scale for Children* (TABC) by S. B. Sarason, et al. (1960) Children are asked to respond "yes" or "no" to each of a series of statements describing feelings about being tested. An expanded version is given by Feld and Lewis (1969).	Dunn (1964, 1965), Feld & Lewis (1967, 1969); Forhertz (1970), Loughlin, et al. (1965), Nighswander & Beggs (1970, 1971), Rhine & Spaner (1973), S. B. Sarason, et al. (1958, 1960).
12. *Test Anxiety Inventory* by Spielberger, et al. (1978) Subjects respond to items on a four-point scale. Reports separate emotionability and worry scores as well as a total score.	Spielberger, et al. (1978).
13. *Suinn Test Anxiety Behavior Scale (STABS)* by Suinn (1969) Consists of a series of statements describing testing situations. The subject is supposed to indicate how frightening each situation is. Intended for college students.	Suinn (1969a,b, 1971, 1972).
14. *What I am Like* by Wallach and Kogan (1965) Elementary school children check which statements describe themselves. *What I am Like* has six scales, one of which is test anxiety.	Shriberg (1974), Wallach & Kogan (1965).

Note: Information in this table obtained from Tryon (1980) and Wildemuth (1977). Wildemuth's bibliography lists more tests and many more references on test anxiety than are shown above.

2. Self-controlled relaxation and desensitization A person learns not to terminate the anxiety provoking situation but to cope with it and use it as a stimulus for triggering a relaxation response.
Note: Frequently this is a more effective treatment than desensitization alone in reducing the emotionality component. The worry (cognitive) component is perhaps less well-treated.

3. Cognitive procedures These teach a person to attend to the task at hand (i.e., answering the test items) rather than the self-

oriented anxiety responses which interfere with completing the task.
Note: This type of treatment is directly concerned with the worry (cognitive) test anxiety response.

4. Observational learning A person observes the therapist who models how to deal with anxiety or observes another subject who is undergoing desensitization training. The treatment is based on the research finding that high test-anxious persons are more sensitive to modeling stimuli than are low test-anxious persons.
Note: The treatment seems to be more directed

toward the emotionality than the worry component of test anxiety. Research on the effectiveness of this treatment method is mixed (Tryon, 1980).

5. Study skills Counseling and teaching is directed toward improving study habits and test-taking skills.
Note: When combined with another treatment, such as desensitization or relaxation, this seems to both reduce test anxiety and improve grades.

The above treatments usually require the services of a trained professional, often a counselor or psychologist. A teacher can, however, apply some of the techniques to those pupils who suffer from debilitating test anxiety. For example, the teacher can present effective study skills and test-taking skills and encourage pupils to focus attention on the task at hand rather than on their self-deprecating feelings. For further reviews of test-anxiety and its treatment, see I. G. Sarason (1980), Tryon (1980), Wine (1971), and Zuckerman and Spielberger (1976).

Correction for Guessing

Correction for Guessing Formulas

When true-false and/or multiple-choice items are used, a correction for guessing is sometimes applied to scores by subtracting from the number of right answers a fraction of the number of wrong answers. The usual formula is:

$$\text{Corrected score} = R - \frac{W}{n-1} \quad \text{[Eq. 12.1]}$$

where

R means the number of items answered correctly,

W means the number of items marked wrongly, and

n means the number of options in each item.

If there are two choices per item (e.g., true-false), the

$$\text{corrected score} = R - W.$$

If there are four options per item, the

$$\text{corrected score} = R - \frac{W}{3}.$$

The intention of the correction formula is to eliminate the advantage an examinee might have as a result of guessing correctly.

For example, suppose Jim took a 50 question multiple-choice test with four options per item. Further, suppose Jim's test results were: 40 items marked correctly, 6 items marked wrongly, and 4 items omitted. Applying the formula we find:

$$\text{corrected score} = R - \frac{W}{n-1}$$

$$= 40 - \frac{6}{3}$$

$$= 40 - 2 = 38.$$

Notice that the number of omitted items is *not* used in this correction formula: only the number of answers marked wrongly *(W)* and the number marked correctly *(R)*.

A complementary version of the above correction formula does use the number of omitted items: Instead of penalizing an examinee for responding wrongly, it rewards the examinee for omitting items (i.e., for refraining from guessing). This formula is:

$$\text{Adjusted score} = R + \frac{O}{n} \quad \text{[Eq. 12.2]}$$

where

R means the number of items answered correctly,

O means the number of items omitted, and n means the number of options in each item.

(I use the term "adjusted" instead of "corrected" to distinguish this formula from the previous one. This is not standard practice. The generic term is "formula scoring.")

To return to Jim's test performance: Recall that on a 4-option multiple-choice test he marked 40 items correctly, 6 items wrongly, and omitted 4 items. Applying the adjusted score formula we obtain:

$$\text{Adjusted score} = R + \frac{O}{n}$$

$$= 40 + \frac{4}{4}$$

$$= 41.$$

This formula credits the examinee with the number of points to be expected if random responses were substituted for the omitted responses. If an examinee omitted every item, the score would be equal to the average score expected if the examinee guessed blindly on every item.[4] Thus, the scores obtained by the "adjusted score" formula will be higher than the scores of the same persons had they been obtained from the "corrected score" formula. However, the scores under the two methods are perfectly correlated (e.g., Gulliksen, 1950): The relative ordering of persons is the same regardless of which formula is used.

The uncorrected score *(R)* is simply the number of items marked correctly. When every examinee marks every item, the uncorrected scores are perfectly correlated with the corrected or adjusted scores (e.g., Gulliksen, 1950)

---

[4]This is called the *expected chance score* and is equal to k/n, where k = number of test items and n = number of options for each item (assumed to be the same from item-to-item). For a 10-item four-option test the expected chance score is 10/4 = 2.5; for a 10-item true-false test, 10/2 = 5; and so on.

so that here, too, the relative ordering of persons is the same, whether or not the scores are corrected for guessing.

Rationales for Formula Scoring

One way to consider what happens when a person is faced with a true-false or multiple-choice item is shown in Figure 12.4. The formula [12.1] essentially considers only interpretations (a), (b), (e), and (j). The formula assumes that examinees follow the directions which caution against blind guessing and which enjoin examinees to answer only if they are sure they know the right answer. Since wrong answers are assumed to represent unlucky guesses and omitted items to represent lack of knowledge (if they are the only factors related to examinee's responses), the correction formula can be derived from probability theory. Because wrong answers are viewed as evidence of guessing, the number of wrong answers on a person's test paper is used to estimate the number of lucky (correct) guesses made. This estimate of the number of lucky guesses is equal to the quantity $W/(n - 1)$, the fraction subtracted from a person's number right score.

Another rationale can be offered (Lord, 1975) which, although it can be applied to formula [12.2], rewards omissions by adding a fraction of the number of omitted items to the number right score. This formula considers interpretations (a), (b), (c), (e), and (j). It is assumed that examinees are given (and follow) directions which convince them that the best strategy is to answer all items which they feel they have a better than random chance of getting right and to omit an item only when they feel that their response would be not better than blind guessing. Their reward for doing this is to credit their papers with the expected blind guessing score (i.e., $O \div n$); wrong answers receive no reward, no punishment, and no credit. The difference between the two formulas in terms of credits for right and wrong responses and omissions is summarized here:

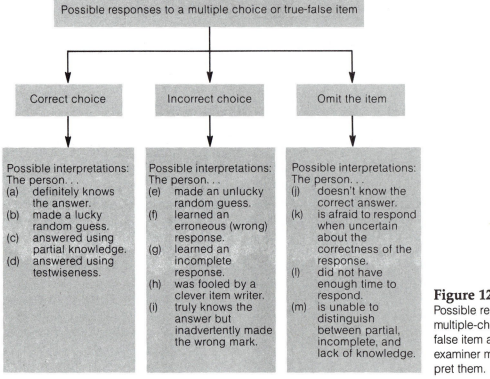

Figure 12 • 4
Possible responses to a multiple-choice or true-false item and how an examiner might interpret them.

Response to an item:	Credit given for that item under:	
	"Corrected score"	*"Adjusted score"*
right answer	+1	+1
wrong answer	$-1/(n-1)$	0
omit the item	0	$+1/n$

Things to Consider When Deciding Whether to Use a Correction Formula

Table 12.3 lists a few things to keep in mind when deciding whether to use a correction formula. Some of the points mentioned in the table are discussed earlier in this chapter in Chapter 6.

There is no correction for luck It isn't intuitively obvious that the correction formula does not correct for luck: When Lady Luck smiles, the gambler makes a point; when she frowns the gambler craps out. The correction formula corrects for the average, *long-run*, expected gain from blind guessing. Sometimes blind guessing is better than this average and sometimes worse. Rather than remove the influence of these fluctuations in luck, the correction formula tends to amplify them. Lucky persons keep at least some, if not all, of their gains, while the unlucky lose, as is illustrated in Box 12.2.

Directions to students about guessing For classroom tests, the directions to students should describe not only the scoring proce-

1. A correction formula does not correct for good luck nor compensate for bad luck.	6. Responding to an item on a rational basis, even when lacking complete certainty of the correctness of the answer, provides useful information on general educational achievement.
2. The relative ordering of pupils is usually the same for uncorrected as for corrected scores.	7. Using a correction-for-guessing penalty may discourage slower students from guessing blindly on items near the end of a test when time is short.
3. The chance of getting a good score by random guessing is very slim.	8. Correction-for-guessing directions do not seem to discourage the test-wise or risk-taking examinee from guessing, but do seem to discourage the reluctant, risk-avoiding, or non-test-wise examinee.
4. Pupils who want to do well on the test, and who are given enough time to attempt all items, will guess on only a few items.	9. A formula score makes the scoring more complicated, offering additional opportunities for the teacher to commit scoring errors.
5. Encouraging pupils to make the best choice they can, even if they are not completely confident in their choice, does not seem to be morally nor educationally wrong.	

Robert L. Ebel, *Measuring Educational Achievement,* © 1965. Adapted by permission of Prentice-Hall, Inc., Englewood Cliffs, N.J.

Table 12 • 3 Factors to keep in mind when deciding whether to use a formula for correction for guessing

dure but also the strategy they should use in order to obtain the highest score possible. There should be no attempt to state or imply that a penalty will be applied to wrong answers when simply the number right will be counted. Simply inform the pupils that their score will be the number right and that they should answer *every* item on the test, even if they are not completely sure of the correctness of their responses. Examinees should be made aware that with number-right scoring they are at a decided *disadvantage* if they omit some items.

One set of directions to use with Formula [12.1] which describes the response strategy a student should use is given below (Davis, 1967; Bliss, 1980, p. 148):

> Your score will be the number of questions you answer correctly minus a fraction of the questions you answer incorrectly. You should answer questions even when you are not sure that your answer is correct. This is especially true if you know one or more of the choices is wrong, or if you have a "feeling" about which choice is correct. However, it is better to leave a blank than to guess wildly.

These directions may have to be modified or explained in different terms to elementary and junior high students.

Don't use phrases in the directions such as, "Mark an answer only if you are sure of it" (Thorndike, 1971). Such phrases tend to inhibit pupils from displaying the knowledge they actually have, because each is free to use personal standards to define what "sure" means and because "risk-avoiding" pupils and insecure pupils may interpret this as an additional caution.

Even when examinees seem to understand the directions, many are reluctant to mark items which they have a better than random chance of getting right (Bliss, 1980; Crehan, Candor, & Beckett, 1976; Cross & Frary, 1977; Poggio, Asmus, and Levy, 1978; Sheriffe & Boomer, 1954; Slaker, Juliano, & Sarnacki, 1976; Whitney, 1974). These findings have led some, such as Bliss (1980), to conclude that, "The consistency with which this test taking behavior has been found across ages [of pupils] and the finding that formula scoring may especially tend to penalize more able students raises an ethical question about the advisability of using formula scoring directions" (p. 152). Other experts have noted that if better test instructions cannot induce pupils to use their best test-taking strategy, it may be necessary for children to be taught effective test-taking behavior in schools (Lord, 1975).

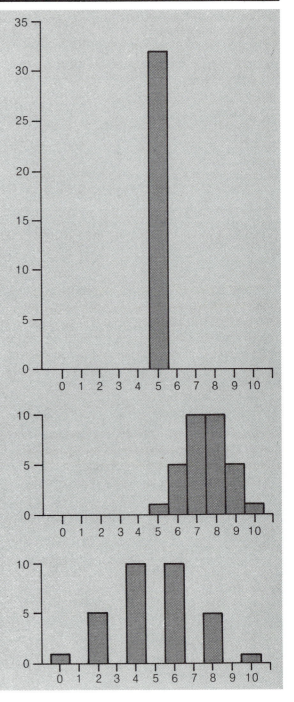

Suppose 32 pupils were given 10 true-false questions. Further, suppose each student actually knew the answer to only 5 of the 10 items. Thus, each of the 32 pupils should get a score of 5. This is graphed at the right.

Now, suppose every student guessed on those items he or she didn't know. Not all students would be lucky guessers. Some student would be extremely lucky and get all items guessed right: This person's score would be 10 (= 5 known + 5 lucky guesses). Someone would be extremely unlucky and get all items guessed wrong: This person's score would be 5 (= 5 known + 0 lucky guesses). The mathematics of probability indicates that we would expect the 32 pupils' scores to be distributed as is shown at the right.

Now suppose each of the scores in the middle distribution were corrected for guessing by the usual formula. The distribution at the right shows the results after applying the correction. Notice what happened to the lucky and unlucky guessers described above: One-half of the class gets penalized; the lucky guessers get extra rewards. "To him that hath luck a high score shall be given, even after correction for guessing. From him that hath not luck, even that score which is rightfully his shall be taken away!" (Ebel, 1965, p. 226).

Source: Based on information in Ebel (1965, p. 226).

Box 12 • 2

Current practices among test publishers Differences exist among test publishers concerning the use of correction for guessing. Most commercially available achievement and aptitude batteries taken by elementary and high school youngsters simply use the number right score. This is probably due to practical concerns rather than to psychometric considerations: The additional task of correcting for guessing adds one more burden and another possible source of clerical error (Thorndike, 1971).

No matter what the teacher decides to do with a classroom test, when a standardized test is used, the instructions in the manual should be followed exactly. Failure to apply the intended correction, to apply it when the test developer didn't intend it to be used, or otherwise to alter the instructions to students at the time of testing will make the test's norms unusable because the alterations, in effect, make a new test situation.

Directions to Students about Changing Answers

Is it beneficial for examinees to change their answers once they have been marked on the answer sheet? Despite popular opinion, it *does* pay to change answers if changing them is based on a thoughtful reconsideration of the item. A summary of the research findings on this issue is given below (Pike, 1978):

1. Most test takers and many educators believe it does not pay to change answers.
2. Most examinees, however, do in fact change their answers to about four percent of the items.
3. Research studies show that it does, in fact, pay to change answers. Typically two out of three answers changed will become correct.
4. The payoff for changing answers diminishes as the items become more difficult for the examinee.

5. Lower scoring examinees benefit less from changing answers than higher scoring examinees do.

Ways to Prepare to Take a Test

Most of the ideas in this chapter relating to preparing a student to take a test are summarized in Table 12.4. Most likely all except number seven would be considered appropriate ways to prepare for a test. Not all are equally effective, however, nor are all needed by every pupil.

It seems obvious that learning the specific topic(s) and skill(s) which will appear on a test will be the most helpful. We distinguish here the learning of the skills and topics (number 2), from learning the answers to only the specific items that appear on the test (possibly a variant of number 7 in the table). "Teaching to the test" seems to be a legitimate and even desirable practice *if* (a) the test measures important skills and knowledge of important

1. Learning about the general topic(s) or area(s) to be covered by the test.
2. Learning the specific topic(s) or skill(s) covered by the test.
3. Taking similar tests for practice.
4. Learning test-wiseness principles about: (a) general test-taking skills, (b) taking advantage of test construction flaws, and/or (c) special strategies to answer certain kinds of items.
5. Learning to handle test-related worry and emotionality (i.e., test anxiety).
6. Learning to respond to intrinsic and/or extrinsic motivational factors related to successful performances on test.
7. Cheating: Obtaining and using unauthorized information related to the specific items and answers comprising a test.

Adapted from "Coaching, Test-Wiseness and other Extraneous Factors in Ability Testing," by Nancy S. Cole, Programs in Educational Research Methodology, University of Pittsburgh. Used by permission of Nancy S. Cole.

Table 12 • 4 Various kinds of learning associated with preparing for a test.

content, and (b) the instruction is geared to a general level of skill and knowledge development. Test items represent a sample from a larger domain of performance to which the teacher wishes to generalize an individual's behavior. Thus, performance on the specific items of a test often is not an end in itself. In this sense, teaching to the test helps focus a student's learning and is quite different from "teaching the *specific items* on the test." The latter can be an unethical practice since it is a deception leading to a false generalization about the pupil's performance in the broader domain of interest. Since a teacher frequently makes decisions about pupils' capabilities in an area using information obtained from tests, the consequences of such deception can be quite serious.

Since much of the learning depicted in Table 12.4 occurs informally, perhaps serendipitously, large individual differences among pupils in the degree to which they are prepared to take any test are likely. Even if everyone "studies hard" for the test, individuals are apt to distribute their study efforts differently. Some teacher sensitivity about the various kinds of learning that contribute to successful test performance will help when interpreting pupils' test results and may suggest ways of helping individuals lacking preparation in certain of these areas.

Summary

The following are the main points of this chapter.

1. Pupils should demonstrate their maximum performance on classroom tests; the way the testing situation is handled can facilitate this demonstration of maximum capability.

2. Facilitation of maximum test performance begins with the test itself and includes its appearance, the arrangement of the copy of the test, and the way the teacher presents the test to pupils.

3. When designing the format and procedures for test administration, the teacher should be sensitive to the visual and auditory characteristics of the pupils and how these characteristics may affect their test performance.

4. The items in a test should be arranged to facilitate students doing their best.

5. Before an upcoming test, pupils should know (a) the number and kind of items, (b) the test's time limits, (c) how the teacher expects them to answer questions, (d) the penalty, if any, for guessing, and (e) whether there is a general strategy they should follow when responding to the items.

6. The teacher should prepare the procedures for scoring and a scoring key before administering the test to pupils.

7. I recommend that students have at least 48 hours notice before testing them in a subject. "Surprise quizzes" do not seem to have the motivating effects frequently attributed to them, and pupils sometimes view them as unfair.

8. A list of nine test-taking skills is presented. These appear to be minimum skills needed beyond subject-matter knowledge for students to display maximum capabilities on a test.

9. Test-wiseness refers to an examinee's ability to use the characteristics of both the test and the test situation to attain a higher score.

10. Test-wiseness knowledge can be classified into two broad areas: (a) skills and knowledge which students can use regardless of who developed the test or the purpose for taking the test and (b) skills and knowledge students can use with tests developed by certain persons or for certain purposes. These skills and knowledges are outlined in Table 12.1.

11. Test-wiseness and general test-taking skills are learned and exhibited with increasing sophistication as students progress through the grades and experience more tests, but students vary greatly in these abilities. Those with few skills and little knowledge in these areas are usually at a disadvantage when they take tests along with more skilled pupils.

12. Anxiety associated with taking a test is thought to elicit in examinees: (a) task-relevant responses, which facilitate performance on the test and (b) task-irrelevant responses, which interfere with test performance.

13. Task-irrelevant thoughts can debilitate highly test-anxious persons who are preoccupied with their own inadequacy, helplessness, and/or possible failure.

14. Text anxiety consists of (a) a cognitive, worry component and (b) an emotionality component.

15. Highly test-anxious persons seem to have difficulty focusing their attention on the test task at hand. Training programs which teach persons to attend to the task-relevant aspects of taking tests appear to be successful in reducing test anxiety. Several types of treatments are briefly reviewed.

16. A number of the many different measures of test anxiety are listed in Table 12.2.

17. Correction-for-guessing formulas attempt to discourage examinees from guessing blindly on multiple-choice and true-false items, but only a few of the many explanations of why a pupil marked or didn't mark an answer appear to fit the rationales needed for using a correction formula. Further, applying a correction-for-guessing does not correct for pupil's good luck nor compensate for bad luck.

18. A list of things to consider before deciding whether to use a correction-for-guessing formula on a classroom test is given in Table 12.3.

19. A test's directions to students should clearly indicate whether a correction will be employed and what the students' best strategy is when responding to the items.

20. Although teaching the important skills that will appear on a test is a desirable practice, teaching pupils only to answer the specific items on a test appears to be an undesirable, unethical practice.

Themes

- Many systems and procedures exist for evaluating and assigning grades and marks to pupils.

- Most school systems use a combination of several pupil progress reporting methods, and different combinations of methods are often used at different grade levels within the same school system.

- Among the major bases for assigning marks are group-referencing, self-referencing, and task-referencing. Each has advantages and disadvantages, and a teacher may find a need to use more than one of these for particular purposes.

Terms and Concepts

continuous evaluation of pupil progress
grading (marking) vs. reporting pupil
    progress
evaluating pupils
assessing pupils
pupil progress reporting systems (letter
    grades, numerals, percentages, two
    category, checklist, rating scale,
    pupil-teacher conferences, parent-
    teacher conferences, letter to
    parents)

multiple marking and reporting system
group-referenced scheme
task-referenced scheme
ranking method
standard deviation method
grading a composite vs. grading a single
    assignment or test

13
MARKS AND GRADING

This chapter describes the many methods of reporting pupil progress and how the teacher may go about assigning grades. The chapter opens with a discussion of the many functions of grading and progress reporting systems. A questionnaire gives you the opportunity to express your own attitude toward grading and measuring pupil progress. You can compare your responses to those given by student teachers and professional educators. I discuss the issue of whether and under what conditions grades can motivate pupils and present a survey of the many criticisms of grades. Next I describe the many methods used by schools to report pupil progress along with the frequency with which they tend to be used at each level of schooling and the strengths and weakness of each. Since schools tend to use more than one method of reporting progress, I also describe multiple marking systems and suggestions for multiple reporting systems. The last part of the chapter discusses various ways to assign letter grades to pupils, emphasizing group-referenced systems and systems using absolute standards.

Functions Served by Marks and Pupil Progress Reporting Systems

What are Your Attitudes toward Marks and Grades?

Before going any further in this chapter, consider how *you* feel about assigning grades and marks. Read each of the measurement statements in the box and next to each one check "A" if you agree, "D" if you disagree, or "U" if you are undecided. Compare your answers with your classmates. The responses of other groups are summarized in Table 13.7.

Instruction Requires Continuous Evaluation of Pupil Progress

A teacher continuously assesses and evaluates the progress of pupils, incorporating the information and judgments into the instructional process. Many teacher assessments are not systematically recorded and reported (although they perhaps could be) and most are not based on formal paper-and-pencil tests. A teacher's assessment of pupils during instruction provides information for answering a wide variety of questions such as these:

Before a lesson begins

1. Has each pupil acquired the necessary readiness skills?
2. To what extent has each of the pupils already acquired the lesson's learning objectives?
3. What previously learned material should the class review?
4. What new material should the class cover during a particular time period?
5. What teaching approach or style should be used with this lesson for each pupil?

While carrying out a lesson

6. Is each pupil paying attention?
7. Does each pupil seem to be learning?
8. Does each pupil seem sufficiently motivated to learn the lesson's material?
9. What (if any) are some of the difficulties each pupil is experiencing in learning the lesson's objectives?

After a lesson has been presented

10. Has each pupil acquired the important objectives of the lesson?

Box 13 • 1

11. Is each pupil's degree of learning sufficient so that new, more advanced learning can begin?
12. Are certain pupils experiencing so much difficulty that they are ready to "crash"?
13. To what extent is each pupil's progress normal relative to other pupils in the class?

14. Should certain pupils be progressing faster relative to their stage of development or their abilities?

This chapter is concerned with the process of formally recording and reporting only some of these evaluations of pupil progress, so keep in mind distinctions between such terms as grading (marking), reporting, evaluating, and assessing. *Grading* or *marking* refers primarily to the process of using a system of symbols for reporting various aspects of a pupil's progress. These marks or grades are *reported* to pupils and parents through various devices such as report cards, conferences, or letters and are reported to the school administration on a permanent record card or folder. The grades or symbols reported represent a teacher's *evaluations* or judgments about the quality or worth of each pupil's progress. To arrive at these evaluations, teachers use various means of *assessment:* They observe and/or test pupils to obtain the information needed to judge performance quality.

A total pupil progress reporting system is likely to require the teacher to report a judgment on a pupil for each of a large number of questions, similar to the fourteen listed above. However, the teacher does not formally record all such evaluations on a report card or a permanent record card. Many are reported directly to the student (e.g., "Megan, I want you to pay special attention to the lesson today" or "Bob, Monday we are going to learn how to do word problems. Please review the number facts with your Dad this weekend."); other evaluations are discussed with parents in a personal conference, by telephone, or in a letter or note to the home.

As you can see from the variety of the questions, it is highly unlikely that any *one* set of symbols, or report card format can effectively communicate the necessary information to parents, pupils, and administration. You should keep in mind, as you read this chapter, that the teacher may need to use several methods of communicating evaluations.

Why is it so Hard to Give Marks?

For many teachers, the assignment of marks or grades is one of the most difficult and troublesome aspects of the teaching process. Why

is this? Among the reasons are these (Ebel, 1979):

1. Educational achievements are difficult to measure: There is neither an accepted unit nor a standard, accepted set of accomplishments to measure, and measuring is inherently complex.
2. Marking systems are often objects of educational controversies. Differing educational opinions and philosophies among teachers and others imply different methods for evaluating and reporting pupil progress.
3. Grading and marking require teachers to judge pupils, and many of these judgments are difficult and/or unpleasant to make. Teachers want to be helpful: to teach and to guide learning. Giving a low grade to a pupil who has not learned can be very unpleasant.

Information, Decisions, and Pupil Progress Reports

Table 13.1 gives examples of information frequently found on pupil progress reports and of various kinds of decisions which may be based on such information. Pupil progress reports communicate to pupils and parents, however, more than information about an individual pupil. The kinds of marks and grades a pupil receives communicate to the pupil a teacher's (and school's) values. If obedience to a teacher's rules is rewarded by an "A" or "performing satisfactorily" in *reading*, while "fooling around" during class means the reading grade is lowered in spite of successful reading performance, the teacher communicates that obedience is valued more than reading behavior. The teacher who gives a low grade to the pupil whose academic performance is satisfactory and then says, "I warned you about passing notes during class!" is perhaps communicating vindictiveness. A teacher may value both social behavior (e.g., conformance) *and*

Information in report	Decisions that can be made			
	Selection	**Placement, remediation**	**Guidance, counselling**	**Course improvement**
1. Content or objectives learned	Promotion, probation, graduation, admissions	Selection of courses to take, remedial help needed	Next courses to take, additional schooling needed, career-related choices	Where instruction can be improved
2. Comparison of performance in different subjects	Admission	Selection of advanced and/or remedial courses	Pattern of a pupil's strengths and weaknesses	Areas which are strong points of school
3. Performance relative to other people	Scholarships, prizes, admission	Estimating likely success, eligibility for special programs	Estimating likely success in certain areas	
4. Social behavior		Matching personal characteristics to course and teacher placement	Need for adjustment, likes/dislikes, ability to get alone with others	Identify problems with a course or with a teacher

Table 13 • 1   Examples of the kinds of decisions about a pupil made from report card information.

achievement, but if the grade reported intertwines the two, it becomes unclear which is to be the basis for future educational efforts.

Do Marks Motivate Pupils?

From purely the measurement and institutional viewpoints, marks should objectively describe a pupil's level of attainment in each subject area—that is, what a pupil's performance warrants when compared to some professionally defendable standard such as the curriculum's objectives. But as Cronbach (1977, p. 680) says, ". . . no one regards them that way. Students treasure them or worry over them; parents beam or scold. Teachers use marks deliberately to goad, reward, and punish."

Can and should marks be used to motivate pupils? Educational measurement experts are divided on the issue of whether it is appropriate to use the traditional marking system

(A, B, C . . .) to motivate pupils. Robert L. Ebel (1979), for example, states that marks serve as important motivators for students. In order to serve this function, he feels that they must validly and accurately reflect achievement—students who attain the course objectives to the highest degree should receive the highest grades.

Lee J. Cronbach (1977) offers another view of the motivating effects of grades. He tenders four principles of motivation: (1) There should be goals which students seek to attain, (2) students should be convinced these goals can be attained, (3) students should be able to judge the extent to which they are attaining these goals, and (4) attainment of classroom goals should lead to applications of the learning in nonschool settings. His analysis of traditional A, B, C, . . . grading in terms of these principles states that: (1) Grades can serve as goals which at least some students seek to attain; (2) grades do not motivate students who feel

Table 13 • 2 Commonly expressed criticisms of grades.

high grades are out of reach—a condition likely to exist when grades reflect solely final level of attainment, rather than progress in a course which takes initial readiness into account; (3) whether grades can be used by students to judge their progress depends on whether the teacher continually gives students the results of assessments; and (4) grades (A, B, C, . . .) tend to be holistic judgments rather than descriptions of strengths and weaknesses and thus do not tell students what they need to do better to improve their future learning. Cronbach's conclusion: "Teachers must evaluate, but in my view they should do as little comparison and as little summary rating of individuals as the institutional setting allows" (p. 687).

Criticisms of Grades and Marks

Some educators have voiced a number of criticisms of grades over the years. Many of these criticisms can be summarized under the four headings in Table 13.2.

The following comments are offered in response to these criticisms (Ebel, 1974):

1. Grades are essentially meaningless There is some truth in each of the criticisms under this heading. However, Criticisms 1, 2, 4, and 5 can be used as arguments for improving and strengthening grading practices rather than for eliminating them. Criticism 3 attributes to grades more than they were ever intended to convey: Grades are summary reports of the general level of achievement; they were never intended to substitute for the complex details of achievement needed for daily instructional planning.

2. Grades are educationally unimportant

Criticisms here are a mixture of value statements and unnecessary comparisons. Certainly grades are symbols, but it doesn't follow that symbols are unimportant. Within some persons' value systems, concrete, tangible rewards are more important; other persons work with and for symbolic rewards. To value intangible outcomes exclusively would be to hold that nothing of any value in education can be observed or assessed. This seems untenable. To pit a teacher's grades against a pupil's self-evaluations implies that only one or the other can be used, but there is reason to believe that both should be used. Further, external evaluations help individuals to realistically evaluate themselves. Grades do predict subsequent academic achievement (i.e., subsequent grades), and they do predict some types of out-of-class accomplishments. Grades cannot be expected to be perfect or near perfect predictors, however, because much goes into subsequent accomplishment including opportunity, effort, quality of instruction, and luck.

3. Grades are unnecessary

The above discussion and the Cronbach analysis show that although not necessary for all evaluative functions, grades cannot be entirely eliminated. Some type of summary report is needed for guidance and counselling and for purposes of accountability—both of the pupil to the school and the school to the pupil. Human information processing is such that masses of data need to be capsuled before they are understood; thus, imperfect as they are, grades serve summary and recordkeeping functions. Parents need to know, for example, how their children are doing in arithmetic, on the whole, as well as the specific kinds of arithmetic competence the child possesses. Overly detailed

reports, however, will be incomprehensible (see "Dallas Monster," Box 4.1). A high school student wants to know whether to register for "advanced placement" calculus or for "regular" calculus: The counselor reaches for this semester's pre-calculus course grade, not a list of specific mathematic concepts acquired in the last nine weeks. A pupil wants to know whether he or she is progressing satisfactorily; the school is obliged to offer its judgment, not simply a description of placement in a curriculum.

4. Grades are harmful

Some teachers use grades punitively and vindictively as weapons rather than as tools. Some parents overstress the importance of grades, putting undesirable pressure on their children to achieve at all costs. But to what extent this pressure is occurring is not clear. For example, are one or two or ten parents per classroom overly ambitious for their children? Are all teachers vindictive? One in twenty? No one knows for sure. A real concern among teachers of elementary pupils is the discouraging effect of low grades. Cronbach's analysis of the motivating effects of grades suggests some ways in which teacher evaluations can be improved to avoid discouragement. Even though grades may only report learning failure and cannot be entirely to blame for this failure, still, it is important to consider the effects such reports can have on children.

Methods of Reporting Pupil Progress

What Methods of Reporting are Schools Using?

Figure 13.1 summarizes the results of a nationwide survey and provides an overview of the ways schools are reporting pupil progress. Table 13.3 summarizes the advantages and disadvantages of each method. Note in connection with Figure 13.2 and Table 13.3 that

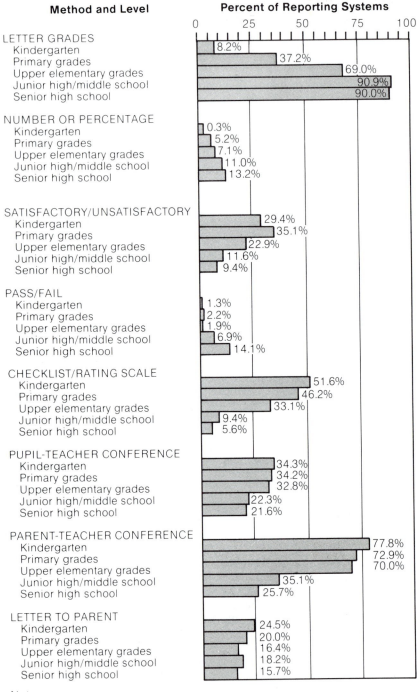

Method and Level

Percent of Reporting Systems

0   25   50   75   100

LETTER GRADES
- Kindergarten — 8.2%
- Primary grades — 37.2%
- Upper elementary grades — 69.0%
- Junior high/middle school — 90.9%
- Senior high school — 90.0%

NUMBER OR PERCENTAGE
- Kindergarten — 0.3%
- Primary grades — 5.2%
- Upper elementary grades — 7.1%
- Junior high/middle school — 11.0%
- Senior high school — 13.2%

SATISFACTORY/UNSATISFACTORY
- Kindergarten — 29.4%
- Primary grades — 35.1%
- Upper elementary grades — 22.9%
- Junior high/middle school — 11.6%
- Senior high school — 9.4%

PASS/FAIL
- Kindergarten — 1.3%
- Primary grades — 2.2%
- Upper elementary grades — 1.9%
- Junior high/middle school — 6.9%
- Senior high school — 14.1%

CHECKLIST/RATING SCALE
- Kindergarten — 51.6%
- Primary grades — 46.2%
- Upper elementary grades — 33.1%
- Junior high/middle school — 9.4%
- Senior high school — 5.6%

PUPIL-TEACHER CONFERENCE
- Kindergarten — 34.3%
- Primary grades — 34.2%
- Upper elementary grades — 32.8%
- Junior high/middle school — 22.3%
- Senior high school — 21.6%

PARENT-TEACHER CONFERENCE
- Kindergarten — 77.8%
- Primary grades — 72.9%
- Upper elementary grades — 70.0%
- Junior high/middle school — 35.1%
- Senior high school — 25.7%

LETTER TO PARENT
- Kindergarten — 24.5%
- Primary grades — 20.0%
- Upper elementary grades — 16.4%
- Junior high/middle school — 18.2%
- Senior high school — 15.7%

Note:
The figure represents approximately 300 school districts per grade level. Many school systems used more than one method of reporting pupil progress.
Source: Kunder and Porwoll, ERS, (1977, p. 19)

Figure 13 • 1 Percentage of school systems at each grade level using the various methods of reporting pupil progress.

YOUR CHILD CAN:	1st				2nd				3rd				4th			
	Excellent Progress	Satisfactory	Improvement Needed	Skill not yet introduced	Excellent Progress	Satisfactory	Improvement Needed	Skill not yet introduced	Excellent Progress	Satisfactory	Improvement Needed	Skill not yet introduced	Excellent Progress	Satisfactory	Improvement Needed	Skill not yet introduced
Identify familiar objects																
Describe pictures																
Identify pictures that are alike																
Identify pictures that do not belong																
Identify missing parts																
Choose a likely ending to a story																
Tell if letters are the same or different																
Put things in the right order from memory																
Recognize familiar sounds																
Tell whether sounds are the same or different																
Tell whether words sound exactly the same or different																
Tell if words rhyme or do not rhyme																
Copy geometric shapes																
Copy numerals																
Copy letters																
Tell the names of different colors																
Make comparisons about length, age, weight and height																
Understand words that give direction , ie, up, down, left, right, etc.																
Recognize shapes which are alike but different in size																
Pick out a pattern within a group of patterns																
Identify equivalent and empty sets																
Match sets which have the same number of members																
Count up to ten the number of members in a set																
Identify fractional parts																
Identify an object that is in a stated ordinal position (1st, 2nd, etc.)																
Identify a clock face which gives the time asked for (in hours)																
Substract a smaller number from a larger number of objects																
Add two small sets of objects																
Measure a line with a measuring unit																
Use what he/she knows about objects to decide which is heavier or lighter																
Identify an open curve																
Identify pictures of workers named																
Identify a worker and the equipment he uses																
Recognize activities which might be dangerous																
Identify the best way to travel to do certain things																
Recognize the flag of the United States																
Identify common American coins																
Indicate most direct route on a simple map																
Participate in music activities																
Use various art materials																

Source: Reprinted directly from Leon County Public Schools

Figure 13 • 2   A section of a checklist report card for kindergarten.

a particular school district may use more than one method of reporting pupil progress.

Study of this table and figure reveals that teachers use some methods of reporting pupil progress more frequently at certain grade levels. Letter grades, for example, are used with high frequency in the upper elementary, junior high, and senior high school levels. Parent-teacher conferences do not occur often in junior and senior high schools. Another point to note is that often schools use combinations of methods to report pupil progress. For example, letter grades may report on subject-matter learning while rating scales may report pupil attitudes and deportment. A parent-teacher conference may convey information on both achievement and behavior. Conceivably, some schools use some combination of nearly all methods. A third point to consider is that conflicts may arise between methods. School administrators need a concise summary of each pupil's progress for purposes of accountability and record keeping. Parents and teachers may need more detailed explanations of the objectives taught and mastered and/or how a pupil's educational development compares with members of a peer group.[1] The most detailed method of reporting identified in the table and figure is the checklist. Figure 13.2 shows an example of a checklist one school used to report progress of kindergarten pupils. You can find useful summaries of the practical pros and cons of various pupil reporting methods in the sources listed at the end of this chapter.

Parent-Teacher Conferences

Parent-teacher conferences need to be carefully and skillfully conducted if they are to be productive. Table 13.4 lists some of the things

to do before and during the conference to keep it moving along on target. Additional suggestions are given in Gronlund's (1974) *Improving Marking and Reporting in Classroom Instruction.*

Parent-teacher conferences are not without their drawbacks, however. (a) They are time consuming for the teacher both in preparation time and in actual contact time. Schools frequently schedule one or two days to hold conferences during school hours; some schedule evening hours for the convenience of working parents. Sometimes schools neglect to give teachers time to plan and prepare for the conferences, however, assuming that teachers either need little or no planning time, or that they will do the necessary preparation after hours. Some parents (and teachers) talk too much and use up more than their share of time. (b) Parent-teacher conferences can be frustrating and produce anxiety for both teacher and parent especially if the parties lack confidence in each other. (c) Not all parents will come to conferences for various reasons. Parents may be: unwilling to attend, working, ill, or otherwise unable to come. While some parents are courteous and notify the teacher that they cannot attend, the teacher should not expect most parents to do this. (d) Teachers and/or parents may have too much information, too many issues, or too many concerns to discuss in the brief time allotted to the conference, and scheduling another conference with the parents may be necessary.

Parent conferences should be private and between one teacher and the parents of one pupil. Facilities should be such that discussions are confidential. Avoid holding a conference where other teachers, other students, or other parents can overhear what is being said. This protects the rights of all involved. It may be difficult to arrange to limit the conference to one teacher and the parents, especially in schools where pupils have different teachers for different subjects. Little privacy and helpful communication can occur, however, if a "gang" of six or eight teachers face a parent in an inquisition-like arrangement.

[1]Note that parents often seek group-referenced information because they have had little experience with pupils of a given age or grade. After five years of teaching, for example, a teacher may have experienced hundreds of pupils of a given grade. After 20 years of parenting, parents have experienced only their own children plus a few children of friends, relatives, and neighbors.

Name	Type of code used	Advantages	Disadvantages
Letter grades	A, B, C, etc., also "+" and "−" may be added.	a. Administratively easy to use b. Believed to be easy to interpret c. Concisely summarize overall performance	a. Meaning of a grade varies widely with subject, teacher, school b. Do not describe strength and weaknesses c. Kindergarten and primary school children may feel defeated by them
Number or percentage grade	Integers (5, 4, 3 . . .) or percentages (99, 98, . . .)	a. Same as (a), (b), (c) above b. More continuous than letter grades c. May be used along with letter grades	a. Same as (a), (b), (c) above b. Meaning not immediately apparent unless explanation accompanies them
Two-category grade	Pass-Fail, satisfactory-unsatisfactory, credit-entry	a. Less devastating to younger students b. Can encourage older students to take courses normally neglected because of fear of lowered GPA	a. Less reliable than more continuous system b. Does not communicate enough information about pupil's performance for others to judge progress
Checklist and rating scales	Checks (✓) next to objectives mastered or numerical ratings of degree of mastery	a. Gives the details of what the pupil achieved b. May be combined with letter grades or with group-referenced data	a. May become too detailed for parents to comprehend b. Administratively cumbersome for record keeping
Pupil-teacher conference	Usually none, but any of the above may be discussed	a. Offers opportunity to discuss progress personally b. Can be an on-going process that is integrated into instruction	a. Teacher needs skill in offering positive as well as negative comments b. Can be time consuming c. Can be threatening to some pupils d. Doesn't offer the institution the kind of summary record desired
Parent-teacher conference	None, but often one or more of the above may be discussed	a. Allows parents and teachers to discuss concerns and clarify misunderstandings b. Teachers can show samples of students' work and explain basis for judgments made c. May lead to improved home-school relations	a. Time consuming b. Requires teacher to prepare ahead of time c. May provoke too much anxiety for some teachers and parents d. Inadequate means of reporting large amounts of information e. May be inconvenient for parent to attend
Letter to parents	None	a. Useful supplement to other progress-reporting methods	a. Short letters inadequately communicate pupil progress b. Requires exceptional writing time and much teacher time

Table 13 • 3   Advantages and disadvantages of some commonly used methods of reporting pupil progress.

Preparing for the conference:	Sharing information with parents during the conference:
1. Have a clear grasp of the purpose of the conference.	1. Begin by describing the pupil's strong points.
2. Review the pupil's school records for general background information.	2. Describe the areas needing improvement in a positive and tactful manner.
3. Assemble a folder of specific information concerning the pupil's present learning progress.	3. Encourage parents to participate in the conference.
4. Organize the information for parents in a systematic manner.	4. Be cautious about giving advice.
5. Make a tentative list of questions to ask parents.	**Planning a course of action with parents during the conference:**
6. Anticipate parents' questions.	1. Begin the concluding phase of the conference with a brief overall summary.
7. Provide a comfortable, informal setting, free from interruption.	2. Have parents participate in planning a course of action.
Establishing and maintaining rapport during the conference:	3. Review your conference notes with parents.
1. Create a friendly, informal atmosphere.	4. End the conference on a positive note.
2. Maintain a positive attitude.	
3. Use language that parents understand.	
4. Be willing to listen to parents.	
5. Be honest and sincere with parents and do not betray confidence.	

Adapted with permission of Macmillan Publishing Co., Inc. from *Improving Marking and Reporting in Classroom Instruction*, pp. 39–43, by Norman E. Gronlund. Copyright © 1974 by Norman E. Gronlund.

Table 13 • 4   Suggestions for organizing and conducting a parent-teacher conference.

(Teachers wouldn't want several parents ganging up on one teacher either.) Such "gang conferences" threaten many parents and inhibit expression of their concerns. A really aggressive and articulate parent, on the other hand, can say things that will embarrass one teacher in front of the others. The principal has a responsibility to make arrangements which preserve these privacy principles.

Multiple Marking Systems

When a school uses more than one method, it employs what is called a *multiple reporting system*. Sometimes a school uses a report card with several kinds of marks or symbols, referred to as a *multiple marking system*. Figure 13.3 shows a report card employing a multiple marking system for an elementary school. A number code is used for the achievement level and a letter (S, U, N) rating scale for other

areas. Most schools rate citizenship, behavior, etc. separately from achievement, but this provision varies with the grade level (Kunder & Porwoll, 1977). For kindergarten, primary, and upper elementary grades, 80 to 90% of the schools provide this separation; about 78% of the junior high schools and 68% of the senior high schools do so. Gronlund's suggestions for developing a multiple code report are shown in Table 13.5.

Using a Multiple Reporting System

Committees of teachers, school administrators, and parents frequently form to review, critique, and/or redesign a school district's report card. As you may know already, it takes about 15 minutes of the first committee meeting to discover that everyone has a different view concerning the particular information which is "most important" to report and the

EXPLANATION OF GRADES

1—EXCELLENT ACHIEVEMENT
2—ABOVE AVERAGE ACHIEVEMENT
3—AVERAGE ACHIEVEMENT
4—BELOW AVERAGE ACHIEVEMENT
5—UNSATISFACTORY ACHIEVEMENT
(FAILING WORK)

S—SATISFACTORY PROGRESS
U—UNSATISFACTORY PROGRESS
N—NEEDS IMPROVEMENT

NAME_____ GRADE _____

IF THE GRADE OR CHECK MARK APPEARS IN THE "S" COLUMN, THE ACHIEVEMENT GRADE IS CONSISTENT WITH ABILITY. IF THE GRADE OR CHECK MARK APPEARS IN THE "N" COLUMN, THE GRADE IS LOWER THAN THE STUDENT IS CAPABLE OF ATTAINING.

HABITS AND ATTITUDES	1st PERIOD	2nd PERIOD	3rd PERIOD	4th PERIOD
GENERAL CONDUCT				
ACCEPTS RESPONSIBILITY				
RESPECTS RIGHTS OF OTHERS				
OBSERVES RULES AND REGULATIONS				
FOLLOWS DIRECTIONS				
WORKS WITH OTHERS				
WORKS WELL INDEPENDENTLY				
NEATNESS & ACCURACY				
MAKES GOOD USE OF TIME				

REPORT PERIOD

ACHIEVEMENT IN SPECIAL SUBJECTS

ARTS AND CRAFTS				
HANDWRITING				
CLASSROOM MUSIC				
PHYSICAL EDUCATION AND HEALTH				
A "√" INDICATES A PARENT CONFERENCE IS DESIRED				

ACHIEVEMENT IN BASIC SUBJECTS	1st PERIOD S	N	2nd PERIOD S	N	3rd PERIOD S	N	4th PERIOD S	N
READING								
VOCABULARY								
COMPREHENSION								
INDEPENDENT READING								
ENGLISH								
GRAMMAR ORAL								
GRAMMAR WRITTEN								
SPEAKING ABILITY								
SPELLING								
WEEKLY LESSON								
USE IN WRITTEN WORK								
MATHEMATICS								
REASONING								
NUMBER FACTS								
COMPUTATION								
ACCURACY								
SOCIAL STUDIES								
HISTORICAL CONCEPTS								
GEOGRAPHICAL CONCEPTS								
CIVICS								
SCIENCE								
CONCEPTS								
PARTICIPATION								
INTEREST								

Source: Courtesy of Kansas City, Kansas Public Schools

Figure 13 • 3 Example of a section of a multiple-marking system report card for grades 4, 5, and 6.

particular method which is the "best way" of reporting that information. Sometimes members of a committee spend hours trying either to convince other committee members that their views are inappropriate or to derive a compromise view—the One Best System, to borrow a phrase from Tyack (1974).

As I describe in the next section, information about pupils needs to be interpreted. Among the basic referencing schemes to be described are group-referencing, task-refer-

encing, and self-referencing.[2] Each of these ways of referencing provides a different perspective on a pupil. Each has advantages and disadvantages (see below). Different constituencies (parents, teachers, etc.) will want different combinations of information from these referencing schemes; thus the problem is to

[2]Group-referencing is sometimes called *norm-referencing*, while task-referencing is sometimes called *objectives-referencing* or *criterion-referencing*.

1. Analyze the needs of each of the persons (pupils, parents, teachers, counselors, and administrators) who will use the system, and delineate the kinds of marks and reports each will find most useful.	5. Balance desire for diagnosis and detail with practical concerns for (a) the amount of time the system will require from teachers; (b) the degree to which parents, teachers, pupils, and other school personnel can understand the system; and (c) the ease with which teachers can summarize the report for school records.
2. Develop the marking and reporting system cooperatively with pupils, parents, teachers, counselors, and school administrators.	
3. Base the system on clear statements of the learning objectives of the local school district and each particular course.	6. Design the system to include parent-teacher conferences as well as formal report cards.
4. Limit the items on the final report form to those for which teachers can obtain valid and reliable information.	

Adapted with permission of Macmillan Publishing Co., Inc. from *Measurement and Evaluation on Teaching*, Fourth Edition, by Norman E. Gronlund. Copyright © 1981 by Norman E. Gronlund.

Table 13 • 5 Guidelines for developing and using a multiple marking and reporting system.

design a system of reporting information to parents and pupils as well as teachers and school administrators. In an information delivery system, providing certain kinds of information only to those parents who want it may be desirable. Further, the method or medium of delivery (e.g., report card, letter to parent, checklist, parent-teacher conference, etc.) may not necessarily need to be the same for all types of information.

Consider this hypothetical example as one possibility for a certain school district. The report card for the elementary level may contain short lists of major developmental objectives[3] in each subject area along with information about the teacher's view of the child's social development, attitude toward learning, and classroom deportment. The report card may also contain a place for parents to indicate if they want additional information. If some parents want to see a checklist of the specific objectives their child mastered in mathematics during the preceding marking period, such a checklist can be sent home and returned. Other parents may want to know if the teacher thinks their children are working

up to their capabilities. Still others may want to know if the child's performance in a subject ranks in the upper, middle, or lower third of the class. Some may want to know what the child's letter grade *would be*, even though letter grades are not reported on the report card or permanent record card. Within practical limits of cost and teacher time the task is to design a system to deliver a variety of kinds of information to a variety of persons. With the advent of microcomputers in the schools and computer literary courses for teachers, such multiple reporting systems seem quite feasible.

Not all information needs to appear on a child's permanent record card. Assigning letter grades to pupils at the elementary level is controversial since letter grade assignment usually occurs at the junior and senior high school levels. However, pupils and parents may become upset if, for the first time in junior high, a pupil receives a "C" (or lower) in a subject, when previously the pupil has received only "performing satisfactorily" checks on the elementary report card. Yet many educators (and some professional associations) argue that reporting or recording grades at the elementary level is inappropriate. Some intermediate coding position may help a pupil

[3]Developmental objectives are distinguished from mastery or "can do" objectives (Gronlund, 1973; Forsyth, 1976). See Chapter 4 for a discussion of these.

Educational level	Stipulated school board policy			No policy stipulated by board	Number of districts
	Task referencing	Self-referencing	Group-referencing		
Kindergarten	38 13.7%	120 43.2%	36 12.9%	104 37.4%	278
Primary grades	57 18.6%	145 47.2%	56 18.2%	87 28.2%	307
Upper elementary grades	60 19.8%	136 44.9%	67 27.1%	86 28.4%	303
Junior high/ middle school	76 25.5%	86 28.9%	93 31.2%	90 30.2%	298
Senior high school	83 28.0%	76 25.7%	100 33.8%	88 29.7%	296

Note: Some schools reported more than one method; the number of districts reporting (last column) does not equal the row sum.
Source: Kunder, L. H. and Porwoll, P. J. "Stipulated School Board Policy Standards for Reporting Pupil Progress." *Reporting Pupil Progress: Policies, Procedures, and Systems*, pp. 26–27, Table 8. Copyright 1977 by Educational Research Service, Arlington, Va.

Table 13 • 6   Number and percent of school districts having stipulated policies for using particular referencing schemes for grading.

with this transition from the elementary school marking code to a new marking code at the junior high. A school may decide, for example, to have teachers prepare letter grades for fifth and sixth graders, but not to report them on report cards nor on permanent record cards. Parents, however, are apprised of these grades. Thus, a "performing satisfactorily" can mean a "C" for some students and a "B" for others. At the end of the year, the letter grades records are destroyed.

The ideas and suggestions in this section are opinions; no evidence suggests they will solve pupil progress reporting problems. Schools will have to try out and to evaluate a variety of creative approaches in order to find those which report the kinds of information professional educators and community members want reported. Perhaps little is to be gained by either closing off one channel of communication, limiting the kinds of information to that which only one party feels is appropriate, or forcing all parties to conform to a particular medium or method of communication. There are no prescriptions; there is no one best system.

Suggestions for Assigning Letter Grades

Schemes for Referencing Pupils' Performance

Grades reflect, among other things, a teacher's judgment of the quality of a pupil's performance in relation to the pupil's own abilities, the performance of others in the class, and/or a specified set of standard tasks or objectives. Thus, grades take on meaning when the referencing scheme on which they are based is clearly specified. Which referencing scheme(s) you use depend(s) mostly on (a) your personal value system and (b) the policies of the school district in which you work. Table 13.6 summarizes the results of one nationwide survey of school districts. Notice that from a quarter to a third of the school districts have no stipulated school board policy, although particular schemes may be entrenched. A number of school districts use more than one referencing scheme (Kunder & Porwoll, 1977).

Group- or norm-referencing This approach assigns grades on the basis of how a pupil's performance compares with others in the class: Pupils performing better than their classmates receive the higher grades. Persons advocating group-referencing center their arguments on (a) the necessity of competition in life, (b) the value of knowing a pupil's standing in relation to peers, and (c) the idea that relative achievement is more important than absolute. Arguments against norm-referenced grading center on (a) the ill-effects of competition, (b) the knowledge of standing in a peer group does not describe what a pupil has learned, and (c) ascertaining the absolute level of achievement is more important than ascertaining relative achievement. See Bellanca and Kirschenbaum (1976) for a more detailed summary of these arguments.

Self-referencing Here grades are assigned by comparing a pupil's performance with the teacher's perceptions of the pupil's capability: Pupils performing at or above the level at which the teacher believes them capable of performing receive the better grades, regardless of their absolute levels of attainment. A student judged to be less capable may be given the same grade as another student judged more capable, even though the former completed less work, because the less capable one was "working to capacity" while the other was not. Arguments in favor of self-referenced grading center on (a) the possibility of reducing competition among pupils and (b) the concept that grades can be adjusted to motivate and meet the needs of students. Arguments against the system center on (a) the unreliable nature of teachers' judgments of capability, (b) the need for parents and pupils to know standing relative to peers, (c) the idea that this procedure tends to be applied mostly to lower ability pupils, and (d) the possibility that this system may eventually lead to grading based solely on effort or improvement (Dunbar, Float, & Lyman, 1980). From a statistical viewpoint a negative correlation tends to exist between initial level of achievement and growth: Students coming into class with the highest levels of achievement tend to have the smallest amount of measurable improvement or change, even though their final levels of achievement remain the highest. (See Terwilliger [1971] for an illustration of how this can happen.)

Task-referencing This is sometimes referred to as using *absolute standards* or *criterion-referencing*. Teachers assign grades by comparing a pupil's performance to a defined set of tasks to be done, behaviors to be learned, or knowledge to be acquired: Students who complete more of the tasks or acquire more of the objectives are given the better grades, regardless of how well other pupils perform, or whether they have worked up to their potential. If teachers define the domain of tasks to be learned well, this approach may be called criterion-referenced (see Chapter 17), but usually neither the teacher nor the school defines the domain to be learned well. Thus, task-referencing is not criterion-referencing in the strictly technical usage of the term. To grade on a task-referencing basis, however, a teacher must explicitly define the tasks for which pupils are held accountable and use these tasks as the basis for assigning marks. Task-referenced grading is sometimes referred to as "absolute grading." Arguments both for and against task-referencing, in general, center on whether it is of value to know exactly what the pupil has learned independently of the pupil's own capability and the learning of others. Bellanca and Kirschenbaum (1976) give a summary of these arguments.

A teacher or a school probably finds some merit in each of these systems of referencing because each addresses a somewhat different aspect of a pupil's performance: self, others, and the curriculum. Thus, in the long run, a report card may need to contain all three types of information. A given school district will likely emphasize one of the referencing schemes at a particular grade level. Thus at the primary grade level, for example, a report card may be mainly task-referenced, but secondarily contain self-referenced and group-referenced information. All three types of information are likely to interest many parents.

Deciding What to Include in the Grade

Although grades are assigned within the context of a particular referencing scheme, an important step prior to the actual assignment of grades is to decide on *what* will count toward the grade and *how much* each will count. Will the grade be based on only test scores? On homework and tests? Class participation? Attendance? Will all homework assignments count? How much weight will be assigned each of the performances that enter into the grade? Will a student be allowed to redo an assignment or retake a test? How often? Under what conditions?

Ideally, the teacher will know the answers to questions such as these and tell the students at the start of the course or grading period. One procedure is to put this information in writing and either post it or give each student a copy. It may be unethical for a teacher to fail to inform students ahead of time about the basis on which they will be graded.

The decisions about how much weight to assign to homework, various tests and quizzes, term papers, etc. are made in relation to their importance to the objectives of instruction. Pupil activities may be related to a variety of learning objectives, but each objective may not be equally important in terms of the ultimate goals of instruction. More than likely, however, several activities (e.g., homework, quiz, mid-term exam) relate to the *same* objectives (i.e., teacher can use the several activities to infer achievement of several common objectives). So that if you give equal weight to each activity, you weight the common objective more heavily, since more activities relate to it. You need to make a list, then, of all the pupil activities (performances) you take into consideration in the assigned grade, decide how these performances relate to the various learning objectives, and determine how important each is (and thus how heavily each will weigh) in relation to the overall grade.

Assigning Group-Referenced Letter Grades

One method of group-referencing uses *ranks:* Pupil's performances are expressed as ranks or percentile ranks (see Chapter 3) and grades (A, B, C, etc.) are assigned on the basis of this ranking. Another method uses the *standard deviation* (see Chapter 3) as a unit: A teacher computes the standard deviation of the scores and uses this number to mark off segments on the number line; these segments become the basis for grade assignment. The two methods do not necessarily give the same results. Further, the group to which the grades are referenced may be a single classroom, a section of a course, or a larger group formed by combining several classes or sections of the same course.

Grading a single test or assignment To use the *ranking method* to assign letter grades, you decide on the percentage of As, Bs, Cs, etc. to award. For example, you may decide that the top 20% of the students get A, the next 30% B, the next 30% C, the next 15% D, and the lowest 5% F. One set of percentages based on dividing the range of a normal curve[4] into five equal intervals is: the top 3.6%, A; next 23.8%, B; next 45.2%, C; next 23.8%, D; lowest 3.6%, F (Blommers & Lindquist, 1960). This set of percentages assumes that the true amount of achievement in the group at hand

[4]See Chapter 14.

is normally distributed, an assumption which, in my view, may be hard for you to justify. Notice that (a) the percentages are completely arbitrary, (b) the test scores must be valid measures of the desired achievement, and (c) there is no reference to the particular skills or competence the grades represent except in the sense that higher ranked students have more competence than lower ranked students. Some logical reasoning should justify the particular percentages that you use; otherwise, the grading scheme is likely to be capricious.

To use the *standard deviation method* you first decide how many multiples of a standard deviation the lower limit of A will lie above the median (PR = 50) of the group (Ebel & Stuit, 1954; Ebel, 1965). After you decide this, you mark the score scale off into five[5] segments, with each one a standard deviation wide beginning at the lower limit of A and going downward. The steps for doing this, along with an example, are shown in Box 13.2.

The method Ebel outlines in the box adjusts the distribution of letter grades to suit the general level of scholastic ability of the group at hand. Thus, the first step is to estimate the ability level of the group (poor to exceptional) using either (a) their previous grade point average (GPA) or (b) a common ability test they have taken. With this method, the interval width (= numerical value of the standard deviation) and the lower limit for A are arbitrary just as the percentages in the previous method were arbitrary. Further, as with the ranking method, reference is made only to the person's relative achievement rather than to an absolute description of the skills the person may possess. The method assumes that "average" ability pupils should exhibit a normal distribution of actual achievement, even though they may not show the distribution on the test or assignment being graded. The assumptions about the actual distribution of

achievement for above and below average pupils are represented by the "percentage of marks" in the rows of tables in the box. A decided advantage of this approach is that it helps to make grades more comparable among all teachers who use it.

Grading a composite of several scores
Usually a grade is based on a pupil's performance on several assignments, quizzes, reports, and perhaps an examination. A teacher usually wants to weight each of these according to their importance for the final grade. Some may, for example, count homework and quizzes equally, written reports twice that of quizzes, and exams three times the value of quizzes. There is no agreement as to what should constitute proper weighting.

When a group-referenced grading scheme is adopted, the principle to follow is that the weights should be chosen so that the most important[6] scores contribute the most to the final standings of the persons in the group. This principle is likely to be violated if the teacher simply multiples the scores by some arbitrary weights and then adds the weighted scores to form a composite. The reason is that the rank of a composite score is influenced by the standard deviations of the components making up the composite.[7] To take an extreme example, suppose that the final grade is based on the sum of the grades on one homework assignment and on one exam. Suppose that every pupil gets 100% on the homework, but that there is a wide range of scores on the exam. Since everyone receives the same score on the homework, the student's final *ranking* depends entirely on their exam score. The standard deviation of the homework scores is equal to zero, and thus, the influence of the homework scores on the final ranking is zero as well. In general, the larger the standard deviation of a set of component scores, the

---

[5]This assumes an A, B, C, D, F scale. If there are six grades, the intervals would be narrower; if three letter grades, wider; and so on.

[6]As decided by the teacher.
[7]Also the intercorrelations among the components.

Letter Mark Distribution Statistics for Classes at Seven Levels of Ability

	Lower limit of A's	Percent of marks					Ability measures	
		A	B	C	D	F	GPA	Percentile
Exceptional	0.7	24	38	29	8	1	2.80	79
Superior	0.9	18	36	32	12	2	2.60	73
Good	1.1	14	32	36	15	3	2.40	66
Fair	1.3	10	29	37	20	4	2.20	58
Average	1.5	7	24	38	24	7	2.00	50
Weak	1.7	4	20	37	29	10	1.80	42
Poor	1.9	3	15	36	32	14	1.60	34

Four steps are involved in this process of assigning marks.
1. Select from [the above table] . . . a distribution of marks appropriate to the level of ability of the class being graded.
2. Calculate the median and the standard deviation of the scores on which the marks are to be based.
3. Determine the lower score limits of the A, B, C, and D mark intervals, using the median, the standard deviation, and the appropriate lower limit factor from [the table].
4. Assign the designated marks to the students whose scores fall in intervals determined for each mark.

Sample Problem in Letter Mark Assignment

A. **Data for the problem**
   1. Class ability levels measures:
      a. Mean GPA on previous years' courses: 2.17
      b. Mean percentile on aptitude test: 56.3
      c. Appropriate grade distribution [from above table]: *fair*

   2. Achievement scores (number of students = 38):

112	100	93	84	78	72	66	51
109	97	91	83	75	71	62	47
106	97	90	82	75	70	59	44
105	95	89	81	75	69	59	
104	95	84	80	74	68	58	

B. **Calculations from the data:**

   1. Median $\dfrac{81 + 80}{2} = 80.5$

   2. Standard deviation $\dfrac{636 - 318}{19} = 16.7$

Marks	Lower Limits	Intervals	Number	Percent
A	$80.5 + (1.3 \times 16.7) = 102.2$	103–112	5	13
B	$102.2 - 16.7 = 85.5$	86–102	9	24
C	$85.5 - 16.7 = 68.8$	69–85	15	39
D	$68.8 - 16.7 = 52.1$	53–68	6	16
F		44–52	3	8
			38	100

Source: Robert L. Ebel, *Essentials of Educational Measurement*, 3rd ed., © 1979, pp. 248–251. Reprinted by permission of Prentice-Hall Inc., Englewood Cliffs, N.J.

Box 13 • 2 Ebel and Stuit method of assigning group-referenced letter grades.

more that component contributes to the rankings of the persons when the composite is formed.

To preserve the desired influence (weights) of the components comprising a composite, a group-referenced system should take into account the numerical values of the standard deviations of the components. One way to do this is to first change all of the scores on each component into z-scores (see Chapter 3) and then multiply the z-scores by the weights desired. Finally, add these products to form the composite for each student. The formula below summarizes these steps.

$$C = \Sigma wz \qquad \text{[Eq. 13.1]}$$

where
  C = composite score

  Σ = sum of

  w = weight of the component

  z = the linear z-score for the component.

Changing the raw scores on each component to z-scores assures that each component has the same standard deviation, since the standard deviation of the z-scores equals 1. The weights by which the component z-scores are multiplied become the new standard deviations of the components.

An alternate procedure for forming composite scores is to first convert each person's component raw score to a normalized standard score (Ahmann and Glock, 1981) such as a stanine or T-score using Table BC.1 at the back cover. Then multiply by the desired weights before adding to form the composite. This can be expressed by the following formula:

$$C = \Sigma wS \qquad \text{[Eq. 13.2]}$$

where
  C = composite score

  Σ = sum of

  w = weight given to a component

  S = normalized standard score on a component.

To illustrate, suppose Bob's scores are as follows:

	Raw score	Percen- tile rank	Rank (N = 30)
Quizzes	87	85	5
Homework	55	75	8
Term paper	48	50	15.5
Exam	96	91	3

Further suppose the teacher wants to give the following weights to these components:

	Quizzes	Home- work	Term paper	Exam
	20%	10%	20%	50%
weights =	2	1	2	5

Percentile ranks can be used to obtain the T-scores. Thus, Bob's composite score is computed as follows:

	T-score (S)	Weight (w)	Product (wS)
Quizzes	60	2	120
Homework	57	1	57
Term paper	50	2	100
Exam	63	5	315
		$C = \Sigma wS =$	592

Note that these composite scores are not themselves T-scores or stanines, but these composite scores do provide a basis on which to rank pupils, so that the weightings will have the desired influence on the final standings.

Assigning Letter Grades in a Task-Referenced System

In a task-referenced or criterion-referenced grading system a grade reflects a pupil's status with respect to a well-defined domain of tasks. To assign grades in this system you usually compute the percent of the domain that the pupil is able to do correctly. Since a test and/or any assignment is only a sample of a pupil's behavior, you consider scores obtained in this manner only as estimates of the true percent of the domain a pupil is able to perform.

Grading a single test or assignment Teachers frequently use percents as bases for marking and grading papers. Note that a percent begs the question, "Percentage of what?" Often, the only answer is that the score

Statement	Opinion								
	% Agree			% Undecided			% Disagree		
	ST	K	NCME	ST	K	NCME	ST	K	NCME
1	74	70	45	22	18	38	4	12	16
2	71	70	50	21	14	24	8	15	26
3	9	25	30	15	16	9	76	59	61
4	72	35	51	18	24	25	10	41	24
5	44	35	54	42	21	20	14	44	26
6	13	20	13	20	38	60	67	42	27
7	64	27	76	22	10	12	14	63	12
8	19	79	80	43	9	9	38	12	11
9	66	64	54	19	21	21	15	15	25
10	71	32	13	14	19	18	15	49	69
11	14	46	76	13	33	14	73	21	19
12	39	43	38	41	17	21	20	40	41
13	46	40	38	36	37	26	19	23	36
14	36	36	37	41	23	17	23	41	46
15	19	50	55	34	13	24	47	37	21
16	60	17	22	23	18	20	17	65	58
17	37	37	43	38	34	40	25	29	17
18	41	41	69	36	21	18	23	37	13
19	32	52	45	35	16	15	33	32	40
20	54	28	33	22	20	21	24	52	46
21	24	30	51	19	13	21	57	56	27
22	48	38	15	21	23	18	31	39	67
23	52	40	64	17	25	15	31	35	21
24	54	59	35	15	14	19	31	27	46

Note: ST = 202 student teachers from Southern Illinois University (Boykin & Pope, 1977); K = 406 readers of *Phi Delta Kappan* magazine (53% were teachers; 21% were administrators, 8% were students) (Gephart, 1977); NCME = 145 members of the National Council on Measurement in Education (47% were college teachers, 10% were college administrators, 23% school psychologists, researchers, data analysts) (Harris, 1973).
Source: Adapted from W. J. Gephart, "Editor, Take A Test on Taking A Test on Grading," © 1977 Phi Delta Kappan, Inc., p. 767 and W. S. Harris, "Agreement Among NCME Members on Selected Issues in Educational Measurement." *Journal of Educational Measurement*, 1973, Vol. 10, pp. 65–68. Copyright 1973, NCME, Washington, D.C.

Table 13 • 7 A comparison of student teachers' (ST), *Kappan* (K) readers', and measurement specialists' (NCME members) responses to the grading and marking statements in Box 13.1.

represents the percent of the maximum score on the test or the assignment. This answer ignores the broader concern: The test should be a representative sample from a well-defined domain of tasks. If you have not defined this domain and have not built the test to sample the domain, then you cannot use the percent grade to accurately estimate the pupil's performance on a broader domain. Such tests (or assignments) and, consequently, such scores cannot be considered criterion-referenced.

The relationship between percent correct and letter grade is rather arbitrary. In some schools, 80% is "A," in others 85% is "A," while still in others, 90% is "A." Some school boards have a policy on this matter (see Table 13.6), but many do not. The percentage that defines each grade should represent not only a teacher's judgment, but also a teacher's experience with (a) the kinds of pupils being taught, and (b) the difficulty of the tests the teacher develops. Thus, group-referenced information plays a role in establishing a task-referenced system. It may take a teacher several years to work out a percent grading scheme that is both fair to the students and represents reasonable standards of scholarship. The new teacher should check with colleagues to be sure that the grading scheme is a reasonable one and is not unnecessarily "out of line" with the rest of the teachers.

Grading a composite of several scores As with group-referenced grading, you must be careful when using weights, otherwise the results will not reflect the importance of each component you seek to maintain. One way to do this is to first change all component scores to percentages, then multiply the percentages by the desired weights. Add these products together and divide by the sum of the weights. This procedure may be summarized by the following formula:

$$C = \frac{\Sigma wP}{\Sigma w} \qquad \text{[Eq. 13.3]}$$

where
$\quad C$ = composite percentage (weighted)

$\quad \Sigma$ = sum of

w = weight given to a component

P = percent score on a component

To illustrate, consider Bob's scores again along with the same weights used before.

	Raw score	% score[8] (P)	Weight (w)	Product (wP)
Quizzes	87	63%	2	126
Homework	55	70%	1	70
Term paper	48	40%	2	80
Exam	96	95%	5	475
			10	751

$$C = \frac{\Sigma wP}{\Sigma w} = \frac{751}{10} = 75.1\%$$

This procedure should not be used with group-referenced grading because the weights assigned here do not reflect the standard deviations of the components.

[8]Divide each raw score by the maximum number of points for that component. For example, if the Exam had 101 points, $P = 96 \div 101 = 95\%$. I have not shown the maximum number of points for each component.

Summary

The main points of this chapter follow.
   1. Marks and grades are difficult for many teachers to assign because (a) educational achievement is difficult to measure, (b) marking systems are frequently objects of controversies, and (c) grading may require difficult or unpleasant decisions about pupils.
   2. The ways teachers and schools assign grades communicate their values and attitudes as well as pupil progress information.
   3. Teachers assess and evaluate pupil progress before, during, and after each lesson. Grades are symbols for periodically reporting some of these evaluations to parents and pupils. Many methods of reporting seem necessary.

4. Measurement specialists are divided on the issue of whether traditional grades are effective motivators of academic performance. One analysis indicates that traditional grades (a) can serve as goals for some students, (b) reduce motivation when they are perceived by a student as being out of reach, (c) seldom provide continuous information the student can use to judge progress, and (d) provide little information the pupil can use to improve learning. If conditions (b), (c), and (d) exist, then grades are less likely to be effective motivators of pupil learning.

5. Grades have been criticized on many different grounds. These are summarized in Table 13.2.

6. Among the methods of reporting pupil progress in the United States the most popular are letter grades, numbers or percentages, two-category systems, checklists and rating scales, pupil-teacher conferences, parent-teacher conferences, and letters to parents.

7. Schools often use more than one method of reporting pupil progress, and different methods are used at different educational levels. The results of one survey of schools are summarized in Figure 13.1. The strengths and weaknesses of each method are summarized in Table 13.3.

8. Suggestions for conducting parent-teacher conferences are summarized in Table 13.4.

9. Multiple-marking systems are needed when a school reports several kinds of symbols and marks pupils on several kinds of objectives. Suggestions for developing multiple-marking systems are given in Table 13.5.

10. It is unlikely that one best system for reporting pupil progress exists. Schools might consider the total informational needs of different students and parents and design multiple reporting systems tailored to community circumstances. The availability of microcomputers in schools may make this a practical approach to solving several pupil progress reporting problems.

11. Letter grades are assigned within certain referencing frameworks: group-referencing, self-referencing, and task-referencing (absolute standards).

a. A *group-referenced* approach assigns grades to pupils on the basis of how well their performances compare with one another.

b. A *self-referenced* approach assigns grades on the basis of the teacher's perception of the pupil's capability.

c. A *task-referenced* approach assigns grades on the basis of a comparison of a pupil's performance with a defined set of tasks to do, behaviors to learn, or knowledge to acquire. This approach can be considered criterion-referenced only if the teacher uses a well-defined domain of tasks and draws representative samples from the domain on which to observe and test pupils. Most teachers do not do this.

PART THREE

BASIC PRINCIPLES OF INTERPRETATION

Themes

● All test scores require external referencing to be interpreted. Two such schemes of referencing are norm-referencing and criterion-referencing.

● Norm-referencing provides a way to interpret the relative test performance of a pupil and how the pupil compares with others in a defined group.

● A pupil is a member of several groups, and often the pupil's relative standing in more than one group needs to be known to interpret performance on a test.

● Norm-referenced interpretation of tests is often facilitated by using several different types of scores, each derived from the raw or number right score on a test. Understanding the concepts represented by each type of norm-referenced score is necessary to use such a score to interpret a pupil's test performance properly.

Terms and Concepts

norm-referencing vs. criterion-referencing

norm-groups (local, national, special)

modal-age norms

school averages norms

empirical norming dates

relevance, representativeness, and recency of norm data

percentile ranks

linear standard scores (z, SS, CEEB)

normal distributions

areas under the normal curve

normalized standard scores (z_n, T, DIQ, NCE)

"normalizing" a set of scores

stanine scores

extended normalized standard score scales

grade-equivalent scores

interpolation vs. extrapolation

"normal" growth

14

NORM-REFERENCED INTERPRETATIONS

This chapter describes various ways to interpret a pupil's score by referencing it to the performance of other pupils. The first section explains why referencing is necessary and the difference between norm-referencing and criterion-referencing. The next section describes the various kinds of norm-groups to which scores can be referenced and suggests criteria for evaluating the adequacy of norm data provided by test publishers. The third section describes many of the important norm-referenced scores used to interpret test performance including: percentile ranks, linear standard scores, stanines, normalized standard scores, expanded scale standard scores, and grade-equivalents. The chapter closes with a case study and guidelines for interpreting scores on a norm-referenced test battery.

The Need for Referencing[1]

Suppose that just before you began reading this chapter, I administered a spelling test to you. Your *raw score* on the test—found by counting up the number of right answers or points credited—for example, one point for each word spelled correctly—was 45. How well would you have performed? Knowing only that the test was "a spelling test" and that your raw score was "45" you will be unable to interpret your performance.

Two Referencing Schemes

Practically all educational and psychological tests require using some type of referencing scheme to interpret an examinee's performance on them. A referencing scheme is a way to compare an examinee's performance to something external to the test itself. Usually, interpretation of an examinee's test results is enhanced when this external information is brought to bear on the test score. Often the referencing is done by developing a different type of score derived from the raw score.

Norm-referencing   After a great many proposals and trials during the late nineteenth

[1]This section is adapted from Nitko (1980, pp. 35–37).

and early twentieth centuries, a more or less standard set of derived scores are now rather routinely reported for most published tests in education:

1. *Percentile Rank*—a number telling the percentage of persons in a defined group scoring lower than the particular raw score,
2. *Linear Standard Score*—a number telling the location of the particular raw score in relation to the mean and standard deviation of a defined group,
3. *Normalized Standard Score*—a number telling the location of the particular raw score in relation to a normal distribution defined in terms of a particular group,
4. *Grade-Equivalent Score*—a number telling the grade placement for which the particular raw score is the average for a defined group.

The derived scores mentioned above tell an examinee's location in a defined group of other examinees and are called *norm-referenced scores*. The defined group itself is called the *norm group*, and tests built to make these kinds of derived scores especially useful are called *norm-referenced tests*. I consider the advantages and limitations of a variety of norm-referenced scores in subsequent sections of this chapter.

To make a norm-referenced interpretation, return to your spelling test score. Suppose your raw score of 45 meant that your percentile rank was 99—ninety-nine percent of the persons to whom I have administered my spelling test have scored lower than 45. Before you congratulate yourself, you should determine who the persons are to whom your score has been referenced. The interpretation would be different if the norm-group were comprised of third graders than if the norm-group were comprised of adults. Norm-referencing of test scores is meaningless if the norm-group is not well-defined. The better the norm-group is defined, the better able you are to interpret a norm-referenced score. Consider the difference in interpretation, for example, between a group of "adults in general" and "adults who have won prizes in national spelling contests."

Norm-referencing is not enough   But norm-referencing is not enough to fully interpret your score. You may be a better speller than other people—whoever they happen to be— but what can you spell? At a minimum you would need to know the nature of the pool of words from which those appearing on the spelling test were selected, the number of words selected, and the selection process. Were they really "words" or were they "nonsense" syllables? Were they English words? Were they selected from a list of the most difficult (or easiest) English words? Were there 45 words or 500 words on the test? Were the words on the test representative of some larger class or domain? Did spelling the words require certain mental processes or certain applications of rules or procedures?

These latter questions become especially important when absolute interpretations of test performance are required—for example, when instructional decisions about learners need to be made. Norm-referencing provides information helpful for relative interpretations of scores, but frequently these are not sufficient. Relative achievement scores such as ranks, for example, may be helpful in picking the best readers, or in sectioning a class into "better,"

"good," and "poor" readers, but to plan an appropriate instructional experience eventually we would need to know the kinds of reading performances an individual could do, and the particular types of difficulties an individual was experiencing. When diagnosis and prescription are based on pupils' error patterns or on an analysis of their faulty cognitive processes, norm-referenced scores are seldom helpful.

Criterion-referencing   The derived scores in norm-referencing schemes convey an examinee's relative standing in a defined group of other examinees, but other schemes, called *criterion-referencing* schemes, are possible for some tests. These schemes use derived scores or other procedures which reflect an examinee's behavior repertoire—the kinds of things an examinee can do—rather than the examinee's relative standing in a group. Criterion-referencing schemes are described in detail in Chapter 17. It is possible to report both criterion-referenced and norm-referenced scores from certain tests and many publishers of criterion-referenced tests do so. This dual referencing is illustrated in Figure 1.5.

Various Types of Norm-Groups

The performance of a norm-group on a particular test represents the present, average status of that group of persons on that particular test. A group's current test performance does not represent a standard, nor does it establish a desirable goal for schools or pupils to attain. Comparisons of pupils and schools to norm-groups can be helpful, however, in deciding the general range of performance to expect from the present group provided the present group is similar to the norm-group. As you can see below, test publishers may provide information on a variety of groups when norm-referencing test scores.

Norm-Groups to which Pupils Can Be Compared

Multiple norm-group comparisons Ordinarily, a person is a member of more than one group. For example, a fourteen year old, hearing handicapped, eighth grade male took a standardized mathematics concepts test and obtained a raw score of 32. This may represent a percentile rank of:

99 in a national group of deaf 8th graders
96 in the test publishers national 8th grade standardization sample
90 in the group of 8th graders in his local community
80 in the group of 8th graders currently enrolled with him in an advanced mathematics course.

Depending on the decisions an educator must make, referencing a student's score to several norm-groups may be in order. Vocational counseling decisions, for example, may require that a counselee's profile of different abilities and achievements be compared to each of several occupational or vocational groups about which the counselee is seeking career information. Comparing the person only to "students in general" may offer less information for career exploration.

Local norms For many educational test interpretations the most appropriate group with which to compare a pupil is the group of students in the same grade in the same school district: It is this group with which the pupil and teacher will interact the most. Local percentile ranks or standard scores are easy to compile for a school's testing program. Test publishers offer this service for their customers, frequently at extra cost.

National norms Most norm-referenced, standardized achievement and aptitude batteries have what are called national norms. In principle, the national norm-groups are supposed to be representative of the country in some way, and some publishers spend a great deal of money on this effort. But each publisher will use a somewhat different definition of what constitutes a truly representative national sample and will conduct the sampling processes somewhat differently. The result is that the norms from different publishers are not comparable. It should be noted that no publisher's norming sample is truly representative of the nation's schools. A school's participation in a publisher's norming sample is voluntary. This creates a self-selection bias in a given publisher's norms which may distort the norms in favor of those schools which have used that publisher's tests in the past (Baglin, 1981). A more detailed description of how publishers obtain norming samples is given in Chapter 18.

National norms need not be composed simply of "students in general at a grade level." A developer may provide separate male/female norms or may provide separate norms for minorities. Frequently, *modal-age norms* are provided: From among all pupils at a particular grade level, only those near the most typical chronological age of that grade are included.

Special norm-groups For some tests special norm-groups are formed. Examples include the deaf or blind, the mentally handicapped, those enrolled in a certain course of study or curriculum, special occupational groups, regional schools, large city schools, parochial schools, private schools, and applicants to a certain type of school or college. A student may be a member of more than one special group.

School averages norms If a school principal wants to know how that school's third grade average test score compares with that of other schools, then the principal needs school averages norms. So far, only individual pupil norms have been discussed: For individual pupil norms, a distribution of individual pupil's scores is made and used as the basis for norm-referencing. But individual pupils vary widely in their scores—so much so that comparing a *school's average* to that group may lead to misinterpretations. School averages norms consist of a tabulation of the average (mean) score from each school building in a national sample of schools and provide information on the relative ordering of these averages (means). This distribution of averages is much *less variable* than the distribution of individual pupil scores.

To get some idea of what a system may gain from school averages norms, suppose that in School A the average 5th grade score on the *Iowa Test of Basic Skills* (Language subtest) is 65. A teacher who erroneously looks up this number in the individual pupil norms concludes that the school ranks higher than eighty percent ($PR = 80$ for individuals) (Hieronymus & Lindquist, 1974a, p. 91). Actually, the school is much better, ranking at the top two percent ($PR = 98$ *for school averages*) (Hieronymus & Lindquist, 1974b, p.61). In general, if individual norms are used erroneously, above average schools will underestimate their standing among other schools, while below average schools will overestimate their standing in the norms for school averages.

Using a Publisher's Norms

Empirical norming dates   The most accurate estimate of a pupil's standing in a norm-group is obtained when a pupil is tested on a date nearest the time of year the publisher establishes the norms; otherwise, the obtained norm-referenced score will be less accurate. Publishers commonly interpolate and extrapolate to develop norm tables and may provide spring norm tables, for example, even though no tests were actually administered to the norm group in the spring. Each publisher's empirical norming date(s) is different, but the date(s) should be mentioned in the test manual or technical report.[2] In order to be most accurate, tests should be administered within two or three weeks to either side of the midpoint date of their empirical norming period.

Criteria for evaluating norms data   It is generally accepted (APA, 1974) that published norms data should satisfy three R's: relevance, representativeness, and recency. First, the norm-group(s) the publisher provides should be relevant; they should be the group(s) to which you will want to compare the examinee. Second, the test manual should tell you clearly that the norm data was based on a carefully planned sample and should provide you with information about the subclassifications (e.g., sex, age, socioeconomic level, etc.) used to assure that the sample was "re-presentative" of the relevant population (see Chapter 18). Remember, the size of the sample is not crucial, but the representativeness is. (Of course, for some populations, a representative sample will have to be relatively large.) Third, the norms must be based on recent data. As the knowledge base, the schooling, the workplace, and other social and economic factors change, so will the performance of persons on tests. If the norms are not recent, they will be misleading.

Overview of Types of Norm-Referenced Scores

As I mentioned previously, norm-referenced scores are derived from the raw scores of a test. You should be aware that many norm-referenced scores exist, some of which Howard B. Lyman names in Figure 14.1. Space permits me to discuss only the ones you will most

---

[2]Telephone the publisher's service representative to obtain this information if it is not in the printed materials accompanying the test.

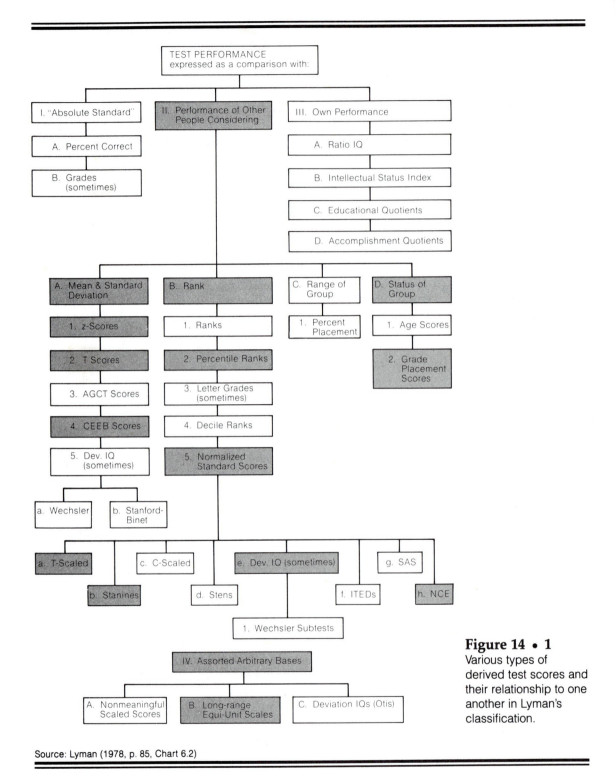

Figure 14 • 1
Various types of derived test scores and their relationship to one another in Lyman's classification.

Source: Lyman (1978, p. 85, Chart 6.2)

often encounter, represented by the shaded boxes in Figure 14.1. If you are interested in pursuing the study of norm-referenced scores in greater detail, you should consult a very readable book by Lyman (1978) titled *Test Scores and What They Mean.*

Norms tables   Test manuals contain tables—called *norms tables*—for connecting raw scores to a variety of norm-referenced scores. No computation is required; you need "only" look up the score. I put "only" in quotes because, as trivial a task as it may seem, looking up scores in a table and copying them on a student's record is something people seem to have a hard time doing correctly. Studies of the kinds of errors found in Title I evaluations indicate that using the wrong norms table, and misreading a table are common problems (Crane and Bellis, 1978; Finley, 1977; Johnson and Thomas, 1979; Moyer, 1979). Specimen tables (14.1, 14.4, 14.6) are shown with the scores discussed in this chapter so that you can practice using them.

Notice there are two sets of percentile ranks in Table 14.1—one for the middle of the grade and one for the end. This is common practice for norm-referenced achievement tests. You should use the set that corresponds to the time of year during which the pupil takes the test. In our example, a score of 49 in the middle of the year corresponds to a percentile rank of 92 instead of 78. The lower percentile rank for the same score in the end-of-year norms table reflects the fact that pupils learn rather quickly during the early grades.

As with all scores, percentile ranks should not be interpreted too precisely, since pupils with percentile rank 44 and pupils with percentile rank 46 differ little. Some publishers, to reflect the fact that all scores contain measurement error, report "percentile bands" or uncertainty intervals instead of a single percentile rank. These "percentile bands" are based on the test's standard error of measurement (see Chapter 15). The advantages and disadvantages of percentile ranks are summarized in Table 14.2.

Percentile Ranks

Perhaps the most useful and easiest to understand norm-referenced score is the percentile rank. *The percentile rank tells the percentage of the persons in a defined group that have scored lower than the raw score in question.* Percentile ranks are introduced and discussed in Chapter 3. Appendix A shows how to compute them.

Table 14.1 is an example of a percentile rank norms table. The raw score obtained from the test is located in the correct column in the body of the table; in the marginal columns the corresponding percentile rank is read out. For example, suppose a first grader, Veronica, takes this test on May 23rd and scores 49 in Total Mathematics. Her percentile rank from Table 14.1 is 78. She is above average in the norm group in first grade mathematics; her raw scores exceeds 78% of the standardization group.

Linear Standard Scores

Linear standard scores tell how far a raw score is from the mean of the norm-group, the distance being expressed in terms of standard deviation units. Linear standard scores are not as easily understood as percentile ranks because the educator needs to understand the concept of the standard deviation. In general, linear standard scores (a) have the same shaped distribution as the raw scores from which they are derived (this is not true of percentile ranks and nonlinear standard scores) and (b) can be used to make two distributions more comparable by placing them on the same numerical scale. Linear standard scores are called "linear" because if you make a graph plotting each raw score against its corresponding linear standard score and then connect these points, you will always have a straight line.

Middle of Grade 1

TOTAL NUMBER RIGHT

%ile Rank	Complete Battery*	Total Auditory	Total Reading	Total Mathematics	%ile Rank
99	243-274	59-63	141-147	56-64	99
98	233-242	55-58	134-140	54-55	98
96	221-232	53-54	127-133	52-53	96
94	211-220	52	118-126	50-51	94
92	205-210	51	113-117	49	92
90	201-204	50	111-112	48	90
89	198-200	49	109-110	47	89
88	195-197	48	107-108	46	88
86	192-194	47	103-106	45	86
84	187-191	46	101-102	44	84
82	184-186		98-100	43	82
80	181-183	45	97	42	80
78	179-180	44	96	41	78
77	177-178		95		77
76	175-176		93-94	40	76
74	171-174	43	92		74
72	169-170		91	39	72
70	167-168	42	89-90		70
68	164-166	41	88	38	68
66	162-163		86-87	37	66
64	160-161	40	84-85	36	64
62	158-159	39	83		62
16	—107	25	55		16
14	101-103	24	53-54	20	14
12	99-100		51-52	19	12
11	96-98	23	50		11
10	93-95		48-49	18	10
8	89-92	22	46-47	17	8
6	84-88	21	42-45	16	6
4	79-83	19-20	38-41	15	4
2	72-78	17-18	32-37	13-14	2
1	63-71	16	29-31	12	1

*Does not include Spelling.

End of Grade 1

TOTAL NUMBER RIGHT

%ile Rank	Complete Battery*	Total Auditory	Total Reading	Total Mathematics	%ile Rank
99	257-274	60-63	145-147	59-64	99
98	252-256	58-59	144	58	98
96	248-251	56-57	142-143	56-57	96
94	245-247	55	141	55	94
92	243-244	54	140	54	92
90	240-242		138-139		90
89	238-239	53	137	53	89
88	236-237		136		88
86	233-235	52	135	52	86
84	230-232		134	51	84
82	229	51	132-133		82
80	225-228	50	130-131	50	80
78	224		129	49	78
77	222-223		128		77
76	220-221	49	127		76
74	219		125-126	48	74
72	215-218	48	123-124	47	72
70	213-214		121-122		70
68	211-212	47	119-120	46	68
66	208-210		117-118	45	66
64	206-207	46	115-116		64
62	203-205	45	113-114	44	62
16	134-13?	28	65-67	26-27	16
14	130-133	27	63-64	25	14
12	124-129	26	61-62	24	12
11	122-123	25	60	23	11
10	117-121	24	58-59	22	10
8	111-116	23	54-57	21	8
6	106-110	21-22	50-53	20	6
4	94-105	19-20	45-49	18-19	4
2	80-93	16-18	35-44	15-17	2
1	53-79	14-15	30-34	13-14	1

*Does not include Spelling.

Table 14 • 1 Percentile norms table for converting raw scores to percentile ranks for the *Stanford Achievement Test*, Primary Level I Battery, Form A.

Examples of Types of Linear Standard Scores

z-scores The fundamental linear standard score is the z-score introduced in Chapter 3; other linear standard scores are computed from z-scores. Equation 3.7 shows what it is:

$$z = \frac{X - M}{SD}$$

where

X represents the raw score,

M represents the mean raw score of the group, and

SD represents the standard deviation of the raw scores for that group.

The z-score tells the number of standard deviations a raw score is above or below the mean. A z-score is negative when the raw score

Advantages	Limitations
1. Easily understood by pupils, parents, teachers, and others 2. Clearly reflect the norm-referenced character of the interpretation 3. Permit a person's performance to be compared to a variety of norm-groups 4. Can be used to compare a pupil's relative standing in each of several achievement or ability areas	1. Can be confused with percentage correct scores 2. Can be confused with some other type of two-digit derived scores 3. Differences between PR's in the middle of the scale tend to be overinterpreted; differences of the same magnitude near the tails of a distribution tend to be underinterpreted

Table 14 • 2   Summary of advantages and limitations of percentile ranks.

is below the mean; positive when the raw score is above the mean; and equal to zero when the raw score is exactly equal to the mean. Examples of computing and interpreting z-scores are given in Chapter 3, which also discusses the advantages and disadvantages of z-scores.

SS-scores   To remedy some of the disadvantages of z-scores some publishers apply a modification (transformation) designed to eliminate both the negative scores and the fractional portion of the scores. I shall refer to these as SS-scores. The SS-score is defined as:

$$SS = 10z + 50$$
$$= (10 \text{ times the } z\text{-score}) + 50 \quad \text{[Eq. 14.1]}$$

First z-scores are computed; then, each z-score is transformed to an SS-score: The z is multiplied by 10, and the product rounded to the nearest whole number, and finally 50 is added. Multiplying by 10 and rounding eliminates the decimal. Adding 50 eliminates the negative values.

As an example, suppose Tammy's z-score was computed to be 1.37. To convert this to an SS-score, multiply it by 10 and add 50 to the result. Thus,

$$SS = 10(-1.37) + 50$$
$$= -13.7 + 50 = -14 + 50$$
$$= 36$$

The result of applying this conversion to the z-scores is that the distribution of SS-scores will have a mean of 50 and a standard deviation of 10. Once you know this fact, you can interpret anyone's SS-score, essentially by doing a mental conversion back to a z-score. For example, Tammy's SS-score was 36; a score of 36 is 1.4 standard deviations below the mean. Thus, Tammy's z-score is −1.4.

SS-scores have the advantages of (a) not changing the shape of the original raw score distribution, (b) always having a mean of 50 and a standard deviation of 10, and (c) being interpretable in terms of standard deviation units, while avoiding negative numbers and decimal fractions. A disadvantage is that an understanding of the concepts of standard deviation and linear transformation are needed to interpret them.

CEEB scores   A frequently encountered type of linear standard score is the one employed by the College Entrance Examination Board (CEEB) on such tests as the Scholastic Aptitude Test (SAT). The SAT's report scores on a scale ranging from 200 through 800. The SAT-verbal scale is based on a group of 10,654 candidates tested in April of 1941 for whom the mean was set at 500 and the standard deviation set at 100; the SAT-mathematical scale began a year later (Donlan and Angoff, 1971). The formula for this is:

$$CEEB = 100z + 500. \quad \text{[Eq. 14.2]}$$

You can see that this is a linear standard score. A score of 450, for example, is interpreted as being one-half of a standard deviation below the mean of this 1941 applicant group.

Tests given after 1941 were statistically equated to this group's performance, thus placing all subsequent scores on the same scale. The purpose of scaling and equating to an anchor group is ". . . to ensure that the score system would have the same meaning from year-to-year—that is, any given scaled score would represent the same level of ability regardless of the difficulty characteristics of the form of the test on which it was earned, the nature of the group taking the test, or the time of the year when the test was administered" (Donlon & Angoff, 1971, p. 32). Percentile ranks corresponding to each current year's scores are provided to test users to facilitate interpretations for the current year.

Comparison of linear standard scores It may be helpful to display the relationship between the linear standard scores discussed above. Since all linear standard score systems reflect essentially the same information, interpreting the meaning of any linear standard score will be easy for you once you know the multiplier and the added constant. The examples below show how each type of score is related to the other and to the raw scores.

Raw score in a group[3] with M = 41 and SD = 3	Corresponding linear standard score on:		
	z-score scale	SS-score scale	1941 CEEB scale
32	−3.00	20	200
35	−2.00	30	300
38	−1.00	40	400
41	0.00	50	500
44	+1.00	60	600
47	+2.00	70	700
50	+3.00	80	800

[3]The values of M and SD have been set arbitrarily.

Normal Distributions

Test developers have found it advantageous to transform the scores to a common distributional form: *a normal distribution.* A normal distribution, sometimes called a *normal curve,* is a mathematical model, invented in 1733 by Abraham deMoivre (1667–1754) (Pearson, 1924). It is defined by a particular equation that depends on two specific numbers: the mean and the standard deviation,[4] signifying that many normal distributions exist and each has a different mean and/or standard deviation. Figure 14.2 shows several different normal curves. Each of these was obtained by using the normal equation and plotting points on a graph. In Figure 14.2(A) each normal distribution has the same mean but a different standard deviation. Although each is centered on the same point on the X-scale, some appear to the eye to be flatter and more spread out because their standard deviation is larger. Figure 14.2(B) shows three normal curves, each with the same standard deviation but each with a different mean. The degree of spread is the same for each, but each is centered on a different point on the score scale.

Every normal curve is smooth and continuous; each has a symmetrical, bell-shaped form. In theory, a normal curve never touches the base line (horizontal axis) but is asymptotic to it, extending out to infinity in either direction from the mean. Graphs of actual raw score distributions are nonsymmetrical and jagged; the lowest possible score is 0, and the highest possible score would be equal to the total number of items on the test. An idea of how an actual distribution compares to the mathematically defined normal curve may be obtained from Figure 14.3. Both distributions

[4]One version of this equation is:

$$\text{height of graph} = \frac{1}{\sigma\sqrt{2\pi}}\, e^{-\frac{(X - M)^2}{2\sigma^2}}$$

where $\pi = 3.1416\ldots$, $e = 2.7183\ldots$, M = the mean, and σ = the standard deviation.

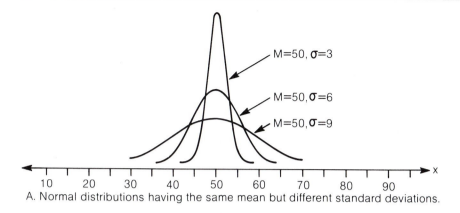

A. Normal distributions having the same mean but different standard deviations.

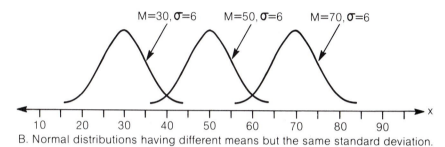

B. Normal distributions having different means but the same standard deviation.

Figure 14 • 2
Illustrations of different
normal distributions.

Source: Lindvall and Nitko (1975, p. 87, Figure 5.3)

have the same mean and the same standard deviation. This normal curve approximates the actual distribution but does not match it exactly.

Early users of normal curves believed that somehow there were natural laws in which nearly all human characteristics were distributed in a random or chance fashion around a mean or average value. This view of the applicability of the normal curve was, perhaps, begun by deMoivre (1756), but it was adamantly held to be true for intellectual and moral qualities by Quetelet (1848) (Dudycha & Dudycha, 1972; Landau & Lazarsfeld, 1968).

The thought that somehow abilities are naturally distributed normally has carried over to mental measurement. It is frequently held, too, that because test scores have a bell-shaped distribution, this indicates that the abilities *underlying* the scores are normally distributed. This converse statement is, of course, not true. The test's score distribution depends, not only on the characteristics of the persons tested, but also on the characteristics of the test items administered. In principle, a test developer can, by judicious selection of items, make the test have any shape: rectangular, skewed, bimodal, symmetrical, and so on (Lord, 1953). This would be true, for example, even though the actual ability of the group is normal in form. From your own experience you know that if all of the items on a test are easy, there will be a lot of high scores and few low scores—that is, the distribution will be negatively skewed (see Chapter 3). A very difficult test would be positively skewed.

If we cut up a normal distribution into sections, each section one standard deviation wide, then no matter to which normal distri-

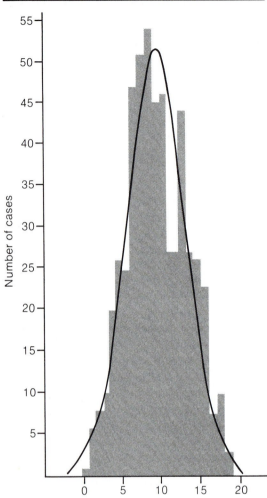

Source: Lindvall and Nitko (1975, p. 88, Figure 5.4). Histogram based on data obtained from Lohnes and Cooley (1968, pp. 248–252).

Figure 14 • 3 Illustration of the actual distribution (histogram) of creativity test raw scores for 505 twelfth-grade students and a normal curve (smooth curve) that has the same mean and standard deviation.

bution we refer, each section will have a fixed percentage of cases. This is shown in the figure on the inside of the back cover (Figure BC.1). For example, a section that is one standard deviation wide and located just above the mean, contains approximately 34% of the

cases. The comparable section just below the mean contains, by symmetry, 34% as well. Together those two sections contain 68% of the cases. About two-thirds of the cases in a normal distribution will be within one standard deviation of the mean; 95% are within two standard deviations; and 99.7% of the cases are within three standard deviations. Thus, if a distribution is normal, nearly all of the scores will span a range equivalent to a distance of six standard deviations.

These facts about the percentage of cases in various segments can be used to determine the correspondence between percentile ranks and z-scores in a normal distribution. It is this correspondence, the same for all normal distributions, which permits an easy interpretation of standard scores in normal distributions. Look at Figure BC.1. The percentage of cases below $z = -2.00$ is 2.27% ($= 0.13 + 2.14$). Thus, in a normal distribution the percentile rank corresponding to $z = -2.00$ is (rounded) 2. Other z-scores' percentile ranks can be computed similarly from Figure BC.1 as is shown below:

z	PR (rounded)	How computed
−3.0	0.1	= 0.13
−2.0	2	= 0.13 + 2.14
−1.0	16	= 0.13 + 2.14 + 13.59
0.0	50	= 0.13 + 2.14 + 13.59 + 34.13
+1.0	84	= 50 + 34.13
+2.0	98	= 50 + 34.13 + 13.59
+3.0	99.9	= 50 + 34.13 + 13.59 + 2.14

The table on the back cover (Table BC.1) provides a more complete table of z-score-to-normal curve percentile rank correspondences.

Normalized Standard Scores

Scores can be transformed in such a way that, after the transformation, they are distributed normally (or nearly so). Such a transformation changes the shape of the original distribution, squeezing and stretching the scale to make it conform to a normal distribution. Once this is accomplished, various types of standard scores can be derived, and each can have an appropriate normal curve interpretation. The derived scores obtained by such a transformation are called *normalized standard scores*. These are also termed *area transformations* as opposed to linear transformation. We will review a few of the common varieties.

Normalized z-scores (z_n)   When the z-scores have percentile ranks corresponding to what we would expect in a normal distribution, they are called normalized z-scores and the following symbol will be used:

z_n = the z-score corresponding to a given percentile rank in a normal distribution

If a distribution is *not normal* in form, the percentile ranks of its z-scores will not correspond to what would be expected in a norm distribution. One can, however, derive a set of "normalized" z-scores for any non-normal distribution, such that this new set of scores is more nearly like a normal distribution. This is done in the following way: (1) Determine the percentile rank of each score in the norm group, and (2) look up each percentile rank in a normal curve table (e.g., Table BC.1) and read out the z_n-value that corresponds to each. The resulting z_n-values are "normalized." That is, they are the z-scores that *would have been attained if the distribution had been* normal in form. Table 14.3 illustrates how each percentile rank was looked up in Table BC.1, and the corresponding normalized z-score was read out and recorded in Table 14.3. For the sake of comparison, the actual, linear z-scores were computed via Equation 3.7 using $M = 26.75$ and $SD = 3.8$. The difference between the normalized and linear z-scores represents the "stretching and squeezing" necessary to make the original distribution correspond more nearly to a normal distribution.

Raw score	%ile rank	Normalized[a] z-score (z_n)	Linear[b] z-score (z)
36	98	2.05	2.43
33	96	1.75	1.65
32	94	1.55	1.38
31	90	1.28	1.12
30	88	1.18	0.86
29	84	0.99	0.59
28	72	0.58	0.33
27	54	0.10	0.07
26	32	−0.47	−0.20
25	16	−0.99	−0.46
24	10	−1.28	−0.72
22	8	−1.41	−0.99
21	6	−1.55	−1.51
15	4	−1.75	−3.09
14	2	−2.05	−3.36

[a] z_n-values obtained by looking up the percentile ranks in Table BC.1.

[b] z-values based on the actual distribution: $z = \dfrac{X - M}{SD}$, where $M = 26.75$ and $SD = 3.80$.

Table 14 • 3   Illustration of normalized z-scores and (actual) linear z-scores for the distribution of test scores in Table A.1 (Appendix A).

Normalized T-scores (McCall's T)[5]   The normalized T-score is the counterpart to the linear SS-score. Thus,

$$T = 10z_n + 50 \qquad [\text{Eq. 14.3}]$$

The difference between this equation and Equation 14.1 (i.e., $SS = 10z + 50$) is that z_n is a normalized z-score instead of a linear z-score.

Normalized T-scores have the same advantages over normalized z-scores as SS-scores have over linear z-scores, with the additional advantage that T-scores have the percentile rank interpretations of a normal curve. For example, if Joey's T-score is 40, he is one standard deviation below the mean of the norm-group, *and* his percentile rank is approximately 16. If Betty's percentile rank is

[5]Invented by William A. McCall (1922). McCall named it "T" after Terman and Thorndike.

84, her T-score is 60 *and*, she is a distance of one standard deviation above the norm-group mean.

Table BC.1 shows the correspondence between percentile ranks, T-scores, and z_n-scores in a normal distribution. That table can help you convert percentile ranks directly to T-scores without using Equation 14.3.

Deviation IQ scores *(DIQ)* One type of normalized standard score is the deviation IQ score used with certain tests of mental ability. The norm-group is usually made up of all those pupils with the same chronological age regardless of grade placement. The test developer sets the mean at 100 and the standard deviation at 15 or 16. For example, if the standard deviation is set at 16, *DIQ*s are given by

$$DIQ = 16z_n + 100. \quad \text{[Eq. 14.4]}$$

These *DIQ*s are interpreted in a way similar to T-scores. If Megan has *DIQ* = 116, this means she has scored one standard deviation above the mean of her age group and has a percentile rank of 84. Usually, tables are provided in test manuals that permit the direct conversion of test scores to *DIQ*s.

Normal curve equivalents *(NCE)* This is a normalized standard score developed primarily for use with federal Title I evaluation efforts (Tallmadge & Wood, 1976). Although some publishers present norm tables for *NCE*s in their test manuals, these scores are not recommended for use in reporting individual pupil scores because they are too easily confused with percentile ranks. *NCE*-values are found by the following formula. Their highest possible value is 99 and their lowest possible value is 1.

$$NCE = 21.06z_n + 50 \quad \text{[Eq. 14.5]}$$

Stanines A potentially more useful normalized standard score is the stanine. Figure 14.4 illustrates the meaning of a stanine score. A normal distribution is divided into 9 segments numbered from a low of 1 through a high of 9. Scores falling within the boundaries of these segments are assigned one of these nine numbers (hence, the term "stanine" from *standard nine*). Each segment is one-half a standard deviation wide, except for stanines 1 and 9. The percentage of the cases in a normal curve falling within each segment is shown in the figure, along with the range of percentile ranks associated with each.

All persons with scores falling within an interval are assigned the stanine of that interval. For example, all persons with scores having percentile ranks from 11 through 22 are assigned a stanine of 3; all from 23 through 29 a stanine of 4; and so on. Twelve percent of the persons in the norm-group would be assigned a stanine of 3 and seventeen percent a stanine of 4.

Test publishers frequently recommend stanines for norm-referenced interpretation of achievement and aptitude tests. Among the advantages claimed for them are that stanines (a) are single digit numbers only, (b) have approximately equal units all along the score scale, and (c) do not imply an exactness greater than that warranted by the test. In normal distributions, stanines have a mean of 5 and a standard deviation equal to 2. Not all test experts agree that using stanines for norm-referenced tests is appropriate. Some hold that stanines present more difficult interpretative problems than percentile ranks, especially for reliable tests, because they reflect rather coarse groupings of scores (Lindquist and Hieronymus, 1964).

Qualitative, verbal interpretations are often recommended for use with stanines. Below are two examples.

Comprehensive Tests of Basic Skills:[6]

9—Highest level (top 4%)
8—High level (Next 7% lower)

[6]CTB/McGraw Hill (1974, p. 36).

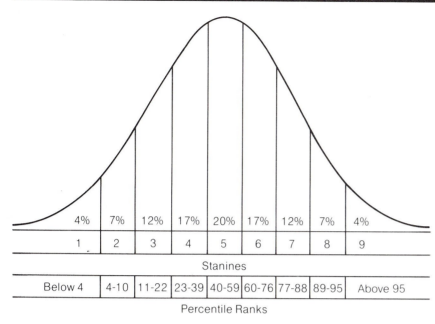

	4%	7%	12%	17%	20%	17%	12%	7%	4%	
	1	2	3	4	5	6	7	8	9	

Stanines

Below 4	4-10	11-22	23-39	40-59	60-76	77-88	89-95	Above 95

Percentile Ranks

Figure 14 • 4
Illustration of a normal distribution showing stanines, percentile rank intervals, and percentage of cases in each stanine.

Source: Adapted from Prescott, Balow, Hogan, and Farr (1978, p. 44, Figure 4).

7—Well above average (next 12% lower)
6—Slightly above average (next 17% lower)
5—Average (middle 20%)
4—Slightly below average (next 17% lower)
3—Well below average (next 12% lower)
2—Low level (next 7% lower)
1—Lowest level (bottom 4%)

Metropolitan Achievement Tests:[7]

1. *Stanines 7, 8, and 9—Above Average.* Pupils whose scores fall consistently within these levels should be given enriched instructional experience.
2. *Stanines 4, 5, and 6—Average.* Pupils scoring consistently in this category can benefit from instruction appropriate to their grade.
3. *Stanines 1, 2, and 3—Below Average.* By and large, these are pupils for whom a specialized curriculum is desirable.

[7]Prescott, Balow, Hogan, and Farr (1978, p. 45).

Strictly speaking, these verbal interpretations apply only when scores are normally distributed. If a test is very easy or very hard, the resulting distribution is likely to be highly skewed. Some tests, for example, are intended to be "diagnostic" in the sense that they identify only the poorest students in an area of a curriculum. Intentionally, the test wouldn't distinguish among the able and very able students. Figure 14.5 shows an example of such a norms table for a diagnostic reading test along with a histogram of the frequency distribution. Notice that a perfect score of 40 has a stanine of 8; a student missing one item obtains a stanine of 7; and so on. The skewed nature of the distribution permits students at the lower end to be identified and given remediation. The verbal labels presented above for stanines of 7, 8, and 9 do not characterize the performance of high scoring students very well on such tests. With a very hard test, scores will be skewed positively; then, stanines of 1, 2, and 3 may have to be interpreted cautiously.

TEST 3 Phonetic Analysis		
Raw Score	%-ile Rank	Stanine
40	93	8
39	84	7
38	74	6
37	66	
36	59	5
35	54	
34	49	
33	45	
32	41	
31	38	4
30	36	
29	34	
28	32	
27	30	
26	28	
25	26	
24	24	
23	21	3
22	19	
21	17	
20	16	
19	14	
18	12	
17	11	
16	9	2
15	7	
14	6	
13	5	
12	3	1
11	3	
10	2	
9	1	
8	1	
7	1	
Below 7	1	

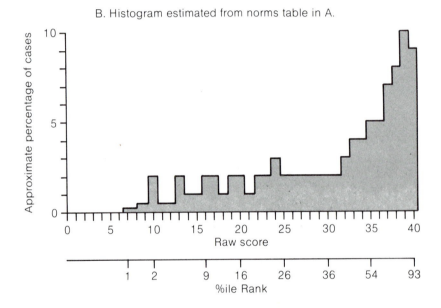

B. Histogram estimated from norms table in A.

Figure 14 • 5   Percentile ranks and stanines for second graders corresponding to raw scores on the Phonetic Analysis subtest of the *Stanford Diagnostic Reading Test,* Red Level, Form A, 1976. Skewed distributions may not yield all stanine scores.

Source: Karlsen, Madden, and Gardner (1976, p. 38, Table 6)

Note, however, meaningful diagnosis can be made only after examining each pupil's reading performance in detail.

Extended normalized standard score scales
The normalized standard score scales discussed so far are specific to a particular group. For example, the stanines of the *Stanford Diagnostic Reading Test* (Figure 14.5) are specific to second grade children in a national standardization sample. The content of survey test batteries[8], however, spans several grades, say 2nd through 8th, or 9th through 12th. If the score scale of such batteries does not link the tests from several grade levels to the same score scale, there is no way in which pupils' growth could be reflected in their scores. For example, a pupil may place at the 84th percentile in grade five, in grade six, and in grade seven. This pupil would be growing in skills and knowledge, even though the location in a distribution as reflected by the percentile rank may change very little over time. Since the pupil's group would also be progressing through the grades, the percentile rank, remaining at 84, would not of itself reflect growth. Similarly, a *T*-score determined separately for each grade level could remain nearly the same from year-to-year, say about 60, while the pupil in fact exhibited educational growth.

A "ruler" or scale of scores extending over a wide range of grades on which a pupil's progress can be measured year-to-year can be useful. Publishers refer to this type of score with a variety of names, for example: obtained scale score (*California Achievement Tests*), scale score (*Comprehensive Tests of Basic Skills*), extended standard score (*Gates-MacGinite Reading Tests*), standard score (*Iowa Tests of Basic Skills; Metropolitan Achievement Tests*), or growth scale values (*Iowa Tests of Educational Development*). Sometimes the general term "absolute scaled score" is applied to these procedures.

While each test developer prepares expanded scales somewhat differently,[9] and while the numbers obtained are not comparable from publisher to publisher, absolute scaled scores share the same goals and the same general method of development: (a) a base or anchor group is chosen and normalized z-scores are developed which extend beyond the range of scores for this group; (b) a series of tests is administered with common items given to adjoining groups (e.g., 2nd and 3rd graders take a common set of items, then 3rd and 4th graders, 4th and 5th, and so on); (c) distributions of scores are tabulated and normalized for each grade; and (d) through these overlapping items all of the groups are placed on the extended z-score scale of the anchor group. This extended z-scale becomes the "ruler" or "growth" scale spanning the several grades. The expanded z-scale is then transformed to a scale that removes the unpleasant properties (i.e., negative numbers and decimals) of the z-scores. The new scale may range from 00 to 99, 000 to 999, or any other set of numbers, depending on the publisher; there are no standards for what this range should be. Figure 14.6 illustrates the establishment of such scales in a hypothetical case. Table 14.4 is an example of a table provided in an actual test manual.

Although expanded standard scores are generally preferable for research and for evaluating educational programs, their meaning is not immediately apparent to teachers, parents, and pupils. Some consider this an advantage because it lessens the chance of overinterpreting scores. On the other hand, if no one knows what they mean, they will not be used and, therefore, the scores will be underinterpreted. Note that expanded standard scores show different variability from test to test and progressively increasing variability

[8]For examples see Chapter 19.

[9]Basic proposals for such scales were originated by McCall (1922), Thurstone (1925), Flanagan (1939), Gardner (1949), and Swineford and Fan (1957). For summaries see Gulliksen (1950) and Angoff (1971). Latent trait scaling methods are not discussed here.

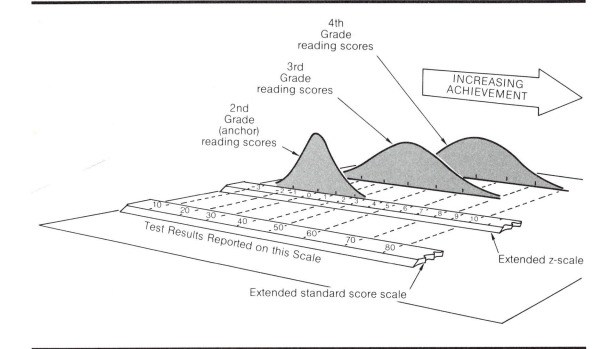

Figure 14 • 6 A hypothetical example of how scores on a series of achievement tests are converted to a common extended score scale. The successive groups are located horizontally by using overlapping tests in a special administration.

from grade to grade. Thus, expanded test scores are not comparable from subtest to subtest and, thus, share a common property with grade-equivalent scores, which I shall now discuss.

Grade-Equivalent Scores

Grade-equivalents are used often with achievement tests at the elementary school level. The grade-equivalent score is then reported as a decimal fraction such as 3.4 or 7.9. The whole number part of the score refers to a grade level, and the decimal part refers to a month of the school year within that grade level. Thus, a grade-equivalent score of 3.4 is

read as "third grade fourth month"; similarly 7.9 is read as "seventh grade ninth month." The *grade-equivalent score* is designed to report the grade placement for which the raw score on a test is average.[10] For example, a raw score of 31 may have a grade-equivalent of 6.3. This would be interpreted to mean that the average for all those who took this test during the third month of sixth grade was 31.

The month of the school year to which the decimal part of a grade-equivalent refers is illustrated here. The time between June and September (i.e., the summer months) are

[10] Grade-equivalents were invented by B. R. Buckingham (1920). Early educational measurement books (e.g., McCall, 1923; McCall and Bixler, 1928; Monroe, 1923; Odell, 1930) called them "grade scores," "G-scores," or "B-scores" (after Binet and Buckingham).

SCALED SCORES

GE	Reading	Mathematics	Language	Basic Battery	GE
PHS*	843	813	828	824	PHS*
12.9	841	812	827	822	12.9
12.8	839	811	825	820	12.8
12.7	837	810	824	818	12.7
12.6	836	809	822	817	12.6
12.5	835	808	821	816	12.5
12.4	834	807	819	815	12.4
12.3	833	806	818	814	12.3
12.2	831	805	816	813	12.2
12.1	830	804	815	812	12.1
12.0	828	803	813	811	12.0
11.9	827	802	812	810	11.9
11.8	825	801	810	809	11.8
11.7	824	800	809	808	11.7
11.6	822	799	808	807	11.6
11.5	821	798	806	806	11.5
11.4	819	797	805	805	11.4
11.3	818	796	804	804	11.3
11.2	816	795	802	803	11.2
11.1	815	793	801	802	11.1
11.0	813	792	800	801	11.0
10.9	812	791	798	800	10.9
10.8	810	789	797	798	10.8
10.7	809	788	796	797	10.7
10.6	807	787	794	796	10.6
10.5	805	785	793	795	10.5
10.4	803	784	791	793	10.4
10.3	801	782	790	791	10.3
10.2	799	781	788	790	10.2
10.1	797	779	787	788	10.1
10.0	795	778	785	787	10.0
9.9	793	776	784	785	9.9
9.8	791	775	782	783	9.8
	789		780		9.7

GE	Reading	Mathematics	Language	Basic Battery	GE
2.6	616	46.	507		2.6
2.5	608	478	499	525	2.5
2.4	599	469	491	517	2.4
2.3	590	460	482	508	2.3
2.2	580	450	472	499	2.2
2.1	570	440	462	489	2.1
2.0	558	430	452	479	2.0
1.9	545	420	441	468	1.9
1.8	531	410	430	456	1.8
1.7	516	401	418	443	1.7
1.6	500	392	405	429	1.6
1.5	483	383	392	414	1.5
1.4	465	375	378	398	1.4
1.3	447	368	363	381	1.3
1.2	428	360	349	365	1.2
1.1	409	352	336	350	1.1
1.0	391	345	323	336	1.0
K.9	374	338	311	323	K.9
K.8	358	331	300	311	K.8
K.7	342	323	290	300	K.7
K.6	327	316	281	291	K.6
K.5	314	308	273	283	K.5
K.4	302	301	266	275	K.4
K.3	291	293	259	268	K.3
K.2	281	284	253	261	K.2
K.1	272	274	247	255	K.1
K.0	264	264	242	250	K.0
PK**	256	253	237	245	PK**

* PHS = Post-High School

** PK = Pre-Kindergarten

If a particular Scaled Score does not appear on these tables, read to the next higher Scaled Score.

Table 14 • 4 A table relating grade-equivalents to expanded standard scores for the *Metropolitan Achievement Tests*, 1978.

				Month of school year					
September	October	November	December	January	February	March	April	May	June
.0	.1	.2	.3	.4	.5	.6	.7	.8	.9

Decimal part of G.E.

assumed to represent an increment of one-tenth (or one month) on the grade-equivalent scale.

Administrators, teachers, parents, and pupils frequently misinterpret grade-equivalents. Understanding how the test publisher obtains grade-equivalents helps prevent misinterpretation. (There is no need, of course,

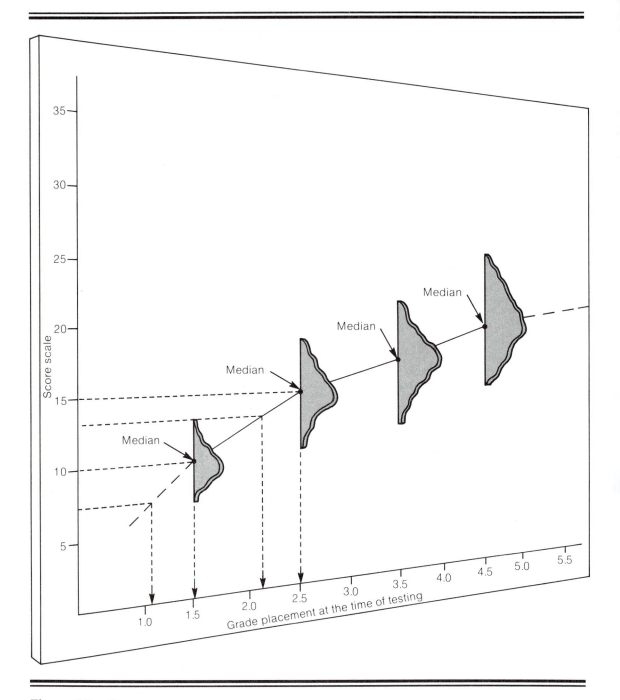

Figure 14 • 7   Hypothetical example of data used to obtain grade-equivalent scores.

for teachers to compute them since test manuals provide the needed conversion tables.)

Suppose a developer wishes to test reading from grades one through eight and to develop grade-equivalents. What a publisher does is to develop a series of *overlapping tests* that spans the desired grades: one test for first and second grades, one for third and fourth, and so on. Each test is appropriate for specific grade levels. A large national sample at each grade level is administered the appropriate test of the series, usually once or twice during the year (fall and/or spring), since it is impossible to administer them continuously throughout the year. Because large individual differences in reading exist, a distribution of scores occurs at each grade level. These are shown in Figure 14.7. In this illustration, the tests were administered only once during the year—in February (0.5).

The first step is to locate the median[11] score in each distribution. For instance, first graders taking the test in February have an average (median) score of 10. The grade-equivalent corresponding to the raw score 10, therefore, is 1.5. Second graders in February have an average score of 15, and their corresponding grade-equivalent is 2.5.

Interpolation and extrapolation Actual grade-equivalents can be obtained only for those points in time when the tests were administered. Grade equivalents for other points are obtained by interpolation or extrapolation. In Figure 14.7, notice that the median of the actual distributions are connected by a solid line. This solid line is used to *interpolate* and thereby estimate the values of the in-between grade-equivalents. For example, the raw score 13 is not an actual median of a distribution. However, we draw a horizontal line from 13 across the graph until it intersects with the solid line and then drop a perpendicular line down to the grade-placement scale. The grade-place-

[11]The mean score is used sometimes instead of the median.

ment corresponding to this vertical line (i.e., 2.1) becomes the (interpolated) grade-equivalent score.

Consider a raw score of 8. A grade-equivalent for this score can be obtained only by *extrapolation*—by extending the line beyond the groups tested according to the trend of the medians. This extension is represented by the dashed lines in Figure 14.7. Thus, the estimated grade-equivalent of the raw score 8 is 1.1. If the extrapolation is incorrect, so will be the grade-equivalent. Table 14.5 summarizes what has been said so far. An actual conversion table from a published test is shown in Table 14.6.

Spring-to-fall drops: summer losses One concern in the process of interpreting grade-equivalents is the phenomenon of summer achievement losses. In some subject areas, arithmetic, for example, students' performance is at its best near the end of the school year and at its worst at the beginning of the school year (Beggs & Hieronymus, 1968; Tallmadge, 1973; Tallmadge & Horst, 1974; Tallmadge & Wood, 1976; DeVito & Long, 1977). A performance difference such as this has

Raw score	Grade equivalent	How obtained
9	1.4	extrapolation
10	1.5	actual data
11	1.7	interpolation
12	1.9	interpolation
13	2.1	interpolation
14	2.3	interpolation
15	2.5	actual data
16	2.8	interpolation
17	3.2	interpolation
18	3.5	actual data
19	4.0	interpolation
20	4.5	actual data
21	4.6	extrapolation

Table 14 • 5
Raw score to grade-equivalent conversion table for the hypothetical data in Figure 14.8.

GE	Reading			Language				Mathem	
	Vocab	Compr	Total	Spell	Mech	Expr	Total	Compu	Cncpt
7.5			48			20		24	
7.6	23		49				52		
7.7		28	50					25	14
7.8	24		51	19			53		
7.9			52			21		26	
8.0		29	52				54		
8.1	25		53				55	27	15
8.2			54						
8.3	26		55			22	56	28	
8.4		30	56	20				29	
8.5			57		13		57	30	16
8.6	27		57						
8.7		31	58			23			
8.8	28		59				58	31	
8.9				21				32	17
9.0			60				59	33	
9.1			61						
9.2	29	32						34	
9.3			62			24	60	35	18
9.4								36	
9.5	30		63						
9.6			64		14		61	37	
9.7	31	33	65	22				38	19
9.8	31		66			25	62		
9.9							63		
10.0		34	67	23				39	
10.1	32					26	64		20
10.2			68				65		
10.3	33	35						40	
10.4			69				66		
10.5			70	24		27			
10.6	34	36			15		67	41	
10.7			71						
10.8							68		
10.9			72						
11.0	35							42	
11.1		37		25		28	69		
11.2			73						
11.3									
11.4							70		22
11.5	36		74						
11.6		38						43	
11.7					16				
11.8						29	71		
11.9			75						
12.0				26					
12.1									
12.2	37	39							
12.3			76				72		
12.4								44	
12.5									
12.6									
12.7									
12.8									
12.9	38-40	40-45	77-85	27-30	17-20	30-35	73-85	45-48	23-25

Table 14 • 6
Part of a raw score to grade-equivalent conversion table for the *Comprehensive Tests of Basic Skills, Level 3, Form S.*

Source: From *Comprehensive Tests of Basic Skills, Form S. Level 3*. Reproduced by permission of the publisher, CTB/McGraw-Hill, Del Monte Research Park, Monterey, Ca. 93940. Copyright © 1974 by McGraw-Hill, Inc. All rights reserved.

several meanings: (a) the assumption of an over-the-summer growth of one month is generally not true, (b) educational growth is not regular and uniform for many children, and (c) using fall-to-spring gains in grade-equivalent scores to evaluate an instructional program can lead to erroneous conclusions.

Grade-equivalents and curriculum correspondence Believing that students ought to have the same placement as their grade-equivalent scores is a misconception. To understand why, first, recall Figure 14.7 and how grade-equivalents are based on the median. By definition half the pupils actually at a particular grade-placement will have scores above the median. Thus, half the pupils in the standardization sample will have grade-equivalent *scores* higher than their grade-*placement*. Second, recall that a series of tests, rather than a single test, is used to establish grade-equivalents. A third grader's grade-equivalent score of, say, 5.7 on an arithmetic test covering *third grade content* cannot be interpreted to mean that this pupil ought to be placed in fifth grade arithmetic. The pupil did very well on third grade content, but the pupil did not take a test on fifth grade arithmetic. Many factors, of course, besides a single test score determine whether an accelerated placement is warranted. Presumably, these include the results of a test covering fifth grade arithmetic.

Grade-equivalents and mastery Sometimes grade-equivalents are misinterpreted to mean mastery of a particular fraction of a curricular area. For example, a grade-equivalent of 3.5 in mathematics might be erroneously thought to mean the pupil has mastered five-tenths of the third grade mathematics curriculum. The most that can be said is that on this test the pupil's score is equal to the average score of those in the norm-group taking this test in the fifth month of third grade. The more closely the test items match what material emphasized in the classroom, the more likely pupils are to score well *above* grade-level. This points out the norm-referenced character of grade-equivalents and illustrates that criterion-referenced interpretations cannot be made from them.

Noninterchangeable nature of grade-equivalents from different publishers' tests Grade-equivalent (and other norm-referenced) scores depend on the particular items placed on a test and the particular norm-group used. It is a misinterpretation to say that a grade-equivalent of say, 3.7 on the *ABC Reading Test* means the same thing as a grade-equivalent of 3.7 on the *DEF Reading Test*. The test results on two different tests are simply noncomparable except under special conditions (Jaeger, 1973; Bianchini & Loret, 1974a, 1974b; Angoff, 1971).

Noncomparability of grade-equivalents from one subject (subtest) to another Another misinterpretation is to use grade-equivalents to compare a pupil's mathematics grade-equivalent with the pupil's reading grade-equivalent. Consider the following hypothetical third grade pupils' test results.

		Survey subtest:	
		Reading	Mathematics
John	G.E.	4.9	4.9
	P.R.	78	90
Howard	G.E.	4.9	4.3
	P.R.	78	78
Susan	G.E.	4.9	4.6
	P.R.	78	84

Notice that two identical grade-equivalents can have different percentile ranks (John), two different grade-equivalents can have identical percentile ranks (Howard), and one grade-equivalent can be higher than another, yet it can be associated with a lower percentile rank than the lower grade-equivalent (Susan).

The reason for the phenomena described above is that the scores for one subject area are more variable than those of another, resulting in different patterns of interpolation. Expanded standard scores cannot be used to compare a student's performance in different areas, either.

"Normal" growth Sometimes grade-equivalents are used to answer questions of normal or expected educational growth. The results of doing this are not satisfactory. One view of normal growth is this: "A pupil ought to exhibit a growth of 1.0 grade-equivalent units from

Grade placement at time of testing	Metropolitan Achievement Tests, Survey Battery, Mathematics Subtest							Comprehensive Tests of Basic Skills, Form S, Mathematics Total						
	Level	Pupil A		Pupil B		Pupil C		Level	Pupil A		Pupil B		Pupil C	
		GE	PR	GE	PR	GE	PR		GE	PR	GE	PR	GE	PR
2.3	Primary 1	1.3	9	2.3	50	3.3	86	C	1.3	5	2.3	47	3.3	87
3.3	Primary 2	2.3	17	3.3	54	4.3	79	1	1.3	14	3.3	47	4.3	76
4.3	Elementary	3.3	33	4.3	57	5.3	75	1	3.3	23	4.3	47	5.3	72
5.3	Intermediate	4.3	34	5.3	56	6.3	76	2	4.3	27	5.3	47	6.3	67
6.3	Intermediate	5.3	35	6.3	55	7.3	69	2	5.3	31	6.3	48	7.3	63
7.3	Advanced 1	6.3	34	7.3	53	8.3	68	3	6.3	35	7.3	48	8.3	61
8.3	Advanced 1	7.3	35	8.3	52	9.3	62	3	7.3	38	8.3	49	9.3	62

Source: Some data are reproduced by permission from the *Metropolitan Achievement Tests, Teacher's Manual for Administering and Interpreting*. Copyright © 1978 by Harcourt Brace Jovanovich. All rights reserved. Other data are from *Comprehensive Tests of Basic Skills, Form S*. Reproduced by permission of the publisher, CTB/McGraw-Hill, Del Monte Research Park, Monterey, Ca. 93940. Copyright © 1973, 1975 by McGraw-Hill. All rights reserved.

Table 14 • 7 Changes in percentile ranks for three hypothetical persons as each "gains" one year in grade-equivalent units from second through eighth grade.

one grade to the next." A pupil taking the test in second grade and scoring 1.3, for example, would, under this view, need to score 2.3 in third grade, 4.3 in fifth, and so on to show "normal" or expected growth. Such a view of grade-equivalents cannot be supported. Table 14.7 illustrates this view for three hypothetical pupils on the mathematics subtest of two published tests. The "pupils" have these characteristics: Pupil A is "one year behind" in terms of grade-equivalents, Pupil B is "at grade level," and Pupil C is "one year ahead." Each year, the pupils' grade-equivalents show a one year "growth" over the preceding year. But look at the percentile ranks corresponding to their scores: Pupil A, who starts out "one year behind," has to *exceed more* persons in the norm-group in order to maintain a "one year behind" grade-equivalent. Being "one year behind" in second grade means being at the fifth or tenth percentile. However, "one year behind" in grade eight means being around the *thirty-sixth* percentile. One has to move from the bottom of the group toward the middle. An opposite phenomenon occurs for Pupil C who begins "one grade ahead" at around the eighty-sixth percentile.

An alternate norm-referenced definition of "normal growth" might be that: "A pupil shows normal growth if that pupil maintains the same position (i.e., percentile rank) in the norm from year-to-year." Table 14.8 shows what happens to a pupil's grade-equivalent score if that pupil's percentile stays the same each year. While middle scoring pupils (such as Pupil B) remain "at grade level," low scoring pupils (such as Pupil A)—even though they don't change their position in the norm group—have grade-equivalents indicating they are further and further behind. An opposite trend occurs for initially high scoring pupils. The exact magnitude of this "falling behind" phenomenon will (a) vary from test to test and (b) depend on the pupil's percentile rank. The grade-equivalent scales of some tests are developed in such a way that the "falling behind" effect is held to a minimum. Students close to the 50th percentile will exhibit less of the effect than will those further from the center of the distribution. The reasons for this effect are two: (a) the line connecting the medians of the distributions at each grade level (see Figure 14.7) tends to curve or flatten out at higher grades rather than being a diagonal

Grade placement at time of testing	Stanford Achievement Test, Form A, Reading Comprehension				Iowa Tests of Basic Skills Forms 5 & 6, Reading Comprehension			
	Pupil D(PR = 16) "Grades behind"		Pupil E(PR = 84) "Grades ahead"		Pupil F(PR = 16) "Grades behind"		Pupil G(PR = 84) "Grades ahead"	
	GE		GE		GE		GE	
3.1	2.0	−1.1	4.4	+1.3	2.1[a]	−1.0	4.4	+1.3
4.1	2.5	−1.6	5.9	+1.8	2.7[a]	−1.4	5.5	+1.4
5.1	3.1	−2.0	7.3	+2.2	3.6	−1.5	6.6	+1.5
6.1	4.0	−2.1	9.3	+3.2	4.6	−1.5	7.7	+1.6
7.1	4.4	−2.7	10.7	+3.6	5.2	−1.9	8.8[a]	+1.7
8.1	5.0	−3.1	11.8	+3.7	5.9	−2.2	9.9[a]	+1.8

[a]Developers recommend that GEs below 3.1 and above 8.1 not be interpreted strictly as "grades and months" due to extrapolation errors.

Source: Some data are from Madden, Gardner, Rudman, Karlsen, and Merwin, *Stanford Achievement Tests*. Copyright © 1973 by Harcourt Brace Jovanovich, Inc. All rights reserved. Other data are from Hieronymus and Lindquist, *Iowa Tests of Basic Skills*. Copyright 1974 by the University of Iowa. Used with permission of Riverside Publishing Co.

Table 14 • 8 Year-to-year changes in grade-equivalent scores as pupils' percentile ranks remain the same.

line and (b) scores at upper grades become more variable, spanning a larger range.

Unequal units It should be mentioned that the grade-equivalent "ruler" doesn't have equal units. This means, for example, that pupils in the middle of the distribution who get one more item correct are likely to raise their grade-equivalent scores by only one-tenth (i.e., one "month"). For students in the upper part of the distribution, however, one additional correct item may result in an increment of several tenths (i.e., several months of growth).

Recommendation In light of the problems with grade-equivalents, you may wonder why they are used at all. Indeed, many test specialists feel they should be eliminated. The APA (1974) test standards, in fact, call for their abandonment. Yet such scores are popular with school people, who are generally unaware of the complex criticisms. There is apparently a real need for at least some crude measure of educational development or growth that can be related to years of schooling. In spite of the technical difficulties in doing so, grade-equivalents or grade-placement levels seem intui-

tively to be a "natural metric." Extended standard scores are sometimes recommended as measures of growth, but they possess many of the same interpretive problems as grade-equivalents.

Grade-equivalents should be used only as coarse indicators of educational development or growth and, then, only when they are accompanied by corresponding percentile ranks. Grade-equivalents are norm-referenced growth indicators. If information about the content of a pupil's behavioral repertoire is sought, criterion-referenced interpretations are needed. I discuss these in Chapter 17.

As a summary of grade-equivalent scores, consider the situation in which a published, norm-referenced achievement test has been administered to a group of third graders during May of the school year. Further, assume that the test has been judged valid and appropriate by the school and that the test publisher's norms are appropriate. Then each of the following statements[12]—except the first—are *false*.

[12]Statements 1 through 6 are from Lindvall and Nitko (1975, p. 98). Statements 7 and 8 have been adapted from Hills (1976, pp. 87–88).

1. Pat's Reading Subtest grade-equivalent score is 3.8. This suggests that she is an average third grade reader.
2. Ramon's Arithmetic Subtest grade-equivalent is 4.6. This means that he knows arithmetic as well as the typical fourth grader who is at the end of the sixth month of school.
3. Melba's Arithmetic Subtest grade-equivalent is 6.7. This suggests that next year she ought to take arithmetic with the sixth graders.
4. Debbie's Reading Subtest grade-equivalent is 2.3. This means she has mastered three tenths of the second grade reading skills.
5. John's grade-equivalent profile is: Vocabulary = 6.2, Reading = 7.1, Language = 7.1, Work-Study Skills = 7.2, Arithmetic = 6.7. This means that his weak areas are vocabulary and arithmetic.
6. Two of Sally's grade-equivalents are: Language = 4.5 and Arithmetic = 4.5. Since her language and arithmetic grade-equivalents are the same, we conclude that her language and arithmetic ability are about equal.
7. Half of this school's third graders have grade-equivalents below grade level. This means that instructional quality is generally poor.
8. This year Mrs. Murray was assigned all of the pupils whose test scores were in the bottom quarter. The average of her class' grade-equivalents this May was further below grade-level than the class' average last year. This means that Mrs. Murray's instruction has been ineffective for the class as a whole.

Comparison of Various Norm-Referenced Systems

Table 14.9 summarizes the various norm-referenced scores discussed above. While each type of score describes the pupil's location in a norm-group, each does so in a somewhat different way. The easiest type of score to explain to parents and students is a percentile rank. Various types of linear standard scores require an understanding of the mean and standard deviation in order for their meaning to become clear. Normalized standard scores are usually interpreted in conjunction with percentile ranks. From test to test, normalized standard scores will have the same percentage of cases associated with them. Consequently, their meaning remains fairly constant as long as a normal distribution can be assumed. Grade-equivalents and expanded standard scores attempt to provide scores along an educational growth continuum, but because of their inherent technical difficulties, they are subject to frequent misinterpretation. The use of grade-equivalents is limited to gross estimates of yearly pupil growth. They should be used only when accompanied by percentile ranks.

General Guidelines for Score Interpretation

Educators should consider the following points when interpreting pupil scores on norm-referenced tests (Prescott, Balow, Hogan, and Farr, 1978):

1. **Look for unexpected patterns of scores** A test should confirm what a teacher knows from daily interactions with a pupil; unusually high or low scores for a pupil should be a signal for exploring instructional implications.

2. **Seek an explanation for patterns** Ask why a pupil is higher in one subject than another. Check for motivation, special interests, special difficulties, etc.

3. **Don't expect surprises for every pupil** Most pupils' test results should be as you expect from their performance in class. A valid test should confirm your observations.

Type of score	Interpretation	Score	Examples of interpretations
Percentile rank	Percentage of scores in a distribution below this point.	$PR = 60$	"60% of the raw scores are lower than this score."
Linear standard score (z-score)	Number of standard deviation units a score is above (or below) the mean of a given distribution.	$z = +1.5$	"This raw score is located 1.5 standard deviations *above* the mean."
		$z = -1.2$	"This raw score is located 1.2 standard deviations *below* the mean."
Linear standard score (SS-score or 50 ± 10 system)	Location of score in a distribution having a mean of 50 and a standard deviation of 10. (Note: For other systems substitute in these statements that system's mean and standard deviation).	$SS = 65$	"This raw score is located 1.5 standard deviations *above* the mean in a distribution whose mean is 50 and whose standard deviation is 10."
		$SS = 38$	"This raw score is located 1.2 standard deviations *below* the mean in a distribution whose mean is 50 and whose standard deviation is 10."
Stanine	Location of a score in a specific segment of a normal distribution of scores.	Stanine = 5	"This raw score is located in the middle 20% of a normal distribution of scores."
		Stanine = 9	"This raw score is located in the top 4% of a normal distribution of scores."
Normalized standard score (T-score or normalized 50 ± 10 system)	Location of score in a normal distribution having a mean of 50 and a standard deviation of 10. (Note: For other systems substitute in these statements that system's mean and standard deviation [e.g. *DIQ's* have a mean of 100 and a standard deviation of 16; this is a 100 ± 16 System.])	$T = 65$	"This raw score is located 1.5 standard deviations above the mean in a normal distribution whose mean is 50 and whose standard deviation is 10. This score has a percentile rank of 84."
		$T = 38$	"This raw score is located 1.2 standard deviations below the mean in a normal distribution whose mean is 50 and whose standard deviation is 10. This score has a percentile rank of 12."
Expanded standard score	Location of a score on an arbitrary scale of numbers that is anchored to some reference group		(No interpretation is offered here because the systems are so arbitrary and unalike)
Grade-equivalent score	The grade placement at which the raw score is average.	$GE = 4.5$	"This raw score is the obtained or estimated average for all those pupils whose grade placement is at the 5th month of the 4th grade."

Source: Adapted from *Measuring Pupil Achievement and Aptitude*, Second Edition, p. 99, Table 5.4, by C. Mauritz Lindvall and Anthony J. Nitko, © 1975 by Harcourt Brace Jovanovich, Inc. Reproduced by permission of the publisher.

Table 14 • 9   Summary of various norm-referenced scores.

4. Small differences in subtest scores should be viewed as chance fluctuations Use the standard error of measurement (Chapter 15) to help decide whether differences are large enough to have instructional significance.

5. Use information from various tests and observations to explain performance on other tests Pupils low in reading comprehension may perform poorly on the social studies subtest, for example.

You may wish to try your hand at implementing these general guidelines by reviewing the case presented in the box. Your interpretations of Joseph James may be different than that of Mrs. Arlington.

STANFORD Achievement Test
1973 Edition

INDIVIDUAL RECORD for James Joseph

Teacher	Arlington Mrs	Date of Testing	4/75	DUPLICATE
School	Jackson Elementary	Grade	4	
System	Jacksonville Sch. Dist.			Scoring Service

Number Right/Possible	Scaled Score	%ile Rank Local	%ile Rank Nat'l	Grade Equiv.	TESTS	NATIONAL STANINE PROFILE	Local Stanine
19/50	139	2	20	3.6	Vocabulary	-3-	1
					Reading - Part A		
					Reading - Part B		
38/72	160	30	62	5.6	Reading Comprehension	-6-	4
42/55	159	29	60	5.7	Word Study Skills	-6-	4
27/32	183	89	94	7.9	Math Concepts	-8-	8
35/40	179	77	92	7.5	Math Computation	-8-	7
34/40	170	71	84	6.5	Math Applications	-7-	6
39/50	167	54	76	6.1	Spelling	-6-	5
45/79	163	31	66	5.7	Language	-6-	4
37/60	164	42	72	5.8	Social Science	-6-	5
43/60	174	70	89	6.9	Science	-8-	6
34/50	154	26	56	5.2	Listening Comprehension	-5-	4
					AREA TOTALS		
80/127	159	30	62	5.7	Total Reading	-6-	4
96/112	180	83	94	7.6	Total Mathematics	-8-	7
53/100	145	7	36	4.5	Total Auditory	-4-	2
					BATTERY TOTAL		
393/588	163	42	74	5.9	Complete Battery	-6-	5

| SCORE DETAIL | | | | | OTIS - LENNON MENTAL ABILITY TEST | 1 2 3 Below Average | 4 5 6 Average | 7 8 9 Above Average |
| Mental Age Yrs. Mos. | Raw Score | Grade Norms PR S | Age Norms %ile Rank Local Nat'l | Dev. I.Q. | | | | |

OTHER PUPIL DATA:

Age **9** yrs. **11** mos.

Other Information

Pupil Number

TEST INFORMATION:

Level   Form   Norms Used

Stanford   **Intermed 1 A   Grade 4.8**

Otis-Lennon

Local Norms based on **510** pupils.   Process No.

TEACHER NOTES:

See back for aids for interpretation.

Figure 14 • 8 An example of an individual score report for a fourth grade pupil on the *Stanford Achievement Test*, Intermediate I Level, 1973.

Courtesy of Harcourt Brace Jovanovich, Inc.

Joseph James is an exceptionally bright, hearing handicapped, fourth grader who has a bilateral loss of about 90 decibels over the speech range. Joey has worn a hearing aid since age 3 and has been totally mainstreamed since kindergarten. In the past year Joey has had the services of an academic tutor for one and a half hours a week and of a hearing therapist for one hour a week. He took all of his subjects with his classmates in a standard classroom.

Mrs. Arlington, Joey's teacher, is reviewing his scores on the *Stanford Achievement Test* because she will be meeting with his parents and the district's child study team to review Joey's education plans for next year. Figure 14.8 shows Joey's test results. Of course, Mrs. Arlington will use much information about Joey to make a decision about his placement, but here I will only discuss the standardized test.

The first thing she notices is that on the whole Joey did generally average or slightly above average work. This does not exactly confirm Mrs. Arlington's impression, since in class he has been a solid student, perhaps one of her top five or so. She knows that Joey is one of the top math students, grasping concepts easily and doing computations rapidly. (In eighth grade, Joey will be recommended for advanced mathematics courses.) She is pleased to see that he did well on the *Stanford*. Math Application was a bit lower, but he performed well, nevertheless. These results confirmed what she knew about Joey's classroom performance: His language deficit was such that at times he had difficulty understanding some of the vocabulary associated with word problems. This subtest, she knew, contained all word problems.

His science score was also high. Mrs. Arlington had a special interest in teaching science at this level. She knew Joey had been enthusiastic with the class work and especially the laboratory demonstrations she had used.

Her attention now turned to Vocabulary and Listening Comprehension. She knew of Joey's hearing impairment, of course, and she had taken pains during the year to seat him where he could read her lips. She had made special arrangements to have these two subtests individually administered to him (the total Auditory score is the sum of the two subtest scores). Vocabulary is a dictated test; the examiner reads a sentence and the student selects the word that best completes the sentence. She expected his worst performance to be on this test. She took special notice of the local percentile rank. During the planning meeting she would be sure to suggest to next year's teacher that Joey's tutor should teach him new vocabulary or technical words. Pre-familiarizing Joey with new terms to be used in class would allow him to benefit more from the class discussions. Listening Comprehension was in the average range, and this surprised her somewhat since she expected him to perform much lower. The test requires the examiner to read aloud both passages and corresponding multiple-choice questions. Perhaps the individual administration and the context of the passage helped. She didn't know why he scored higher than expected here, but she decided that she would ask the hearing therapist.

Although for many students she would be pleased with the reading subtest results, she thought Joey should have placed a little higher, perhaps near the middle of the local group. There seemed to her a rather large discrepancy between the local and national percentile ranks. Further, Joey was in her top reading group. Perhaps his performance was related to his general language and vocabulary deficit which in turn was linked to his hearing loss. While it was clear to her that Joey could function well in a standard class—she knew his intellectual ability was superb—she expected that he could improve his reading skills. She would review his responses to individual questions to see if she could identify any particular pattern of skill deficiency.

Although Spelling and Language were not exceptionally high scores in the local norm group, she was not particularly concerned with this for Joey. She figured that his use of the mechanics of language would improve as he became older and more aware of his usage. She knew, too, that in this school system, systematic, formal instruction in English usage continued into high school and that spelling instruction continued on through sixth grade.

*This is an actual student's test results. The names have been changed and the story is somewhat fictionalized.

Box 14 • 1

Summary

Of themselves, raw scores on educational and psychological tests are difficult to interpret; they need to be referenced to something outside the test. One type of referencing scheme is called criterion-referencing. This chapter discusses norm-referencing whereby a raw score is interpreted by comparing it to one or more norm-groups. New scores, called derived scores, have been developed to communicate the norm-referenced interpretation more directly. Among the many varieties of norm-referenced scores, the most commonly used in education are percentile ranks, linear standard scores, normalized standard scores, expanded normalized standard scores, and grade-equivalent scores. These scores and their interpretations are summarized in Table 14.9.

It is important to decide whether norm-referenced scores will help the teacher make a particular decision about a pupil. For many classroom decisions norm-referenced scores are not necessary, and frequently you need a more detailed description of the pupil than a single score can "capture." When norm-referenced scores are needed, you should make sure the norm-group is relevant, recently tested, and representative of the population for which you want or need generalization. Frequently, local norms and specialized norms are more informative to score interpretation than are national, pupil-in-general norms.

Teachers should review the pattern of a pupil's scores on standardized achievement tests with an eye toward confirmation of what they already know about the pupil through daily interaction. In general, the student's profile should be examined (a) for unusually high or low scores, (b) with a questioning attitude as to "why" a particular score was obtained, (c) with an expectation that confirmation rather than "surprises" are usual, (d) without overemphasizing small differences in scores, and (e) in light of other knowledge the teacher has about the pupil's performance on other tests and in the classroom.

Themes

● Reliability refers to scores, rather than tests, and concerns the consistency of scores from one measurement to another.

● All test scores have some degree of inconsistency resulting from factors such as instability of persons' behavior, fluctuations in the content of test items from form to form, and inconsistent application of scoring rules.

● Reliable scores are a necessary, but not sufficient, condition for valid scores.

● Knowledge of the degree or magnitude of errors of measurement likely to be found in the test scores of pupils helps teachers to better interpret scores and make better decisions using tests.

Terms and Concepts

reliability
error scores, true scores, obtained
    scores
reliability coefficient
factors influencing score inconsistency
types of reliability coefficients (alternate
    forms [same occasion], parallel
    forms, split-halves, Spearman-
    Brown formula, odd-even split-
    halves, Kuder-Richardson formulas
    20 and 21, coefficient alpha, test-
    retest, alternate forms [delayed])

homogeneous items
scorer reliability
standard error of measurement
uncertainty interval (score band)
underinterpreting vs. overinterpreting
    score differences
decision consistency
percent agreement
kappa coefficient

15
RELIABILITY
OF
TEST SCORES

This chapter is concerned with the fallibility or inconsistency of test scores—the nature of score inconsistency, methods of estimating the magnitude of score inconsistency, and ways to interpret these estimates in relation to test scores. The first section discusses the nature of the concept of score reliability and why this concept is important for the interpretation of test scores, the nature of measurement error, and the concept of a reliability coefficient. The second section describes many ways of estimating the reliability of test scores, most of which are used and presented in manuals of published standardized tests. Each contributes somewhat different information about the effects of various sources of inconsistency of scores from particular tests.

A third section describes the standard error of measurement, an index of the likely size of measurement errors, and ways to use this index to interpret test scores. The fourth section describes additional factors which affect the interpretation of reliability information presented in test manuals. The final section describes the concept of decision consistency and ways this concept might be used to ascertain the likelihood of misclassifying pupils when making mastery and/or minimum competency decisions in schools.

Nature of the Concept of Reliability

Reliability refers to the consistency of test scores. Test scores may be inconsistent because persons' behaviors are unstable, varying unpredictably from moment-to-moment or occasion-to-occasion; because the sample of test items or content of the observation procedures vary; because the persons or procedures employed in scoring are inconsistent; and so on. This implies that when interpreting test scores we need to have some understanding of the sources or factors which cause their inconsistency.

Why Reliability is Important

Consistent measurement is a necessary condition for high quality educational and psychological testing. If the scores from a test are very inconsistent, exhibiting large fluctua-

tions from one sample of performance to the next, then the teacher has no valid basis for using these scores to decide a student's general status on the entire performance domain. A necessary condition for a test score to be valid is that it have an acceptable degree of reliability. We cannot realistically expect, however, that any test will yield perfectly consistent or reliable scores. Nevertheless, as the degree of reliability of test scores diminishes, so does their degree of validity.

Note that although reliability is a necessary condition for valid test scores, it is not a sufficient condition. I discuss validity at greater length in the next chapter. Note here, however, that you could observe some behavior with great consistency, but that observation could be entirely invalid for making the inference intended. You could observe with great consistency, to take an extreme example, the hand that a pupil uses to write arithmetic computations. Such a consistent observation is not a valid basis, however, for inferring a student's computational skill.

The reliability of test scores affects the quality of decisions. Suppose a teacher sets a passing or mastery score for a test at 80%, for example. Unreliable test scores make it likely that some pupils who actually know 80% or more of the material will score below 80% and thus be erroneously classified; some pupils knowing slightly less than 80% are likely to pass the tests as well. As another example, a counselor may want to know whether a pupil's mathematical ability or verbal ability is higher. If a test of each ability is administered, a pupil's scores on them are likely to differ. The question is, "Do these scores represent a true difference in the two abilities?" When test scores are unreliable, observed differences, as well as observed equalities, are likely to represent rather large measurement errors, rather than to reflect the pupil's true abilities. Errors of measurement are a special concern to persons needing to interpret a pupil's profile of scores such as is done in diagnostic testing or in vocational counseling.

Error Scores, True Scores, and Obtained Scores

The numbers obtained when applying a particular measurement procedure are called *obtained scores*. Obtained scores can be ratings, raw scores, derived scores, or norm-referenced scores. All scores contain some amount of measurement error. If you could quantify the amount of error in an obtained score, you could have another number or measurement called an *error score*. If you knew both the obtained score and the error score, subtracting the two would yield a score without error, called a *true score*:

true score = obtained score − error score

or

$$T = X - E \qquad \text{[Eq. 15.1]}$$

This relationship is often expressed as an equivalent addition sentence:

$$X = T + E \qquad \text{[Eq. 15.1a]}$$

or

obtained score = true score + error score.

An obtained test score is conceptualized as being composed of the sum of two scores: a true score and an error score.

An error score is often referred to as an error of measurement. An error of measurement may be either positive, negative, or zero. Errors of measurement cause obtained scores to be higher or lower than true scores. Thus, obtained scores do not rank persons in the same order as if there were no errors of measurement.

Table 15.1 shows true, error, and obtained scores for a hypothetical group of students, along with means, standard deviations, and variances. Notice that Sueann and Georgia

Student	Obtained score X	=	True score T	+ +	Error score E
Sueann	52		53		−1
Georgia	52		50		+2
Ira	46		47		−1
Fred	48		47		+1
Peter	50		50		0
Anne	48		50		−2
Mary	44		44		0
Nick	56		56		0
Charles	54		53		1
Totals	450		450		0
Means	50		50		0
Variances	13.33		12.00		1.33
Standard Deviations	3.65		3.46		1.15

Table 15 • 1
True, error, and obtained scores for a hypothetical group of students.

have the *same obtained score*, X = 52. Sueann's score resulted from a negative measurement error, while Georgia's resulted from a positive measurement error: Sueann's obtained score is 1 point lower than her true score; Georgia's score is 2 points higher. On the other hand, Ira and Fred have the *same true score*, T = 47, but Fred's obtained score of 48 ranks him ahead of Ira because of measurement error.

Concept of a Reliability Coefficient

Since observed test scores tend to be inconsistent, some of the individual differences in test performance we observe can be attributed to chance measurement error, rather than to differences in true ability. A *reliability coefficient* quantified the relationship between individual differences in true scores and individual differences in obtained scores. A perfectly reliable test would yield obtained scores with no measurement error. In this case, all observed individual differences would be identical to all true differences among the persons measured, and the reliability coefficient would equal 1.00. A completely unreliable test would yield obtained scores that contained nothing but measurement error: Observed individual differences would bear no relationship to the true individual differences among the persons, and the reliability coefficient would equal 0.00. A reliability coefficient for any test, then, is a number between 0.00 and 1.00 that reflects the degree of consistency of the test's scores. It can be interpreted as a fraction—the fraction of observed individual differences among persons that can be attributed to true differences among them.

A quantitative index of the individual differences in *true* scores among persons is the true score variance, σ_T^2; a quantitative index of the individual differences in *obtained* scores among persons is the obtained score variance, σ_X^2. (Recall this discussion of variance and standard deviation in Chapter 3.) These two indices suggest that a reliability coefficient can be defined as the ratio of the variance of the true scores to the variance of the observed scores:

Reliability

= the extent to which observed score

differences reflect true score differences

$$= \frac{\text{Index of true score differences}}{\text{Index of observed score differences}}$$

$$= \frac{\text{variance of true score}}{\text{variance of observed scores}}$$

$$= \frac{\sigma_T^2}{\sigma_X^2} \qquad \text{[Eq. 15.2]}$$

To apply this equation to the data in Table 15.1, first we find at the bottom of the table that $\sigma_X^2 = 13.33$ and $\sigma_T^2 = 12.00$.[1] Thus,

$$\text{Reliability} = \frac{\sigma_T^2}{\sigma_X^2} = \frac{12.00}{13.33} = 0.90$$

This application of the equation indicates that for the test scores in Table 15.1, 90% of the individual differences among observed scores can be attributed to individual differences in true scores, rather than to errors of measurement.

What is a True Score?

In the discussion above, the word "true score" was used a lot. What is a true score? First note that neither true scores nor error scores can be "seen." Obtained scores are all that you have at your disposal. Most people believe that obtained scores are influenced in some way by a combination of true scores and error of measurement.

The belief that a true score is something quite apart from the measuring process itself

[1]Notice from Table 15.1 that 13.33 = 12.00 + 1.33. In general, $\sigma_X^2 = \sigma_T^2 + \sigma_E^2$. However, $\sigma_X \neq \sigma_T + \sigma_E$ (i.e., 3.65 ≠ 3.46 + 1.15); rather $\sigma_X = \sqrt{\sigma_T^2 + \sigma_E^2}$ (i.e., 3.65 = $\sqrt{12.00 + 1.33}$).

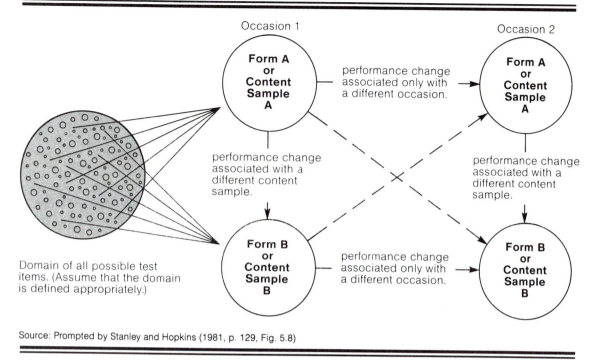

Occasion 1

Form A
or
Content
Sample
A

performance change
associated only with
a different occasion.

Occasion 2

Form A
or
Content
Sample
A

performance change
associated with a
different content
sample.

performance change
associated with a
different content
sample.

Domain of all possible test
items. (Assume that the domain
is defined appropriately.)

Form B
or
Content
Sample
B

performance change
associated only with
a different occasion.

Form B
or
Content
Sample
B

Source: Prompted by Stanley and Hopkins (1981, p. 129, Fig. 5.8)

Figure 15 • 1 A schematic diagram illustrating how changes in test
performance relate to content samples and occasions of testing.

is not unusual. For example, what is your "true spelling ability"? Is it some number assigned to you at the time of your birth or, perhaps, some ability which can be manifest only under some unspecified set of ideal conditions? Some feel that a true score is an inherent individual property that tests seek to discover.

The true score concept here, however, is not an ". . . ultimate fact in the book of the recording angel" (Stanley, 1971, p. 361). Rather, a person's true score on a particular test is the average (mean) of the observed scores the person would obtain over repeated testings. This is an operational definition of true score (Lord & Novick, 1968).

Consider the following situation. Suppose all of the possible items that might be tested in an area are delineated. This delineation of possible items is called a *domain*. For example, the domain could be all items that

test knowledge of simple addition facts, as the large circle at the left of Figure 15.1 illustrates.

Now, suppose you want to determine the percentage of the domain of items a pupil knows. Rather than administering all possible items, you might select a random sample of 10 of these items and administer them to the pupil. Clearly, the pupils' score on the 10 item test depends on which items the test happens to sample. A different sample of 10 items might be easier or harder than the first sample, resulting in a higher or lower score for the pupil. But what is a pupil's true score on the test? Suppose the results are 50% right on the first sample and 80% right on the second. What is the true percentage of the domain of which the pupil has command?

Now consider this: Suppose you administer the first sample of 10 items on Tuesday and that this is a "bad day" for the pupil. Perhaps the pupil has an upsetting encounter on the playground before class, has eaten no breakfast, or the pupil's allergies are "acting up" and making concentration difficult. For whatever reason, Tuesday is a day on which the pupil's performance is "off." If the *10 exact same items* had been administered on Thursday instead of Tuesday, perhaps this child would have been very "up" and could have performed much *better than* normal. Again, you ask, what is the pupil's true score? Is Tuesday's or Thursday's (or neither) performance indicative of the domain percentage of which the pupil has command?

The above description considers two of the *factors influencing consistency of test performance:* (a) The content or particular sample of items appearing on any form of the test and (b) the occasion on which the test is administered. Solid arrows in the schematic diagram of Figure 15.1 indicate these factors. The figure also shows (via the dotted arrows along the diagonal) the additional possibility that *both* content and occasion may work together to influence test performance.

Figure 15.1 implies there are several kinds of true scores. Form A of a test, for example, could be repeatedly administered on several different occasions. An examinee's average Form A score over all possible occasions is the examinee's true score for Form A. In a similar way, there are different true scores for Forms B, C, D, etc. Now consider only Occasion 1 and the possibility of administering many forms of the test to an examinee only on this occasion. The average score for all possible test forms taken on this occasion is the examinee's true score for Occasion 1. In like manner, the examinee would have true scores for Occasions 2, 3, 4, etc. Thus an examinee may have many different true scores: A true score for each content sample (test form)—defined as the average observed score over all occasions—and a true score for each occasion—defined as the average observed score over all content samples. The diagonal arrows of Figure 15.1 represent still another type of true

score. This true score would be the average score over all possible occasions *and* all possible content samples. This true score is not specific to any particular occasion or test form.

Thus, because a reliability coefficient is defined in part in terms of the variance of true scores in a group of persons, you should be clear about which of the several kinds of true scores you refer to in order to be sure you interpret the appropriate coefficient. Since many kinds of true scores exist, so do many kinds of reliability coefficients, some of which I describe in the next section.

Types of Reliability Coefficients

In this section I discuss procedures for estimating a variety of reliability coefficients in each of three categories: reliability on a single occasion, reliability over different occasions, and scorer reliability. These varieties are most frequently reported for published standardized tests. All the procedures estimate the reliability coefficient from data on obtained scores; they do not require knowledge of true scores. Understanding each variety is important because these reliability coefficients give us information that helps us interpret pupils' observed test scores. Some of these reliability coefficients are relatively easy to calculate, so a teacher may want to use them for a teacher-made test. An explanation of computational procedures appears in Appendix B.

Estimating Reliability on a Single Occasion

When attempting to interpret pupils' test scores you may wonder whether pupils' scores would have been different had you administered a different but similar sample of test items. The concern then is the consistency of two sets of scores (one set from each of two comparable forms of a test) obtained on the same occasion.

Test level	Grade	Number of pupils	Number of items	Raw scores Form J		Raw scores Form K		r
				Mean	SD	Mean	SD	
Primary II	1	1,047	55	40.66	8.66	41.62	8.30	.87
Elementary II	4	1,004	80	41.08	15.87	40.56	16.37	.89
Intermediate	9	1,198	80	53.44	16.50	52.85	16.29	.93
Advanced	10	1,002	80	45.91	16.41	45.62	16.08	.94

Table 15 • 2 Alternate forms reliability coefficients, means, and standard deviations for raw scores on Forms J and K of the *Otis-Lennon Mental Ability Test*.

Alternate forms reliability (same occasion) One way to provide the type of reliability information implied by the above question is to administer two forms of a test to the same group of persons on the same (or nearly the same) occasion and to correlate the scores. This correlation is known as the *alternate forms reliability coefficient.* If "A" is used to designate one form of the test, and "B" designates the other, then the formula for this correlation would be

$$r_{AB} = \frac{\Sigma z_A z_B}{N} \qquad \text{[Eq. 15.3]}$$

As you can see, this equation is the Pearson product-moment correlation coefficient (Equation 3.8). Since teachers usually do not build two forms of a test, this coefficient is seldom used with teacher-made tests.

When interpreting this coefficient, remember that only inconsistencies due to fluctuations in content samples are counted as measurement error; testing factors such as practice effects, fatigue, and boredom are considered part of the examinees' true scores. A teacher seeks information about alternate forms reliability when true scores are considered to be the average of obtained scores on all possible content samples administered on a particular occasion (see Figure 15.1). Because Equation 15.3 is usually computed for only

two samples of content, the resulting coefficient is only an estimate of the reliability coefficient defined by Equation 15.2.[2] Table 15.2 gives examples of alternate forms of reliability information, as well as means and standard deviations of each test form.

Two forms of the test made up of items carefully matched to the same test blueprint are called *parallel forms* (APA, 1974). In this case, the correlation coefficient is referred to as a *parallel forms reliability coefficient.* Ideally, two parallel forms should (a) have equal observed score means and standard deviations, (b) measure people equally accurately (i.e., have equal error score variances), and (c) correlate equally with other measurements. Each form would measure the same attribute in precisely the same way. Alternate forms that are "built" by drawing *random* samples of items from the same domain are not strictly parallel in the sense described above because chance will determine the composition of each form.

Empirical evidence is needed to justify using two test forms interchangeably—that is, to support the claim that it doesn't matter which form the examinee is administered on a given occasion. Form-to-form differences are

[2]Note that because of cost and other practical concerns, alternate forms reliability coefficients are frequently computed from much smaller sizes than those upon which the test's norms are based (e.g., see Hieronymus and Lindquist, 1974).

especially important when an individual's score is to be interpreted on its own merits rather than on the basis of relative standing in a distribution as, for example, when a pretest and posttest are used in a mastery learning situation to decide placement into and release from instruction. Pupils are not served well when pretest and posttest lack equivalence. The consequences of using a pretest that samples a larger proportion of more difficult content than the posttest is that more pupils than necessary are placed into instruction. The less difficult posttest has an obverse consequence: Many pupils are released from instruction prematurely. A correlation coefficient won't reveal such consequences.

Evaluating a test's form-to-form equivalence requires examining: (a) the alternate forms *reliability coefficient* to establish the degree to which persons' relative ordering (i.e., z-scores) are the same on the forms; (b) the extent to which the *means and standard deviations* are the same on the two forms to establish whether the general level of performance is likely to be the same on the forms; (c) the *content of the forms* to establish whether they cover the same material in the same proportion or balance and can be considered interchangeable; and (d) the *frequency distributions* of each to establish whether they are sufficiently similar that the consequences of a decision based on the scores of one form would be the same if the other form were used instead. If the frequency distributions are not the same, then setting a "passing score," for example, at z = 1.0 may result in passing 20% of the persons when Form A is used and, perhaps, only 10% when using Form B.

Although in principle many alternate forms of a test might exist, in practice many tests have no alternate form, and those that do seldom have more than two or three forms. Reasons for this include:

a. The test is to be used only once with each examinee and repeated testings for practical decisions are not anticipated.

b. The test is obtrusive or reactive: The very act of taking the test may change the examinee (Thorndike, 1951). For example, if a test is designed to assess the strategies examinees use to solve unfamiliar problems, responding to the items may change an examinee's ability to identify appropriate problem solving strategies.

c. Only one way exists to test the behavior of interest (Thorndike, 1951).

d. It may be too costly to build an alternate form of the test.

Methods other than alternate forms reliability assess the extent to which content sampling affects observed scores when situations such as these arise. These methods follow.

Split-halves reliability coefficients Reliability may be estimated from a single form of a test administered on one occasion by a method known as the *split-halves procedure*. In the split-halves procedure a single test is split into two equivalent halves and *each half* is considered to be a separate (albeit smaller) sample of items. Every examinee receives a score for each half of the test; these half-test scores form the basis for estimating the extent of error due to content sampling in a way analogous to the alternate forms method. Of the various possible split-halves procedures[3] I discuss only one here: the Spearman-Brown double length formula (Spearman, 1910; Brown, 1910).[4]

Spearman-Brown double length formula (sometimes called the Spearman-Brown prophecy formula) is an estimate of the alternate forms correlation. Examinees' scores on the halves are correlated, but since this correlation reflects the correspondence of two sets of scores from tests only half as long as the test of interest, this correlation is adjusted or

[3]See Thorndike (1951) and Stanley (1971) for summaries of various procedures.
[4]Appendix B provides a computing guide for the Spearman-Brown formula as well as for another split-half method, the Rulon (1939) method.

"stepped-up" to estimate the reliability of the whole test. In the formula below r_{hh} stands for the correlation between the halves and r_{SB} represents "Spearman-Brown double length reliability estimate."

$$r_{SB} = \frac{2r_{hh}}{1 + r_{hh}}$$

$$= \frac{2 \times \left(\begin{array}{c}\text{correlation between} \\ \text{half-tests scores}\end{array}\right)}{1 + \left(\begin{array}{c}\text{correlation between} \\ \text{half-test scores}\end{array}\right)} \quad \text{[Eq. 15.4]}$$

For example, assume that the correlation between the half-test scores is 0.60. The Spearman-Brown double length reliability estimate for the full length test is found from Equation 15.4 as follows:

$$r_{SB} = \frac{2 \times 0.60}{1 + 0.60} = \frac{1.20}{1.60} = 0.75$$

The double length formula is often used as an estimate of a parallel forms reliability coefficient, but to do so properly requires that the test be split into parallel halves, making the halves equivalent in terms of content coverage, difficulty level, and variability in essentially the same manner as when two parallel forms are constructed.

A test may be split into halves in many ways,[5] but not all prove satisfactory when applying split-halves procedures. The most commonly accepted procedure to split a test consider that the odd-numbered items (1, 3, 5, 7, . . .) comprise one of the halves and the even-numbered (2, 4, 6, 8, . . .) comprise the other half. This is known as the *odd-even split-halves procedure*. Splitting the test into halves

[5]For a 4-item test there are 3 possible ways to split the test into halves. A 6-item test may be split into halves 10 ways. An 8-item test, 35 ways; and a 10-item test, 126 ways. For a general formula see Thorndike (1951, p. 579) or Stanley (1971, p. 408).

this way works fine as long as (a) the "odd half" and the "even half" can be considered as comparable samples of content, and (b) the test is not speeded. If a test is speeded, agreement among the scores on the two halves of the test is spuriously high. In general, split-halves procedures should not be used with speeded or partially speeded tests unless precautions are taken to separately administer and separately time each half. The odd-even split-halves procedure is inappropriate when groups of items are linked together such as when a cluster of items requires answers based on the same reading selection (or on the same data table, figure, graph, etc.) or when items are grouped in homogeneous clusters in a matching exercise (Thorndike, 1951).

Kuder-Richardson reliability coefficients Another way to obtain a reliability estimate from a single form of the test is by using one of the Kuder and Richardson (1937) procedures. The two discussed here, Kuder-Richardson formula 20 (*KR*20) and Kuder-Richardson formula 21 (*KR*21), are designed for use when test items are scored dichotomously (0 or 1). The names of these procedures derive from the numbering scheme Kuder and Richardson used to identify the formulas in their 1937 paper.

The more widely used of the two procedures, especially for published tests, is *Kuder-Richardson formula 20*:

$$KR20 = \frac{k}{k-1}\left[1 - \frac{\Sigma p(1-p)}{(SD_X)^2}\right]. \quad \text{[Eq. 15.5]}$$

Here, k represents the number of items in the test; p represents the proportion or fraction passing each item (see Chapter 11); and $(SD_X)^2$ is the variance of the total test scores. In addition to the variance of the total test scores, you need the proportion of persons in the group passing each item to use this formula. For each item, compute the product $p(1 - p)$ and then sum all of these products to get the quantity $\Sigma p(1 - p)$. Insert the three quantities $(k, \Sigma p(1 - p),$ and $SD_X)^2)$ in the formula and compute $KR20$. An illustration of its computation appears in Appendix B.

The *Kuder-Richardson formula 21* gives a computationally simpler approximation to $KR20$.

$$KR21 = \frac{k}{(k - 1)} \left[1 - \frac{M(k - M)}{k(SD_X)^2} \right]$$

$$= \left[\frac{\text{No. of items}}{\text{No. of items} - 1} \right] \times$$

$$\left[1 - \frac{\text{Mean} \times (\text{No. of items} - \text{Mean})}{\text{No. of items} \times \text{Variance}} \right]$$

[Eq. 15.6]

Here, k and $(SD_X)^2$ have the same meaning as in $KR20$; M represents the mean of the test. As an illustration, if a 4-item test has a mean of 2.0 and variance of 1.67, then you would compute $KR21$ as follows:

$$KR21 = \left[\frac{4}{4 - 1} \right] \left[1 - \frac{2(4 - 2)}{4(1.67)} \right] = 0.53.$$

This procedure is straightforward enough to compute for classroom tests, although it is seldom used for published tests. Appendix B gives a complete illustration of the *Kuder-Richardson formula 21*.

For the same test data, $KR21$ gives a lower value than $KR20$, except for the special case when all the items have equal difficulty (i.e., when all p-values are identical). In this case $KR21 = KR20$. The discrepancy between $KR20$ and $KR21$ becomes larger when the items vary greatly in difficulty. The discrepancy is more serious for short tests that are relatively easy (Cronbach & Azuma, 1962).

Kuder-Richardson formulas 20 and 21 are used only with dichotomously scored items. Not all tests contain items scored that way: Items on essay tests are scored more continuously; attitude scales require a respondent to rate each item on a scale of, say 1 to 4; several judges may rate a pupil's performance on

a scale from, say 1 to 9. In situations such as these, a more general form of $KR20$ is used. This reliability estimate is known as *coefficient alpha* (α) (Cronbach, 1951):

$$\alpha = \frac{k}{k - 1} \left[1 - \frac{\Sigma(SD_i)^2}{(SD_X)^2} \right]$$

$$= \left[\frac{\text{No. of items}}{\text{No. of items} - 1} \right] \times$$

$$\left[1 - \frac{\text{sum of item variances}}{\text{variance of total scores}} \right]. \quad \text{[Eq. 15.7]}$$

The formula is exactly like Equation 15.5 except[6] for the symbol $\Sigma(SD_i)^2$. Here, $(SD_i)^2$ represents the variance of the scores of all the students on one item or from one rater, and $\Sigma(SD_i)^2$ means to add together the variance from all items or from all raters. An example of how to compute the value of coefficient alpha is given in Appendix B. Coefficient alpha is interpreted in essentially the same way as $KR20$.

The three procedures above are founded on the idea that the consistency with which persons respond from one item to the next within a test can provide a basis for estimating the reliability coefficient for the total test scores. Note, however, that consistency of responses to items within a test means that something in addition to content sampling is contributing to inconsistency. These three procedures are sensitive to the *homogeneity* of the items as well as to their specific content. *Homogeneous items* all measure the same trait or attribute; a test that contains items measuring more than one trait is said to be *heterogeneous*. If a test's items are homogeneous, the $KR20$ and α procedures will give results that are nearly the same as the split-halves procedure. When the

[6]In the $KR20$ formula, the quantity $p(1 - p)$ is the variance of one dichotomously scored item, and $\Sigma p(1 - p)$ is the sum of all of the item variances of the test. Thus, $KR20$ is really a special case of the more general coefficient alpha. When items are scored 0 or 1, $(SD_i)^2 = p(1 - p)$, and $\alpha = KR20$.

items are heterogeneous, results from the *KR*20 and α procedures are lower than the split-halves procedure. For this reason, *KR*20 and α are often called lower bound estimates of reliability.

It should be noted that *KR*20 and α are equal to the average of all possible split-half reliability coefficient[7] which could be computed for the test in question (see, e.g., Cronbach, 1951). All possible split-halves mean not just the odd-even split but all different splits that could divide a test into halves.

Another thing to note about *KR*20 and α is that their numerical value is influenced by the length of the test as well as its homogeneity. Longer tests will tend to have higher values of *KR*20 or α, even though they may be heterogeneous. The *KR*20, *KR*21, and α coefficients are influenced by speed in the same manner as split-halves coefficients and are not recommended for use with speeded or partially speeded tests because the spuriously high coefficients overestimate the consistency of scores since content samples vary.

Estimating Reliability Over a Time Period

The question posed by the teacher cited at the beginning of the previous section concerns the consistency of two sets of scores obtained on a single occasion. Thus, occasion is constant, and error is attributed to content sampling. Here we ask another question: "To what extent are scores likely to be different because the occasion is different rather than the sample of test items?" (Recall Figure 15.1.) If a student teacher is observed on a Monday, would it be likely that the same ratings would be given if the observations occur on Wednesday? Similarly, one could ask, "If Dr. Adams rates the teacher on Monday and Dr. Meyers rates on Thursday, would such ratings be likely to agree?" The latter question is concerned with

[7]The split-half reliability coefficients referred to here are not the Spearman-Brown of Equation 15.4, but the Rulon (1939) formula. See footnote 5 of this chapter and Appendix B.

the effects of sampling both occasions (days of the week) and content (observers or raters). Procedures for estimating reliability for these two situations are the subject of this section.

Test-retest reliability If a reliability question centers on the stability of scores on a particular sample of items over a time period, then studying data obtained from administering the identical items to a group of persons on two separate occasions will answer the question. Since the *same* test form (rather than equivalent forms) is administered at two different times, the correlation between the scores on the two occasions is known as the *test-retest reliability coefficient*. This paradigm looks like this:

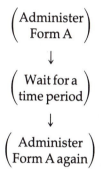

$$\begin{pmatrix} \text{Administer} \\ \text{Form A} \end{pmatrix}$$
↓
$$\begin{pmatrix} \text{Wait for a} \\ \text{time period} \end{pmatrix}$$
↓
$$\begin{pmatrix} \text{Administer} \\ \text{Form A again} \end{pmatrix}$$

Of importance when interpreting these test-retest coefficients is (a) the length of the interval between the two administrations of the test and (b) the expected stability of the performance being measured. For example, students' attitudes toward a particular school subject may not remain stable if a special intervention program is initiated to change those attitudes. Similarly, some performances of infants and young children are not consistent from one occasion to the next. Some tests measure traits such as general scholastic aptitude, which educators expect to remain stable over longer time periods (e.g., a semester or a year) and which educators expect, consequently, to be useful in predicting future performance over these periods. The validity of a test's score as a predictor of future performance is diminished when that score lacks stability. The teacher's concern with whether a student is having an "off day or days" would concentrate on the consistency or inconsistency of scores over a relatively short time interval, a week or two or perhaps as long as a month. Inconsistency of performance over a longer time interval would likely reflect actual changes in pupil ability rather than fluctuations due to particular occasions or "off days." Such actual changes reduce the consistency of scores obtained on two occasions because different persons have different rates of changes or growing.

Alternate forms reliability (different occasions) Another procedure for estimating reliability is to administer one form of a test on one occasion and an alternate form on another occasion. This permits both content and occasion to vary. The correlation between the scores on the two occasions is influenced by differences in both content and in occasion. This paradigm may be depicted as:

$$\left(\begin{array}{c} \text{Administer} \\ \text{Form A} \end{array}\right)$$

$$\downarrow$$

$$\left(\begin{array}{c} \text{Wait for a} \\ \text{time period} \end{array}\right)$$

$$\downarrow$$

$$\left(\begin{array}{c} \text{Administer} \\ \text{Form B} \end{array}\right)$$

The correlation is computed in the same manner as indicated by Equation 15.3; the only difference between this procedure and Equation 15.3 is that a time interval is introduced here. The comments about the length of the time interval for the test-retest reliability estimate apply to the alternate forms procedure as well. However, a new sample of items eliminates the effects of remembering specific test questions (but does not eliminate general practice effects). As with alternate forms

administered on the same occasion, an obtrusive or reactive testing method may systematically affect performance on the second administration.

The type of true score of interest when you follow a delayed alternate forms procedure is illustrated by the number in the lower right corner of Table 15.2.

Delayed alternate forms reliability is significant when you want to generalize about occasions *and* content samples: "How well does this test measure the attribute regardless of form used or occasion on which it is administered?" A good many educational decisions may be cast into this framework. For example, in estimating the "teaching ability" of a student teacher, you may want to focus on the consistency of ratings obtained on different occasions *and* from different raters. Usually, there is less interest in defining "teaching ability" in terms of only a single occasion (e.g., many supervisors' ratings on Tuesday, October 5th) or in terms of only a specific supervisor's ratings over several occasions (e.g., Mr. Washington's ratings of teachers throughout the year).

Another point to stress here is that "occasions" need to be carefully specified when interpreting delayed alternated forms reliability coefficients. For instance, if children are observed while learning a subject they happen to enjoy very much or when they are with an exceptionally enthralling teacher, there may be little variation in observed attentiveness from day-to-day. But there might be relatively large fluctuations in attentiveness within the *same day* as students move, say, from mathematics instruction to language arts to gym, etc. These moment-to-moment or subject-to-subject fluctuations in attentiveness might be larger than day-to-day fluctuations (e.g., Goodwin cited in Cronbach, et al., 1972).

Rules based strictly on testing and measurement methodology, while frequently helpful, are insufficient bases for judging the appropriateness of particular reliability estimation procedures. Deciding the appropriateness of a particular time interval and a particular stability coefficient is a professional judgment calling for substantive considerations *and* experience. A teacher needs to be knowledgeable about (a) the domain of behavior that is of interest, (b) the theory and facts concerning which factors influence performance in that domain, and (c) the purpose(s) for which behavior from that domain are to be observed. In addition, a teacher needs to bring to bear on this judgmental process knowledge gained through experience with the particular population of pupils about which the teacher is concerned. A teacher has a wealth of knowledge that is relevant to test score interpretation. The combination of knowledge and professional experience permits the teacher to evaluate the usefulness of a particular test and its accompanying reliability information.

Estimating Scorer Reliability

Yet another source of measurement error arises from those persons (or machines) scoring a test. Here concern focuses on such questions as, "To what extent would a pupil obtain the same score if a different person had scored the paper or judged the performance?" and "To what extent might the test be said to be objective?" and "Are the results obtained from different scorers (observers, raters, judges) interchangeable?"

The most straightforward way to estimate this type of reliability is to have two persons score each pupil's paper or rate each pupil's performance.[8] The two scores for each pupil—one score from each scorer—are then correlated using Equation 15.3. The correlation coefficient serves as an index of the extent to which the scorers were consistent—consistency being defined here as similarity of z-scores. The group of four students' ratings given below illustrate this point in an admittedly exaggerated situation.

	Ratings from:		Ratings converted to z-scores:	
	Rater A	Rater B	z_A	z_B
Tony	4	8	1.34	1.34
Marya	3	7	0.45	0.45
Bobby	2	6	−0.45	−0.45
Megan	1	5	−1.34	−1.34
Mean	2.5	6.5	$r_{AB} = 1.00$	
SD	1.12	1.12		

The ratings in this example don't "agree" in the *absolute* sense, but they do "agree" perfectly in the *relative* sense because the z-scores are in perfect agreement; the correlation coefficient of 1.00 reflects this.

Agreement in the absolute sense happens as a result of two scorers assigning the identical scores to each examinee. The extent to which this identical assignment of scores occurs is sometimes expressed as a *percent of agreement*.[9] If scorers always agree in their assignment of scores there is 100% agreement; if they never agree, the percent of agreement is zero; partial agreement is expressed as a percent falling between these two values.

Percent of agreement is quite different in conception than a correlation coefficient; in general, the numerical value of the two will be different. The choice between a percent of agreement index and a correlational index of scorer consistency depends on whether the absolute or the relative score level is important for a particular decision. Suppose that in the example above, a rating of 5 or better was needed to "pass." If the scores of Rater A were used then everyone "failed," but if the scores of Rater B were used, everyone "passed." For

---

[8]More informative procedures are described in Cronbach et al. (1972). These procedures require more statistical sophistication than is assumed here and are, consequently, beyond the scope of this text.

[9]Indices describing percent of agreement are given in the last section of this chapter.

such decisions, the absolute score level is important, and a serious source of error (in this example) is the particular scorer or rater employed. Suppose, on the other hand, that only relative score level is important. In this case, the two observers agree perfectly on whom the "best" and the "next best" are.

Summary of Estimating Reliability

This section describes various methods for estimating reliability coefficients. These methods were organized around three views of true scores and errors of measurement: (a) single occasion reliability, viewing content sampling as a major source of error; (b) reliability over time, viewing occasion sampling (and, perhaps, content sampling as well) as a major error source; and (c) scorer reliability viewing, the persons assigning scores as major error sources. The choice of interpreting one or more of these coefficients depends on the particular concern(s) the educator interpreting test scores may have and the substantive knowledge and professional experience the educator can bring to bear on the problem. Table 15.3 summarizes information about the various reliability estimation procedures that have been discussed in this section.

Standard Error of Measurement

Since no test measures persons with perfect consistency, taking the likely size of errors of measurement into account when interpreting test scores is useful. One way to describe the inconsistency of test scores is to measure a pupil repeatedly and note the extent to which scores vary. If teachers could test a pupil many times (without changing the pupil's ability with respect to the trait being measured), they would obtain a collection or distribution of obtained scores. While some would be higher than others, most would cluster around a mean or average value. This mean is the true score to which we referred earlier. The standard deviation of this distribution is the *standard error of measurement* (SEM) and is an index of the extent to which pupils' obtained scores are likely to differ from their true scores. In practice it is not possible to repeatedly retest persons without changing them, so the standard error of measurement is not calculated by retesting but is estimated by using the equation:

$$SEM = SD_X \sqrt{1 - \text{reliability coefficient}}$$
[Eq. 15.8]

where SD_X is the standard deviation of the obtained scores of the test. The standard error of measurement computed by Equation 15.8 is an estimate of the standard deviation of the errors of measurement resulting from repeated testing as described above. For example, if SD_X was equal to 10 and the reliability coefficient equaled 0.84, then

$$SEM = 10\sqrt{1 - 0.84} = 10\sqrt{0.16}$$
$$= 10(0.4) = 4.0$$

The standard error of measurement helps to understand the size of measurement error for a particular testing procedure. One interpretation is that *SEM* gives a sense of the average amount a person's observed scores are likely to deviate from their true scores. Thus, in the above example, $SEM = 4.0$ can be interpreted to mean that persons' obtained scores are likely to be about 4 points above or below their true scores.[10] Another interpretation of SEM involves using a normal distribution. It is assumed that the hypothetical distribution of obtained scores resulting from repeatedly testing a person is normal in form. The mean of this distribution is the person's true score, while the standard deviation is the standard error of measurement. Using the relation

[10] Although it is useful to think of *SEM* in these terms, this interpretation is not true in a technical, mathematical sense (see Chapter 3).

Types	Major question(s) answered	What is counted as measurement error or inconsistency
Alternate forms (no time interval)	**I. Influence of different content samples** a. Are scores affected by sampling different content on the same occasion? b. Are two carefully matched test forms interchangeable (equivalent, parallel)?	Content sampling
Spearman-Brown double length	a. Same as above. b. What is an estimate of the alternate forms reliability coefficient?	Content sampling
Kuder-Richardson formula 20	a. Same as above except equivalence or parallelism of forms may not be a concern to investigator. b. What is a crude estimate of test homogeneity? c. How consistent are responses from item to item?	Content sampling and homogeneity
Kuder-Richardson formula 21	a. Are scores affected by content sampling on the same occasion?	Same as *KR*20.
Coefficient alpha	a. Same as *KR*20.	Same as *KR*20.
Test-retest	**II. Influence of occasions** a. How are scores on the identical content sample affected by testing of another occasion? b. How stable are scores on this particular test form over time?	Time or occasion sampling
Alternate forms (with time interval)	a. How consistent are the test scores regardless of form used or occasion on which it is administered? b. How stable are scores on this trait over time (and content samples)?	Time or occasion sampling and content sampling
Scorer reliability	**III. Influence of different scorers** a. To what extent will the scores be different if different scorers (raters, judges) are used? b. To what extent is the test objective? c. Are the results from different scorers (observers, raters, judges) interchangeable?	Scorer sampling

Table 15 • 3 Summary of types of reliability estimation procedures.

between standard deviation and percent of cases under the normal curve from Chapter 14, it can be said that 68% of the time the person's obtained score will be within a distance of one *SEM* from the true score. This one *SEM* difference is illustrated in Figure 15.2 for a hypothetical examinee with true score = 52 and *SEM* = 4.0. Following this normal curve interpretation, one third (32%) of the time a person is retested the obtained score might be outside these bounds: It will be greater than 56 (= 52 + 4) about one sixth (16%) of the time and less than 48 (= 52 − 4) about one sixth of the time.

Note that the smaller the standard error of measurement, the more consistent are the scores (i.e., the smaller are the measurement errors). The size of the standard error of mea-

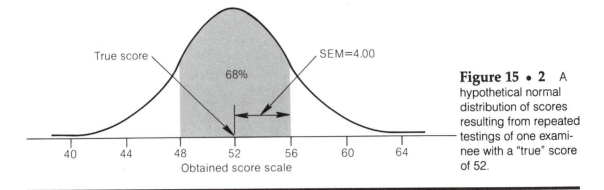

Figure 15 • 2 A hypothetical normal distribution of scores resulting from repeated testings of one examinee with a "true" score of 52.

surement, however, depends on both the reliability coefficient and the standard deviation of the test. In the preceding example, if SD_X = 5 instead of 10, then SEM = 2.0. Thus, while the reliability remained at 0.84, SEM became smaller. This smaller SEM illustrates the point that the standard deviation of the test should be taken into account when interpreting the consistency of test scores. Because different tests have different units of measurement as well as different standard deviations, it is usually true that the only way to compare the consistency of the scores from two *different* tests is by way of looking at their reliability coefficients. The relationship between the SD_X, the reliability coefficient, and the SEM is shown in Table 15.4. Notice that for a fixed value for the reliability coefficient, SEM becomes larger as SD_X increases and that for a fixed value for the SD_X, SEM becomes smaller as the reliability coefficient becomes larger. If a test manual does not report SEM, Table 15.4 can provide a rough estimate once the SD_X and the reliability coefficient are known.

Study of the standard error of measurement indicates that obtained test scores should not be interpreted as if they had great precision. An obtained score is likely to fall within a band or range around the person's true score. For example, grade-equivalent scores from a standardized achievement test may have equivalent forms reliability coefficients around

0.83 and standard deviations around 1.0 (on the grade-equivalent scale); thus SEM is likely to be 0.4. Shifts up or down the scale of four months (0.4) in grade-equivalents upon retesting with another form of the test would be quite likely. Two pupils with identical true scores are likely to show a larger than four-months difference.

Although the above comments direct you to be cautious about *overinterpreting* small differences in scores, you should not be so conservative as to err by *underinterpreting* test results, ignoring meaningful score differences. Some measurement specialists recommend, for example, that the value of SEM be added and subtracted from each pupil's obtained score, thus forming the boundaries of a "score band" or *uncertainty interval* for scores. If such bands are formed for two examinees, and if these score band boundaries overlap (or if the bands overlap for the same student on two different tests such as verbal ability and quantitative ability), some specialists recommend making a "no difference between the true scores" interpretation because differences the size of those observed could arise simply by error of measurement 68% of the time. But perhaps a more widespread problem than overinterpreting scores is a "do-nothing pattern": failing to interpret score changes or ups and downs of profiles because of overdemanding criteria of 68%, 90%,

Reliability coefficient	Standard deviation					
	5	10	15	20	25	30
.98	.7	1.4	2.1	2.8	3.5	4.2
.95	1.1	2.2	3.4	4.5	5.6	6.7
.90	1.6	3.2	4.7	6.2	7.9	9.5
.85	1.9	3.9	5.8	7.7	9.7	11.6
.80	2.2	4.5	6.7	8.9	11.1	13.4
.75	2.5	5.0	7.5	10.0	12.5	15.0
.70	2.7	5.5	8.2	11.0	13.7	16.4
.65	3.0	5.9	8.9	11.8	14.8	17.7
.60	3.2	6.3	9.5	12.6	15.8	19.0
.50	3.5	7.1	10.6	14.1	17.7	21.2
.20	4.5	8.9	13.4	17.9	22.4	26.8
.10	4.7	9.5	14.2	19.0	23.7	28.5

Table 15 • 4
Standard error of measurement for various standard deviations and reliability coefficients.

or 95% uncertainty bands (Feldt, 1967). To avoid wasting valuable test information, a teacher should corroborate the hints obtained from test scores with evidence from other sources, thereby reducing the probability of errors of overinterpretation (Feldt, 1967).

Additional Factors Affecting Interpretation of Reliability Information

You should keep a number of factors in mind when interpreting reliability information, especially when you compare the reliability coefficients from two or more tests.

1. **Longer tests are more reliable than shorter tests** The greater the number of observations (i.e., items, judges, occasions of observation, etc.) that enter into the formation of a score, the more reliable that score will be. This means, for example, that a teacher should put little confidence in a pupil's response to one item on a test, even to responses on clusters of two or three items. The relation between lengthening a test by adding similar items and the reliability of the resultant test given by the *general Spearman-Brown formula:*

$$r_{nn} = \frac{nr_{11}}{1 + (n - 1)r_{11}} \quad \text{[Eq. 15.9]}$$

where r_{nn} is the reliability of a test n times as long as the original test, r_{11} is the reliability of the original test, and n is the number of times the original test was lengthened. Appendix B shows a computational example.

2. **The numerical value computed for a reliability coefficient will fluctuate from one sample of persons to another** The reliability coefficients reported in a test manual are based on samples of examinees. These numerical values will fluctuate from one sample to the next, so that any one published number can be considered only as an estimate of what the reliability coefficient would be if the entire population were tested. Sampling fluctuations are greater for small samples drawn from the population than from large samples.

3. **The narrower the range of ability of a group, the lower the reliability coefficient tends to be** It is much easier to distinguish individual differences in ability when persons in fact differ widely from one another than when their abilities are very similar. Many educational situations involve using test scores to decide about pupils whose abilities, grade levels, and ages are relatively close together. Therefore, look in test manuals for reliability coefficients based on data from pupils whose abilities are in the ranges within which you

must deal. Put less stock in higher reliability coefficients derived from pooling samples from several grades, ability, and/or age levels when your situation calls for measuring a group of pupils whose abilities are rather close together.

4. **Persons at different ability levels may be measured with different degrees of accuracy** The *SEM*, being a single number for a test, represents only an average amount of score inconsistency. It is probable that the consistency of a test's scores varies with the ability level of the pupil tested. You have to study carefully the manual or technical report of the test you are using to determine this because there is no general rule to tell you what to expect in advance. As an illustration, consider the *Iowa Tests of Basic Skills*, Vocabulary Subtest, which reports the following standard errors of measurement for different raw score levels for the fourth grade (Hieronymus & Lindquist, 1974, p. 61):

Score level	SEM at each level[11]
10–19	4.0
20–29	4.6
30–39	4.8
40–49	5.2
50–59	5.4
60–69	5.2
70–79	4.0

Weighted average *SEM* = 5.1

As can be seen, *SEM* is larger in the middle of the score range than at the extremes. Thus, very high and very low scoring pupils are measured on this subtest with somewhat more consistency than are average students.

5. **The longer the time interval between testings, the lower will test-retest and alternate forms reliability coefficients tend to be** Given that persons actively interact with their environments, their status on an attribute changes with time. One study found, for example, that

[11] Based on parallel forms reliability coefficients.

first graders' *Metropolitan Achievement Test (MAT)* composite scores correlate 0.73 with their second grade MAT composite scores, but correlate 0.60 with their ninth grade composite scores on the *Iowa Tests of Educational Development* (Bracht & Hopkins, 1972). Test-retest and delayed alternate forms reliability coefficients are often called *stability coefficients* since they reflect persons' relative standing in a distribution over time.

Indices of Decision Consistency

Likelihood of Misclassification on Mastery Tests

A pupil's score on a test is frequently used to judge whether a skill or an instructional objective has been mastered. We may obtain some idea of the extent to which misclassifications can occur on mastery tests by assuming a domain sampling model.[12] You can conceive of a large pool of items all measuring the same objective. The degree of proficiency a pupil has with respect to this domain is quantified by the fraction of items in the entire domain which the pupil can answer correctly; this fraction is considered to be the pupil's true score. Frequently, an arbitrary decision is made as to which domain true score level should constitute mastery: for example, "80% is mastery."[13] Pupils whose domain true scores are greater than or equal to 80% are called masters; the others nonmasters.

Often the domain of items is so large that only a sample of items is administered to the

[12] The misclassification error rate discussed in this section applies when passing the test is the sole criterion for deciding a pupil's mastery status. We have emphasized throughout this book that a teacher needs to take into account all information, not just test scores when making decisions. When the teacher considers all information, the rate of misclassification is likely to be much lower than described here.

[13] There seems to be no pedagogical or psychological justification for 80%, yet it is the percentage commonly used.

		True status of a pupil with respect to the degree of domain proficiency	
		Master	Nonmaster
Conclusion drawn from the test about the pupil's domain status	Passing the test is interpreted as mastery.	*There is no misclassification:* Both the pupil's true status and the conclusion from the test agree.	*An error of classification:* Pupil is a nonmaster, but passed the test.
	Not passing the test is interpreted as non-mastery.	*An error of classification:* Pupil is a master, but the test was not passed.	*There is no misclassification:* The conclusion drawn from the test is correct.

Figure 15 • 3   Relationship between a pupil's true mastery status and possible errors of classification when drawing conclusions from a test.

pupil. In this way the teacher estimates the pupil's domain true score from the sample of items constituting a test. To decide "mastery," a passing score is set on the test. If mastery is defined as a domain true score of 80%, for example, teachers usually apply the same percent to the test. Thus, on a 5-item test "mastery" would be declared if a pupil answered 4 or 5 items correctly; on an 8-item test the mastery score may be 7 or more correctly answered items.

Some pupils, whose domain true scores are less than 80%, may actually pass the test and be erroneously declared "masters" because the sample of items on the test may happen, by chance, to contain a great many items for which they know the answers. On the other hand, other pupils whose domain true scores are greater than 80% may not pass the test and be erroneously classified as "nonmasters" because the sample contained too many items which they could not answer correctly. The situation with correct and incorrect classification decisions is summarized in Figure 15.3.

Examples of estimates of the probabilities of committing the two types of classification errors shown in Figure 15.3 are given in Table 15.5 for the special case where mastery is defined as knowing 80% of the items in the

domain.[14] Suppose a pupil's true score on the domain is 70%. What is the probability of this pupil passing a 7-item test (passing = 6 or more correct)? The table shows this to be 0.33—one third of the pupils with true scores of 70% would be misclassified as masters because their obtained test scores would be 6 or more. What is the probability of a pupil whose true score is 80% *failing* the test and thereby being mislabeled as a nonmaster? The table shows this probability to be 0.42—two out of five pupils whose true scores equal 80% will be misclassified because their test score was less than 6. Results such as these suggest not only that the teacher should use longer, more reliable tests, but also that the teacher should bring to bear on such decisions all available information. Using test scores alone is likely to result in higher rates of misclassification. Notice, too, that errors of misclassification are highest for pupils with true scores close to the defined mastery criterion (80%). This illustrates a psychometric truism: *Errors of classification are greatest for persons with true scores at or near the cutoff score on a test.*

[14] Table 15.5 is based on the binomial probability distribution and assumes tests are independent random samples from a large domain of items.

Percent Agreement and Kappa Coefficient

The data in Table 15.5 describes the likelihood of erroneously classifying particular pupils. It is sometimes useful to compute indices that describe the consistency with which all the pupils in *a particular group* are classified. Two are described below: percent agreement and Cohen's kappa coefficient.

Suppose two forms of a test, A and B, were administered to a group of 25 pupils and that the mastery criterion on each form was 80 percent. Table 15.6 summarizes how consistently the two tests classified these pupils. Eleven pupils were classified as masters on both forms, nine as nonmasters by both forms, and the others as masters on one and nonmasters on the other.

Percent agreement (P_A) One simple index of decision consistency for the above situation is *percent agreement*:

$$P_A = \begin{pmatrix} \text{percent consistent} \\ \text{mastery decisions} \end{pmatrix} \qquad \text{[Eq. 15.10]}$$
$$+ \begin{pmatrix} \text{percent consistent} \\ \text{nonmastery decisions} \end{pmatrix}$$

Equation 15.10 is usually expressed as a decimal fraction. For the example in Table 15.6:

$$P_A = \frac{11}{25} + \frac{9}{25} = \frac{20}{25} = 0.80.$$

The value 0.80 is the ". . . total proportion of consistent classification that occurs *for whatever reason* on the two tests" (Subkoviak, 1980, p. 152).

Cohen's kappa coefficient (k)   Consistency of classification depends not only on the extent of measurement error, but also on the relative numbers of "true masters" in the group. The percent of classification consistency that can

Advance-ment score	Number of test items	Student's true level of functioning*									
		50	55	60	65	70	75	80	85	90	95
6	7	6	10	16	23	33	45	42	28	15	4
7	8	4	7	11	17	26	37	50	34	19	6
8	9	2	4	7	12	20	30	56	40	23	7
8	10	6	10	17	26	38	53	32	18	7	1
9	11	3	7	12	20	31	46	38	22	9	2
10	12	2	4	8	15	25	39	44	26	11	2
11	13	1	3	6	11	20	33	50	31	13	2
12	15	2	4	9	17	30	46	35	18	6	—
17	20	—	1	2	4	11	23	59	35	13	2
19	22	—	—	1	3	7	16	67	42	17	2

Percent of students incorrectly classified as masters | Percent of students incorrectly classified as nonmasters

*The percent of items a student would be able to answer correctly if the entire domain of items were administered.
Source: From M. R. Novick and C. Lewis. "Prescribing Test Length for Criterion-Referenced Measurement." *Problems in Criterion-Referenced Measurement*, Harris et al. (eds.), Center for the Study of Evaluation, University of California, Los Angeles, 1974. Used by permission.

Table 15 • 5   Estimates of the percent of students misclassified when mastery is defined as being able to answer correctly 80% of the items in a domain.

		Results from Form A		Marginal totals
		Mastery	Nonmastery	
Results from Form B	Mastery	11	4	15
	Nonmastery	1	9	10
	Marginal totals	12	13	25

Table 15 • 6 Hypothetical example of how twenty-five pupils were classified on two forms of a test.

be expected by virtue of the group's composition is given by the equation:[15]

$$P_C = \begin{pmatrix} \text{percent} \\ \text{masters} \\ \text{Form A} \end{pmatrix} \times \begin{pmatrix} \text{percent} \\ \text{masters} \\ \text{Form B} \end{pmatrix}$$
$$+ \begin{pmatrix} \text{percent} \\ \text{nonmasters} \\ \text{Form A} \end{pmatrix} \times \begin{pmatrix} \text{percent} \\ \text{nonmasters} \\ \text{Form B} \end{pmatrix} \quad \text{[Eq. 15.11]}$$

For the data in Table 15.6:

$$P_C = \frac{15}{25} \times \frac{12}{25} + \frac{10}{25} \times \frac{13}{25} = \frac{310}{625} = 0.50.$$

The fraction 0.50 is interpreted to mean that in this group you would expect 50% consistent classifications on the basis of chance alone because of the nature of the group.

Two sources contribute to the magnitude of percent agreement, P_A: (a) the quality of the tests and (b) the composition of the group. Cohen's (1960) *kappa coefficient* (κ) removes from P_A the chance effects of the group's composition (P_C) in order to estimate the amount of consistency of decisions contributed by the measuring procedure:

$$\kappa = \frac{P_A - P_C}{1 - P_C} \quad \text{[Eq. 15.12]}$$

[15]What is estimated is the degree of consistency expected to occur by chance when the marginal totals are as specified by the data.

For the group represented by the data in Table 15.6:

$$\kappa = \frac{0.80 - 0.50}{1 - 0.50} = \frac{0.30}{0.50} = 0.60.$$

The fraction 0.60 is interpreted to mean that the tests contribute 60% consistent classification beyond that which is expected by the group's composition.

Both P_A and κ need not be limited to the simple, dichotomous case illustrated here: More than two categories could be used for classifying persons. Formulas for computing them in such cases can be found in Cohen (1960) and Swaminathan et al. (1974). You can also use a test-retest paradigm or judges instead of the alternate forms paradigm illustrated here. The choice between using P_A or κ depends on whether you wish to focus on the total consistent classification, regardless of course of consistency; then you use P_A. If you are mainly concerned about the degree of consistency contributed by the measurement procedure, use κ. Both indices are sensitive to the particular group's composition, the cutoff score used to establish mastery, and errors of measurement. Properties of κ in relation to mastery decisions are reviewed by Subkoviak (1980) and Huynh (1976, 1978).

Summary

This chapter has described the concept of score consistency or reliability and the nature and impact of errors of measurement and several procedures for estimating the reliabilities of a test (Table 15.3). I note that the choice among these various coefficients depends on the kinds of questions the teacher might ask about pupils' scores. Some questions concern the effects of testing at different times or on different occasions, and still other questions express a concern for both of these aspects. Another source of unreliability is score inconsistency resulting from persons scoring a test or judging a performance.

Much of the chapter is devoted to ways in which reliability information can be interpreted. The standard error of measurement estimates the likely size or magnitude of errors. Information from the standard error of measurement should be incorporated into the processes by which pupils' scores are interpreted. Uncertainty intervals, which reflect the likely size of measurement error, should be incorporated into procedures for deciding whether a pupil's true score is above the passing score on a test, or whether the differences observed between two scores reflect true differences or true growth, rather than simply measurement error. I also discuss the possibility that a test may measure some persons more accurately than others. The implication is that the teacher needs to become acquainted with the idiosyncratic nature of the tests that are frequently used, since it is possible that these tests may not conform to the concept of "uniform error" implied by the standard error of measurement. Knowing at which ability levels a test is more (or less) accurate should facilitate interpreting test scores.

The chapter reviews several factors affecting the magnitude of reliability coefficients. Among the factors which result in larger coefficients are the use of better items and longer tests. More homogeneous tests are generally more reliable, for the same length, than heterogeneous tests. Using tests in groups with narrow ranges of ability and/or increasing the time interval between testings are among the factors which result in lowered reliability. Reliability coefficients are statistics computed from samples of examinees drawn from populations and, therefore, are likely to be subject to sampling fluctuations.

I also review how errors of measurement affect classifications, such as, mastery decisions on classroom tests or passing decisions on competency-based examinations in this chapter as well as various procedures for estimating the effects of such errors of classification for individuals and for groups.

Themes

• Validity relates to the soundness of test score interpretations and the usefulness of scores for making decisions about people.

• The validity of a test is specific to particular purposes or decisions and forces the teacher to clearly articulate the decision or purpose intended before selecting the testing procedure to use.

• Evidence from various aspects of validity need to be integrated in order for the teacher to interpret scores meaningfully. Teachers should avoid separate "types of validity" interpretations.

• The teacher, being a professional educator and interpreter of test scores, bears a special responsibility for employing rudimentary principles of validity when using test results.

Terms and Concepts

validity
aspects of validity (content, construct, criterion-oriented)
criteria for judging representativeness of test content
test user's domain vs. test developer's domain
curricular relevance
content taught vs. content tested
procedures used to gather construct validity evidence (logical analysis, correlational studies, experiments)
passage dependency
predictive vs. concurrent validity criterion
judging the worth of criteria

validity of selection decisions
steps in validating selection tests
cross-validation
validity coefficient
predictor test
multiple correlation coefficient
expectancy table
decision consequences (valid, positive, valid negative, false positive, false negative)
selection ratio
base rate
validity for placement decisions
regression line(s)
aptitude treatment interaction

16
VALIDITY
OF
TEST SCORES

This chapter is concerned with the interpretive quality of test scores—the nature of score validity and its various aspects, the kinds of inquiry and evidence needed for each aspect, and the manner in which this evidence is related to specific test uses, decisions, and interpretations. The first section discusses the general nature of test score validity, why validity is necessary for making informed judgments about students, the importance of validity compared to reliability, and an overview of the various aspects of validity. Section two describes content validity, its general nature and the types of judgments one makes to establish the degree of content validity in a test. The section distinguishes two domains of content—the test developer's and the test interpreter's—and stresses the importance of judging a test in relation to its relevance to the test interpreter's content domain.

Section three discusses construct validity and the procedures used to gather evidence about this validity aspect. The concepts in this section are illustrated by applying them to testing a pupil's status in a trait widely used in education. The nature of a teacher's judgments in relation to construct validity is also described. The fourth section describes criterion-oriented validity: the nature and quality of criteria, the validity of selection decisions, and the validity of placement decisions. Emphasis is on judgmental and data interpretation principles. The final section relates the various aspects of validity to one another to show that to meaningfully interpret test scores integrating information from different validity aspects is necessary as is avoiding the mistake of assuming that one aspect of validity is sufficient for making inferences from test scores.

General Nature of Validity Questions

Validity refers to the soundness with which test scores can be interpreted in a particular way or to the usefulness of test scores for a particular purpose. Tests are not unconditionally valid or invalid. The answer to the general question, "Is this test valid?", depends on the purpose for the test and the context in which the test is intended to be used. A test may be valid for some specific purposes or some specific intended interpretations but less valid for others. Therefore, clearly specifying the kinds of interpretations of scores you would like to make or the types of decisions you want to make before investigating a test's validity is important.

To ask about the goodness of scores from a test means to ask if you can expect the scores to give you information about pupils that enables you to make better decisions concerning them. The decisions you make are ultimately informed judgments about the pupils for some purpose or goal. As a professional, your judgments are improved if they are based on sound interpretations of relevant information of known quality: the validity of the information obtained from educational and psychological tests should be expressed in terms of the purpose(s) for which that information is to be used. Since different educational contexts can be identified, it is unlikely that a test which provides valid information in one context can be unconditionally recommended in another. Because of practical requirements, schools frequently use one test for several purposes. Schools may employ a single score, for example, to judge a particular pupil's progress, to divide a class into groups for instructional purposes, and to evaluate the effectiveness of a targeted intervention program, such as Title I. A consequence of using a single test for several purposes is that the particular test will serve some decisions well and others less well.

Precedence of Validity Over Reliability

To be sure, reliability is important, but validity is more important. Reliable test scores need not be valid for a particular intended use. The validity of a test's scores, however, is constrained by the scores' reliability. A seemingly valid test may function poorly because its scores have low reliability. High validity necessitates high reliability. The converse is not true: A test with high reliability may not be valid for a particular purpose.

For example, a teacher wants to measure arithmetic computational skill and could measure this skill very consistently by using a test with a moderately large number of items. But knowing that test scores are consistent is not enough. Before the teacher could judge validity, additional information would be necessary such as: whether the test items sample appropriate arithmetic computation tasks, whether the sample represents the domain of computation tasks, whether the directions are clear, and whether test performance is substantially affected by the examinee's reading skills. Any number of factors might potentially affect test performance; to the extent they operate in a given situation our interpretations of the scores are affected.

Aspects of Validity

Because there is no single validity question, there is no single "validity index" or "validity coefficient." However, different kinds of validity questions do exist. Each question views the test from a somewhat different perspective; each emphasizes a different aspect of the test. Both qualitative and quantitative information answer each question, but the degree of validity a test has for a specific purpose is ultimately a matter that requires your professional judgment as an informed teacher and educator. In the end, you have to integrate a wide variety of kinds of information to decide whether a test is valid for a given set of decisions.

This chapter deals with three basic aspects of validity:

a. *content validity*—the extent the items on a test are representative of the domain or universe that they are supposed to represent.
b. *construct validity*—the extent a test measures the trait, attribute, or mental process it should measure, and whether descriptions of persons in terms of such constructs can follow using the scores from that test (cf. Cronbach, 1971).
c. *criterion-related validity*—the extent scores on a test can be used to infer an individual's likely standing on some other test or variable called a criterion (APA, 1974).

In some books these are called "kinds of validity" rather than aspects of validity.[1]

Content Validity

Example of a Single-Objective Test

Consider this very specific elementary school arithmetic objective (Instructional Objectives Exchange, 1973, p. 11):

> The student will be able to solve a multiplication problem involving a one-digit numeral and a four-digit numeral.

[1]"Many other terms have been used. Examples include synthetic validity, convergent validity, job-analytic validity, rational validity, and factorial validity. In general, such terms refer to specific procedures for evaluating validity rather than to new kinds of interpretative influences. . . . So-called 'face' validity, the mere appearance of validity, is not an acceptable basis for interpretive inferences from test scores" (APA, 1974, p. 26).

A sample test item would be:

$$3{,}175 \times 6$$

The objective implies there would be 90,000 of these multiplication problems in the domain (assuming that only the vertical format of the example was to be used). Any one form of a test of this objective, therefore, would have only a few problems on it. When a test to measure this objective is developed, we, as teachers, can ask: "How representative of the domain is the sample of items comprising the test?" The sample may lack representativeness in the following ways.

The test may include items that are outside of the domain such as the following:

$$6 \times 3{,}175 \qquad 315 \times 27 \qquad 3{,}175 \times 6 = \underline{\hspace{1.5cm}}$$

Although each of these types of items may represent important learning outcomes, they fall outside of the domain of the objective as stated. Hence, a test including them is not representative of the domain and reduces content validity.

The test may include only items from within the boundaries of the domain, but the items included may be unrepresentative "A 'representative' sample is one that re-presents or reproduces the essential characteristics of the universe in their proper proportion and balance" (Lennon, 1956, p. 301). Several ways of "re-presentation" are possible. For example, types of items may appear on the test in proportion to their occurrence in the domain (ecological representation), item-types may appear in proportion to the frequency with which the skills they represent will be used in future instruction or in terms of their general educational importance (cf. Cronbach, 1971). Of the 90,000 problems in this example, only 146 would not involve carrying (renaming). A test consisting mostly or entirely of items from among these 146 would be unrepresentative of the 90,000-item domain implied by the objective. Again, the content validity of the test would be reduced.

Even though the items fall within the boundaries of the domain and have some degree of representativeness, there may be too few items to support a reasonable claim of representativeness Among other things, judgments about the number of items to be included on a test need to take into account the homogeneity of the domain. For example, if all of the 90,000 potential items were essentially alike, each requiring the pupil to use the same mental processes to basically the same degree, then it is likely that a pupil would respond to a large number of items in much the same way as a few items. (See Chapter 4.) Administering a few items then, would support a generalization about how well the pupil would perform on the entire domain. Since in this example such a situation is unlikely, a longer test would be needed before a high degree of content validity could be claimed.

General Nature of Content Validity

As the above example illustrates, content validity involves a judgment about the adequacy of the test as representative of the domain of objectives the test developer claims to be sampling. Content validity judgments are made for tests measuring several objectives as well as those measuring a single, narrow objective. The concept applies to all sorts of tests: achievement tests, aptitude tests, personality tests, student teacher observation schedules, and rating scales. In this chapter, the focus is mostly on achievement tests.[2] The teacher needs to be concerned about the content validity of both published tests and teacher-made tests.

[2]For broader views see APA (1974); CSC, EEOC, DOJ, and DOL (1977); Cronbach (1971); and Guion (1977).

Although a clear description of the domain from which the test developer claims to have sampled is a necessary condition for the assessment of a test's content validity, it is *not a sufficient* condition: Simply writing clear behavioral objectives does not guarantee a test's content validity. As the arithmetic example in this section illustrates, judgments of content validity are based on actually inspecting a test's items and deciding whether: (a) all test items are within the domain boundaries, (2) the test items "represent" the essential characteristics of the domain, and (3) there are enough items on the test to support the intended generalization from test performance to domain performance. Further, judgments need to be made about whether (4) the items and their keyed answers are accurate from the point of view of the content specialist (Cronbach, 1971). This last point implies, among other things, that the content validity of a test will erode over time as the knowledge base of the discipline matures.

Curricular Relevance vs. Content Validity

Test developer's vs. test user's domain   A question closely related to constant validity is whose definition of a domain is the appropriate one: the test developer's or the test user's? A reading test, for example, may emphasize paragraph and sentence reading while not directly measuring word attack skills or vocabulary. A test user, on the other hand, may want these latter areas included in the definition of reading upon which a test battery is built. The disagreement here between user and developer concerns the definition of the domain: what is or is not to be included on the reading test. Content validity as defined here does not deal with this type of disagreement. Rather, *content validity begins with the test developer's domain definition* and asks whether the items on the test represent that domain. If a user's definition of the domain of reading is different from that of the test developer's, then the user needs to find another test devel-oper whose definition corresponds more nearly to that of the user's. The distinction made here is not conventional. Frequently an achievement test manual will request the user to examine the test's items in relation to the local curriculum and to judge the content validity of the test on that basis.

Curricular relevance of a test   To the extent that a particular *test* matches a school's curriculum objectives, the test is relevant to that school's definition of the domain. We call this judgment of the degree of overlap between curriculum and test items the *curricular relevance* of the test.[3] Studying Figure 16.1 may help to clarify the distinction between content validity and curricular relevance. The developer's domain definition and a particular test are shown in the center of the figure. The test is judged content valid if the items on it (shown by both the solid *and* broken *straight* lines) adequately represent the developer's domain. But a particular school's curriculum will not coincide exactly with the developer's domain. Some (but not all) commercial test developers will base a domain definition on material likely to be common to a wide variety of school systems (see Chapter 18), information generally abstracted by reviewing textbook series, syllabi, curriculum guides, and recommendations by professional organizations, teachers, and curriculum experts. As can be seen from Figure 16.1, School A's curriculum matches (overlaps) the developer's domain more than that of School B: we would conclude that the test has more curricular relevance for School A than for School B. School A may or may not decide to use the test depending, among other things, on whether the test's degree of curricular relevance is sufficient for its purposes. It should be obvious from Figure 16.1 that not all of a school's curriculum objectives in a given subject will be covered by a published test.

[3]Similar proposals have been made by others (e.g., Cronbach, 1971; Guion, 1977).

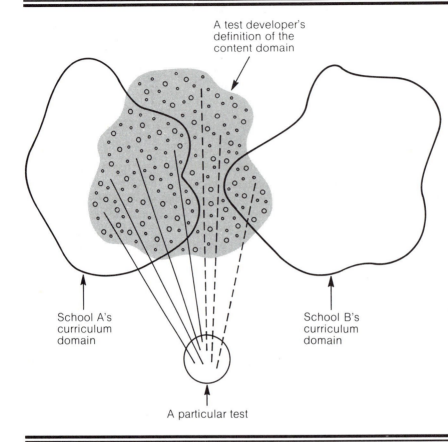

A test developer's definition of the content domain

School A's curriculum domain

School B's curriculum domain

A particular test

Figure 16 • 1 A schematic illustration of the relationship between a test, a test developer's content domain, and the curricular domains of two schools. A test may have content validity, yet may lack curricular relevance for some schools.

Review the actual test items When describing test content to a user, a test developer frequently focuses on the original domain definition used to develop the general test specifications; the fact that item selection procedures may result in a different definition is seldom mentioned. This means it is important to carefully examine the actual test before purchasing it. A checklist for doing this review is given in Table 18.3. The way items for the test are selected may alter the developer's initial domain definition. If item analysis data are used to systematically select test items, certain items are systematically excluded from ever appearing on any form of the test. This may result in lack of domain representativeness and, in effect, redefines the domain (Buros, 1935,

1949, 1977; Cox, 1965; Cronbach, 1971; Kwansa, 1972, 1974; Osburn, 1968). Matching test items to curriculum objectives is not necessarily a simple task but can be done systematically. A useful and relatively easy procedure to learn for doing this is given in Figure 4.3.

Content taught vs. content of the test A question that comes up from time to time is how closely a test should match what was actually taught or what pupils had an opportunity to learn at a particular school. A teacher examining a published test will notice that there will be items covering behaviors the pupils have not been taught. Further, if pupils are grouped within a classroom, or if a pupil's rate through the curriculum is individualized, it is likely that all pupils will not have been exposed to exactly the same curriculum content during a given time period. Even if there is neither grouping or individualization, there are frequently significant teacher-to-teacher differences in content emphasis and in the amount of time pupils spend actively learning and practicing specific content. In studies of the various factors influencing achievement test performance, a persistent research result indicates that the amount of time pupils are actually engaged in learning objectives measured by the tests is correlated with their test scores (Berliner, 1979; Cooley, 1977; Fisher, Berliner, Filby, Marliave, Cahen, Dishaw and Moore, 1978; Fisher, Filby, Marliave, Cahen, Dishaw, Moore, and Berliner, 1978; House, Glass, McLean, and Walker, 1977; Kowal, 1975; Rosenshine, 1979; Walker and Schaffarzick, 1974).

Figure 16.2 illustrates the extent to which four standardized tests differ with respect to their emphases on various arithmetic topics. The data in the figure were obtained by reviewing each test and classifying items in a two-way table of topic-by-arithmetic operation (Freeman, Kuhs, Knappen, & Porter, 1982). Only the topic classifications for one grade level appear in the table. These differences in content coverage point out the importance of carefully reviewing a test before using it to be sure that classroom teaching objectives in class match test emphasis. Otherwise, the test may provide misleading information about both student learning and quality of instruction.

A final point to mention here is that for *some* purposes an over-concern about whether items on a published test cover specific classroom learnings may lead to improper decisions. Presumably a school chooses a published achievement test because the school agrees with the educational importance of the objectives the test measures and accepts the premise that the items adequately sample these important areas. If so, the school may wish to test these objectives even though students may not have received formal classroom instruction in all areas covered in the test. Curriculum specialists and educational evaluators can glean useful information about pupils' status on outcomes deemed important even though they have not had specific instruction in specific areas. On the other hand, it would be unfair to judge a student a poor learner, if that student has had no opportunity to learn the material asked for on the test. Similarly, it would be unfair to judge teachers on material they were not responsible for teaching. (This does not imply that it is fair to judge teachers on the basis of their pupils' test scores in areas for which teachers were responsible. Many factors besides the adequacy of the teacher affect pupil performance on tests.)

Construct Validity

General Nature of Construct Validity

It is not unusual to raise questions about what a test "really measures." You can take a midterm exam in a course, for example, and even though your teacher has explained the nature and content, you may have questions about the exam: "Did the test offer me the opportunity to demonstrate my knowledge of each topic completely? Some items seemed tricky; did my performance depend on my ability to perceive this trickiness? I had hardly enough time and had to rush; was my performance affected by this degree of speediness?" Because a test is seldom a pure measure of the attribute it claims to measure, identifying the factors which affect students' performances on it is necessary before educators can properly interpret scores (e.g., Cronbach, 1970).

When we raise questions about how we should interpret a test result or about what the test really measures, we are actually asking a question about the validity of the test in term of the constructs used to interpret scores on it (Cronbach, 1971; Cronbach and Meehl,

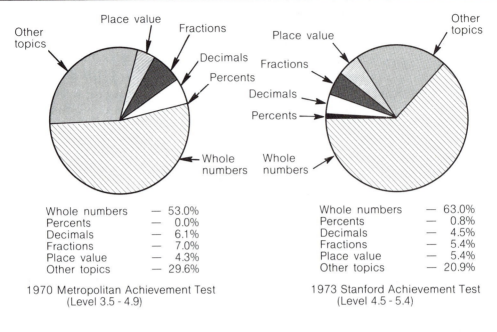

Whole numbers	—	53.0%
Percents	—	0.0%
Decimals	—	6.1%
Fractions	—	7.0%
Place value	—	4.3%
Other topics	—	29.6%

1970 Metropolitan Achievement Test
(Level 3.5 - 4.9)

Whole numbers	—	63.0%
Percents	—	0.8%
Decimals	—	4.5%
Fractions	—	5.4%
Place value	—	5.4%
Other topics	—	20.9%

1973 Stanford Achievement Test
(Level 4.5 - 5.4)

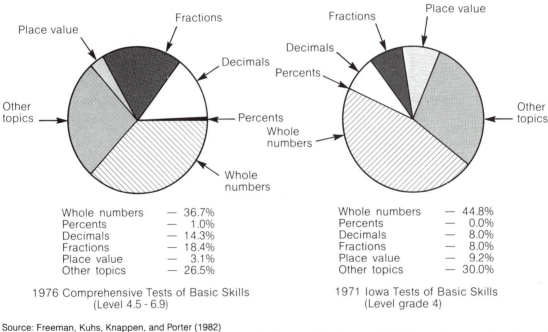

Whole numbers	—	36.7%
Percents	—	1.0%
Decimals	—	14.3%
Fractions	—	18.4%
Place value	—	3.1%
Other topics	—	26.5%

1976 Comprehensive Tests of Basic Skills
(Level 4.5 - 6.9)

Whole numbers	—	44.8%
Percents	—	0.0%
Decimals	—	8.0%
Fractions	—	8.0%
Place value	—	9.2%
Other topics	—	30.0%

1971 Iowa Tests of Basic Skills
(Level grade 4)

Source: Freeman, Kuhs, Knappen, and Porter (1982)

Figure 16 • 2   The percent of items covering various arithmetic topics on each of four standardized achievement tests which might be administered in the spring to a fourth grade class. Note that each test would have a different degree of curricular relevance for a particular school.

1955). This type of validity has come to be known as *construct validity*.[4] Educational terminology abounds with constructs used to interpret test results such as: verbal ability, intelligence, reading readiness, mastery, minimum competence, spelling ability, and self-concept. For our purposes here, constructs are terms and phrases used to explain and/or organize ideas, experiences, or observations within a particular logical framework. Constructs are more than isolated verbal labels; propositions link constructs to one another forming part of a theory[5] and link constructs with observable phenomena in the real world (APA, 1974; Cronbach, 1971; Lord & Novick, 1968; Torgerson, 1958).

Procedures Used as Evidence for Construct Validation

Construct validation consists of constantly looking for evidence that scores on a test which claims to measure a particular construct cannot be explained by other factors unrelated to the construct in question. No single study nor single study method provides all the information needed. Both theories of performance and empirical evidence are used in the process. In general, evidence from three broad methods of inquiry need to be integrated in order to check on the validity of an intended interpretation (Cronbach, 1971):

1. **Logical analysis** By carefully examining a test and the performance it requires and integrating this with knowledge of theory and experience with examinees who have performed in similar situations, you can raise questions about the plausibility of the proposed construct interpretation. As a result, you can often hypothesize explanations for good or poor test performance other than the originally proposed interpretation.

2. **Correlation studies** The theoretical or logical framework which forms the basis for interpreting scores on a test implies that persons with certain scores will behave in certain ways. In the logical framework within which the construct is defined, the construct can be related to certain other constructs and can be predicted to be unrelated to still others. Correlational studies investigate whether these postulated relationships are obtained. If the relationships postulated are not obtained in these correlational studies, the interpretation of test scores in terms of the construct is open to question and doubt.

3. **Experimental studies** Experiments are designed attempting to deliberately modify test scores by introducing certain conditions. If experimental conditions theoretically unrelated to the construct interpretation intended can change test scores, modification of the proposed interpretation is necessary.

Although we can imagine a process through which the test is constructed, hypothesized interpretations and counter-interpretations listed, and studies conducted, the process is not so linear nor logical. A test is developed, revised, and used over a number of years. Experience accumulates and theories develop and change, sometimes long after the test is available for use. As a professional, this means you need to be continually abreast of developments in psychology and education which may lead to a modified interpretation of a test you are using.

Construct Validity of Reading Comprehension Tests

To show the complex and abstract ideas above I have chosen an illustration, based in part on an example in Cronbach (1971), of a common type of test, a reading comprehension test. In

---

[4]The concept of construct validity had its beginnings in the late 1940s and early 1950s; it was formalized by the APA Committee on Psychological Tests (APA, 1954) and has continued to be refined to the present.
[5]Perhaps a primitive theory.

addition to the following example, you should read Chapter 12 to obtain an idea of how factors such as teacher actions, administrative conditions, testwiseness, and test anxiety affect scores. Various methods are used to measure reading comprehension. In this example we focus on a rather typical format: A passage of one or two paragraphs is presented, followed by several multiple-choice questions. The test directions call for the examinee to read each passage and to answer the questions which follow the passage by marking a separate answer sheet. At first glance, it appears that the examinee needs to read and understand the passages in order to answer the questions.

Vernon (1962) did a thorough logical analysis of this type of reading comprehension task; that analysis led to hypothesizing several factors which might account for an examinee's test performance beside reading comprehension. If these factors do alter an examinee's score, then one cannot interpret the test as a pure measure of reading comprehension. Among the factors are the following:

1. *Technical bias*—A passage may refer to a specific topic or theme about which an examinee may have a lot of prior knowledge. For such an examinee, the test is a different kind of task than for another examinee who lacks this specific knowledge. (*Passage dependency* is the term used to describe the degree to which answers to the questions depend on reading and comprehending the passage.)
2. *Speediness*—Many tests are timed. If the time limits are not generous enough, the score may depend on reading speed rather than reading comprehension only.
3. *Attitudes and motivations*—If the way the test is presented or the way the examiner administers the test affects performance, the test will not be a pure measure of reading comprehension. Highly motivated students are likely to score much better than poorly motivated ones.

4. *Sophistication of the examinee*—Examinees who are "test-wise" or who have command of good test-taking strategies are likely to score higher than their peers of equal ability who do not have such test-taking skills.
5. *Test directions*—If an examinee misunderstands the test's directions, it is likely that performance will be adversely affected.
6. *Ability to mark answers*—Most published tests of the type described here require the use of separate answer sheets that can be machine scored. Examinees will differ in the speed and accuracy with which they can mark the correct answer. Frequently, the type of answer sheet used affects the score on the test.

The list above is by no means exhaustive; questions such as these stand as counter-hypotheses to the intended interpretation of a test as a straightforward measure of reading comprehension. In construct validation research, each of these questions is investigated and the data is used to either confirm or reject each as a plausible influence on test performance.

As an example, consider the hypothesis that the examinee's motivation will influence scores on a reading comprehension test. Motivation (itself a construct) is complex, and, of course, no simple "one-shot" study can give a definite answer as to what incentives, under which conditions, can influence scores on a particular test. But a series of investigations with a test can shed considerable light on the influence of motivating factors. One such experiment, which sought to determine the influence of offering prizes on reading scores, is reported in the box. You shouldn't assume that simple incentives, such as "pep talks," prizes, and money will influence the scores of all tests or all types of examinees, nor that they are the only factors which influence test performance (see e.g., Kirkland, 1971).

Can test scores go up if prizes are offered?

Tuinman, Farr, and Blanton (1972) sought to determine the extent to which reading test scores could be increased by offering prizes immediately before giving a posttest which followed an instructional period. Non-problem readers in the seventh and eighth grades were randomly selected and randomly assigned to either an experimental (E) or control (C) group. All students took the *Nelson Reading Test*, Form A (1962) twice; there was a four week interval between testings. Between the two testing sessions, students took their regular school program.

Directions for retesting the E and C groups were different. The C group was told that the reason they were to be retested was to find out how much they had learned. The E group was shown prizes (6 transistor radios @ $4.95, 9 Indiana University sweatshirts, and large candy bars @ 25¢) and given the following directions (p. 217):

"A few weeks ago you took a test and we have now scored your test. We would like to have you try to beat your first test score. We have some prizes for you if you can do better on this than you did on the last test. We don't care who makes the highest score. We want to see who can make *more points* on this test than on the first test. All you need to do is *raise your own score* by as many points as you can. The students who raise their scores the most will win prizes. *Remember,* it's not the student that scores highest that wins; it's the student who *raises his score the most.*

If you are one of the top six students who gain the most points you will win a transistor radio—NOT the six highest scores but the six who improve the most.

If you are one of the next nine students who raise their scores the most points, you will win one of these IU shirts.

And if you raise your score even as little as one point, you get one of these candy bars. So everyone who gets even just one point higher will get a prize.

If you do not score any higher on this test than the first test there are no prizes.

It's not hard, just try to beat your own score. Compete with no one but yourself. All you have to do is work harder and try to do more items and more of them correctly than you did last time. Raise your score and take home one of the prizes."

Some of the results of the study appear here.

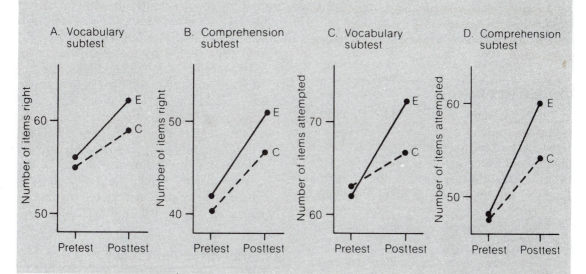

A. Vocabulary subtest B. Comprehension subtest C. Vocabulary subtest D. Comprehension subtest

Source: Based on data reported by Tuinman, J. J., Farr, R., and Bianton, B. E. "Increases in Test Scores as a Function of Material Rewards." *Journal of Educational Measurement,* Vol. 9, 1972, pp. 218–220, Tables 1, 5. Copyright 1972, National Council on Measurement in Education, Washington, D.C.

Box 16 • 1

Correlational studies could be conducted as well.[6] A researcher may, for example, correlate the scores obtained by pupils on a multiple-choice test of reading comprehension with scores of the same pupils from an individually administered oral test given after they have read similar passages. If both procedures measure reading comprehension, then one would expect a positive and significant correlation. If the correlation were low, the scores on the two measures would be unrelated: Apparently they would be measuring different attributes. Additional research would be needed to determine the cause of the low correlation, and which procedure—the multiple-choice test or the oral test—truly measures reading comprehension.

Keep in mind that the magnitude of a correlation coefficient may be lowered by several conditions that are extraneous to the relationship between the traits (see Chapter 3). The reliability of the measures used in correlational construct validation studies is of special concern: The relationships predicted to exist by a logical framework or theory may fail to be detected by correlations because of measurement errors which lower the correlation coefficient.

The Teacher's Role

A teacher cannot be expected to conduct extensive studies to validate the interpretations given to test scores. But test developers and test publishers can be expected to provide information in the test manual concerning the intended interpretation, its theoretical basis,

and the extent to which the intended interpretation has been substantiated (APA, 1974). One example of the kind of research program underlying an achievement test is listed in the Additional Readings at the end of this book. There are limits to what the developer and publisher can provide: It is unreasonable to expect exhaustive evidence on all aspects of construct validity or on all possible counter-interpretations. It is desirable, however, that the test manual provide data on the extent to which test scores are influenced by constructs different from those the developer intends (APA, 1974).

Professional teachers will need to use a great deal of judgment when interpreting test results in terms of the various constructs taught in their teaching methods courses. For example, the validity of such interpretations as reading comprehension, mathematical ability, or intelligence is always open to question in a particular group of students. The possibility of bias in test content or in the testing process toward (or against) certain pupils should form part of the construct interpretation of tests as well. But the teacher should not be overly cautious and avoid test interpretations entirely. The teacher should have a sensitivity or an awareness of the strengths and limitations of particular tests and a willingness to examine the tests carefully and to consider reasonable counter-interpretations of test performance for certain students. Professional journals that deal with measurement topics and with current developments in the substantive area of the tests are resources; reading them will help keep the teacher informed. Additional discussion of construct validity is found in Chapter 17.

Criterion-Oriented Validity

Criterion-oriented (or criterion-related) validity questions concern the extent to which scores on a test permit inferences about examinees' likely standing on another measure called a criterion. A familiar example is the use of a

---

[6]No single correlation coefficient can establish the construct validity of a particular interpretation of a test's scores. Among the methods of studying construct validity via correlations are multitrait-multimethod studies (Campbell & Fiske, 1959), multimethod factor analysis (Jackson, 1969, 1975, 1977), confirmatory factor analysis (Werts, Jöreskog, & Linn, 1972), and path analysis (e.g., Blalock, 1964). An introduction comparing several methods may be found in Lomax (1978; Lomax & Algina, 1979); more complex treatments are found in Boruch, Larkin, Wolins, and McKinney (1970) and in Schmitt, Coyle, and Saari (1977).

scholastic aptitude test and the high school grade-point average (HSGPA) to help a college admissions committee estimate each applicant's future performance during the first year of college. The criterion measure most often used in this situation is the college grade-point average (CGPA) at the end of the first term or first year. Thus, HSGPA and the scholastic aptitude test are used to predict each applicant's standing on the criterion, the CGPA. One sort of criterion-oriented validity concerns the evidence related to the validity of such selection procedures. Less familiar, perhaps, but also in the realm of this aspect of validity are procedures to validate tests used with placement and classification decisions such as assigning pupils to different instructional groups. A third variety of criterion-oriented validity concerns whether evidence supports using a new or abbreviated test as a substitute for an older or more elaborate procedure.

Distinctions are frequently made between two types of criterion-oriented validity: predictive validity and concurrent validity (APA, 1974). *Predictive validity* evidence relates to the extent to which a person's future performance on a criterion can be estimated or predicted from prior test performance. *Concurrent validity* evidence concerns the extent to which current standing on a criterion can be estimated from a score obtained from a currently administered test. The distinction is important because the time interval between administering the test and obtaining criterion measures may affect the observed degree of relationship between the two measures.

Note that criterion-oriented validity is different than criterion-referenced testing. I explain the latter in the next chapter.

As with other aspects of validity, no single number is sufficient evidence. Correlation coefficients are the basic statistical indices used in criterion-oriented studies (but often other statistical indices are equally appropriate). You should not accept a single coefficient as sufficient validity evidence for at least four reasons (APA, 1974): (a) conditions change so that the exact circumstances under which the initial study was conducted no longer exist; (b) no single, most appropriate criterion against which a test can be validated for all situations exists; (c) a single study seldom uses a sample of examinees that is representative of every test user's population; and (d) many times a small number of examinees has been used in the validity study for practical reasons making the results subject to large sampling fluctuations.

The Criterion

Your judgments about whether the test developer has provided enough evidence for the criterion-oriented validity of the test scores depend on your decision about whether an appropriate criterion has been used. It is so difficult to obtain suitable criterion measures against which tests can be validated that this has been dubbed "the criterion problem" (Thorndike, 1949).

Kinds of criteria A variety of criteria have been used in validation studies. Personnel classification and selection research in government and industry have tended to use the four general types: production (quantity and quality of goods, sales), personal data (accidents on the job, length of service, group membership, training course grades), samples of job performance, and judgments by others (checklists, supervisors' ratings) (Lawshe & Balma, 1966). In education, criterion measures frequently tend to be of three types: achievement test scores; ratings, marks, and other quantified judgments; and career data. A common example of the first is when a reading test given at the end of the first grade serves as a criterion for a reading readiness test. Using grade-point averages to validate an admissions test has been mentioned already. Sometimes teachers' ratings of pupils' self-concept, sociability, and so on are used as criterion measures. Among other procedures, the developers of the *California Test of Personality*, for example, compared teachers' ratings of their pupils' personality adjustment with the responses these pupils made to the adjustment items on the personality questionnaire (Thorpe, Clark, & Tiegs, 1953). Vocational interest inventories and sometimes tests of general mental ability use career data as criteria. College out-of-class accomplishments served as a criterion in a series of studies by Holland (summarized by American College Testing Program, 1973) in an effort to validate a high school out-of-class accomplishments checklist. These out-of-class accomplishment scales in areas such as art, leadership, music, science, speech, and writing eventually became part of a college admissions test battery of the ACT program. Table 16.1 displays some of these validity coefficients. It should be noted, too, that nearly all criterion measures are incomplete; they represent only part of the attainment of the ultimate behavior series the test would like to predict.

Judging the worth of criteria Criterion measures are evaluated in four broad areas (Thorndike, 1949): (a) relevance to the long-term or ultimate real-life criterion, (b) degree of reliability, (c) extent of bias against individuals or groups, and (d) practical problems of availability and/or convenience. What is most often of predictive interest is one or more ultimate criteria (Thorndike, 1949; Lindquist, 1951; Cronbach, 1971). But such ultimate criteria frequently don't occur until many years after the initial measurements on the predictor test have been taken. In such cases, intermediate criteria are used, and a rationale similar to construct validation is needed to justify their use (Thorndike, 1949; Cronbach, 1971). In educational testing direct measurement of the ultimate criterion behavior series is seldom possible (see Lindquist, 1951).

If test scores have low reliability, their correlation with other measures will be lowered. Frequently, a test may be quite reliable but the measures of the criterion against which it is to be correlated will be unreliable. Error of measurement is considered to be unsystematic: If the scores on a criterion are simply "noise" or random error, no test will be able to predict them.

Other types of errors can be systematic, rather than random such as, when supervisors' ratings favor males over females or when a criterion measure unnecessarily favors those persons with high verbal skills. Systematic bias leads to criterion measures which are biased against certain types of individuals or certain groups: Irrelevant factors such as these lower the validity of the criterion measures.

Finally it should be noted that, while practical considerations will place a limit on the degree to which the ultimate criterion can be

Area of accomplishment	Correlations			
	Freshman year		Sophomore year	
	503 Men	592 Women	1,373 Men	1,419 Women
Art	.41	.49	.44	.51
Leadership	.29	.25	.28	.35
Music	.41	.35	.49	.39
Science	.31	.22	.40	.24
Speech	.34	.44	.33	.39
Writing	.43	.44	.45	.46

Note: This table is constructed from data presented by Richards, Holland, and Lutz (1969).
Source: From *Assessing Students on the Way to College: Technical Report for the ACT Assessment Program*, Vol. 1, p. 157, Table 5.26. Copyright © 1973 by the American College Testing Program. Used by permission of the ACT.

Table 16 • 1
Relation of ACT out-of-class accomplishment scales to college out-of-class accomplishments.

measured, they should not be the driving forces. Sometimes convenient and available measures are used as surrogates for criterion measures that are more appropriate and which could have been obtained by the investigator. As a result, criterion-oriented validity is lessened.

Validity for Selection Decisions

Selection decisions follow the pattern depicted by Figure 1.2: Of those who apply, some are selected, while others are rejected; those rejected are no longer of concern of the institution. Familiar examples of selection situations include admissions to colleges and universities, scholarship competitions, and hiring persons to fill job openings. In each of these situations one or more tests are used to obtain information and this (along with other) information is used to accept some persons while rejecting others. Rejection for a job can occur at any point in the selection process: after a preliminary interview, by examining the application blanks, after obtaining test results, after an in-depth interview, after investigating previous experience or employment, and after screening by the person or department directly in charge of the job (Uhrbrock, 1936). Having a "reject" category is the key to distinguishing selection decisions from others. The following are placement or classification decisions, rather than selection decisions: assigning students to reading groups; giving some kindergarteners additional training in perceptual skills and others only the regular curriculum; tracking students; and assigning some students to remedial programs and others to advanced placement programs. In each of these decision contexts, all pupils are assigned to some type of "treatment" and/or "program of instruction"—the school system (institution) is accountable for pupils; no rejection per se occurs. This section of the chapter applies to selection decisions and not to these latter types of decisions.

Ideally, a systematic and rational process is used to validate the procedures ultimately used for selection. The procedure below is frequently recommended (e.g., Cronbach, 1970). An overview appears in the diagram in Figure 16.3.

1. *Job or task analysis*—An analysis is made of the job or task for which persons are to be selected to identify the abilities, skills and knowledge needed for successful performance as well as specifying what criteria operationally define successful performance.

2. *Choose or develop measures*—Particular tests or measurement procedures are identified which appear to measure the job requirements or appear to be able to predict success. Among these categories of variables used to predict educational outcomes are (Schwarz, 1971): entry skill levels, achievement tests, school grades, general scholastic aptitude tests, specific aptitude tests, biographic information, interest questionnaires (e.g., preferences for certain occupations or activities), and personality tests. Measures of the criterion are identified at this stage, too. If the desired tests are not available, they have to be constructed.

3. *Administer experimental selection tests*—A representative sample of applicants is chosen, and the potentially useful selection tests are administered. *Ideally, this group is then admitted to the job or school without regard to their performance on the tests because the tests—and not members of the group—are under study.* To select on the basis of these experimental tests would bias the results, not allowing the empirical relationship between test performance and criterion success to be clearly determined. Frequently, this step is short-circuited due to pressures of cost, convenience, or practicality. Concurrent validity studies, for example, frequently administer the experimental tests to those already on the job

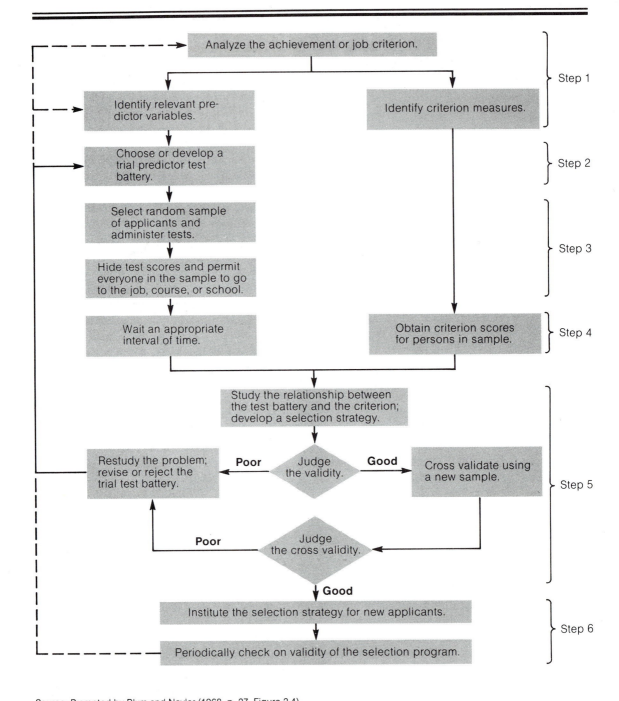

Source: Prompted by Blum and Naylor (1968, p. 27, Figure 2.4).

Figure 16 • 3   Schematic diagram of the idealized process of validating
selection tests.

and collect criterion measures nearly at the same time. As I have said before, the time interval between measures and the range of talent in the group often affect the observed degree of relationship between the predictor tests and the criterion measures.

4. *Criterion data are collected*—After persons have been in school or on the job some time, their criterion performance is measured. When there is a time interval between the administration of the trial battery of selection tests and the measurement of criterion performance, the study is often referred to as a **predictive validity study**.

5. *Study the relationship between (criterion) success and each test in the trial battery*—This step permits the establishment of an empirical relationship between one or a combination of selection test scores and the criterion measures. This study of a relationship will ultimately lead to the elimination of the tests that fail to predict criterion scores satisfactorily and which, therefore, will not be useful as selection tests. Eliminating one-half of the trial tests because of a failure to predict the criterion or because they provide redundant information is not unusual (Cronbach, 1970). Frequently a statistical equation called a *regression equation* is used to estimate applicants' criterion scores from knowledge of their selection test scores. The procedure calls for tailoring the equation of the results obtained from the experimental group in order to minimize errors of estimation. However, when this equation is applied to a second sample, errors of estimation are larger because the equation is not tailored to it. The process of checking the validity of a prediction equation tailored to one sample by applying it to a second sample from the same population is called *cross-validation*.

6. *Instituting and periodically checking on the selection procedure*—Once examiners have identified and cross-validated the best predictor tests and procedures, they can put the selection program in place. But as persons and conditions change over time, the initial validities will erode. Periodically checking and revalidating the procedures used will assure that the initial goals of selection are maintained or modified appropriately.

Interpreting validity coefficients The usual procedure when studying the **predictive or concurrent validity of a test is to compute correlations between the test scores and the criterion scores**. Such a correlation is sometimes referred to as a *validity coefficient*, although, as I have said, no single number is appropriate to judge the merits of a test. Chapter 3 introduced the correlation coefficient and the scatter diagram and noted that the higher the correlation, the more accurately could the scores on a second variable be predicted from the scores on a first. In the selection decision context, concern is with how well the criterion scores can be predicted from the selection test[7] scores. One would examine the correlations of various tests with the criterion to judge this aspect of validity. If Test A correlates with college grades better than Test B, Test A would likely be chosen because all things being equal, it has the highest predictive validity.[8] Note that realistically one wouldn't expect perfect validity nor a correlation of 1.00.

Some examples of validity coefficients are given in Table 16.2. To interpret whether a particular test has a relatively "good" validity coefficient, you need to become familiar with

[7]The selection test is sometimes called the *predicator test*.

[8]Note that you cannot judge from the correlation coefficient the likely size of the errors that may be made when a test is used to predict a criterion score. (This is analogous to the idea that a reliability coefficient cannot be used to judge the likely size of errors of measurement.) An index that can estimate the likely size of errors of prediction is called the *standard error of estimate* and is given by the equation $SD_{Est} = SD_y \sqrt{1 - r_{xy}^2}$. For an elementary discussion see Anastasi (1982, p. 159).

Test	Sample	Criterion	Validity coefficient	Confidence interval[a]
American College Testing Program Composite	4100 freshmen at a highly selective university	1st semester college GPA	.27[b]	.24–.30
College Entrance Examination Board Scholastic Aptitude Test Total	1750 freshmen at university above	1st semester college GPA	.29[b]	.24–.33
Percentile rank in high school graduating class	4280 freshmen at university above	1st semester college GPA	.43[b]	.41–.45
Differential Aptitude Tests: Verbal Reasoning	72 twelfth graders in a Texas school	Spring semester grades in an enriched English course	.39[c]	.17–.57
Numerical Ability	236 eighth grade boys in a Texas school	Spring semester grades in a general mathematics course	.63[c]	.55–.70
Modern Language Aptitude Test Total	176 adults in USAF intensive spoken Mandarin Chinese course	Grades after 1 week	.62[d]	.52–.70

[a]95% confidence interval using Fisher's z; [b]Aleamoni and Oboler (1977); [c]Bennett, Seashore, and Wesman (1974); [d]Carroll and Sapon (1959); see also Chapter 21.

Table 16 • 2 Examples of validity coefficients for different paper-and-pencil tests.

the types of criteria typically used, the population being tested, and the typical correlations past investigators have found. In Table 16.2, for example, the first three correlations are lower than what you might find in other schools—schools that may be less selective and, therefore, have a wider range of scholastic aptitude among their freshmen. See the extent of college-to-college fluctuations in correlation coefficients in Figure 3.9. Also, the correlations in Table 16.2 are based on *enrolled freshmen*, rather than *applicants;* this further restricts the range of ability and lowers the correlation. You can get an idea of the difference between the number of applicants and the number of enrolled freshmen (for a different college) from the graph in Box 16.2. If all who applied to a college were admitted and persisted through the first term, the correlation between the admissions test scores and college GPA might be, say, 0.75 or 0.80. On the other hand, if only the top-scoring 30% are admitted and persist, the observed correlation for this group might be 0.50. Most schools have data for this type of restricted group rather than for the full applicant population. Since it is the full applicant population on which validity information is needed, data on the restricted group underestimate the validity of the test for selection decisions.[9] (Other examples appear in Table 3.6.)

Each correlation shown in Table 16.2 reflects the relationship between one predictor test and one criterion measure. When several predictor tests are available, combining the scores on the different tests for each person is possible as is computing the correlation between this combination of predictor test scores and the criterion. Such a correlation coefficient is called a *multiple correlation coefficient* or *a multiple R*.

[9]A statistical procedure which estimates the effect of restriction in range is available (e.g., Lord & Novick, 1968), but in some cases such estimates may be inadequate (Novick & Thayer, 1969).

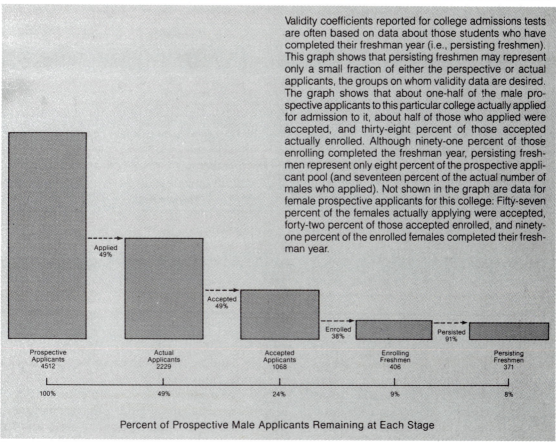

Validity coefficients reported for college admissions tests are often based on data about those students who have completed their freshman year (i.e., persisting freshmen). This graph shows that persisting freshmen may represent only a small fraction of either the perspective or actual applicants, the groups on whom validity data are desired. The graph shows that about one-half of the male prospective applicants to this particular college actually applied for admission to it, about half of those who applied were accepted, and thirty-eight percent of those accepted actually enrolled. Although ninety-one percent of those enrolling completed the freshman year, persisting freshmen represent only eight percent of the prospective applicant pool (and seventeen percent of the actual number of males who applied). Not shown in the graph are data for female prospective applicants for this college: Fifty-seven percent of the females actually applying were accepted, forty-two percent of those accepted enrolled, and ninety-one percent of the enrolled females completed their freshman year.

Percent of Prospective Male Applicants Remaining at Each Stage

Source: "New Graphs" (1979, p. 4)

Box 16 • 2

Although a weighted combination of several tests, each measuring different abilities and each correlating with the criterion, usually improves the prediction, there are limits. Intuitively, you might conclude that, say, a combination of 10 different predictor test scores would predict a person's criterion score better than would 3 or 4 predictor tests. However, there is seldom any significant improvement in prediction (correlation) when more than 3 or 4 predictor tests are combined, as the results shown in Table 16.3 illustrate. High school standing (percentile rank) is the best single

predictor but little predictive validity is gained after the combination of SAT: Total score and ACT: English score is added to the predictor battery. The best combination of predictor tests occurs when one chooses tests that correlate little or zero with each other, but each of which correlates highly with the criterion.

Expectancy tables Another way to interpret predictive validity data is to make an expectancy table. An *expectancy table* is a grid or two-way table that permits one to say how likely it is for a person with a specific selection test

A. Correlation of single measures with first semester GPA for college freshmen	
Predictor	**Correlation**
High school percentile rank (HSPR)	.429
CEEB Scholastic Aptitude Test	
Verbal score (SAT:V)	.268
Total score (SAT:T)	.290
American College Testing Program	
English score (ACT:E)	.259
Cooperative School and Ability Tests	
Quantitative score (SCAT:Q)	.201
Total score (SCAT:T)	.272

B. Multiple correlations with GPA for various combinations	
Tests	**Multiple R**
HSPR	.429
HSPR + (SAT:T)	.449
HSPR + (SAT:T) + (ACT:E)	.453
HSPR + (SAT:T) + (ACT:E) + (SCAT:Q)	.455
HSPR + (SAT:T) + (ACT:E) + (SCAT:Q) + (SCAT:T)	.456
HSPR + (SAT:T) + (ACT:E) + (SCAT:Q) + (SCAT:T) + (SAT:T)	.459

Table 16 • 3
What happens to the multiple correlation when additional tests are added to the predictor battery at a particular college?

Source: Aleamoni and Oboler (1977, pp. 9–10, Tables 1, 2). Used by permission of Dr. Aleamoni.

score to attain each criterion level. Table 16.4 can be used to illustrate how an expectancy table is developed. First a table is constructed, such as Table 16.4A, in which each cell contains a frequency telling the number of persons with a particular test score who attained a particular criterion measure (i.e., course grade). For example, 15 students had test scores between 60 and 69. Three of these 15 students attained a course grade of "D," 5 students a grade of "C," 6 a grade of "B," and 1 student attained an "A." Second, each cell frequency in Table 16.4A is divided by the corresponding *row* total, converted to a percent, and put in an expectancy table such as Table 16.5B. The percents are interpreted as probabilities to answer such questions as, "What is the probability at this school that a person with a predictor test score of 65 will succeed in this course?" Referring to Table 16.4B, it is seen that of those individuals with scores between 60 and 69, 33% (5 persons) obtained a grade of "C," 40% (6 persons) obtained a grade of "B," and 7% (1 person) received an "A." Three

"Ds" and no "Fs" were given to persons with scores between 60 and 69.

Expectancy tables such as this help parents and students interpret predictor test scores as well. Thus, if an expectancy table is made for a particular college relating admissions test scores to freshmen grades, an educator can interpret the scores in terms of a student's chances of obtaining various grade point averages. Such an interpretation of scores gives more information than a norm-referenced score such as a percentile rank gives. Note that when interpreting test results via expectancy tables, you should observe common sense cautions. For example, predictor tests seldom (if ever) measure student initiative, persistence, or motivation. Thus, they cannot predict with certainty what *this particular* student will do. Rather, the table represents the experience of other students in the past and can offer some guidance only.

Decision consequences Still another way to interpret validity for selection decisions is in

A. Frequency of grades for each predictor score level

Predictor test score	Number of pupils receiving each grade					
	F	D	C	B	A	Totals
80–89			1	3	1	5
70–79		1	4	5	2	12
60–69		3	5	6	1	15
50–59		4	8	5	1	18
40–49	1	5	8	4		18
30–39	1	6	5	3		15
20–29	2	5	4	1		12
10–19	1	2	1			4
0–9	1					1
Totals	6	26	36	27	5	100

B. Expectancy table made by converting frequencies into percents

Predictor test score	Percent of pupils receiving each grade					
	F	D	C	B	A	Totals
80–89			20	60	20	100
70–79		8	33	42	17	100
60–69		20	33	40	7	100
50–59		22	44	28	6	100
40–49	6	28	44	22		100
30–39	7	40	33	20		100
20–29	17	42	33	8		100
10–19	25	50	25			100
0–9	100					100

Table 16 • 4
The development of an expectancy table for a hypothetical set of 100 pupils. The expectancy table tells the probability of pupils at each predictor test level getting each grade level of the course.

terms of whether using a particular test will lead to more correct decisions than simply choosing the persons either at random or by another means. Administrators ask in effect, "If we accept a person by using a test, how likely is it that the person will be successful; if we reject a person, how likely are we to be correct in asserting that the person will be unsuccessful?" The answer to these questions will depend on three things: (a) the proportion of the applicant population who can be successful (called the *base rate*), (b) the proportion of the applicant population which must be selected to fill the available slots (called the *selection ratio*), and (c) the correlation between the selection test and the criterion.[10] With

[10]Compare this statement to the one made with respect to the consistency of mastery (classification) decisions in Chapter 15.

respect to base rate, for example, if the entire applicant population can perform successfully on the criterion, then no matter how persons are selected, those accepted will always be successful; conversely, if no person in the applicant population can ever perform successfully on the criterion, no selection procedure would be useful. With respect to selection ratio, for example, if one must accept 95 out of 100 applicants, no selection test is going to offer much improvement over merely selecting persons at random. But, if one has to select only 5% of the applicants, even a test of modest validity offers substantial improvement over chance selection.

Ideally, in order to study the decision consequences of using a test for selection, a special study is conducted in which a random sample of applicants takes the proposed selec-

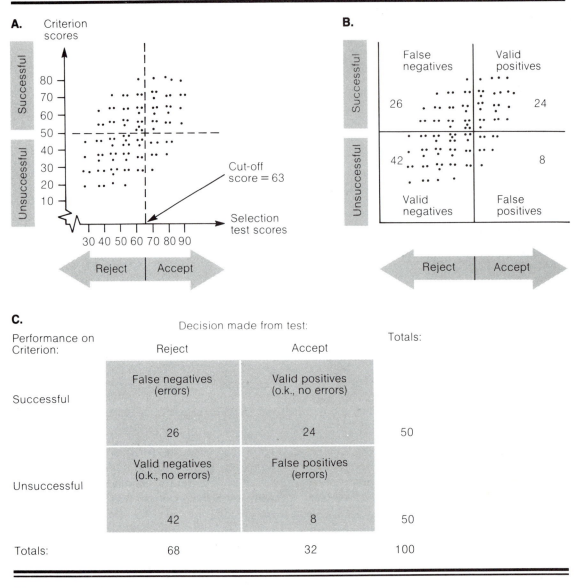

Figure 16 • 4   Hypothetical data illustrating the interpretation of validity coefficients by examining the consequences of acceptance and rejection.

tion test, and all these applicants are permitted to go to the job, school, course, or whatever (see Figure 16.4). After an appropriate time interval, criterion measures are obtained for each person. A scatter diagram is made to show the relation between selection test scores and criterion scores.[11] The consequences (to the institution) of selecting and rejecting various people are studied by marking the min-

[11]Other, more statistically sophisticated means of studying decision consequences in selection are beyond the scope of this book.

imally acceptable criterion score and the cut-off score on the selection test on the scatter diagram.

Consider the scatter diagram in Figure 16.4 in which it is assumed that (a) the correlation between the selector test and the criterion is $r = 0.60$, (b) "minimal success" is defined as having a criterion sccore of 50 or higher, (c) fifty percent of the applicants can be successful (i.e., score above 50 on the criterion) and (d) that 32 percent of the applicants are to be accepted (i.e., the cut-off score is 63 on the selection test). Figure 16.4(A) shows dotted vertical and horizontal lines drawn perpendicularly from the cut-off score and minimal success score, respectively, dividing the scatter diagram into quadrants. These quadrants are labeled in Figure 16.4(B) and the number of persons in each is tallied.

In the upper right quadrant are found those persons who can be successful, *and* who were accepted. These 24 persons are called *valid positives. False positives* are the 8 persons in the lower right quadrant: They were accepted, but fail to perform successfully on the criterion; these represent one type of selection error. In the lower left quadrant are 42 *valid negatives:* Persons who, because of low test scores, would be rejected, and who also fail to perform successfully on the criterion. Finally, in the upper left quadrant are *false negatives:* These persons scored below the cut-off score and, consequently, would be rejected but can perform successfully. These 26 represent yet another type of error in selection: failing to choose qualified persons when a particular cut-off score is used. Figure 16.4(C) summarizes this in tabular form.

The relationship between the magnitude of the validity coefficient, the proportion of the applicants selected (selection ratio), and the overall percentage of correct decisions is shown in Table 16.5. This table assumes that the base rate is 50 percent. Notice that for any particular selection ratio, there is an increase in the percentage of correct decisions as the test validity increases. The table shows that

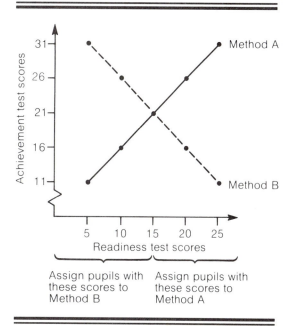

Figure 16 • 5   A hypothetical relationship between readiness test scores and average achievement scores under two different methods of instruction. This is one pattern of results that provides evidence for placement validity.

generally the highest overall percentage of correct decisions is made when about half of those who apply are selected. The reason why *overall* benefits decline as the selection ratio gets smaller is that the number of *false negatives gets larger* when the cut-off score is set higher. Not shown in the table is the fact that as the cut-off score gets higher (i.e., a smaller selection ratio), there are *fewer false positives.* Raising the cut-off score increases false negatives and decreases false positives. Lowering the cut-off score will have the opposite effect.

When an institution focuses only on those selected, and ignores talent or "opportunity" lost, then the values in Table 16.5 are not so important. In education, however, false negatives are likely to be of social concern. Persons not selected but who could succeed represent a potential loss to society. Thus, from

Validity coefficient	Percentage of overall correct decisions when the selection ratio is:		
	.50	.30	.10
.00	50	50	50
.20	56	55	53
.40	63	61	56
.50	67	64	57
.60	70	67	57
.70	75	71	59
.80	80	74	60
1.00	100	80	60

Table 16 • 5
Percentage of correct decisions for various selection ratios and validity coefficients when the base rate is fifty percent.

Note: Percent of correct decisions includes both valid negatives and valid positives. Percentages derived from Taylor and Russell (1939) tables.

this perspective, Table 16.5 represents a broader view of the value of selection tests.

Validity for Placement Decisions

Placement decisions, introduced in Chapter 1, are characterized by: (a) the assignment of students to different levels of the same general type of instruction, (b) there is no rejection, those not placed at one level are assigned to another, and (c) in the end everyone is accounted for and remains within the concern of the institution. The classic example at the elementary school level is the practice of grouping for reading at the beginning of first grade: Those with low readiness scores are given one method of instruction (i.e., the instruction they receive is different) while those scoring high are given another. At the end of first grade, a reading achievement test is administered. The end-of-year criterion test for both methods is generally the same, but the methods (often called instructional treatments) vary somewhat in pace and content.

The placement test in this example is a readiness test and the appropriate validity question to ask is: Does the differential assignment of students to the methods of instruction on the basis of test scores lead to increased learning? The increase is measured against what would have resulted if there had been no differential assignment—everyone

being assigned to one of the methods. Unlike selection tests, which seek to predict success under one treatment or job setting at a time, placement tests seek to predict to which one of several treatments a student should be assigned in order to make the most progress.

Evidence to support validity for placement To get an idea of the kind of evidence needed to support the validity for placement decisions, consider the following experiment. Suppose first you administer a readiness test to everyone, and then you assign half of the students at random to Method A (an accelerated pace instruction) and the remaining half to Method B (a slower paced instruction). At the end of the year, you administer the same achievement test to both groups. This achievement test serves as the criterion. If you compute the average achievement test score for each group, you might find the following:

Mean for Method A = 21
Mean for Method B = 21.

Your intuition might lead you to conclude that the methods work equally well, and, therefore, you should assign all students to one method; the other method should be eliminated. But, before you conclude this, suppose you study how the pupils' achievement results related to their readiness test scores. You might find the following:

Mean for:	Readiness score level: 5 10 15 20 25	Overall mean for each group
Method A:	11 16 21 26 31	21
Method B:	31 26 21 16 11	21

It is clear from this data that the two methods are not equally effective for all pupils. Those with readiness score 5, for example, do much better with Method B (mean = 31) than with Method A (mean = 11). The opposite occurs for those with high readiness scores. It is only those with middle-level readiness scores (i.e., 15) for whom the two methods average the same. The readiness test provides *additional information* that indicates which students should be assigned to the different methods. Figure 16.5 graphs these results.

The lines (called *regression lines*) relate final achievement results to initial readiness scores. They cross at a readiness score of 15; thus, those scoring above 15 on this test should be assigned to Method A because, on the average, Method A leads to higher achievement for these students. Those scoring below 15 on the readiness test should be assigned to Method B. If a readiness test developer provided evidence of the type in this hypothetical example, then there would be support for the validity of the readiness test as an aid to placement decisions.

Practically no test follows the pattern of Figure 16.5 because little is known about how different kinds of abilities interact with various treatments or methods of instruction and because it is difficult to design instructional procedures that capitalize on specialized, rather than general, pupil aptitudes. Figure 16.6(A to F) shows some possible results of studies which investigate the placement validity of tests. Notice that only certain general patterns of results (illustrated by Panels C and F) provide the evidence needed to support differ-

ential placement. Another name for these placement supporting patterns is *disordinal aptitude treatment interaction*.[12]

Research evidence for differential placement validity is generally discouraging to date mainly because of the ways in which research has been conducted. Further, when treatments and abilities do interact, their relationship tends to be much more complex than the simple figures in this section depict. Given the vast range of possible variations in teachers, pupils, and methods of instruction, probably no test will possess the kind of *placement* validity outlined in this chapter in a variety of school situations. It is likely, however, that instruction can be differentiated on the basis of the specific prerequisite skills and knowledge needed (Cronbach & Snow, 1977), and that this can form the basis for placement.

Relating the Aspects of Validity in order to Meaningfully Interpret Test Scores

Content, criterion-oriented, and construct validities are not separate types of validity, but aspects of a broad process of validating the interpretations and uses we make of test scores. In the daily lives of pupils and tests, a teacher is constantly faced with the questions, "What do Megan or Bob's test scores mean?" and "How shall they be interpreted?" The discussion of the preceding sections separately examined several specific questions of interpretation, focusing on different aspects of the general question, "Is this test valid?" Table 16.6 summarizes these separate aspects, the questions to which they are specifically addressed, and the techniques often used to answer them.

There is a danger in considering each aspect separately: By gathering evidence about only one aspect of validity you may come to

[12]For more information on the relation of aptitudes and instructional methods see Cronbach and Snow (1977).

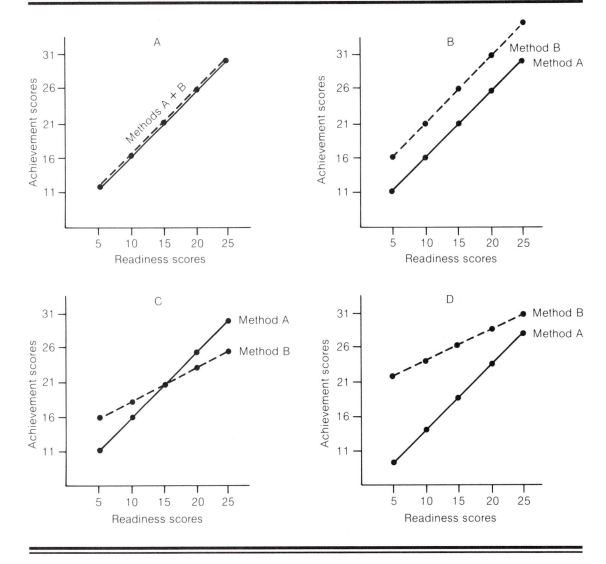

Figure 16 • 6 Examples of possible results of placement test validation studies.

the false conclusion that all interpretations of the test have been validated (Cronbach, 1971; Guion, 1974; Messick, 1981a,b). It is better to speak about evidence showing a test can be used for a specific interpretation or purpose than to speak about the validity of a test for general purposes.

Most educators interpret test scores very broadly, going beyond the mere description of which behaviors or items on the test or in the domain the examinee answered correctly. They often forget the exact content of the test and use a shorthand construct label such as "reading comprehension" or "mathematics con-

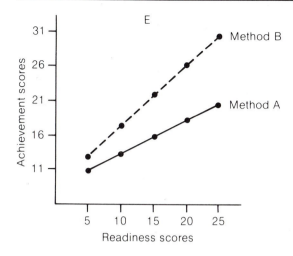

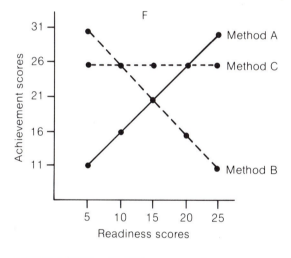

A. No differential placement indicated: Methods equally effective.

B. No differential placement indicated: Method B uniformly better for all persons.

C. Differential placement is possible: Method B for lower readiness levels, Method A for higher levels.

D. No differential placement indicated: Method B better for all (but not uniformly so).

E. No differential placement indicated: Method B better for all (but not uniformly so).

F. Differential placement is possible: Method B for low levels, Method C for middle levels, Method A for upper levels.

cepts" to describe the test and a pupil's performance on it. Therefore, construct validation is an extremely important aspect to consider when evaluating an education or psychological test. Construct validation needs to subsume and to integrate much of the same evidence used for the other aspects of validity (Messick, 1981a). In a certain sense, content validity, curricular relevance, and criterion-oriented validity are part of construct validity. This relationship is illustrated in a schematic way in Figure 16.7.

Aspect of validity	Examples of questions needing to be answered	Techniques often used to obtain answers
Content validity	a. To what extent are the items a representative sample of content (behavior) from the test publisher's domain? b. To what extent are the psychological processes required by the test items representative of the processes required by the test developer's domain?	The test manual and descriptive material is studied to obtain a description of the developer's domain. Each test item is checked to see if it matches the domain, and if the ensemble of items adequately represents the domain.
Curricular relevance	To what extent are the test items and their required psychological processes representative of the domain as *we* define it (e.g., our school curriculum, our view of intelligence, and/or our view of a certain personality trait)?	The test user articulates a definition of the relevant domain. Each test item and the entire ensemble is checked as above but with respect to the user's domain description.
Construct validity	To what extent can the test scores be interpreted as meaningful beyond the mere level of items to the level of construct interpretations which are believed to underlie observed performance on the test items?	a. Logic, substantive knowledge, and experience are used to generate explanations for high or low test performance. Not all explanations should be consistent with the intended construct interpretation. b. Empirical studies, both experimental and correlational, are conducted to support or refute the explanations generated in (a) above. c. Information from all the aspects of validity is integrated to come to an interpretive meaning of test scores.
Criterion-oriented validity a. validity for selection (predictive, concurrent) b. validity for placement	To what extent can scores on the test be used to infer a person's standing on a second measure (criterion)? a. To what extent can the scores be used to select persons for jobs, schools, etc.? What is the magnitude of error? b. To what extent can the test be used to assign pupils to different levels of instruction?	a. The criterion tasks are analyzed, tests are developed and tried on samples of applicants, correlations with criteria are computed, and studies of various classification errors are made. b. The test developer analyzes the tasks to be learned and the requirements of the different levels of instruction. A test to predict differential success in various treatments is developed, and experiments are conducted to study whether differential assignment to treatments on basis of test scores is warranted.

Table 16 • 6   Summary of the different aspects of test validity.

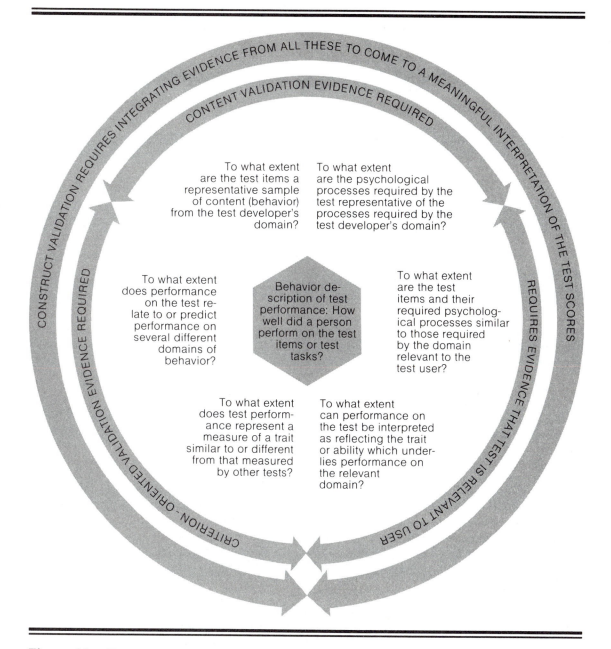

Figure 16 • 7 Schematic diagram illustrating the relation among the various aspects of test validation which are required in order to interpret the meaning of educational and psychological test scores.

Summary

The answer to the general question, "Is this test valid?" depends on the purpose for which the test is being used and the context in which it is used. A test may be valid for some specific purposes and may not be valid for others. It is important, therefore, to clearly specify the decisions you want to make before searching for validity information about it.

One aspect of validity discussed in the chapter is called content validity and concerns the extent to which a particular test can be considered an adequate sample of content or behavior from the test developer's domain. Content validity is determined principally by judging the representativeness, accuracy, and currency of the test items in relation to the test developer's domain description. A test's curricular relevance is judged by examining the extent to which test items represent the objectives of a local school's curriculum.

A second aspect of validity is construct validity concerned with the extent to which certain educational and psychological constructs can help educators to interpret a pupil's test performance meaningfully. Construct validation necessitates a logical framework in which the constructs and their interpretations are embedded and connected to one another and to the real world. Construct validity is judged by making a logical analysis of the test and postulating potential counter-interpretations to the intended interpretation, then verifying or negating these interpretations through empirical research.

Criterion-oriented validity is another aspect. It relates to the extent to which scores on a test can be used to predict or forecast a person's standing on a second measure called a criterion. Criterion-oriented validity is judged after studying the relevance, practicality, and reliability of the criterion to be predicted and the manner in which the test is empirically related to the criterion. The criterion-oriented validity aspect is especially important when a test is to be used for purposes of selection or placement. In judging the adequacy of a test for use in selection decisions, correlational data are examined as well as the rates of errors of classification. When interpreting correlation data, educators should keep in mind the various factors described in Chapter 3 which indeed affect this data. Using a test for placement purposes requires evidence that using the test scores to assign pupils to different levels of instruction will result in better pupil learning than giving all pupils the same level of instruction. This usually requires an experiment rather than a correlation coefficient.

Since most persons interpret test scores in a broad way that implies an inference about an examinee's status on a trait or an ability that underlies the observed performance, construct validity is an important aspect for educational and psychological testing. To judge construct validity necessitates integrating a rather large and diverse amount of information concerning the factors which influence an examinee's test performance. Such factors include, for example, the test's content, its relation to other abilities, and the consistency or reliability of the scores. For this reason, construct validity is sometimes viewed as subsuming the evidence from the other aspects of validity.

Themes

● All test scores require external referencing in order to enhance their interpretation.

● Just as many ways of norm-referencing scores exist, so do many ways of criterion-referencing them exist.

● Criterion-referenced tests are distinguished in that performances on them can be referenced to a well-defined domain of behavior.

● Many traditional principles of reliability and validity can and should be applied to criterion-referenced tests to improve their quality.

● Nothing in the inherent nature of criterion-referencing requires the use of cut-off scores, but educators frequently use cut-off scores with criterion-referenced tests.

● Several practical methods for setting passing scores on mastery or minimum competency tests are available. These methods do not have a high degree of acceptance and require careful justification and professional judgment when applied.

Terms and Concepts

criterion-referencing
criterion-referenced tests
domain of instructionally relevant tasks
    (well-defined domain)
ordered vs. unordered domains
ways of ordering domains (social or
    aesthetic quality, difficulty or
    complexity, proficiency of
    performance, prerequisite hierarchy,
    and empirically defined latent trait)
ways of delineating unordered domains
    (stimulus properties; verbal
    statements of stimuli and responses;
    diagnostic categories; and
    abstractions, traits, or constructs)

criterion level confusion
criterion measure confusion
domain-referenced testing
objectives-referenced testing
single-objective testing
mastery test (mastery decision and
    relative mastery)
cut-off score setting methods (using
    norm data, "feet on the desk,"
    contrasting groups, Nedelsky, and
    Ebel)

17

CRITERION-REFERENCED INTERPRETATIONS*

*Much of this chapter has been adapted from Nitko, 1980a.

This chapter discusses an additional set of procedures for enhancing the interpretation of test scores—criterion-referencing. Norm-referencing (Chapter 14) and criterion-referencing are the two major schemes used to enhance the meaning of educational tests. The first section describes the general nature of criterion-referencing and how the need for criterion-referencing arose. Section two describes and illustrates the many varieties of criterion-referencing. I adopt a broad definition and describe and illustrate categories of criterion-referencing. The third section discusses certain concepts closely related to criterion-referencing: domain-referenced testing, objectives-referenced testing, and mastery testing. The next section discusses specific issues surrounding the reliability and validity of criterion-referenced tests. These are of special concern because, as the criterion-referenced testing movement developed in reaction to the dominant norm-referenced testing viewpoint, many useful techniques were unnecessarily disregarded. This led to poorly constructed criterion-referenced tests. The final section discusses several methods commonly used to establish cut-off scores for mastery decisions and offers some practical suggestions for establishing cut-off scores in instructional settings.

General Nature of Criterion-Referencing

As Chapter 14 describes, raw test scores obtained by counting up the number of right answers or number of points earned are difficult to interpret. To aid in the process of interpreting scores for decision-making, test scores need to be referenced to something external to the test itself. Chapter 14 describes several kinds of norm-referencing schemes which reference an examinee's test performance to the performance of other examinees in a relevant norm-group. Also Chapter 14 explains that norm-referencing is not enough to interpret scores for a number of important educational and psychological decisions, especially those requiring adaptation of learning conditions to the individual learner. For many instructional decisions, the information required consists of knowing such particulars as the kinds of skills a learner has already acquired and the degree to which these skills

can be performed, the patterns of errors a learner habitually makes with respect to performing an assigned task, or the cognitive process a learner can or cannot use to solve relevant problems. Test performance referenced only to norms does not provide such specific information about what individuals can do or how they behave.

Criterion-Referencing

It is possible for some tests to use other than norm-referencing schemes. Through the use of derived scores or other procedures, a test user may be able to reference examinees' test performances to the examinees' behavioral repertoire—the kinds of things each examinee can do—rather than only to their relative standing in a group. Such schemes are called *criterion-referencing* schemes.

Although there have been efforts, especially by educators, to develop tests that were capable of being interpreted in other than relative terms, most measurement specialists in the first half of this century, influenced by the prevailing psychological theories of mental abilities, focused on improving norm-referencing schemes. In 1962, however, Robert Glaser and David Klaus called for criterion-referenced measurement. Their concern at the time was with the development of measures of proficiency in military and industrial training. A year later, however, Glaser, who was beginning a program of research and development that applied psychological principles to the design of school learning environments, expanded the original notion in his now widely known *American Psychologist* article (1963, p. 519):

Underlying the concept of achievement measurement is the notion of a continuum of knowledge acquisition ranging from no proficiency at all to perfect performance. An individual's achievement level falls at some point on the continuum as indicated by the behaviors he displays during testing. The degree to which his achievement resembles desired performance at any specified level is assessed by criterion-referenced measures of achievement or proficiency. The standard against which a student's performance is compared when measured in this manner is the behavior which defines each point along the achievement continuum. The term "criterion," when used in this way, does not necessarily refer to final end-of-course behavior. Criterion levels can be established at any point in instruction as to the adequacy of an individual's performance. The point is that the specific behaviors implied at each level of proficiency can be identified and used to describe the specific tasks a student must be capable of performing before he achieves one of these knowledge levels. It is in this sense that measures of proficiency can be criterion-referenced.

Along such a continuum of attainment, a student's score on a criterion-referenced measure provides explicit information as to what the individual can or cannot do. Criterion-referenced measures indicate the content of the behavioral repertoire, and the correspondence between what an individual does and the underlying continuum of achievement. Measures which assess student achievement in terms of a criterion standard thus provide information as to the degree of competence attained by a particular student which is independent of reference to the performance of others.

The idea of criterion-referencing does not exclude the use of norm-referencing. Figure 1.5, which shows how a hypothetical elementary school addition test can be both criterion-referenced and norm-referenced, illustrates this point. As Chapter 19 illustrates, many commercially available criterion-referenced tests also provide norm-referenced scores. You should be aware, however, that for certain types of testing, the same test will be probably not be optimal for providing both kinds of information (Hambleton & Novick, 1973; Nitko, 1970).

Varieties of Criterion-Referencing

There are many kinds of criterion-referenced tests, each kind designed to reference an examinee's score to a different behavior domain. In fact, there have been so many criterion-referencing schemes proposed that it's hard to keep track of them. In 1960, the term criterion-referenced testing was unknown to educators, psychologists, and measurement specialists; in 1971 Glaser and Nitko's book states ". . . although preliminary work has begun, no substantial literature is exact (p. 652)." By 1978, however, over 600 references existed on the subject (Hambleton, and others, 1978), and many school people and a great many testing specialists were using the term.

But there is no single agreed upon definition of criterion-referencing, and there is no single prototype criterion-referenced test. A recent content analysis of 57 descriptions of criterion-referencing revealed that it was not unusual for different authors to use the term differently, and that the same author was sometimes inconsistent within the same article (Gray, 1978). In some ways, criterion-referencing is in a state of development similar to the state in which norm-referencing was at the beginning of this century: The more or less standard ways of criterion-referencing have not become firmly established.

Broad Definition

In this chapter, I adopt a broad definition of criterion-referencing. This definition encompasses a wide variety of criterion-referencing schemes to be described later.

The following definition is useful to distinguish criterion-referenced tests from other kinds (Glaser & Nitko, 1971, p. 653):

A criterion-referenced test is one that is deliberately constructed to yield measurements that are directly interpretable in terms of specified performance standards. Performance standards are generally specified by defining a class or domain of tasks that should be performed by the individual. Measurements are taken on representative samples of tasks drawn from this domain, and such measures are referenced directly to this domain for each individual measured.

[Criterion-referenced tests] . . . are specifically constructed to support generalizations about an individual's performance relative to a specified domain of tasks . . . (In the instructional context, such a domain of tasks may be termed a *domain of instructionally relevant tasks*. The insertion of the qualifiers "instructionally relevant" serves to delimit the domain to those tasks, the learning of which is the goal of instruction. The term tasks includes both content and process).

Many kinds of achievement tests seem to fit this definition. To distinguish among them first look at how each defines the domain of tasks or behaviors to which the examinee's test score will be referenced. A test developer defines the domain of performance in one of

three ways: *well, poorly,* or *not at all.* Tests with poorly defined or undefined performance domains do not qualify as criterion-referenced tests under the definition adopted here, even though the test developer might claim otherwise. A well-defined domain of performance is a requirement for criterion-referencing. Attempting to criterion-reference the scores from a test developed from an undefined or ill-defined domain is analogous to trying to norm-reference the scores to an undefined or ill-defined norm-group. Norm-referencing is meaningless unless the norm-group is well-defined; criterion-referencing is meaningless unless the behavior domain is well-defined.

A domain is *well-defined* when both the person(s) developing the test and the person(s) using the test are clear about which categories of performance (or which kinds of tasks) are and which are not potential test items. Since the basic idea of criterion-referencing is to generalize from the few items that happen to be on the test to the broader domain of performance from which the test items were sampled, a well-defined domain seems a necessary condition for criterion-referencing. But test building involves much more than simply defining the domain of behaviors. Thus, while defining the domain of behaviors is a necessary condition, it is not sufficient.

Two Broad Categories of Criterion-Referenced Tests

We can distinguish between two broad categories of criterion-referenced tests: those based on *well-defined but ordered* behavior domains and those based on *well-defined but unordered* domains (Nitko, 1980b). This distinction is a fundamental one and stems from the notion that in some cases behaviors in the domain can be ordered along an achievement continuum of the kind that Glaser and Klaus (1962; Glaser, 1963) and others have spoken. Figure 1.5 showed an example of an ordered domain— elementary arithmetic behaviors were ordered

How the domain of behavior for achievement testing is characterized			
Well-defined and ordered domains	**Well-defined but unordered domains**	**Ill-defined domains**	**Un-defined domains**
Ordering based on judgments of the social or aesthetic quality of an examinee's product or performance.	Specifying the stimulus properties of the items to be included in the domain.	Poorly articulated behavioral objectives.	No attempt to define a domain to which test performance is referenced.
Ordering based on the level of difficulty or complexity on which a topic or subject is learned.	Specifying the stimuli and the response in the domain.	Defining the domain only in terms of the particular items on the test.	Using a cut-off score but not defining a performance domain.
Ordering based on degree of proficiency with which a complex skill is performed.	Specifying the "diagnostic" categories of the domain.		
Ordering based on prerequisite sequences for acquiring an intellectual or psychomotor skill.	Specifying the abstractions, traits, or constructs that define the domain.		
Ordering based on an empirically defined latent test.	Other ways of specifying the domain are possible.		
Ordering on other bases are possible.			

(Left vertical label: **Basis for test development**)

Source: Adapted from A. J. Nitko, "Distinguishing the Many Varieties of Criterion-Referenced Tests." *Review of Educational Research*, 1980, Vol. 50, No. 3, p. 466, Table 1. Copyright 1980, American Educational Research Association, Washington, D.C.

Table 17 • 1 A scheme for classifying and distinguishing the many varieties of tests that have been called criterion-referenced.

along a scale of difficulty or complexity of performance.

Not all behavior domains can be ordered, however. For example, if the domain is defined as a rather narrow one such as the ability to add three single-digit addends involving carrying in a vertical format, the test items for this domain probably cannot be ordered along a scale. Narrow domains and domains that are very homogeneous contain items that are essentially interchangeable, so that ordering is not possible. For some domains no one has yet discovered the basis on which a domain might be ordered. You should note, too, that some domains are both ordered *and* unor-

dered, as when several narrowly defined domains are organized into a broader, scalable domain, for example, to obtain the ordering of the addition domain upon which the example in Figure 1.5 was based (see Cox and Graham, 1966; also, see Ferguson, 1969, 1970).

Sub-Categories of Criterion-Referenced Tests

Table 17.1 shows various categories of criterion referenced tests according to the distinctions made above. The column headings of the table describe the way the performance

Basis for scaling or ordering the defined domain of behavior[a]	Examples[b]
Judged social or aesthetic quality of the performance	Rev. George Fisher's Scale Books (1864) E. L. Thorndike's Handwriting (1909) and Drawing (1913) Scales
Complexity or difficulty level of the subject-matter	Ayres' Spelling Scale (1915) Glaser's Criterion-Referenced Measures I (1962, 1963) Cox and Graham's Arithmetic Scale (1966)
Degree of proficiency with which complex skills are performed	Harvard-Newton English Composition Scales (1914) Glaser's Criterion-Referenced Measures II (1962, 1963) Perhaps certain sports events or physical fitness tests
Prerequisite sequence for acquiring intellectual and psychomotor skills	Gagné's Learning Hierarchies (1962) Piagetian Development Scales (Gray, 1978) Infant Development Scales (Uzgiris & Hunt, 1966)
Location on an empirically defined latent trait	Connolly, Nachtman, and Prichett arithmetic tests (1971) ⌈ Other tests build with latent trait models (e.g., Rasch, 1960 or Birnbaum, 1968) provided they are referenced to well-defined and ordered domains of behavior. ⌋

[a]Other bases for scaling are possible as well.
[b]Examples are meant to be illustrative rather than representative or exhaustive.
Source: Adapted from A. J. Nitko, "Distinguishing the Many Varieties of Criterion-Referenced Tests." *Review of Educational Research*, 1980, Vol. 50, No. 3, p. 468, Table 2. Copyright 1980, American Educational Research Association, Washington, D.C.

Table 17 • 2 Various categories of criterion-referenced tests based on well-defined and ordered domains.

domain may be characterized; only well-defined domains are considered the basis for criterion-referencing. Within the ordered and unordered categories several subcategories of tests are listed. Each subcategory describes the basis for developing the tests. The next sections will describe these varieties. I have presented a more detailed description of this classification scheme elsewhere (Nitko, 1980b).

Tests Referenced to Well-Defined and Ordered Domains

Table 17.2 presents examples of the varieties of criterion-referenced tests based on ordered domains. Most of these examples are discussed and illustrated, but for purposes of this book some will be omitted. You should check the original sources listed in the references. Some of the older tests are illustrated in early testing and measurement books such as Starch (1916) or Chapman and Rush (1917) which may be in your college library. Of course, you wouldn't expect these early tests to be called criterion-referenced since the term wasn't invented until 1962.

Ordering on Social or Aesthetic Quality

One of the earliest ways used to order achievement was on the basis of its aesthetic quality. As early as 1864 various "scale books" were developed by the headmaster of an English school (Chadwick, 1864). Among the scales developed was one for handwriting in which specimens of various quality were ordered in a scale book and assigned numerical values. A student's work was compared to the scale book until a close match to a specimen was found. The student then received the "mark" or "merit rating" of that specimen.

In 1909, Edward L. Thorndike and his students began to develop a variety of tests and scales; two well-known ones were for handwriting (Thorndike, 1910) and drawing (Thorndike, 1913). Thorndike used the then current psycho-physical scaling techniques to locate specimen writing samples (or drawing samples) on a numerical scale (see Figure 17.1). Thorndike (1918) once reported that thousands of his handwriting scales hung on classroom walls.

Ordering on Difficulty or Complexity

The arithmetic problems in Figure 1.5 are essentially ordered on the basis of the difficulty or complexity of the problems. Adding two-digit addends with carrying is more difficult and complex for youngsters than adding single-digit numbers. This type of scale is one of those referred to by Glaser and his co-workers (Glaser and Klaus, 1962; Glaser, 1963; Glaser & Cox, 1968) and so has been referred to as "Glaser's criterion-referenced measures I." Unlike the previous category of tests, scores on these tests cannot be interpreted as being more "aesthetic," etc. Further, difficulty or complexity scales do not necessarily lend themselves to an interpretation of prerequisite learning sequences (see below). Rather, they stand as psychometric scales, ordering behaviors or tasks on the basis of their difficulty.

Ordering on the Basis of Degree of Proficiency

Glaser and Klaus mentioned another type of ordering—an ordering based on the degree of proficiency with which a complex performance is done. This type of scaling has been referred to as "Glaser's criterion-referenced measures II." There aren't very many (if any) of these scales around for measuring academic performance, but you can imagine that they could be built for complex physical performance such as the proficiency with which a bicycle or skateboard is ridden. Marks for "technical merit" of ice skating seem to come close to this, too.

New developments in cognitive psychology, however, may lead to the development of this category of scales in the future for measuring academic performance. Cognitive psychologists are now studying the mental processes used by skilled or proficient "experts" to solve complex intellectual tasks such as physics problems or chess matches. "Experts'" intellectual performances are contrasted with those used by "novices" to see the manner in which they are qualitatively different. Chi and Glaser (1980; Glaser, 1979) summarize the implications of these newer cognitive theories for educational test development.

Ordering Based on Prerequisite Learning or Development

Another way to order the domain of performance is in terms of its hierarchy of prerequisite learnings or developmental sequence. Behaviors are ordered in a learning sequence when it can be demonstrated that being able to perform the lower level task facilitates the learning of higher level tasks in the sequence (Glaser & Nitko, 1971). As I indicated above, the fact that behaviors or test items can be scaled in terms of their difficulty does not necessarily mean that they are arranged in a prerequisite sequence which facilitates learning. Performances of students on criterion-referenced tests linked to prerequisite learning hierarchies are interpreted as placements in a learning sequence or as indicators of which parts of a curriculum sequence students have acquired. An example of a criterion-refer-

Quality 18
showed that the rise and fall of the tides the attraction of the moon and sun upon

Quality 17
Then the carelessly dressed gentleman stepped lightly into Warren's carriage and held out a small card, John vanished be-

Quality 14
Then the carelessly dressed gentlemen stepped lightly into Warren's carriage and held out a small card, I

Quality 9
Then the carelessly dressed gentlemen stepped lightly into Warren's carriage and held out a small card, John Vanished behind the

Quality 5
bushes and the carriage moved along down the driveway. The audie

Quality 4
seated on the curb was my driver and

Figure 17 • 1 E. L. Thorndike's scale for measuring handwriting. A series of handwriting specimens were scaled on a numerical "quality" scale. To use the scale a student's sample of writing is matched to the quality of one of the specimens and assigned the given numerical value. This figure shows only some of the specimens.

Source: Thorndike (1910)

enced test of this type was given in Figure 5.3. Other examples of learning hierarchies are given by Gagné (1962, 1968; Gagné and others, 1962; Gagné and Paradise, 1961).

Domains of performance may be ordered in terms of developmental sequences, too. Examples include scales of Piagetian developmental levels (Gray, 1978) and infant development scales (e.g., Uzgiris and Hunt, 1966; 1968; Hunt, 1975). Developmental scales present special interpretative problems unless there is convincing evidence of their sequentiality (Kohlberg, 1969; Loevinger, 1979). For example, that the developmental behaviors in the domain occur for virtually all persons in the postulated sequence must be demonstrated.

Ordering on the Basis of a Latent Trait

Some domains of behavior can be ordered according to an underlying dimension or hypothetical factor called a *latent trait*. If the domain is orderable and if the assumptions of the latent trait statistical model are met, then test items (which operationally define the subcategories of behavior in the domain) can be placed along a numerical scale of "latent ability." A person's test score can be referenced via the latent dimension to the behavior domain. The techniques for doing this lie beyond the scope of this book, but you can obtain an introduction to the topic of latent trait theory in issue Number 4 of the 1979 *New Directions for Testing and Measurement*. Another introductory source is the special issue of the *Journal of Educational Measurement* (Volume 14, No. 2, 1977). An example of such a scale for elementary arithmetic is the one developed by Connolly, Nachtman, and Pritchett (1971) described in Chapter 19.

Tests Referenced to Well-Defined and Unordered Domains

Table 17.3 shows the categories of criterion-referenced tests based on well-defined but unordered domains. Most of the literature on criterion-referenced testing and most of the available tests have dealt with unordered domains. Since there have been so many of these kinds of tests, they cannot all be described in detail in this book. Again, you should check the references.

Domain Delineation Focused on Stimulus Properties

The tests in the first category of Table 17.3 attempt to define the stimulus properties of the items in the domain in great detail. In this context, the term stimulus properties refers to the surface features of the items in the domain which the test developer believes will alter the probability that a given examinee will respond correctly to a given item (for example, the type of word used in a vocabulary item or "borrowing" required in an arithmetic problem). Once these stimulus properties are identified, an attempt is made to identify those properties which may affect performance. This information is then used to form a plan for sampling items from a domain so that an examinee's performance on them will be representative of the performance to be expected if the entire pool of items in the domain were administered. This is an ideal situation, of course, and not every test will accomplish this degree of representative sampling. (One reason is that limited knowledge is available about how the stimulus properties of items relate to performance).

One early approach was to define the content very precisely. For example, one could define the content as the words in a specific dictionary and draw a systematic sample of words and definitions from that dictionary to put on a test. An examinee's score on such a test could be interpreted as an estimate of his or her vocabulary knowledge operationally defined by the particular dictionary.

More precise methods have been developed for specifying the properties of the items in the domain. One of these was proposed by

Basis for delineating the behavior domain[a]	During test development emphasis is placed on:	Examples[b]
Stimulus properties of the domain and the sampling plan of the test	Defining content and content strata	Starch's English Vocabulary Test (1916) Ebel's Content-Standard English Vocabulary Test (1962)
	Specifying stimulus properties of item domains	Hively's Item Forms (1966, 1968) Osburn's Item Forms (1968)
	Specifying the precise relationship between instructional content and item domain	Bormuth's Transformational Rules (1970)
Verbal statements of stimuli and responses in domain	Behavioral objectives with or without the cut-off score ("criterion") specified	Tests based on Mager's Type of Objectives (1962) Curriculum Embedded Tests of IPI Mathematics (Cox & Boston, 1967) Popham and Husek's Criterion-Referenced Testing (1969) Harris and Stewart's Criterion-Referenced Testing (1971)
	Elaborated descriptions of behaviors and stimuli	Popham's Criterion-Referenced Tests (1975, 1978a, c) IOX Objectives-Based Tests (Popham, 1972): Amplified Objectives IOX Test Specifications (Popham, 1978a, c)
"Diagnostic" categories of performance	Identifying entry level behaviors	Hunt and Kirk's Tests of School Readiness (1974)
	Identifying behavior components missing from a complex performance	Tests build on Resnick's Component Analysis (1973) Gagné's Two Stage Testing (1970a)
	Identifying and categorizing erroneous responses	"Tab-Item" Technique (1954) Nesbit's CHILD Program (1966) Hsu's Computer-Assisted Diagnostic Tests (1972)
	Identifying erroneous processes	Beck's Blending Algorithm (1972) Interviews to determine what processes were used in responding
Abstractions, traits or constructs	Specifying specific behaviors or categories of behaviors that delimit the abstraction, trait, or construct	Tests based on the *Taxonomy of Educational Objectives* (1956) Certain basic skills survey tests, e.g., ITBS, MAT

[a]Other bases for delineating exist.
[b]Examples are meant to be illustrative rather than representative or exhaustive.
Source: Adapted from A. J. Nitko, "Distinguishing the Many Varieties of Criterion-Referenced Tests." *Review of Educational Research*, 1980, Vol. 50, No. 3, pp. 472–473, Table 3. Copyright 1980, American Educational Research Association, Washington, D.C.

Table 17 • 3 Various categories of criterion-referenced tests based on well-defined but unordered domains.

Wells Hively (1966; Hively, Patterson, and Page, 1968; Hively, 1970; Hively, Maxwell, Rabehl, Sension, and Lundin, 1973) and others (e.g., Osburn, 1968). The stimulus dimensions of the items are used to develop *item forms*, which are sort of "generic" versions of items. An item form specifies an unchanging part of an item along with (a) variable parts, (b) elements that are used in these variable parts; and (c) rules for selecting the elements. Following the rules results in selecting an element to put into the invariant part of the "generic" item, and, thus, a specific item is generated. A simple example may help to clarify this:

generic   *specific item when:*
item $a_1 = 4, a_2 = 3, b_1 = 1,$ and $b_2 = 2$

$$\begin{array}{r} a_1a_2 \\ -b_1b_2 \end{array} \quad \begin{array}{r} 43 \\ -12 \end{array}$$

The rules (not shown) for the above example would specify the particular digits that would be permitted for a_1, a_2, b_1, and b_2. Depending on how the rules are specified, "borrowing," for example, may or may not be permitted for items in the domain. Consult Hively and others (1968; 1973) for specific examples.

Another way of delineating the domain of items was described by John Bormuth (1970). Certain transformational rules (analogous to linguistic transformational grammar rules) were developed and applied to verbal instructional content. The rules generated certain kinds of comprehensive questions which had a precise relationship to the verbal text. The application of all the rules generates a domain of questions that applies to the particular verbal text at hand.

Verbal Statements of Stimuli and Responses Delineate the Domain

Most people associate criterion-referenced tests with this category. In fact, most people believe that behavioral objectives or some variant of them are necessary for criterion-referenced testing. The citations in Table 17.3 give a number of examples of criterion-referenced testing in this category (also see Appendix G).

Recently Popham (1978a) has argued that behavioral objectives, as usually stated, are not sufficient to delineate the domain properly because they are too vague. Items written for a typical behavioral objective vary considerably in their form, content, and difficulty. To remedy this, Popham suggests writing "IOX Test Specifications." This is an elaborated verbal statement which describes the stimulus and response characteristics of the items in the domain. An IOX Test Specification contains the following parts (Popham, 1978c): (1) *general description*—the general statement about the domain looks much like an elaborate behavioral objective, (2) *sample test item*—this serves to illustrate the general domain description and provides item writers with a format illustration, (3) *stimulus attribute description*—this states the properties that constrain the items in the domain (by delimiting their content and general physical properties), and (4) *response attribute description*—this states whether the examinee's responses are to be multiple-choice or constructed responses and details the rules for generating distractors or scoring constructed responses. An example of an IOX Test Specification for testing a secondary school reading objective appears in Appendix E. For additional information see Popham (1978c) or Popham and Lindheim's (1980), *The Practical Side of Criterion-Referenced Test Development*.

Diagnostic Categories Can Define the Domain

Some criterion-referenced tests are designed to make "diagnostic interpretations" especially for decisions about remedial instruction. Emphasis in these tests is on (a) identifying entry level behavior (e.g., a preschooler's concept of position, shape, or color); (b) identifying behavior components missing from a complex performance (e.g., identifying which subconcepts are unknown and, therefore, causing the examinee to be unable to solve a problem); (c) identifying erroneous responses (e.g., determining that a youngster's arithmetic errors on certain problems are all due to an inability to "borrow" across the hundreds place); and (d) identifying erroneous processes used to solve a problem. An example of (d) is shown in Figure 17.2 for a short test used to determine if a beginning reader can make "phonemes" from "graphemes" and blend them together to form words. A further discussion of diagnostic testing is given in Chapter 19.

Defining the Domain by Abstractions, Traits, or Constructs

Certain tests define the domain in terms of abstractions, traits, or constructs as well as by more fine-grain behavioral objectives. The categories of Bloom and others (1956), *Taxonomy of Educational Objectives*, for example, refer mainly to internal processes or psychological constructs (e.g., see Cronbach, 1971). Reading comprehension, work-study skills, and spelling ability are other examples of constructs or traits.

If it is clear (and that's usually a "big if" for these tests) which items would or would not be included in the domain, then they would be called criterion-referenced tests. Examples of some of these criterion-referenced tests appear in Chapter 19 and Appendix G. If the domain definition is vague (ill-defined) then they would not be called criterion-referenced tests. Popham (1974) has called tests based on ill-defined domains "cloud-referenced."

Concepts that are Not Equivalent to Criterion-Referencing

In this section I discuss some concepts which are often confused with criterion-referencing in order to clarify the kinds of test interpretations that criterion-referencing implies.

The Criterion Level Confusion

Many persons confuse the meaning of criterion-referencing with the idea of having a *passing score* or *cut-off score*. Sometimes the cut-off score is called the "mastery level" or the "minimum competency level." An older usage of the term "criterion level," stemming mainly from learning research in experimental psychology, may have created this confusion with criterion-referenced testing.

Any test can have a cut-off score: All you have to do is declare the score. Certainly just learning that 85% is passing or "mastery," will not automatically mean you can reference an examinee's score to a well-defined behavior domain in a manner which permits an inference about that examinee's performance in that domain. So don't confuse cut-off scores with criterion-referencing. Any test (even a criterion-referenced test) can be given a cut-off score, but it is the ability of a test to be referenced to a well-defined domain that makes it criterion-referenced.

The Criterion Measure Confusion

Another usage of the word criterion that is sometimes confused with criterion-referencing stems from a selection testing context. When a test such as a scholastic aptitude test is built for selecting college applicants, it needs to be validated as a predictor of future success. This second measure of future success that is external to the test and to be predicted by it is called the *criterion measure*, as I discuss in Chapter 16. For example, freshman grades may serve as a criterion measure for a scholastic aptitude test. In order for a selection test to be useful, results of empirical research would have to establish that it is a valid and unbiased predictor of scores on one or more kinds of criterion measures of interest to test users. (A test is unbiased if it measures the same characteristics, to the same degree, for every subgroup of the population in which it is used.) Research designed to determine the degree to

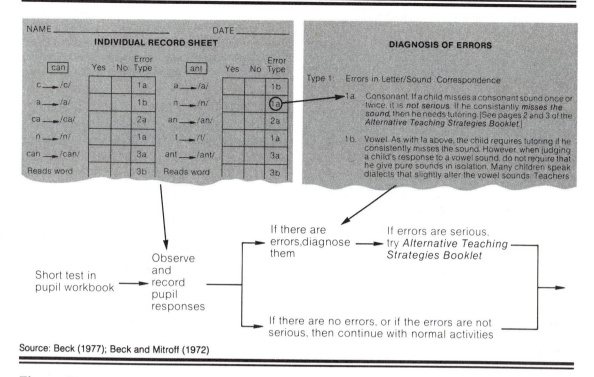

Figure 17 • 2 Example diagnostic testing by examining the process or procedure a pupil uses to perform a synthetic decoding task in a beginning reading program.

which scores on a test can be used to infer a person's likely standing on other criterion measures is called *criterion-related* (or criterion-oriented) *validity* research (American Psychological Association, 1974). But such criterion measures are not necessarily criterion-referenced tests.

Any test used to infer status on criterion measures should be subject to appropriate validation studies. Thus if a criterion-referenced test is used to infer examinee's present or future status on criterion measures, criterion-oriented validity studies should be conducted to demonstrate the appropriateness of this test usage. If, for example, a criterion-referenced test is used to place pupils into various instructional treatments, then criterion-oriented validation research is needed. If you place different students into different treat-

ments on the basis of their pre-instructional test performance, you are inferring that by so doing their posttest scores will be better. That is, you are making a prediction about their scores on the posttest. Criterion-oriented validity studies would have to demonstrate that the pretest can be validly used for such placement purposes.

Concepts Closely Related to Criterion-Referenced Testing

Domain-Referenced Testing

One of the concepts most closely related to criterion-referenced testing is *domain-referenced testing*. If a test is built so that scores on it can be referenced to a well-defined domain of behaviors in a way that permits an examinee's status on that domain to be estimated, then that test is called a domain-referenced test. When this rather broad notion of domain-referencing is used, little difference exists between this notion and criterion-referencing. For a variety of reasons, however, testing specialists have come to the conclusion that criterion-referencing should remain the preferred term (e.g., see Popham, 1978c; Hambleton et al., 1978).

In the context of instructional testing, note Wells Hively's (1970, 1973; cf. Hively, Patterson, & Page, 1968) specific use of the term. For the kind of instructional design and evaluation in which Hively and his associates engaged, defining a domain by using behavioral objectives proved too vague. The solution was to operationally define a domain by using item forms. This led to the following description of domain-referenced testing (cited in Hively, Maxwell, Rabehl, Sension, & Lundin, 1973, p. 15):

> The basic notion underlying domain-referenced achievement testing is that certain important classes of behavior in the repertoires of experts (or amateurs) can be exhaustively defined in terms of structured sets or *domains* of test items. Testing systems may be *referenced* to these domains in the sense that a testing system consists of rules for sampling items from a domain and administering them to an individual (or sample of individuals from a specified population) in order to obtain estimates of the probability that the individual (or group of individuals) could answer any given item from the domain at a specified moment in time.
>
> Domains of test items are structured and built up through the specification of stimulus and response properties which are thought to be important in shaping the behavior of individuals who are in the process of learning to be experts. These properties may be thought of as stratifying large domains into smaller domains or subsets.
>
> Precise definition of a domain and its subsets makes statistical estimation possible. This

provides the foundation for precise diagnosis of the performance of individuals over the domain and its subsets. In addition, clear specification of the properties used to structure the domain makes possible inductive generalization beyond the domain to situations which share those properties. That is, once we have diagnosed a student with respect to a defined domain we may be able to predict his behavior (in a non-statistical, inductive fashion) in natural situations which have some properties in common with the test items within the domain (Hively, 1970).

Objectives-Referenced Testing

A test that has behavioral objectives associated with specific test items can be called an *objectives-referenced test*. This term originated in the late 1960s and early 1970s when criterion-referencing was just becoming popular and some advocates were calling for the use of behavioral objectives in the development of criterion-referenced tests.

From the point of view of this chapter, objectives-referenced tests may or may not be criterion-referenced. If objectives are written to describe a domain, and if items are then written to sample the behaviors in this domain, then this would fit the description of unordered criterion-referenced tests found in Table 17.3. You can, however, "make up" objectives for any existing collection of items—after the items are written. This is done by writing a general statement describing the performance required by an examinee when responding to a test item. Such a collection of objectives and items, however, is likely to be a poor basis on which to generalize about an examinee's test performance. In Table 17.1, these kinds of domains are called ill-defined and are not considered to lead to appropriate criterion-referenced test interpretations.

Single-Objective Testing

A test developed to infer an examinee's status on the domain of tasks implied by a single behavioral objective is a *single-objective test*. This kind of test would generally be criterion-referenced and would reference scores to an unordered domain (but see the section on objectives-based tests). Single-objective tests are most closely associated with the tests in the second major category in Table 17.3.

Mastery Testing

A test used to provide information to make a decision about whether a particular pupil has "mastered" a given instructional goal is called a *mastery test*. The term "mastery" is likely to mean different things in different contexts. In the instructional context, one view of mastery is that (Glaser & Nitko, 1971, p. 641):

> . . . an examinee makes a sufficient number of correct responses on the sample of test items presented to him in order to support the generalization (from this sample of items to the domain or universe of items implied by an instructional objective) that he has attained the desired, pre-specified degree of proficiency with respect to the domain.

This definition of mastery seems to be more closely associated with the idea of criterion-referencing to unordered domains. Perhaps a different formulation of mastery would be needed for criterion-referencing to ordered domains. If one views mastery as an examinee's location or a number line representing a trait or dimension, then yet another formulation is needed.

Note that a mastery test need not be a criterion-referenced test as described in this chapter, although it would be difficult to imagine that a mastery test shouldn't be criterion-referenced. Answering the question, "Mastery of what?," would be difficult without linking the answer to a well-defined performance domain. But purely from a decision-making viewpoint, a *mastery decision* could be made by virtually any kind of procedure. (No one advocates this, however!) Given the pres-

ent state of criterion-referencing, the "mastery of what" question seems to be best answered by clearly specifying the domain of instructionally relevant behaviors which a learner commands.

Mastery is verbally encumbered. Frequently it carries with it the idea that perfect or near perfect performance is desirable or required. Sometimes mastery is viewed in absolute terms quite apart from a particular instructional sequence. A concept of *relative mastery* can be employed, however. For example, given that a learner desires to attain some instructional outcome, and that a learning sequence leading to that outcome has been developed, the question can be phrased as, "What level of test performance is required at each point in the learning sequence in order to increase the likelihood of successful learning at the next point in the learning sequence?" The question is asked again at each point in the learning sequence leading to the final learning outcome (Nitko, 1970). This is a kind of transfer of learning problem. Viewed in this way, the decision about a "passing" or "mastery" score becomes neither a purely subjective judgment nor a purely statistical matter. Huynh has suggested one technical approach to setting passing scores in a manner consistent with this relative mastery approach (1976; Huynh & Perney, 1979). Numerous additional questions can be raised about the topic of mastery testing, but to do so goes beyond the scope of this chapter.

Reliability and Validity of Criterion-Referenced Tests

Many of the technical procedures for ascertaining test score reliability and validity were developed during the first fifty or sixty years of this century. This period of technical innovation coincided with the development and widespread use of norm-referenced score interpretations. Criterion-referencing was formally developed and proselytized during the

1960s and 1970s, in part as a reaction to the fact that norm-referencing alone was not serving some very important instructional needs of daily classroom practice. The reaction against norm-referencing was so severe in some quarters, that it left many test users with the impression that none of the technical developments of the preceding sixty years had merit for criterion-referenced interpretations. Note, however, that nearly all of the basic concepts presented in the last two chapters apply to both norm-referenced and criterion-referenced tests: Teachers and other professional educators should insist that test developers provide meaningful empirical evidence to support claims for reliable and valid use of their tests for the purpose(s) for which they are advertised. I briefly describe a few special concerns about the reliability and validity of criterion-referenced tests below and urge the reader to consult the references for a more detailed and technically complete treatment.

Reliability

A person's test performance is subject to a variety of influences which cause it to vary from one test administration to the next: the items on one form may be a bit harder than another, the person may have permanently or temporarily changed between testings (become fatigued, learned more, etc.), a different test administrator may alter conditions (rapport, motivation, etc.), and/or physical conditions of the environment may impact the examinee (e.g., power outage, or other sudden disturbance). These and other factors combine to contribute to measurement error and, hence, introduce some degree of unreliability to the test scores. Many of the techniques described in Chapter 15 are directed to assessing the degree of measurement error attributed to factors such as those above and are generally applicable to both criterion-referenced and norm-referenced tests.

Often educators choose criterion-referenced tests in situations requiring pass-fail or mastery-nonmastery decision. In such cases, decision consistency is usually a specific concern of test users. Many of the "criterion-referenced reliability estimates" found in the literature deal with decision consistency, rather than the reliability of estimating a person's true score on the entire domain from which the test items sample. Elementary procedures for estimating decision consistency are discussed in Chapter 15. Most techniques for estimating decision consistency have been developed for use with tests referenced to *unordered* domains. You may check the following sources to obtain information about estimating decision consistency in ways more sophisticated than the elementary ways described in this book: Berk (1980); Hambleton, Swaninathan, Algina, and Coulson (1978); Huynh and Saunders (1980); Millman (1979); Subkoviak (1980); and Traub and Rowley (1980).

Validity of Criterion-Referenced Tests

Test validity refers to the soundness of the interpretations of test scores for a particular purpose. Validity is specific to a purpose: A test is not valid in general. A test has a certain degree of validity for one purpose while, simultaneously, having a different degree of validity for other purposes.

Concepts of validity were initially developed in the context of norm-referencing, since this context was more consistent with the dominant focus of test specialists on individual differences and relative ability during the first part of this century. When the ideas associated with criterion-referencing were first advocated in the late 1960s and early 1970s, some educational test specialists felt that anything related to norm-referenced testing should be abandoned. Today, however, only a few hold this position.

Various concepts or aspects of validity have developed over the years. *Content validity* concerns the extent to which the items on a test are representative of the domain or universe they are supposed to represent. *Construct validity* concerns the extent to which a test measures the trait, attribute, or mental process it is intended to measure and whether descriptions of persons in terms of such constructs can be made using the scores from that test (cf. Cronbach, 1971). *Criterion-oriented validity* concerns the extent to which scores on a test can be used to infer an individual's likely standing on some other test or variable called a criterion (American Psychological Association, 1974).

Content validity If a domain of behaviors is well-defined, you should be able to judge a test's content validity relatively easily. But you should not assume content validity.

Sometimes a test developer will claim that a test has content validity *just because* the test is criterion-referenced or *just because* it is based on a well-defined domain. Specifying the domain definition is only the initial step. A sufficient and representative number of items (observations) need to be on the test in order to claim content validity. Thus, even though the domain is well-defined, a test can lack content validity (see Chapter 16).

A related issue concerns the *curricular relevance* of the test. A test may contain a representative sample of items from the domain which the test developer defined, but the developer's domain may not represent the test user's domain. Criterion-referenced test developers usually specify the domain very precisely, and the test could be a representative sample from it. However, the test could lack curricular relevance if the curriculum in a school focuses on an entirely different domain of performance. Curricular relevance is an important concern when purchasing achievement tests (see Chapter 15).

Construct validity Many construct interpretations are advanced for criterion-referenced tests. For example, criterion-referenced tests are used to infer mastery, minimum competence, expert (vs. novice) performance, status with respect to a learning hierarchy, etc. Also,

they are sometimes used as a basis for assigning students to certain diagnostic categories—these categories having a number of construct interpretations.

A score on a criterion-referenced test may, for example, be used to infer the mastery status of a pupil. But the scores on the test may be subject to a variety of influences which may invalidate this mastery (or nonmastery) interpretation. Among the counter-interpretations that can be advanced are the following:

1. *Poor motivation* may cause a pupil to score low even though the pupil may, in fact, have attained a mastery status on the domain.
2. *Poorly written items*, containing irrelevant sources of difficulty, may lower a pupil's score. Or the items may contain unnecessary clues which raise the scores of nonmasters.
3. *Lack of content validity or lack of curricular relevance* may make scores of "masters" lower than they might have been otherwise.
4. *Mastery implies a transfer of learning* so that high scorers should learn advanced material more easily than low scorers. Do they?

Undoubtedly, you can think of other interpretations counter to the intended mastery interpretation. Each of these counter-interpretations stands as an hypothesis that needs to be verified or rejected. If these additional factors are found to influence scores significantly, then the intended interpretation of "mastery of a domain" cannot be made in a simple way; at the minimum, the counter interpretations need to be taken into account (see Chapter 16).

Criterion-oriented validity One example of the need for this type of validity evidence is in the context of using criterion-referenced tests as posttests for instructional units arranged in a learning sequence leading to some desired outcome. I outline this above when discussing the concept of relative mastery. A measure of the final learning outcome to be attained serves as the criterion, and criterion-oriented validity studies are conducted to validate using each unit's criterion-referenced posttest as a mastery test that predicts attainment of the final learning outcome. (For an example, see Huynh and Perney, 1979.)

Another example stems from the use of criterion-referenced tests as means for assigning students to different instructional procedures or to remedial treatments for what I call placement decisions in this book. Students at a particular point in an instruction sequence may be tested to decide which ones should receive "remedial instruction" while others proceed with "regular instruction." This interpretation of test scores implies that pupils with low scores will ultimately perform better on the final outcome measure if they have had remedial instruction first, while those with high scores will ultimately perform well on the final outcome measure without this additional remedial help. A test developer and/or test user may suggest using a criterion-referenced test for such purposes solely on the basis of logical deduction. However, more than good thinking is needed. You need evidence which bears on the question of whether assigning students to particular treatments on the basis of test scores will, in fact, lead to greater achievement than will random assignment to the various treatments or assigning everyone, regardless of test score, to one of the treatments (e.g., everyone continues on with regular instruction). Such differential assignments imply that the test user is expecting an *aptitude treatment interaction* (see Chapter 16).

Establishing Cut-Off Scores for Mastery Decisions

Even though there is nothing inherent in a criterion-referenced test which requires a cut-off score, if a test is to be used to help decide mastery, it is necessary to establish a cut-off score or passing standard. No entirely satisfactory method exists for establishing a passing standard to which all parties will agree because there are numerous factors to consider. The following methods are among the many ways suggested and used to make mastery and/or minimum competency decisions (for a more comprehensive discussion see Glass [1978], Hambleton [1978], Huynh and Saunders [1980; Huynh et al., 1981]; Millman [1973], Meskauskas [1976], and Bunda and Sanders [1979]).

1. **Using norm data** Data concerning the performance of the target norm-group are used for setting the passing score. Among the cut-off scores that have been used in the past are: (a) the mean or median test score of those who received a "C" in the course, (b) the mean or median test score of those whom a teacher (or other expert) has judged as borderline between master and nonmaster, (c) the 25th percentile of all those who have taken the course and passed, and (d) a grade-equivalent score that is two or three grade levels below the current grade placement (e.g., setting a grade-equivalent of 9.0 as a minimum passing score for twelfth graders).

2. **"Feet on the desk" procedure** Since most people feel that 100% on a test is too strict to be a passing score, the person(s) in charge keeps lowering the passing score until reaching a percent with which most people are comfortable. This often results in 80% or 85% being used as the passing standard.

3. **Contrasting groups method (Zieky & Livingston, 1977)** Teachers (or other experts) judge pupils and separate them into two groups: masters and nonmasters. A test is administered to both groups, and the two overlapping frequency polygons are plotted on the same graph. The score point at which the two curves cross is used as the cut-off score. Slight upward or downward adjustments may

This is *not* a validated list of guidelines. It is a list of practical guidelines that I have evolved over the years through my work with numerous school districts.

1. The determination of cut-off scores should be done by several groups working together. These groups include teachers, parents, curriculum specialists, school administrators, and (if the tests are at the high school level) students. The number from each group will depend upon the importance of the tests under consideration and the number of domain specifications. . . .
2. I usually introduce either the Ebel method or the Nedelsky method. Following training in one of the methods, I have the groups work through several practice examples. Differences between groups are discussed and problems are resolved.
3. The domain specifications (or usually, but less appropriately, the objectives) are introduced and discussed with the judges.
4. I try to set up a schedule so that roughly equal amounts of time are allotted to a consideration of each domain specification. If some domain specifications are more complex or important I usually assign them more time.
5. I make sure that the judges are aware of how the tests will be used and with what groups of students.
6. If there exist any relationships among the domain specifications (or objectives), the information is noted.

For example, if a particular objective is a prerequisite to several others, it may be desirable to set a higher cut-off score than might otherwise be set.

7. Whenever possible I try to have two or more groups determine the cut-off scores. Consistency of their ratings can be studied and, when necessary, differences can be studied and a consensus decision reached.
8. If some past test performance data are available, they can be used to make some modifications to the cut-off scores. . . .
9. As test data become available, the percentage of "masters" and "nonmasters" on each objective should be studied. If performance on some objectives appears to be "out of line," an explanation can be sought. . . .
10. Whenever possible I try to compare the mastery status of uninstructed and instructed groups of examinees. Instructed groups ought to include mainly "master" students. . . .
11. It is necessary to review cut-off scores occasionally. Curriculum priorities change and so do instructional methods. These shifts should be reflected in the cut-off scores that are used.

The list above is something of a fantasy since I have never had the opportunity to implement it fully. Nevertheless, I do feel that the set of guidelines (or even a subset) if followed carefully will produce more valid cut-off scores.

Source: Hambleton, R. K. "On the Use of Cut-off Scores with Criterion-Referenced Tests in Instructional Settings." *Journal of Educational Measurement*, 1978, Vol. 15, pp. 288–289. Copyright 1978, National Council on Measurement in Education, Washington, D.C.

Table 17 • 4 Hambleton's practical suggestions for establishing cut-off scores for achievement tests in instructional settings.

be made in an attempt to minimize certain classification errors.

4. Judging how minimally competent pupils will perform on the test A group of experts (teachers, curriculum experts, citizens) reviews each test item and comes to a judgment about the score expected from a minimally competent examinee. One of two methods have been used: (a) The Nedelsky (1954) procedure[1] or (b) the Ebel (1972, 1979) procedure. The Nedelsky procedure is limited to multiple-choice

items. It requires the judge to state which foils on each item the minimally competent person could eliminate, and then, assuming that this minimally competent person will guess blindly on the remaining items, the educator computes an expected chance or guessing score (see Chapter 12, Note 4) which in turn serves as the passing score. The Nedelsky procedure has found successful application in setting passing standards for examinations in medical education (Gross, 1982; Guerin & Smilansky, 1976; Taylor & Reid, 1972; Taylor, Reid, Senhauser & Shively, 1971). The Ebel method is also judgmental, asking the experts to first classify items as to difficulty and importance,

[1] A similar procedure has been presented by Angoff (1971).

then stating the percent of each category that minimally competent students should pass, and finally, from these percents, computing the total number of items that students should pass on the whole test. This final figure becomes the passing score. The Ebel procedure may be used with non-multiple-choice items. The Ebel and Nedelsky procedures use different criteria to judge the performance of a hypothetical minimally competent student and, as you might expect, give different results (e.g., Andrew and Hecht, 1976; Glass, 1978) especially if judges work independently rather than working toward a consensus (Gross, 1982).

Each of these procedures is unsatisfactory in some way. All require teachers to develop a careful rationale for using the particular cut-off score. Some critics will view all methods as too arbitrary. All methods result in a certain number of misclassifications (see Chapter 15).

The justification of any method must include the educational and/or pedagogical reasons for using the *specific* cut-off score. Although these reasons can be presented in the context of a particular instructional practice for school situations, they are not likely to be widely accepted—especially by those parties who will be adversely affected by a nonpassing decision—as the legal actions described in Chapter 2 attest.

You should check the references mentioned in the first paragraph of this section before you decide how to set passing scores, especially if you must make crucial decisions about pupils. Table 17.4 offers a practitioner's advice on how to establish cut-off scores in instructional settings.[2]

[2]See also Hambleton (1980) for a review of various standard-setting methods.

Summary

Criterion-referencing is a way to enhance the interpretation of test scores by referencing them to well-defined behavior domains. If the domain of reference is ill-defined or undefined, then you cannot accomplish criterion-referencing, just as you cannot accomplish the enhancement of scores through norm-referencing using a poorly defined or undefined norm-group.

There is no single prototype criterion-referenced test. A variety of criterion-referenced tests have been proposed over the years. Generally, two broad groups of criterion-referenced tests exist: those based on ordered behavior domains and those based on unordered behavior domains. Within each of these there are several varieties. Each variety is likely to be useful for some decision contexts but not others. Thus, one has to be careful to distinguish one type of criterion-referenced test from another and one decision context from another. I have discussed a variety of concepts closely related and unrelated to criterion-referencing.

A pressing need exists for test developers to provide validity evidence for the different uses of criterion-referenced tests they recommend. This evidence should be specific to each use or interpretation a test developer claims for the test. Users of criterion-referenced tests have an obligation to validate the specific applications they employ in the local settings, especially if published evidence cannot be generalized to the local setting.

Several methods for establishing cut-off scores to be used with mastery tests exist, yet none of these procedures is entirely satisfactory. The professional educator and citizen alike will have to use considerable judgment and study the consequences of using cut-off scores for mastery and/or minimum competency decisions.

PART FOUR

USE AND INTERPRETATION OF PUBLISHED TESTS

Themes

● Standardized tests should be the products of carefully conducted programs of research and development. Evaluating a test requires an examination of the accompanying research and development program as well as the test itself.

● Before adopting a test for use in a decision context, a school or agency should thoroughly review the practical and technical merits of the test and compare it to other tests available to serve the same function.

● Numerous print (and other) sources are available to help locate and review a particular test.

● The test user bears a special responsibility to acquire the requisite competence and qualifications to administer and interpret a particular test.

Terms and Concepts

test specifications
curriculum analysis
tryout version of the test
item analysis (item difficulty, item
    discrimination, grade progression of
    easiness, distractor analysis)
item selection procedures
standardization phase
concurrent standardization
local norms (vs. publisher's norms)
scaling phase

equating studies (equipercentile
    method, anchor test)
special norms
test manual (technical manual)
specimen set
sources of irrelevant difficulty
Mental Measurements Yearbooks (MMY)
CSE test evaluations
test publisher's catalogue
APA *Standards*
qualifications for test purchase

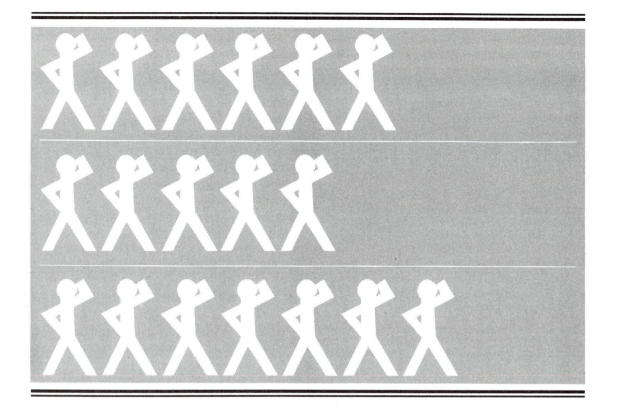

18
SELECTING AND EVALUATING PUBLISHED TESTS

This chapter is designed to help you locate and evaluate a particular published test you may want to use for a specific educational purpose. The chapter is consumer-oriented, providing criteria that you can use to thoroughly review and critique a particular test and opens with a discussion of how a standardized test is developed. The chapter describes the major steps along with various kinds of research which need to be built into the development process. Part of evaluating a test is related to judging how well this research and development are conducted. The chapter details a systematic procedure for evaluating a test. You may want to follow this outline when collecting information about a test. A set of guidelines will help you rate the quality of certain kinds of criterion-referenced tests. The chapter also presents a systematic procedure for searching for a test and a list of various sources which will help you find information about specific tests and test reviews. Finally, the chapter explains the qualifications for test purchase.

How a Standardized Test is Developed

A standardized test should be the product of a carefully conducted program of research and development. Such a program involves the work of many persons and includes the following steps (Robertson, 1978).

1. Considering preliminary planning and marketing.
2. Developing test blueprint and item drafts.
3. Designing and professionally producing test items, materials, answer documents, and directions.
4. Pretesting items; collecting and analyzing data on them.
5. Selecting items for the final forms and professionally producing standardization editions.
6. Locating schools willing to participate in standardization and conducting standardization testing.
7. Collecting and analyzing standardization data and preparing norms tables, collecting and analyzing data for reliability and validity studies.
8. Professionally producing the final forms of the test and writing test manuals.

9. Marketing and selling the final edition.
10. Conducting post-publication special studies and developing special technical publications.

As a consumer of tests, you should be aware of what activities are involved in each of these steps and should base part of your judgment of the quality of a test on how well the test producer followed the steps when developing the test. The activities involved in each step are briefly described below.

Note, however, that many tests available in the marketplace do not follow all steps because to do so is quite costly and time-consuming. If a test publisher omits steps during the developmental process, they will probably be those concerned with collecting and analyzing data used (a) to improve the quality of the test and/or (b) to validate the claims made for the test.

Preliminary Steps

Depending on the test publisher, the ideas for a particular kind of test come either from within the publishing organization itself or from an author external to the organization. Larger test publishers tend to conduct their own needs analyses or market surveys to identify the kinds of tests users would purchase. Some publishers seek or accept (unsolicited) proposals from outside authors. Before an idea gets too far along, however, the developer must prepare some type of formal proposal which outlines the major features of the test, for whom it is intended, and how it compares to similar existing tests (i.e., the competition). The publisher then determines the likely size of the market for the test, the projected costs for developing and bringing the test to market, and the profitability of the project. Once the publisher decides to go ahead with the project, contracts with the test authors are negotiated (if this is necessary), and a schedule for development is prepared.

Planning and Drafting the Initial Version

Test specifications Once the general purpose of the test is decided, developing a test blueprint or set of *test specifications* is necessary. An early step in this process is to identify the content the test will include. "Content" is used broadly here and means: (a) the subject matter and/or behavioral objectives the test will include (if it is to be an achievement test), (b) the kinds of factors or abilities the test will tap (if it is to be an aptitude test), and (c) the kinds of careers or jobs for which the test will provide information (if it is to be a vocational guidance or interest inventory).

When developing a survey achievement test for national use, the developer conducts a *curriculum analysis*. This ". . . requires the detailed summarizing of published textbook series, syllabuses, outlines of objectives, and other current curricular material from across the country. . . . In addition to analyses of current texts and course outlines, curriculum experts in each of the skills and subject matter areas to be tested are consulted for suggestions as to what trends the curriculum might be taking in the future" (Burrill, n.d., p. 1). Although this type of analysis has been com-

mon for survey achievement test developers, there is some indication that criterion-referenced test developers are also doing something similar. If the content of a test drifts too far from what is being taught in the schools, the test will not sell.

In their final form, the test specifications are similar in form to the blueprint arrangement shown in Figure 5.2 but broader in scope. Any format which describes in detail the content, behavior, and numbers of items in each area will do.

Item writing Once the test specifications are developed, draft items are written. These items will undergo several editorial reviews and empirical data will be collected to see how well they function. Frequently, between two and four times as many items are written as will eventually appear on the test. Item writing frequently involves a team of content experts and professional item writers. Some publishers will contract with subject matter experts (such as teachers, curriculum coordinators, and college professors) to write a specified number of items. Experienced members of the test publisher's staff then edit and/or revise these items to conform to existing item writing standards (see the item writing suggestions in Chapters 6 through 9). Items need to be reviewed to make sure that the content is both up-to-date and accurate and that the items do not appear to be biased or offensive to any group of persons (e.g., that the written or pictorial materials do not reflect ethnic or sexual stereotypes).

Professionally Designed and Produced Tryout Materials

The publisher prepares a preliminary or tryout version of the test to administer to sample groups to obtain information on how the items function. Experts also prepare a preliminary version of the test manual containing directions for administration and answer documents.

People who live at or near sea level become short of breath at high altitudes because the concentration of

(A) *their* white cells ~~in their blood~~ *count* is low

(B) carbon dioxide is ~~greater~~ *more concentrated* at high altitudes

(C) carbon dioxide is less at high altitudes *more concentrated*

(D) oxygen is ~~greater~~ at high altitudes *barometric pressure*

(E) ~~oxygen~~ is less at high altitudes

People who live at or near sea level become short of breath at high altitudes because

(A) their white cell count is low

(B) carbon dioxide is more concentrated at high altitudes

(C) carbon dioxide is less concentrated at high altitudes

(D) atmospheric density is less at high altitudes

(E) oxygen is more concentrated at high altitudes

Box 18 • 1

Need for tryout sample to be representative The preliminary versions of the test are tried out on fairly large and representative samples from the target population of pupils for whom the test is intended. For example, if a language development test is intended for national use with pupils in the first three grades, then testing only pupils from one or two midwestern states is inadequate. In designing for a "representative sample" of pupils, the test developer needs to take into account regional differences (e.g., the Far West, New England, the South, etc.) as well as other differences such as dialect (e.g., Southern vs. New England or standard vs. black English). Securing agreement of schools around the country to try out tests, to find willing test administrators, to transport the test materials, and to collect the completed test forms is a difficult task.

Item analysis Every item should be subjected to item analysis, much as I suggest for teacher-made tests (see Chapter 11). Among the types of statistical information collected for each item are these four:

1. *Item difficulty* indicates the percentage of the tryout groups answering an item correctly. The publisher uses item difficulty information to (a) keep the final form of the test within the range of difficulty suitable for the intended examinees, (b) make sure that alternate forms of the test have the same degree of difficulty, and (c) arrange items within a test in order of difficulty. Items will be selected for norm-referenced *achievement* tests if they (a) match the test blueprint, (b) tend to be answered correctly by approximately 20 to 80% of the pupils at the grade level for

	Item Numbers					
ITEM DIFF	Level 9 Grade 3 Fall	Level 10 Grade 4 Fall	Level 11 Grade 5 Fall	Level 12 Grade 6 Fall	Level 13 Grade 7 Fall	Level 14 Grade 8 Fall
98						
96						
94						
92						
90						
88						
86						
84						
82		11				
80	1		28			
78						65
76			24	39		
74	5	28 14		48	60 65	70 96
72	7	22 13 19	32 26 25	60		68 73 69 76
70				40 42 49 65		78
68		24 12 21	33		56 59	64
66	9	25	29	53	68 69 70	88 74
64		18	38 31	43 44	73 61 76 96	82
62	11	20 15 23	34 36	51 47	58	71 77 85
60	6 2	32 26	48 30 40 49	56 69 59		80 72 84 91
58			60 35 42		82 74 57	66 75 67
56	8	33	27 39	68 50 70	88 71 64 77 85	81 89 98
54	4	34 17		45 73 57	78 63 84	
52	19 14	36 29 31	53	52 58	80 91	99 92 104
50	22 13	38 30	56 37 43	55 74 61	66 75 67 72	94 93 87
48	28 3 25		51 57	54 76	81	101
46	10	16 40	45 44	71 64 77 67 72	89	86 95
44	15	35	47 59	63	93 87	90
42	24 20 18 12 21			66 41	86 98 62	83
40	23	27	55 50	78 75 46	94 92	102
38		39	52	80 62		103
36	26	45 37 42			83 95	79
34		43 44	54		90	106
32			58			105
30	17		41 46 61			97
28					79	
26	30 29		63 62			100
24						
22		41		79	97	107
20	16 27					
18		46				
16						
14						
12						
10						
8						
6						
4						
2						

Table 18 • 1 The distribution of item difficulties (% of pupils getting the item right) for a spelling test (national item norms).

Source: A. N. Hieronymus, E. F. Lindquist, and H. D. Hoover, *Iowa Tests of Basic Skills, Manual for School Administrators*, p. 103, © 1982 by University of Iowa. Reproduced by permission of Riverside Publishing Co.

which the test is intended, and (c) meet certain other statistical criteria described below. Although individual items on the final form of the test differ greatly in their difficulty levels, their average difficulty level tends to be between 55 and 65%. An example of how items on a test tend to differ in difficulty appears in Table 18.1. In Grade 3 on this test, for example, items range in difficulty from 20 to 80%. Some publishers, in addition to computing the difficulty of an item in the entire group, check the difficulty of each item within each of several subgroups of pupils (e.g., boys vs. girls, blacks vs. whites, etc.) to see if an item favors (i.e., is easier for) one group over another.

2. *Item discrimination* is an index telling how well the item distinguishes between high-scoring and low-scoring students. I describe a discrimination index for teacher-made tests, using the upper-scoring 27% and the lower-scoring 27% of the pupils, in Chapter 11. Most test developers use another index, the correlation between each item score (usually equal to zero or one) and the total score on the test. The total score is assumed to be an indicator of overall ability on the domain being tested. Thus, the correlation for each item tells how well the item distinguishes persons at various ability levels. Items with low or negative discrimination indices are eliminated from the test.

3. *Grade progression of easiness.* If an item is used for several successive grades, the publisher will often check to see that progressively larger proportions of pupils pass an item at each higher grade level. For example, 36% of the fifth graders answered Item 26 in Table 18.1 correctly. The rationale for selecting items showing such an increasing percentage of pupils passing is the belief that items on a test should include content on which pupils become more skilled as they progress through school. Such a rationale is also the basis for the development of growth scales, such as the grade equivalent scale. However, some items may not become easier for higher grade children for several reasons: The skill may not continue to develop, remaining at the same level; lack of practice may result in poor performance at higher grades; and/or students may learn the content (knowledge) only at one grade level and forget it at higher levels.

Not all measurement specialists agree with this practice of selecting achieve-ment test items which become progres-sively easier (e.g., Buros, 1949, 1977; Guttman, 1950; Popham & Husek, 1969; Anderson, 1972; Linn, 1980), and many criterion-referenced tests makers ignore this aspect entirely.

4. *Analysis of distractors.* For multiple-choice tests, the percent of examinees choosing each foil or incorrect option is tabulated separately for upper-scoring and lower-scoring groups. The rationale for this information was explained in connection with teacher-made tests in Chapter 11.

Selecting items for the final form(s) There are no prespecified, set standards for select-ing items for standardized tests, especially standardized achievement tests. Each test publisher will follow a somewhat different practice. Usually a test developer will weigh all four kinds of statistical information along with information about the importance of the item content before deciding to select a par-ticular item. Given several items of equal dif-ficulty and measuring the same content, pref-erence is usually given the item with the highest discriminating power, as explained in Chapter 11. With achievement tests it is im-portant that the items match the content spec-ifications, even if they do not meet "ideal" sta-tistical standards. The teacher should be wary of a test whose developer says that the items were selected purely "objectively" using sta-tistical criteria alone: *The statistical tail should never wag the intellectual dog.*

Standardization Phase

In order to permit schools and other test users to compare the performance of pupils in one school or classroom with a larger reference group, a test publisher administers the final version of the test to a large group of pupils representative of the population at the age and/or grade level for which the test is intended. This procedure occurs during the *standardiza-tion phrase* of test development.

Representativeness is the goal. The extent to which a publisher's standardization sample is representative of a specific population varies from test to test. Some publishers take great care to be sure that a test represents the national school population. Among the various characteristics a publisher might consider representing in a sample from a national school population are: characteristics of individual pupils (e.g., age, sex, general scholastic ability), characteristics of school systems (e.g., public-parochial-private, teachers' salaries, curriculum emphasis), and characteristics of communities in which the schools are located (e.g., geographical location, population of city, socioeconomic status of neighborhood) (Burrill, n.d.). A general rule is that a publisher should attempt to represent within practical limits those characteristics of a population related to test scores. As a test user, you should examine a publisher's descriptions of how the normative data were collected to see if the standardization sample is representative of the population to which *you* want to reference pupils' scores. It is not only the size of the sample used that is most important, but, rather, how representative that sample is of the population to which you intend to compare scores. However, I point out in Chapter 14 that because schools themselves choose whether or not to participate in a publisher's standardization phase, no publisher's norm group is truly representative of the nation's schools (see, e.g., Baglin, 1981).

Trend toward twice a year standardization With the increased use of standardized achievement tests for evaluating federally funded education programs, achievement test publishers have tended toward both a fall and spring standardization program.

Concurrent standardizations A publisher may concurrently standardize a general scholastic ability test and an achievement test. This was done, for example, in October and November of 1977 with the *Iowa Tests of Basic Skills*, the *Tests of Achievement and Proficiency*, and the *Cognitive Abilities Test*. This is how the standardization samples were selected (Hieronymus, Lindquist, & Hoover, 1982, p. 55):

Three primary stratifying variables were used to classify school districts across the nation: district enrollment, geographic region, and socioeconomic status of the community. Within each of the five geographic regions (Southeast, Southwest, North Central, Northeast, and Far West), school districts were stratified into seven categories on the basis of enrollment. The third stratifying variable, community socioeconomic status, was determined from 1970 census data. The socioeconomic facts were (1) median years of education of the population 25 years old and over, and (2) median family income in thousands of dollars. To derive the socioeconomic status index, the median years-of-education figure was multiplied by two and added to the median family-income figure. This gave approximately equal weights to education and income. The resulting index was used to stratify school districts within the thirty-five enrollment-by-region units. Within each unit, school districts were ranked by the socioeconomic index and divided into three strata.*

Then, within each socioeconomic stratum three districts were selected at random; these were designated as first, second, and third choices. The chief administrative officers of selected districts were contracted by representatives of the publisher. Districts selected by these random procedures were, of course, free to decline participation. When a district declined, the next choice district was contacted.

Once a district within the stratum agreed to participate, one of three sampling plans was

*Because large-enrollment districts (over 25,000) include the major cities, in addition to many smaller cities, special sampling procedures were used for the nation's largest cities. In order to take into account the wide variations in socioeconomic characteristics of these schools and to obtain representative large-city pupil and school (building) norms, a disproportionate number of large-city *districts* were contacted. Within-district sampling procedures were developed so that the number of pupils from these large districts is proportionate to large-district enrollments nationally.

used to select buildings within multibuilding school districts. The three different sampling plans insured that when all the districts were combined, the group of pupils was truly representative of achievement in respect to both central tendency and variability. . . .

This sampling procedure was designed to produce: (1) a national probability sample representative of the nation's pupils; (2) a sample of the nation's school buildings to provide the basis for school building norms; and (3) the data on which to base special regional, large city, high and low socioeconomic, and Catholic school norms.

Publisher's vs. local norms A data table showing the results of the standardization sampling process—describing the various demographic features of the sample including grade level, school district size, geographic representation, socioeconomic status, and ethnic composition—should be available in either the general user's manual or the technical manual which accompanies each test. Examining such tables helps a prospective test user to judge the representativeness of the norms. Note, however, that seldom does the composition of the student population of a local school correspond exactly to a test publisher's national standardization sample. This means that the local school district may need to collect data and construct its own norms in order to make certain meaningful norm-referenced comparisons among the local students. Often, test publishers provide this data analysis service for a school district.

Scaling Phase

Data collected during the standardization phase is used to develop various kinds of norm-referenced information to be tabulated and reported in the test's manual. This aspect of test development is sometimes referred to as the *scaling phase.*

The tables of norm-referenced data which appear in the test manual are referred to as norms. Chapter 14 describes the various norms

typically reported for achievement tests and general scholastic ability tests.

Special Studies and Preparing the Manual

Publishers sometimes supplement data collected and analyzed during the standardization phase by conducting additional special studies. Among the studies ultimately reported are: reliability and validity studies, studies to link together various levels of multilevel edition of a test (i.e., studies designed to put scores from all levels on a common measuring scale), test bias studies, and equating studies.

Equating studies Alternate forms of the same test will not naturally yield raw scores that are on the same scale of measurement. As a result, special statistical analyses serve to relate raw scores on one form to their equivalents on the other form. This is called *equating*. A rather typical process used with achievement tests is called the *equipercentile method:* A raw score on one form is said to be equivalent to a raw score on another form, if those two raw scores will result in the same percentile rank in the norm-group. Scores of 12 on Form A and 15 on Form B, for example, are equated if both have the identical percentile rank in their respective distributions. When applying the equipercentile method, a publisher selects a special sample of pupils, administers both forms of the test to them, and uses the results to establish the equipercentile relationships. Sometimes, to prevent practice effects from interfering with the equating results, two different groups of pupils will be involved, one taking Form A, the other Form B. In order to establish the relationship between the test forms, each group may take an additional—common—test called an *anchor test*. Forms A and B will then be equated indirectly through the common anchor test. In the future it is likely that special latent trait techniques will be used to equate test forms by using statistical calibration data from the items, the data originating from previous item tryouts.

A. **Purpose for which a test is sought.**
   1. General school setting.
   2. Specific decisions or uses.
   3. How test will solve the problem.
B. **General description of the test under review.**
   1. Identifying information.
   2. Type of test.
   3. General description of content.
   4. General administrative features.
C. **Practical evaluation.**
   1. Quality and appropriateness of test material.
   2. Judgments about administrative features.
   3. Cost and usefulness of scores and scoring.
   4. Evaluation of overall costs of the test.
   5. Summary evaluation of practicality of test.
D. **Content evaluation.**
   1. Publisher's description of test content.
   2. Publisher's rationale for including item types.
   3. The test as representative sample from publisher's domain.
   4. Currency of item content.
   5. Breadth or range of content coverage.
   6. Item bias, sources of irrelevant difficulty.
   7. Quality and clarity of items.
   8. Overlap of test content and user's domain.
   9. Summary evaluation of test content.
E. **Technical evaluation.**
   1. Normative quality.
      a. Decisions requiring norm-referencing.
      b. Kinds of norm-referenced scores publisher provides.
      c. Population(s) standardization sample(s) intend(s) to represent.
      d. Evaluation of representativeness of standardization sample.

   e. Evaluation of overall normative quality in relation to purposes.
   2. Reliability
      a. Summary of reliability data provided.
      b. Summary of likely size(s) of errors of measurement.
      c. Identification of most important sources of error in relation to purpose.
      d. Evaluation of test reliability in relation to intended decisions.
   3. Validity
      a. General summary of validity data provided.
      b. Identification of most important aspects of validity in relation to purpose.
      c. Summary of publisher's evidence for aspects noted in b.
      d. Evaluation of test's validity in relation in intended decisions.
   4. Summary evaluation of technical merits of the tests.
F. **Comments from other reviewers.**
   1. List of important positive and negative evaluative comments from persons who have used the test.
   2. Conclusions drawn from published reviews.
G. **Overall evaluation of the test for the specific use intended.**
   1. Brief recapitulation of intended use.
   2. Identification of most important data and information to this review.
   3. Summary of overall evaluation giving reasons for conclusions made.
H. **References used and cited.**

Table 18 • 2   A suggested outline for reviewing a test intended for a specific use in a school.

Special norms   Additional information which may be compiled during this phase is used to prepare special norms: large city norms, regional norms, and parochial school norms (see Chapter 14). Item norms (see Table 18.1) may be prepared at this time as well. Various correlational studies bearing on the validity of the interpretations claimed for the test may also be conducted.

Test manuals, score reports, and specimen sets   All of the above information along with descriptions of the background, purposes, development, and interpretation of the test are written into the *test manual(s)*. Some test publishers prepare several manuals, some only one, so you can't be sure you have all of the necessary information to evaluate a test if you simply request a "manual" from the publisher. Professional organizations concerned with testing have prepared special standards describing what kinds of information are essential, very desirable, and desirable to include in test manuals. These *Standards* are described later in the chapter.

An important part of the development of a test is the designing of score reporting materials and services. These materials and services help to make the test scores usable for schools, parents, students and school boards. If a test does not have usable score reporting materials, schools are not likely to purchase it.

You can obtain information about a test by ordering a *specimen set* from the publisher (cost is listed in the publisher's catalogue). This set includes a sample of the test booklet, an answer sheet, the scoring key, the manual for administering, some technical material, various promotional materials, and price lists. Having a copy of the test is essential if you are to properly evaluate it.

A Procedure for Reviewing and Evaluating a Test for a Specific Purpose

Tests should be carefully examined, compared with each other, and evaluated before you adopt them. This section describes a procedure for proceeding in a systematic way. Usually a committee of teachers, school administrators, and/or citizens reviews and decides whether to adopt a test. Table 18.2 gives a suggested outline for such a review, and I describe each part below. If parts of the outline are not applicable to the particular test, you may omit them in a review. Since no test is perfect, comparing the merits of one test with another is important if you are to choose the better product relative to others available.

Purposes for Which a Test is Needed

You look for a test because you perceive the need for a specific kind of test. First, then, you need to pinpoint the specific purposes for which the scores will be used and find out who will be using them to make decisions. The clearer you are about the purposes and conditions under which a test will be used, the better you will be able to select the appro-

priate test. Some of the information to summarize in this part of an evaluation are:

1. *A description of the general school setting in which the test will be used:* type of community, ages or grades of pupils, person or persons who will be helped by an appropriate test, and persons who, generally, will be directly in charge of using the test scores.

2. *A list of the specific decisions, purposes, and/or uses intended* for a test, such as: identification of specific reading skills needing remediation, appraisal of a pupil's emotional needs or areas of anxiety as a prelude to counseling, appraisal of a pupil's relative aptitude for mechanical activities which to discuss during guidance sessions, and/or a survey of general levels of reading and mathematics achievement for purposes of reporting evaluation information to the school board.

3. *A description of how using test scores or test information will help to improve the decision, serve the purpose, or solve the problem.* This is an articulation of what the user, from the outset, expects to accomplish by using a test in this particular decision context. Articulating the expectations for a test helps to focus the evaluation.

General Description of the Test Being Reviewed

1. *List identifying information:* title, author(s), institutional affiliation of author(s), publisher, date of latest revision, age or grade levels covered by the test, age or grade levels to be used in this decision context, number of alternate forms, and group or individually administered.

2. *State type of test* (e.g., general survey achievement battery, reading readiness test, general scholastic aptitude test, language aptitude test, individually administered diagnostic mathematics test, etc.)

and publisher's description of the intended purpose of the test.

3. *Give a general description of the content*: variable(s), trait(s), or characteristic(s) measured; listing of the subtests, number of items on each, and time required to administer each (including the total number of testing sessions required, if applicable); and description of the kinds of items (including format, general nature of their content, and processes required of the examinee in order to respond to them).

4. *Query the general administrative features*. Who can administer the test? How is it to be scored? What special training requirements are there? In what form are the test results (scores) reported?

You can obtain much of the information summarized in this section from the test publisher's catalogue, promotional materials, and the manual for administering the test. Information noted in point 3 above often necessitates actually examining the test materials and taking the test yourself.

Practical Evaluation of the Test

For most school situations, a test cannot be used unless it meets certain practical requirements concerning its appearance, ease of administration, ease of recording and reporting pupils' scores, and overall cost. This part of the review should address the following points.

1. *Quality and appropriateness of materials*. Are the materials professionally prepared and produced? Are they pleasant and appealing to the student? Are the size of the type and the spacing appropriate for the pupils for whom they are intended? (Pupils with certain physical disabilities or learning difficulties may do poorly on a test, for example, simply because the format is "too busy," there are too many items on a page, or the answer-marking process is too

complex). Are the administration directions to the examiner printed clearly so students can follow them? Are all the materials needed to administer the test easy to handle? Store? Transport? What kind(s) of score reporting services and interpretive materials accompany the test?

2. *Judgments about administrative features*. This is an overall evaluation of whether the test is practicable from the examiner's viewpoint: ease of administration, quality of directions for administering, special concerns about the psychosocial situation that the test creates for the examinee, special concerns about the need for training and supervising examiners and scorers.

3. *Evaluative questions about the cost and usefulness of the scoring*. Is the test easy to score? What will it cost to score each test used? How much will it cost to score the entire group of tests? How quickly will the test results get back to the persons who will be expected to use them? How useful are the various score-reporting services the publisher provides (e.g., individual examinee reports and labels, profiles, class or school rosters, subtest and total score reports, summaries by building or system, etc.)? Are the scores and reports easy to interpret for the person who will use the results?

4. *Evaluative questions and comments about the overall cost of using the test*. What is the initial cost (outlay) for booklets and materials? How long can the test be used? What are the continuing costs if the test is used during this period? What expenses are involved to administer the test? What are the overall costs for scoring and reporting results? What is the nature and extent of instructional time lost if testing is implemented and is this justifiable? What is the total cost (per year) per pupil affected by the testing? Note that actual costs can differ from those listed in a publisher's catalogue depending on (a) the publisher's general discount policy, (b) whether there

are reduced prices for purchasing materials and services together, and (c) whether there are complimentary services and materials (Iwanicki, 1980).

5. *Summary evaluation of the practical aspects of this test*. Given all of the practical considerations above, is it feasible to use the test? Explain why or why not.

Content Evaluation

It is very important to carefully examine the content of a test before reaching a judgment about adopting it. This is true whether the test is an achievement test, an aptitude test, an interest inventory, or a personality test. Many claimed benefits for a test are never realized because the content and quality of the test items are inappropriate or just plain poor. You can obtain information to evaluate the content of the test in several ways: carefully examining copies of the test (test specialists highly recommend actually taking the test), carefully reviewing the test manual and accompanying interpretative materials, contacting the test publisher to obtain additional reports and explanations, noting the comments made in published reviews of the test, contacting subject matter experts, and contacting experienced users of the test. Among the factors to keep in mind when reviewing the test's content are:

1. *Publisher's description of the test content*. A test contains a sample of behavior from some broader domain of content, skills, developed abilities, personality characteristics, vocational interest, or, in general terms, behaviors. The test reviewer should judge the adequacy with which the test publisher has described this domain so that it is clear what the test is intended to measure. The description can be evaluated in terms of its clarity, completeness, and usefulness to the user in understanding what the test measures.

2. *Publisher's rationale for including various kinds of items*. A variety of kinds of items can be used to measure characteristics of pupils. The publisher should select the particular kinds of items appearing on the test on some reasoned basis rather than simply for the sake of convenience. For example, if a test should measure usage of written English, the test developer should explain why the particular mix of multiple-choice and essay items is used and what contribution each is intended to make in the overall assessment of a student in this domain.

3. *The test as a representative sample of the publisher's domain*. You should judge whether the particular items that appear on the test adequately represent the domain *as the publisher of the test describes it*. (Judgments about whether the publisher's description is in agreement with the user's conception of the domain appear separately below.) Information relevant to making this judgment can be presented by the publisher as logical and/or statistical analyses. Examples of logical analyses for achievement tests include showing how the items on a test are classified according to the test specifications; describing how experts have written, edited, reviewed, and revised the items; and showing model responses for essay or performance items. Examples of statistical analyses for achievement tests include summarizing the ratings given to items by panels of content specialists, item analysis data obtained from administering the items to representative samples of pupils from the intended reference population, and summaries of ratings for particular essay responses. After studying the available information and carefully examining the test, you should make an overall judgment about whether the items represent the domain claimed by the publisher (see the content validity section of Chapter 16).

4. *Currency of item content*. The items should represent the current state of the art in an area. For an achievement test, do the items represent what is currently taught in the particular school(s) for which it is being considered? Will the curriculum change soon? For aptitude tests, do the items represent the current conceptions of the tasks which should be on such tests? For interest inventories, do the items contain statements about activities and occupations that are actually in existence (not out of date)?

5. *Breadth or range of content coverage*. An achievement test generally should represent the range of values, issues, and knowledge of the subject area which the publisher claims to be assessing. Sometimes the content of the test represents only certain aspects of the content or a certain author's views, often the case for tests in a specific subject area rather than for general achievement surveys. An evaluation of the breadth of the content is necessary.

6. *Item bias and sources of irrelevant difficulty*. The items on a test should be free from sources of *irrelevant* difficulty which may (a) lead to erroneous measurement, (b) be ambiguous to knowledgeable examinees, and (c) be offensive or unfair to particular groups of persons. The publisher should provide information about the procedures used to consider these factors. For example, some publishers employ a panel of judges to review the items. Another may conduct special studies which compare the performance of various groups on each item. Among the factors which may contribute to unfairness or be irrelevant sources of difficulty are size and color of printing (e.g., to those with sight problems), male-oriented problems on science and mathematics achievement tests, reading selections with white-middle-class orientations, items portraying sexual or ethnical stereotypes, ease with which test-

wise examinees can obtain higher scores with the same subject knowledge as less test-wise examinees, and extent to which reading ability intrudes on tests which are not supposed to measure primarily reading skill.

7. *Quality and clarity of items*. Use the item writing rules in Part II of this book to judge the professional quality of the items. It is important in *achievement* tests, for example, to be sure that examinees who do not have the requisite knowledge cannot obtain the correct answer simply on the basis of general information, general vocabulary knowledge, general verbal reasoning, and/or specific test-wiseness skills. Conversely, the test should not prevent those having the requisite knowledge from choosing the right answer because an item is poorly constructed. Table 18.3 contains a checklist that might be used for an in-depth review of the quality of each item.

8. *Overlap of test content with the user's concept of the domain*. The test may match the publisher's specified domain very well, but may miss a particular test user's concept of the domain by a wide margin. With respect to achievement tests, I refer to this overlap as *curricular relevance* in Chapter 16. The idea applies equally well to other domains. A test user may, for example, have an entirely different concept of creativity than the developer of a particular creativity test. Although the test may match the developer's domain very well, it may not prove useful for that particular user's purposes. Thus, you should evaluate the extent to which the test being reviewed matches the curriculum, school goals, and "theory" to be employed in the decisions described in the above section under "Purposes for which a test is sought."

9. *Summary evaluation of test content*. From an examination of the test's content, does it

A. Judge each stated behavioral objective on the following: 1. Does it state a behavior? 2. Is the behavior overt or covert? 3. What is the main intent of the objective? Is the main intent clear? 4. If the objective is classified in a taxonomy of some kind, does the objective fit into the taxonomy category under which it is listed? **B. Judge each item on the following:** 1. Does the item test important content? 2. Are the answer to—and other information in—the item accurate and/or correct?	3. Rate the quality of the *idea* behind the item. 4. Does the item match the objective it should test? 5. Does the item contain things which could be sources of irrelevant difficulty? (Name them.) 6. Does the item contain any material biased toward or against a particular group? Does it contain material which reflects sexual or ethnic role stereotypes? Or does the item contain material which may offend one or more groups? (Name them.) 7. Rate the overall design and layout of the item. 8. What are some of the item's good points?

Note: If you are using this checklist with items to be rewritten, suggest several ways for improving them.

Table 18 • 3 Checklist for reviewing objectives and items on achievement tests.

appear that the test can be used for the purposes initially specified? Explain why or why not.

Technical Evaluation

If the test is practical and the content is appropriate, the test *may* be useful for the specific purpose(s) intended. More detailed information is required, however, concerning the technical merits of the test and the extent to which the claims for the test can be supported by empirical evidence.

1. *Quality of norms.* Most test users will want norm-referenced information about the scores on a test even if criterion-referenced interpretations are the major concern. You should, therefore, review and judge the quality of the normative data the test publisher provides.
   a. *Decisions requiring norm-referencing.* Before judging the norms, the reviewer should briefly articulate the decisions which require norm-referenced information and the kind(s) of norm group(s) and norm-referenced score(s) considered important to these decisions.
   b. *Kinds of norm-referenced scores the publisher provides.* List these types of scores.

   c. *The population(s) which the standardization sample(s) are supposed to represent.* Describe the population which the publisher claims (explicitly or implicitly) to have represented by the standardization sample. The administrator's manual usually provides this information.
   d. *Evaluate the representativeness of the standardization sample.* Judge the standardization sample in terms of (i) how well it represents the population the publisher claims it to represent and (ii) how well it represents the particular population to which you would like to reference the scores. A publisher does not always describe the standardization sample completely in the administrator's manual. You may need to consult the technical manual or supplementary technical reports which you should obtain from the publisher.
   e. *Evaluate the overall normative quality of the test in relation to the initially stated purposes and uses.*
2. *Reliability of the test.* Before you adopt a test, you should determine whether the scores will be sufficiently reliable for the intended purposes. If you intend a test for program evaluation rather than individ-

ual pupil assessment, for example, you may tolerate a somewhat lower level of reliability. I discuss the concepts of reliability, error of measurement, and standard error of measurement in Chapter 15.

This section of the test review should contain the following information.

a. *Summarize reliability data*. Describe the types, procedures, sample size, and magnitudes of each of the reported reliability coefficients. (Averages or ranges of values may be used to summarize if the data are numerous.) Include the following types of reliability coefficients if they are applicable to your purpose: test-retest with no delay, long term stability coefficients, internal consistency, alternate forms, and scorer reliabilities.

b. *Estimate the likely sizes of the errors of measurement.* Use the standard error of measurement to infer the likely size of errors of measurement.

c. *Identify important sources of error.* Describe the kind(s) of errors of measurement that seem particularly important to the kind of accurate decisions listed in the initial statement of the test purposes. For example, if the scoring of the test is subjective and several persons in a school will participate in scoring, then scorer errors (or degree of disagreement) will be one of the important sources of error to consider.

d. *Evaluate the reliability of the test in relation to the intended uses and decisions using the above information.*

3. *Validity*. A test needs to be not only reliable, but valid. I discuss various aspects of validity in Chapter 16, and these are applied at this point in the test review. Content validity, however, is one aspect of validity that I discuss in "D" in Table 18.2 and do not need to repeat in this section.

a. *General summary of validity data*. Describe in general terms the kinds of validity

evidence the publisher provides for the test. Much of this evidence and data appears in technical manuals or supplementary technical reports), rather than in a "teacher's manual."

b. *Identify the most important aspects of validity.* Describe the aspects of validity which seem most important for making the decisions which initially motivated the selection of this test for review.

c. *Summarize the publisher's evidence.* State the evidence the publisher provides for each of the important aspects of validity identified in "b" above. Include such information as descriptions of the samples used and magnitudes (or ranges) of the correlation coefficients.

d. *Evaluate the test's validity in relation to the decisions or purposes initially described*.

4. *Summary evaluation of the technical evaluation of the test*. Given all the technical considerations outlined above, can you recommend the test for the specific decision-making purposes described in the section on "Purposes for which a test is sought"? Explain.

Comments from Other Reviewers

Measurement and/or substantive experts have professionally reviewed a number of tests. The potential user of the test should locate and read these reviews in addition to making a personal examination and evaluation of the test. You should also try to talk with persons who have used the test in practical situations.

1. *List important positive and negative evaluation comments* by current test users or extracted from reviews published in such sources as the *Mental Measurements Yearbooks*, professional journals, anthologies and bibliographies of tests, testing and measurement textbooks, and publications from state and county educational agencies. Judge the importance of the review-

ers' comments in relation to the way you intend to use test results.

2. *Conclusions drawn from published reviews.* What can you conclude about the quality of the test after studying the comments of other reviewers?

Overall Evaluation of the Test for the Specific Use Intended

1. *Briefly recapitulate the specific use intended* for the test.
2. *Describe the most important data and information.* Of all the data and information reviewed for this evaluation, which are the most important for the purposes of evaluating the test for the initially stated purposes? Are there any unintended negative effects of using the test?
3. *Final overall evaluation and recommendation.* You should write a brief summary of an overall judgment of the quality of the test for the specific purposes initially delineated. You should support evaluative statements with reference to the specific facts which summarize the major strengths and weaknesses of the test. If possible, compare the test with other tests or with other nontest sources of relevant information to point out the advantages or disadvantages.

Guidelines for Evaluating Certain Criterion-Referenced Tests

The procedure outlined above can be used to review and evaluate most tests likely to be used in a school. Some persons, however, may feel more comfortable if a set of review guidelines are specifically tailored to particular kinds of tests. One set of guidelines has been developed for objectives-referenced tests by Hambleton and Eignor (1978, pp. 322–324). These guidelines consist of a series of questions organized around 10 major aspects of test quality: objectives, test items, administration, test layout, reliability, cut-off scores, validity,

norms, reporting test score information, and test score interpretations. The reader should look up this source for specific details.

How to Locate a Test and Obtain Information About It

A Systematic Procedure for Searching for a Test

Suppose you want to use a certain kind of test (e.g., attitude toward reading or an individually administered diagnostic mathematics test). How do you find out what tests of this type are available and obtain a copy? Table 18.4 which shows one approach to finding tests in a systematic way assumes you know essentially nothing about the test you seek. Of course the more you know, the fewer steps you need to follow.

Searching the Specialized Testing Literature

You can consult a number of sources to find information about specific tests. I describe some of these below; you can find most in a college library, a testing and measurement office of a college campus, or in a school's testing office.

Publication of the Buros Institute of Mental Measurements Among the most useful resources for locating information on tests are the publications of the Buros Institute of Mental Measurements (which recently relocated at the University of Nebraska in Lincoln). The late Oscar K. Buros who began a series of test bibliographies and *Mental Measurements Yearbooks* (MMY), the latter of which critically review tests printed in the English language founded the Institute.

The *Mental Measurements Yearbooks* (Buros, 1938 through 1978) are a series of eight yearbooks which critically evaluate most of the currently available published tests. Each yearbook supplments rather than replaces the ear-

Table 18 • 4 One procedure for systematically searching for measurement procedures.

lier editions, so that it is occasionally necessary to consult earlier volumes to obtain complete coverage of a test. One or more experts review tests especially for the MMYs, and the yearbook gives excerpted journal reviews as well. The *Eighth Mental Measurements Yearbook* (Buros, 1978), for example, contains 898 original reviews of 638 tests and 140 excerpts from journal reviews of 96 tests. In addition, each review entry contains test title, age or grade levels, publication date(s), special comments, number and type of part scores, author(s), publishers, references, and bibliographic information. There are 1,184 tests listed. The MMYs also list recent books on testing and include excerpted book reviews.

Names and addresses of 309 test publishers are listed in the 8th MMY. The 9th MMY is being prepared as of this writing. A disadvantage of the MMYs is that because of the publication lag editions of tests reviewed may not correspond to publishers' new editions.

Publications of the Center for the Study of Evaluation The Center for the Study of Evaluation (CSE) at the University of California at Los Angeles publishes monographs which evaluate a number of tests. Tests are rated on criteria of validity, appropriateness, usability, and quality of norms and an overall (average) rating is provided as well. You should use the latter cautiously, since average ratings could be moderately high even though a test is rated low in crucial areas such as validity or reliability. The following are the presently available CSE test evaluations: (1) Hoepfner, R. and others, *CSE Elementary School Test Evaluations* (1976 Revision); (2) Hoepfner, R. and others; *CSE Secondary School Test Evaluations: Grades 7 and 8* (1974); (3) Hoepfner, R. and others, *CSE Secondary School Test Evaluations:* Grades 11 and 12 (1974); (4) Hoepfner, R., Stem, C. and Nummedal, S. G., *CSE-ECRC Preschool/Kindergarten Test Evaluations* (1971); (5) Hoepfner, R. and others, CSE-RBS Test Evaluations: *Tests of Higher-Order Cognitive, Affective, and Interpersonal Skills* (1972); and (6) CSE Test Evaluation Project Staff, *CSE Criterion-Referenced Test Handbook* (1979).

News on Tests Educational Testing Service (ETS) publishes *News on Tests* (formerly the *Test Collection Bulletin*). ETS maintains a collection of published and unpublished tests, many of which are available in microfiche form through your library's ERIC collection. *News on Tests* is a periodic listing and annotation of recent additions to this collection but contains no reviews.

Bibliographies of tests Numerous bibliographies exist which list and describe both published and unpublished tests. These are usually specialized lists in a particular area as, for example, the following titles suggest: *Women and Women's Issues* (Beere, 1979), *The Assessment of College Performance* (Miller, 1979), *Tests and Measurements in Child Development* (Johnson & Bommarito, 1971; Johnson, 1976), and *Assessing Reading Behavior: Informal Reading Inventories* (Johns, Garton, Schoenfelder, & Skirba, 1977). You can find such books frequently in the reference section of the library, and selected volumes may be held by the testing and measurement office of a local college, professors in an area, or in a school's testing office. Two *directories* containing listings of about 90 of these bibliographies of tests are Backer (1977) and Aaronson (1974). (Also see the Additional Readings at the back of this book.)

Professional journals Professional journals in a field often review tests that have potential application in a particular area such as reading, mathematics, child development, or learning disabilities. Specialized testing and measurement journals review tests that have a wide appeal to school practitioners and psychologists. Among the journals frequently reporting test reviews are (Buros, 1978): *Developmental Medicine and Child Neurology, Journal of Educational Measurement, Journal of Learning Disabilities, Journal of Personality Assessment, Journal of Reading, Journal of School Psychology, Journal of Special Education, Measurement and Evaluation in Guidance, Modern Language Journal, Psychological Reports, Psychology in the Schools,* and *Reading Teacher.*

Bibliographic information about these and other journals (including those which review testing books) appears at the back of each *Mental Measurement Yearbook.* Journal references are indexed in such sources as the *Education Index, Dissertation Abstracts, Research Studies in Education, Psychological Abstracts,* and *Research in Education* (ERIC).

The test publisher's catalogue An important way to get information about a test is directly from the test publisher. Most test publishers have catalogues which describe the various tests which they publish in considerable detail. A publisher's catalogue is especially helpful for finding out about current editions of various tests along with information about various scoring services and costs and how to obtain specimen sets, test manuals, and technical reports. Current information of this sort is seldom found in other print sources. The local public school's testing office and the testing and measurement office of a college or university usually maintain collections of recent catalogues. The publisher's catalogue will list any restrictions on test purchasing: The sale of certain tests, especially individually administered intelligence and personality tests, is restricted to qualified psychologists. The catalogues provide prices and ordering information also.

Textbooks on testing and measurement A number of textbooks list, describe, and/or review selected tests. If you are looking for a test in a specific area, looking through textbooks may be a useful way to see which tests are frequently used. A textbook, however, is not a comprehensive source for information about tests because (a) tests are often selected for inclusion primarily for their merits in illustrating an author's point, (b) space permits only a few tests being mentioned, (c) often only the most popular or easily available tests are mentioned or illustrated, and (d) no single author is aware of all available tests.

Professional contacts A few professional contacts may make locating a test easier. The director of the school testing office or the school psychologist is frequently a useful resource. Testing and measurement professors at colleges and universities usually work in departments of educational research, educational psychology, measurement and statistics, counseling and guidance, or psychology. Many larger colleges and universities have testing offices designed to help their faculties and students with testing problems, and such offices are usually available to answer questions from the public, as well. Larger testing companies and agencies usually have an information and/or advisory office to answer questions over the telephone (use the 800-number). Professional organizations can sometimes help by referring you to a member who can be of assistance in your local area. Professionals in educational measurement and testing usually belong to one or more of the following organizations: American Educational Research Association, American Psychological Association, Association for Measurement and Evaluation in Guidance (which is a division of the American Personnel and

Guidance Association), National Council on Measurement in Education, or the Psychometric Society. In some areas, federally funded research and development centers and regional laboratories have technical assistance offices which can help with testing problems. In some states, county-based school agencies or state-related school agencies are specially organized to offer technical assistance in review and using tests.

The test Standards A useful publication for evaluating educational and psychological tests in the *Standards for Educational and Psychological Tests* (APA, 1974). This is a set of standards for publishers and users of tests prepared by a joint committee from the American Psychological Association, The American Educational Research Association, and the National Council on Measurement in Education. The *Standards* describe as "essential," "very desirable," or "desirable" various kinds of information which a publisher might provide in a test manual and accompanying materials.

The ideas and concepts in the *Standards* are directed to the professional tester rather than to measurement students and the public. An explanation of the 1974 *Standards*, written in nontechnical language for those associated with education, has been prepared by the National Council on Measurement in Education under the title *Guidelines for Test Use* (Brown, 1980). A revision of the 1974 *Standards* by a joint committee of the three forementioned organizations was underway at the time of this writing.

Qualifications for Test Purchase

Tests are ordered through a publisher's catalogue. In an effort to guard against test abuse, some publishers restrict the sale of test materials. The previously mentioned *Standards for Educational and Psychological Tests* give the test publisher the responsibility for telling the user what qualifications are needed to interpret test results properly. However, the *Standards* state that, "A test user should know his own qualifications and how well they match the qualifications required for use of specific tests" (p. 58).

Sales restrictions vary with the test publisher, each implementing a somewhat different policy on establishing a purchaser's qualifications and selling tests. Some publishers are very explicit about stating the professional qualifications a customer needs before being permitted to purchase a test, and such statements appear in their test catalogues. Most publisher's catalogues of psychological tests contain statements about the need for purchasers to be qualified for administering and interpreting a test. It is the responsibility of the test user to be sure to acquire the requisite training and experience before purchasing a test.

Summary

These are the main points of this chapter.

1. One aspect of evaluating a standardized test is judging the care with which it was built.

2. A professionally developed test should have gone through several research and development steps before being made available to consumers. Among the major steps are these:

    a. *Carefully planned initial version*—Test specifications are built after thoroughly analyzing the area or skills to be tested and professionally writing, reviewing, and editing test items.

    b. *Tryout and item analysis*—The items are tried out on samples of pupils representative of those for whom the items are intended, and empirical data is used to improve and/or select the better items for inclusion on the final version of the test.

    c. *Standardization*—The final version of the test is administered under standardized conditions to a representative sample from the population of students for whom the test is intended. Data are gathered for developing norms.

    d. *Scaling*—Various tables of norm-referenced scores are developed from the standardization sample.

    e. *Special studies*—Data are gathered, analyzed, and written into the test manual concerning reliability, validity, equivalence of forms, and special norms.

3. The information about how a test is built and about its technical qualities can be found in the test's manual. You may order specimen sets from the test publisher for review and evaluation before you make the decision to adopt a test.

4. The chapter provides a systematic procedure for reviewing a test for a specific educational purpose. This procedure is outlined in Table 18.2.

5. A systematic procedure for searching for a test is summarized in Table 18.4.

6. Sources for finding information about specific tests are described: publications of the Buros Institute for Mental Measurements, publications of the Center for the Study of Evaluation, *News on Tests*, various bibliographies on tests, professional journals, test publishers' catalogues, textbooks on testing and measurement, and professional contacts.

7. Qualifications for test purchase were discussed. Although the publisher is obliged to tell the prospective user what qualifications are necessary to use and interpret a test, the user bears the ultimate responsibility of knowing his or her own qualifications and whether they match those required for use of a test.

Themes

● Many achievement tests can be purchased in the marketplace, but unless the test has been standardized and empirically documented, its quality cannot be completely judged.

● Standardized achievement tests in the marketplace can be both criterion-referenced and norm-referenced.

● Some criticisms of standardized achievement tests can be overcome by properly selecting and using them. When used properly, standardized achievement tests provide one type of information that can be used both within and outside the classroom.

Terms and Concepts

standardized test
multilevel test vs. single-level test
survey battery
subtest
empirically documented
types of diagnostic tests

special norms
test level
in-level vs. out-of-level
computer-prepared reports (item
    analysis report, building report,
    narrative profile report)

19
PUBLISHED ACHIEVEMENT TESTS

T his chapter is concerned with published achievement tests used in the schools. The first section identifies the various kinds of achievement tests in the marketplace, discusses their general characteristics, and compares them with teacher-made tests. The second section discusses the uses and misuses of standardized achievement tests. Administrative, outside-the-classroom uses are illustrated by the actual ways in which administrators of an urban school district reported they used the test data. Three categories of criticisms of tests and four categories of test misuse are discussed. The teacher's role in preventing misuse of test results at the classroom level is of special concern.

The third section gives examples of survey achievement batteries designed to span several grade levels, discussing both group and individually administered batteries. The next section gives examples of multilevel criterion-referenced tests, both group and individual. The final two sections describe other multilevel tests and single-level tests designed to measure achievement in specific subjects, including tests used for granting credit-by-examination and the GED high school equivalency testing program.

Published Achievement Tests in the Marketplace

In Chapter 18 we discuss the way in which a published test is developed and evaluated. In this chapter we discuss a variety of published achievement tests and the ways they differ from each other and from teacher-made tests.

Kinds of Published Achievement Tests

There are a great many published achievement tests. These tests vary in their purpose, usefulness, and quality. To acquire an overview of their variety, classifying them is helpful; here is one classifying scheme:

I. Published achievement tests in the marketplace

A. *Standardized, empirically documented tests.*[1] This group of tests has a high degree of

standardization of procedures and follows the development procedures outlined in Chapter 18, using empirical data to document their effectiveness.

1. *Multilevel survey batteries.* The familiar annually administered tests survey pupils' general educational growth or basic skill development in each of several curricular areas. *Multilevel* means that the test content spans several grade levels.

2. *Multilevel criterion-referenced tests for a single curricular area.* These tests provide detailed information about pupils' status for a well-defined domain of behavior in a single curricular area (e.g., mathematics).

3. *Other multilevel tests for a single curricular area.* Noncriterion-referenced tests for a curricular area provide a broader content-sample than a subtest of a sur-

---

[1] We are breaking with tradition here. In the history of testing, standardized tests in education usually had norm-referenced interpretations. The criterion-referenced "movement" of the 1960s argued strongly against this norm-referencing as the sole interpretive device of test scores. Hence, a norm-referenced/criterion-referenced dichotomy currently exists in the minds of many people, even though a test can be referenced in both ways (see Chapter 17).

vey battery and measure educational development (growth) in that area.

4. *Single-level standardized tests for one course or subject.* These tests are directed toward measuring achievement at only one level or for one course (e.g., Algebra I) and usually are not coordinated with tests from other courses.

B. *Nonstandardized, not empirically documented tests.* Tests in this group make little or no attempt to standardize testing procedures and do not follow the procedures outlined in Chapter 17 to develop or empirically document the effectiveness of the tests.

1. *Criterion-referenced tests.* These tests estimate pupils' status with respect to some well-defined domain of behavior (usually specified by specific behavioral objectives) but lack standardization and empirical documentation of worth.

2. *Textbook or curricular accompaniments.* Tests or test items which are found in teachers' editions, end of textbook chapters, back-of-the-book, or built into instructional materials. Often called pretests, posttests, placement tests, progress checks, review tests, and/or curriculum embedded tests. They lack standardization and empirical documentation and are seldom the products of professional item writers.

II. Teacher-made tests Tests constructed by a teacher measure the specific objectives the teacher emphasizes and help in day-to-day instructional decisions.

Characteristics of Standardized, Empirically Documented Achievement Tests

As I discuss in Chapter 1, standardization of testing procedures is necessary if the results are to be comparable from time to time, place

to place, and person to person. Standardization is often a necessary characteristic for the interpretation of both norm-referenced tests and criterion-referenced tests. The quality of a test is verified by collecting *empirical data to document* the test's effectiveness. Empirical data contribute to test quality by providing a basis for: (a) item improvement and selection, (b) establishing a test's reliability and validity, (c) describing how the test functions in the target population of pupils, and (d) developing a variety of norm-referenced scores.

Multilevel survey batteries consist of *subtests,* each covering a specific curricular area such as: reading, mathematics, listening skills, English usage (mechanics), spelling, vocabulary, social studies, general science, work-study skills, and skills in using reference materials. Subtests are organized so that there is a coordinated series of levels spanning the grades. For example, there may be one level for grades 1–2, another for 3–4, one for 5–6, and so on. Each level measures essentially the same characteristic (e.g., reading comprehension) but at a more advanced grade level. Because the development and empirical scaling of the tests are coordinated, it is possible to use multilevel tests to measure pupils' growth or year-to-year learning progress. If the multilevel subtests for the various curricular areas are part of a survey *battery,* there is the additional characteristic that all subtests have been normed in the same population of pupils. This allows a comparison between a pupil's relative strengths and weaknesses in different curricular areas (via percentile rank comparisons).

Multilevel criterion-referenced tests provide information about a pupil's status with respect to the specific behaviors in a domain. Although some survey batteries provide this criterion-referenced information, most surveys provide measurements of broadly or globally defined growth or educational development in each of the several curricular areas. Note that virtually all published standardized norm-referenced and criterion-referenced tests cover content and objectives judged to be common to many schools (see Chapter 18), and, therefore, such tests are not specific to the teaching emphasis of one teacher, one school, one text or one set of curricular materials. Therefore, it is imperative that (a) a school system carefully study a test's content before deciding to adopt it and (b) a teacher use tests especially geared to the specific learning objectives of the classroom for day-to-day instructional decisions requiring test information (e.g., whether a pupil has mastered a specific concept).

Multilevel tests not part of a survey battery are usually "stand alone" products, covering one curricular area such as reading or mathematics. These tests provide a deeper and broader sampling of content than a corresponding subtest of a survey battery. Thus, the amount of time devoted to testing in the single curricular area is generally longer than a survey battery subtest. This increased time expenditure may be either an advantage or disadvantage. Some publishers of survey batteries sell certain subtests (e.g., reading) for separate administration. If the stand alone multilevel test has not been concurrently normed with tests from other curricular areas using the same standardization sample, it cannot be used to compare a pupil's relative strengths and weaknesses in different curricular areas.

The term *diagnostic tests* has been associated with some tests classified as multilevel, single subject tests. There exist, however, several distinct kinds of diagnostic tests. One kind is built on a strictly *individual differences model* and uses norm-referencing as a primary method of score interpretation. Using this approach, a mathematics diagnostic test, for example, may have several separate subtests: one for each of the four basic operations ($+$, $-$, $\times$, $\div$), one for basic concepts of numeration and place value, one for fractions, and one for word problems. A person's status in each of these separate areas is ascertained by referencing the subtest scores to norms (usually percentile ranks) and using these norm-referenced scores to plot a profile of strengths and weaknesses in mathematics. This is analogous to what is done in survey batteries, but here all comparisons are within a single curricular area rather than between curricular areas. This kind of diagnostic test is not criterion-referenced.

A second kind of diagnostic achievement test is built on a *behavioral objectives model* and uses criterion-referencing to interpret scores. The content of an area is described by fine-grained, specific behavioral objectives. Diagnosis consists of testing and reporting whether each behavior is mastered. It seeks to go beyond describing a pupil as "weak in subtraction." Rather, it attempts to describe the pupil with terms such as "mastery of single-digit subtraction," and/or "nonmastery of two-digit subtraction requiring borrowing from the tens' position." This kind of diagnostic test is frequently a multilevel test. A third kind of diagnostic test is also criterion-referenced. This kind attempts to *identify and classify the kinds of errors* a pupil makes. Taking mathematics as an example again, these tests may help a teacher describe a pupil's erroneous performance such as "renames subtrahend incorrectly and subtracts original numbers." A fourth type of diagnostic test helps a teacher describe a pupil in terms of the *basic prerequisites* which the pupil may be lacking (e.g., "The pupil lacks a basic understanding of place value and numeration necessary to proceed with subtraction problems involving borrowing." You may want to look at the diagnostic section of Table 17.3 at this point.)

If a measure of growth or development is not desired, a single-level test may be useful. Rather than cover several grade or age levels, such tests are directed toward a particular level or a particular course. Usually such tests are built for high school and college courses, rather than for elementary curricular subjects because the skills learned in the latter are developed over several years. There are, for example, tests for Algebra I, first year college chemistry and first year college French. Each test is generally designed to "stand alone" and is not coordinated with other tests. Thus, comparing a pupil's relative standing in several subjects is generally not possible. Also, a test in this area frequently does not provide scores for different subtopics of a course, but there are some exceptions. A foreign language test, for example, may provide separate scores for subareas such as idioms, vocabulary, grammar, paragraph reading and listening comprehension. Scores on tests in this category of achievement tests are most often interpreted using norm-referencing schemes.

Most publishers of standardized, empirically documented tests provide materials which help to interpret and use the test scores. Teachers' manuals often describe in considerable detail the intended purpose and uses of the test results, often suggesting ways to improve pupils' skills by using test information for instructional planning. Some publishers provide separate manuals for curriculum coordinators and school administrators to help them use test information for purposes of evaluation and reporting to the school board. Most publishers provide score reports to be used both within the school and for reporting scores to pupils and parents.

Characteristics of Nonstandardized, Not Empirically Documented Achievement Tests

Without trying out the tests and without collecting data concerning how well they are functioning, there is little a test developer can do to either improve the test or verify that its intended purposes are in fact being accomplished. A great many of these kinds of tests, however, are published and used by teachers. One kind is advertised and sold as a criterion-referenced test. The major purpose of criterion-referencing is to describe a person in terms of a well-defined domain of performance (see Chapter 17), and the developers of these tests often define the instructionally relevant domain in terms of specific behavioral objec-

tives. Criterion-referencing, however, precludes neither (a) the development of norm-referencing schemes as an aid to additional score interpretation nor (b) the collection of empirical data to improve the test or to validate the claims made for it. Further, normative data are required if the test is intended to be used for either (a) comparing a pupil with others or (b) comparing a pupil's growth in one area with growth in other areas. (The state of the art at this time does not permit us to compare one area with another in any absolute sense. For example, can you answer a question such as, "How many reading objectives would a pupil have to attain before that pupil's reading status is equal to the pupil's arithmetic status?") These *may* be good tests, but no one knows for sure. As you read in Chapter 16, the validity of a test should not be an article of faith, but should be judged on the basis of empirical data. Unfortunately, many persons purchase such tests, so these publishers continue to stay in business.

Teacher's editions of texts often contain items: items appear at the end of chapters or at the back of some books; some curricular materials have tests incorporated into the learning exercises. These tests appeal to a teacher because they are very closely matched to what the students have been taught. The quality of such tests varies widely, however, and most of the time they have not been improved on the basis of tryout data. A textbook author is seldom an expert item writer, and the editorial office of the textbook publisher seldom edits the items for their technical merit. Such tests may not pass muster if judged by the item writing rules presented in Chapters 6 through 9, yet important decisions about a pupil's daily progress in a curriculum are often based on scores obtained from them. One suggestion is to edit the items yourself, revising them when necessary, and improving them as you discover their flaws when you use them in the classroom. (This may be done by teacher committees or by one teacher, a little at a time, over several years.)

Comparison of Published and Teacher-Made Tests

For most day-to-day instructional decisions a teacher will have to rely on curricular accompaniments or teacher-made tests. These will more nearly match the curriculum and the teacher's emphasis. Exceptions exist, of course, as when the teacher is unable to diagnose a pupil's difficulty in, for example, reading or mathematics; then using a published diagnostic test may be necessary.

Survey batteries and multilevel single area tests do give a broad picture of a pupil's general educational development which extends beyond the specifics of what is taught in the classroom. However, the more nearly a test covers skills and content emphasized by a teacher, the higher the pupils can be expected to score.

Uses and Misuses of Standardized Achievement Tests

Within Classroom Uses

These are among the most frequently listed purposes of achievement testing for within classroom decisions (Hieronymus, 1976):

1. To describe the educational developmental levels of pupils so that instruction can be modified or adapted to accommodate individual pupil's needs.
2. To describe specific qualitative strengths and weaknesses in pupils' educational development in order to remediate deficiencies and capitalize on strengths.
3. To describe the extent to which a pupil has attained the prerequisites needed to go on to new or advanced learning.
4. To describe commonalities among pupils in order to group pupils for more efficient instruction.
5. To describe pupils' performances with respect to specific instructional objectives

in order to make immediate instructional decisions.

6. To provide pupils with an operational description of what kinds of performances are expected of them.
7. To provide pupils with feedback about their progress toward learning goals.

Not all of these purposes are served equally well by any one particular test. Survey tests, for example, measure broad, long-term educational goals, rather than specific objectives or immediate learning outcomes. It may take all year for a pupil to learn to read well enough, for example, to show some sign of improvement on a survey test. In the interim, however, the pupil may learn many specific skills and reading strategies and perform well on tests measuring these immediate learning objectives. Further, norm-referenced survey information is not likely to be very useful to teachers for purposes of designing an individual pupil's instructional plans and procedures. Standardized tests (or teacher-made tests) which provide criterion-referenced information on specific objectives or on less global, more delimited skill areas are likely to be more useful to the teacher for instructional planning than are ordinary survey tests.

An important concern about standardized tests is not only whether they correspond closely to the objectives actually taught in the classroom, but also whether the test results are available to a teacher at the time decisions have to be made. Standardized tests are often administered in the fall, after the teacher has organized the class, and the tests are sent away for scoring. By the time a teacher receives pupils' results, several weeks of schooling have already passed. Circumstances such as these work against the possibility of using standardized tests for immediate instructional decisions.

A within classroom use of standardized test results not mentioned above is that the test can serve to confirm or corroborate a teacher's judgment about a pupil's general educational development. It is important to realize that no single source of information about pupils is entirely accurate—be that source a teacher's observations, results on teacher-made tests, or results on standardized tests. Standardized tests can provide additional information that may alert a teacher of the need to consider a particular pupil further.

Use of Tests for Purposes External to the Classroom

Standardized survey tests are most useful for extra-classroom purposes (Airasian, 1979). Among these extra-classroom uses of tests are (Hieronymus, 1976):

1. To describe the strengths and weaknesses of a group (class, building, or school system) in order to help make decisions about curricular or instructional procedure changes.
2. To describe the relative effectiveness of alternate methods of instruction and some of the factors moderating their effectiveness.
3. To describe the relative effectiveness of innovations or experiments in education.

To this list add:

4. To describe the general educational development of children to their parents.
5. To describe to school boards and other "publics" the relative effectiveness of the educational enterprise.

All of these purposes relate in some way to accountability. But accountability purposes are not served well if the tests used do not correspond to what is happening in the classroom. Further, a possibility exists that when standardized tests are overemphasized they may intrude into classroom practices so that having the pupils "pass the test" becomes more important than teaching them the important

skills the test samples. Young and Ayrer (1979) reported on how administrators in the School District of Philadelphia used the results of their citywide standardized testing program. At the time of their study, the district had eight sub-districts and over 200,000 pupils. Figure 19.1 shows the line organization of the particular administrators they interviewed. This figure will be helpful in understanding the roles of the administrators. Below is a summary of what the various administrators said about how they used the standardized testing results sent to them by the district's testing division.

1. *Executive superintendent:* Reviews summary reports on a school-by-school basis to confirm or identify exceptions of what the superintendent perceived to be a school's expected performance.
2. *Associate superintendents:* Use the test results in a variety of ways dependent on their role and function. Among the ways are:
   a. *communications:* Reporting to school board, to individual school's parent advisory board, and to various community groups; and disseminating results to media and to each school building.
   b. *student management decisions:* Identifying students that are eligible for special programs and services (e.g., Title I) and distributing students to other buildings when a school closes.
   c. *resource allocation:* Initiating a test-taking skills program in a school; allocating additional teachers, coordinators, and/or staff to particular schools.
   d. *conflict resolution:* Discussing test results with community and/or parent groups when asked to do so by the groups.
   e. *evaluating and planning for specific programs:* Judging whether the district as a whole attained its goals in reading and mathematics; judging whether individual schools attained the goals set by the district; clarifying and setting goals for low-achieving schools; devel-

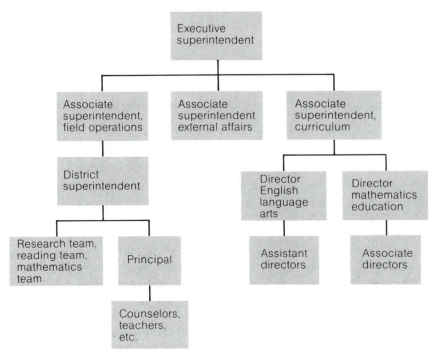

Figure 19 • 1
Line organization of school administrators interviewed by Young and Ayrer (1979).

Source: Adapted from Young and Ayrer (1979, p. 7)

oping plans for improving reading in schools and in the district; and guiding the development and implementation of a new reading program.

f. *staff development and information:* Presenting a particular school's test results to its principal and staff and presenting district-wide results to supervisory and central administration staff.

3. *Principals:* Use test results in ways similar to superintendents, except the scope of their uses were limited to their own schools. Among the specific uses were: deciding how to group pupils, identifying pupils eligible for Title I programs, making changes in curriculum and instructional emphasis, discussing test results with curricular department chairpersons, and discussing test results with parents.

Young and Ayrer found that the district's standardized achievement test results were used most by the associate superintendents and other central administration staff, and that teachers used the test results very little. They attributed this to two things: (a) support staff to help teachers organize the test information into a usable form was lacking and (b) the tests were administered in the fall after the schools had their classrooms organized.

Misuses of the Standardized Achievement Test Results

Criticisms Criticisms of the standardized achievement tests abound, especially of norm-referenced survey batteries. For some persons, the very idea of a commercial, external,

A. **Criticisms directed toward an intrinsic test characteristic:**
  1. Tests assume that everyone values the skills tested.
  2. Tests assume a homogenous culture and/or a common curriculum.
  3. Tests are biased, favoring white, middle class pupils.
  4. Tests assume that approximately half the pupils are below average.
  5. Tests are too impersonal, vague, undemocratic, and/or irrelevant.
  6. Tests cover only a small fraction of what schools try to accomplish.
  7. Tests are invalid measures of behaviors specifically learned in schools.

B. **Criticisms directed toward a characteristic not measured by a test:**
  1. Tests are not diagnostic.
  2. Tests do not measure the objectives of innovative instructional programs.
  3. Tests do not measure creativity, interest, initiative, and/or values.
  4. Tests compare students rather than measure an individual's learning.

C. **Criticisms directed toward the effects of using a test:**
  1. Children are "labeled" (or "mislabeled").
  2. Test use alters the school curriculum by encouraging teaching toward the test.
  3. Tests result in competition among learners.
  4. Tests cause fear.

Table 19 • 1

Examples of three domains of criticisms of standardized, norm-referenced, survey tests.

Source: Based on P. W. Airasian, "A Perspective on the Uses and Misuses of Standardized Achievement Tests." *Measurement in Education*, 1980, Vol. 10, No. 3. Copyright 1980, National Council on Measurement in Education, Washington, D.C.

norm-referenced, summative, and/or quantitative device for measuring educational outcomes is repugnant and incredulous. Tests—standardized or not, norm-referenced or criterion-referenced, formative or summative, external or teacher-made, qualitative and quantitative—can be misused. Much of this misuse, moreover, stems not from characteristics inherent in a particular test, but from (a) the unvalidated claims made for some tests and (b) the unscrupulous way(s) in which the test might be used. Throughout this text, I discuss appropriate uses and emphasize the need to validate claims made for tests and for using professional judgment in administering and interpreting tests.

Table 19.1 gives a summary of some of the many criticisms of standardized achievement tests, especially survey batteries. As the table shows, criticisms may be directed (a) toward some intrinsic characteristic of a test, such as its content coverage, (b) toward something which is not part of a test, such as its failure to test certain pupil characteristics, or (c) toward the effects of using a test, such as inappropriately classifying or labeling a pupil.

Airasian (1979) mentioned several things about these three domains of criticisms:

1. *Perceived misuses of tests are often described by criticisms from more than one of the three domains*, for example, that tests (a) measure only a small portion of what is taught in the classroom (intrinsic characteristic), (b) do not measure the real goals of an educational program (characteristic not measured), *and* (c) foster undesirable changes in school curricula or teacher emphasis (effects of testing).

2. *Some criticisms are contradictory.* The same test may be criticized, (a) by some persons because its focus is too narrow and (b) by others because scores on it are influenced by too broad a range of human characteristics.

3. *Many of the criticisms can be overcome* by either (a) using the test in the way it was intended to be used or (b) by choosing another, more appropriate test.

4. *A single test cannot be expected to measure the "whole person."* Human qualities are too rich and too diverse to be observed by any one

set of procedures. It is an open question, furthermore, if some human characteristic (e.g., interest, attitudes, values, emotional states, etc.) *ought* to be measured by the school.

5. *A criticism of a test may or may not be the same things as a misuse of a test.* Educators can criticize a test for not measuring a certain pupil characteristic (e.g., feelings toward someone), but such a failure may not be a misuse. Sometimes, *measuring* a characteristic may be the misuse (e.g., by violating a pupil's privacy).

Misuses Rather than enumerating a lengthy list of specific misuses or abuses, four broad categories will be considered (Airasian, 1979): (1) interpreting the observed test score as if it contained no error of measurement, (2) using a single test score as the only criterion for making important decisions about individual pupils and programs, (3) uncritically interpreting a test as a pure measure of the trait or characteristic it claims to measure, and (4) interpreting test performance as if it were caused solely by the pupil, solely by a school, or solely by a teacher, rather than interpreting it as a measure of a complex set of antecedent conditions.

As you read in Chapter 15, any single test score is likely to contain error of measurement. For many standardized, empirically documented tests, such measurement errors are not extremely large. A study of the test's standard error of measurement will give an indication of the likely size of such errors of measurement (see Chapter 15).

A second type of misuse of tests occurs when the only criterion used to make a decision is a test score. Examples of such misuses include sectioning a class based only on reading readiness test scores, putting a pupil into an educable mentally retarded class only on the basis of an intelligence test score, putting a pupil into a gifted and talented program only on the basis of an intelligence test score, granting a high school diploma only on the basis of a test score, judging one teacher better than another only on the basis of the average achievement test results. Using several sources of information along with test scores more often than not will improve the total pool of relevant information that is brought to bear on the decision and, thus, improve the quality of the decision itself.

A third misuse concerns uncritically interpreting what a test measures. It is a common practice to assume that a test, for example, of reading comprehension or science, is a pure measure of those traits and to forget that the scores may be seriously influenced by other factors such as general school ability, home background, motivation, item content or format, and so on. Concerns of this sort are directed toward the construct validity of the test (see Chapter 16). To be sure, all test users will need to make inferences about pupils which go beyond the items on the test, but such interpretations should be made carefully and only after first examining the research evidence and understanding the processes which led to a particular individual's score. The ability to make careful, thoughtful, and well-founded inferences is an important characteristic that distinguishes a professional teacher's approach to testing from the approaches of less than professional colleagues.

The fourth misuse concerns attributing poor test performance solely to one cause. Sometimes a score is interpreted as though it were entirely the result of a particular pupil's failing rather than the result of several interacting conditions such as the quality of previous teaching, the nature of a home environment, or other personal experiences the pupil has had. A similar situation arises when some persons try to blame the teacher if the class does poorly on a test. Before a person can attribute the rise (or fall) of a group's test scores solely to a particular teacher, that person would have to consider the influence on the scores of each of several factors by answering such questions as the following: (a) Did the content of the test match the breadth and emphasis of what was taught in the classroom? (b) Did the pupils in this year's class have, on the whole, better or worse general school aptitude than classes in the past (or classes assigned to other teachers)? (c) Were students in this (or another) class taught the answers to the items or otherwise given unfair advantages? (d) Did last year's teacher do an exceptionally good (or poor) job of teaching and did this influence carry over to this year? (e) What home factors related to the pupils' successes (or lack thereof)? (f) Did the school principal (or other instructional leader) facilitate or inhibit the teacher's teaching or the pupils' learning? The reader can probably name other factors to consider when ascertaining the reasons why a class did well or poorly on a test. Unlike an automobile manufacturer or an owner of a pizzeria, schools and teachers have relatively little control over the raw materials with which and conditions under which they must operate (Feldt, 1976).

"We've taught him very little. We figured you would like to train him in your own way."

Source: Reprinted courtesy of C. A. Murphy, 1980.

Multilevel Survey Batteries

There are a great many achievement survey batteries available in the marketplace. The *Eighth Mental Measurements Yearbook* listed 38 different tests and, during the two years following its publication, the Buros Institute of Mental Measurements received an additional 25 new or revised editions (Mitchell, Reynolds, & Elliott, 1980). Below, in alphabetical order, are the most widely used batteries. The grade ranges they cover are listed in parentheses.

> *California Achievement Tests* (K–12)
> *Comprehensive Assessment Program Achievement Series* (K–12)
> *Comprehensive Tests of Basic Skills* (K–10)
> *Iowa Tests of Basic Skills* (K–9)
> *Iowa Tests of Educational Development* (9–12)
> *Metropolitan Achievement Test* (K–12)
> *Peabody Individual Achievement Test* (K–adult)
> *Sequential Test of Educational Progress* (K–12)
> *SRA Achievement Series* (K–12)
> *Stanford Achievement Test Series* (K–12)
> *STS Educational Development Series* (2–12)
> *Tests of Achievement and Proficiency* (9–12)
> *The 3-R's Test* (K–12)
> *Wide Range Achievement Test* (K–adult)

All of the above are group administered tests except for the "Peabody" and the "Wide Range" which are individually administered. Publishers of these tests are listed in Appendices F and G. Details about each battery can be obtained from the publishers' catalogues. Critical reviews are found in the *Mental Measurements Yearbooks* and other sources identified in Chapter 18.

Group Administered Survey Batteries

Group administered survey batteries have several *subtests*, each designed for assessment in a separate curricular area. Although there are differences among the tests in the number of subtests and areas covered, the following list is descriptive of areas typically measured. Separate scores are provided for several (usually 6 to 8) areas; different publishers may have different names for an area.

Basic Skill Areas

Vocabulary (knowing the meanings of words)
Reading
  Decoding Skills (visual discrimination, sound/symbol relationships)
  Comprehension (sentence and paragraph reading)
Spelling (usually recognition of misspelled words)
Language
  Mechanics (use of capitalization and punctuation conventions)
  Grammar (usage of parts of speech, correct expressions, sentence structure, etc.)
Mathematics
  Computation (use of basic operations with whole numbers, fractions, decimals)
  Concepts (recognizing the meaning of mathematical terms and concepts)
  Applications (solving word problems, reading mathematical data)

Additional Areas

Listening Skills (comprehending what is said, but not written by the teacher)
Study Skills:
  Library and Reference Skills (knowing how to use library and reference materials)
  Maps, Graphs, and Tables (reading and comprehending the information contained in these)
Social Studies (some tests are mostly reading comprehension in this area, others measure knowledge of specific facts and concepts)
Science (similar to the social studies area except the content is general science).

The above list is meant to be suggestive of the breadth of coverage of survey batteries.

You should not assume that every survey battery covers every topic or subtopic listed. Further, it is important to note that the specific behaviors actually required of pupils on a particular survey battery vary quite widely from survey battery to survey battery. *Survey batteries of different test authors are not interchangeable, even though they have similar sounding names.*[2] One example of how widely the mathematics content of four batteries varies appears in Chapter 16 (Figure 16.2). An analysis of the other subtest areas would reveal similar differences. Such content variability makes actually inspecting a test and matching its content and emphasis in each area to that of the local curriculum before adopting it imperative.

Most group administered survey batteries have several features in common (Iwanicki, 1980):

1. Test development features Manuals and other materials provide the following information about test development for each subtest: (a) content and behavioral objectives covered, (b) type of norms and how developed, (c) type of criterion-referencing provided, (d) reliability data, and (e) techniques used to screen items for offensiveness and possible sex, ethnic, and racial bias.

2. Test administration features Tests generally (a) have two equivalent forms, (b) require a total administration time of 2 to 3 hours spread among several testing sessions over several school days (Note: tests vary widely in length and administration time), (c) provide practice booklets for pupils to use before being tested, (d) have separate, machine scorable answer sheets for upper grades, while pupils in lower grades mark answers directly on the machine scoreble test booklets,

---

[2]This false assumption is called the "jingle fallacy"; assuming that tests with different sounding names in fact measure different things is called the "jangle fallacy" (Kelly, 1927).

and (e) permit both *in-level* and *out-of-level* testing.[3]

3. Test norming features Tests generally (a) use broadly representative national sampling for norms development (but see Chapter 14) and (b) provide both fall and spring individual pupil norms. Sometimes *special* norms such as the following are provided: (a) large city norms, (b) Title I norms, (c) norms for high SES communities, (d) norms for nonpublic schools, (e) regional norms, and (f) norms for school building averages.

4. Test score features Tests provide raw scores for each subtest and the following norm-referenced scores: percentile ranks, normal curve equivalents, stanines, extended normalized standard scores, and grade-equivalents (or some similar grade level indicator score). Attitudes among publishers toward using grade-equivalents varies from encouraging their use (e.g., *Iowa Tests of Basic Skills*), through remaining rather neutral (e.g., *California Achievement Tests*), to discouraging their use (e.g., *Metropolitan Achievement Test*) (Iwanicki, 1980). Some tests provide instructional reading level scores which are keyed to commonly used basal readers (e.g., *Metropolitan Achievement Tests*).

5. Test score reporting and interpretation features Tests generally have interpretive manuals for teachers, school administrators, and/or counselors. Most group tests provide computer-generated score reports. Examples of these reports include: (a) analysis of class performance on clusters of items (Figure 19.2), (b) building report for one grade level on all subtests (Figure 19.3), (c) a narrative report specially tailored to an individual pupil which interprets the test results to the teacher or parent (Figure 19.4). Some tests have narrative reports which interpret the results for each grade level or for each school building. Such reports are not free, of course.

Although each of the survey batteries have interpretive information included in their manuals or other materials, a feature of the *California Achievement Tests* (CAT) is the inclusion of a special guide book which presents a step-by-step procedure for the teacher to use in analyzing the test results and for translating these results into lesson plans. The procedure is summarized in Figure 19.5.

Several of the tests contain suggested strategies for teaching the skills tested. The CAT guidebook appears to be more extensive than others, providing a teacher with several teaching activities that can be used to teach each of the tested skills and concepts. The activities are directed toward skill and concept development; they do not give practice or training directly related to the items. A sample page from this guidebook is shown in Figure 19.6.

Individually Administered Survey Batteries

Individually administered achievement batteries are usually administered to pupils with special needs, for example, pupils with learning disabilities or handicaps who otherwise would have difficulty taking tests in group settings. Pupils unable to be tested in group settings often can be validly tested in individual sessions where the test administrator can provide the special testing conditions they need (e.g., ease of lip-reading or freedom from distractions) and can establish greater rapport. Sometimes individual achievement batteries are used as "screening" tests to identify pupils with learning difficulties or as part of a broader

---

[3]Test booklets are organized by *level;* each level is designed for use with several grades. The *California Achievement Test,* for example, has five levels: (1) grades 1.5–2.9, (2) 2.0–4.9, (3) 4.0–6.9, (4) 6.0–9.9, and (5) 9.0–12.9. A pupil is said to be tested *in-level* if the level of the test booklet corresponds to the pupil's actual grade placement. If a pupil's level of academic functioning is either above or below the actual grade placement, the school may elect to administer the test level that more nearly corresponds to the pupil's functioning level. This is called *out-of-level* testing. A pupil is measured best when a test is tailored to the pupil's functioning level.

A set of reports (single copy, 14" x 11") is produced for each test designated. Each set consists of a report for each class, a report for each grade in each school, and, when appropriate, a report for each grade for all schools combined. The reports present:

Ⓐ Objective measured by each item

Ⓑ Percent correct for each item with the comparable national percent correct; flag if percent is significantly above or below national value

Ⓒ Number (class) or percent (school & system) selecting each wrong option and omitting each item

Ⓓ Pupil test scores

Ⓔ Responses to each item (shown only on class reports)

Ⓕ Summaries for clusters of items measuring similar objectives or skill areas; number and percent of pupils at or above national median for the cluster

There are two important notes to be considered in ordering this option:

— When a level of Metro has been used in a grade or at a time for which no national item data are available, the comparison of local to national percent correct figures may not be appropriate.

— By its very nature, a given item analysis report can display data for only one form of one level. If forms or levels are mixed within grades in a school or across schools, separate reports must necessarily be produced for each form/level combination.

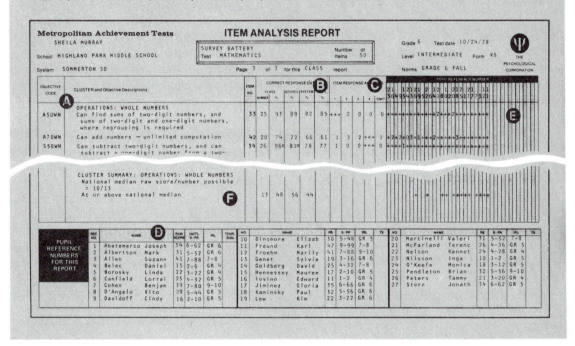

Figure 19 • 2 An example of a computer-prepared item analysis report for one classroom which took a multilevel survey achievement test.

series of individual tests when a general psychological evaluation is conducted. Individual achievement survey batteries may be used to assess the general educational development of a pupil newly transferred to a school or as a "double check" on a previously adminis-

tered group survey test, the results of which are being questioned for a particular pupil. Because both the content and norms of an individual test are different than the group test, this latter use should proceed very cautiously. You can expect a pupil's results from

This option provides a duplicate report (11" x 8½") for each grade for each school, and for each grade for all schools combined if more than one is covered by the order. Each report includes:

A Means, Standard Deviations, and Quartile Points in terms of Raw Scores

B Means, Standard Deviations, and Quartile Points in terms of Scaled Scores

C Grade Equivalents of Scaled Score Percentile Points

D Number and Percent in each national Percentile Rank quarter

E Number and Percent obtaining each IRL

F Stanines based on norms for schools or systems

Otis-Lennon School Ability Test scores are also summarized when the combination Survey/OLSAT is involved.

Source: The Psychological Corporation (1978, p. 25)

Figure 19 • 3 An example of a computer-prepared administrator's building report for one grade which took a multilevel survey achievement test.

the two types of tests to correspond only very roughly.

Two commonly administered individual survey achievement tests are the *Wide Range Achievement Test* (WRAT) and the *Peabody Individual Achievement Test* (PIAT). Such tests are wide-range achievement tests. That is, a single instrument contains items that span many ages or grades (essentially ages 5 to adult). Thus, by their very nature, they contain few items specifically associated with a given age

or grade level. Such tests do not have as broad or as in-depth coverage as group survey tests that have separate instruments for each age or grade level. This is not necessarily a criticism of these tests. The intent of the developers of such wide-range tests is to provide a means of obtaining a quick survey of a pupil's strengths in several curricular areas. This quickly obtained information is used to direct the practitioner to the appropriate relatively weak areas for a more in-depth diagnostic fol-

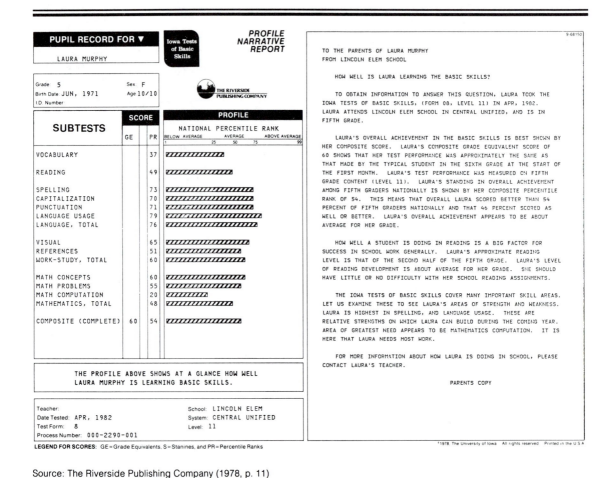

Figure 19 • 4   An example of a computer-prepared narrative report of a pupil's performance on a multilevel achievement survey battery.

low-up. Also, the subtests of a group survey battery do not contain enough test items for detailed diagnostic decisions. This is often why single area tests (to be discussed subsequently) are necessary.

The PIAT is administered using an easel format. The pupil need not write responses to the multiple-choice items; they need only say or point to the option. Within each subtest the items are arranged in order of difficulty. A pupil does not take each item but a starting point (called a *basal level*) and an ending point

(called a *ceiling level*) are established based on the pupils' pattern of correct answers and errors. This is shown in Figure 19.7.

Consideration When Selecting and Using Survey Batteries

Suggestions for using survey battery information in the classroom instructional process are outlined in Figure 19.5. Other procedures for teachers to use in reviewing test scores

Steps of a Classroom Management System as Applied to CAT C and D	
Step 1: Assessing Needs Use CAT C and D reports to determine strengths and weaknesses of the class and of individuals. Diagnose further if necessary. Use other test instruments or teacher evaluation. **Step 2: Assigning priorities** Use CAT C and D reports to establish initial instructional priorities. Use classroom knowledge to re-evaluate and refine priorities. **Step 3: Establishing groups** Use CAT C and D reports to help group students with similar instructional needs.	**Step 4: Planning instruction** Use CAT C and D reports to identify objectives and skills to help organize instructional units. Develop a variety of instructional methods and materials. Use CAT C and D suggested instructional activities as a resource. **Step 5: Monitoring progress** Develop a method to record progress of individuals and groups toward specified goals. Use CAT C and D reports to help record or monitor progress. **Step 6: Evaluating results** Use written materials, short tests, or conferences to determine the results of instruction. Retest with CAT C and D to determine growth.

Source: CTB/McGraw-Hill (1978, p. 65)

Figure 19 • 5 The steps of a procedure recommended by one publisher for using survey test results to plan instruction for a class.

when they are received appear in Chapter 14. You should review these at this time.

As I have mentioned, each test has to be examined and reviewed individually in order to decide whether it is appropriate for use in a particular school. School officials should keep the following advice in mind before deciding to adopt an elementary school survey battery (Gronlund, 1976):

1. Survey batteries measure only part of the outcomes desired for elementary schools. Additional procedures are needed to evaluate the other outcomes.
2. Specific content in subjects such as social studies and science may become dated quickly. Tests designed to measure broad cognitive skills or levels of educational development become less quickly dated.
3. Tests measuring broad cognitive skills or levels of educational development need to

be supplemented by teacher-made or standardized tests of specific content.
4. Each battery has a different mix and emphasis of content and behavior; each is accompanied by various kinds of interpretive aids. Because of this, examining a test battery carefully before deciding to purchase is necessary.

Because so much variation exists in high school curricula, choosing a survey battery for this educational level is difficult. To choose a test at this level requires a rather complete knowledge of the major curriculum emphasis and philosophy of a school. School officials should keep the following points in mind before selecting a high school test battery (Gronlund, 1976):

1. Survey batteries that emphasize basic skills (reading, mathematics, language) may be

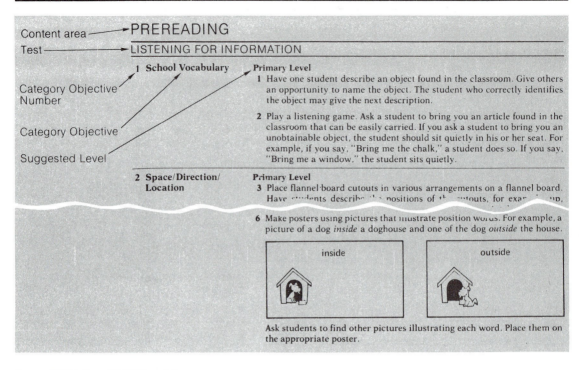

Content area ⟶ PREREADING

Test ⟶ LISTENING FOR INFORMATION

Category Objective Number

Category Objective

Suggested Level

1 School Vocabulary

Primary Level

1 Have one student describe an object found in the classroom. Give others an opportunity to name the object. The student who correctly identifies the object may give the next description.

2 Play a listening game. Ask a student to bring you an article found in the classroom that can be easily carried. If you ask a student to bring you an unobtainable object, the student should sit quietly in his or her seat. For example, if you say, "Bring me the chalk," a student does so. If you say, "Bring me a window," the student sits quietly.

2 Space/Direction/Location

Primary Level

3 Place flannel-board cutouts in various arrangements on a flannel board. Have students describe the positions of the cutouts, for example, up,

6 Make posters using pictures that illustrate position words. For example, a picture of a dog *inside* a doghouse and one of the dog *outside* the house.

| inside | outside |

Ask students to find other pictures illustrating each word. Place them on the appropriate poster.

Source: CTB/McGraw-Hill (1978, p. 70)

Figure 19 • 6 Example of a page from a guidebook which one test publisher provides for helping teachers to teach the skills and concepts tested on an achievement survey battery.

more useful as measures of high school readiness than as measures of high school outcomes (unless a high school program was especially directed toward basic skill development) because such basic skills are prerequisite to learning specific course content.

2. Some tests are more oriented toward testing specific content than educational development broadly defined. If a content-oriented test is desired, a careful review of *each item* on the test is necessary to see if the test measures what the school intends (see Chapter 18).

3. Tests stressing the measurement of levels of educational development which cut across several subject areas rather than measure knowledge of specific content tend to measure more complex skills and global processes.

4. The variety of course offerings at the high school level makes careful examination of the content of each survey battery more necessary than at the elementary level.

5. Supplementing a high school survey battery with tests designed to measure content knowledge of specific subjects may be necessary.

6. A practical consideration is the continuity of measurement from elementary to secondary levels. This often means purchasing a high school battery from the same publisher as the elementary school battery used.

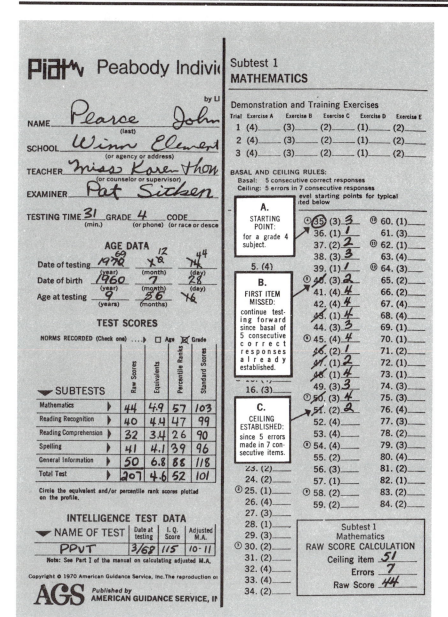

Figure 19 • 7 A sample page from the individual record form of the PIAT showing how the basal and ceiling levels are established.

Multilevel Criterion-Referenced Tests

Since a survey test is designed to cover several curricular areas within a given time limit, it must do so with relatively few items. Seldom do survey tests include more than one or two items per objective and seldom are a great many specific objectives for a subject covered at a particular level. While survey tests do have an advantage for assessing global or general growth, using a more in-depth multilevel test that covers only a single area is often desirable. A few examples of criterion-referenced tests appear in this section. Others are listed in Appendix G.

Examples of Group Administered Multilevel Criterion-Referenced Tests

The *Metropolitan Achievement Tests* described in the previous section are survey tests. A second component of this series consists of three separate criterion-referenced tests—reading, mathematics, and language—and is known as the *Instructional Tests*. Each test has five levels, ranging from Primer (grades K.5–1.4) through Advanced 1 (grades 7.0–9.9). Within each level there are several subtests. Table 19.2 gives the subtest titles and number of items for the Intermediate Level. Notice, for example, that the Reading Instructional Test has seven subtests each with between 18 and 60 items: a total of 223 items for this fifth and sixth grade reading test. By contrast, the Reading Subtest of this level of the *Metropolitan Survey Battery* has 60 items. There are at least three items per objective on the *Instructional Tests*. Each test is group administered. The administration is broken into several "sittings" of about one class period each during which one or two subtests are taken. Thus it may take several school days to administer a complete test.

As with most criterion-referenced tests, the major benefit comes from obtaining a score for each pupil on each objective. Forms such as the one in Figure 19.8 greatly facilitate this process, permitting the teacher to see at a glance a pupil's overall test performance. The "+ +" in Figure 19.8 indicates that the pupil has "reached criterion" or has "sufficiently mastered" the objective in question, so that instructional planning can proceed for those remaining objectives which the teacher feels are important. Forms are also available for summarizing the entire class' performance, to facilitate planning for the entire group. It is important to keep in mind that three to five items per objective, while better than one item, are still a small and likely unreliable sample of behavior, especially when multiple-choice items are used. The teacher will have to use (a) professional judgment and (b) knowledge of each pupil to make a final decision about a child's instructional needs. In practice, tests derive their value from their use (a) as part of a (sequential) series of observations and (b) for formulating hypotheses (requiring follow-up) about what constitutes a particular person's difficulty (Meehl, 1954; Cronbach & Gleser, 1965).

Tests such as the METRO *Instructional Tests* cover a broad range of objectives some of which may not be appropriate for a given classroom. Second, as I discuss in Chapter 4, the concept of mastery of specific objectives may be of limited usefulness for some educational programs. Third, teachers may have little control of the scheduling of tests, so that such detailed information, even if appropriate, may not be available when needed for planning instruction. Fourth, a teacher may have available or may be able to construct more narrowly focused tests covering the instructional objectives that are to be taught next (see also Chapter 5). These considerations are among those which you should take into account when reviewing a test such as this and before making a decision to use it.

The following suggested guidelines for reviewing and interpreting objectives-referenced profiles such as that in Figure 19.8 seem applicable for a variety of tests which are like

Area/subtests	Number of Items	Actual working time (minutes)
Reading		
Phoeneme/Grapheme: Consonants	24	20
Phoneme/Grapheme: Vowels	42	25
Vocabulary in Context	24	15
Word Part Clues	18	10
Skimming and Scanning	20	20
Rate of Comprehension	35	4
Reading Comprehension	60	40
	223	134
Mathematics		
Numeration	30	20
Geometry and Measurement	42	30
Problem Solving	24	20
Operations: Whole Numbers	39	35
Operations: Laws and Properties	27	20
Operations: Fractions, Decimals	24	20
Graphs and Statistics	18	20
	204	165
Language		
Punctuation and Capitalization	54	30
Usage	30	15
Grammar and Syntax	45	30
Spelling	40	15
Study Skills	36	30
	205	120

Metropolitan Achievement Tests. Copyright © 1978 by Harcourt Brace Jovanovich, Inc.

Table 19 • 2

Structure of the Intermediate Level (Grades 5.0–6.0) *Metropolitan Achievement Tests Instructional Tests.*

the *Metropolitan Instructional Tests* (Hogan, Farr, Prescott, & Balow, 1978):

1. *First form an overall picture of a pupil's achievement in an area* and then go on to consider specific tests and objectives. Be sure to consider the total context: placement in each curricular area, both last year and this year's test results, factors which affect performance the day the test is administered, etc.

2. *Keep in mind that each pupil can learn more.* Use test results to individualize a pupil's program so it leads to new learning and new successes.

3. *Use both norm-referenced and criterion-referenced information, if available.* Rate each objective as to whether it (a) should have

been learned before the test was administered, (b) should be learned in the forthcoming instructional period, (c) is not expected to be learned in the immediately forthcoming period, or (d) is not important for your school. Use item norms (Figure 18.1) to aid your judgment as to the appropriateness of learning certain objectives at a particular grade level.

4. *Interrelate a pupil's performance in different topics within a subject area.* Examine performance on clusters of objectives that go together or that are prerequisites for later learning, rather than looking only at one objective at a time.

5. *Consider a pupil's interests and attitudes.* Knowledge of these can help in motivating a pupil and tailoring instruction.

PROBLEM SOLVING

Addition or Subtraction (N¹R / R²C)

		N¹R	R²C
5ND	Sums to 18; number sentence; dictated	3	++
5NR	Sums to 18; number sentence; read	3	++
5SD	Sums to 18; solve; dictated	3	++
5SR	Sums to 18; solve; read	2	++
6SX	2d & 1d; no regrp.; extraneous info.; solve; read	2	++

Multiplication or Division

7ND	Basic facts 1-9; number sentence; dictated	1	
7NR	Basic facts 1-9; number sentence; read	0	
7SD	Basic facts 1-9; solve; dictated	2	++
7SR	Basic facts 1-9; solve; read	1	

Add., Subt., Mult., and Div.

| 8SM | A&S 2d & 1d; M&D basic facts 1-9; multi-step; sol.; read | 0 | |

NUMERATION

18	Can count by 2's, 5's, and 10's	2	++
19	Determines which of 3 nos. is between other 2 in value	3	++
21	Determines ordinal position thru 100	3	++
22	Recognizes numbers as odd or even	3	++
23	Uses < or > to compare 2 numbers less than 1000	3	++
24	Determines value of any digit in 4-digit numeral	1	
25	Recognizes no. of 1's, 10's, 100's, 1000's in 4-digit numeral	1	
26	Determines expanded form of 3- or 4-digit numeral	0	
27	Can determine the union of sets	1	
28	Associates number-words with numerals (thru millions)	1	

¹ Number Right
² Reached Criterion

OPERATIONS: WHOLE NUMBERS

Addition

		N¹R	R²C
A4	2d and 1d; 2d and 2d; no regrouping	0	
A5	2d and 1d; 2d and 2d; regrouping required	3	++

Subtraction

S4	2d and 1d; 2d and 2d; no regrouping	1	
S5	2d and 1d; 2d and 2d; regrouping required	1	
S6	Zeros in 1's or 10's place	2	++

Multiplication

M1	Basic facts 1-5	1	
M2	Basic facts 6-9	0	
M4	2d and 1d; no regrouping	2	++
M5	2d and 1d; regrouping required	0	

Division

| D1 | Basic facts 1-5 | 1 | |
| D2 | Basic facts 6-9 | 0 | |

OPERATIONS: LAWS & PROPERTIES

		N¹R	R²C
01	Knows role of zero in addition and subtraction	1	
02	Can use Commutative Property of Addition	2	++
03	Can supply relational symbol for 2 quantities; <, >, =	2	++
04	Can use number line for addition and subtraction	1	
05	Recognizes addition and subtraction as inverses	2	++
06	Sees mult. as repeated addition; div. as reptd. subt.	1	
07	Can use arrays to show multiplication & division	1	
08	Uses Comut. Prop. of Mult. & knows div. is non-commutative	1	

GEOMETRY & MEASUREMENT

		N¹R	R²C
12	Can obtain information from a calendar	3	++
14	Can tell time to the minute	1	
15	Knows relationships among seconds, minutes, hours & days	1	
16	Identifies sphere, cone, cube, cylinder	3	++
17	Using ½'s, ⅓'s, ¼'s, can determine fractional parts	2	++
18	Finds value of any group of coins	3	++
19	Determines amount change due on purchase $1 or less	0	
20	Knows relationships betw. cups, pints, and quarts	0	
21	Can use non-standard units to express measures	0	
22	Determines perimeter of squares, rectangles & triangles	1	
23	Identifies shapes resulting from simple paper folding	1	
24	Knows relationships among inches, feet, and yards	0	
25	Selects English units for expressing measurements	0	
26	Selects metric units for expressing measurements	0	
27	Knows metric prefixes & relationships among them	0	

Name DEBBI STARR
Teacher LYNN CARLIN Grade 4
School HAMILTON
Date of Testing 10/16/77

Percentile Ranks and Stanines based on tables for
Fall [X] Spring [ ]

Score Summary Box

	Number Possible	Number Right	Scaled Score	Percentile Rank	Stanine	Reached Criterion
Numeration	30	18	591	38	4	5 / 10
Geom & Meas	45	15	588	12	3	4 / 15
Problem Solving	30	17	617	32	4	6 / 10
Operations: Whole No.	33	11	546	8	2	3 / 11
Operations: Laws & Prop.	24	11	564	23	4	3 / 8
Total Mathematics	162	72	504	22	3	Grade Equivalent 2.8

Figure 19 • 8
Example of a hypothetical profile of a fourth grader on the Mathematics Instructional test of the MAT.

Source: Hogan, Farr, Prescott, and Balow (1978, p. 71)

6. *Give pupils opportunities to practice the behaviors they have already acquired.* Avoid focusing only on the material not yet learned to the neglect of already acquired behavior. Practice is needed to maintain skills already acquired; pupils may enjoy demonstrating their previously acquired competence.

7. *While reviewing each pupil's test results, keep in mind questions of how the results can be*

38 *DRP* Units	81 *DRP* Units
A bird's wings are well-shaped for flight. The wing is curved. It cuts the air. This helps lift the bird. The feathers are light. But they are strong. They help make birds the best fliers. A bird can move them in many directions. Birds move their wings forward and down. Then they move them up and back. This is how they fly. The tail feathers serve as a brake. They also aid in steering.	Thomas Jefferson's belief in man's ability to govern himself is well known, but his views concerning the conditions under which this ability can be successfully realized are less familiar. Jefferson believed that a natural moral sense—which he assumed to be a universal characteristic of mankind—was the initial and basic prerequisite for self-government. The effective operation of this moral sense was then influenced, he believed, by environmental factors, in particular by economic circumstances.

Source: From *The Degrees of Reading Power: Readability Report* 1980–81 (New York: The College Board, 1980), pp. 9–10. Used by permission of The College Board.

Table 19 • 3   Examples of passages having different *Degrees of Reading Power (DRP)* readability scores.

used during instruction. What do the results suggest about (a) *what* should be taught, (b) *how* it should be taught, (c) what should be *reviewed*, and (d) in what *sequence* it should be taught?

8. *Coordinate class and individual plans, matching these with your personal teaching style.* Integrating these three aspects, while not an easy task, is important and necessary if instruction is to succeed.

9. Plan follow-up testing to check on the progress being made. Teacher observations, homework assignments, and classroom quizzes help to monitor daily pupil progress, but comprehensive assessment of the degree to which broader goals are being attained is essential. Don't leave this to serendipity, plan for it.

Another example of a multilevel, group administered criterion-referenced test is the *Degrees of Reading Power (DRP)* (College Entrance Examination Board, 1980d). Unlike the METRO *Instructional Tests,* however, the *DRP* does not report a pupil's performance on specific behavioral objectives. The purpose of testing is to determine the most difficult nonfiction passage a person can read with comprehension, the passages being ordered on a scale of reading difficulty. Multiple-choice cloze

items (called MAZE items in Chapter 9) test comprehension. Levels of the test span grades 3 through 12.

The readability of each passage on the difficulty scale is measured by using the Bormuth (1969) formula and each is assigned a number of *DRP* Units of difficulty.[4] This number estimates the average cloze score (percent correct) to be expected for the passage if it were given to a population of students whose reading abilities vary widely (College Entrance Examination Board, 1980c). Table 19.3 shows examples of passages at two different readability levels. Raw scores on the test are converted to *DRP* Units, thus referencing a pupil's performance to a particular level of reading comprehension. This example is a criterion-referenced test using an ordered performance domain (see Chapter 17). The publisher of the *DRP* has measured the readability (in *DRP* Units) of many textbooks, basal readers, and learning materials in various curricular areas for grades 4 through 12. This permits the test user to determine the suitability of various print materials for a learner.

[4]*DRP* Units = $(1 - R) \times 100$. Readability = $R = .886593 - .083640\,(L \div W) + .161911\,(D \div W)^3 - .021401\,(W \div S) + .000577\,(W \div S)^2 - .00005\,(W \div S)^3$. Here L = number of letters in passages, W = number of words in passage, D = number of Dale Long List words in passage, and S = number of sentences in passage.

Note that you can also use the *Metropolitan Instructional Tests* to determine an instructional reading level. Further, the publisher of those tests has identified the instructional reading levels of basal reading series, too. The METRO, however, uses different techniques for determining readability and for determining reading comprehension. Readability levels for METRO test passages below grade 6 are determined using vocabulary control; for grade 7 and above the Dale/Chall formula is used (Farr, Prescott, Balow, & Hogan, 1978).

An Example of an Individually Administered Criterion-Referenced Test

KeyMath Diagnostic Arithmetic Test (Connally, Nachtman, & Prichett, 1976). This test is designed for preschool through sixth grade (and beyond for remedial) students. The test items are presented to the pupil on an easel (like the PIAT) for individual administration. A pupil gives nearly all the answers orally, except for the computation items which are done with a pencil on the record form. The arithmetic content of this test is divided into 14 topical areas:

A. *Content*
   1. Numeration
   2. Fractions
   3. Geometry and symbols
B. *Operations*
   4. Addition
   5. Subtraction
   6. Multiplication
   7. Division
   8. Mental computation
   9. Numerical reasoning
C. *Applications*
   10. Word problems
   11. Missing elements
   12. Money
   13. Measurement
   14. Time

Each of these areas is represented by a subtest of from 10 to 27 items arranged on the easel in order of difficulty. When testing a pupil, a basal and ceiling approach similar to that described earlier with the PIAT is used. The idea behind the test is to obtain a "diagnostic profile" over these 14 areas which can be used for further instructional planning. Items within each subtest are "scaled," that is, ordered on a number line according to a special statistical model, called the Rasch (1960) model. Once items have been placed along a number line according to their numerical scale values, using norm-referenced scores is unnecessary. (Norm-referenced scores are included, however, and can be used.) A behavioral objective represents each item, so that in some sense the domain of behaviors represented by each of the 14 areas has been ordered along the scale.

Although tests such as *KeyMath* provide more in depth information about a pupil's mathematics skills than does an overall survey test, they frequently can offer only rather gross insight into the specific difficulties a pupil is experiencing. Each item is keyed to a behavioral objective, but there is only one item per objective. *This makes diagnosis on the basis of objectives very unreliable.* Recently, some psychologists and educators have focused attention on diagnosing the processes or procedures a pupil uses when answering arithmetic problems (e.g., Brown & Burton, 1978), rather than simply describing a pupil in terms of a profile or the behavioral objectives mastered. These kinds of process diagnosis procedures are not readily available to educational diagnosticians; they await future test development efforts (Glaser, 1980).

Examples of Other Criterion-Referenced Tests

Appendix G lists a variety of criterion-referenced tests along with their publishers and some places where reviews of them can be found. A rather complete listing and reviews of criterion-referenced tests are found in the

CSE Criterion-Referenced Test Handbook (1979). You should consult test publishers' catalogues for more recent editions of tests.

Other Multilevel Tests

Reading tests are among the most numerous of all tests: The *Eighth Mental Measurements Yearbook* and *Tests in Print II* list 149 different reading tests, roughly 9% of all tests printed in the English language. (Not all of these are multilevel tests.) I have mentioned two reading tests already: *Metropolitan Reading Instruction Tests* and *Degrees of Reading Power*. The *Mental Measurement Yearbooks* list several categories of reading tests: survey, diagnostic, oral, readiness, special fields, speed, study skills, and miscellaneous. Appendix G gives examples of reading survey readiness and diagnostic tests. Readiness tests are discussed in Chapter 21 also. One of the major differences between the reading survey and reading diagnostic tests listed in Appendix G is the number of subscores the tests report, diagnosis being interpreted to mean obtaining a profile on several traits or "dimensions" of reading ability. As I indicate at the beginning of this chapter diagnosing via a profile on several trait dimensions is quite different from diagnosing in terms of behavioral objectives (e.g., *METRO Instructional Tests*) or identifying errors or erroneous processes (Figure 17.2). Most reading survey tests in Appendix G use a normed-referenced basis for describing reading ability: they identify a pupil's reading ability in terms of the person's location in a norm group. This norm-referenced description might be contrasted with the criterion-referenced approach of, for example, the *Degrees of Reading Power* tests, which identify a person's reading ability in terms of the difficulty level of printed passage a person can read.

Other single area tests This book cannot provide a complete cataloguing of multilevel single area achievement tests. Many of these tests are in basic skills areas such as mathematics and language arts. The best way to get an overview of the variety of these tests is to look at the Scanning Index of a recent edition of the *Mental Measurements Yearbook*. This index, organized by subject area, gives the test title, grade levels, publication dates, and number of reviews of the tests in that yearbook.

Note that a survey/diagnostic distinction exists for many multilevel tests. The survey versions of tests provide only a few subscores (usually only one or two), while the diagnostic versions provide several subscores (sometimes as many as 20 or more). The same general pattern illustrated with reading tests in Appendix G applies here.

Single-Level, Specific Subject Tests

Uses for Specific Subject Tests

A teacher of a given subject is often interested in assessing how well students are performing in just that subject. Although there are exceptions, most often multilevel tests are directed toward basic curricular areas (reading, mathematics, language arts, or social studies) rather than toward specific subjects such as Algebra I or Nineteenth Century English Literature. Multilevel tests are often inappropriate for such courses because they span several grades with relatively few items and thus lack content relevance for a particular course. For many purposes a teacher-made test for a subject is most appropriate: It is closest to the course content and contains the emphasis the teacher desires. Single subject or course tests have been found most useful for such purposes as pretesting to determine the general background of students coming into a course, advanced placement in college courses, exemption from required or introductory courses, contests and scholarship programs directed toward general knowledge of a particular subject, and granting college credit for knowledge acquired by independent study or other types of nontraditional education. Many tests for specific subjects are listed in the *Mental Measurements Yearbooks.*

A useful resource for those concerned with credit granting and credentialing policies and practices of postsecondary institutions is the Office on Educational Credit and Credentials (OECC) of the American Council on Education in Washington, D.C. This office serves postsecondary institutions in several ways related to the measurement and evaluation of competence, knowledge, and skills associated with granting college credit. For example, the OECC evaluates and makes credit granting recommendations for courses and training programs operated by the armed forces, business corporations, government agencies, professional associations, and labor unions.

The OECC evaluates credit-by-examination tests which test developers submit to it for review. This includes such national testing programs as the College-Level Examination Program (CLEP) and the Subject Standardized Tests of the armed forces in its program called Defense Activity for Nontraditional Educational Studies (DANTES). It also reviews tests with less widespread usage such as the American Chemical Society examinations and the California State University and Colleges English Equivalency Examinations. Each test is reviewed by a panel of six or more persons: three subject matter specialists and three testing specialists. A test is recommended for granting college credit if it passes both a content review and a technical review. Tests recommended by the OECC are listed in the *Guide to Credit by Examination* (ACE, 1981). The *Guide* contains summaries of the content and technical panel reviews.

It should be noted that the OECC administers the General Educational Development (GED) Testing Program which is used by about 500,000 adults each year to obtain high school equivalency certificates in all U.S. states and territories and in several countries. The GEDs are not specific subject tests, however. The GEDs were begun by E. F. Lindquist after World War II under the auspices of the United States Armed Forces Institute (now DANTES). The GEDs are multiple-choice tests covering five areas: writing skills (mechanics), social studies, science, reading comprehension, and mathematics (General Educational Development, 1979).

Summary

These are among the main points of this chapter.

1. There are a variety of published achievement tests in the marketplace. The chapter distinguished two broad groups: (a) standardized, empirically documented tests and (b) nonstandardized, not empirically documented tests.

2. Standardized, empirically documented tests include multilevel tests designed to span several grade levels or age levels and single-level tests designed for only one grade level or course.

3. Multilevel tests include (a) achievement survey batteries and (b) criterion-referenced and/or norm-referenced tests in particular curricular areas such as mathematics or reading.

4. Single-level tests measure achievement in a particular subject or course such as Algebra I, French II, etc.

5. Nonstandardized, not empirically documented tests do not employ empirical data from samples of subjects to improve and refine tests and to document their degree of reliability and validity.

6. There are several kinds of *diagnostic achievement* tests in the marketplace: (a) One type, built using an individual differences model, employs a norm-referenced profile of scores as a primary means of score interpretation. (b) A second type, built using a behavioral objectives model, employs criterion-referencing and constructs such as "mastery" as a primary means of score interpretation. (c) A third type also uses criterion-referencing but seeks to classify the kinds of errors a pupil makes. (d) A fourth type seeks to describe the prerequisite skills and knowledge a pupil lacks.

7. Standardized achievement tests can be used for a variety of within classroom and extra-classroom purposes. The usefulness of a particular standardized achievement test for any of these purposes depends on its curricular relevance to a given school.

8. Criticisms of standardized achievement batteries have been directed toward their (a) intrinsic properties, (b) missing properties, and/or (c) effects on pupils and school curricula. Many criticisms can be overcome by proper test selection and use.

9. Among the misuses of achievement test scores are: (a) failing to consider the possibility of measurement error, (b) using a single score as the only criterion for important decisions, (c) uncritically accepting a score as a pure measure of a characteristic, and (d) failing to recognize that pupils' test performances are caused by a complex set of antecedent conditions.

10. The features of group administered and individually administered multilevel achievement tests were described and illustrated along with suggestions for interpreting scores and using test results for instructional planning. Specific tests are listed in Appendix G.

Themes

• Measurement of general scholastic aptitude is important when estimating a student's likely success in an academic learning situation that cannot adapt to the student's idiosyncratic pattern of specific abilities and interests.

• Information about a student's aptitude comes from many sources, not only from "aptitude tests."

• Tests of scholastic aptitude reflect how well a student can adapt to mainstream schooling, but they are not a measure of fixed ability.

• Comprehensive assessment of general mental ability must take into account a person's ability to cope in a broader social context and not only simply to master skills related to school learning.

Terms and Concepts

scholastic aptitude
general vs. specific intellectual skills
aptitude (vs. achievement)
fixed vs. adaptive learning conditions
mental age
chronological age
deviation IQ vs. ratio IQ
basal age, ceiling age
performance IQ vs. verbal IQ
verbal-performance discrepancy

fluid vs. crystallized intelligence
field dependence vs. field independence
sequential vs. simultaneous mental processing
medical model, social model, pluralistic model
anglo-conformity model vs. structural pluralism model
adaptive behavior

20
TESTING
SCHOLASTIC
APTITUDES:
INDIVIDUAL TESTS

T his chapter describes a number of individual testing procedures for the measurement of general scholastic aptitudes. By way of introduction, the chapter begins with a discussion of the nature of scholastic aptitude, the importance of general intellectual skills, the view that aptitude tests measure learned behavior, and the importance of learning conditions for the development of scholastic aptitudes. This is followed by a brief history of the development of tests of general mental ability. The remainder of the chapter describes individual tests of general scholastic ability: The *Stanford Binet Intelligence Scale*, the *Wechsler Intelligence Scale for Children—Revised*, the *Kaufman Assessment Battery for Children*, and the *System of Multicultural Pluralistic Assessment*. There is also a brief discussion of methods of assessing adaptive behavior. A selected list of other individual tests is given in Appendix G. The next chapter discusses group tests of scholastic abilities.

Aptitudes for Learning

General vs. Specific Intellectual Skills

Tests of the kind discussed in this chapter have as their chief function describing a learner's general intellectual skills, rather than describing the specific skills needed in, say, next week's geometry lessons. When the achievement, knowledge, or skill to be learned in an upcoming lesson is specific and narrow, success in learning it is best predicted by a person's present level of prerequisite knowledges and skills. For most of these specific, day-to-day instructional decisions, teachers will have to develop their own procedures for gathering this information.

Importance of Measuring General Intellectual Skills and Aptitudes

A measure of specific past performance such as the achievement level in a specific course is less helpful in predicting future success or in establishing expectations for learning new material when (a) a student must learn behaviors that are quite different from those learned in the past, (b) a student's past performance

has been very erratic, (c) a student's previously obtained test scores or school grades are known to be very unreliable or invalid, or (d) a student simply does not have an available record of past performance. Consider a high school freshman, for example, who wants to study Spanish for the first time, having had no previous foreign language training or experience. For such a student, a test of Spanish language knowledge provides no information about the student's chances of succeeding in an upcoming Spanish course. In such cases, a test of more general intellectual skills and abilities related to language learning may measure the extent to which the pupil has (a) learned English language skills and concepts, (b) acquired auditory learning skills, and (c) can apply memory skills. Similarly, a student transferring from another school system or moving from one educational level to the next, may have complete records, but the meaning of these records may be unclear. To clarify the meaning of these records of past achievement, a school may test the student with an instrument measuring broad intellectual skills or scholastic aptitude.

There are any number of predictors of a person's likely success in attaining an academic achievement. Three examples are (1) the level of past achievement of the same specific type as the new performance to be learned, (2) the level of general scholastic ability attained, and (3) the levels attained on several specific aptitudes related to the performance to be predicted. The validity of these predictors is related to the specificity of the achievement to be predicted. If the achievement to be predicted is very specific (e.g., solving quadratic equations), then the order of predictions is: prior achievement of a very similar kind is the best predictor followed by general scholastic aptitude, and finally specific aptitudes; if the achievement to be predicted is very general (e.g., general school performance as measured by, say, freshman grade point average) then the order of predictors is general scholastic aptitude, then tests of prior specific achievement, then tests of specific abilities (Snow, 1980).

Aptitude Tests Measure Learned Behavior

Capacity is not fixed   *Tests* measuring aptitude or intellectual skills reflect only past learning and do *not* directly measure innate ability or "capacity." Since we cannot obtain a sample of behavior from the future, we have to be content to use past learning and present behavior to predict future learning. Note that a person has an ability or aptitude for learning under a specific type of instructional approach. This aptitude is influenced by a number of facts of development including biological makeup, experience in the environment (including other persons), and a complex interaction of the two. The idea of "capacity" as some upper limit is likely to be true in only a very specific way. For example, a student's capacity to do algebra may depend on the way algebra is currently taught, on previously learned mathematics concepts, and on the motivational level a teacher stimulates, as well as on some kind of native endowment. It seems reasonable to conclude that both developmental (life history) and instructional condi-

tions affect the particular potentials realized by a person: "So long as a way is open to invent better conditions of development, no one knows the limit of human potentialities" (Cronbach, 1977, p. 274).

Aptitude-achievement distinctions   It sometimes troubles persons to see tests bearing titles such as readiness, intelligence, general mental ability, or aptitude for "X" containing items closely resembling items found on achievement tests. The troublesome aspect appears to be related in part to a failure to distinguish between the *abstract concepts* of aptitude and achievement and the *observations* we make to infer the state of a person's aptitude and achievement. We can define *an aptitude for "X" as the present state of a person which indicates the future performance in "X" which we expect of the person if the conditions of the past and present continue into the future* (cf. Carroll, 1974). The person's present aptitude (or state) could be indicated in many ways. Thus (Carroll, 1974, p. 287):

> . . . [an] "aptitude test" is only one indicant of aptitude. Other indicants of aptitude could include scores on achievement tests, data on prior performance in activities similar to those for which we wish to predict success, and information derived from procedures for assessing personality, interest, attitude, physical prowess, physiological state, etc.

Interestingly, the *Pimsleur Language Aptitude Battery* (Pimsleur, 1966) directly reflects this broad definition of aptitude, for it includes not only a series of tests of cognitive abilities, but also indicants of previous academic success and of interest in studying modern foreign languages. The latter consist of simple scales by which the examinee reports his school grades in English, social studies, mathematics, and science, and rates his interest in studying foreign languages. Although the reviewers in Buros' yearbook have raised questions about the validity and propriety of using self-report data, it is still noteworthy that this aptitude battery attempts to measure interest and prior school achievement as components of aptitude.

It might be helpful in this regard to think of a large domain of all possible indicators of a person's aptitude for a particular learning, only some of which would appear on an "aptitude test." Those items appearing on an aptitude test presumably would be more predictive of a relevant future performance than other items that might appear on an "achievement test."

Importance of the Learning Conditions for Aptitude Development

An important part of the definition of aptitude given above concerns the continuance of past learning conditions into the future. One thing that makes aptitude tests useful predictors of future school success is that schools are generally not very adaptive to individual learners. Thus, the conditions under which pupils learn this year are usually quite similar to last year's learning conditions.

When learning conditions are fixed from year to year, a danger that the results of scholastic aptitude testing will be viewed deterministically is present: Once an individual's present aptitude level has been ascertained, little will be done to modify learning conditions so that this aptitude level can be both accommodated and increased. There is a pressing need for present pedagogical practice to overcome the tendency to hang onto past psychological conceptions of the learner. Past psychological conceptions of the learner have led educators to *overemphasize* the (a) consistency of the general scholastic ability of learners, (b) passivity of learners as receivers of information, and (c) categorical placement of learners into educational tracks having narrow ranges of instructional options and to *underemphasize* the (a) adaptivity and plasticity of learners, (b) learners' ability to actively construct information during problem solving, and (c) responsibility of educational systems to adapt to learners' initial performance levels (Glaser, 1977a). Unfortunately, aptitude tests for matching optimal instructional methods with specific learners are not available today.

By and large, the aptitude tests described in this chapter and the next have not been validated for use in assigning pupils to different kinds of instructional methods. Rather, they have been designed to predict how well a student will perform when the student must adapt to the fixed instructional setting. You should view the tests' helpfulness for decision-making in that light.

Brief History of Tests of General Mental Ability[1]

Perhaps contemplation of the nature of intelligence has been undertaken since the beginning of civilization. Until the 19th century, however, intelligence was studied mainly as a philosophical rather than a scientific topic. The first systematic, scientific efforts to quantify and measure intelligence probably can be attributed to Sir Francis Galton (1822–1911) of England and James McKeen Cattell (1860–1944) of the United States (Boring, 1929). Cattell studied experimental psychology under Wundt in Leipzig, Germany and then spent his early postdoctoral years working with Galton. Eventually he came to Columbia University to head its psychology department. Cattell (1890) was the first to use the term "mental test." His views, however, that general mental ability could be ascertained from measures of sensory discrimination and reaction time were quite unlike the measures of general mental ability that have become popular today.

The first practical and widely accepted test of intelligence was developed by two Frenchmen: the psychologist Alfred Binet (1857–1911) and the psychiatrist Theophile Simon (1873–1961). Binet was a tireless worker and a prolific writer, being credited with 277 publications (Dennis, 1954). From 1880 until his death Binet studied many aspects of psychology including mental illness, mental retardation, sensation, perception, memory, reaction time,

[1]See the inside front cover also.

spatial perception, suggest-ability and hypnosis, mental fatigue, judgment, and a variety of pedagogical problems (Pollack & Brenner, 1969; Wolf, 1973). In 1904 Binet was appointed by the Minister of Public Instruction to a commission of citizens, educators, medical men, and academic scientists given the task of recommending ways of improving the prospects of children unable to learn from the existing school program. It was through their work with this commission that Binet and Simon developed their first mental ability scale (Binet & Simon, 1905).

Binet sought to identify children who couldn't profit from normal schooling so they might be given special instruction. Because teachers might want to have troublesome pupils removed from their classes or want to keep those children from "better" families, a more objective, easily administered procedure was needed.

> At first, he tried to develop measures that provided the possibilities of differential diagnosis so that instruction could be adapted to . . . different capabilities, but he abandoned this attempt. After vainly trying to disentangle and separately measure various intellectual functions, Binet decided to test them in general, in their combined functional capacity, without any pretense of measuring the exact contribution of each to the total product (Glaser, 1977b, p. 44).

Based on empirical results obtained from using the tests in Paris, Binet and Simon revised their test in 1908 and again in 1911.

Psychologists around the world, particularly those working with children and schools, greeted the Binet-Simon tests enthusiastically. Several American translations of the tests were used: H. H. Goddard[2] (1910, 1911), F. Kuhlman (1912), L. M. Terman (1911; Terman & Childs, 1912; Terman, 1916); G. M. Whipple

(1910); R. M. Yerkes, J. W. Bridges and R. S. Hardwick (1915). Some other early translations include K. L. Johnston (1910) in England, O. Bobertag (1911, 1912) in Germany, and Z. Treves and U. Saffiotti (1910, 1911) in Italy. By 1916, the Binet-Simon Scale had been used also in Australia, Canada, China, Japan, New Zealand, Russia, South Africa, Switzerland, and Turkey (Goddard, 1916).

The history of the development of group tests of mental ability began with World War I. The first group intelligence test (the Army Alpha) was not developed until 1917. Within the next four years, however, over 2,000,000 children had been tested with them (Terman, 1922). By 1922 at least 44 group intelligence tests were listed in the *Yearbook of the National Society for the Study of Education* (Whipple, 1922a). Contributing to this rapid acceptance and use of group intelligence tests were factors such as (a) compulsory education (Tyler, 1976), (b) centralization of the school administration and adoption of businesslike school management procedures (Tyack, 1974), (c) acceptance of scientific management and quantitative analysis as a means of improved school management (Callahan, 1962), and (d) the popularization of social Darwinism and belief that the child, not the school, was to blame when learning failed to occur (Calhoun, 1973).

The influence of compulsory education laws on the increased use of general mental ability tests in schools in this country and in Europe should not be underestimated (Tyler, 1976, p. 14):

> Obviously what the legislation did was to assemble in one place, probably for the first time in human history, almost the full range of human intellects, and to make it necessary for educators to struggle with this diversity. Society has not yet met this challenge. People still blame the schools or tests for the magnitude of the variation that compulsory attendance reveals. The first mental-test developers and their successors were at least attempting to cope with the problem.

---

[2]Goddard (1916, p. 10) can be given the dubious distinctions of coining the word "moron" (greek Moros, foolish) which was for years associated with those exhibiting slight mental retardation.

Through the 1920s and 1930s schools clamored for general mental ability tests in the hopes that using them would help solve the problems they faced. The *Twenty-first Yearbook of the National Society for the Study of Education* (Whipple, 1922b), for example, was devoted to explaining the benefits of using intelligence tests for such purposes as admitting pupils to first grade, identifying both gifted and mentally slow children, forming homogenous ability groups, and admitting students to colleges and universities. Early intelligence tests were also used to foster social Darwinism and to rationalize existing prejudices about various racial and ethnic groups (Kamin, 1974). Such views generated considerable debate among both white and nonwhite intellectuals (see Box 20.1).

Early in the 1920s there were perhaps 40 or 50 different English language intelligence tests. In 1978 there were about 130 intelligence tests published in the English language; they represented about 8% of the test titles listed in the *Eighth Mental Measurements Yearbook* (Buros, 1978). Only a handful of those listed, however, are widely used.

Today's intelligence tests are based on nearly the same principles as used early in the century. Sometimes the name of a test will be changed to clarify its purpose or in an attempt to reduce improper interpretations of test scores. As one publisher said in relation to its own test, "The change in the name of the series, from *mental ability* to *school ability*, does not signify a radical or marked departure from the rationale underlying previous editions, or major differences in the nature of the abilities being measured (Otis & Lennon, 1979, p. 6)."

Individually Administered Tests of General Scholastic Aptitude

The Stanford-Binet Intelligence Scale

The *Stanford-Binet Intelligence Scale* is a widely used, individually administered test of general scholastic aptitude. First prepared in 1916 by Lewis M. Terman as a translation and revision of the Binet-Simon Scale, the test was revised in 1937 (with Maud A. Merrill), revised again in 1960, and renormed in 1972 (Terman & Merrill, 1973). The 1960 version combined into a single form the two forms (L and M) of the 1937 edition. A revision and renorming is currently underway and is expected to be completed in 1983.

Nature and content of the test   The *Stanford-Binet* is designed for a wide range of ages: from 2 years old through adult. Some idea of the nature of the items in the test can be obtained by studying Table 20.1 which describes the subtests used at four of the age levels. "Age level" represents the ages at which about 60 or 70% of the children typically pass those types of items. The objective of testing is essentially to determine the age level of the tasks (items) which a given child can perform successfully.

There are six subtests for each age level and each subtest has one or more items. The same subtest (e.g., Vocabulary) is sometimes used at several age levels, higher passing standards being associated with older ages.

As can be seen from Table 20.1, there are qualitative differences between the tasks at different age levels. For example, tasks designed for older examinees require greater use of verbal reasoning skills than the tasks at younger age levels. Unlike the Wechsler tests (which are described in the next section), the *Stanford-Binet* reports only one global score to represent an examinee's composite performance on all varieties of tasks. The arrangement of the subtest in an age scale is such that the tasks at each age represent what the average examinee of that age in the norming sample was able to perform successfully. Thus, examinees are considered "normal" if they are able to perform about as well or better than their age peers; "subnormal" if they perform considerably below the level of the age peers.

Box 20 • 1

Special administrative conditions The *Stanford-Binet* as all other individual intelligence tests mentioned in this chapter must be administered by a specially trained psychologist who has had supervised experience administering, scoring, and interpreting it. (Some states have laws which require schools to accept individual intelligence test reports only from state-certified psychologists.) The psychologist should make every effort to establish rapport with the subjects and to motivate the subjects to do their best.

Skill in administering individual tests lies not in mechanically following "procedures" but in understanding that testing involves a psychosocial relationship between examiner and examinee (Schafer, 1954). Both the examinee and the examiner have hopes, fears, anxieties, and expectations which are present in this face-to-face test situation, and which, if unattended by the examiner, may result in subtle psychological mechanisms operating in a way that causes an examinee to give less than a top performance.

Although teachers do not administer the *Stanford-Binet*, they should be aware of the influence of factors such as those above which may influence pupils' scores when interpreting the psychological reports from a psychologist. They should realize, too, that these subtle influences of examiner on examinee are not limited to situations in which psychologists administer tests. They operate with the teacher in the daily class situation as well.

Mental age The immediate objective of testing with the *Stanford-Binet* is to establish an examinee's *mental age* (MA): the age level at which the examinee's general scholastic abilities operate. The examiner need not administer every item on the test to an examinee because the items are arranged in order of their difficulty. Usually, the first step is to determine a person's *basal age*, the highest age level

7-year level	13-year level
1. Picture absurdities I (5 pictures on cards) [.64]* Child is asked to tell what is foolish or funny about each picture.	**1. Plan of search (drawing of a diamond-shaped figure) [.47]** Uses pencil to mark the path that would be used to search for an object lost in the "field" represented by the diamond.
2. Similarities: Two things [.65] Child is asked to describe the way in which two things (e.g., ship and automobile) are alike.	**2. Abstract words II [.72]** Defines abstract words such as "compare" and "obedience" (6 words).
3. Copying a diamond (Picture of diamond-shape) [.62] Child draws the shape when shown the model.	**3. Memory for sentences III [.65]** Examiner reads 15-word sentence, and child repeats it verbatim (two sentences).
4. Comprehension IV [.48] Child answers questions such as, "What's the thing to do when you have broken something that belongs to someone else?" (six questions asked)	**4. Problems of fact [.53]** A few sentence story is read, and the child is asked to infer a fact or conclusion about it.
5. Opposite Analogies III [.62] Completes word analogies (e.g., "Snow is white; coal is . . .")	**5. Dissected sentences (cards on which are printed disarranged words) [.79]** Child is asked to rearrange the words into a sentence.
6. Repeating 5 digits forward [.59] Examiner says five random digits, and child repeats them in order said.	**6. Copying a bead chain from memory (48 beads; equal numbers of round, square, and cylindrical; string) [.70]** Child watches examiner make a 9-bead chain of a certain pattern. After chain is removed from sight, child is asked to make one like it.

*Numbers in brackets represent the correlation with the total test score.

Source: Adapted from L. M. Terman and M. A. Merrill, *Stanford-Binet Intelligence Scale: Manual for the Third Revision* (Iowa City: Riverside Publishing Co., 1973), pp. 7ff, 342 ff. Used by permission of the publisher.

Table 20 • 1 Examples of tasks appearing on the *Stanford-Binet Intelligence Scale.*

at which the person can pass all of the subtests assigned to it. If before the testing begins, a person is judged to be above average, the examiner will likely begin testing one year below the person's *chronological age*. If the examinee experiences difficulty with the tasks at that age level, the examiner will go back to an earlier, more appropriate age level to begin testing. If the person passes all six subtests at a particular age level, the examiner will move upward. Once the basal age is established, the examiner keeps administering all tasks above that level until a *ceiling* is reached at which the person is unable to answer any of the items correctly. When this ceiling is reached, testing stops. The mental age is determined by adding to the person's basal age a credit of two months[3] for every subtest passed at levels above the basal age. This is illustrated below:

Person's performance	Credit given
Passes all subtests at year 9	9 years (basal age)
Passes 2 of 6 subtests at year 10	4 months
Passes 3 of 6 subtests at year 11	6 months
Passes none at year 12 (test stops)	0 months
MA =	9 years, 10 months

[3]Applies to age levels 6 through 14 only.

IQ scores   Originally, performance on this test was reported as a ratio IQ (intelligence quotient)[4] defined as:

$$IQ = \frac{\text{mental age}}{\text{chronological age}} \times 100$$

However, for a number of technical and interpretive reasons, modern day testing has abandoned reporting intelligence test performance in this way. The IQ obtained from the current version of the *Stanford-Binet* (and most other modern day tests of scholastic aptitude) is a normalized standard score called a deviation IQ (see Chapter 14). The mean deviation IQ is 100 and the standard deviation is 16 at each age level in the 1972 norming sample. As was illustrated above, the score obtained when the test is administered is a mental age (MA). Tables, arranged according to chronological age (CA), are provided in the manual for converting MAs to deviation IQs. Adults are considered to have a CA of 18 for purposes of determining the deviation IQ.

Since the deviation IQ is a standard score, it is not based on the older notion that children's mental ages should be equal to their chronological ages. The old ratio IQ would assign, for example, an IQ of 100 to a child tested at CA = 5 years and 0 months who had an MA = 5 years 0 months. However, the actual IQ score in the *Stanford-Binet* would be different: ". . . a child on his fifth birthday who achieves an MA of 5–0 does not receive an IQ of 100, but rather one of 91. In order to be credited with an IQ of 100, he must achieve an MA of 5–6" (Terman & Merrill, 1973, pp. 360–361).

Norm-referenced character of the test   Tests of scholastic aptitude report ability as a location in a norm-group having the same age as the person. If the person's intellectual development does not keep pace with others in the norm-group, a lower IQ will result. Norms become outdated and from time to time a test will have to be renormed. The effects of shifts in the norm-group are illustrated in Table 20.2. This table shows the average IQs of a group tested in 1972 when the scores are referenced to the 1937 norm-group. These averages all would be around 100 for each age if the scores of the persons tested in 1972 were referenced to their own group. The table illustrates that the average youngster in 1972 has a higher mental age than a comparably aged youngster in 1937. The differences between the 1937 and 1972 IQs reflect changes both in the norm-group characteristics (the 1937 group was limited to primarily English-speaking adults) and in American culture.

The Wechsler Intelligence Scales

Another widely used set of individual tests is the Wechsler intelligence scales. This set consists of three intelligence scales, each designed for use with a different age level: (1) *Wechsler Preschool and Primary Scale of Intelligence* (WPPSI) [4 to 6½ years], (2) *Wechsler Intelligence Scale for Children—Revised* (WISC-R) [6 to 6½ years], and (3) *Wechsler Adult Intelligence Scale—Revised* (WAIS-R) [16 to 74 years].

Background   This series of tests was developed by David Wechsler, a psychologist at the Bellevue Psychiatric Hospital in New York City, who needed a means to assess the intellectual abilities of adults seen at Bellevue in the 1930s. He saw inadequacies in the then existing individual intelligence tests: (a) The content of the items was more relevant to children than to adults which interfered with establishing rapport with adult examinees, (b) other tests' norms reflected school age children rather than adults, and (c) tests designed for school age children tended to emphasize verbal ability rather than maintaining a balance of several different indicators of intellectual ability (Wechsler, 1939). In addition, as a clinical psy-

---

[4]The *ratio IQ* was invented by a German psychologist William Stern who called it the "mental quotient" (Stern, 1914). Binet and Simon preferred to use only the term "mental level."

Age	Mean IQ score	Age	Mean IQ score
2-0	110.4	8-0	103.3
2-6	110.6	9-0	102.1
3-0	110.7	10-0	101.9
3-6	110.8	11-0	102.2
4-0	110.7	12-0	102.5
4-6	110.0	13-0	102.9
5-0	109.7	14-0	103.3
5-6	108.4	15-0	103.9
6-0	107.1	16-0	104.7
7-0	105.0	17-0	105.7
		18-0	106.9

Table 20 • 2

Estimates of the average *Stanford-Binet* IQ of those tested in 1972 when their scores are referenced to the 1937 norms.

From L. M. Terman and M. A. Merrill, *Stanford-Binet Intelligence Scale: Manual for the Third Revision*, p. 359, Table 11, © 1973 by Riverside Publishing Co. Reproduced by permission of the publisher.

chologist, Wechsler needed more from a mental ability test than a single global score. In order to make a diagnosis and recommendation for treatment, Wechsler saw a need to interpret a person's pattern or profile of abilities. A profile of the strengths and weaknesses on several different facets of mental ability serves as a source of clinical hypotheses about the nature of a patient's illness. By conducting more intensive testing, observation, and interviewing, the clinician eventually rejects false hypotheses, comes to some conclusion about the patient's mental functioning, and makes a diagnosis.

The first form of the test, called the *Wechsler-Bellevue Intelligence Scale* (published in 1939), was revised in 1955 and in 1980, and is now known as the *Wechsler Adult Intelligence Scale—Revised* (WAIS-R). Another outgrowth of the *Wechsler-Bellevue* was the *Wechsler Intelligence Scale for Children* (WISC). Published in 1949 and revised in 1974, it is now known as the *Wechsler Intelligence Scale for Children—Revised* (WISC-R). Still another version was published in 1967 for use with children ages 4 through 6: The *Wechsler Preschool and Primary Scale of Intelligence* (WPPSI).

General design of the Wechsler tests All the Wechsler tests have the same general design although the items are not identical. This design is different from the *Stanford-Binet* in several respects. First, the content of the test is not organized around age levels as is the *Stanford-Binet*. Second, there are 10 subtests (more counting the optional subtests) organized into two groups: Verbal and Performance. The items within a subtest are similar in content but differ in level of difficulty. Third, all examinees take all subtests, and like the *Stanford-Binet*, the items are arranged in the order of difficulty, so that testing within a subtest can stop when the items become too difficult. Fourth, three types of IQs are reported: Performance IQ, Verbal IQ, and Full Scale IQ. As with the *Stanford-Binet*, these are normalized deviation IQs (mean = 100, but standard deviation = 15).[5] The concept of mental age is essentially abandoned (Wechsler, 1949). Fifth, a normalized standard score (mean = 10, standard deviation = 3) is reported for each of the 10 subtests administered and an attempt is usually made to interpret this profile.

The WISC-R You can obtain some idea of the content of the Wechsler tests from Table 20.3 which describes the subtests for the WISC-R.

---

[5]It was Wechsler, in fact, who first broke away from the traditional ratio IQ for individual intelligence tests and used the deviation IQ (Wechsler, 1949).

Verbal-performance discrepancy By and large, a child's WISC-R Verbal IQ will not be exactly equal to the child's Performance IQ. There are many reasons for this, and often a psychologist will attempt to interpret the discrepancy and explore its educational implications. Before doing so, however, the psychologist would be aware that many of the small differences observed can reasonably be attributed to errors of measurement—essentially random fluctuations in both Performance and Verbal IQ scores. Most psychologists would follow traditional 95% uncertainty interval rules (see Chapter 15) and not interpret a discrepancy unless it was 12 points or larger. Wechsler (1974) considers a difference of 15 or more points quite important, warranting further explanation.

For large discrepancies, the psychologist seeks a more substantive explanation. A discrepancy is like a symptom; there are many different reasons why it could have come about. A psychologist would investigate further to see which explanation is the most plausible for the particular child at hand. Table 20.4 lists several of the more common interpretations of the V-P discrepancy.

Abilities measured by the WISC-R subtests Although the WISC-R reports a verbal and performance IQ, these are not pure indicators of independent abilities as is evidenced by their average correlation of .67. Further, a factor analysis of the WISC-R standardization sample indicates that the test may measure three broad factors, rather than two (Kaufman, 1979): (1) verbal comprehension—defined by the Information, Similarities, Vocabulary, and Comprehension subtests; (2) perceptual organization—defined by the Picture Completion, Picture Arrangement, Block Design, Object Assembly, and Mazes subtests; and (3) freedom from distractability—defined by the Arithmetic, Digit Span, and Coding subtests.

It should be noted, also, that scores on the individual subtests can be influenced by a number of specific abilities and experiences which need to be considered when interpreting a score for an individual pupil. For example, the Arithmetic subtest score of a pupil can be influenced by specific abilities such as computational skill, numerical reasoning, freedom from distractibility, verbal comprehension, general acquired knowledge, specific knowledge acquired in school, memory, and/or anxiety, and the ability to work within time limits (Kaufman, 1979). Consult Kaufman's book for specific factors influencing each subtest.

Kaufman Assessment Battery for Children[6]

The **Kaufman Assessment Battery for Children (K-ABC)** is an individually administered test of both intelligence and achievement first published in 1983. Its authors are Alan S. Kaufman and Nadeen L. Kaufman. The K-ABC differs in several ways from other approaches to measuring scholastic aptitude described thus far: (a) the intelligence scales focus on the *process* used to solve a problem rather than on the *content* (e.g., verbal comprehension) processed, (b) the subtests were derived from psychological and neuropsychological theory, (c) mental processing ("intelligence") is tested separately from learning of school-related material ("achievement"), (d) both verbal and nonverbal achievement is tested, (e) norms include both normal and exceptional children, and (f) supplemental norms separating blacks and whites are provided. The K-ABC is designed for use with children ages 2½ through 12½ years.

The K-ABC contains 16 subtests: 10 subtests associated with the intelligence scale and 6 with the achievement scale. Not all subtests are administered to every age level (e.g., 2½ year olds are administered 7 subtests; 7–12½ year olds are administered 13 subtests. The intelligence scale divides the 10 subtests into

[6]This section is based on prepublication information made available to the author by the American Guidance Service.

<table>
<tr><th>Verbal Scale[a]</th><th>Performance Scale[a]</th></tr>
<tr><td>

1. **Information[b] (30 items) [1.19][c]:** Child is asked a number of general information questions relating to simple science, geography, history, calendar and seasons, and so on.

3. **Similarities (17 items) [1.34]:** Child is given two words and asked to state the way in which they are alike. Word pairs are either concrete (e.g., saw-hammer) or abstract (fear-love).

5. **Arithmetic (18 items; card with trees imprinted, word problems, three of which are printed on cards) [1.38]:** Lowest ages (6–7 years) use card with trees printed on it and do simple arithmetic problems. Upper ages have word problems read to them or, for complex word problems, read them themselves.

7. **Vocabulary (32 items) [1.15]:** Child is asked to state the meaning as each word is read. Words range from relatively easy to difficult.

9. **Comprehension (17 items) [1.39]:** A series of "why" questions, such as, why copper is used in electrical wiring, why money is kept in a bank, and so on.

11. **Digit Span (14 items) [1.44]:** Seven items request the child to repeat digits in the exact order the examiner says them (digits forward); seven item request the child to repeat the digit in exactly the reverse order the examiner says them (digits backward). The most difficult digits forward is nine digits; for digits backward it is eight.

</td><td>

2. **Picture Completion[b] (26 cards with printed picture) [1.45]:** Child is shown pictures one at a time and asked to tell what part of the picture is missing.

4. **Picture Arrangement (13 sets of cards with pictures. Within a set, the pictures can be arranged in a sequence that tells a story, much like the panels of a cartoon strip.) [1.57]:** Child is presented a set of pictures in a mixed-up order and asked to arrange them in an order that tells a sensible story.

6. **Block Design (11 cards, one design printed on each; nine cubes with red and white sides) [1.17]:** Child is shown a printed design and asked to make the design using the cubes.

8. **Object Assembly (5 cardboard object shapes (e.g., apple) cut-up as a puzzle) [1.70]:** Child is presented the pieces in a pre-determined, mixed-up arrangement and is asked to put them together to make an object.

10. **Coding (page on which are printed symbols and corresponding codes) [1.63]:** Child is shown the pairs of symbols and then codes, and is given a page with symbols in a random arrangement. The task is to write the correct code that goes with each symbol.

12. **Mazes (Nine mazes printed on pages) [1.70]:** Child uses a pencil to indicate the "way out of the maze" without crossing lines or going into "blind alleys."

</td></tr>
</table>

[a]Average standard error of measurement in IQ units are: (Verbal IQ 3.60, Performance IQ 4.66, Full Scale IQ 3.19).
[b]The number in front of the subtest name is the order in which the subtest is administered. Thus, verbal and performance subtests are alternated during administration.
[c]The numbers in brackets represent the (average) standard error or measurement for each subtest expressed in scaled score units.

Table 20 • 3 Description of the subtests of the *Wechsler Intelligence Scale for Children—Revised.*

two groups: sequential processing (3 subtests) and simultaneous processing (7 subtests). Table 20.5 describes the subtests and states the ages for which they are intended to be used.

An essential aspect of the K-ABC is its provision for separate measures of sequential processing and simultaneous processing of information. Subtests on the Sequential Processing Scale require examinees to solve problems by *mentally* arranging the stimuli in a sequential or serial order. Subtests on the Simultaneous Processing Scale contain mostly spatial or analogic stimuli which examinees have to *mentally* integrate and must simultaneously organize in order to solve the problem. The authors acknowledge that intelligent behavior requires an integration of both sequential and simultaneous processing abilities, so the tasks on the two scales are not sure measures of these two abilities. The authors suggest that organizing information into the three scales (sequential processing, simultaneous processing, and achievement) provides a better way to understand the learning disabled and mentally retarded child. They further suggest that teaching processing skills

1. **Verbal vs. nonverbal intelligence.** The traditional Wechsler view is that some individuals are better at expressing their intelligence in response to verbal stimuli (thus, V > P), while others express intelligence better in response to concrete stimuli (thus, P > V).
2. **Fluid vs. crystallized intelligence.** Based on Cattell's theory that fluid intelligence involves general reasoning using adaptation and flexibility (thus, P > V), while *crystallized intelligence* involves breadth of knowledge, experience, and acculturation of the mainstream culture's intellectual skills (thus, V > P).
3. **Psycholinguistic deficiency.** A deficiency in receptive or expressive communication ability or in some other psycholinguistic process may cause a score discrepancy. Children with hearing losses, for example, may have P > V.
4. **Bilingualism or nonmainstream dialect.** If standard English is a second language, then P may be greater than V.
5. **Coordination problem.** Since many of the performance subtests require motor coordination and speed, a poorly coordinated child may have V > P.

6. **Time pressure.** Anxious, distractable, reflective, and/ or compulsive children may not work well under time constraints. Since only one verbal subtest (Arithmetic) is timed, and all performance subtests are timed, for such children, V may be greater than P.
7. **Field dependence vs. field independence.** These are considered to be the extremes on a continuum of "cognitive style." Field-independent persons easily overcome the "field" and separate embedded elements from their surrounding contexts, while field dependent persons do this with great difficulty.* Field independent persons may have P > V, while field dependent persons may have V > P.
8. **Socioeconomic influences.** Children from advantaged, professional families tend to have V > P.
9. **Guilford's evaluation factor.** Some psychologists believe that a V > P which can be attributed to a very high Comprehension subtest score reflects high ability on the evaluation factor of Guilford's Structure of Intellect Model.

*For a review of this area and its educational implications see Witkins and Goodenough (1977) and Witkins, Moore, Goodenough, and Cox (1977).

Source: Based on A. S. Kaufman, *Intelligence Testing with the WISC-R* (New York: John Wiley and Sons, 1979). Used by permission of the publisher.

Table 20 • 4   Examples of possible explanations for Verbal (V) − Performance (P) discrepancies in WISC-R IQ scores.

will have pay-off in the form of improved academic achievement.

Because the K-ABC is a new instrument, its validity as a diagnostic and placement test in the practical affairs of schooling has yet to be demonstrated. Since not all of the evidence is in, teachers are likely to hear or read both enthusiasm for and disparagements against the K-ABC in the next few years.

The System of Multicultural Pluralistic Assessment

Another relatively new individual assessment procedure, called the *System of Multicultural Pluralistic Assessment* (Mercer & Lewis, 1978) or SOMPA, appeared in 1978. The SOMPA is a system of several different kinds of measures used together to come to a more comprehensive evaluation of a child's general scholastic ability. As can be seen from the overview of the SOMPA shown in Table 20.6,

there are two main parts: the Student Assessment and the Parent Interview. The Student Assessment, conducted by a psychologist and other trained professionals, involves administering the WISC-R[7] as well as several psychomotor and physical tests. Trained paraprofessionals may conduct the Parent Interview. All the results are integrated in an attempt to obtain a comprehensive, holistic picture of the child's potential for learning in a standard school environment. Box 20.2 contains an illustrative case study taken from SOMPA's promotional materials. Read this case study to get an idea of how SOMPA is used.

Background and rationale of the SOMPA   The SOMPA grew out of the work of sociologist Jane R. Mercer who studied the ways in which school children in Riverside, California came to be labeled mentally retarded

[7]Or WPPSI if the child is under six years old.

Sequential Processing Scale	Achievement Scales
Hand Movements (2½–12½) Child performs series of hand movements in same sequence as the examiner performed them.	**Picture Vocabulary** (2½–4 yrs. 11 mo) Stating the name of an object in a photograph.
Memory for Numbers (2½–12½) Repeating digits in same sequence as presented by the examiner.	**Famous Faces and Places** (2½–12½) Naming the well-known person, place, or thing in a photograph.
Memory for Words (4–12½) Child touches silhouettes of common objects in same sequence as examiner orally names them.	**Arithmetic** (3–12½) Knowing school-related arithmetic concepts and skills.
	Riddles (3–12½) Naming a concrete or abstract concept after being presented with a list of its characteristics.

Simultaneous Processing Scale / (continued Achievement Scales)

Simultaneous Processing Scale

Magic Window (2½–4 yrs. 11 mo.) Child identifies a picture which is partially exposed when the examiner moves it behind a narrow window.
Memory for Faces (2½–4 yrs. 11 mo.) One or two faces are exposed briefly and child has to find them when a group photograph is presented.
Gestalt Closure (2½–12½) Naming the object or picture in a partially completed drawing.
Triangles (4–12½) Arranging identical triangles to match a pattern in a given model.
Matrix Analogies (5–12½) Selecting the picture that best completes a visual analogy.
Memory for Places (5–12½) Recalling location of pictures on a page that was briefly exposed.
Photo Series (6–12½) Arranging photographs in chronological order.

Reading Decoding (5–12½) Naming letters; reading words.
Reading Understanding (7–12½) Reading sentences and following the commands presented in them.

Source: American Guidance Service. Courtesy of Randy W. Kamphaus.

Table 20 • 5 Subtests and age levels of the K-ABC.

(Mercer, 1973). Her study documented that: (a) a disproportionate number of black, hispanic, and poor children were labeled mentally retarded and placed in special education classes, (b) public schools were the primary agency in the community for labeling children, (c) teachers played a significant role in initiating the referral *and the labeling* process, (d) the label "mental retardation" was attached principally on the basis of scores on an IQ test with little or no regard for a child's adaptive behavior outside the school setting,[8] and (e) seldom did the school obtain information other than scholastic ability test scores before labeling a child mentally retarded.

[8]This led Mercer to speak of the "six-hour retardate": A child who was considered retarded only by the school, but whose family, neighbors, and peers accepted the child and considered the child normal in all other facets of life.

Mercer (1979) presents a sociological analysis of the acculturation process, in which two models are juxtaposed: the Anglo-conformity model and the cultural and structural pluralism model. In the *Anglo-conformity model*, a major goal is the anglicization of all ethnic and cultural groups; those persons not able to be anglicized are viewed by the dominant society as less valuable. In the *structural pluralism model*, distinct ethnic and cultural groups are accommodated in society without necessarily demanding they be anglicized.

This sociological analysis provides the rationale for including many of the SOMPA measures. The WISC-R, consistent with the Anglo-conformity model, is a measure of how well a child can function in the mainstream school setting. The *Adaptive Behavior Inventory for Children* (ABIC) and the *Sociocultural Scales*

	Student Assessment	Parent Interview
Medical Model*	**Physical Dexterity Scales:** Ambulation Scale Equilibrium Scale Placement Scale Fine Motor Sequencing Scale Finger-Tongue Dexterity Scale Involuntary Movement Scale Physical Dexterity Average Scale Score **Bender-Visual-Motor Gestalt Test** **Weight by Height Scales** **Visual Acuity (Snellen Test)** **Auditory Acuity (audiometer)**	**Health History Inventories:** Prenatal/Postnatal Trauma Disease and Illness Vision Hearing
Social System Model*	**School Function Level (SFL) (Wechsler Intelligence Scale for Children-Revised: [WISC-R]):** Verbal IQ Performance IQ Full Scale IQ	**Adaptive Behavior Inventory for Children (ABIC):** Family Scale Community Scale Peer Relations Scale Nonacademic School Rules Scales Earner/Consumer Scale Self-Maintenance Scale ABIC Average Scale Score
Pluralistic Model*	**Estimated Learning Potential (ELP) (WISC-R regression estimate):** Verbal IQ (estimated) Performance IQ (estimated) Full Scale IQ (estimated)	**Sociocultural Scales:** **Own ethnic group:** Family Size Scale Family Structure Scale Socioeconomic Status Scale Urban Acculturation Scale **School Culture Group:** Family Size Scale Family Structure Scale Socioeconomic Status Scale Urban Acculturation Scale

*See text for an explanation.

Table 20 • 6 An organization of the tests on the SOMPA: *System of Multicultural Pluralistic Assessment.*

assess the extent to which children and their families have been acculturated and can function in the mainstream culture. The "Estimated Learning Potential" (ELP) estimates a pupil's school success *if* the pupil were enrolled in an educational program especially adapted to the child's sociocultural background.[9]

[9]The ELP is a multiple-regression estimate based on data from California. It is not necessarily valid for other places. SOMPA users should conduct their own validity studies (see Chapter 16).

The three assessment models of the SOMPA The SOMPA presents information about a child from the viewpoints of three assessment models: a medical model, a social system model, and a pluralistic model. A *medical model* looks for organic abnormalities that interfere with a child's school functioning. As can be seen from Table 20.6, six SOMPA measures are reported in this model: Physical Dexterity, *Bender Visual-Motor Gestalt*, Weight by Height, Visual Acuity, Auditory Acuity, and

Bernice's scores on the *Physical Dexterity Tasks, Weight by Height, Visual Acuity,* and *Auditory Acuity* are well within the normal range. Her performance on the *Bender Visual Motor Gestalt Test* is low, but not critically so, and her scores on the *Health History Inventories* are no cause for concern.

Her scores on the *Adaptive Behavior Inventory for Children* show that Bernice is unusually capable for her age in caring for herself and in performing the role of earner/consumer. However, her School Functioning Level (SFL) as measured by her *WISC-R Full Scale IQ* is only 68. Academically, she is performing at the level of the lowest 2 percent of the dominant school population. In most schools she would be eligible for placement in classes for the mentally retarded.

Bernice's scores on the *Sociocultural Scales* reflect a socioeconomically impoverished background. She lives with her mother, three brothers, and one sister. Her parents are separated but not divorced. Her mother, who is the head of the household and is unemployed, was reared in a small community in the South and completed nine years of schooling. The family is supported entirely by state and federal aid.

When Bernice's *WISC-R IQs* are interpreted relative to her own sociocultural group, the picture that emerges is a more positive one. The average *WISC-R Full Scale IQ* earned by children having Bernice's configuration of scores on the *Sociocultural Scales* is 77. Her *WISC-R Full Scale IQ* of 68, therefore, is only 9 points below the mean for her normative group. This is not an important variation from the mean, and her Estimated Learning Potential, expressed as an ELP Full Scale score of 89, argues against placing Bernice in a class for the mentally retarded.

In Bernice's case, there is much to build on. She does not have a history of serious health problems, her sensory-motor abilities do not appear to be impaired, and her vision and hearing are good. As evidenced by her scores on the ABIC, Bernice exhibits a degree of personal independence and social responsibility greater than one ordinarily finds among children her age. Although her *WISC-R IQs* are low, her ELP scores are within the normal range. When all of these factors are considered, it seems likely that Bernice can benefit from a program of educational instruction that takes differences between her background and the culture of the school into account.

Box 20 • 2

Health History. The Physical Dexterity Tasks provide information about motor coordination and balance for the identification of neurological impairments. The *Bender Visual Motor Gestalt Test* (Bender, 1946) requires the child to copy nine designs and provides an indication of perceptual maturity and neurological functioning. Visual Acuity is the standard *Snellen Test;* Auditory Acuity is tested with an audiometer.

The *social system model* looks at adaptation to the various social roles in which the child is expected to engage within family and community and within the school. Two instruments provide information to be interpreted within this model: the WISC-R and the *Adaptive Behavior Inventory for Children* (ABIC). Although the WISC-R is used both in this model and in the pluralistic model, in the social system model scores are referenced to national norms and are interpreted as measures of the degree to which a child is succeeding in an

academic role (Mercer & Lewis, 1978). To emphasize this point, Mercer and Lewis dub the WISC-R IQ-score the School Functioning Level (SFL). The ABIC consists of 242 age-graded questions, the answers to which describe the child's degree of success as: a family member (e.g., How well does the child get along with siblings?), a consumer and earner (e.g., Does the child lose money?), a nonacademic member of a school group (e.g., Is the child often late for school?), a person interrelating with adults and peers (e.g., Does the child visit nearby neighbors or relatives?), and a person capable of caring for personal health and physical needs (e.g., Does the child get a drink for himself or herself when thirsty?). Answers to these questions are obtained by trained interviewers from a parent.

The *pluralistic model* describes how well a child has adapted to unique sociocultural circumstances. The measures are norm-referenced; the object of the measures is to compare a child with other children of the same age and sociocultural background. This model uses the *Sociocultural Scales* and the WISC-R. The *Sociocultural Scales* measure sociocultural characteristics of a child's family in order to re-interpret the WISC-R by comparing the child's Verbal, Performance, and Full Scale IQs with others of the same sociocultural circumstances. The *Sociocultural Scales* cover four areas: family size, family structure (i.e., the interrelationship between the persons in the household and the child), socioeconomic status (i.e., occupational level of the head of the household) and degree of urban acculturation (i.e., sense of efficacy, community participation, degree of anglicization, and degree of urbanization).

Information from the *Sociocultural Scales* is used to obtain a norm-referenced score called the *Estimated Learning Potential* (ELP). The ELP is really a deviation IQ score for the WISC-R, but instead of being based on the child's location in the national standardization norm-group, it is based on an estimate of the child's location in a norm-group with ethnic and sociocultural characteristics identical to those of the child being tested. This provides a clue as to whether a special school program that is adapted to the child's unique sociocultural background might be especially useful.

Limitations of the SOMPA There is always the temptation to claim more merit for a new educational technique or tool than hard evidence can support. Much of this stems from the real and pressing problems of children in schools and the hope that one can contribute in some small way to the solution of these problems. Since the SOMPA is quite new and not all the evidence is in, the teacher is likely to hear both enthusiasm for its use as well as disparagements against it.

As of this writing there is not widespread clinical use of the SOMPA in schools, even though some of the measures within it are widely used. The sociological rhetoric of the SOMPA is likely to be a barrier to its imme-diate acceptance by school psychologists who have been trained to interpret test performance in traditional psychological ways which are generally consistent with the anglo-conformity and social system models. The criticisms and counter-responses to the issues and claims of the SOMPA are too numerous to catalogue here (but not more numerous than those associated with the S-B or WISC). The main issue is whether one can, in practice, design better educational programs by using the SOMPA. In other words, an experience base needs to be developed to provide evidence that the promise the SOMPA holds up for children hitherto served badly by the schools is not an empty one, incapable of fulfillment. The reader interested in a fuller discussion of this point is referred to the *School Psychology Digest*, Volume 8, Issues 1 and 2, 1979, in which Mercer and her critics exchange views.

Assessing Adaptive Behavior

Tests such as the *Stanford Binet*, the WISC-R, and the K-ABC measure general scholastic ability. A school setting is not, of course, the only environment in which persons are expected to cope. The SOMPA recognizes this by providing other measures of a child's functioning, particularly the *Adaptive Behavior Inventory for Children*. Another instrument for assessing the extent mentally retarded individuals cope with the demands of their environment is the *Adaptive Behavior Scale* (see Appendix G). An older instrument for assessing individuals' ability to care for themselves is the *Vineland Social Maturity Scale* (Doll, 1953, 1965).

A revision of the *Vineland*, the *Vineland Adaptive Behavior Scales* (VABS) (authored by Sara S. Sparrow, David A. Balla, and Domenic V. Cicchetti), was standardized in 1981–1982 and is to be published in 1983.[10] The VABS is

[10]This description of the VABS is based on prepublication information from the American Guidance Service courtesy of Patti L. Harrison.

a developmental checklist which assesses adaptive behavior in five areas: Communication, Daily Living Skills, Socialization, Motor Skills, and Maladaptive Behavior. The first three areas are assessers for children from birth through 19 years (and low functioning adults). The Motor Skills area assessment is limited to children younger than 9 years and the Maladaptive Behavior area to children 5 years and older. A child's parent or caregiver completes the VABS checklist. There are three editions: (a) Interview Edition, Survey Form, which provides standard scores for each of the five areas as well as a total adaptive behavior score; (b) Interview Edition, Expanded Form, which in addition to the standard scores, provides specific, detailed information for preparing educational and habilitation programs; and (c) Classroom Edition, for ages 3 to 13, which a teacher completes, and which provides standard scores for four adaptive behavior areas as well as a total adaptive behavior score. The VABS provides national norms for all three editions. For the two Interview Editions, special supplementary norms are available for mentally retarded adults (residential and non-residential), hearing impaired children, visually handicapped children, and emotionally disturbed children (the latter three groups in residential settings).

Summary

The following are the main points of this chapter.

1. Tests of general scholastic ability or intelligence describe a learner's general intellectual skill rather than the specific abilities needed to learn a particular lesson or task.

2. Information about general intellectual skill becomes important when trying to forecast a pupil's future academic performance in a general way when the conditions for future learning are expected to remain similar to the past learning conditions.

3. The validity of general scholastic ability test scores for predicting very specific kinds of academic learning is apt to be less than their validity in predicting more global kinds of academic accomplishments.

4. A person's capacity to learn is a function of biological makeup, experience in the environment, and a complex interaction of environment and biological makeup. The capacity of a person to learn something new will depend on previous learning, the way the new material is taught, the pupil's motivation, and a host of other factors, as well as the pupil's native endowment.

5. Both achievement tests and aptitude tests can reflect a person's present aptitude level. Test items that best predict future attainment, however, would tend to be found on aptitude tests.

6. All predictions made from aptitude test scores assume that the same learning conditions that existed in the past will extend into the future.

7. The first persons to attempt systematic, quantitative, and scientific measurement of intelligence were Sir Francis Galton and James McKeen Cattell.

8. The first practical and widely accepted test of intelligence was developed by Alfred Binet and Theophile Simon as part of their work with the Ministry of Public Instruction in Paris, France. The Binet-Simon tests were quickly translated and used in several countries including Australia, Canada, China, England, Germany, Japan, New Zealand, Russia, South Africa, Switzerland, Turkey, and the United States.

9. World War I stimulated the development and widespread use of group intelligence tests but the rapid acceptance and use of group intelligence tests in schools during the first twenty years of this century was likely due to such factors as (a) legislated compulsory education which, for the first time, placed the full range of human talent in the schools, (b) centralization of school administration with its accompanying adoption of businesslike school management procedures, (c) the school administration's acceptance of scientific management with its accompanying quantitative analyses, and (d) the popularization of social Darwinism with its accompanying belief that the child, rather than the school, was to blame when the child failed to learn.

10. The *Stanford-Binet Intelligence Scale,* unlike the Wechsler tests, reports only a single global IQ score. The tasks on the test are arranged in an age scale: At each age level tasks which average examinees of that age can perform successfully are included. The immediate objective of testing is to locate an examinee's mental age— that age level on which the examinee's general scholastic abilities are operating. The *Stanford-Binet* score is a deviation IQ: At each age level in the norming sample the deviation IQs have a mean of 100 and a standard deviation of 16.

11. The *Wechsler Intelligence Scale for Children—Revised,* unlike the *Stanford-Binet,* contains 10 subtests, each of homogeneous content: Items within a subtest are of the same type but are arranged in order of difficulty. The WISC-R reports a separate standard score for each subtest, a verbal deviation IQ, a performance deviation IQ, and a full-scale deviation IQ.

12. The *Kaufman Assessment Battery for Children* (K-ABC) contains both intelligence and achievement measures. The K-ABC intelligence test separately measures the ability to sequentially process and simultaneously process information. Unlike the *Stanford-Binet* and the Wechsler tests, the K-ABC focuses on the manner in which examinees process stimuli. The K-ABC is a new and not widely accepted test.

13. The *System of Multicultural Pluralistic Assessment* (SOMPA) includes the WISC-R, but attempts to go beyond the WISC-R to provide a rather comprehensive holistic assessment of the child. To do so, the SOMPA is organized around three assessment models: (a) A medical model looks for abnormalities of organic origins that might interfere with school functioning, (b) a social systems model looks at how well a child is able to adapt to various social roles (family and community member and role as student in school), and (c) pluralistic model looks at how well the child has adapted to special sociocultural circumstances. A unique feature of the SOMPA is that it makes clear the sociological analysis of the acculturalization process on which it is based. The SOMPA is a new system not yet widely accepted by school psychologists.

14. Behavior checklists are available to help psychologists assess the extent to which a child has acquired normal, age-appropriate adaptive behavior. Adaptive behaviors are the behaviors which indicate a child can cope with the natural demands of the social and physical environment, especially outside the academic learning context. In a comprehensive assessment of a pupil, ascertaining the developmental level of the pupil's adaptive behavior as well as the level of general intellectual (academic) skills is necessary.

Themes

- Group administered tests of scholastic aptitude provide an efficient means of measuring general school ability.

- Several approaches have been tried to develop tests to disentangle cultural effects from general mental ability, but it is apparent that scores on nearly all tests are influenced by a person's sociocultural background.

- Growth of intellectual skills in the early years is enhanced when a child has an emotionally supportive and accepting environment in which a child experiences considerable success with cognitive tasks.

- School ability tests are often used to set expectations and place pupils. To use tests in this way demands considerable professional judgment and integrating several types of nontest information into the decision process. No test can be used in a mechanical way for making these decisions.

Terms and Concepts

omnibus test
nonverbal tests
multiple aptitude tests
spiral format
norms for a pupil's age (norms-by-age)
verbal analogies
figural analogies
verbal classification
figural classification
series completion (number, letter, figure)
figural pattern matrix
mechanical reasoning
space relations
profile of scores
uncertainty interval

culture-free vs. culture-fair vs. culture-specific
common-culture approach
equal representation approach
test-train-retest approach
developmental stages approach
overlap hypothesis
cross-sectional studies
longitudinal studies
homogeneous ability grouping (tracking)
gifted and talented
predicted achievement score
underachiever
overachiever
regression effect

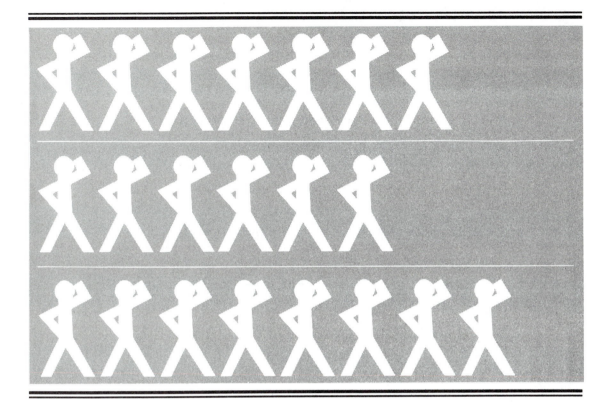

21
TESTING SCHOLASTIC APTITUDES: GROUP TESTS

The previous chapter described individually administered aptitude tests, especially those used by school psychologists in clinical practice. A teacher will not administer such tests but will encounter them when reading psychological reports or in discussions with school psychologists. In this chapter attention turns to the kinds of scholastic aptitude tests a teacher is more likely to administer and be required to interpret: group tests. The chapter describes three kinds of general school ability tests: a single-score omnibus test, a three-score test, and a multiple-aptitude test. Next described are tests used for special purposes: readiness tests, high school and college admissions tests, and aptitude tests for specific school subjects. The chapter concludes with a discussion of certain issues which surround the use of scholastic aptitude tests: culture-fair testing, whether pupils' aptitude test scores change much, using tests for ability grouping and placement of pupils, and means of identifying underachievers. A selected list of group administered aptitude tests is presented in Appendix G.

Group Tests of Scholastic Aptitude

The principal advantage of group testing over individual testing is the testing efficiency and cost savings gained by testing many persons at the same time. This was the principal motivation for the development of the *Army Alpha* and *Army Beta* tests during World War I. The ease with which these tests could be administered and scored contributed greatly to schools adopting tests like them after the war and to the subsequent development of other varieties of scholastic aptitude tests.

There are a variety of types of group aptitude tests. The *omnibus* test does not measure different kinds of abilities that comprise general scholastic aptitude separately. Rather, like the *Stanford-Binet*, it contains items measuring different aspects of general scholastic aptitude, but provides a *single* ability *score*. A *two-score* test also measures several different kinds of specific abilities, but *reports* only two scores, usually verbal/quantitative or verbal/nonverbal. There may be several kinds of specific verbal abilities measured by the items on the verbal section of the test, for example, but only

one general verbal ability *score* is reported. Some group school ability tests report *three scores* such as verbal, quantitative, and nonverbal. Nonverbal tests measure how well examinees process symbols or content that has no specific verbal labels (e.g., discerning spatial patterns and relation or classifying patterns and figures). (See Chapter 1 for the distinction between verbal and performance tests. Group tests are usually not performance tests.) *Multiple aptitude* tests measure each of several different abilities separately and provide an ability score for each. Multiple aptitude tests, for example, may provide separate scores for each of several abilities such as: verbal reasoning, verbal comprehension, numerical reasoning, and figural reasoning.

As with all tests, the type of group scholastic aptitude test to use in a school should depend on the decisions to be made with the scores. Multiple aptitude tests are useful, for example, when a student seeks information about a profile of strengths and weaknesses in order to make better decisions about further schooling and/or planning a career. Omnibus tests are useful, for example, in

Ability category	Type of item	Elementary Level		Intermediate Level		Advanced Level	
		Number	Percent	Number	Percent	Number	Percent
Verbal compre- hension	Synonym-definition, opposite meanings, sentence completion, scrambled sentences.	13	19	15	19	15	15
Verbal reasoning	Word-letter matrix, verbal analogies, verbal classification, inference, logical selection.	26	37	30	38	30	38
Figural reasoning	Figure analogies, series completion, pattern matrix.	13	19	15	19	15	19
Quantitative reasoning	Number series, arithmetic reasoning.	18	26	20	25	20	25
TOTAL		70	101	80	101	80	101

Source: Courtesy of The Psychological Corporation, Michael Beck, Project Director, 1981.

Table 21 • 1   Number and percent of items in each category of ability on three levels of the *Otis-Lennon School Ability Test* (Forms R and S).

ascertaining the general level of school ability for purposes of predicting future success under standard classroom conditions. Examples of these types of aptitude tests are given below, and others are listed in Appendix G.

An Omnibus Test: The Otis-Lennon School Ability Test

This is the most recent edition of the test that Arthur S. Otis first developed during his graduate studies at Stanford University during World War I.[1] The test is organized into five levels (Otis & Lennon, 1977c): Primary

(grade 1), Primary II (grades 2 and 3), Elementary (grades 4 and 5), Intermediate (grades 6, 7, and 8), and Advanced (grades 9, 10, 11, and 12).

Items in the primary level are pictorial and do not require reading. Items in the other three levels are described in Table 21.1 and some of them are illustrated in Figure 21.1. Similar types of items are *not* grouped together into subtests, however, but are arranged similarly to Figure 21.1 in a *spiral format:* One item of each type is presented, then the sequence is repeated but with more difficult items.

Omnibus tests are designed to report a single raw score measuring general scholastic ability but this raw score is given several different norm-referenced interpretations (see Chapter 14). The publishers of the Otis-Lennon, for example, provide tables which reference a pupil's raw score to either (or both) of two norm-groups and through these tables

[1]It was Otis' paper-and-pencil multiple-choice format that was adopted as a basis on which the *Army Alpha* was built (Yoakum & Yerkes, 1920; Yerkes, 1921). Otis developed what was likely the first multiple-choice intelligence test (Robertson, n.d.). Multiple-choice achievement tests were already available (Thorndike, 1914; Kelly, 1915; Starch, 1915).

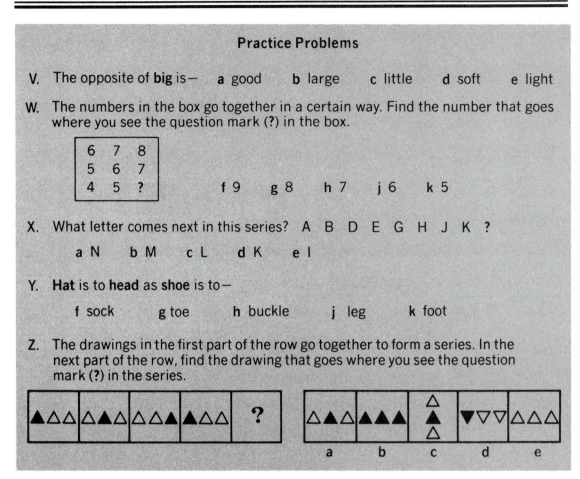

Figure 21 • 1 Sample items from *Otis-Lennon School Ability Test*, Elementary Level. (Types of items represented are: (V) opposite meaning, (W) number series in matrix form, (X) letter series, (Y) verbal analogy, and (Z) figure series completion. The test includes more varieties of items than are illustrated.)

obtain five norm-referenced interpretations: (1) *norms for a pupil's age* that provide percentile ranks, stanines, and a school ability index (SAI); and (2) *norms for a pupil's grade* that provide percentile ranks and stanines. The SAI is a normalized standard score with a mean of 100 and a standard deviation of 16 (i.e., SAI $= 16z_n + 100$). The change to SAI in the recent edition is an attempt ". . . to reduce the possible overinterpretation of the Otis-Lennon results by persons unfamiliar with the scope and purpose of such instruments" (Otis & Lennon, 1979, p. 13).

Two norm-groups are provided because a one-to-one correspondence between a pupil's age and grade placement does not exist. If a pupil has been accelerated or held back, the pupil's age is likely to be different than that of the bulk of the youngsters in the classroom. For such over or underage pupils, a more comprehensive norm-referenced interpretation is obtained if scores are referenced to both groups. Jane, for example, is a 10 year 1 month old fifth grader. At the time of testing (fall) the bulk of her classmates were eleven year olds. Suppose Jane received a raw score of 55 on Form R of the Otis-Lennon. Consulting the tables in the test manual will provide the following results:

Norms by Age (10 yrs. 0–2 mos.)	Norms by Grade (5th grade)
(1) SAI = 113	
(2) PR = 79	(4) PR = 76
(3) Stanine = 7	(4) Stanine = 6

In general, pupils who are over or underage for their grade placement will have percentiles and stanines closer to "average" when compared to norms by grade than when compared to norms by age.

A Three-Score Test: The Cognitive Abilities Test

This test is organized into levels as follows (Thorndike & Hagen, 1978a): Primary I (grades K and 1), Primary 2 (grades 2 and 3), and Levels A through H (grades 3 through 12). Items in the primary levels are pictorial and do not require reading, but as with the *Otis-Lennon* they do require listening comprehension skills. Levels A through H have a variety of item types, but unlike the *Otis-Lennon*, similar items on the *Cognitive Abilities Test* are grouped together into subtests. A subtest at each level contains 25 items. Further, subtests are grouped together into three batteries: Verbal Battery, Quantitative Battery, and Nonverbal Battery. These subtests and batteries are

described in Table 21.2 and examples of items from the Nonverbal Battery are shown in Figure 21.2.

An interesting feature of the *Cognitive Abilities Test* (CogAT) is its arrangement in a multilevel edition. Items within each subtest range in difficulty from very easy for average third and fourth graders to very difficult for the average twelfth grade student. The test booklet contains 60 items for each subtest area. Each pupil, however, takes only 25 items, depending on that pupil's grade placement and level of cognitive development. A fourth grader, for example, whose level of cognitive development can be considered typical for grade 4 would take Level B of a subtest: This would be the 25 items beginning with Item 6 and ending with item 30. On the other hand, a slower developing fourth grader would take Level A of the same subtest: This would be a somewhat easier set of 25 items, beginning with Item 1 and ending with Item 25. Since the time limits and directions for administering are the same for a subtest, regardless of level, both youngsters could, if the teacher desired, take the two different levels of the subtest in the same room at the same time.

The advantages of a multilevel arrangement for ability tests are the same as those for out-of-level achievement testing (see Chapter 19): Pupils are tested with items matched to their own level of development thus increasing the reliability of the scores and avoiding boring advanced students with very easy items or frustrating slower students with items that are too difficult. Tables in the examiner's manual permit converting all scores to the same scale, regardless of the level pupils were administered.

The CogAT yields three raw scores measuring verbal, quantitative, and nonverbal abilities. *Each* of these raw scores can be referenced to either (or both) of two norm groups and, through the publisher's tables five norm-referenced interpretations can be obtained for each battery: (1) *norms for a pupil's age* provide

Subtest	What is measured	Description of items
Verbal Battery		
1. Vocabulary	Word knowledge, ability to identify specific word meanings.	Examinee selects which one of five words means most nearly the same as the stimulus word given in the item stem
2. Sentence Completion	Knowledge of sentence structure, ability to comprehend sentence meaning.	Sentence is presented with one word omitted. Examinee selects which one of five words best completes the sentence.
3. Verbal Classification	Ability to apply verbal concept memory to identify the common element among several verbal stimuli.	Three or four stimulus words, all of which are alike in some way (e.g., animals) are presented. Examinee selects which one of five other words belongs with the stimulus words.
4. Verbal Analogies	Ability to identify relationships between a pair of words and use that relationship to complete the analogy in a second pair.	Three stimulus words are presented. The first two words are related in some way (e.g., antonyms) while the third is the final word of a second pair. Examinee selects which one of five other words best completes the second pair.
Quantitative Battery		
1. Quantitative	Knowledge of mathematical concepts, ability to judge relative size or amount of quantitative material.	Two quantities are presented, and examinee selects which is greater or whether they are the same. Quantities may be sets of objects, portions of geometric figures, numbers, number sentences, lines, etc.
2. Number Series	Ability to identify the relationships in a series of numbers.	A series of five or six numbers is presented. Examinee selects which one of five other numbers comes next, to best complete the given series.
3. Equation Building	Knowledge of arithmetic operations and ability to use quantitative concepts to discover, construct, and solve number sentences.	Several numerals and/or fractions are presented along with one or more arithmetic operation symbols $(+, -, \times, \div, \sqrt{\ }, ())$. Examinee must discover how to put together all of the stimulus numerals and symbols to obtain one of the five answer choices given.
Nonverbal Battery		
1. Figure Classification	Ability to apply figural and/or shape concept memory to identify the common element among several figural stimuli.	Three geometric shapes or figures, all of which are alike in some way (e.g., composed only of straight lines), are presented. Examinee selects which of one of five other figures belongs with the stimulus figures.
2. Figure Analogies	Ability to identify relationship among a pair of figures and use that relationship to complete the analogy in a second pair.	Some as Verbal Analogies except that items contain only figures (no words).
3. Figure Synthesis	Ability to mentally organize parts of a geometric figure into a whole and ability to mentally manipulate shapes and geometric figures.	Separate parts of a geometric shape are presented along with five completed shapes. Examinee decides whether each completed geometric shape could be constructed by an arrangement of the given pieces.

Source: Based on descriptions from R. L. Thorndike and E. P. Hagen, *Cognitive Abilities Test*, Form 3, a) *Examiner's Manual* and b) *Multilevel Booklet for Grades 3–12*, © 1978 by Riverside Publishing Co. Used by permission of the publisher.

Table 21 • 2 Description of the subtests in the Verbal, Quantitative, and Nonverbal batteries of the *Cognitive Abilities Test* (Form 3).

Figure Classification: "Find the drawing on the right that goes with the first three" (p. 46).

A B C D E

Figure Analogies: "From the five lettered figures that follow on the right, find the one that goes with the third figure in the same way that the second goes with the first" (p. 54).

F G H J K

Figure Synthesis: Decide whether each completed shape can be made by arranging all of the given pieces.

Given pieces

Complete shapes

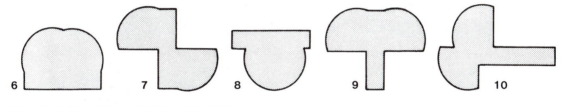

6   7   8   9   10

Source: Thorndike and Hagen (1978b, pp. 46, 54, 66)

Figure 21 • 2 Sample items from the *Cognitive Abilities Test* (Form 3).

percentile ranks, stanines, and standard age scores (SAS); and (2) *norms for a pupil's grade* provide percentile ranks and stanines. The SAS is a normalized standard score with a mean of 100 and a standard deviation of 16 (i.e., SAS $= 16z_n + 100$). The CogAT does not provide total or composite scores combining all three batteries.

Note that both the *Otis-Lennon* and the CogAT have norms-by-age and norms-by-grade and that they provide these two norms for the same reasons. You may also want to note that the SAI of the *Otis-Lennon* and SAS of the CogAT are similar normalized standard scores. This does not mean, however, that pupils' scores on the *Otis-Lennon* and the CogAT are identical or interchangeable. The reasons why scores will not be interchangeable are that (1) the test items comprising the tests are different, and (2) different samples of pupils are used in the norms.

An advantage of a test such as the CogAT, which provides scores in more than one area of scholastic aptitude is that the teacher may obtain separate information on a pupil's ability to use different kinds of symbols. A pupil's performance on a single score omnibus test does *reflect* abilities in several areas, of course, but the single score does not permit a closer examination of a pupil's relative strengths in using verbal, quantitative, or nonverbal symbols. The authors of the CogAT point out how the differential information from these tests might be used to adapt instruction to individuals (Thorndike & Hagen, 1978a, p. 47):

1. Students scoring high on the Verbal and Quantitative Batteries have good memory and reasoning skills since these relate to the most commonly used school symbols: words and numbers. These students are likely to have the ability to succeed in fast-paced instruction.

2. Students scoring low on the Verbal and Quantitative Batteries may lack both a store of verbal and quantitative concepts and an ability to quickly retrieve such concepts. Teachers may need to explicitly teach these students certain verbal and quantitative concepts which other students already know as well as how to use these concepts to solve problems. Low scoring students may need slower paced instruction with more practice than do higher scoring pupils.

3. Students scoring higher on the Nonverbal Battery than on the Verbal and Quantita-

tive batteries have good reasoning skills and can manipulate complex nonverbal stimuli to solve problems, identify relations and patterns, and recall information. However, they apparently process information differently from pupils who score high on the Nonverbal Battery may require the teacher to use special instructional tactics to take advantage of their well-developed abilities.

Note that the interpretation of profiles of scores in different areas depends to a considerable extent on how different the areas are from one another: whether the subtests measure unique abilities rather than a single ability which happens to be called different names by a test author. The CogAT, for example, reports the following average (median) intercorrelations among the batteries for samples from the 1970 standardization: Verbal vs. Quantitative, $r = 0.75$; Verbal vs. Nonverbal, $r = 0.66$; and Nonverbal vs. Quantitative, $r = 0.72$ (Houghton, Mifflin, 1978). This shows that the three batteries do measure some common or general ability. However, the battery reliabilities are relatively high, so some cautious interpretation of large differences (15 points or greater on the SAS scale) in the profile of a pupil's scores is justified.

A teacher who receives a class list of scores from a test which measures two or three abilities should carefully examine the list to discern pupils' patterns of abilities and to think about ways to use each pupil's pattern to foster improved learning in the student. The following suggestions may help you in reviewing a class list of ability scores (Thorndike & Hagen, 1978a): (1) look at each pupil's level and pattern of scores, (2) note each pupil's strong area(s), (3) identify pupils showing uneven patterns of abilities (as indicated by large differences in their standard scores), (4) identify students who marked few answers but whose answers marked were mostly correct (i.e., slow but accurate workers) for possible special attention, (5) compare a pupil's

Case 6: L.B. Male			Chronological Age 9 Years 4 Mos.			Grade 4	
			Norms by Age			Norms by Grade	
	Number of answers marked	Number of answers correct	Standard age score	Percen- tile rank	Stanine	Percen- tile rank	Stanine
V	50	48	98	45	5	38	4
Q	41	39	108	69	6	62	6
NV	80	78	137	99	9	99	9

At first glance, L. B. appears to be extremely strong in spatio-visual reasoning and only about average in verbal and quantitative reasoning. But look at the number of items he *attempted* on the verbal and quantitative batteries and the number he answered correctly. He answered only 50 out of 100 items on the Verbal Battery and he got 48 of the 50 right. On the Quantitative Battery he answered 41 out of 60 items and got 39 of the 41 right. He is much slower in processing verbal and quantitative symbols than geometric or spatial symbols, but he is equally *accurate* with all three kinds of symbols. The average scores on the verbal and quantitative batteries probably represent the lower level of his ability in these two areas. His true verbal and quantitative abilities may be above average. It would be worthwhile to study L. B. to determine why he is slow in processing verbal and quantitative symbols. It would also be desirable to give him an individually administered test to determine the upper limits of his verbal and quantitative abilities. L. B. may be a gifted individual and one would *not* want to overlook him.

Source: Reproduced with permission from R. L. Thorndike and E. P. Hagen, *Cognitive Abilities Test, Form 3: Examiner's Manual*, p. 45. Copyright © 1978 by Riverside Publishing Co.

Box 21 • 1

standing in both norms for age and norms for grade, and (6) interpret ability scores only in relation to other information available for a pupil (e.g., achievement test scores, class performance, relations with peers, teacher's observations).

A Multi-Score Test: The Differential Aptitude Tests

This battery of tests was originally developed in 1947 to satisfy the needs of guidance counselors and consulting psychologists working in schools, social agencies, and industry (Bennett, Seashore, & Wesman, 1974). The test was revised in 1962, 1972, and 1982. The primary purpose of the tests is to provide information about profiles of different abilities for guiding and counseling students in junior and senior high schools (grades 8 through 12) as they prepare for career decisions. The *Differential*

Aptitude Tests (DAT) report scores for each of the 8 subtests shown in Figure 21.3. An additional ninth score, Verbal Reasoning and Numerical Ability, is reported: This score is used to measure general scholastic aptitude. Figure 21.3 also shows examples of items from each subtest.

The DAT has separate male and female norms, because males and females score differently on some subtests and the authors believe reporting percentiles separately for each gender encourages fair interpretations of the results (The Psychological Corporation, c. 1982). The results of the national standardization show that: (a) males and females score *essentially the same* on the Verbal Reasoning, Numerical Ability, and Abstract Reasoning Subtests, (b) males score *higher* than females on the Mechanical Reasoning and Space Relations Subtest, and (c) males score *lower* than females on Clerical Speed and Accuracy, Spelling, and Language Usage Subtests. When

Verbal Reasoning: Find the pair of words that will fill the blanks to make a sensible and true sentence. (50 items, 30 minutes)

. . . . is to water as eat is to . . . .

- A   continue — drive
- B   foot — enemy
- C   drink — food
- D   girl — industry
- E   drink — enemy

Numerical Ability: Find the answer to each numerical problem. (40 items, 30 minutes)

Add
	A	14
13	B	16
12	C	25
	D	59
	N	none of these

Abstract Reasoning: Find which one of the Answer Figures would be the next one (fifth) of the Problem Figures. (45 items, 20 minutes)

Problem Figures

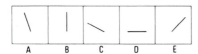

Answer Figures

A   B   C   D   E

Language Usage: Read each sentence and mark the part of the sentence that has an error. Some sentences have no errors, then mark "N." (50 items, 20 minutes)

1. I just / left / my friends / house
   A   B   C   D

2. Ain't we / going to / the office / next week?
   A   B   C   D

Clerical Speed and Accuracy: One of the five letter and number combinations in each item is underlined. Find that same combination after the item number on your answer sheet and mark it. (100 items, 3 minutes)

Items:

1.	AB	AC	AD	AE	AF
2.	A7	7A	B7	<u>7B</u>	AB

Answer Sheet:

	AB	AF	AD	AC	AE
1.	0	0	0	0	0
	AB	A7	B7	7B	7A
2.	0	0	0	0	0

Mechanical Reasoning: Look at the picture and answer the question. (70 items, 30 minutes)

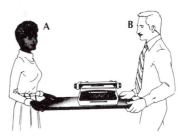

Which person has the heavier load? (If equal, mark C.)

Space Relations: The pattern at the left can be folded into a figure. Find the one figure at the right that can be made from the pattern shown. (60 items, 25 minutes)

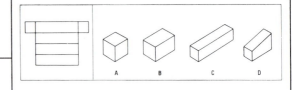

Spelling: Mark whether each word is spelled right or wrong. (90 items, 10 minutes)
1. man
2. gurl

Source: Adapted from Bennett, Seashore, and Wesman (1982, pp. 3, 9, 15, 21, 27, 42, 57, 59).

Figure 21 • 3   The eight subtests and examples of items on the *Differential Aptitude Tests*. (The number of items on each subtest as shown in parentheses.)

one gender obtains scores considerably higher on a subtest than another, the use of combined norms (i.e., males and females) may encourage persons to enter occupations traditionally associated with specific genders. For example, suppose

> Larry and Linda both have raw scores of 50 in Mechanical Reasoning. Combined norms would place both . . . [at] the 65th percentile. [However,] comparing Larry's score with males in his grade, [indicates] he is only . . . average [50th percentile]. Comparing Linda's score with females in her grade [indicates] she is [at] the 90th percentile. This information can have significance in counseling Linda. . . . If Linda wants to pursue a career requiring mechanical ability, . . . she should know [how her score compares] . . . with the norm for young men in her grade. Linda should be given a realistic picture of the challenges to be met but should be encouraged by her high same-sex standing (The Psychological Corporation, c. 1982, p. 7).

The results of the DAT are reported to students in terms of a *profile* such as that shown in Figure 21.4 for a 9th grade male. The raw scores on each subtest are listed in the leftmost column. The column of percentile ranks at the left tells how the pupil ranks in terms of other pupils of the same gender in the same grade (9th grade males in this example), whereas the column of percentile ranks at the right compares the pupil to pupils of the opposite gender in the same grade (9th grade females in this example).

For each subtest, the same-gender percentile rank is plotted on the chart as a bar of Xs (the percentile rank in the left column is located at the center X of the bar). The bars represent the fact that the scores are not perfectly reliable. The length of the bar reflects the standard error of measurement and is an *uncertainty interval* (Chapter 15). A student's ability levels in any two areas are considered essentially the same if the ends of the bars for those two areas overlap. If the bars for two areas do not overlap, the student's ability in

the higher scoring area is most likely higher. In Figure 21.4, for example, numerical ability is interpreted as significantly higher than spelling ability since the bars do not overlap. If bars overlap, but less than half of their length, the difference in scores *may* be significant, but additional information about the pupil is needed before a decision can be made.

The publisher also offers the DAT Career Planning Program which combines the scores of the DAT with the results of a questionnaire students complete indicating their grades, school subjects they like, educational level to which they aspire, and occupational areas they like. Each student receives a computer printout with interpretive statements relating the DAT and questionnaire. These statements show how well a student's educational and career goals match that student's DAT results and expressed occupational interests.

Group Tests of Specific Aptitudes

The kinds of general scholastic aptitude tests illustrated above are widely used in schools, but other types used for special decisions should be mentioned, too. Among these are readiness tests, high school and college admissions tests, and tests of aptitude for specific subjects.

Readiness Testing

Schools often use readiness tests as supplemental information to make instructional decisions for first grade pupils. Often such tests are used to supplement a kindergarten teacher's judgment about a youngster's general developmental and readiness level for first grade work, especially reading, where grouping by readiness level is a common practice. Since readiness tests measure a child's acquired learning skills, they are frequently classified as achievement tests rather than aptitude tests. The reader is referred to the discussion at the

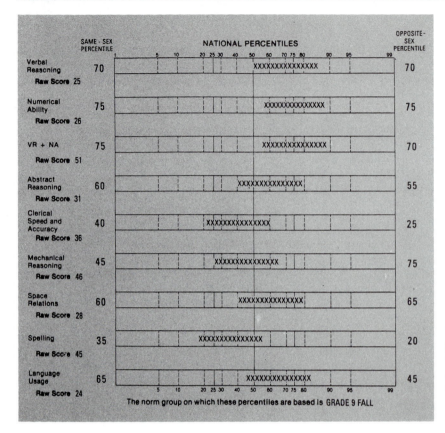

Figure 21 • 4 A portion of the Career Planning Report for the DAT showing the subtest score profile of a ninth grade male student.

Source: The Psychological Corporation (c. 1982, p. 4).

beginning of Chapter 20 concerning the distinction between aptitude and achievement used in this book.

As an illustration of the kinds of abilities tested on such tests, I shall discuss one readiness test: the *Metropolitan Readiness Tests* (Nurss & McGauvran, 1976). These tests originated in 1933 with Gertrude H. Hildreth. The tests were revised in 1949, 1964, and 1976. Currently, the tests function as one of four components of a readiness assessment and instruction program: (1) *Metropolitan Readiness Tests* (MRT)—these are formal group administered tests of readiness skills (see below); (2) *Early School Inventory*—teachers observe pupils during the early weeks of school, talk with parents, and complete a checklist of specific physical, language cognitive, and socio-emotional development behaviors to gather information about a child's readiness for school learning; (3) *Parent-Teacher Conference Report*—the teacher uses these sample items, a description of each MRT subtest, and a record of a child's MRT performance when the teacher meets with parents; (4) *Handbook of Skill Development Activities for Young Children*—This list of curriculum objectives and suggested games and activities facilitates learning in the areas of audition, language development, quantification, and visualization.

Level I Content	Level II Content
Test 1. Auditory Memory (12 items): Immediately recalling what the teacher said. Pupils close their eyes while the teacher says words, then pupils open their eyes and find the pictures of what the teacher said.	**Test 1. Beginning Consonants (13 items):** Discriminating the beginning sound of a word.
Test 2. Rhyming (13 items): Hearing and discriminating middle and ending sounds. The teacher says a word; pupils mark a picture of something that rhymes with the spoken word.	**Test 2. Sound-Letter Correspondence (16 items):** Identifying the letter with which a spoken word begins.
	Test 3. Visual Matching (10 items): Visually matching two letters, word-like forms, and other forms.
Test 3. Letter Recognition (11 items): Recognizing names of upper and lowercase letters. The teacher says a letter name; pupils mark the printed letter.	**Test 4. Finding Patterns (16 items):** Visually locating letters, numerals, and other forms embedded in a string of similar characters.
Test 4. Visual Matching (14 items): Visually matching letters, words, numerals, and other forms. Pupils find the picture that matches the form appearing at the beginning of a row of several pictures.	**Test 5. School Language (9 items):** Comprehending standard spoken American English.
	Test 6. Listening (9 items): Listening to a story read by the teacher and integrating the information, drawing inferences, and evaluating.
Test 5. School Language and Listening (15 items): Comprehending standard American English. The teacher reads a short passage; pupils mark the picture which corresponds to the story.	**Test 7. Quantitative Concepts (9 items):** Knowing of number-numeral correspondence, part-whole relations, and quantitative reasoning.
Test 6. Quantitative Language (11 items): Counting, recognizing numerals, comparing size and shape, and knowing other quantitative concepts.	**Test 8. Quantitative Operations (15 items):** Counting, adding, and subtracting.

Table 21 • 3 Description of the subtests of the *Metropolitan Readiness Tests.*

The readiness tests themselves are organized into two levels: Level I (beginning through middle kindergarten) and Level II (end of kindergarten through beginning grade 1). The content tested at each level is described in Table 21.3. Tests of copying skill are optional.

Various norm-referenced scores are used as an aid to interpreting this readiness test. For Level I, each subtest score is norm-referenced as High (= stanines 9, 8, or 7), Average (= stanines 6, 5, or 4), or Low (= stanines 3, 2, or 1); and percentile ranks and stanines are provided for composites: visual skill area (= Test 3 and Test 4), language skill area (= Test 5 and Test 6), and pre-reading skills composite (= Tests 1 through 6). For Level II, percentiles and stanines are reported for five skill areas—auditory (= Test 1 and Test 2), visual (Test 3 and Test 4), language (Test 5 and Test 6), and quantitative (Test 7 and Test 8)—and for pre-

reading skills composite (= Tests 1 through 6). National norms are also available for a full battery composite (= Tests 1 through 8). Thurstone absolute scaled scores (see Chapter 14) are used to measure growth, permit out-of-level testing, and to provide a common scale for linking Level I and Level II scores.

Readiness tests are frequently used to help teachers form instructional groups (for example, for reading instruction). When used in this way, they should be considered placement tests for purposes of validation, as placement is described in Chapter 16. Since readiness tests are frequently used in the context of (implicitly) predicting a pupil's likely success in instruction, I have classified them as aptitude tests in this book, although they may also be classified as achievement tests.

Keep in mind the test author's point of view when reviewing one of the many available readiness tests. This viewpoint of what constitutes "readiness to learn X" will determine the test content (as does an author's viewpoint for every test, of course). If scores on a readiness test are to be used as indicators of whether a child has mastered specific prerequisites, the teacher will have to carefully examine the actual test items to see if they measure the kinds of skills and abilities the teacher expects each child to have acquired before entering the new instruction.

High School and College Admissions Testing

Test scores, previous grades, letters of recommendation, interviews, and biographical information on out-of-school accomplishments are among the kinds of information used by colleges and selective high schools to make admissions decisions. Some private and parochial high schools, for example, use a battery of achievement and aptitude tests to screen applicants. Testing sessions are usually held at the local high school and the tests are generally administered by its staff. One test used for this purpose is the *Closed High School Placement Test* (Scholastic Testing Service, 1976). This battery contains the following tests: (1) Verbal Ability (60 verbal analogy items), (2) Quantitative Ability (52 items: number series, letter series, figure classification, figure analogies), (3) Reading (40 reading comprehension items), (4) Vocabulary (22 synonym items), (5) Mathematics Concepts (24 general mathematics concept items), (6) Problem Solving (40 word problem items), and (7) Language (60 items testing error checking ability, grammar, spelling, and punctuation).

Two widely used college admissions testing programs are the College Entrance Examination Board's *Scholastic Aptitude Test* (SAT) and the American College Testing Assessment Program. The College Entrance Examination Board (CEEB), currently located in New York City, was formed around 1899 to help selective colleges in the northeastern United States

coordinate their admissions testing requirements. The SAT developed out of that effort around 1926, being created by Carl Brigham, Associate Secretary for the CEEB (Donlon & Angoff, 1971). The test is currently developed for the CEEB by Educational Testing Service in Princeton, New Jersey.

The *Scholastic Aptitude Test,* generally taken during senior year of high school, has three parts: verbal, mathematics, and a test of standard written English. The English test is both multiple-choice (the mechanics of English) and essay (a short essay written on one of several topics). Tests are administered in local centers around the country (usually high schools and colleges) at pre-established times during the year. The test booklets and answer sheets are sent to the Educational Testing Service for scoring, recording, and processing to the colleges the student designates. With the passage of the recent "truth-in-testing" legislation, examinees can obtain copies of their answer sheets and test booklets.

The American College Testing (ACT) Assessment Program was formed in 1959, with the ideas and help of E. F. Lindquist among others. This admissions testing program is of a different character than the SAT. Whereas initially CEEB was concerned primarily with the private selective colleges of the northeast, the ACT Program initially sought to service midwestern public colleges and universities. What these colleges needed was help in (a) eliminating the few incapable students applying, (b) providing guidance services for those admitted, and (c) measuring broad educational development rather than narrower verbal and quantitative aptitudes (Lindquist in Feister & Whitney, 1968). Today the ACT Program in Iowa City is as active a research and test development enterprise as is the Educational Testing Service.

The ACT Assessment has two sections: the ACT tests and the Student Profile Section. The ACT tests are multiple-choice tests in English (mechanics), mathematics, social sciences (reading comprehension). The developers view the test items as "work samples"—simulations of the kinds of learning activities typically required of the college freshman (Cole & Hanson, 1973). In addition to these tests, students taking the ACT Assessment are asked to report their most recent grades in English, mathematics, social studies, and natural science for use by colleges along with students' test scores to predict college grades. The Student Profile Section includes an out-of-class accomplishments checklist and a short career interest inventory. The checklist permits the student to indicate any special talents and accomplishments not reflected in course grades (e.g., winning a state debate). The career interest inventory helps the student get a better idea of how his or her career interests fit into the mainstream of various major areas of college. The ACT tests are, of course, subject to the same truth-in-testing requirements as all other admissions tests. As with the SAT, test booklets and answer sheets are returned to the test developer for scoring, recording, and processing for the college(s) the student designates.

Testing Aptitudes for Specific Subjects

Over the years a number of tests have been developed which measure aptitudes for specific subjects such as algebra, typing and shorthand, foreign language, music, and art. The *Modern Language Aptitude Test* (MLAT) (Carroll & Sapon, 1959) can be used to illustrate an aptitude test for a specific subject.

The MLAT is designed as a selection test for use in situations in which the pupil has had little or no experience in formal foreign language instruction. (It is assumed, however, that the pupil is literate and speaks English with a native fluency.) In such situations, past grades in language courses are nonexistent, and pupils would score zero on language achievement tests (except for luck in blind guessing). The test authors' factor analytic research with high school students and adults indicates that five abilities are predic-

tive of successful foreign language learning and also can be tested before a person begins learning a foreign language (Carroll & Sapon, 1959): (1) auditory alertness and memory, (2) ability to associate sounds and symbols, (3) ability to derive meaning from symbols, (4) sensitivity to grammatical structure, and (5) rote memory. These abilities are tested on the MLAT. The test is administered with the help of a tape recorder which presents the words and sounds of both English and an artificial language. A similar version of the test, especially designed for 8 to 11 year old children, is also available.

The authors describe the MLAT's use in selection in the following way (Carroll & Sapon, 1959, p. 20):

> The MLAT does *not* predict *whether* an individual can learn a foreign language if he is given enough time and opportunity to do so; what it *does* predict is how well he can learn a foreign language in typical foreign language courses in the usually allotted time. The use of the MLAT in selecting students for foreign language courses, therefore, is based on the premise that only students with reasonable promise of rapid learning and success at a high level of proficiency are worth the time and expense of training. This premise will hold true for many situations in the government, in industry and business, and in education, particularly where individuals are being trained in a foreign language with a view to immediate practical use.

After selection, a teacher may want to be appraised of the kinds of learning difficulties a pupil may experience during the language course. The authors describe the way the results may be used for such diagnostic purposes below (Carroll & Sapon, 1959, p. 20):

> While it will generally be true that the experienced instructor will quickly become aware of the student's particular learning difficulties without the use of any aptitude test, it will sometimes save time and effort to forecast such difficulties by use of the part scores from the

MLAT. Thus, low scores on Part II tend to mean that the individual will have difficulty learning the phonology (sound system) of a foreign language and also difficulty in mimicking spoken sentences accurately. Low scores on Part IV probably mean that the individual will have particular difficulty in learning the grammar and structure of the foreign language, and low scores on Part V may suggest that the individual may have to spend more time with the rote memory aspects of learning a foreign language.

The MLAT is only one of a number of tests which have been developed to measure aptitude for a specific subject. Although the manuals of these tests provide data on their validity for predicting measures of achievement, establishing a test's validity *locally* is often necessary. A test's validity for predicting grades in a subject varies from school to school because (a) course requirements differ, (b) grading policies differ, and (c) the composition of the student group taking a course differ. A test manual only gives a general idea of the likely predictive validity of a test. The responsibility for conducting local validation studies usually resides with a school's central administration, but a teacher should be alert to the central question of such research: Does using that particular aptitude test provide any more useful information to the process of making decisions about pupils than already available information such as general scholastic aptitude test scores, achievement test scores, records of past pupil performance, or careful observations made by the teacher?

Culture-Free, Culture-Fair, and Culture-Specific Tests

There have been various attempts over the years to reduce the influence of culture-specific experience on test performance by either modifying already existing tests or by attempting to create culture-free or culture-fair tests. Some have sought, on the other hand, to capitalize on the specific knowledge of a given cultural subgroup and create culture-specific tests. Mercer (1978) has summarized these four approaches to multicultural testing as follows.

Culture-Free Tests

At one time it was thought a test could be created essentially free of all cultural influence. Since all tests require the person to use learned behavior, today it is generally considered impossible to create a culture-free test (Wesman, 1968; Williams, 1975b).

Culture-Fair Tests

With the realization that it was impossible to build a culture-free test, some have attempted to build tests which, while not entirely free from cultural influence, are "fair" (or "fairer") to different cultural groups. Four different approaches are described here.

Common-culture approach Test developers using this approach seek to include on a test only items in which the content is common to all cultures. Included among such tests are the *Davis-Eells Games* (1953), *Cattell Culture Fair Test* (Cattell & Cattell, 1960), and *Goodenough Draw-a-Man Test* (Harris, 1963). Among problems with such tests are that: (a) differences among culturally distinct groups still exist, (b) paper-and-pencil tests present special problems in many cultures, and (c) the psychosocial character of the testing situation makes it difficult to claim that the test is measuring the same trait in all cultures.

Equal representation approach Developers using this approach include on a test equal numbers of items from each of the cultures that would be taking the test. A problem with such tests, in addition to those mentioned above, is that they do not have predictive validity in any one culture.

Test-train-retest approach Persons employing this approach "teach the common culture

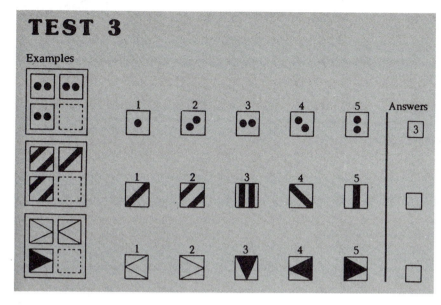

TEST 3

Examples

Figure 21 • 5
Sample item from the *Cattell Culture Fair Intelligence Test.*

Source: Bobbs-Merrill (1980, p. 14)

items" by training persons in how to perform the tasks on nonverbal tests such as the *Raven Progressive Matrices* (e.g., Budoff, 1972). It is not clear exactly what such an approach actually measures.

Developmental stages approach This usually means using Jean Piaget's (1896–1980) stages of intellectual development as a means of developing culture-fair tests. It remains to be proven that this approach is culture-fair.

Adapting Existing Tests

Since the invention of the Binet-Simon scales, psychologists have attempted to adapt tests developed in one culture for use in another. Among the methods of adaptation have been: (a) direct translation, (b) weighing the nonverbal portion of a test more heavily into the total, and (c) varying the speed and power components of a test. Direct translation usually is not successful, especially for verbal items, since concepts represented in them fre-

quently have either no direct counterparts or different meanings in the second culture. Items may become more difficult if the words are less frequently used in the second culture. Some persons have attempted to adapt a test by giving the verbal portion of a test less weight than the nonverbal portion, but there is no guarantee that this makes a test culture-fair. Nonverbal items are not culture-fair ipso facto. Furthermore, such weights are often applied arbitrarily and, thus, it is questionable whether the altered scoring measures the same traits as the original tests. Any modification of a test nullifies using its standardization data, of course, and thus alters its interpretive framework.

Culture-Specific Tests

It is possible to develop a test which is specific to each particular subculture of the larger society. Each such test would in some sense be fair for the group for whom it is designed. Williams (1975a), for example, developed a vocabulary test measuring knowledge of black slang: the *Black Intelligence Test of Cultural Homogeneity* (BITCH). As expected, he demonstrated that black high school pupils scored considerably higher on it than white pupils. The major difficulty with using such culturally specific tests in schools is that these tests face the same problems as anglocentric tests: A need exists to show that the tests validly measure important characteristics of pupils which the schools can use in the process of making instructional decisions.

The Stability of Scholastic Aptitude Test Scores

An important school concern is whether a pupil's measured scholastic aptitude remains constant or stable over a period of time. Although on a pupil-by-pupil basis scores may systematically rise or decline, a definite tendency exists for pupils to maintain similar relative positions in a norm-group throughout their schooling years. In other words, a pupil's z-score in a distribution of aptitude test scores tends to remain *roughly* the same.

The Constancy of Scholastic Aptitude Test Scores

The index which reflects the agreement between persons' z-scores on two measurements is, of course, the correlation coefficient. In general, test-retest correlations for general scholastic aptitude tests (a) tend to be lower as the time interval between the two testings becomes longer and (b) for a fixed interval of time between testings tend to be lower for younger children. For example, the test-retest correlations on an individual intelligence test such as the WPPSI or WISC-R tend to be around 0.85 to 0.95 when retesting occurs between one and six months after the original testing (Wechsler, 1967; 1974). For most tests the correlations will probably drop to the 0.40

to 0.60 range for a longer retesting interval of ten years.

Among the factors which contribute to the stability of persons' aptitude test scores over time are these (Anastasi, 1976): (1) *intellectual skills are cumulative*—what is learned at an earlier age tends to be retained along with newly acquired skills [called the *overlap hypothesis* (Anderson, 1940)], (2) most persons have a long term, *stable environment*—the advantages or disadvantages of socioeconomic level, family configuration, and sociocultural influences tend to remain the same over relatively long periods of time, and (3) the *generative nature of earlier acquired prerequisite skills* tends to facilitate future intellectual development—previously learned skills are not only retained but actually facilitate the subsequent learning of new skills.

Changes in Scholastic Aptitude Test Scores

While as a group pupils generally tend to maintain their relative positions in the distribution of scores, important changes in individuals' statuses do occur. We cannot be very confident about whether a particular pupil's score will remain the same from year to year. There are often large fluctuations in pupil's scores over time.[2]

Reasons for Aptitude Score Changes

Among the reasons why a person's aptitude test score may not remain the same from one testing to another are:

1. *Errors of measurement.* Even if the person's "true score" were to stay the same, the obtained score is likely to be different due to a test's unreliability (see Chapter 15).
2. *Tests and norm differences.* When trying to explain why an individual's scholastic

[2]Anastasi (1982, p. 326) cites thirteen examples of studies reporting large fluctuations in individuals' IQ scores.

aptitude test scores have increased or decreased, considering the test(s) on which those scores were obtained is important. The content of different tests will vary, and often the content of the same test may vary with the age level of the person taking the test, being somewhat more concrete and perceptual for young children and more abstract and verbal for older children. Further, the norms of different publishers' tests are not comparable. Since mental ability scores are norm-referenced, differences in scores may be due to differences in norms. For example, in one study comparing scores on several scholastic aptitude tests (Hieronymus & Stroud, 1969), a 7th grade pupil with an IQ = 106 on *Lorge-Thorndike Intelligence Test* (1963) would need to obtain an IQ = 114 on the Kuhlman-Anderson Test (1960) in order to have a score equivalent in the norm-referenced sense.

3. *Special interventions and enriched environments.* If a person's environment dramatically and persistently becomes more intellectually nurturing over a period of time, that person's scores on a scholastic aptitude test are likely to increase. Conversely, if the person becomes physically or emotionally ill or deprived in a way that interferes with intellectual development, then aptitude scores may decrease.

Changes during childhood Examples of changes in individual children's ability test scores are shown in Figure 21.6. The cases were specially selected to represent high, middle, and low ability persons. Notice that at younger ages persons' scores tend to fluctuate wildly, but although the undulations tend to decrease after the onset of school age, the graph of a person's ability score is not necessarily a horizontal line. Some individuals tend to systematically increase their scores, while others' scores decrease. Among the factors associated with increased aptitude scores for individuals are: (a) amount and quality of

schooling, (b) stable and supportive home life, (c) curiosity and tendency to explore the environment, (d) high achievement drive, and (e) intellectually rewarding environment (e.g., Haan, 1963; Härnquist, 1978; Kagan & Freeman, 1963; Kagan, Sontag, Baker, & Nelson, 1958; McCall, Appelbaum, & Hogarty, 1973).

Changes during adulthood In the past it was generally held that on the average general mental ability increased until age twenty-five, then declined rather rapidly. Data which supported this hypothesis have been criticized because they were based on cross-sectional sampling. *Cross-sectional* research studies compare the average scores of one age group with another age group, both being tested at the same point in time (e.g., testing all age levels in 1983). Any differences observed in these averages cannot be attributed solely to age because they are influenced by any cultural conditions which impact on one age group but not on the other. *Longitudinal* studies which retest the same persons as they become older tend to overcome this shortcoming because persons presumably carry the impact of cultural conditions with them as they get older. But longitudinal studies are not without criticism, since the influence of aging on the test scores is confounded with the influences of practice due to retesting and any special factors that may be associated with a particular point in history. Currently, research studies on the influence of aging on general mental ability tend to include both longitudinal and cross-sectional data in an attempt to separate the influence of these two confounding factors as much as possible.

Anastasi (1982) summarizes much of the current thought on the matter of intellectual decline with age:

> In general, the results of the better designed studies of adult intelligence strongly suggest that the ability decrements formerly attributed to aging are actually intergenerational or cohort differences, probably associated with cultural changes in our society. Genuine ability decre-

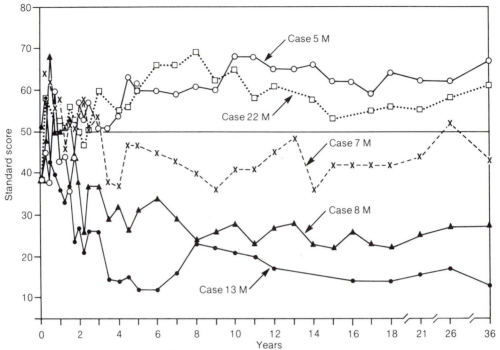

A. Five males from the Berkeley Growth Study

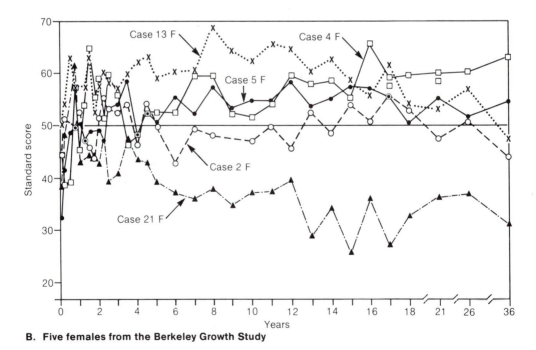

B. Five females from the Berkeley Growth Study

Source: Bayley (1970, p. 1174, 1175, Figs. 1, 2)

Figure 21 • 6   Examples of individual curves of relative mental ability expressed in standard scores (see Chapter 14) from birth to 36 years old.

ments are not likely to be manifested until well over the age of 60. Moreover, any generalization whether pertaining to age decrement or cohort differences must be qualified by a recognition of the wide individual variability found in all situations. Individual differences within any one age level are much greater than the average difference between age levels. . . . Thus, some 80 year-olds will do better than some 20 year-olds [and vice versa] (p. 336–337).

This conclusion is not without controversy, however. A reanalysis by Horn and Donaldson (1976) of the data[3] upon which much of this conclusion is based indicates that different kinds of abilities decline at different ages, but most abilities have begun to decline by age 40 or 50. The question of the nature of intellectual development in adulthood, as Horn and Donaldson point out, is that

> Our state of knowledge about adulthood development . . . is not sufficient to permit authoritative assertions that there is, or that there is not, important intellectual decrement associated with aging. . . . If it turns out that these functions do not deteriorate, but only seem to because of some defect in study design, the mistake can be absorbed without much real loss. On the other hand, if study of true decrement is neglected on the wishful assumption that it doesn't exist, then the possibilities for amelioration of an undesirable condition are reduced and real loss does result (p. 718).

Using Scholastic Aptitude Tests for Ability Grouping and Placement

Ability Grouping

Ability grouping in this context means to use a test of general scholastic ability to organize

[3]Much of the conclusion is based on data collected and analyzed by Baltes, Labouvie, and Schaie (Baltes, Labouvie, 1973; Schaie, Labouvie, & Buech, 1973; Schaie & Labouvie-Lief, 1974). A response to the Horn and Donaldson (1976) criticism is found in Baltes and Schaie (1976).

pupils into groups of "homogeneous ability" for purposes of instruction. In its extreme form, this practice is known as *tracking:* An entire school is organized into "tracks" such as "college prep," "general high school," and "remedial." Those employing homogeneous ability grouping assume that (1) pupils learn better when placed into homogeneous ability groups, and (2) forming homogeneous groupings is, in fact, possible (Tyler, 1974). For the majority of cases in which normal children have been grouped, there seems to be very little, if any, gain in achievement (Findley & Bryan, 1971).

> . . . It appears that the usual ways in which test results are employed to group students for instruction neither produce homogeneous groups nor greatly increase student learning. Furthermore, ability grouping is now under attack by those seeking to eliminate school segregation. They point out that as children from different racial and ethnic groups are enrolled in the same school, they are assigned to segregated classrooms on the basis of test results. In this way, the effort to facilitate social interaction among racial and ethnic groups is thwarted by the separation of children into different tracks or so-called ability groups (Tyler, 1974, p. 67).

Placement into Special Classes

A closely related matter is the use of general scholastic aptitude tests to place pupils in special education classes. Past practices of placement based primarily on scores from these tests led to many abuses, such as excluding from mainstream classrooms physically handicapped pupils who, with minor adaptations on the part of the school, can perform satisfactorily, and including large numbers of black, native American, and Spanish-speaking children in special classes. With the passage of the Rehabilitation Act of 1973 (Public Law 93-112) and the Education for All Handicapped Children Act of 1975 (Public Law 94-142), federal regulations have attempted to remedy these abuses by requiring that the tests used with physically handicapped children reflect the specific aptitude or achievement claimed to be measured as opposed to having the scores on the test reflect primarily a pupil's impairment or language skills; and, also, that no single test score shall be the sole criterion for a placement decision (U.S. Office of Education, Department of Health, Education, and Welfare, 1977). Implicit in such regulations is the necessity for persons administering standardized tests to special pupils to have experience and training in the techniques of testing these children. Without such special training, inappropriate decisions are likely to be made.

Identifying the Gifted and Talented

Another common use of scholastic aptitude test scores is as one piece of information in the process of identifying gifted and talented pupils. The use of a scholastic aptitude test alone as a determiner results, of course, in a very narrow conception of students' "gifts and talents." Among the characteristics that can be included in a broad definition of gifted and talented are: (1) general mental ability, (2) aptitude for a specific academic subject, (3) creative thinking ability, (4) ability to lead others, (5) aptitude for a visual and/or performing art, and (6) ability for outstanding psychomotor accomplishments (Marland, 1972). Although some pupils may be accomplished in several areas, it is unlikely that anyone would be equally strong in all areas. Thus, to use only one measure such as that obtained from a scholastic aptitude test as the basis for identifying such gifted and talented youngsters seems inappropriate. Further, students scoring high on tests of *general* school ability often do not have high aptitude for learning a *particular* subject because students can obtain high general school ability test scores in several ways. For example, if an educator takes a group of students with very high IQs and places them into an accelerated mathematics class, some students will probably lag behind because they lack the high aptitude for math-

ematics which others with the same IQ have (Stanley, 1977). Some teachers who may be unaware that a high IQ score does not necessarily imply that a pupil has a high aptitude for a specific subject may misdiagnose the problem and accuse those who lag behind of being poorly motivated (Stanley, 1977). A related issue is whether some standardized, multiple-choice achievement tests which measure mostly information about a subject can identify students who have unusually high ability to apply knowledge to a wide variety of situations or have a deep understanding of the abstract concepts in the subject (Gallagher, 1979).

Overachievement and Underachievement

According to this practice, scholastic aptitude tests are used to set expected or predicted achievement levels (usually defined to be a grade-equivalent score on an achievement test). Those pupils performing above these predicted achievement levels are termed *overachievers*, while those performing below predictions are *underachievers*. It is important to realize that the *predicted achievement score* is really an estimated average—the average achievement score of all those having an identical scholastic aptitude score.[4] Since averages are generally in the middle of a distribution, you can expect that about one-half of those having a particular aptitude score will have above average achievement scores (and, hence, be labeled overachievers), while one-half will score lower than the predicted score (and, hence, be labeled underachievers). In practice, an uncertainty interval is often placed around the predicted achievement score. Thus, the actual achievement scores of about two-thirds of the pupils will be near enough to their predicted achievement scores to fall within

[4] A statistical equation, known as a *regression equation*, is used to estimate this average from the scholastic aptitude score and (sometimes) other measures such as chronological age and achievement test scores.

---

this uncertainty interval: These pupils are said to be performing as expected.

Although labeling a pupil an "underachiever" is an oversimplification, a useful first step in attempting to identify pupil difficulties is to examine the discrepancy between a pupil's general scholastic ability and specific ability in a curriculum area such as reading or mathematics. One recommendation is for the teacher to identify pupils for further exploration whose achievement test score is in the bottom 20% of the distribution for pupils who have the *same* scholastic aptitude score as that pupil (Hieronymus, 1976). Not all publishers provide the teacher with information to do this, however.

Although it is possible to invoke many reasons why pupils do not achieve their estimated potential, there are several technical, statistical reasons why one can expect to observe a discrepancy between actual achievement levels and predicted achievement levels (Ahmann & Glock, 1981):

1. *The limited nature of scholastic aptitude tests* means that only a few of the abilities needed for achievement in a subject are measured. Thus, the correlation (and, hence, the prediction) will always be less than perfect and there will always be a discrepancy observed. But this does not mean that the person is necessarily failing to achieve as he or she should.
2. *Error of measurement* in the aptitude test score means that the predicted achievement score will also be in error. Conversely, the observed achievement score may be in error and may account for a large part of the discrepancy observed.
3. *Differences in norms.* The discrepancy could be entirely misplaced unless the prediction equation is based on the identical persons taking both the aptitude and the achievement tests. This means, for example, that unless the local school conducts a special study, educators cannot use the scholastic aptitude test from one publisher to set the expected score on another publisher's achievement test. Many publishers concurrently standardize (Chapter 18) aptitude and achievement tests, and thus the school ability tests can be used to estimate achievement levels.
4. *Regression effect.* Since two tests do not correlate perfectly, there is a tendency for a *regression effect* to operate: Those scoring high on one test (e.g., aptitude test) will tend to have less extreme (lower) scores on the second test (e.g., achievement test), while those scoring low on one test will tend to score somewhat higher on the second test. This means that a statistical artifact is built into the discrepancy for very high and very low scorers, an artifact which has very little to do with their capacity. Pupils with very high aptitude scores will tend to be labeled underachievers, while pupils with very low aptitude scores will tend to be labeled overachievers just because there is not a perfect correlation between the tests.

Although there are compelling reasons for deciding whether pupils are capable of learning more than their current performance indicates, the means of making this decision is neither straightforward nor mechanical. The decision will require a teacher to use considerable judgment and to integrate several types of information; a simple "decision-prescription" is not available.

The concept of *"overachiever"* seems not only an oversimplification but also misplaced. It conveys the idea that a pupil has a certain limited capacity to learn a subject and, by implication, the "overachieving" pupil has somehow achieved more than that limit. The logical question is, "How can a person be already attaining that which is beyond that person's capacity?" If the pupil is doing something already, the pupil must have the capacity to do so. Thus, "overachiever" seems to be a logical contradiction of terms.

Summary

The following are the main points of this chapter.

1. This chapter discusses three general types of group administered scholastic aptitude tests: an omnibus test, a three-score test, and a multiple-aptitude test. Suggestions for using these test scores appear.

2. School readiness tests are also described and an example of the kinds of skills and abilities found on one given.

3. High school and college admissions tests are designed to predict success at the next higher level of schooling. The chapter describes one high school and two college admissions tests.

4. Tests exist to measure a person's aptitude for quickly learning a particular subject, such as algebra or a foreign language. These tests usually test the elemental processes and prerequisite skills and knowledges needed to progress rapidly in the new course. A foreign language aptitude test serves as an example.

5. When attempting to measure general mental ability of all persons, educators soon become aware that a person's sociocultural background influences scores on nearly all tests. Several approaches have been tried in an effort to disentangle cultural effects from "general ability" or "intelligence": culture-free tests, culture-fair tests, culturally-adapted tests, and cultural-specific tests.

6. As a group, pupils' scholastic aptitude test scores tend to be stable over time. This means that, on the whole, pupils' z-scores in an aptitude test score distribution remain *roughly* the same over time.

7. In general, test-retest correlations for scholastic ability tests (a) tend to become lower (less stability) as the time interval between the testings becomes longer and (b) for a fixed interval between testings tend to be lower for younger children than for older children.

8. Among the factors which contribute to the relative stability of persons' aptitude scores are: (a) the cumulative nature of intellectual skills, (b) the stable environment which persons experience, and (c) the generative nature of earlier acquired prerequisite skills.

9. Among the factors which contribute to changes in a person's aptitude scores are: (a) errors of measurement, (b) test and norm differences, and (c) special interventions and enriched environments.

10. Growth in intellectual skills in early years seems to be associated with an environment that is emotionally supportive and accepting and in which there are many opportunities for experiencing and reinforcing a person's cognitive successes.

11. How to interpret the evidence on decline of mental ability in adulthood is unclear. Within any age group there appear to be wide individual differences, so that even if an older group shows lower scores on the average, many older individuals will have substantially higher scores than a younger group. There is a tendency for average declines in ability to begin in the late 40s or 50s. These declines in test scores may be associated with physiological factors such as speed of responding.

12. Scholastic aptitude tests have been used to "track" pupils or place them into "homogeneous" groups for instruction. No evidence seems to support unequivocally the ideas that pupils learn very much better in homogeneous scholastic aptitude groups or that the groups that are formed are in fact homogeneous in this regard. Further, the practice of using tests to group pupils has been criticized because it tends to result in segregated classrooms and thereby work against the goal of increasing racial and ethnic interaction in the school.

13. In the past, a score on a scholastic aptitude test frequently has been the sole basis for placing pupils in special classes. Recent state and federal legislation and court decisions seem to be directed toward remedying this abuse.

14. Scores on scholastic aptitude tests are often used to place pupils into gifted and talented programs. Such tests seem to be too narrow in their measurement of "gifts and talents." A broad conception of gifts and talents would include not only those with high general mental ability, but individuals who excel in (a) specific academic subjects, (b) creative thinking, (c) leadership, (d) visual and/or performing arts, or (e) psychomotor accomplishments.

15. Most standard tests of either general mental ability or specific subject matter knowledge do not seem to provide opportunities for gifted students to display unusual comprehension of or insight into a subject which they may have acquired.

16. Scholastic ability tests are sometimes used to identify over- and underachievers. The term overachiever seems illogical since it implies that a pupil is doing something which is beyond that pupil's capacity to do it.

17. Before concluding that a pupil's actual achievement is really out of line with the predicted or expected achievement for that pupil, a teacher would have to collect evidence that discounts the following counter-explanations for the observed discrepancy: (a) the scholastic aptitude test measures too narrow a set of skills, (b) one or both test scores reflect large errors of measurement, (c) the scholastic ability test and the achievement test are referenced to different norming samples, and (d) the observed discrepancy reflects only a regression effect.

Themes

- Teachers should be aware of the wide variety of noncognitive variables which have been defined and measured and which have bearing on educational decisions.

- Of special concern to junior and senior high school teachers and counselors is the nature and measurement of knowledge, interest, maturity, and career decision-making processes.

- Attitudes of individual pupils and of the public toward school and school-related issues can be measured and used to inform educational decision-making.

- Personality measurement is important in helping psychologists and counselors in the psychotherapeutic process, but such measurement is less useful to teachers who generally lack the specialized training and time to use them.

Terms and Concepts

noncognitive (affective) domain
areas of the noncognitive domain
    (experiential factors, affects,
    attitudes, beliefs, interests, motives,
    temperaments, social sensitivities,
    coping strategies, cognitive styles,
    creative abilities, values, curiosities)
vocational interest inventories
forced-choice item format
empirical scales
homogeneous (single factor) scales
people-similarity rationale vs. activity-
    similarity rationale
expressed interests, manifested
    interested, tested interests,
    inventoried interests

career maturation
Holland's hexagonal model of
    personality types (realistic,
    conventional, enterprising, social,
    artistic, investigative)
bias in interest measurement
affective, cognitive, and behavioral
    components of attitudes
methods of attitude scale construction
    (Thurstone, Likert)
projective personality test
structured (self-report) personality test

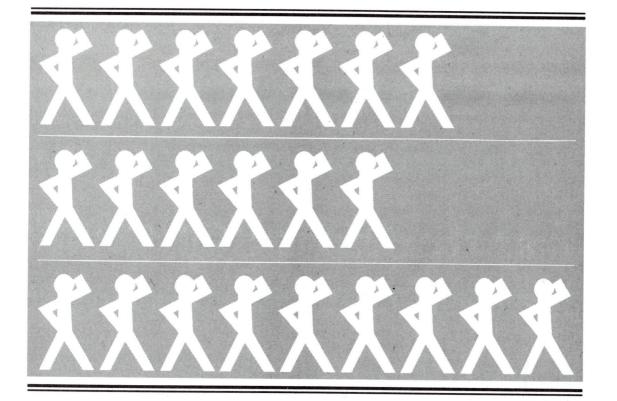

22
MEASURING NONCOGNITIVE VARIABLES: INTERESTS, ATTITUDES, AND ASPECTS OF PERSONALITY

This chapter describes how several different kinds of noncognitive dimensions of a pupil can be measured and how such measurements can be used for educational decisions. There are a great many aspects of a person that are lumped together and called "noncognitive." The first part of this chapter presents a kind of map of this domain. It lists, defines, and describes the general usefulness of these variables. The second section discusses the measurement and use of vocational and career-related interests. That section is organized around several questions: What are vocational interest inventories? Why and how are they used? What are career interests and how are they related to career decision-making skills and career maturity? Are different interest inventories similar? What of bias in interest inventories? A third section discusses how attitudes are measured and includes a discussion of public opinion surveys. The last section briefly describes measuring personality by means of projective and structured techniques.

A Map of the Domain of Noncognitive Measures Having Potential Uses in Education

Variety and Importance of Noncognitive Variables

Up to this point we have discussed the measurement of variables that emphasize the cognitive features of a pupil's personality such as general educational development, specific achievements, general school aptitudes, and specific abilities. However, a vast array of human characteristics remain which have relevance to education. One large group of these is often referred to as the *noncognitive* or *affective domain*. As Messick (1979) points out, however, a comparison between cognitive and noncognitive is difficult because the distinction is essentially artificial: Nearly all behavior is subject to influence by both the cognitive and the noncognitive aspects of a person. Thus, a sharp distinction between the two domains cannot be made. To say that we are testing a cognitive capability does not imply that only cognition influences a pupil's performance; to say we are testing a noncognitive capability does not imply that cognition is absent from a pupil's response.

Table 22.1 displays one panoramic view of the noncognitive domain.[1] Fourteen broad areas are depicted, each area encompassing a variety of specific traits or variables often studied in the educational context. These traits are listed in the far right column. Note that the fourteen areas are not entirely separate or independent of one another, but overlap considerably in many cases (Messick, 1979). These areas do, nevertheless, represent different facets of personality that have often been considered important to education.

These noncognitive variables are important to education in several ways (Messick, 1979): (a) some of them, such as those in the areas of affect and motivation, can be used to predict a pupil's success in a particular instructional environment; (b) some seem to function as mediating variables, facilitating (or hampering) either the rate a pupil learns new material, the level of learning a pupil attains,

[1]The reader should also refer to Appendix D.

---

or both; (c) others appear to act as moderator variables, determining the differential effects which certain kinds of instructional procedures have on different students; and (d) some are viewed as either desired outcomes of education or as valued individual characteristics which, at a minimum, education should not undermine. Note that in most cases the exact influence of each of these variables on pupil learning is unknown.

Potential Roles of Noncognitive Variables

Educational decisions There are several varieties of educational decisions which need to be made, as described in Chapter 1. Messick (1979) examines the potential roles that could be played by measures of noncognitive variables in connection with these decisions.

1. *Access.* The essential concern here is with *who* is admissible to particular educational opportunities. Traditionally, cognitive variables have been used in these decisions, but broadening the domain of variables measured to include noncognitive types may offer expanded educational opportunities to nontraditional students.

2. *Objectives and standards.* This class of decisions is concerned with *what* educators should teach and *which* of several domains they should address. Many noncognitive variables seem to fit into a broadened definition of educational goals. Some variables, such as curiosity, interests, and values, have direct implication for the particular subject-matter objectives that should be taught.

3. *Guidance.* This class of decisions involves the student choosing one educational program or alternative over another. Interest, values, and motivations are among the noncognitive variables which play roles here along with cognitive variables such as aptitudes and achievements.

4. *Selection.* These decisions focus on *whether* a particular person is permitted to enter a program and *where* the person may need to go in order to reach the desired program goals. Again, the tradition has been to use cognitive variables to make decisions, but certain noncognitive variables might be added: experiential learning, social sensitivity, creativity, interests, and motivations.

5. *Placement.* These decisions refer to vertical grouping of students either for remediation or advanced placement. Interests, motivations, affects, experiential learning, and creative and talent accomplishments are among the noncognitive variables which have potential roles to play in placement decisions.

6. *Instructional approach.* One of the decisions to be made in instruction concerns *how* the educator is to teach. Motivations and cognitive styles may be variables of potential worth. Measuring cognitive variables is necessary, however, to identify the content to be learned.

7. *Evaluation of programs.* This class of decisions concerns *how well* an educational program has accomplished its various espoused goals, and whether the program has had side effects. Outcome measures may need to include noncognitive as well as cognitive variables.

Misuses of noncognitive variables Note that while, on the one hand, educators generally agree about the value and desired emphasis of many cognitive variables, especially those associated with general educational development or with basic educational skills, on the other hand, educators agree much less on the value and emphasis to place on each of the noncognitive areas. Messick points to this lack of consensus as a potential invitation for misuse. Thus, for example, issues of *which* values to support arise. He recommends that persons make explicit which values—those of the state, school, parent, teacher, pupil—will be used to decide which noncognitive variables to measure and use in decision-making. We

Area measured and general description	Variables measured and related to education
Experiential background factors a. work experience, educational history, and talent accomplishments, and b. demographics (age, sex, social class, ethnic background, and bilingualism).	a. often used as proxy measures for "prior learning." b. often used as proxies for functional characteristics of the learner.
Affects Positive and negative feelings that can be either: a. affective *states* (specific to specific circumstances), or b. affective *traits* (characteristic way(s) in which an individual generally behaves).	Included are such variables as joy, surprise, fear, anger, euphoria, vague uneasiness, feelings about: school, a subject, being tested, and/or being a learner.
Attitudes Positive and negative feelings directed toward particular social objects, situations, institutions, persons, and/or ideas. Attitudes ". . . possess cognitive (beliefs or knowledge), affective (emotional, motivational), and performance (behavioral or action tendencies) components (Aiken, 1980, p. 2).	Includes attitudes toward learning, school, a subject matter, and/or self as a learner.
Beliefs The relationship an individual expects to hold between one object and another object (concept, value, goal) (Fishbein & Ajzen, 1975).	Includes "locus of control" or the degree to which persons feel responsible for their own actions; self-motivation felt to be a consequence of this variable.
Interests Patterns of selective attention toward and of choice among alternative activities when not subject to external pressures. Usually expressed as a like or dislike for particular activities.	Includes interests in a particular subject area and vocational or career interests.
Motives Impulses, emotions, or desires that spark a person to an action.	Includes need for achievement; need for social approval in learning contexts; curiosity; need for affiliation, aggression, autonomy, change, cognitive structure, dominance, endurance, exhibition, impulsiveness, order, play, sentience, social recognition, succorance, and understanding.

Source: Based on "Potential Uses of Noncognitive Measurement in Education," by S. Messick, *Journal of Educational Psychology,* 1979, *71.* Courtesy of the American Psychological Association.

Table 22 • 1   The different areas of the domain of noncognitive measurement in the educational context.

need to know how various sets of values are operating because these values influence (a) the particular noncognitive variables the school will emphasize and (b) the consequences, to both society and the individual, which result when various educational decisions are made using measures of the variables as sources of information.

Measurement of Vocational and Career Interests

What are Vocational Interest Inventories?

Vocational interest inventories are formal paper-and-pencil questionnaires that help persons express their likes and dislikes about a very

Area measured and general description	Variables measured and related to education
Temperaments Characteristics or dispositions which influence a person's tempo, rhythmicity, adaptability, energy expenditure, mode, and focus of attention (Thomas, Chess, & Birch, 1968).	Includes traits such as confidence vs. inferiority, impulsiveness vs. deliberateness, cheerful vs. depression, nervousness vs. composure, ascendance vs. timidity, friendliness vs. hostility, tolerance vs. criticality, masculinity vs. femininity, extroversion vs. introversion (Guilford, 1959).
Social sensitivities Interpersonal competence and ability to get along with others.	Includes empathy, interpersonal participation, social adroitness, leadership, persuasiveness, modeling, and tolerance (Weinstein, 1969).
Coping strategies Patterns and strategies for adapting to the requirements imposed by the (social) environment and for dealing with stress and threats (Lazarus, 1966).	Includes the ability to formulate and use effective and flexible strategies to deal with the learning and social environment.
Cognitive styles Consistent, habitual information-processing strategies that characterize a person's usual way of perceiving, remembering, thinking, and problem solving.	Includes leveling vs. sharpening, scanning vs. focusing, cognitive complexity vs. simplicity, field independence vs. field dependence. Are viewed as influencing how pupils learn, teachers teach, and vocational choices are made (Messick, 1976; Witkin, Dyk, Faterson, Goodenough, & Karp, 1962).
Creative abilities Measured or judged by observing a. predisposing personal characteristics such as divergent thinking, openness, and sensitivity. b. creative products or talented accomplishments.	Includes originality, flexibility, fluency, novelty, excellence and/or beauty of accomplishment.
Values A long-lasting belief that a particular manner of conduct or state of existence is personally or socially preferable to a converse or alternate manner of conduct or state of existence (Rokeach, 1973).	Includes athletic, social, economic, political, intellectual, moral, and religious values.
Curiosities Exploratory behavior thought to be induced by novelty, uncertainty, or insufficient information.	Includes measures designed to ascertain the extent to which persons seek to understand the nature and course of events (Berlyne, 1976).

Table 22 • 1 continued

wide range of particular kinds of work and other activities. A person's pattern of interests is then determined from the responses. This profile or pattern of interests becomes one source of information a person can use for career exploration, career counseling, and career decision-making.

Methods of measuring interests Table 22.2 shows sample items from several vocational interest inventories. Notice that the items from the first two inventories (ACT, *Strong-Campbell*) ask persons to rate each activity or statement on a like/dislike continuum. The Hall inventory asks persons to rate how important certain job characteristics and activities are to them. The last inventory *(Kuder)* presents activities in sets of three (triads). These latter items ask the person to make the one activity in the triad most ("M") liked and the one activ-

Table 22 • 2

Examples of items on various vocational interest inventories.

*M = most desirable, D = desirable, N = not important, U = undesirable, V = very desirable
Source: The test item from the *Act Interest Inventory* is © 1980 by the ACT; the *Strong-Campbell Interest Inventory* is © 1974 by the Stanford University Press: the *Hall Occupational Orientation Inventory* is © 1971 by *Hall Occupational Inventory Booklet*. Reprinted by permission of *Scholastic Testing Service, Inc.* from Lacy G. Hall; *Kuder Occupational Interest Survey* is © 1976 by G. Frederic Kuder. Used by permission.

ity least ("L") liked. In other words, each person ranks the three activities from most liked to least liked. The latter approach, called a *forced choice item format*, was designed to overcome the tendency for some persons to have very high personal standards for "like" while others have very low standards. When this occurs, two persons who may in fact have the same order of likes or dislikes for an activity may mark their answer sheets differently. The forced-choice format has been criticized, however, because using it results in a statistical artifact that causes a negative correlation among the scales of the inventory.

The content of the items The pioneers of the interest inventory technique used a variety of content to survey interests including asking examinees likes and dislikes of job titles, school subject matter, hobbies, leisure activities, work activities, types of persons, and type of reading material and assessing examinees' personal characteristics (Davis, 1980). Over time, however, the concept of interests narrowed to the world of work and careers so that today the content of most inventories is limited exclusively to lists of activities and most are concerned with work activities. An exception is the *Strong-Campbell Interest Inventory* (SCII). Of the 325 items on the SCII, 131 deal with occupational titles, 36 with school subjects, 51 with activities (both work-related and nonwork related), 39 with amusements, 24 with types of people, and 14 with personal characteristics.

Two rationales for describing a person's interests The traditional view of describing a person's inventoried interests is a variation on the "birds of a feather flock together" theme (Darley & Hageneh, 1955). This rationale has been called the *people-similarity rationale* (Cole & Hanson, 1975, p. 6):

> *Rationale 1.* If a person likes the same things that people in a particular job like, the person will be satisfied with the job.

Certain parts of the *Strong-Campbell Interest Inventory* and the *Kuder Occupational Interest Survey* (Kuder DD) follow this rationale. The Occupational Scales of the SCII (see below), for example, are *empirical scales,* made up of items especially selected because of their ability to empirically *differentiate* between persons who are currently and happily employed in a particular occupation and people in general. The developers of the Kuder DD, on the other hand, select items to form *homogeneous* or *single factor scales* within a particular occupational group.

A second rationale has been called the *activity-similarity rationale* (Cole & Hanson, 1975, p. 6):

> *Rationale 2.* If people like activities similar to the activities required by a job, they will like those job activities and consequently be satisfied with their job.

Inventories built using this rationale develop lists of activities that are similar to those required by certain jobs and assume that if a person has a pattern of like and dislikes common to a particular job, that person will be satisfied with that job. Among the inventories developed using this rationale are the *Ohio Vocational Interest Survey,* the *Self-Directed Search,* and the *ACT Interest Inventory* (see Figure 10.7).

Why are Vocational Interests Inventories Used?

Students want career counseling A national survey of junior and senior high school students revealed some rather striking findings about students' perceptions of their needs for career guidance and counseling (Prediger, Roth, & Noeth, 1973): (1) Almost 75% of the nation's 11th graders, and nearly the same percentage of 8th graders, would like help in making career plans, (2) about 50% of the 8th and 11th graders felt they had received little or no help with their educational and job planning through the school (13% said they received a lot of help), (3) 85% of the 11th graders recognized that their career plans must begin before they finish high school and, (4) 84% of the 11th graders said they could see a guidance counselor nearly anytime they want. Thus, at least from the students' viewpoint there is a need for career counseling but, even though students have access to counselors, apparently they are not receiving the help they feel they need.

Knowledge and skill needed to make decisions No single piece of information is sufficient for a person to use in making a vocational decision. Table 22.3 lists but a few of the many kinds of knowledge and information that are relevant for exploring career choices. Beside these knowledge aspects, a number of personality and attitude characteristics are related to career choice and maturity (Crites, 1974; Super, 1955; Super, Crites, Hummel, Moser, Overstreet, & Warnath, 1957). Interest inventories provide one source of information a person can use in making educational and vocational decisions.

How interest inventories are used Among the uses made of scores on vocational interest inventories are these: "(1) to reassure people about tentative choices; (2) to give people a structure for understanding the world of work; (3) to help people resolve conflicting alternatives; (4) to help people plan their personal development; (5) to call attention to desirable alternatives that the average person usually does not know about or overlooks; (6) to help people understand their job dissatisfaction; (7) to help employers select people who will be

I. Occupational Awareness	III. Career Planning and Decision Making

A. Occupational knowledge
   1. Characteristics of various occupations
      a. duties of particular jobs
      b. psychosocial aspects of particular occupations
      c. abilities, interests, and skills needed for a job
      Amount of preparation/training needed for an occupation
B. Exploratory occupational experiences
   1. Formal experience in a particular occupation
   2. Informal experience related to the occupation
	A. Career planning knowledge
	   1. Knowledge of basic career development principles
	   2. Knowledge of the realities of jobs and the labor market
	   3. Knowledge of the career planning process (when and how to plan)
	B. Current involvement in career planning
	   1. Seeking information
	   2. Work and experience related to career planning
	   3. Actually formulating career plans

II. Self-Awareness
A. Preferred job characteristics
   1. What a person values in a job
   2. Working conditions preferred
B. Current plans for a career
   1. Amount and type of education planned
   2. Preferences for particular job families
   3. Degree of certainty about current preferences
C. Perceived need for help in career planning
	IV. Perceptions of the extent to which current resources can be used

Source: Adapted from D. J. Prediger, J. D. Roth, and R. J. Noeth, *Nationwide Study of Career Development: Summary of Results*, pp. 4–6. Copyright © 1973 by the American College Testing Program. Used by permission.

Table 22 • 3   An outline of types of knowledge a person is likely to find useful in exploring career opportunities and choices.

better workers; (8) to help people plan their career advancement; (9) to aid in the scientific study of the world of work and to link this research to other research in the social sciences" (Holland, 1975, p. 22).

What are Career Interests?

Psychological definitions of interests   After reviewing the many definitions of career interests, Cole and Hanson (1975) concluded that career interests have three aspects: "First, they are a constellation of likes and dislikes leading to a consistent pattern of types of behaviors. Second, they may involve some mix of genetic and environmental causes, but they are certainly related to environmental influences. Third, although the explanations of interest relate to satisfaction with activities, they are not derived from a clear explication of the

link between interests and satisfaction. . . . Thus, the problem of the link between measured interests and job satisfaction remains a central problem for interest-measurement technology" (pp. 4–5).

Inventoried interests   Interest inventories of the type described in this section view the concept of interests quite narrowly. That is, they are limited to only vocational interests or career interests. Even career interests are narrowed even further. Super (1947, 1949), for example, distinguished between expressed, manifested, tested, and inventoried interests. *Expressed interests* are those obtained when persons are asked directly about their interests. The interests a person verbally professes when asked directly may not express the person's true preferences: A youngster may express an interest in, say, being a doctor, because it is perceived to be something parents expect of the child. Or, a teenager may say she wants to be a prostitute, (or a nun, for that matter) just to see the reaction of her parents. *Manifested interests* are those deduced from what a person actually does or the activities in which the person actually engages. Deductions about a person's interests from their activities are also subject to error, as when observers conclude a girl is interested in athletics because she participates in the junior high track team but later find out she wants only to be with her friends after school. *Tested interests* are those inferred from an information or knowledge test about a particular area. For example, an interest in science, it is hypothesized, would lead a person to have more "scientific information" than someone who was not interested in science. Such measures are not used very often in current vocational counseling practice. *Inventoried interests* are those identified through various paper and pencil tests or interest inventories. A limitation here is that the interests inventoried do not represent all interests or even all career interests. Further, as with other forms of educational and psychological tests, you should not assume that the interest patterns identified with one interest inventory are the same ones that could be identified with others. When counseling, keep in mind that all three interests—expressed, manifested, and inventoried—should be used to ascertain a person's interest pattern is important (Davis, 1980).

Career maturation Related to the concepts of career interests and career decision-making is the concept of career maturation. In recent times career decision-making has come to be viewed as part of a developmental process, rather than as a single decision. This process, called *career maturation*, was studied in a 20-year longitudinal Career Pattern Study by Super (1955) and (Super, Crites, Hummell, Moser, Overstreet, & Warnath, 1957), and five principle dimensions of career maturation were identified (Crites, 1973, pp. 2–3):

1. *Orientation to Vocational Choice:* One mark of career maturity is the extent to which a young person is aware of the need to choose an occupation and the factors which enter into this decision.
2. *Information and Planning:* Another criterion of career maturity is the amount of reliable information an individual has to make decisions about occupations and then to plan logically and chronologically for the future.
3. *Consistency of Vocational Preferences:* Still another index of career maturity is how consistent an adolescent is in his/her preferences for different occupations from one point-in-time to another.
4. *Crystallization of Traits:* In mature career development, the psychological attributes of the individual relevant to decision-making, e.g., differentiable interest patterns, explicit values, and increasing independence, develop at a pace with the tasks which have to be accomplished.
5. *Wisdom of Vocational Preference:* More generally known as realism of vocational choice, this dimension of career maturity reflects how closely an individual's career decisions agree with various aspects of reality, such as the prerequisite ability for the preferred occupation, the appropriate interest for the chosen career field, and the availability of financial resources for relevant training.

Crites (1978) has developed the *Career Maturity Inventory* to measure vocational choice, attitudes, and vocational choice competence. The *Career Maturity Inventory* is designed to measure the *process* variables of career maturation: competence in choosing careers and attitudes toward work and career choice. The components of the process of career choice are shown on the right side of Figure 22.1.

Measures of career maturation differ from measures of career interests. Crites views interest inventories, ability tests, and personality tests as providing a person with information about the content of an eventual career choice. But a person arrives at the eventual career choice through some process and must, according to Crites' theory, have certain skills, knowledge, and attitudes in order for this

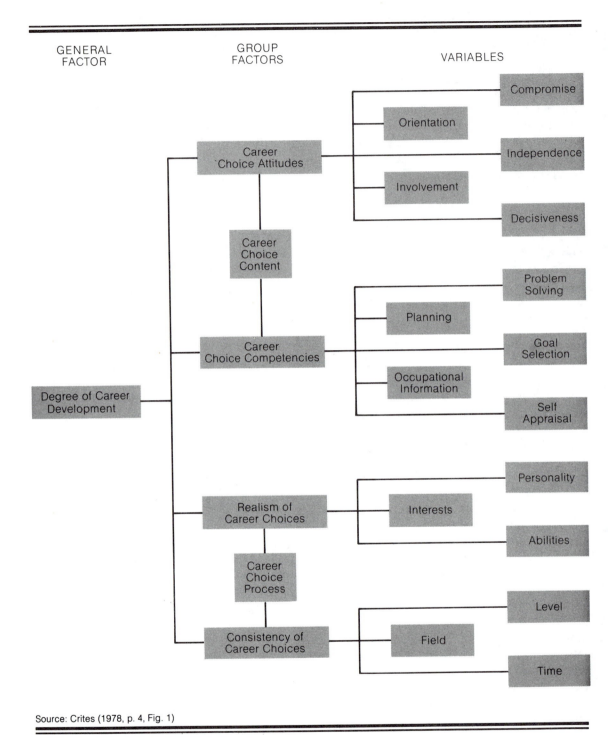

GENERAL
FACTOR

GROUP
FACTORS

VARIABLES

Source: Crites (1978, p. 4, Fig. 1)

Figure 22 • 1 The Crites model of the components of career maturity in adolescence.

process to operate in a way that will lead to a satisfying career choice. It is the purpose of the *Career Maturity Inventory* to measure this process.

An Example of a Vocational Interest Inventory: The SCII

A number of vocational interest inventories are listed in Appendix G along with references to their reviews in the *Mental Measurements Yearbooks*. I will briefly describe one of the inventories, the *Strong-Campbell Interest Inventory*, here.

Edward K. Strong, Jr. (1884–1963) began work on the problem of interest measurement when as a graduate student he attended C. S. Yoakum's seminar at Carnegie Institute of Technology[2] after World War I. Later as a faculty member at Stanford University

> . . . he collaborated with T. L. Kelly in supervising K. M. Cowdery's doctoral dissertation on the differential measurement of the interests of lawyers, physicians, and engineers. Cowdery drew his terms from the Carnegie item pool and used an item-weighting formula suggested by Kelly. . . . Strong . . . revised the items, and added many new ones. This set of about 400 items was first published as the *Strong Vocational Interest Blank* (SVIB) in 1927 and was to endure for more than four decades as the most successful measure of vocational interests and as one of the most heavily researched psychological instruments in the history of the science (Davis, 1980, p. 78).

The current version, revised by David P. Campbell and Jo-Ida C. Hansen, is composed of 325 items. A person rates the activity described in each item as "like," "dislike," or "indifferent" (or "can't decide"). The responses are then scored via a computer (tests can't be scored locally) and reported as standard scores on various *scales*. The results of the SCII are reported to the examinee in three ways: (1) six

[2]Now called Carnegie Mellon University.

General Occupational Themes which describe a person's overall pattern of occupational interests, (2) 23 Basic Interest Scales which describe the somewhat narrower categories of activities a person likes, and (3) 162 Occupational Scales which describe the extent to which a person's likes and dislikes are similar to persons in specific occupations.

General Occupational Themes There are six themes or personality types adapted from John L. Holland's (1973) hexagonal model of six personality types. These are described in Table 22.4 and shown in Figure 22.2. The themes next to each other in the figure are most similar, while themes across from each other are most dissimilar. On the SCII, the examinee is given a standard score for each one of these themes.

Basic Interest Scales There are 23 scales, but they are grouped according to their relationship to the six themes. For example, five Basic Interest Scales (Teaching, Social Service, Athletics, Domestic Arts, Religious Activities) are associated with the Social theme. The Basic Interest Scales are considered to be intermediate between the General Occupational Themes and the more specific Occupational Scales: They describe the clusters of activity a person likes. These activity areas may be common to several specific occupations.

Occupational Scales One hundred sixty-two occupations are listed (e.g., farmer, air force officer, advertising executive, artist, math-science teacher, etc.). The person receives a standard score for each occupation. This score describes how similar the person's pattern of likes and dislikes are to persons who are experienced and satisfied in each occupation.

Special Scales Two other "nonoccupational" scales are used: the Academic Orientation Scale and the Introversion-Extroversion Scale. The first is designed as a measure of the extent to which a person likes intellectual activities. The

Type of personality	Occupational preference	Occupational avoidance	Competencies used to solve problems	Self-perception	Achievement valued
Realistic (R)	realistic occupations (e.g., construction, skilled trade)	social occupations	realistic competencies (e.g., physical skills)	Have mechanical and athletic ability; lack in human relations.	Concrete, tangible attainments (money, power, status)
Conventional (C)	conventional occupations (e.g., office work, accounting)	artistic occupations	conventional competencies (e.g., following orders)	Orderly, have clerical ability, dependable; lack artistic ability.	Business and economic attainments
Enterprising (E)	enterprising occupations (e.g., sales promotion)	investigative occupations	enterprising competencies (e.g., leadership skills)	Aggressive, popular, self-confident, sociable, having leadership and speaking ability; lack scientific ability.	Political and economic attainment
Social Type (S)	social occupations (e.g., counselor)	realistic occupations	social competencies (e.g., group process skills)	Enjoy helping others, understand others; lack mechanical and scientific ability.	Social and ethical problem solution
Artistic (A)	artistic occupations (e.g., author, artist)	conventional occupations	artistic competencies (e.g., using artistic media to express ideas)	Have ability to act, write, draw, or speak; independent, nonconforming, disorderly; lack conventional skills.	Esthetic attainment
Investigative (I)	investigative occupations (e.g., scientist, scientific writer)	enterprising occupations	investigative competencies (e.g., using abstract problem solving skills)	Scholarly, intellectual, have mathematical and scientific ability; lack leadership ability.	Scientific attainment

Source: John L. Holland, *Making Vocational Choices: A Theory of Careers*, © 1973, pp. 14–18. Adapted by permission of Prentice-Hall, Inc., Englewood Cliffs, N.J.

Table 22 • 4 Holland's six personality types that form the basis of the SCII General Occupational Themes.

second is designed to measure the extent to which a person likes to interact and work with other people as contrasted with being content to work alone.

Male-female differences Although the SCII has a single booklet used with both males and females, there are separate norms for each gender. The authors have kept the norms sep-

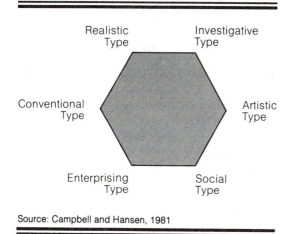

Source: Campbell and Hansen, 1981

Figure 22 • 2 Holland's hexagonal model of personality types.

arate because (a) there are large differences in the strength of interests in the two genders in many areas and (b) combined-sex (unisex) scales appear less valid for many occupations. Such differences in interest patterns appear no matter how the samples of persons are selected. Thus, the authors feel that to use combined-gender scales and norms would lead to error and deny persons useful information about themselves. The results of the SCII report a person's standing via standard scores in both male and female norm-groups on each of the scales. The authors emphasize that the counselor should help the client to interpret the entire pattern of scores on the inventory rather than to focus on the one or two high scoring areas and to consider career choice as a long term developmental process.

Similarities Among Interest Inventories

Each of the interest inventories in the marketplace have different items, are built by somewhat different procedures, have different norms, and espouse somewhat different theories of the nature of career interests. In short, the results obtained from one inventory are not interchangeable with those

obtained from another. It is possible, however, to show that they are all similar in their basic configuration or pattern of interests measured.

Cole and Hanson (1971) analyzed several of the then current interest inventories using a statistical technique which allowed the scales of the different inventories to be compared and related to Holland's six types. The practical implications of their study for counseling are:

[1] . . . correspondence of the scores on two or more interest inventories can best be determined by *considering patterns of scales rather than individual scales*. If a person scores high on several Intellectual scales on one instrument, he will likely score high on another. However, he may be highest on Chemist on one instrument and on Physicist on the other, [2] Most occupational titles, such as engineer, physician, lawyer, and salesman, do not represent narrowly defined occupations. Instead many different types of activities occur under the same occupational title. While the activities have common aspects and reflect many common interests, in the Holland scheme the bridge builder [engineer, for example,] represents almost typical Realistic interests while the electrical engineering professor combines Intellectual interests with Realistic ones. . . . Thus, the circular configuration of interests provides a possible explanation for differences in performance on scales having the same name possibly based on groups reflecting somewhat different vocational interests (Cole & Hanson, 1971, p. 485. Italics added).

Bias in Interest Measurement

The use of interest inventories for career exploration and counseling presents special problems for women. Traditionally, interest inventories have reported to clients how well their pattern of likes and dislikes have matched the patterns of likes and dislikes of those persons already employed in certain occupations. Also, it can be said that a person's current interests are to a large extent developed as a result of the socialization process this person has experienced. The special concerns are these (Cole & Hanson, 1975):

1. Interest inventories provide limited information for women because the occupational scales are based on persons already in the occupations, and many occupations have few women. A similar situation arises for men when considering female-dominated occupations such as nursing. Thus, the sex differences in interest patterns that are observed may reflect only sex characteristics, not real job satisfaction differences. We don't know what the pattern of interests would be if women were to participate fully in certain occupations.

2. Another concern is whether the socialization process for girls results in an interest pattern that is as predictive of job satisfaction as the same socialization process is for boys. If it suddenly became socially acceptable for girls to have access to the full range of occupations, would their current interest patterns predict their future job satisfaction?

Both of these concerns may limit or misdirect the usefulness of interest inventories for the career counseling of adolescent women because these adolescents are not encouraged to explore occupations which traditionally have been closed to them. Although there is considerable disagreement about the validity of the above two propositions, the developers of most major interest inventories have begun to take steps to reduce the potential for sex bias in their instruments. The National Institute for Education (NIE) has given direction to the movement to "unisex" or "unsex" interest inventories by publishing a set of guidelines for ascertaining the sex fairness of career interest inventories. The developers of several interest inventories have published statements describing the extent to which they have adhered to the NIE guidelines.

Measurement of Attitudes

Attitudes and Their Characteristics

Attitudes are characteristics of persons which describe their positive and negative feelings toward particular objects, situations, institutions, persons, or ideas. Although attitudes are frequently considered noncognitive or affective aspects of a person, they can also be considered as having cognitive and behavioral components as well (Wagner, 1969; Zimbardo, & Ebbeson, 1970). The *affective component* relates to a person's liking of or emotional response toward the object. The *cognitive component* of an attitude relates to a person's beliefs or perceptions about the facts concerning the object. The *behavioral component* concerns the person's actions or overt behavior toward the particular object in question. Most attitude instruments have focused on the affective component of attitudes.

Even focusing on the affective aspect of attitude allows considerable leeway in the characteristics of a person's attitudes that can be measured. A person's attitudes toward something or someone can be described in terms of (Scott, 1968):

1. *Direction:* Whether the attitude is positive or negative.
2. *Magnitude:* The degree to which the positive or negative feeling is held.
3. *Intensity:* The importance or strength of feeling the person holds with respect to the object.
4. *Ambivalence:* The extent to which a person holds conflicting attitudes toward different aspects of the same object.
5. *Salience or Centrality:* Whether this particular attitude is central to explaining a wide variety of a person's attitude.
6. *Affective Salience:* The degree to which a person becomes highly emotional in expressing attitudes toward a particular object.

7. *Flexibility:* The extent to which the person will change or modify his or her attitude toward an object.
8. *Imbeddedness:* The extent to which an attitude is imbedded as part of a person's network of attitudes.

Scott points out that most attitude measurement has focused on the magnitude or intensity characteristic.

How Attitude Scales are Built

Thurstone method Most paper-and-pencil attitude scales have been built using either the Thurstone (1928; Thurstone & Chave, 1929) or the Likert (1932) techniques. To build a scale using the Thurstone technique,[3] the investigator writes or locates a large number of statements (e.g., about 200) reflecting various degrees of attitude toward a particular object. Thurstone and Chave, for example, measured attitude toward the church with such statements as, "I feel the need for religion but do not find what I want in any one church." A group of judges sort the statements into 11 categories from least favorable ($=1$) to most favorable ($=11$). Each judge is directed to think of each category as being equally distant from the adjacent categories when they are placed on a continuum. Not all judges will agree on how to categorize each statement, so a frequency distribution (see Chapter 3) is tabulated for each statement, showing the number of judges who placed the statement in each category. Then the median of this frequency is computed (see Chapter 3). This median becomes the "scale value" that locates a statement on the 1 to 11 scale. About 20 statements are selected from the large pool for the final form of the test. The items selected have the following characteristics: (a) together their scale values cover the full range (i.e., 1 to 11), (b)

the numerical differences ("distances") between successive scale values are about equal, and (c) the variability[4] in the distribution to the judges' scale placement is as small as possible.

Persons respond to the final 20-item attitude scale by marking "agree" or "disagree" for each statement. The median scale value of the statements a person marks "agree" becomes the attitude "score" for that person.

Likert method This method, sometimes called the *method of summated ratings,* also begins with a large set of approximately 200 statements representing clearly favorable or unfavorable attitudes toward an object. The second step is to have a group of expert judges sort these statements into three categories: favorable, neutral, unfavorable. Statements in the neutral category are eliminated. The third step is to ask a large sample of persons from the target population to rate each statement on a four- to nine-point scale according to the extent to which they agree or disagree with it. The rating scale for each item (statement) usually has verbal "anchors" associated with each number. A five point scale, for example, may be anchored by these words: 1 = strongly disagree, 2 = disagree, 3 = undecided or neutral, 4 = agree, 5 = strongly agree. (The number of points on a scale can vary upward from 2 [i.e., agree vs. disagree]. When the attitudes of people in a population are very similar, the overall attitude scale will be more reliable if more categories [say, 5 or 7] are used for each statement; if attitudes in the population vary widely among people, the number of categories doesn't matter very much [Masters, 1974].) The fourth step consists of computing a discrimination index for each statement: the correlation between the ratings given a statement and the total score on the scale. The fifth step is to select for the final form of the scale about 20 statements with the highest discrim-

---

[3] Also known as the method of *equal appearing intervals.*

[4] Thurstone used the semi-quartile range as the measure of variability.

ination indices. Selecting items this way helps to make the final version of the scale homogeneous (i.e., measuring only one attitude dimension). A person's score on the final version of the attitude test consists of the sum of the ratings the person assigned to each of the items.

An Example of a Likert Scale: The Survey of School Attitudes

The *Survey of School Attitudes* (Hogan, 1975a, b) consists of four sets of 15 Likert-type items. Each set of 15 items represents activities in a curriculum area: reading/language arts, mathematics, science, and social studies. Each activity is rated "like," "not sure or don't care," or "dislike." The survey has two levels: Primary (grades 1 through 3) and Intermediate (grades 4 through 8). The primary level does not require reading: Pupils look at pictures of activities while the teacher reads a description of the activity. The pupils mark one of the "smiley faces" to indicate their likes or dislikes. Figure 22.3 gives an example of a few intermediate level items which the pupils read for themselves. (These items have "smiley faces," too.)

The scores for the survey are: raw scores, "level" scores, and percentile ranks. For each item, "like" is scored 2; "don't know or don't care," omitted items, and double marked items are scored 1; and "dislike" items are scored 0. A pupil's raw score is the sum of the item scores. Separate raw scores are obtained for each curriculum area. Each raw score is converted to a percentile rank using the publisher's national norm table. Also, "Level scores" are obtained as per Table 22.5.

The author of the Survey reports the following research findings using this instrument (Hogan, 1975c):

1. Students' attitudes toward school are generally favorable, on the average, even though there are wide variations among individuals.

2. There is a change in attitude across grades: The eighth grade average is lower than the early grades.

3. There are differences among the four curricular areas: Science activities are best-liked, mathematics activities least liked.

4. The variability of scores seems about the same in different grades and curricular areas.

5. Reliability of attitude scores increases through the grades: Alternate forms retest reliabilities for the first three grades are between .52 and .65; for grades 4 through 8, they are between .74 and .83.

6. Boys' and girls' attitudes are different: Girls score higher in reading/language arts; boys are higher in science at the intermediate level; boys and girls average about the same in science at the primary level, and in mathematics and social studies at both levels.

7. Attitudes toward the different curricular areas become more differentiated across grades: The median correlation among the four areas is about .60 at the primary level; this median correlation drops to .45 at the intermediate level.

8. Correlations between attitude scores in the different curricular areas and scores on achievement tests in corresponding content areas are essentially zero.

The Public Opinion Survey

The focus of a test such as the *Survey of School Attitudes* is on the attitude patterns of individual persons. Public opinion polls such as those conducted by the Gallup organization, the Harris organization, and the University of Michigan Institute for Social Research, to name a few, are directed toward surveying the attitudes of larger groups or populations of persons. The Institute for Development of Educational Activities (IDEA), for example, sponsors an annual spring survey of the attitudes of Americans toward education conducted by the Gallup organization; the results

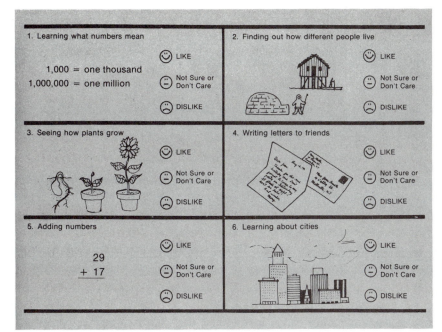

Figure 22 • 3
Example of items from the Intermediate Level of the *Survey of School Attitudes*.

Source: Hogan (1975a, p. 2)

Raw score	Level score	Verbal description
26–30	5	Expresses a liking for all or nearly all aspects of the curricular area.
19–25	4	Expresses a liking for most aspects of the area, but may dislike or be indifferent to some aspects of the curricular area.
12–18	3	Is indifferent to most aspects of the curricular area or expresses about an equal number of likes and dislikes.
5–11	2	Expresses a dislike for most aspects of the area, but may like or be indifferent to some aspects of the curricular area.
0–4	1	Expresses a dislike for all or nearly all aspects of the curricular area.

Table 22 • 5
Relationship of "level scores" to raw scores on the *Survey of School Attitudes*.

are published in the September issue of *Phi Delta Kappan* magazine.

Small-scale surveys are sometimes conducted by a local community, church, or school group (e.g., the PTA). Some communities conduct phone surveys (see box), others send questionnaires, and still others have interviewers personally contact a sample of people in the community. The Charles F. Kettering philanthropic foundation publishes a little pamphlet describing how a group can replicate the national Gallup education attitude

Box 22 • 1

survey in a local community.[5] A useful resource for designing and conducting a mail questionnaire survey is the book, *Questionnaires: Design and Use* (Berdie & Anderson, 1974).

Measurement of Personality Dimensions

A variety of techniques have been developed to measure various noncognitive aspects of personality. Of the 1,650 different tests listed in *Tests in Print II* and in the *8th MMY*, 269 (16.25%) are personality tests. Personality tests and vocational tests are the two most numerous varieties of tests. The user of personality tests must be trained in psychological interpretation of the results. This usually requires not only extensive graduate work in clinical counseling or school psychology but also a rather lengthy supervised internship. Thus,

[5]The pamphlet is entitled *A Look Into Your School District* (CFK Ltd. Publications, 3333 Bannock Street, Englewood, Colorado 80110).

for the most part, teacher-training programs leave teachers unqualified to administer and interpret personality tests. Teachers will encounter the results of such tests, however, if they are part of a child study team or if they read psychological reports of pupils. Thus, some familiarity with a few basic concepts of personality measurement is in order.

Approaches to the Measurement of Personality Characteristics

The kind of personality tests used depends primarily on the psychological orientation of the particular psychologist. At the present time, no standard model or conception of personality exists nor do psychologists agree on which particular aspects of personality are most important to measure. Table 1.5, for example, lists (a) six different models of personality, (b) the typical dimension or aspect of personality that is considered important by psychologists in identifying themselves with a particular model, and (c) some specific tests used with each model. The implication of this diversity is that the kind(s) of personality tests used in psychological reports a teacher may encounter depend(s) on the background and training of the psychologist assigned to a given pupil's case.

Projective tests Two broad categories of methods for assessing personality dimensions are projective techniques and structured techniques. *Projective techniques* present the examinee ". . . with a number of ambiguous stimuli and . . . [then invite the examinee] to respond to these stimuli. By such means it is assumed that the subject projects his own needs and press and that these will appear as responses to the ambiguous stimuli" (Bellak, 1959, p. 9).[6] Examples of projective personality tests are the *Rorschach Test*, the *Thematic Apperception Test* (TAT), various sentence completion tests, and various figure drawing tests. The *Rorschach Test*, for example, consists of presenting several cards on which inkblots are printed, one at a time, to the subject. The subject is asked to tell what each inkblot means or to describe the things seen in the inkblot. The psychologist analyzes the content of the responses as well as the process and manner in which the subject responds. As a result of this analysis, the psychologist generates hypotheses about the subject's personality dynamics which can be explored and confirmed or rejected during subsequent interview sessions. The TAT pictures are more structured than the Rorschach inkblots, showing surrealistic pictures of scenes involving one or more persons. The subject is asked to tell a story about the picture: What happened before the event pictured; what is happening at the moment; who are the characters, and what are their feelings; and how the story will end. The psychologist analyzes the

content of the story in terms of H. A. Murray's personality theory of "needs" and "press," generating hypotheses about the subject's personality for further exploration during interviews. Sentence completion techniques ask the examinee to complete sentences related to various aspects of self and of interpersonal relations relations (e.g., "Compared with most families, mine . . ."). The results of a content analyses are used similarly to generate hypotheses about a subject's personality.

In general, projective techniques are characterized by (Vernon, 1964): (1) test materials intended to stimulate projective responses; (2) ambiguous or unstructured stimulus materials and directions intended to encourage freedom of responses; (3) an unawareness on the part of the subject concerning how the response will be scored in order to minimize the subject's displaying an "acceptable" personality; (4) no predetermined right or wrong answers; (5) an assumption that the subjects' responses will reveal their latent personality dispositions; (6) the viewpoint that each response capsules the whole personality; and (7) a much longer analyzing, scoring, and interpreting process than with objective or structured tests. Vernon points out that projective techniques were originally developed to counteract the influence of the behavioral and statistical personality studies of the 1920s and as a means of obtaining clues about personality dynamics so that the lengthy interview process can be shortened.

Structured personality measurement techniques usually follow a response-choice format: yes-no, true-false, or multiple-choice. Examples of structured personality tests are the *Guilford-Zimmerman Temperament Survey*, the *Minnesota Multiphasic Personality Inventory* (MMPI), the *California Psychological Inventory*, the *Sixteen Personality Factor Questionnaire* (16PF), and the *Thorndike Dimensions of Temperament*. Each of these is sometimes referred to as a self-report personality inventory because it requires the examinee to respond to the items in a way that describes his or her personal

---

[6]The terminology is that of Henry A. Murray's *Theory of Personality*: Needs are factors within individuals that determine their behavior; press (plural) are factors in the environment that facilitate or hinder individuals' attempts to satisfy their needs. Many clinical psychologists, including the one quoted here, do not entirely agree with the assumption as it is stated.

feelings. For example, the examinee is presented with a list of statements and is asked to state whether the statement describes personal feelings. For instance, examinees may be asked whether the statement, "I usually express my personal opinions to others," is true of themselves.

One characteristic of structured personality inventories is that the items are related to various scales or personality dimensions. The *Guilford-Zimmerman Temperament Survey,* for example, reports an examinee's profile with respect to 10 scales: general activity, restraint, ascendence, sociability, emotional stability, objectivity, friendliness, thoughtfulness, personal relations, and masculinity.[7]

The Limited Usefulness of Personality Tests for the Teacher

Self-report personality inventories require persons to (Thorndike & Hagen, 1977): (1) read and comprehend each item, (2) be able to understand their own actions enough to know whether a given statement is true of them, and (3) be willing to respond honestly and frankly. Reading in the context of personality testing requires more than decoding the words in a statement. This reading requires that

[7]This is the term these authors use.

examinees understand the items well enough to be able to decide the degree to which the statements apply to their own lives. Part of deciding whether a statement applies to the examinee's own behavior requires the ability to view that behavior objectively which may not be within the repertoire of an unsatisfactorily adjusted person. Finally, if a person is not able or willing to respond frankly to the items, a distorted personality description may result. This lack of frankness may occur more often when testing children who feel vulnerable or threatened if they reveal their feelings to the teacher or more generally, to the "school."

Considering the shortcomings of self-report personality and adjustment inventories, some measurement experts answer the question of whether to use them in the following way: ". . . there is little that a classroom teacher can do to dig behind and test the meaning of an inventory score. Accepted uncritically, the score may prove very misleading. We believe that little useful purpose is served by giving an adjustment inventory and making the results available to the teacher, especially the teacher of an elementary school child" (Thorndike & Hagen, 1977, p. 434). This statement should not be taken to mean, however, that personality tests are not helpful to trained psychologists and counselors engaged in intensive therapy with clients.

Summary

These are the main points of this chapter:

1. The distinction between cognitive and noncognitive behavior is somewhat artificial because noncognitive behavior has cognitive components and cognitive behavior is influenced by noncognitive variables.

2. Table 22.1 lists and defines several noncognitive variables thought to be important to education including: experiential background factors, affects (feelings), attitudes, beliefs, interests, motives, temperaments, social sensitivities, coping strategies, cognitive styles, creative abilities, values, and curiosities.

3. Noncognitive variables are considered important in education because educators believe (a) noncognitive variables are predictive of success or failure in certain types of instruction, (b) they function as mediating variables, (c) they function as moderator variables, and (d) some of the variables are desirable outcomes of education and/or personal development.

4. Noncognitive variables may play a role in several educational decisions such as (a) access to certain educational opportunities, (b) setting objectives and standards for what should be taught, (c) guidance toward particular educational options, (d) selection of persons to a particular educational level, (e) placement in a particular instructional procedure, (f) indications of how instruction should be conducted, and (g) evaluation of programs.

5. A potential for misusing noncognitive variables exists because there is no consensus on which variables schools should value and emphasize. Thus, a dangerous potential for arbitrariness and/or capriciousness exists.

6. Vocational and career interest inventories are paper-and-pencil questionnaires for helping individuals express their likes and dislikes about certain work-related activities. Individuals' patterns of likes and dislikes are used to help them in career exploration and career decision-making.

7. Interest inventories contain one or two item formats: (a) a rating format in which persons rate the degree to which they like the activities presented to them and (b) a forced-choice ranking format in which the persons must rank the activities presented from best liked to least liked. (See Table 22.2.)

8. Nearly all vocational interest inventories limit the activities appearing in the items to work-related activities. The *Strong-Campbell Interest Inventory* is an exception because of the diversity of item content it includes (e.g., occupational titles, school subjects, amusements, work and nonwork-related activities, types of people, and personal characteristics).

9. Two rationales have been used to develop or build interest inventories: (a) *People-similarity rationale* states that if a person likes the same kinds of things that persons now in a particular job like, the person will be satisfied with that kind of job; (b) *Activity-similarity rationale* states that if a person likes activities similar to those activities which occur in a particular kind of job, the person will like the job activities themselves and will consequently be satisfied with that kind of job.

10. Specific purposes for which career interest inventories are used are summarized here as well. In addition to understanding interest, a student will also need to acquire specific skills and knowledge about how to explore careers and how to make career decisions. Career counselors distinguish between express, manifested, tested, and inventoried interests.

11. The notion of career maturity is closely associated with career decision-making. Five dimensions of career maturity are: orientation to vocational choice, information and planning, consistency of vocational preference, crystallization of traits, and wisdom of vocational preference.

12. Similarities among the occupational scales on many interest inventories can be described in terms of Holland's six types of personalities summarized in Table 22.4. One implication of the research which demonstrates this similarity is that patterns of scores should be considered, and that occupational titles do not represent narrowly defined occupations.

13. A concern with career interest inventories is whether they are biased toward women and consequently whether they would limit the career choices of women if they used the inventories. If such bias exists, it would limit the career exploration process for women to traditional women-related occupations.

14. Attitudes describe a person's feelings toward particular objects, situations, institutions, persons, or ideas. Attitudes seem to have affective, cognitive, and behavioral components.

15. Two ways of building attitude scales described are: Thurstone's method of equal appearing intervals and Likert's method of summated rating scales. The Likert method has been the most often used.

16. Public opinion surveys often seek to describe the attitudes of large groups of persons rather than individuals.

17. The choice of the particular kind of personality test to use is often dependent on the training and orientation of the psychologist examining the person. Projective tests of personality present ambiguous stimuli and assume that the examinee's responses reflect the person's underlying psychological needs and personality dispositions. Structured personality tests usually use a response-choice format. Examinees are presented with statements which they either rank or rate in terms of how well the statements describe themselves. Structured personality tests give scores describing a person's normative standing on each of several dimensions or aspects of personality.

18. Teachers probably should not administer and interpret personality tests because (a) the tests are subject to distortion by pupils, (b) such tests have limited predictive validity when used alone, (c) paper-and-pencil inventories depend on the examinee's reading ability and insight into his or her own behavior, (d) teachers generally do not have the requisite coursework and supervised training necessary to interpret them, and (e) teachers seldom have the time needed to explore the meaning of a test score with an individual pupil.

APPENDIXES

APPENDIX A
Computational Procedures for Elementary Statistics

Computing the Median

This procedure is described and illustrated with a specific example, then with a formula that summarizes the procedure.

If more then fifteen or so scores exist for which you want to compute the median, first organize the scores into a frequency distribution to facilitate interpreting group performance, computing the median, and doing any additional computations. Look back at the scores of a class organized into the frequency distribution shown in Table 3.2, p. 53.

Score	Frequency
36	1
32	1
31	1
29	2
28	4
27	5 ◄——median will be in this interval*
26	6 ⎫
25	2 ⎬ 11 scores here
24	1 ⎪
20	1 ⎪
14	1 ⎭
	N = 25

*Note that these scores represent *intervals*. For example, 27 represents the interval 26.5 to 27.5; 26 represents the interval 25.5 to 26.5; etc. The bottom or lower limit of each interval is called its *lower real limit*. Thus, the lower real limit for the interval 26.5 to 27.5 is 26.5; for the interval 25.5 to 26.5 the lower real limit is 25.5; etc.

Table A • 1   Frequency distribution of 25 pupils on an arithmetic test.

Step-by-Step

Steps to follow	Numerical illustrations	In symbols
1. Find the total number of scores and divide it in half.	1. $25 \div 2 = 12.5$ (This means that 12.5 scores are below the median)	1. $N = 25$, $N/2 = 12.5$

2. Find the interval in which the median is located. To do this add up the frequencies, starting with the lowest score, until the sum equals nearly one-half the total number.

2. $1 + 1 + 1 + 2 + 6 = 11$. Therefore, the median must be in the interval from 26.5 to 27.5.

2.

---

3. Find the sum of all the frequencies below the interval containing the median.

3. $1 + 1 + 1 + 2 + 6 = 11$ This is the sum of the frequencies below the median interval.

3. sum below $= 11$

---

4. Subtract the sum below from one-half the total number (i.e., Step 1 minus Step 3).

4. $12.5 - 11 = 1.5$

4. $\dfrac{N}{2} -$ sum below
$= (12.5 - 11)$
$= 1.5$

---

5. Find the frequency of the interval in which the median is located and divide this number into the results of Step 4.

5. The frequency of the interval in which the median is located is 5. Thus, $1.5 \div 5 = 0.3$.

5. $\dfrac{\dfrac{N}{2} - \text{sum below}}{\text{frequency of}}$
$= \dfrac{12.5 - 11}{5} = \dfrac{1.5}{5}$
$= 0.3$

---

6. Find the lower real limit of the interval in which the median is located and add to it the results of Step 5.

6. The lower real limit of the interval from 26.5 to 27.5 is 26.5. Thus, $Mdn = 26.5 + 0.3 = 26.8$

6. Mdn
$= L + \dfrac{\dfrac{N}{2} - \text{sum below}}{\text{frequency of}}$
$= 26.5 + 0.3$
$= 26.8$

Formula for the Median

The following formula summarizes the step-by-step procedure:

$$Mdn = L + \frac{\dfrac{N}{2} - \text{sum below}}{\text{frequency of}} \qquad \text{[Eq. A.1]}$$

where

$$Mdn = \text{the symbol for the median}$$
$$L = \text{the symbol for the lower real limit of the interval.}$$
$$N = \text{the total number of scores in the group.}$$
$$\text{sum below} = \text{the sum of the \textit{frequencies} of all of the intervals below } L.$$
$$\text{frequency of} = \text{the frequency of (i.e., the number of scores in) the interval in which the median is located.}$$

For example, in Table A.1, we can compute the median using this formula as follows:

$$Mdn = 26.5 + \frac{\dfrac{25}{2} - 11}{5}$$

$$= 26.5 + \frac{12.5 - 11}{5}$$

$$= 26.5 + \frac{1.5}{5} = 26.5 + 0.3$$

$$= 26.8$$

Thus, 26.8 is the point on the score scale below which one-half of the class lies.

Grouped Data

The procedure in Equation A.1 will work where the frequency distribution is organized into intervals where the real limits span one point (unit). Since this will be the case for most classroom test data and since to do otherwise introduces a source of inaccuracy in the results, this appendix will not present alternative procedures that would be used when a frequency distribution has wider intervals. If you are interested in computing the median for a grouped frequency distribution, you should consult your instructor or an elementary statistics textbook.

Computing the Mean

You can use Equation 3.1 to compute the mean when the number of scores is small or when you do not prepare a frequency distribution. When you do need to prepare a frequency distribution, you can compute the mean directly from it.

The following frequency distribution will illustrate the procedure which is not complicated: First multiply each score by its frequency, then add up all of these products to get the sum of all the scores. Finally, divide by the total number of scores. A formula summarizes this process.

$$M = \frac{\Sigma fX}{N}$$

$$= \frac{\text{sum of the products of each score and its frequency}}{\text{total number of scores}} \qquad \text{[Eq. A.2]}$$

Score (X)	Frequency (f)	Product of frequency and score (fX)	
36	1	(1)(36) = 36	
32	1	(1)(32) = 32	$M = \dfrac{\Sigma fX}{N}$
31	1	(1)(31) = 31	
29	2	(2)(29) = 58	
28	4	(4)(28) = 112	
27	5	(5)(27) = 135	$= \dfrac{36+32+31+58+\ldots+14}{25}$
26	6	(6)(26) = 156	
25	2	(2)(25) = 50	
24	1	(1)(24) = 24	
20	1	(1)(20) = 20	$= \dfrac{668}{25}$
14	1	(1)(14) = 14	
	25	ΣfX = 668	
			= 26.72

Table A • 2   An illustration of applying Equation A.2 to the computation of the mean using the data in Table A.1

If you wish to compute the mean from a grouped frequency distribution, consult an elementary statistics book. The procedure is quite similar to that specified here: interval midpoints replace the score value of column one above; otherwise the procedure is the same.

Computing the Standard Deviation

The formula shown as Equation 3.5 can be used to compute the standard deviation when the number of scores is small. When the number of scores is large, organizing the scores into a frequency distribution first and then using a computational formula such as the one here is easier and more accurate. You can find other computational formulas in an applied statistics text.

Formula for the Standard Deviation

Computational formulas are algebraically equivalent to the definitional formula Equation 3.5. This means that, except for mistakes or rounding error, you should get the answer regardless of formula.

If the scores are arranged in a frequency distribution, then you can use this formula:

$$SD = \sqrt{\frac{\Sigma f(X^2)}{N} - M^2}$$ [Eq. A.3]

Using words for the symbols,

$$SD = \sqrt{\frac{\text{sum of the products of the square of each score and its frequency}}{\text{total number}} - [\text{square of the mean}]}$$

Step-by-Step

This is not as hard to compute as it looks:

Steps	Symbols
1. Square each score.	1. X^2
2. Multiply each square by its frequency.	2. $f(X^2)$
3. Add together all of these products.	3. $\Sigma f(X^2)$
4. Divide by the total number.	4. $\dfrac{\Sigma f(X^2)}{N}$
5. Square the mean. (If the mean has not been computed already, you need to compute it. See Equation A.2.)	5. M^2
6. Subtract the square of the mean from the result found in Step 4. (Stop here if you want only the variance.)	6. $\dfrac{\Sigma f(X^2)}{N} - M^2$
7. Take the square root of the difference. This is the standard deviation.	7. $\sqrt{\dfrac{\Sigma f(X^2)}{N} - M^2}$

The frequency distribution of arithmetic test scores presented in Table A.3 (taken from Table 3.2) can be used to illustrate these computations.

A Quick Estimate of the Standard Deviation   Computing the standard deviation can be quite time-consuming, especially if you do not have access to a calculator. (Some hand-held calculators and microcomputers are pre-programmed to compute the standard deviation with a minimum of effort.) Equation 3.5 gives the definition of the standard deviation, but Equation A.3 is preferred when some degree of accuracy is needed such as when you will use the standard deviation for further calculations (e.g., estimating reliability and validity coefficients) or when you include it in a research report.

A "short-cut" procedure for estimating the standard deviation can serve the teacher well for many classroom purposes. Several short-cut formulas

Score (X)	Frequency (f)	Step 1 (X^2)	Step 2 ($f(X^2)$)
36	1	1296	1296
32	1	1024	1024
31	1	961	961
29	2	841	1682
28	4	784	3136
27	5	729	3645
26	6	676	4056
25	2	625	1250
24	1	576	576
20	1	400	400
14	1	196	196
	N = 25		18,222

The formula is:

$$SD = \sqrt{\frac{\Sigma f(X)^2}{N} - M^2}$$ (Note that $M = 26.72$ [see p. 589])

Putting the numbers into the formula:

$$SD = \sqrt{\frac{18,222}{25} - (26.72)^2}$$

After Steps 4 and 5:
$$SD = \sqrt{728.88 - 713.96}$$

Then Step 6:
$$SD = \sqrt{14.92}$$ (Note that $SD^2 = 14.92 =$ the variance)

Step 7 gives the final result:
$$SD = 3.86$$

Table A • 3 Computing the standard deviation from a frequency distribution.

for estimating the standard deviation are available, but I will discuss only one here.*

The procedure consists of subtracting from the sum of the scores of the highest scoring one-sixth of the students the sum of the scores of the lowest scoring one-sixth of the students. This difference is then divided by one-half of the total number of scores. Equation A.4 summarizes this.

$$\text{est. } SD = \frac{(\text{sum of highest one-sixth}) - (\text{sum of lowest one-sixth})}{\text{one-half of total number}}$$ [Eq. A.4]

*Diederich (1958, 1964) proposed this method. Sabers and Klausmier (1971) review several formulas and offer their own formula which may have a slight advantage in accuracy.

The number of scores in the upper (or lower) one-sixth is rounded to the nearest whole number. An example will help to illustrate.

Consider the distribution of arithmetic scores in Table A.3. There, $N = 25$ so one-sixth of 25 is 4.17; this is rounded to 4. To work the formula, we sum the highest 4 scores and then sum the lowest 4 scores. These two sums are subtracted and the difference is divided by one-half of 25 or 12.5, Thus,

$$\text{est. } SD = \frac{(36+32+31+29) - (14+20+24+25)}{12.5}$$

$$= \frac{128-83}{12.5} = \frac{45}{12.5} = 3.6$$

The estimated value of 3.6 compares favorably with the value of 3.86 computed in Table A.3.

Computing Percentile Ranks

How to Do It With a Frequency Distribution

You can compute the percentile ranks of all the scores in a class rather quickly if you organize them into a frequency distribution. Table A.4 shows how to do this for the arithmetic test scores of Table 3.2 (p. 53).

Recall Equation 3.6 (p. 72) which is repeated below.

$$PR = \frac{\left(\begin{array}{c}\text{number of persons}\\\text{below the score}\end{array}\right) + \frac{1}{2}\left(\begin{array}{c}\text{number of persons}\\\text{having the score}\end{array}\right)}{\text{total number of persons}} \times 100 \quad \text{[Eq. 3.6]}$$

This formula calls for determining both the number of persons having the score and the number of persons below the score. The number having each score is called its *frequency,* and these frequencies appear in the second column of the table. Determining the number below each score is done for all the scores by forming a *cumulative frequency* column first: Add the frequencies consecutively starting at the bottom of the column with the lowest score. These cumulative frequencies appear in the third column.

In books on introductory statistics you will find various formulas and procedures for computing percentile ranks including graphical methods and methods to use with grouped frequency distributions. All of these procedures are either equivalent to or approximations of the procedure above. The method above is always useable when raw scores are available even though under certain circumstances the other procedures may be simpler or more efficient.

Raw score	Frequency (f)	Cumulative frequency	Percentile rank $PR = \dfrac{(\text{number below}) + \frac{1}{2}(\text{number having})}{N} \times 100$
36	1	25	$98 = \dfrac{24 + .5}{25} \times 100$
35	0	24	96
34	0	24	96
33	0	24	$96 = \dfrac{24 + 0}{25} \times 100$
32	1	24	$94 = \dfrac{23 + .5}{25} \times 100$
31	1	23	$90 = \dfrac{22 + .5}{25} \times 100$
30	0	22	$88 = \dfrac{22 + 0}{25} \times 100$
29	2	22	$84 = \dfrac{20 + 1}{25} \times 100$
28	4	20	$72 = \dfrac{16 + 2}{25} \times 100$
27	5	16	$54 = \dfrac{11 + 2.5}{25} \times 100$
26	6	11	$32 = \dfrac{5 + 3}{25} \times 100$
25	2	5	$16 = \dfrac{3 + 1}{25} \times 100$
24	1	3	$10 = \dfrac{2 + .5}{25} \times 100$
23	0	2	8
22	0	2	$8 = \dfrac{2 + 0}{25} \times 100$
21	1	2	$6 = \dfrac{1 + .5}{25} \times 100$
20	0	1	4
19	0	1	4
18	0	1	4
17	0	1	4
16	0	1	4
15	0	1	$4 = \dfrac{1 + 0}{25} \times 100$
14	1	1	$2 = \dfrac{0 + .5}{25} \times 100$
13	0	0	
	$N = 25$		

Table A • 4 Computing percentile ranks from a frequency distribution.

Formula for Correlation Coefficient

Equation 3.8 is a definitional formula for the correlation coefficient. It could be used for calculations, but in practical work you can use the following equivalent formula.

$$r = \frac{N(\Sigma XY) - (\Sigma X)(\Sigma Y)}{\sqrt{[N(\Sigma X^2) - (\Sigma X)^2][N(\Sigma Y^2) - (\Sigma Y)^2]}} \quad \text{[Eq. A.5]}$$

This formula is illustrated below with the test scores for verbal aptitude (here symbolized by X) and reading achievement (here symbolized by Y) from Table 3.5 (p. 79). Computing a correlation coefficient would not generally be undertaken without access to a calculator and/or a table of squares and square roots.*

Steps	Symbols	Examples
1. List everyone's pair of scores.	1. X, Y	1. Pupil A.: $X = 82$, $Y = 59$
2. Square each score.	2. X^2, Y^2	2. Pupil A: $X^2 = (82)^2 = 6724$
		$Y^2 = (59)^2 = 3481$
3. Multiply the scores in each pair.	3. XY	3. Pupil A: $XY = 82 \times 59 = 4838$
4. Sum the X, Y, X^2, Y^2, and XY columns	4. $\Sigma X, \Sigma Y$	4. $\Sigma X = 579$ $\Sigma X^2 = 34{,}359$
	$\Sigma X^2, \Sigma Y^2$	$\Sigma Y = 484$ $\Sigma Y^2 = 22{,}724$
	ΣXY	$\Sigma XY = 27{,}749$

5. Put the sums into Equation A.5:

$$r = \frac{11(27{,}749) - (579)(484)}{\sqrt{[11(34{,}359) - (579)^2][11(22{,}724) - (484)^2]}}$$

$$= \frac{305{,}239 - 280{,}236}{\sqrt{(377{,}949 - 335{,}341)(249{,}964 - 234{,}256)}}$$

$$= \frac{25{,}003}{\sqrt{(42{,}708)(15{,}708)}} = \frac{25{,}003}{\sqrt{670{,}857{,}264}} = \frac{25{,}003}{25{,}900.91} = .965$$

(Slight numerical differences from the example on page 79 are due to rounding errors.)

If you have already computed the standard deviations and means of each variable, then the formula below (which is equivalent to Eq. A.5) will save you some computational labor.

$$r_{xy} = \frac{\dfrac{\Sigma XY}{N} - M_X M_Y}{(SD_X)(SD_Y)} \quad \text{[Eq. A.6]}$$

*Such a table is given in Appendix C.

Pupil	Verbal score (X)	Reading score (Y)	X^2	Squares Y^2	Cross products XY
A	82	59	6724	3481	4838
B	77	54	5929	2916	4158
C	70	55	4900	3025	3850
D	65	58	4225	3364	3770
E	59	51	3481	2601	3009
F	53	44	2809	1936	2332
G	45	38	2025	1444	1710
H	41	34	1681	1156	1394
I	34	35	1156	1225	1190
J	30	30	900	900	900
K	23	26	529	676	598
Sums	579	484	34,359	22,724	27,749

Table A • 5   Computing a correlation coefficient.

To illustrate with the data in Table A.5 above for which

$$M_X = 52.64, \quad M_Y = 44$$
$$SD_X = 18.79, \quad SD_Y = 11.39$$

we have

$$r = \frac{\dfrac{27{,}749}{11} - (52.64)(44)}{(18.79)(11.39)} = .965$$

Computing a Rank-Difference Correlation

Definition and formula   The correlation discussed above is called a Pearson product moment correlation. Another type of correlation coefficient—the *Spearman rank-difference correlation*—can be computed as a quick estimate of the product moment correlation when there are fewer than 30 pairs of scores. Whereas the previously described correlation is an index of the degree of agreement among the pairs of z-scores, the rank-difference correlation is an index of agreement among the rank orders of the pairs.*

---

*The rank-difference correlation is equal to the Pearson r that would be obtained if Equation 3.8 or A.6 were applied to the ranks instead of to the raw scores. The rank-difference correlation is systematically lower than r, the maximum difference being .02 when r = .50 (Guilford & Fruchter, 1978).

The pairs of scores in Table A.6 illustrate the computation of the rank-difference correlation. The formula for Spearman's rank-difference correlation coefficient is:

$$rho = 1 - \frac{6\Sigma D^2}{N(N^2 - 1)} \qquad \text{[Eq. A.7]}$$

Where ΣD^2 = the sum of the squared differences between the ranks of the pairs and N = the number of pairs of ranks.

Step-by-step First make a list of the pairs of scores as shown in the first two columns of Table A.6.

Step 1 Rank the scores on the first variable. If there are ties, use the convention for averaging ranks described on page 72. In Table A.6 these are called Verbal ranks.

Step 2 Rank the scores on the second variable, using the same convention for ties (e.g., Reading ranks in Table A.6)

Step 3 For each person, find the difference between the ranks on each variable. These are shown in the "D" column of Table A.6.

Step 4 Square each difference ("D^2" in Table A.6).

Step 5 Sum these squared differences (ΣD^2). This sum is 10 in the example.

Pupil	Verbal score (X)	Reading score (Y)	Verbal ranks	Reading ranks	Difference in rank (D)	Squared difference in rank (D²)
A	82	59	1	1	0	0
B	77	54	2	4	-2	4
C	70	55	3	3	0	0
D	65	58	4	2	+2	4
E	59	51	5	5	0	0
F	53	44	6	6	0	0
G	45	38	7	7	0	0
H	41	34	8	9	-1	1
I	34	35	9	8	+1	1
J	30	30	10	10	0	0
K	23	26	11	11	0	0
						$\Sigma D^2 = 10$

Table A • 6 Computing a Spearman rank-difference correlation coefficient.

Step 6 Compute the rank-difference correlation by substituting into Equation A.7. For example,

$$rho = 1 - \frac{6\Sigma D^2}{N(N^2 - 1)}$$

$$= 1 - \frac{6(10)}{11(11^2 - 1)} = 1 - \frac{60}{11(120)}$$

$$= 1 - \frac{60}{1320} = 1 - .045$$

$$= .955$$

APPENDIX B
Computational Procedures for Various Reliability Coefficients

Table B.1 Spearman-Brown double length formula and Rulon split-halves formula

Table B.2 Kuder-Richardson formulas 20 and 21

Table B.3 Coefficient alpha

Table B.4 General Spearman-Brown formula

Table B.5 Percent agreement and kappa coefficient

A. Pupil's item scores and total test scores[a]					
	Items on test				**Total score**
Pupils	**1**	**2**	**3**	**4**	**(X)**
Alan	1	0	0	0	1
Issac	1	1	0	0	2
Leslie	0	0	1	1	2
Miriam	0	0	0	0	0
Rebecca	1	1	0	1	3
Robert	1	1	1	1	4

$$M = \frac{\Sigma X}{N} = \frac{12}{6} = 2 \,;\, (SD_x)^2 = \frac{\Sigma(X-M)^2}{N} = \frac{10}{6} = 1.67$$

[a]An item is scored 1 if it is answered correctly; 0 otherwise.

B. Computation for Spearman-Brown formula

	Half-test scores		**Computing correlation between halves**[b]		
	odd items	**even items**	**z-scores for:**		**Product**
Pupils	**(1+3)**	**(2+4)**	**odd**	**even**	**($z_o \cdot z_e$)**
Alan	1	0	0	−1.22	0
Issac	1	1	0	0	0
Leslie	1	1	0	0	0
Miriam	0	0	−1.72	−1.22	2.10
Rebecca	1	2	0	+1.22	0
Robert	2	2	+1.72	+1.22	2.10
Means	1.0	1.0			
SD's	0.58	0.82			

$$r_{hh} = \frac{\Sigma z_o z_e}{n} = \frac{4.2}{6} = 0.70$$

Spearman-Brown
double length
reliability estimate $= \dfrac{2r_{hh}}{1 + r_{hh}} = \dfrac{(2)(.70)}{1+.70} = 0.82$

[b]Other procedures may be used for computing the correlation coefficient (see Appendix A).

Table B • 1   Example of how to compute the Spearman-Brown double length and the Rulon split-halves reliability estimates.

C. Computation for Rulon formula

| Pupils | Half-test scores[c] | | Difference between half-test scores |
	odd items (1 + 3)	even items (2 + 4)	
Alan	1	0	1
Issac	1	1	0
Leslie	1	1	0
Miriam	0	0	0
Rebecca	1	2	− 1
Robert	2	2	0

Variance of differences $= (SD_{diff})^2 = 0.33$

Variance of total scores $= (SD_x)^2 = 1.67$

Rulon split-halves reliability estimate

$$= 1 - \frac{(SD_{diff})^2}{(SD_x)^2}$$

$$= 1 - \frac{0.33}{1.67} = 0.80$$

[c]Neither the Spearman-Brown nor the Rulon formula is restricted to an odd-even split. Other splits may be used (see text).

Table B • 1   Continued

A. Computing KR20

Pupils	Items on test[a]				Total score[b] (X)
	1	2	3	4	
Alan	1	0	0	0	1
Isaac	1	1	0	0	2
Leslie	0	0	1	1	2
Miriam	0	0	0	0	0
Rebecca	1	1	0	1	3
Robert	1	1	1	1	4

Fraction passing each item (p-values)	0.67	0.50	0.33	0.50	$M = 2.0$
(1−p)	0.33	0.50	0.67	0.50	$(SD_x)^2 = 1.667$
p(1−p)	0.222	0.250	0.222	0.250	$\Sigma p(1-p) = 0.944$

$$KR20 = \left(\frac{k}{k-1}\right)\left(1 - \frac{\Sigma p(1-p)}{(SD_x)^2}\right) = \left(\frac{4}{4-1}\right)\left(1 - \frac{0.944}{1.667}\right)$$

$$= (1.333)(1 - .566) = (1.333)(.434) = 0.58$$

[a] An item is scored 1 if it is answered correctly; 0 otherwise.
[b] The mean and variance are computed in Table B.1(A).

B. Computing KR21

Pupils	Total score[a] (X)
Alan	1
Isaac	2
Leslie	2
Miriam	0
Rebecca	3
Robert	4

$M = 2.0; (SD_x)^2 = 1.667$

$$KR21 = \left(\frac{k}{k-1}\right)\left(1 - \frac{M(k-M)}{k(SD_x)^2}\right)$$

$$= \left(\frac{4}{4-1}\right)\left(1 - \frac{2(4-2)}{4(1.667)}\right)$$

$$= (1.333)\left(1 - \frac{4}{6.668}\right)$$

$$= (1.333)(1 - .600)$$

$$= 0.53$$

[a] The mean and variance are computed in Table B.1(A).

C. Comparing the values of various reliability estimates for the same test[a]

Estimating procedure	Numerical value
Spearman-Brown	0.82[b]
Rulon	0.80[b]
KR20	0.58
KR21	0.53

[a] See Table B.1(B,C) also.
[b] Based on an odd-even split.

Table B • 2
Example of how to compute the Kuder-Richardson formula 20 (KR20) and Kuder-Richardson formula 21 (KR21) reliability estimates.

Persons	Questions or Judges				Total score (X)
	I	II	III	IV	
Aaron	4	3	4	4	15
Dorcas	2	5	5	5	17
Katherine	3	5	5	3	16
Kenneth	1	3	1	1	6
Lee	5	5	5	4	19
Peter	4	3	4	4	15
$(SD_i)^2$ values	1.81	1.00	2.00	1.58	$(SD_x)^2 = 16.89$

$\Sigma(SD_i)^2 = 1.81 + 1.00 + 2.00 + 1.58 = 6.39$

$$\alpha = \left(\frac{k}{k-1}\right)\left(1 - \frac{\Sigma(SD_i)^2}{(SD_x)^2}\right) = \left(\frac{4}{4-1}\right)\left(1 - \frac{6.39}{16.89}\right) = (1.33)(1 - .38) = (1.33)(.62) = 0.82$$

Table B • 3
Example of how to compute a coefficient alpha reliability estimate for a set of essay questions or judges' ratings.

A. Formula

$$r_{nn} = \frac{nr_{11}}{1 + (n-1)r_{11}}$$

B. Example

Q. A teacher has a 10-item test with reliability coefficient equal to 0.40. What would be the reliability if the teacher added 15 new items similar to those currently on the test?

A. Here $r_{11} = 0.40$ and $n = \frac{25}{10} = 2.5$. (The new test would be 25 items long and, hence, 2.5 times as long as the original test.) Thus, the new test reliability is:

$$r_{nn} = \frac{(2.5)(0.40)}{1 + (2.5 - 1)(0.40)}$$

$$= \frac{1.00}{1 + 0.6} = \frac{1.0}{1.6} = 0.625$$

C. Results of applying the formula to various values of r_{11} and n.

Original reliability	Number of times original test is lengthened (n)				
	2	3	4	5	6
.10	.18	.25	.31	.36	.40
.20	.33	.43	.50	.56	.60
.30	.46	.56	.63	.68	.72
.40	.57	.67	.73	.77	.80
.50	.67	.75	.80	.83	.86
.60	.75	.82	.86	.88	.90
.70	.82	.88	.90	.92	.93
.80	.89	.92	.94	.95	.96
.90	.95	.96	.97	.98	.98

Table B • 4
Computing the general Spearman-Brown formula.

A. General layout of the data

		Results from Test 1		Marginal totals
		Mastery	Non-Mastery	
Results from Test 2	Mastery	a	b	$a + b$
	Non-Mastery	c	d	$c + d$
	Marginal Totals	$a + c$	$b + d$	$N = a + b + c + d$

B. Formulas

P_A = total percent agreement in table

$$= \frac{a}{N} + \frac{d}{N} = \frac{a + d}{N}$$

P_C = percent agreement expected because of the composition of the group.

$$= \left(\frac{a + b}{N} \times \frac{a + c}{N}\right) + \left(\frac{c + d}{N} \times \frac{b + d}{N}\right)$$

$$\kappa = \frac{P_A - P_C}{1 - P_C}$$

C. Numerical example

		Results from Test 1		Marginal totals
		Mastery	Non-Mastery	
Results from Test 2	Mastery	11	4	15
	Non-Mastery	1	9	10
	Marginal Totals	12	13	25

$$P_A = \frac{11}{25} + \frac{9}{25} = \frac{11 + 9}{25} = \frac{20}{25} = 0.80$$

$$P_C = \left[\frac{15}{25} \times \frac{12}{25}\right] + \left[\frac{10}{25} \times \frac{13}{25}\right] = \frac{180}{625} + \frac{130}{625} = \frac{310}{625} = 0.50$$

$$\kappa = \frac{0.80 - 0.50}{1 - 0.50} = \frac{0.30}{0.50} = 0.60$$

Table B • 5   How to compute percent of agreement and the kappa coefficient.

APPENDIX C
Squares and Square Roots of Numbers from 1 to 500*

N	$\sqrt{N}$	N^2	N	$\sqrt{N}$	N^2	N	$\sqrt{N}$	N^2	N	$\sqrt{N}$	N^2
1	1.00	1	26	5.10	676	51	7.14	2,601	76	8.72	5,776
2	1.41	4	27	5.20	729	52	7.21	2,704	77	8.77	5,929
3	1.73	9	28	5.29	784	53	7.28	2,809	78	8.83	6,084
4	2.00	16	29	5.39	841	54	7.35	2,916	79	8.89	6,241
5	2.24	25	30	5.48	900	55	7.42	3,025	80	8.94	6,400
6	2.45	36	31	5.57	961	56	7.48	3,136	81	9.00	6,561
7	2.65	49	32	5.66	1,024	57	7.55	3,249	82	9.06	6,724
8	2.83	64	33	5.74	1,089	58	7.62	3,364	83	9.11	6,889
9	3.00	81	34	5.83	1,156	59	7.68	3,481	84	9.17	7,056
10	3.16	100	35	5.92	1,225	60	7.75	3,600	85	9.22	7,225
11	3.32	121	36	6.00	1,296	61	7.81	3,721	86	9.27	7,396
12	3.46	144	37	6.08	1,369	62	7.87	3,844	87	9.33	7,569
13	3.61	169	38	6.16	1,444	63	7.94	3,969	88	9.38	7.744
14	3.74	196	39	6.24	1,521	64	8.00	4,096	89	9.43	7,921
15	3.87	225	40	6.32	1,600	65	8.06	4,225	90	9.49	8,100
16	4.00	256	41	6.40	1,681	66	8.12	4,356	91	9.54	8,281
17	4.12	289	42	6.48	1,764	67	8.19	4,489	92	9.59	8,464
18	4.24	324	43	6.56	1,849	68	8.25	4,624	93	9.64	8,649
19	4.36	361	44	6.63	1,936	69	8.31	4,761	94	9.70	8,836
20	4.47	400	45	6.71	2,025	70	8.37	4,900	95	9.75	9,025
21	4.58	441	46	6.78	2,116	71	8.43	5,041	96	9.80	9,216
22	4.69	484	47	6.86	2,209	72	8.49	5,184	97	9.85	9,409
23	4.80	529	48	6.93	2,304	73	8.54	5,329	98	9.90	9,604
24	4.90	576	49	7.00	2,401	74	8.60	5,476	99	9.95	9,801
25	5.00	625	50	7.07	2,500	75	8.66	5,625	100	10.00	10,000

N	$\sqrt{N}$	N	$\sqrt{N}$	N	$\sqrt{N}$	N	$\sqrt{N}$	N	$\sqrt{N}$	N	$\sqrt{N}$
101	10.05	111	10.54	121	11.00	131	11.45	141	11.87	151	12.29
102	10.10	112	10.58	122	11.05	132	11.49	142	11.92	152	12.33
103	10.15	113	10.63	123	11.09	133	11.53	143	11.96	153	12.37
104	10.20	114	10.68	124	11.14	134	11.58	144	12.00	154	12.41
105	10.25	115	10.72	125	11.18	135	11.62	145	12.04	155	12.45
106	10.30	116	10.77	126	11.22	136	11.66	146	12.08	156	12.49
107	10.34	117	10.82	127	11.27	137	11.70	147	12.12	157	12.53
108	10.39	118	10.86	128	11.31	138	11.75	148	12.17	158	12.57
109	10.44	119	10.91	129	11.36	139	11.79	149	12.21	159	12.61
110	10.49	120	10.95	130	11.40	140	11.83	150	12.25	160	12.65

*Megan Nitko calculated the values in this table.

N	$\sqrt{N}$	N	$\sqrt{N}$	N	$\sqrt{N}$	N	$\sqrt{N}$	N	$\sqrt{N}$	N	$\sqrt{N}$
161	12.69	211	14.53	261	16.16	311	17.64	361	19.00	411	20.27
162	12.73	212	14.56	262	16.19	312	17.66	362	19.03	412	20.30
163	12.77	213	14.59	263	16.22	313	17.69	363	19.05	413	20.32
164	12.81	214	14.63	264	16.25	314	17.72	364	19.08	414	20.35
165	12.85	215	14.66	265	16.28	315	17.75	365	19.10	415	20.37
166	12.88	216	14.70	266	16.31	316	17.78	366	19.13	416	20.40
167	12.92	217	14.73	267	16.34	317	17.80	367	19.16	417	20.42
168	12.96	218	14.76	268	16.37	318	17.83	368	19.18	418	20.45
169	13.00	219	14.80	269	16.40	319	17.86	369	19.21	419	20.47
170	13.04	220	14.83	270	16.43	320	17.89	370	19.24	420	20.49
171	13.08	221	14.87	271	16.46	321	17.92	371	19.26	421	20.52
172	13.11	222	14.90	272	16.49	322	17.94	372	19.29	422	20.54
173	13.15	223	14.93	273	16.52	323	17.97	373	19.31	423	20.57
174	13.19	224	14.97	274	16.55	324	18.00	374	19.34	424	20.59
175	13.23	225	15.00	275	16.58	325	18.03	375	19.36	425	20.62
176	13.27	226	15.03	276	16.61	326	18.06	376	19.39	426	20.64
177	13.30	227	15.07	277	16.64	327	18.08	377	19.42	427	20.66
178	13.34	228	15.10	278	16.67	328	18.11	378	19.44	428	20.69
179	13.38	229	15.13	279	16.70	329	18.14	379	19.47	429	20.71
180	13.42	230	15.17	280	16.73	330	18.17	380	19.49	430	20.74
181	13.45	231	15.20	281	16.76	331	18.19	381	19.52	431	20.76
182	13.49	232	15.23	282	16.79	332	18.22	382	19.54	432	20.78
183	13.53	233	15.26	283	16.82	333	18.25	383	19.57	433	20.81
184	13.56	234	15.30	284	16.85	334	18.28	384	19.60	434	20.83
185	13.60	235	15.33	285	16.88	335	18.30	385	19.62	435	20.86
186	13.64	236	15.36	286	16.91	336	18.33	386	19.65	436	20.88
187	13.67	237	15.39	287	16.94	337	18.36	387	19.67	437	20.90
188	13.71	238	15.43	288	16.97	338	18.38	388	19.70	438	20.93
189	13.75	239	15.46	289	17.00	339	18.41	389	19.72	439	20.95
190	13.78	240	15.49	290	17.03	340	18.44	390	19.75	440	20.98
191	13.82	241	15.52	291	17.06	341	18.47	391	19.77	441	21.00
192	13.86	242	15.56	292	17.09	342	18.49	392	19.80	442	21.02
193	13.89	243	15.59	293	17.12	343	18.52	393	19.82	443	21.05
194	13.93	244	15.62	294	17.15	344	18.55	394	19.85	444	21.07
195	13.96	245	15.65	295	17.18	345	18.57	395	19.87	445	21.10
196	14.00	246	15.68	296	17.20	346	18.60	396	19.90	446	21.12
197	14.04	247	15.72	297	17.23	347	18.63	397	19.92	447	21.14
198	14.07	248	15.75	298	17.26	348	18.65	398	19.95	448	21.17
199	14.11	249	15.78	299	17.29	349	18.68	399	19.97	449	21.19
200	14.14	250	15.81	300	17.32	350	18.71	400	20.00	450	21.21
201	14.18	251	15.84	301	17.35	351	18.73	401	20.02	451	21.24
202	14.21	252	15.87	302	17.38	352	18.76	402	20.05	452	21.26
203	14.25	253	15.91	303	17.41	353	18.79	403	20.07	453	21.28
204	14.28	254	15.94	304	17.44	354	18.81	404	20.10	454	21.31
205	14.32	255	15.97	305	17.46	355	18.84	405	20.12	455	21.33
206	14.35	256	16.00	306	17.49	356	18.87	406	20.15	456	21.35
207	14.39	257	16.03	307	17.52	357	18.89	407	20.17	457	21.38
208	14.42	258	16.06	308	17.55	358	18.92	408	20.20	458	21.40
209	14.46	259	16.09	309	17.58	359	18.95	409	20.22	459	21.42
210	14.49	260	16.12	310	17.61	360	18.97	410	20.25	460	21.45

N	$\sqrt{N}$		N	$\sqrt{N}$		N	$\sqrt{N}$		N	$\sqrt{N}$
461	21.47		471	21.70		481	21.93		491	22.16
462	21.49		472	21.73		482	21.95		492	22.18
463	21.52		473	21.75		483	21.98		493	22.20
464	21.54		474	21.77		484	22.00		494	22.23
465	21.56		475	21.79		485	22.02		495	22.25
466	21.59		476	21.82		486	22.05		496	22.27
467	21.61		477	21.84		487	22.07		497	22.29
468	21.63		478	21.86		488	22.09		498	22.32
469	21.66		479	21.89		489	22.11		499	22.34
470	21.68		480	21.91		490	22.14		500	22.36

APPENDIX D
Summaries of Taxonomies of Educational
Objectives: Cognitive, Affective, and Psychomotor domains.

1.00 Knowledge
  1.10 Knowledge of Specifics
    1.11 Knowledge of Terminology   Knowledge of the referents for specific symbols (verbal and nonverbal). . . .
    1.12 Knowledge of Specific Facts   Knowledge of dates, events, persons, places, etc.
  1.20 Knowledge of Ways and Means of Dealing with Specifics
    1.21 Knowledge of Conventions   Knowledge of characteristic ways of treating and presenting ideas and phenomena.
    1.22 Knowledge of Trends and Sequences   Knowledge of the processes, directions, and movements of phenomena with respect to time.
    1.23 Knowledge of Classifications and Categories   Knowledge of the classes, sets, divisions, and arrangements that are regarded as fundamental for a given subject field, purpose, argument, or problem.
    1.24 Knowledge of Criteria   Knowledge of the criteria by which facts, principles, and conduct are tested or judged.
    1.25 Knowledge of Methodology   Knowledge of the methods of inquiry, techniques, and procedures employed in a particular subject field as well as those employed in investigating particular problems and phenomena.

2.00 Comprehension
  2.10 Translation   Comprehension as evidenced by the care and accuracy with which the communication is paraphrased or rendered from one language or form of communication to another.
  2.20 Interpretation   The explanation or summarization of a communication.
  2.30 Extrapolation   The extension of trends or tendencies beyond the given data to determine implications, consequences, corollaries, effects, etc., that are in accordance with the conditions described in the original communication.

3.00 Application   The use of abstractions in particular and concrete situations. The abstractions may be in the form of general ideas, rules of procedures, or generalized methods.

4.00 Analysis
  4.10 Analysis of Elements   Identification of the elements included in a communication.
  4.20 Analysis of Relationships   The connections and interactions between elements and parts of a communication.
  4.30 Analysis of Organized Principles   The organization, systematic arrangement, and structure that hold the communication together.

5.00 Synthesis
  5.10 Production of a Unique Communication   The development of a communication in which the writer or speaker attempts to convey ideas, feelings, and/or experiences to others.
  5.20 Production of a Plan or Proposed Set of Operations   The development of a plan of work or the proposal of a plan of operations.
  5.30 Derivation of a Set of Abstract Relations   The development of a set of abstract relations either to classify or to explain particular data or phenomena, or the deduction of propositions and relations from a set of basic propositions or symbolic representations.

6.00 Evaluation
  6.10 Judgments in Terms of Internal Evidence   Evaluation of the accuracy of a communication from such evidence as logical accuracy, consistency, and other internal criteria.
  6.20 Judgments in Terms of External Criteria   Evaluation of material with reference to selected or remembered criteria.

From *Taxonomy of Educational Objectives: The Classification of Educational Goals: Handbook I: Cognitive Domain*, pp. 201–207, by Benjamin S. Bloom et al. Copyright © 1956 by Longman Inc. Reprinted by permission of Longman Inc., New York.

Table D • 1   Categories and subcategories of the Bloom et al. taxonomy of cognitive objectives.

1.0 Receiving (attending)

    1.1 Awareness . . . be conscious of something . . . take into account a situation, phenomenon, object, or stage of affairs. . . .

        Develops awareness of aesthetic factors in dress, furnishings, architecture, city design, good art, and the like.

    1.2 Willingness to Receive . . . being willing to tolerate a given stimulus, not to avoid it. . . . willing to take notice of the phenomenon and give it . . . attention. . . .

        Appreciation (tolerance) of cultural patterns exhibited by individuals from other groups—religious, social, economic, national, etc.

    1.3 Controlled or Selected Attention . . . the control of attention, so that when certain stimuli are presented they will be attended to. . . . the favored stimulus is selected and attended to despite competing and distracting stimuli . . .

        Alertness toward human values and judgments on life as they are recorded in literature.

2.0 Responding

    2.1 Acquiescence in Responding . . . "obedience" or "compliance" . . . there is a passiveness so far as the initiation of the behavior is concerned. . . .

    2.2 Willingness to Respond . . . the learner is sufficiently committed to exhibiting the behavior that he does so not just because of a fear . . . but "on his own" or voluntarily. . . .

    2.3 Satisfaction in Response . . . the behavior is accompanied by a feeling of satisfaction, an emotional response, generally of pleasure, zest, or enjoyment. . . .

        Finds pleasure in reading for recreation.

3.0 Valuing

    3.1 Acceptance of a Value . . . the emotional acceptance of a proposition or doctrine upon what one considers adequate ground. . . .

        Continuing desire to develop the ability to speak and write effectively.

    3.2 Preference for a Value . . . the individual is sufficiently committed to the value to pursue it, to seek it out, to want it.

        Assumes responsibility for drawing reticent members of a group into conversation.

    3.3 Commitment . . . "conviction" and "certainty beyond a doubt" . . . . acts to further the thing valued . . . , to extend the possibility of . . . developing it, to deepen . . . involvement with it. . . .

        Devotion to those ideas and ideals that are the foundations of democracy.

4.0 Organization

    4.1 Conceptualization of a Value . . . the quality of abstraction or conceptualization is added [to the value or belief which permits seeing] . . . how the value relates to those he already holds or to new ones . . .

        Forms judgments as to the responsibility of society for conserving human and material resources.

    4.2 Organization of a Value System . . . to bring together a complex of values . . . into an ordered relationship with one another. . . .

        Weighs alternative social policies and practices against the standards of the public welfare rather than the advantage of . . . narrow interest groups.

5.0 Characterization by a Value or Value Complex

    5.1 Generalized Set . . . gives an internal consistency to the system of attitudes and values. . . . enables the individual to reduce and order the complex world . . . and to act consistently and effectively in it.

        Judges problems and issues in terms of situations, issues, purposes, and consequences involved rather than in terms of fixed, dogmatic precepts or emotional wishful thinking.

    5.2 Characterization . . . one's view of the universe, one's philosophy of life, one's *Weltanschauung.* . . .

        Develops for regulation of one's personal and civic life a code of behavior based on ethical principles consistent with democratic ideals.

From *Taxonomy of Educational Objectives: The Classification of Educational Goals: Handbook II: Affective Domain*, pp. 176–185, by David R. Krathwohl et al. Copyright © 1964 by Longman Inc. Reprinted by permission of Longman Inc., New York.

Table D • 2   Categories and subcategories of the Krathwohl et al. taxonomy of affective objectives with illustrative statements of objectives.

Classification Levels And Subcategories	Definitions	Behavioral Activity

1.00 Reflex Movements
  1.10 Segmental Reflexes
  1.20 Intersegmental Reflexes
  1.30 Suprasegmental Reflexes
	Actions elicited without conscious volition in response to some stimuli.	Flexion, extension, stretch, postural adjustments

2.00 Basic-Fundamental Movements
  2.10 Locomotor Movements
  2.20 Non-Locomotor Movements
  2.30 Manipulative Movements
	Inherent movement patterns which are formed from a combining of reflex movements and are the basis for complex skilled movement.	Walking, running, jumping, sliding, hopping, rolling, climbing, pushing, pulling, swaying, swinging, stooping, stretching, bending, twisting, handling, manipulating, gripping, grasping finger movements.

3.00 Perceptual Abilities
  3.10 Kinesthetic Discrimination
  3.20 Visual Discrimination
  3.30 Auditory Discrimination
  3.40 Tactile Discrimination
  3.50 Coordinated Abilities
	Interpretation of stimuli from various modalities providing data for the learner to make adjustments to his environment.	The *outcomes* of perceptual abilities are observable in *all purposeful* movement.
		    Examples:
		Auditory — following verbal instructions.
		Coordinated — jumping rope, punting, catching.

4.00 Physical Abilities
  4.10 Endurance
  4.20 Strength
  4.30 Flexibility
  4.40 Agility
	Functional characteristics of organic vigor which are essential to the development of highly skilled movement.	Distance running, distance swimming, weight lifting, wrestling, touching toes, back bend, ballet exercises, shuttle run, typing, dodgeball.

5.00 Skilled Movements
  5.10 Simple Adaptive Skill
  5.20 Compound Adaptive Skill
  5.30 Complex Adaptive Skill
	A degree of efficiency when performing complex movement tasks which are based upon inherent movement patterns.	All skilled activities which build upon the inherent locomotor and manipulative movement patterns of classification level two.

6.00 Non-Discursive Communication
  6.10 Expressive Movement
  6.20 Interpretive Movement
	Communication through bodily movements ranging from facial expressions through sophisticated choreographies.	Body postures, gestures, facial expressions, all efficiently executed skilled dance movements and choreographies.

From *A Taxonomy of the Psychomotor Domain: A Guide for Developing Behavioral Objectives*, pp. 104–106, Fig. 5, by Anita J. Harrow. Copyright © 1972 by Longman Inc. Reprinted by permission of Longman Inc., New York.

Table D • 3   Categories and subcategories of the Harrow taxonomy of psychomotor and perceptual objectives.

APPENDIX E

Example of an IOX Test Specification for Reading: Determining the Main Ideas (Secondary School Level)

General Description

The student will be presented with a factual selection such as a newspaper or magazine article or a passage from a consumer guide or general-interest book. After reading that selection, the student will determine which one of four choices contains the best statement of the central point of selection. This statement will be entirely accurate as well as the most comprehensive of the choices given.

Sample Item

Directions: Read the selection in the [box] . . . below.

Select the best main idea statement for [the] . . . selection.

The Cold Facts

Had you lived in ancient Rome you might have relieved the symptoms of a common cold by sipping a broth made from soaking an onion in warm water. In Colonial America you might have relied on an herbal concoction made from sage, buckthorn, golden-seal, or bloodroot plants. In Grandma's time, lemon and honey was a favorite cold remedy, or in extreme cases, a hot toddy laced with rum. Today, if you don't have an old reliable remedy to fall back on, you might take one of the thousands of drug preparations available without prescription. Some contain ingredients much like the folk medicines of the past; others are made with complex chemical creations. Old or new, simple or complex, many of these products will relieve some cold symptoms, such as a stopped up nose or a hacking cough. But not a single one of them will prevent, cure, or even shorten the course of the common cold.

---

1. Which one of the following is the best statement of the main idea of the article you just read?
   a. Old-fashioned herbal remedies are more effective than modern medicines. (*lacks accuracy—unsupported*)
   b. Throughout history, many remedies but no real cures have been developed for the common cold. (*correct*)
   c. Some of today's cold preparations contain ingredients much like those found in folk remedies of the past. (*lacks appropriate scope—too narrow*)
   d. Simple as well as complex drug preparations and folk medicines have been created to treat a wide variety of health problems. (*lacks appropriate scope—too broad; lacks accuracy—unsupported*)

Stimulus Attributes

1. A test item will consist of a reading selection followed by the question "Which one of the following is the best statement of the main idea of the (article/selection) you just read?" A reading selection will be titled, will be at least one paragraph long, and will contain from 125–250 words.

2. Not more than 1,000 words of reading material will be tested in a set of five items. At least two of the five items in any set of five items will contain reading selections that are more than one paragraph long.

3. Reading selections eligible for testing will be adaptations of passages from factual texts such as newspapers, magazines,

general-interest books, and consumer guides. Care will be taken to pick selections of particular interest to young adults and to avoid selections which may appear dated in the near future.

4. A reading selection will communicate one central idea. This idea may or may not be stated explicitly in the selection.

5. If necessary, the following modifications may be made to a selection used for testing:
   a. A title may be added, if the selection does not have one, or if the selection represents a section of a longer piece whose title would not be applicable to the excerpt. If a title is added, it will be composed of brief, interest-getting and/or summarizing group of words.
   b. A selection may be shortened, but only if the segment which is to be used for testing makes sense and stands as a complete unit of thought without the parts which have been omitted.

6. Reading selections used for testing will be between a seventh grade and a ninth grade reading level, as judged by the Fry readability formula.

Response Attributes

1. A set of four single-sentence response alternatives will follow each reading selection. One of these alternatives will be the correct main idea statement for the selection. The other three will be incorrect main idea statements. All four statements will plausibly relate to the content of the reading selection, either by reiterating or paraphrasing portions of that selection, or by building upon a word or idea contained in the selection.

2. The three incorrect response alternatives will each lack one or both of the two characteristics needed in a correct main idea statement: *accuracy* and *appropriate scope*.

3. A distractor *lacks accuracy* if it:
   a. Makes a statement contradicted by information in the text.

   b. Makes a statement unsupported by information in the text. (Such a statement would be capable of verification or contradiction if the appropriate information were attainable.)
   c. Makes a statement incapable of verification or contradiction; that is, a statement of opinion. (Such statements include value judgments on the importance or worth of anything mentioned in the text.)

4. A distractor *lacks appropriate scope* if it:
   a. Makes a statement that is too narrow in its scope. (That is, the statement does not account for all of the important details contained in the text.)
   b. Makes a statement that is too broad in its scope (That is, the statement is more general than it needs to be in order to account for all of the important details contained in the text.)

5. The three distractors for a selection will include at least one statement that lacks accuracy and one statement that lacks appropriate scope. On a given test, between 10 and 20 percent of the distractors will be sentences taken directly from the text.

6. The correct response for a selection will be a main idea statement that is both *accurate* and of the *appropriate scope*. All the information it contains will be verifiable in the selection upon which it is based. It will encompass all of the most important details contained in that selection.

7. The important points to be included in a main idea statement are those details which are emphasized in a selection by structural, semantical, and rhetorical means such as placement in a position of emphasis, repetition, synonymous rephrasing, and elaboration. Whether any given main idea statement contains all of the important points that it should is always debatable rather than indisputable. The nature of the question asked on this test (i.e., select the *best* main idea statement from among

those given) attempts to account for this quality of relative rather than absolute correctness.

8. If a sentence in the text itself qualifies as the best main idea statement which can be formulated about a selection, that sentence may be reiterated as a response option. No more than 20 percent of the items on a given test will have as their correct answer a main idea statement that is a direct restatement of a sentence in the text.*

*From Popham, W. J. and Lindheim, E. "The Practical Side of Criterion-Referenced Test Development." *Measurement in Education*, Vol. 10, #4, 1980, pp. 5–6. Copyright © 1980, National Council on Measurement in Education, Washington, D.C.

APPENDIX F
List of Publishers of Tests, Collections of Behavioral Objectives, and Made-to-Order Criterion-Referenced Tests

Test Publishers (See current MMY for additional names and addresses.)

AW Addison-Wesley Publishing Co., 2725 Sand Hill Road, Menlo Park, CA 94025

AAMD American Association on Mental Deficiency, 5201 Connecticut Avenue, N.W., Washington, D.C. 20015

ACT American College Testing Program, P.O. Box 168, Iowa City, IA 52240

ACE American Council on Education, 1 Dupont Circle, Washington, D.C. 20036

AGS American Guidance Services, Publishers' Building, Circle Pines, MN 55014

BM Bobbs-Merrill Co., 4300 West 62nd Street, Indianapolis, IN 46268

CTBMH CTB/McGraw Hill, Del Monte Research Park, Monterey, CA 93940

CAL Center for Applied Linguistics, 1611 North Kent Street, Arlington, VA 22209

CEEB College Entrance Examination Board, 888 Seventh Avenue, New York, NY 10019

CPP Consulting Psychologists Press, 577 College Avenue, Palo Alto, CA 94306

EDITS EDITS/Educational and Industrial Testing Service, P.O. Box 7234, San Diego, CA 92107

ERB Educational Records Bureau, Box 619, Princeton, NJ 08540

ETS Educational Testing Service, Rosedale Road, Princeton, NJ 08541

IPAT Institute for Personality and Ability Testing, 1602 Coronado Drive, Champaign, IL 61820

IOX Instructional Objectives Exchange, 11411 West Jefferson Boulevard, Culver City, CA 90230

JA Jastak Associates, 1526 Gilpin Avenue, Wilmington, DE 19806

PC Psychological Corporation, 757 Third Avenue, New York, NY 10017 or 75 Old Oak Blvd., Cleveland, OH 44130

RP Riverside Publishing Co., 8420 Bryn Mawr Avenue, Chicago, IL 60631

RPD Research Psychologists Press, P.O. Box 984, Port Huron, MI 48060

STS Scholastic Testing Services, 480 Meyer Road, Bensenville, IL 60106

SRA Science Research Associates, 155 North Wacker Drive, Chicago, IL 60606

SF Scott, Foresman and Company, Test Division, 1900 East Lake Avenue, Glenview, IL 60025

SPS Sheridan Psychological Services, P.O. Box 6101, Orange, CA 92607

USGPO United States Government Printing Office, Washington, D.C. 20402

WPS Western Psychological Services, 12031 Wilshire Boulevard, Los Angeles, CA 90025

Collections of Behavioral Objectives*

Name and address	Grade level	Topics
Cashier, State Department of Education 515 L Street Sacramento, CA 95814	7,9,11	Proficiency assessment in mathematics, reading, writing, functional skills, applied performance.
Bucks County Public Schools Routes 611 and 313 Doylestown, PA 18901	7	Mathematics, reading, writing
The CO-OP 413 Hills House North University of Massachusetts Amherst, MA 01002	K – 12	Language arts, mathematics, social studies, science, vocational education
Curriculum and Instructional Development Services Greater Phoenix Curriculum Council 2526 West Osborn Road Phoenix, AZ 85017	K – 12	Mathematics, reading, writing
El Dorado County Office of Education Attn: Curriculum Clerk 337 Placerville Drive Placerville, CA 95667	K – 8	Reading
ERIC Document Reproduction Service P.O. Box 190 Arlington, VA 22210	1 – 12	Language arts (ED 116 193; ED 066 498 thru 501) mathematics (ED 066 494 thru 497), social studies (ED 066 thru 502), science (ED 066 505 thru 508)
Greece Central School District Greece, NY 14616. Also available from Clearinghouse for Applied Performance Testing, Northwest Regional Educational Laboratory, 710 S.W. Second Avenue, Portland, OR 97204	K – 9	Mathematics
Institute for Educational Research 794 North Main Street Glen Ellen, IL 60137	1 – 12	See ERIC above (ED 066 numbers)
Uniondale Public Schools Uniondale Union Free School District Uniondale, NY 11553	K – 6	Mathematics

Developers of Made-to-Order Criterion-Referenced Tests*

Comprehensive Achievement Monitoring (CAM), National Evaluation Systems, P.O. Box 226, Amherst, MA 01002

Customized Criterion-Referenced Tests, Multi-Media Associates, P.O. Box 13052, 4901 East Fifth Street, Tucson, AZ 85732

Customized Objective Monitoring Service, Houghton Mifflin Company, 777 California Avenue, Palo Alto, CA 94304

IOX Test Development Service, Instructional Objectives Exchange, P.O. Box 24095, Los Angeles, CA 90025

*Information obtained from *CSE Criterion-Referenced Test Handbook* (1979, pp. 179–201).

Mastery Custom Tests—Reading and Math, Science Research Associates, 259 East Erie Street, Chicago, IL 60611

ORBIT, CTB/McGraw Hill, Del Monte Research Park, Monterey, CA 93940

APPENDIX G
A Limited List of Published Tests

Title	Age/grade level	Publisher[a]	Review[a]
Multilevel survey achievement batteries (group)			
California Achievement Tests	K–12	ETBMH	1977
Comprehensive Assessment Program Achievement Series	K–12	SF	1980
Comprehensive Tests of Basic Skills	K–12	CTBMH	**8**:12
Iowa Tests of Basic Skills	K–9	RP	1978
Iowa Tests of Educational Development	9–12	SRA	**8**:20
Metropolitan Achievement Test	K–12	PC	1978
Sequential Test of Educational Progress, III	K–12	AW	1979
SRA Achievement Series	K–12	SRA	1978
Stanford Achievement Series: Stanford Early School Achievement Test, Stanford Achievement Test, Stanford Test of Academic Skills	K–12	PC	1981
Tests of Achievement and Proficiency	9–12	RP	1978
The 3R's Test	K–12	RP	1982
Wide Range Achievement Test	K–12	JA	**8**:37
Multilevel survey achievement batteries (individual)			
Peabody Individual Achievement Test	K–Adult	AGS	**8**:24

[a]See Appendix F for names and addresses of publishers.
[b]If the test listed has been revised since the last review in the *Mental Measurements Yearbook*, then only the publication *date* is listed; otherwise the reference is to the *Mental Measurements Yearbook* (MMY). The boldfaced number is the number of the MMY volume, the number after the colon is the entry number.

Multilevel criterion-referenced achievement tests

Degrees of Reading Power	Pre K–6	CEEB	1980
Individual Pupil Monitoring System:		RP	
Mathematics	1–8		**8**:274
Reading	1–9		**8**:763
KeyMath Diagnostic Arithmetic Test	Pre K–6	AGS	**8**:305
Mastery: An Evaluation Tool:		SRA	
Mathematics	K–8		**8**:278
Reading	1–9		**8**:766
Metropolitan Achievement Tests:	K–9	PC	1978
Mathematics Instructional Tests			
Reading Instructional Tests			
Language Instructional Tests			
Skills Monitoring System: Reading	3–5	PC	**8**:776

Reading survey tests

Gates-MacGinitie Reading Tests	1–12	RP	1978
Iowa Silent Reading Test	6–Adult	PC	**8**:730
Nelson-Denney Reading Test	9–Adult	RP	**8**:735

Reading diagnostic tests

Diagnostic Reading Scales	1–8	CTBMH	**8**:753
Prescriptive Reading Inventory	K–6	CTBMH	**8**:769
Stanford Diagnostic Reading Test	1–13	PC	**8**:777
Woodcock Reading Mastery Test	1–12	AGS	**8**:779

Adaptive behavior inventories

Adaptive Behavior Scale	3 yrs–Adult	AAMD	**8**:493
Vineland Adaptive Behavior Scales	3–19 yrs	AGS	1983

Individual general ability/scholastic aptitude tests

Bayley Scales of Infant Development	2–30 mo.	PC	**8**:206
Columbia Mental Maturity Scale	3–11 yrs	PC	**8**:210
Concept Assessment Kit: Conservation	4–7 yrs	EDITS	**7**:437
Goodenough-Harris Drawing Test	3–15 yrs	PC	**7**:352
Kaufman Assessment Battery for Children	2–12 yrs	AGS	1983
McCarthy Scales of Children's Abilities	2–8 yrs	PC	**8**:219
Peabody Picture Vocabulary Test: Revised	2–Adult	AGS	1980
Porteus Maze Test	3–Adult	PC	**7**:419
Raven Progressive Matrices	5–Adult	PC	**7**:376
Stanford-Binet Intelligence Scale	2–Adult	RP	**7**:425
System of Multicultural Pluralistic Assessment	5–11 yrs	PC	1977
Wechsler Adult Intelligence Scale: Revised	16–74 yrs	PC	1980
Wechsler Intelligence Scale for Children: Revised	6–16 yrs	PC	**8**:232
Wechsler Preschool and Primary Scale of Intelligence	4–6 yrs	PC	**7**:434

Group administered tests of scholastic aptitude

ACT Assessment	12 grade +	ACT	**8**:469
Closed High School Placement Test	8–9 grade	STS	**8**:26
Cognitive Abilities Test	K–12	RP	1978
Cooperative School and College Ability Test	4–14 grade	AW	**8**:183
Henmon-Nelson Tests of Mental Ability	K–14	RP	**8**:190
Kuhlman Anderson Inteliigence Tests	K–12	PP	**6**:466
Otis-Lennon School Ability Test	1–12	PC	1977
Scholastic Aptitude Test	12+ grade	CEEB(EB)	**8**:182
Short Form Test of Academic Aptitude	1–12 grade	CTBMH	**8**:202
Short Test of Educational Ability	K–12	SRA	**7**:382

Multiple aptitude batteries

Differential Aptitude Tests	8–12 gr	PC	1982
Flanagan Aptitude Classification Test	9–12 gr	SRA	**7**:675
Guilford-Zimmerman Aptitude Survey	9 gr–Adult	SPS	**8**:486
SRA Primary Mental Abilities	K–12 yrs	SRA	**7**:680
USES Nonreading Aptitude Test	9 gr–Adult	USGPO	**8**:491

Vocational interest inventories

ACT Career Planning Program	12 + grade	RP	**8**:989
Hall Occupational Orientation Inventory	3 gr–Adult	STS	**8**:103
Harrington-O'Shea Career Decision-Making System	8 gr–Adult	AGS	1982
Jackson Vocational Interest Inventory	9 gr–Adult	RPD	1977
Kuder, Form DD Occupational Interest Survey	11 gr–Adult	SRA	**8**:1010
Kuder, Form C Preference Record: Vocational	9 gr–Adult	SRA	**8**:1011
Kuder General Interest Survey	6 gr–12 gr	SRA	**8**:1009
Minnesota Vocational Interest Inventory	15 yr + (males)	PC	**7**:1026
Ohio Vocational Interest Inventory	8 gr–12 yr	PC	**8**:1016
Self-Directed Search: A Guide to Educational and Vocational Planning	9 gr–Adult	CPP	**8**:1022
Strong-Campbell Interest Inventory	16 yrs–Adult	CPP	**8**:1023
Vocational Interest, Experience, and Skill Assessment	8 gr–12 gr	RP	**8**:1025

ADDITIONAL READINGS

Chapter 1

Cronbach, L. J. The two disciplines of scientific psychology. *American Psychologist,* 1957, *12,* 671–684.

Cronbach, L. J. Beyond the two disciplines of scientific psychology. *American Psychologist,* 1975, *30,* 116–127.

> Illustrates concern for different educational and psychological decisions, and whether testing and measurement can contribute to their improvement. Read these now, skipping over the technical details.

Glaser, R. & Nitko, A. J. Measurement in learning and instruction. In R. L. Thorndike (Ed.), *Educational measurement* (2nd ed.). Washington, D. C.: American Council on Education, 1971, 625–670.

> Analyzes a particular kind of instructional system, types of decisions necessary and kinds of test information required.

Popham, W. J. *Educational evaluation.* Englewood Cliffs, N. J.: Prentice-Hall, Inc., 1975, Chapter 2, pp. 20–44.

> Gives a brief survey of different ideas of how programs should be evaluated: a useful introduction to program evaluation if you aren't familiar with proposed approaches.

Chapter 2

Committee on Education and Labor, House of Representatives. *Truth in Testing Act of 1979; The Educational Testing Act of 1979: Hearings Before the Subcommittee on Elementary, Secondary and Vocational Education.* Washington, D.C.: U. S. Government Printing Office, 1980.

> Records proposed legislation, testimony, and documents related to H. R. 3564 and H. R. 4949 in 1979 as federal truth-in-testing legislation. Proponents attack and rebut nearly every facet of testing.

Glaser, R. & Bond, L. (Eds.) Testing: Concepts, policy, practice, and research. (Special Issue) *American Psychologist,* 1981, *36* (10) (whole).

> Collects twenty articles on scientific, social, legal, and ethical issues of educational and psychological testing organized around four themes:

(1) scientific, social, and historical foundations of tests; (2) legal and social issues such as minimum competency testing, test bias, and coaching; (3) practical issues such as classification, selection, identification.

The Measuring Cup published by the Public Information and Research Services, Inc., Savannah, Georgia.

The Testing Digest published by the Committee for Fair and Open Testing, New York City.

> Two antitesting periodicals which reprint newspaper articles and news items on abuses and/or harmful consequences of testing.

Chapter 3

Bennett, G. K., Seashore, H. G., & Wesman, A. G. *Manual for the Differential Aptitude Tests* (5th ed.). New York: The Psychological Corporation, 1973.

> The *Differential Aptitude Tests:* a multiple aptitude battery for use with eighth through twelfth grades. Chapters 4 through 8 of the *Manual* contain correlations, means, and standard deviations to interpret.

Blommers, P. J. & Forsyth, R. A. *Elementary statistical methods of psychology and education* (2nd ed.). Boston: Houghton Mifflin Company, 1977.

> Discusses variables and their measurement including the continuous vs. discrete distinction (Chapter 2); details of frequency distribution tabulation and use (Chapter 3); percentile ranks (Chapter 4); indices of central tendency (Chapter 6); measures of variability (Chapter 7); linear standard scores (Chapter 8); a thorough elementary discussion of correlation (Chapter 17); an accompanying *Study Manual* gives practice and extends the concepts.

Kamin, L. J. *The science and politics of I.Q.* Potomac, MD: Lawrence Erlbaum Associates, 1974, Chapter 3.

> Discusses the scientific merit of correlational data frequently cited and used by those advocating the plausibility of the genetic hypothesis of intelligence: reviews major correlational studies on separated identical twins and discusses the interpretation of these correlation

coefficients in light of factors such as errors of measurement, restriction in range, and heterogeneity on a third variable (Chapter 3).

Chapter 4

Bloom, B. S., Hastings, J. T., & Madaus, G. F. *Handbook on formative and summative evaluation of student learning.* New York: McGraw-Hill Book Company, 1971.

(a) Describes the Bloom et al. (1956) cognitive domain-taxonomy in great detail; (b) gives examples of test items and objectives in each taxonomic area; (c) describes mastery learning, formative and summative testing, and placement and diagnostic testing; (d) applies the idea of a test blueprint to eleven different curricular areas, preschool through secondary school.

Lindquist, E. F. Preliminary considerations in objective test construction. In E. F. Lindquist (Ed.), *Educational measurement* (1st ed.). Washington, D.C.: American Council on Education, 1951 (Chapter 5).

Analyzes logically relationships between ultimate objectives of the educational enterprise and achievement tests we build: gives insight into Lindquist's viewpoint on educational measurement which undergirded development of several well known tests of educational development and basic skills.

Mager, R. L. *Measuring instructional intent: Or got a match?* Belmont, CA: Fearon Publishers, 1973.

Uses a programmed format to teach how to: analyze a given instructional objective to identify type of performance stated, analyze a given test item designed to measure that objective and decide whether item and objective match.

Chapter 5

Kryspin, W. J. & Feldhusen, J. F. *Developing classroom tests: A guide for writing and evaluating test items.* Minneapolis: Burgess Publishing Co., 1974.

Teaches how to use the Bloom et al. taxonomy to develop a test blueprint covering a single unit of instruction.

Popham, W. J. *Criterion-referenced measurement.* Englewood Cliffs, NJ: Prentice-Hall, 1978 (Chapters 5 and 6).

Presents a view of how criterion-referenced tests are planned and developed using procedures for precisely defining domains of instructionally relevant behaviors to reduce the ambiguity of what tests measure.

Tinkelman, S. N. Planning the objective test. In R. L. Thorndike (Ed.), *Educational measurement* (2nd ed.). Washington, D.C.: American Council on Education, 1971.

Gives detailed explanations of steps necessary to plan, develop, and produce standardized, objective achievement tests: useful to contrast detailed planning required for standardized test development with planning recommended for teacher-made tests.

Chapter 6

Cooper, C. R. & Odell, L. (Eds.) *Evaluating writing: Describing, measuring, and judging.* Urbana, IL: National Council of Teachers of English, 1977.

Provides overviews of methods of and issues surrounding assessment of general writing ability.

Coffman, W. E. Essay examinations. In R. L. Thorndike (Ed.), *Educational measurement* (2nd ed.). Washington, DC: American Council on Education, 1971 (Chapter 10).

Stalnaker, J. M. The essay type of examination. In E. F. Lindquist (Ed.), *Educational measurement.* Washington, DC: American Council on Education, 1951 (Chapter 13).

Summarizes measurement issues surrounding essay testing in subject-matter areas and in measuring writing ability: some suggestions for construction and scoring.

Hirsch, E. D., Jr. *The philosophy of composition.* Chicago: The University of Chicago Press, 1977.

Engaging essay synthesizing findings and viewpoints of several disciplines (including pedagogy, literary criticism, philosophy, and psycholinguistics) in a unified approach to teaching and assessment of writing ability; considered controversial.

Chapter 7

Ebel, R. L. *Essentials of educational testing* (3rd ed.). Englewood Cliffs, NJ: Prentice-Hall, Inc., 1979 (Chapter 7).

Advocates expanded use of true-false items in achievement testing: presents comprehensive and detailed analysis, offers many suggestions, gives many illustrations of good and poor true-false items.

Wesman, A. G. Writing the test item. In R. L. Thorndike (Ed.), *Educational measurement* (2nd ed.). Washington, D.C.: American Council on Education, 1971 (Chapter 4).

Offers comprehensive treatment of item writing suggestions for all types of response-choice items: abundant illustrations.

Weidemann, C. C. How to construct the true-false examination. *Teachers College, Columbia University. Contributions to Education* (No. 225). New York: Bureau of Publications, Teachers College, Columbia University, 1926.

Old treatment of true-false items: offers some good suggestions for constructing true-false items beyond testing of facts and simple recall.

Chapter 8

Bloom, B. S., Hastings, J. T., & Madaus, G. F. *Handbook on formative and summative evaluation of student learning*. New York: McGraw-Hill Book Company, 1971 (Part 2).

Second part of the book contains numerous illustrations of multiple-choice items at a variety of cognitive levels which may serve as models for your own items. (See annotation under Chapter 4.)

Wesman, A. G. Writing the test item. In R. L. Thorndike (Ed.), *Educational measurement* (2nd ed.). Washington, D.C.: American Council on Education, 1971.

(See annotation under Chapter 7.)

Wood, R. Multiple-choice: A state-of-the-art report. *Evaluation in Education: International Progress*, 1977, *1*, 191–280.

Discusses polemics and empirical research on multiple-choice items, reviewing item analysis methods, using scoring formulas, and techniques of constructing norm-referenced tests.

Chapter 9

Gagné, R. M. & Briggs, L. J. *Principles of instructional design* (2nd ed.). New York: Holt, Rinehart, and Winston, 1979 (Chapters 4, 7, and 12).

Gives more explanations and illustrations of measurement of concept and rule learning, relating this to design of instruction.

Heaton, J. B. *Writing English language tests: A practical guide for teachers of English as a second or foreign language*. London: Longman Group Limited, 1975.

Oller, J. W. Jr. *Language tests at school: A pragmatic approach*. London: Longman Group Limited, 1979.

Concerned with assessing a broad range of English language proficiency via context-dependent test items. May be useful for teachers who teach bilingual pupils or pupils with special language problems.

Hieronymus, A. N. & Lindquist, E. F. *Iowa Tests of Basic Skills: Teacher's guide to administration, interpretation, and use*. Boston: Houghton Mifflin Co., 1971 (pp. 44–50; 57).

Presents an analysis of skills in using reference materials and in reading maps, graphs, and tables tested on the ITBS as well as suggestions for teaching these skills.

Chapter 10

Borich, G. D., & Madden, S. K. *Evaluating classroom instruction: A sourcebook of instruments*. Reading, MA: Addison-Wesley Publishing Co., 1977.

Describes varieties of observation schedules and instruments, especially those relating to classroom events.

Good, T. L., & Brophy, J. E. *Looking in classrooms* (2nd ed.). New York: Harper & Row, Publishers, 1978.

Helps teachers become aware of what events are occurring in the classroom and how they and their students are interacting. Gives examples of categories of behaviors which teachers should observe to improve teaching.

Webb, E. J., Campbell, D. T., Schwartz, R. D., Sechrest, L., and Grove, J. B. *Nonreactive in the social sciences* (2nd ed.). Boston: Houghton Mifflin Co., 1981.

Reviews a variety of techniques used to lessen the obtrusive nature of observation and calls for using several convergent measures to obtain a clear picture of characteristics being measured.

Chapter 11

Berk, R. A. Item analysis. In R. A. Berk (Ed.), *Criterion-referenced measurement: The state of the art*. Baltimore, MD: The Johns Hopkins University Press, 1980 (Chapter 3, pp. 49–79).

Describes procedures for trying out and selecting items for mastery (pass/fail) tests from a different viewpoint than this text.

Cox, R. C. Item selection techniques and the evaluation of instructional objectives. *Journal of Educational Measurement*, 1965, *2*, 181–185.

Gives a vivid demonstration (1) that selecting items only on the basis of item analysis statistics will result in tests being unrepresentative of the domain and (2) that groups on whom data for item analysis has been collected can alter eventual composition of final test forms.

Henrysson, S. Gathering, analyzing, and using data on test items. In R. L. Thorndike (Ed.), *Educational measurement* (2nd ed.). Washington, D.C.: American Council on Education, 1971 (Chapter 5, pp. 130–159).

Comprehensively reviews item selection techniques as these are used to develop tests to measure relative achievement.

Chapter 12

Millman, J. & Pauk, W. *How to take tests*. New York: McGraw-Hill, 1969.

Random House School Division. *Scoring high in . . .* New York: Random House, Inc., 1980.

The first provides comprehensive discussions of test-taking and test-wiseness skills for classroom and standardized tests and the second teaches elementary students skills in taking standardized tests in reading, language, and mathematics.

Sarnacki, R. E. An examination of test-wiseness in the cognitive test domain. *Review of Educational Research*, 1979, *49*, 252–279.

Reviews research literature on test-wiseness.

Tryon, G. S. The measurement and treatment of test anxiety. *Review of Educational Research*, 1980, *50*, 343–372.

Reviews research literature on test anxiety.

Chapter 13

Kunder, L. H. & Porwoll, P. J. *Reporting pupil progress: Policies, procedures, and systems*. (ERS Report) Arlington, VA: Educational Research Services, Inc., 1977.

Reports on a nationwide survey of grading and pupil progress reporting practices. Includes samples of school board policy statements, guides to teachers for using report cards, and samples of report cards and parent conference report forms. May be available through your school's central administration.

Losen, S. *Parent conferences in the schools: Procedures for developing effective partnership*. Boston: Allyn and Bacon, 1978.

Suggestions for improving parent-teacher communications and conferences.

Simon, S. B. & Ballanca, J. A. (Eds.) *Degrading the grading myths: A primer of alternatives to grades and marks*. Washington, D.C.: Association for Supervision and Curriculum Development, 1976.

Reviews strengths and weaknesses of traditional systems and offers suggestions for a variety of alternatives.

Chapter 14

Bradley, J. V. *Distribution-free statistical tests*. Englewood Cliffs, NJ: Prentice-Hall, Inc., 1968 (Chapter 1, pp. 1–14).

Describes history of discovery and early uses of normal distributions and myth of law of normality and how it is easy to enter and remain ". . . in the Gaussian grip of the Normal Mystique" (p. 14).

Ebel, R. L. *The uses of standardized testing* (Fastback 93). Bloomington, IND: The Phi Delta Kappa Educational Foundation, 1977.

Perrone, V. *The abuses of standardized testing* (Fastback 92). Bloomington, IND: The Phi Delta Kappa Educational Foundation, 1977.

Present pro and con discussions of values of norm-referenced testing: useful preludes to forthcoming chapters in this text.

Hieronymus, A. N., Lindquist, E. F., & Hoover, H. D. *Teacher's guide for administration, interpretation, and use: Iowa Tests of Basic Skills, Forms 7 and 8*. Chicago: Riverside Publishing Co., 1979.

Hieronymus, A. N., Lindquist, E. F., & Hoover, H. D. *Manual for administrators, supervisors, and counselors: Iowa Tests of Basic Skills, Forms 7 and 8.* Chicago: Riverside Publishing Co., 1982.

Prescott, G. A., Balow, I. H., Hogan, T. P., & Farr, R. C. *Teacher's Manual for administering and interpreting: Metropolitan Achievement Tests, Complete Survey Battery,* 1978.

Various materials prepared by test publishers to offer teachers suggestions for interpreting norm-referenced scores and suggesting courses of action to follow to teach skills their products test. (You may want to obtain manuals from other test publishers as well.)

Chapter 15

Anastasi, A. *Psychological testing* (5th ed.). New York: Macmillan Publishing Co., 1982 (Chapter 5).

Reviews reliability coefficients of various types. Note especially how information from several types of coefficients can estimate the effects of several sources of error on the scores.

Berk, R. A. A consumer's guide to criterion-referenced test reliability. *Journal of Educational Measurement,* 1980, *17,* 323–350.

Subkoviak, M. J. Decision-consistency approaches. In R. A. Berk (Ed.), *Criterion-referenced measurement: The state of the art.* Baltimore: Johns Hopkins University Press, 1980.

Traub, R. E., & Rowley, G. L. Reliability of test scores and decisions. *Applied Psychological Measurement,* 1980, *4,* 517–546.

Review many ways of computing indices of decision consistency and reliability coefficients for mastery testing. Berk and Subkoviak discuss strengths and limitations of percent agreement and kappa from a practitioner's viewpoint; Traub and Rowley's comprehensive review may be difficult reading for beginners.

Brown, F. G. *Guidelines for test use: A commentary on the Standards for Educational and Psychological Tests.* Washington, D.C.: National Council on Measurement in Education, 1980 (Chapter 3).

Discusses various types of reliability data test publishers should include in their test manuals and how test users should interpret reliability data from published tests.

Chapter 16

Civil Service Commission, Equal Employment Opportunity Commission, Department of Justice, and Department of Labor. Uniform guidelines on employment selection procedures. *Federal Register,* December 30, 1977, *42* (251), 65542-65552.

United States Supreme Court, Willie S. Griggs et al., Petitioners, vs. Duke Power Company March 8, 1971.

Documents Supreme Court decision on a landmark case indicating that employers must provide appropriate validity data to support use of a test for promotion or selection and that the test should not be biased against particular groups. The *Uniform Guidelines* are federal regulations for how selection test validation procedures should be implemented in industry and government to document whether they are unbiased.

Cronbach, L. J. & Snow, R. E. *Aptitude and instructional methods: A handbook for research on interactions.* New York: Irvington Publishers, Inc., 1977.

Treats differential placement of pupils in instructional methods extensively. Surveys available research to the mid-seventies, describes the state-of-the-art and what research should be done next.

Shavelson, R. J. & Stanton, G. C. Construct validation: Methodology and application to three measures of cognitive structure. *Journal of Educational measurement,* 1975, *12,* 67–85.

Shavelson, R. J., Hubner, J. J., & Stanton, G. C. Self-concept: validation of construct interpretations. *Review of Educational Research.* 1976. *46,* 407–441.

Presents two examples of studies, consistent with view taken in this chapter, illustrating how evidence can be organized and integrated to judge construct validity.

Chapter 17

Berk, R. A. (Ed.) *Criterion-referenced measurement: The state of the art* (2nd ed.). Baltimore, MD: The Johns Hopkins University Press, 1983.

Popham, W. J. *Criterion-referenced measurement.* Englewood Cliffs, NJ: Prentice-Hall, 1978.

Criterion-referenced test development and use from the perspectives of several authors.

Ebel, R. L. Some limitations of criterion-referenced measurements. In *Testing in turmoil: A conference on problems and issues in educational measurement*. Greenwich, CT: Educational Records Bureau, 1970.

Ebel, R. L. Criterion-referenced measurements; *Limitations, School Review*, 1971, *69*, 282–288.

Ebel, R. L. The case for norm-referenced measurements. *Educational Researcher*, 1979, *7*, (11), 3–5.

Mehrens, W. A. & Ebel, R. L. Some comments on criterion-referenced and norm-referenced achievement tests. *NCME Measurement in Education*, 1979, *10* (1).

> Leading critic of criterion-referenced testing, Robert L. Ebel, defends the need for both standardized tests and for norm-referenced interpretation of test scores.

Glaser, R. & Klaus, D. J. Proficiency measurement: Assessing human performance. In R. M. Gagné (Ed.), *Psychological principles in systems development*. New York: Holt, Rinehart, and Winston, 1962.

Glaser, R. Instructional technology and the measurement of learning outcomes. *American Psychologist*, 1963, *18*, 519–521.

> Seminal works on criterion-referenced testing which began the "movement."

Chapter 18

Barrow, H. M. & McGee, R. *A practical approach to measurement in physical education* (2nd ed.). Philadelphia, PA: Lea and Febiger, 1971.

Blanton, W., Farr, R. & Tuinman, J. J. *Reading tests for the secondary grades: A review and evaluation*. Newark, DE: International Reading Association, 1972.

Bonjean, C. M., Hill, R. J. & McLemore, S. D. *Sociological measurement: Inventory of scales and indices*. San Francisco: Chandler, 1967.

Braswell, J. S. *Mathematics test available in the United States* (3rd ed.) Washington, D.C.: National Council of Teachers of Mathematics, 1972. (Ed. 067 270)

Buros, O. K. (Ed.) *The eighth mental measurements yearbook*. Highland Park, NJ: The Gryphon Press, 1978.

Cattell, R. B. & Warburton, F. W. *Objective personality and motivation tests*. Urbana, IL: University of Illinois Press, 1967.

Crago, P. H. *Diagnostic tests in reading: An annotated bibliography*. Albany, NY: Bureau of Pupil Testing and Advisory services, New York State Education Department, 1970. (ED 073 426)

Darley, F. L. (Ed.) *Evaluation of appraisal techniques in speech and language pathology*. Reading, MA: Addison-Wesley Publishing Company, 1979.

Goodwin, W. L. & Driscoll, L. A. *Handbook for measurement and evaluation in early childhood education*. San Francisco: Jossey-Bass, 1980.

Grummon, A. H. (Ed.) *Reviews of selected published tests in English*. Urbana, IL: National Council of Teachers of English, 1976.

Hoepfner, R. and others. CSE test evaluation series. (See text for list)

Silverman, R. J., Noa, J. K., & Russell, R. H. *Oral language tests for bilingual students: An evaluation of language dominance and proficiency instruments*. Portland, OR: Northwest Regional Educational Laboratory, 1976.

> Bibliographies of tests on specific topics, some with critical reviews of tests.

Chapter 19

Anastasi, A. *Psychological testing* (5th ed.). New York: Macmillan Publishing Co., 1982 (Chapter 14).

> Discusses and illustrates a number of achievement tests including diagnostic and preschool tests.

Bush, W. J. & Waugh, K. W. *Diagnosing learning problems* (3rd ed.). Columbus, OH: Charles E. Merrill Publishing Co., 1981.

Salvia, J. & Ysseldyke, J. E. *Assessment in special and remedial education* (2nd ed.). Boston: Houghton Mifflin Co., 1981

> Illustrates and describes educational achievement tests which can be used for special populations of children.

Cole, N. S. & Nitko, A. J. Instrumentation and bias: Issues in selecting measures for educational evaluations. In R. A. Berk (Ed.), *Educational evaluation methodology: The state of the art*. Baltimore: Johns Hopkins University Press, 1981.

> Discusses selection and evaluation of achievement tests used to evaluate educational programs: Among issues discussed are out-of-level testing and racial/ethnic bias.

Chapter 20

Block, N. J. & Dworkin, G. (Eds.) *The IQ controversy.* New York: Pantheon Books, 1976.

    Offers a collection of readings on controversial issues of intelligence testing from the Lippman-Terman debates of the 1920's to the critics of Jensen and Herrnstein in the 1970's: attempts to discredit the hereditarian hypothesis of intellectual development.

Mercer, J. R. *System of Multicultural Pluralistic Assessment: Technical manual.* New York: The Psychological Corporation, 1979.

    Analyzes sociologically various testing models and their consequences for measurement concepts and interpretations of pupil performance.

Sattler, J. M. *Assessment of children's intelligence and special abilities* (2nd ed.). Boston: Allyn and Bacon, 1982.

    Comprehensively covers administration and interpretation of the *Stanford-Binet,* WISC, WPPSI, and many other tests of achievement, intelligence, and special abilities. Discussions of testing minorities and handicapped children are special features.

Chapter 21

Bayley, N. Development of mental abilities. In P. H. Mussen (Ed.), *Carmichael's manual of child psychology* (3rd ed.). (Vol. 1) New York: John Wiley & Sons, 1970.

    Bayley reviews her life-long study of the intellectual development of children.

Biondi, A. M. & Parnes, S. J. (Eds.) *Assessing creative growth: The tests (Book One)* and *Measured changes* (Book Two). Great Neck, NY: Creative Synergetic Associates, Ltd., 1976.

    Collects reprinted articles appearing in the *Journal of Creative Behavior* from 1967 through 1975: Book One contains articles on the identification of creative talents in preschool, elementary, and secondary children and in adults;

Book Two articles summarize research and applications of creativity.

Passow, A. H. (Ed.) The gifted and talented: their education and development. *The seventy-eighth yearbook of the National Society for the Study of Education.* (Part I) Chicago: The National Society for the Study of Education, 1979.

    Collects articles reviewing history and current state of the art on identification and education of gifted and talented pupils.

Chapter 22

Anastasi, A. *Psychological testing* (5th ed.). New York: Macmillan Publishing Co., 1982 (Chapters 17, 18, 19, 20).

Cronbach, L. J. *Essentials of psychological testing* (3rd ed.). New York: Harper and Row Publishers, 1970 (Chapters 14, 15, 16, 17, 18, 19).

Thorndike, R. L. and Hagen, E. P. *Measurement and evaluation in psychology and education* (4th ed.). New York: John Wiley and Sons, 1977 (Chapters 11, 12, 13).

    Review specific interest, attitude, and personality inventories in considerable detail.

Payne, D. A. (Ed.) *New directions for testing and measurement: Recent development in affective measurement.* (No. 7) San Francisco: Jossey-Bass, 1980.

    Collects state-of-the-art papers on measurement of attitudes (Aiken), self-concept (Shavelson, Bolus, Keesling), socioemotional development (Ward, Sroufe), educational environments (Walberg, Moos), and interests (David).

Wiggins, J. S. *Personality and prediction: Principles of personality assessment.* Reading, MA: Addison-Wesley Publishing Co., 1973.

    Presents a comprehensive introductory treatment of major techniques and issues in assessment of personality.

REFERENCES

Aaronson, M. *Childhood mental health measurement sources*. Rockville, Md.: Early Child Care Research Center for Studies of Child and Family Mental Health, National Institute of Mental Health, 1974.

Adams, J. A. A closed-loop theory of motor learning. *Journal of Motor Behavior,* 1971, *3,* 111-149.

Ahmann, J. S., & Glock, M. D. *Evaluating student progress: Principles of tests and measurements* (6th ed.). Boston: Allyn & Bacon, 1981.

Aiken, L. R. Attitude measurement and research. In D. A. Payne (Ed.), *New directions for testing and measurement: Recent developments in affective meassurement* (No. 7). San Francisco: Jossey-Bass, 1980.

Airasian, P. W. A perspective on the uses and misuses of standardized achievement tests. *NCME Measurement in Education,* 1979, *10*(3):

Aleamoni, L. M., & Oboler, L. A. *ACT versus SAT in predicting first semester GPA.* Paper presented at the annual meeting of the American Educational Research Association, New York City, April 1977. (ERIC Document Reproduction Service No. ED 139 815).

Alderson, J. C. Review of the cloze procedure as applied to reading. In O. K. Buros (Ed.), *The eighth mental measurements yearbook.* Highland Park, N. J.: The Gryphon Press, 1978.

Alexander, S., & Husek, T. R. The anxiety differential: Initial steps in the development of measures of situational anxiety. *Educational and Psychological Measurement,* 1962, *22,* 325–348.

Aleyideino, S. C. The effects of response methods and item types upon working time scores and grade-equivalent scores of pupils differing in levels of achievement (Doctoral dissertation, University of Iowa, 1968). *Dissertation Abstracts International,* 1968, *29,* 1774A–1775A. (University Microfilms No. 68-16, 773).

Allen, G. J. Effect of three conditions of administration on 'trait' and 'state' measures of anxiety. *Journal of Consulting and Clinical Psychology,* 1970, *34,* 355–359.

Alpert, R. *Anxiety in academic achievement situations: Its measurement and relation to aptitude.* Unpublished doctoral dissertation, Stanford University, 1957.

Alpert R., & Haber, R. N. Anxiety in academic achievement situations. *Journal of Abnormal and Social Psychology,* 1960, *61,* 207–215.

American College Testing Program. The ACT Interest Inventory. In *Taking the ACT Assessment* (1980–81). Iowa City: Author, 1980.

American College Testing Program. *Vocational, Interest, Experience, and Skill Assessment (Self-scored): Career guidebook.* Iowa City: Riverside Publishing Co., 1976.

American College Testing Program. *Assessing students on the way to college: Technical report for the ACT Assessment Program (Vol. I).* Iowa City: Author, 1973.

American Council on Education. *Guide to credit by examination.* Washington, D.C.: Office of Educational Credit and Credentials, American Council on Education, 1981.

American Guidance Service. Prepublication materials describing the *Kaufman Assessment Battery for Children.* Circle Pines, Minn.: Author, 1982. (a)

American Guidance Service. Prepublication materials describing the *Vineland Adaptive Behavior Scales.* Circle Pines, Minn.: Author, 1982. (b)

American Guidance Service. *1980 catalogue.* Circle Pines, Minn.: Author, 1980.

American Personnel and Guidance Association. *Responsibilities of users of standardized tests.* Falls Church, Va.: Author, 1980.

American Psychological Association. *Ethical standards of psychologists.* Washington, D. C.: Author, 1977.

American Psychological Association. *Standards for educational and psychological tests.* Washington, D.C.: Author, 1974.

American Psychological Association. *Ethical principles in the conduct of research with human participants.* Washington, D. C.: Author, 1973.

American Psychological Association. *Casebook on ethical standards of psychologists.* Washington, D.C.: Author, 1967.

American Psychological Association. *Technical recommendations for psychological tests and diagnostic techniques.* Washington, D.C.: Author, 1954.

Anastasi, A. *Psychological testing* (4th ed.). New York: Macmillan, 1976.

Anastasi, A. *Psychological testing* (5th ed.). New York: Macmillan, 1982.

Anderson, J. E. The prediction of terminal intelligence from infant and pre-school tests. In G. M. Whipple (Ed.) *Intelligence: Its nature and nurture. Thirty-ninth yearbook of the National Society for the Study of Education.* Part I, Chicago: National Society for the Study of Education, 1940.

Anderson, R. C. How to construct achievement tests to assess comprehension. *Review of Educational Research,* 1972, *42,* 145–170.

Anderson, T. W., & Sclove, S. L. *Introductory statistical analysis.* Boston: Houghton Mifflin, 1974.

Andrew, B. J., & Hecht, J. T. A preliminary investigation of two procedures for setting examination standards. *Educational and Psychological Measurement,* 1976, *36,* 45–50.

Angoff, W. H. Scales, norms, and equivalent scores. In R. L. Thorndike (Ed.), *Educational measurement* (2nd Ed.). Washington, D.C.: American Council on Education, 1971.

APA Monitor. In the opinion of . . . *APA Monitor*, 1980, *11* (11), 7.

Association of Black Psychologists. *Black consumer's bill of rights and guide to standardized testing*. Washington, D.C.: Author, n.d., (circa 1980).

Ayres, L. P. *A Measuring Scale for Ability in Spelling*. New York: Russell Sage Foundation, 1915.

Backer, T. E. *A directory of information on tests* (TM Report 62). Princeton, N.J.: ERIC Clearinghouse on Tests, Measurements, and Evaluation, Educational Testing Service, 1977.

Baglin, R. F. Does "nationally" normed really mean nationally. *Journal of Educational Measurement*, 1981, *18*, 92–107.

Bajtelsmit, J. W. *The efficacy of test-wiseness and systematic desensitization programs for increasing test-taking skills*. Paper presented at the annual meeting of the National Council on Measurement in Education, Washington, D.C.: April, 1975.

Ballou, F. W. Scales for the Measurement of English Composition. *Harvard-Newton Bulletins* (No. 2). Cambridge, Mass.: Harvard University, 1914.

Baltes, P. B. & Labouvie, G. V. Adult development of intellectual performance: Description, explanation, modification. In C. Eisdorfer & M. P. Lawton (Eds.), *The psychology of adult development and aging*. Washington, D.C.: American Psychological Association, 1973.

Baltes, P. B., & Schaie, K. W. On the pasticity of intelligence in adulthood and old age: Where Horn and Donaldson fail. *American Psychologist, 1976, 31*, 720–725.

Barrett, T. C. Goals of the reading program: The basis for evaluation. In T. C. Barrett (Ed.), *The evaluation of children's reading achievement*. Newark, Del.: International Reading Association, 1967.

Barzun, J. *The house of intellect*. New York: Harper and Row, Publishers, 1959.

Bayley, N. Development of mental abilities. In P. H. Mussen (Ed.), *Carmichael's manual of child psychology* (3rd ed.). (Vol. 1) New York: John Wiley & Sons, 1970.

Beck, I. L. Reading problems and instructional practices. In T. G. Waller & G. E. McKinnon (Eds.), *Reading research: Advances in theory and practice* (Vol. 2). New York: Academic Press, 1981.

Beck, I. L. *Comprehension during the acquisition of decoding skills*. Pittsburgh: Learning Research and Development Center, University of Pittsburgh, 1977. (Publication No. 1977/4)

Beck, I. L., & Mitroff, D. D. *The Rationale and Design of a Primary Grades Reading System for an Individualized Classroom*. Pittsburgh: Learning Research and Development Center, University of Pittsburgh, 1972. (Publication No. 1972/4)

Beck, M. D. Achievement test reliability as a function of

pupil-response procedures. *Journal of Educational Measurement*, 1974, *11*, 109–114.

Beere, C. A. *Women and women's issues: A handbook of tests and measures*. San Francisco: Jossey-Bass, 1979.

Bellak, L. On the problems of the concept of projection: A theory of apperceptive distortion. In L. E. Apt and L. Bellak (Eds.), *Projective psychology: Clinical approaches to the total personality*. New York: Grove Press, 1959.

Bellanca, J. A., & Kirschenbaum, H. An overview of grading alternatives. In S. B. Simon & J. A. Bellanca (Eds.) *Degrading the grading myths: A primer of alternatives to grades and marks*. Washington, D.C.: Association for Supervision and Curriculum Development, 1976.

Beggs, D. L., & Hieronymus, A. N. Uniformity of growth in the basic skills throughout the school year and during the summer. *Journal of Educational Measurement*, 1968, *5*, 91–97.

Bennett, G. K., Seashore, H. G., & Wesman, A. G. *Differential aptitude tests* (Form V). New York: The Psychological Corporation, 1982.

Bennett, G. K., Seashore, H. G., & Wesman, A. G. *Differential aptitude tests* (Standardization edition): *Form V*. New York: The Psychological Corporation, 1980.

Bennett, G. K., Seashore, H. G., & Wesman, A. G. *Fifth edition manual for the Differential Aptitude Tests*. (Forms S and T) New York: The Psychological Corporation, 1974.

Bennett, G. K., Seashore, H. G., & Wesman, A. G. *Manual for the Differential Aptitude Tests* (5th ed.). New York: The Psychological Corporation, 1973.

Berdie, D. R., and Anderson, J. F. *Questionnaires: Design and use*. Metuchen, N.J.: The Scarecrow Press, 1974.

Bergan, J. R. A special scoring procedure for minimizing response bias on the school anxiety questionnaire. *Psychology in the Schools*, 1968, *5*, 210–216.

Berliner, D. Tempus educare. In P. L. Peterson & H. J. Walberg (Eds.), *Research on teaching: Concepts, findings, and implications*. Berkeley, CA: McCutchan Publishing Corp., 1979.

Berlyne, D. E. *Conflict, arousal, and curiosity*. New York: McGraw-Hill, 1976.

Berk, R. A. A consumer's guide to criterion-referenced test reliability. *Journal of Educational Measurement*, 1980, *17*, 323–349.

Berk, R. A. (Ed.) *Criterion-referenced measurement: The state of the art*. Baltimore, Md.: The Johns Hopkins University Press, 1980.

Berk, R. A. Item analysis. In R. A. Berk (Ed.), *Criterion-referenced measurement: The state of the art*. Baltimore Md.: The Johns Hopkins University Press, 1980.

Berry, M. F. *Language disorders of children: The bases and diagnosis*. Englewood Cliffs, N. J.: Prentice-Hall, Inc., 1969.

Bianchini, J. C., & Loret, P. G. Anchor Test Study. Final Report. Project Report (Vol. 1), 1974. (a) ERIC Document Reproduction Service No. ED 092 601)

Bianchini, J. C., & Loret, P. G. *Anchor Test Study Supple-*

ment. *Final Report.* (Vol. 31), 1974. (b) (ERIC Document Reproduction Service No. ED 092 632).

Binet, A., & Simon, T. Méthodes nouvelles pour le diagnostic du niveau intellectuel des anormaux. *L'Année Psychologique,* 1905, *11,* 191–244.

Binet, A., & Simon, T. The development of intelligence in the child. In A. Binet & T. Simon, *The development of intelligence in children (The Binet-Simon Scale).* (H. H. Goddard, Ed. & E. S. Kite, Trans.) Baltimore, Md. Wiliams and Wilkins, Co., 1916 (Originally published in L'Année Psychologique, 1908, Vol. 14, 1–94.)

Binet, A., & Simon, T. New investigation upon the measure of the intellectual level among school children. In A. Binet & T. Simon, *The development of intelligence in children (The Binet-Simon Scale).* H. H. Goddard (Ed.) & E. S. Kite (Trans.), Baltimore, Md.: Williams and Wilkins, Co., 1916. (Originally published in *L'Année Psychologique,* 1911, Vol. 17, 145–201.)

Binstock, L., Pingel, L., & Hsu, T. C. *The design of a computer-assisted mastery testing model for diagnosing inaccurate use of processes underlying problem solutions.* Unpublished report. Pittsburgh: Learning Research and Development Center, University of Pittsburgh November, 1975.

Birnbaum, A. Chapters 17–20. In Lord, F. M. & Novick, M. R. *Statistical theories of mental test scores.* Reading, Mass.: Addison-Wesley Publishing Co., 1968.

Bjerstedt, Äke. The methodology of preferential sociometry: Selected trends and some contributions. *Sociometry Monographs* (No. 37). New York: Beacon House, 1956.

Blalock, H. M. *Causal inferences in nonexperimental research.* Chapel Hill: University of North Carolina Press, 1964.

Bliss, L. B. A test of Lord's assumption regarding examinee guessing behavior on multiple-choice tests using elementary school students. *Journal of Educational Measurement,* 1980, *17,* 147–153.

Blommers, P. J., & Forsyth, R. A. *Elementary statistical methods in psychology and education* (2nd ed.). Boston: Houghton Mifflin Co., 1977.

Blommers, P. J., & Lindquist, E. F. *Elementary statistical methods.* Boston: Houghton Mifflin Co., 1960.

Bloom, B. S., Engelhart, M. D., Furst, E. J., Hill, W. H., & Krathwohl, D. R. *Taxonomy of educational objectives: The classification of educational goals. Handbook I: Cognitive domain.* New York: David McKay Co., 1956.

Bloom, B. S., Hastings, J. T., & Madaus, G. F. *Handbook on formative and summative evaluation of student learning.* New York: McGraw-Hill Book Co., 1971.

Blum, M. L., & Naylor, C. J. *Industrial psychology: Its theoretical and social foundations.* New York: Harper and Row, Publishers, 1968.

Bobbs-Merrill Educational Publishing. *Standardized tests and materials for careers.* Indianapolis, Ind.: 1980.

Bobertag, O. Intelligenzprüfungen an schulkindern. Die Grenzboten, 1911, *70,* 375–384.

Bobertag, O. Quelques réflexions méthodologiques à propos de l'échelle metrique de Binet et Simon. *L'Année Psychologique,* 1912, *18,* 271–288.

Boehm, A. E., & Weinberg, R. A. *The classroom observer: A guide for developing observation skills.* New York: Teachers College Press, 1977.

Bond, G. L., & Dykstra, R. The cooperative research program in first-grade reading instruction period. *Reading Research Quarterly,* 1967, *2,* 5–142.

Borich, G. D., & Madden, S. K. *Evaluating classroom instruction: A sourcebook of instruments.* Reading, Mass.: Addison-Wesley Publishing Co., 1977.

Boring, E. G. *A history of experimental psychology.* New York: D. Appleton Century Company, 1929.

Bormuth, J. R. *On the theory of achievement test items.* Chicago: University of Chicago Press, 1970.

Bormuth, J. R. *Development of readability analyses.* (Final report, Project No. 7-0052, Contract No. OEG-3-7-070052-0326) Washington, D.C.: Office of Education, Bureau of Research, U. S. Department of Health, Education and Welfare, March 1969.

Bormuth, J. R. Comparable cloze and multiple-choice comprehension test scores. *Journal of Reading,* 1967, *10,* 291–299.

Bormuth, J. R. Experimental applications of cloze tests. In the *Conference proceedings of the International Reading Association,* 1964.

Boruch, R. F. Maintaining confidentiality of data in educational research: A systemic analysis. *American Psychologist,* 1971, *26,* 413–430.

Boruch, R. F., Larkin, J. D., Wolins, L., & McKinney, A. C. Alternative methods of analysis: Multitrait-multimethod data. *Educational and Psychological Measurement,* 1970, *30,* 833–854.

Boucher, J. L. Higher processes in motor learning. *Journal of Motor Behavior,* 1974, *6,* 131–138.

Bowles, S., & Gintis, H. *Schooling in capitalist America.* New York: Basic Books, Inc., 1976.

Boykin, A., & Pope, C. Teacher, take a test on grading. *Phi Delta Kappan,* 1977, *59,* 561–563.

Bracht, G. H., & Hopkins, K. D. Stability of educational achievement. In G. H. Bracht, K. D. Hopkins, & J. C. Stanley (Eds.), *Perspectives in educational and psychological measurement.* Englewood Cliffs, N. J.: Prentice-Hall, Inc., 1972.

Brown, F. G. *Guidelines for test use: A commentary on the standards for educational and psychological tests.* Washington, D.C.: National Council on Measurement in Education, 1980.

Brown, J. S., & Burton, R. R. Diagnostic models for procedural bugs in basic mathematical skills. *Cognitive Science,* 1978, *2,* 155–192.

Brown, N. J. *Use of the cloze procedure for monitoring*

elementary students' reading progress. Master's thesis, University of Pittsburgh, 1977.

Brown, R. *Approaches to the evaluation of writing: Some theoretical considerations and practical suggestions.* Unpublished paper, 1979.

Brown, W. Some experimental results in the correlation of mental abilities. *British Journal of Psychology,* 1910, *3,* 296–322.

Brozovich, W. R. Characteristics associated with popularity among different racial and socioeconomic groups of children. *The Journal of Educational Research,* 1970, *63,* 441–444.

Bruininks, R. H. *Examiner's manual: Bruininks-Oseretsky test of motor proficiency.* Circle Pines, Minn.: American Guidance Service, 1978.

Buckingham, B. R. Suggestions for procedures following a testing program—I. Reclassification. *Journal of Educational Research,* 1920, *2,* 787–801.

Budoff, M. *Measuring learning potential: An alternative to the traditional psychological examination.* Paper presented at the First Annual Study Conference in School Psychology, Temple University, Philadelphia, June 1972.

Buros, O. K. (Ed.) *The eighth mental measurements yearbook.* Highland Park, N. J.: The Gryphon Press, 1978. (See also Cloze procedure [Ebbinghaus completion method] and Buros' Introduction.)

Buros, O. K. Fifty years in testing. *Educational Researcher,* 1977, *6*(7), 9–15.

Buros, O. K. Criticisms of commonly used methods of validating achievement test items. In *Proceedings of the 1948 ETS Invitational Conference on Testing Problems.* Princeton, N. J.: Educational Testing Service, 1949.

Buros, O. K. *Review of tests and measurements in the social sciences: Part IV—Report of the Commission on the Social Studies, American Historical Association. Progressive Education,* 1935, *12,* 495.

Burrill, L. E. *How a standardized achievement test is built.* (Test Service Notebook 125) New York: Test Department, Harcourt Brace Jovanovich, Inc., no date.

Calhoun, D. *The intelligence of a people.* Princeton, N. J.: Princeton University Press, 1973.

Callahan, R. E. *Education and the cult of efficiency.* Chicago: University of Chicago Press, 1962.

Callenbach, C. The effects of instruction and practice in content-independent test-taking techniques upon the standardized reading test scores in selected second grade students. *Journal of Educational Measurement,* 1973, *10,* 25–30.

Campbell, R. N. *An account of the principles of measurement and calculations.* London: Longmans, Green, and Co., 1928.

Campbell, D. T., & Fiske, D. W. Convergent and discriminant validation by the multitrait-multimethod matrix. *Psychological Bulletin,* 1959, *56,* 81–105.

Carrier, N. A. & Jewell, D. O. Efficiency in measuring the effect of anxiety upon academic performance. *Journal of Educational Psychology,* 1966, *57,* 23–26.

Carroll, J. B. The aptitude-achievement distinction: The case of foreign language aptitude and proficiency. In D. R. Green (Ed.), *The aptitude-achievement distinction: Proceedings of the Second CTB/McGraw-Hill Conference on Issues in Educational Measurement.* Monterey, Calif.: CTB/McGraw-Hill, Inc., 1974.

Carroll, J. B. The nature of the data or how to choose a correlation coefficient. *Psychometrika,* 1961, *26,* 347–372.

Carroll, J. B., & Sapon, S. M. *Modern language aptitude test: Manual.* New York: The Psychological Corporation, 1959.

Cartwright, C. A., & Cartwright, G. P. *Developing observational skills.* New York: McGraw-Hill, 1974.

Carrier, N. A., & Jewell, D. O. Efficiency in measuring the effect of anxiety upon academic performance. *Journal of Educational Psychology,* 1966, 57, 23–26.

Carver, R. P. Two dimensions of tests: Psychometric and edumetric. *American Psychologist,* 1974, *29,* 512–518.

Cashen, V. M., & Ramseyer, G. C. The use of separate answer sheets by primary age children. *Journal of Educational Measurement,* 1969, *6,* 155–158.

Cattell, J. M. Mental tests and measurements. *Mind,* 1890, *15,* 373–381.

Cattell, R. B., & Cattell, A. K. S. *Cattell culture fair intelligence series.* Indianapolis, Ind.: Bobbs-Merrill Educational Publishing, 1960.

Center for the Study of Evaluation. *CSE Criterion-referenced test handbook.* Los Angeles: Center for the Study of Evaluation, University of California, Los Angeles, 1979.

Chadwick, E. Statistics of Educational Results. *The Museum, A Quarterly Magazine of Education, Literature and Science,* 1864, *3,* 479–484.

Chambers, A. C., & Hopkins, K. D. *Anxiety, physiologically and psychologically measured, and its consequences on mental test performance.* 1966. (ERIC Document Reproduction Service No. 010 407)

Champagne, A. B., & Klopfer, L. E. *Level I teacher's manual, individualized science.* Kankakee, Ill.: Imperial International Learning Corp., 1975.

Chapman, J. C., & Rush, G. P. *The scientific measurement of classroom products.* Boston: Silver, Burdette and Co., 1917.

Charles E. Merrill Publishing Co. *Break through.* Columbus, Ohio: Author 1975.

Chi, M., & Glaser, R. The measurement of expertise: Analysis of the development of knowledge and skill as a basis for assessing achievement. In E. L. Baker & E. S. Quellmalz (Eds.), *Design, analysis, and policy in testing and evaluation.* Beverly Hills, Calif.: Sage Publications, Inc., 1980.

Cleary, T. A. Test bias: Prediction of grades of negro and white students in integrated colleges. *Journal of Educational Measurement,* 1968, *5,* 115–124.

Clymer, T. What is reading? Some current concepts. In H. M. Robinson (Ed.), *Innovation and change in reading instruction. Sixty-seventh Yearbook of the National Soci-*

ety for the Study of Education. Part II, Chicago: University of Chicago Press, 1968.

Coffman, W. E. Essay examinations. In R. L. Thorndike (Ed.), Educational measurement (2nd ed.). Washington, D. C.: American Council on Education, 1971.

Cohen, D. K., & Lazerson, M. Education and the corporate order. Socialism Revisited, 1972, 2, 47–71.

Cohen, J. A coefficient of agreement for nominal scales. Educational and Psychological Measurement, 1960, 20, 37–46.

Cohen, P. A. Student ratings of instruction and student achievement: A meta-analysis of multisection validity studies. Review of Educational Research, 1981, 51, 281–309.

Cohen, S. A., & Foreman, D. I. Scoring high in reading (Teacher's edition). (Books A, B, C & D) New York: Random House, 1978.

Cole, N. S. Coaching, test-wiseness and other extraneous factors in ability testing, (Prepared for the Committee on Ability Testing of the National Academy of Sciences) Pittsburgh: Programs in Educational Research Methodology, University of Pittsburgh, no date.

Cole, N. S. Approaches to examining bias in achievement test items. A paper presented at the annual meeting of the American Personnel and Guidance Association, Washington, D. C.: March 1978.

Cole, N. S. Evaluating standardized tests and the alternatives. In A. J. Nitko (Ed.), Exploring alternatives to current standardized tests: Proceedings of the 1976 National Testing Conference. Pittsburgh: School of Education, University of Pittsburgh, 1977.

Cole, N. S. Bias in selection. Journal of Educational Measurement, 1973, 10, 237–255.

Cole, N. S., & Hanson, G. R. Impact of interest inventories on career choice. In. E. E. Diamond (Ed.), Issues of sex bias and sex fairness in career interest measurement. Washington, D. C.: Career Education Program, National Institute of Education, Department of Health, Education, and Welfare, 1975.

Cole, N. S., & Hanson, G. R. Assessing students on the way to college: Technical report for the ACT Assessment Program. (Vol. 1) Iowa City: The American College Testing Program, 1973.

Cole, N. S., & Hanson, G. R. Analysis of the structure of vocational interests. Journal of Counseling Psychology, 1971, 18, 478–486.

Cole, N. S., & Nitko, A. J. Instrumentation and bias: Issues in selecting measures for educational evaluations. In R. A. Berk (Ed.), Educational evaluation methodology: The state of the art. Baltimore: Johns Hopkins University Press, 1981.

College Entrance Examination Board. Test challenges: Many are called, but very few are chosen. News for Counselors, Fall 1981.

College Entrance Examination Board. Degrees of reading power: Test administration manual. New York: Author, 1980. (a)

College Entrance Examination Board. Degrees of reading power: Test booklet. (Form PX-1). New York: Author, 1980. (b)

College Entrance Examination Board. Degrees of reading power; Readability report. (1980–1981 Academic Year) New York: Author, 1980 (c)

College Entrance Examination Board. Degrees of reading power: User's manual. New York: Author, 1980. (d)

Commission of the Reorganization of Secondary Education. Cardinal principles of secondary education. (Bulletin No. 35). Washington, D.C.: Bureau of Education, Department of the Interior, 1918.

Committee on Education and Labor, House of Representatives. Truth in Testing Act of 1979; The Educational Testing Act of 1979: Hearings before the Subcommittee on Elementary, Secondary, and Vocational Education. Washington, D.C.: U.S. Government Printing Office, 1980.

Connolly, A.J., Nachtman, W., & Pritchett, E. M. Manual: KeyMath diagnostic arithmetic test. Circle Pines, Minn.: American Guidance Service, 1976.

Connolly, A. J., Nachtman, W., & Pritchett, E. M. Manual: KeyMath diagnostic arithmetic test. Circle Pines, Minn.: American Guidance Service, Inc., 1971.

Cook, W. W. The functions of measurement in the facilitation of learning. In E. F. Lindquist (Ed.), Educational measurement. Washington, D. C.: American Council on Education, 1951.

Cooley, W. W. The use and misuse of norm-referenced test scores for decision making at the local school level: The educational researcher's perspective. A paper presented at the annual meeting of the American Educational Research Association, Los Angeles, April, 1981.

Cooley, W. W. Program evaluation in education. An invited address presented at the annual meeting of the American Psychological Association, San Francisco, August, 1977.

Cooley, W. W., & Leinhart, G. The application of a model for investigating classroom processes. (1975/24) Pittsburgh: Learning Research and Development Center, University of Pittsburgh, 1975.

Cooley, W. W., & Lohnes, P. R. Evaluation research in education. New York: Irvington Publishers, 1976.

Cooper, C. R. Holistic evaluation of writing. In C. R. Cooper & L. Odell (Eds.), Evaluating writing: Describing, measuring, judging. Urbana, Ill.: National Council of Teachers of English, 1977.

Cooper, C. R., & Odell, L. (Eds.) Evaluating writing: Describing, measuring, and judging. Urbana, Ill.: National Council of Teachers of English, 1977.

Cowan, J. Is freedom of choice in examinations such an advantage? The Technical Journal, February, 1972.

Cox, R. C. Item selection techniques and the evaluation of instructional objectives. Journal of Educational Measurement, 1965, 2, 181–185.

Cox, R. C., & Boston, M. E. Diagnosis of pupil achievement in the Individually Prescribed Instruction Project. Pittsburgh: Learning Research and Development Center,

University of Pittsburgh, 1967. (Working Paper No. 15)

Cox, R. C., & Graham, G. T. The development of a sequentially scaled achievement test. *Journal of Educational Measurement,* 1966, *3,* 147–150.

Cox, R. C., & Vargas, J. S. *A comparison of item selection techniques for norm-referenced and criterion-referenced tests.* Paper presented at the annual meeting of the National Council on Measurement in Education, Chicago, February, 1966.

Crane, L., & Bellis, D. *Preliminary results of Illinois pilot district edits.* Unpublished memorandum to Technical Assistance Center Directors. October 16, no city, 1978.

Crehan, K.D., Candor, C.A., & Beckett, G.W. *Utilization of partial knowledge on objective exams under formula-and-number-right scoring directions.* Paper presented at the Annual Meeting of the American Educational Research Association, San Francisco, 1976.

Crehan, K. D., Koehler, R. A., & Slakter, M. J. Longitudinal studies of test-wiseness. *Journal of Educational Measurement,* 1974, *11,* 209–212.

Crites, J. O. *Career maturity inventory: Theory and research handbook (2nd ed.).* Monterey, Calif.: CTB/McGraw-Hill, 1978.

Crites, J. O. Methodological issues in the measurement of career maturity. *Measurement and Evaluation in Guidance.* 1974, *6,* 200–209.

Crites, J. O. Career maturity. *NCME Measurement in Education,* 1973, *4* (2).

Cronbach, L. J. *Educational psychology* (3rd ed.). New York: Harcourt Brace Jovanovich, 1977.

Cronbach, L. J. Equity in selection—where psychometrics and political philosophy meet. *Journal of Educational Measurement,* 1976, *13,* 31–41.

Cronbach, L. J. Five decades of public controversy over mental testing. *American Psychologist,* 1975, *30,* 1–14.

Cronbach, L. J. Comment: Dissent from Carver. *American Psychologist,* 1975, *30,* 602–603.

Cronbach, L. J. Test validation. In R. L. Thorndike (Ed.), *Educational measurement* (2nd edition). Washington, D. C.: American Council on Education, 1971.

Cronbach, L. J. *Essentials of psychological testing* (3rd ed.). New York: Harper and Row, 1970.

Cronbach, L. J. Course improvement through evaluation. *Teachers College Record,* 1963, *64,* 672–683.

Cronbach, L. J. The two disciplines of scientific psychology. *American Psychologist,* 1957, *12,* 671–684.

Cronbach, L. J. Coefficient alpha and the internal structure of tests. *Psychometrika,* 1951, *16,* 297–334.

Cronbach, L. J. Further evidence on response sets and test design. *Educational and Psychological Measurement,* 1950, *10,* 3–31.

Cronbach, L. J. Response sets and test validity. *Educational and Psychological Measurement,* 1946, *6,* 475–494.

Cronbach, L. J., & Azuma, H. Internal-consistency reliability formulas applied to randomly sampled single-factor tests: An empirical comparison. *Educational and Psychological Measurement,* 1962, *22,* 645–665.

Cronbach, L. J., & Gleser, G. C. *Psychological tests and personnel decisions* (2nd ed.). Urbana: University of Illinois Press, 1965.

Cronbach, L. J., & Gleser, G. C. Interpretation of reliability and validity coefficients: Remarks on a paper by Lord. *Journal of Educational Psychology,* 1959, *50,* 230–273.

Cronbach, L. J., Gleser, G. C., Nanda, H., & Rajaratnam, N. *The dependability of behavioral measurements: Theory of generalizability for scores and profiles.* New York: John Wiley & Sons, 1972.

Cronbach, L. J., & Meehl, P. E. Construct validity in psychological tests. *Psychological Bulletin,* 1955, *52,* 281–302.

Cronbach, L. J., & Snow, R. E. *Aptitudes and instructional methods: A handbook for research on interactions.* New York: Irvington Publishers, 1977.

Cronbach, L. J., & Warrington, W. G. Efficiency of multiple-choice tests as a function of spread of item difficulties. *Psychometrika,* 1952, *17,* 127–147.

Cross, L. H., & Frary, R. B. An empirical test of Lord's theoretical results regarding formula-scoring of multiple-choice tests. *Journal of Educational Measurement,* 1977, *14,* 313–321.

CSE Test Evaluation Project Staff. *CSE criterion-referenced test handbook.* Los Angeles: Center for the Study of Evaluation, University of California, Los Angeles, 1979.

CTB/McGraw-Hill. *California achievement tests: Class management guide.* Monterey, Ca.: Author, 1978.

CTB/McGraw-Hill. *CTBS: Comprehensive tests of basic skills* (Expanded Edition, Level 4, Form S, Complete Battery). Del Monte Research Park, Monterey, Ca.: Author, 1975.

CTB/McGraw-Hill. *Comprehensive tests of basic skills: Examiner's manual* (Expanded edition, Level 4, Form S). Monterey, Ca.: Author, 1974.

CTB/McGraw-Hill. *fCTBS: Comprehensive tests of basic skills* (Expanded Edition, Level 3, Form S, Complete Battery). Del Monte Research Park, Monterey, Ca.: Author, 1973.

Curtis, F. D. Types of thought questions in textbooks of science. *Science Education,* 1943, *27,* 60–67.

The Dallas Monster. *Time,* February 18, 1974, p. 59.

Darley, J. G., & Hagenah, T. *Vocational interest measurement.* Minneapolis: University of Minnesota Press, 1955.

Darlington, R. B. Another look at "cultural fairness." *Journal of Educational Measurement,* 1971, *8,* 71–82.

Darlington, R. B. A defense of "rational" personnel selection, and two new methods. *Journal of Educational Measurement,* 1976, *13,* 43–52.

Dave, R. H. Quoted in *Developing and writing performance objectives.* Tucson: Educational Innovators Press, 1971.

Davis, A., & Eells, K. *Davis-Eells test of general intelli-*

gence or problem-solving: Manual. New York: World Book Co., 1953.

Davis, B. G., & Trimble, C. S. Consumable booklets vs. single answer sheets with non-consumable booklets. Frankfort: Kentucky State Department of Education, 1978. (ERIC Document Reproduction Service No. ED 160-656).

Davis, F. B. Item selection techniques. In E. F. Lindquist (Ed.), Educational measurement. Washington, D. C.: American Council on Education, 1951.

Davis, F. B. A note on the correction of chance success. The Journal of Experimental Education, 1967, 3, 43–47.

Davis, F. B. Item-analysis data: Their computation, interpretation, and use in test construction. (Harvard Education Papers, No. 2) Cambridge, Mass.: Graduate School of Education, Harvard University, 1946.

Davis, F. B., & Diamond, J. J. The preparation of criterion-referenced tests. In C. W. Harris, M. C. Alkin, & W. J. Popham (Eds.), Problems in the development of criterion-referenced measurement. (CSE Monograph Series in Evaluation No. 3) Los Angeles: Center for the Study of Evaluation, University of California, 1974.

Davis, R. V. Measuring interests. In D. A. Payne (Ed.) New directions for testing and measurement: Recent developments in affective measurement (No. 7). San Francisco: Jossey-Bass, 1980.

Dearborn, W. F., & Rothney, J. W. M. Predicting the child's development. Cambridge, Mass.: Sci-Art Publishers, 1941.

Debra P. v. Turlington, 747 F. Supp. 244 (DC M.D. Fla. Tampa Div. 1979).

Deffenbacher, J. L. Relationship of worry and emotionality to performance on the Miller Analogies Test. Journal of Educational Psychology, 1977, 69, 191–195.

DeHirsch, K., Jansky, J. J., & Langford, W. D. Predicting reading failure: A preliminary study. New York: Harper, 1966.

Dember, W. N., Nairne, F., & Miller, F. J. Further validation of the Alpert-Haber Achievement Anxiety Test. Journal of Abnormal and Social Psychology, 1962, 65, 427–428.

Denmark, T. Scoring high in survival math (Teacher's edition). New York: Random House, 1979.

Dennis, W. Bibliographies of eminent scientists. Scientific Monthly, 1954, 79, 180–183.

DeVito, P. J., & Long, J. V. The effects of spring-spring vs fall-spring testing upon the evaluation of compensatory education programs. A paper presented at the annual convention of the American Educational Research Association, New York City, April, 1977.

Diamond, E. E. (Ed.). Issues of sex bias and sex fairness in career interest measurement. Washington, D. C.: Career Education Program, National Institute of Education, Department of Health, Education, and Welfare, 1975.

Diamond, J. J., & Evans, W. J. An investigation of the cog-

nitive correlates of test-wiseness. Journal of Educational Measurement, 1972, 9, 145–150.

Diederich, P. B. Measuring growth in English. Urbana, Ill.: National Council of Teachers of English, 1974.

Diederich, P. B. Definitions of ratings on the ETS Composition Scale. Princeton, N. J.: Educational Testing Service, no date (mimeo).

Diederich, P. B. Simplified measurement techniques for teachers. In E. M. Huddleston (Ed.), Yearbook of the National Council on Measurements Used in Education. New York: National Council on Measurements Used in Education, 1958.

Division of Industrial and Organizational Psychology, American Psychological Association. Principles for the validation and use of personnel selection procedures. Dayton, Ohio: Author, 1975.

Doctor, R. M., & Altman, F. Worry and emotionality as components of test anxiety: Replication and further data. Psychological Reports, 1969, 24, 563–568.

Doll, E. A. Vineland social maturity scale: Manual of directions (Rev. ed.). Minneapolis: American Guidance Service, 1965.

Doll, E. A. The measurement of social competence. Minneapolis: American Guidance Service, 1953.

Donlon, T. F., & Angoff, W. H. The Scholastic Aptitude Test. In W. H. Angoff (Ed.), The College Board Admissions Testing Program: A technical report on research and development activities relating to the Scholastic Aptitude Test and Achievement Tests. New York: College Entrance Examination Board, 1971.

Donlon, T. F., Ekstrom, R. B., Lockheed, M., & Harris, A. Performance consequences of sex bias in the content of major achievement batteries (RB-77-11). Princeton, N. J.: Educational Testing Service, 1977.

Douglas, H. R., & Tallmadge, M. How university students prepare for new type of examinations. School and Society, 1934, 39, 318–320.

Dudycha, A. L., & Dudycha, L. W. Behavioral statistics: An historical perspective. In R. E. Kirk (Ed.), Statistical issues: A reader for the behavioral sciences. Monterey, Calif.: Brooks/Cole Publishing Co., 1972.

Dunbar, D. A., Float, B., & Lyman, F. J. Report card revision steering committee final report. Mount Lebanon, Pa.: Mt. Lebanon School District, November, 1980.

Dunn, J. A. School anxiety questionnaire: Preliminary results. Proceedings of the Annual Convention of the American Psychological Association, 1970. 5, 155–156. (a)

Dunn, J. A. The school anxiety questionnaire: Theory, instrument and summary results, 1970. (ERIC Document Reproduction Service No. Ed 045–700)

Dunn, J. A. The investigation of children's school anxiety: A theory, procedure, and results, 1969. (ERIC Document Reproduction Service No. Ed 069–698)

Dunn, J. A. The theoretical rationale underlying the development of the School Anxiety Questionnaire. Psychology in the Schools, 1968, 5, 204–210.

Dunn, J. A. Stability of the factor structure of the Test Anxiety Scale for Children across age and sex groups. *Journal of Consulting Psychology*, 1965, *29*, 187.

Dunn, J. A. Factor structure of the Test Anxiety Scale for Children. *Journal of Consulting Psychology*, 1964, *28*, 92.

Dunn, L. M., & Markwardt, F. C. *Peabody individual achievement test: Manual*. Circle Pines, Minn.: American Guidance Service, Inc., 1970.

Durrell, D. Success in first grade reading. *Boston University Journal of Education*, 1958, *3*, 2–47.

Ebbinghaus, H. Ueber eine neue methode zur prüfung geistiger fähigkeiten und ihre anwendung bei schulkindern. *Zeitschrift für Psychologie und Physiologie der Sinnesorgane*, 1897, *13*, 401–457. (Reference from Buros's (1978) *The eighth mental measurement yearbook.*

Ebel, R. L. Writing the test item. In E. F. Lindquist (Ed.), *Educational measurement*. Washington, D. C.: American Council on Education, 1951.

Ebel, R. L. Content standard test scores. *Educational and Psychological Measurement*, 1962, *22*, 11–17.

Ebel, R. L. The social consequences of educational testing. *Proceedings of the 1963 Invitational Conference on Testing Problems*. Princeton, N. J.: Educational Testing Service, 1964.

Ebel, R. L. *Measuring educational achievement*. Englewood Cliffs, N. J.: Prentice-Hall, Inc., 1965.

Ebel, R. L. The relation of item discrimination to test reliability. *Journal of Educational Measurement*, 1967, *4*, 125–128.

Ebel, R. L. Blind guessing on objective achievement tests. *Journal of Educational Measurement*, 1968, *5*, 321–325.

Ebel, R. L. *Essentials of educational measurement* (2nd ed.). Englewood Cliffs, N. J.: Prentice-Hall, 1972.

Ebel, R. L. Shall we get rid of grades? *NCME Measurement in Education*, 1974, *5*, (4).

Ebel, R. L. *The uses of standardized tests*. (Fastback 93) Bloomington, Ind.: The Phi Delta Kappa Educational Foundation, 1977.

Ebel, R. L. *Essentials of educational measurement* (3rd ed.). Englewood Cliffs, N.J.: Prentice-Hall Inc., 1979.

Ebel, R. L. *Practical problems in educational measurement*. Lexington, Mass.: D. C. Heath and Co., 1980.

Ebel, R. L., & Stuit, D. B. *Technical Bulletin No. 8* Iowa City: University Examinations Service, State University of Iowa, 1954.

Education Commission of the States. *NAEP Newsletter*, Vol. 10 (No. 3), June, 1977.

Educational Policies Commission. *The purpose of education in American democracy*. Washington, D.C.: American Council on Education, 1938.

Educational Testing Service. The concern for writing. *Focus 5*. Princeton, N. J.: Author, 1978.

Educational Testing Service. *Suggested procedures for a systematic search for tests and assessment devices*. Princeton, N. J.: Author, n.d.

Educational Testing Service. Where did you ever get those questions? *ETS Developments*, 1978 *25*(3), 1–2.

Einhorn, H. J., & Bass, A. R. Methodological considerations relevant to discrimination in employment testing. *Psychological Bulletin*, 1971, *75*, 261–269.

Elley, W. B. Review of the cloze procedure as applied to reading. In O. K. Buros (Ed.), *The eighth mental measurements yearbook*. Highland Park, N. J.: The Gryphon Press, 1978.

Emery, J. R. *An evaluation of standard versus individualized hierarchies in a desensitization to reduce test anxiety*. Doctoral dissertation, Stanford University, 1966. (University microfilms No. 66–14657)

Emery, J. R., & Krumboltz, J. D. Standard versus individualized hierarchies in desensitization to reduce test anxiety. *Journal of Counseling and Psychology*, 1967, *14*, 204–209.

Epstein, J. L., & McPartland, J. M. The concept and measurement of the quality of school life. *American Educational Research Journal*, 1976, *13*, 15–30.

Equal Employment Opportunity Commission, Civil Service Commission, Department of Labor & Department of Justice. Adoption by four agencies of "Uniform guidelines on employee selection procedures." *Federal Register*, August 25, 1978, *43* (166), 38290–38315.

Equal Employment Opportunity Commission, Office of Personnel Management, Department of Justice, Department of Labor, and Department of the Treasury. Adoption of questions and answers to clarify and provide a common interpretation of the "Uniform guidelines on employee selection procedures." *Federal Register*, 1979, *44*, 11996–12009.

Essays read more than 200,000 times. *ETS Examiner*, January 12, 1978, *7* (20).

Evaluation and Assessment Services. *EAS Test-Taking Skills Kit*, (Primary, Intermediate, and Advanced Levels). Herndon, Va.: Author, 1980.

Evans, K. M. *Sociometry and education*. London: Routledge and Kegan Paul Ltd., 1962.

Family Educational Rights and Privacy Act, P.L. 93–380. (Section 513 of the General Education Provisions Act of 1970) as amended, 1974.

Fan, C. T. On the applications of the method of absolute scaling. *Psychometrika*, 1957, *22*, 175–183.

Farr, R. C., Prescott, G. A., Balow, I. H., & Hogan, T. P. *Teacher's manual for administering and interpreting: Metropolitan achievement tests*. New York: The Psychological Corporation, 1978.

Farr, R. C., Prescott, G. A., Balow, I. H., & Hogan, T. P. *Reading instructional tests (Intermediate Level, Forms JI and KI): Teacher's manual for administering and interpreting*. New York: The Psychological Corporation, 1978.

Feister, W. J., & Whitney, D. R. An interview with Dr. E. F. Lindquist. *Epsilon Bulletin*, 1968, *42*, 17–28.

Feld, S. C., & Lewis, J. Further evidence on the stability of the Test Anxiety Scale for Children. *Journal of Consulting Psychology*, 1967, *31*, 434.

Feld, S. C., & Lewis, J. The assessment of achievement anxieties in children. In C.P. Smith (Ed.), *Achievement-related motives in children*. New York: Russell Sage Foundation, 1969.

Feldt, L. S. A note on the use of confidence bands to evaluate the reliability of a difference between two scores. *American Educational Research Journal*, 1967, *4*, 139–145.

Feldt, L. S. *New uses of Iowa Tests of Educational Development as an instrument for evaluation*. A paper presented at the Sixty-first Annual Education Conference, Evaluation in the Schools, Iowa City, December, 1976.

Ferguson, R. L. *The development, implementation, and evaluation of a computer-assisted branched test for a program of individually prescribed instruction*. Unpublished doctoral dissertation, University of Pittsburgh, 1969.

Ferguson, R. L. A model for computer-assisted criterion-referenced measurement. *Education*, 1970, *81*, 25–31.

Ferguson, R. L., & Hsu, T. C. *The application of item generations for individualizing mathematics testing and instruction*. Pittsburgh: Learning Research and Development Center, University of Pittsburgh, 1971. (Publication No. 1971/14) (ED 053935)

Finley, C. J. *Errors in reporting data in Iowa*. Unpublished memorandums to Technical Assistance Center Directors. October 24, 1977.

Findley, W. G. A rationale for the evaluation of item discrimination statistics. *Educational and Psychological Measurement*, 1956, *16*, 175–180.

Findley, W. G., & Bryan, M. M. *Ability grouping: 1970 status, impact and alternatives*. Athens: Center for Educational Improvement, University of Georgia, 1971.

The fine art of essay testing: More news about December's English Composition Test-with-essay. *The College Board News*, April 1977, p. 31.

Fishbein, M., & Ajzen, I. *Belief, attitude, intention, and behavior: An introduction to theory and research*. Reading, Mass.: Addison-Wesley, 1975.

Fisher, C. W., Berliner, D. C., Filby, N. N., Marliave, R., Cahen, L. S., Dishaw, M. M., & Moore, J. E. *Teaching and learning in the elementary school: A summary of the Beginning Teacher Evaluation Study* (Technical Report VII–1). San Francisco: Far West Laboratory for Educational Research and Development, September 1978.

Fisher, C. W., Filby, N. N., Marliave, R., Cahen, L. S., Dishaw, M. M., Moore, J. E., & Berliner, D. C. *Teaching behaviors, academic learning time and student achievement: Final report of Phase III-B, Beginning Teacher Evaluation Study* (Technical Report V–1). San Francisco: Far West Laboratory for Educational Research and Development, June 1978.

Fisher, T. H. The courts and your minimum competency testing program—A guide to survival. *NCME Measurement in Education*, 1980, *11*(1).

Fiske, D. W. Can a personality construct be validated empirically? *Psychological Bulletin*, 1973, *80*, 89–92.

Fiske, E. B. A second student wins challenge on math tests. *New York Times*, 1981, *130*, (44, 987), Tuesday, March 24, B1, B15. (b)

Fiske, E. B. Youth outwits merit exams, raising 240,000 scores. *New York Times*, 1981, March 17, pp. A1, C4. (a)

Fitzpatrick, R., & Morrison, E. J. Performance and product evaluation. In R. L. Thorndike (Ed.), *Educational measurement* (2nd ed.). Washington, D. C.: American Council on Education, 1971.

Flanagan, J. C. *The Cooperative Achievement Tests: A bulletin reporting the basic principles and procedures used in the development of their system of scaled scores*. New York: American Council on Education, Cooperative Test Service, 1939.

Flaugher, R. L. The many definitions of test bias. *American Psychologist*, 1978, *33*, 671–679.

Foreman, D. I., & Kaplan, J. D. *Scoring high in math* (Teacher's edition). (Books A, B, C, & D). New York: Random House, Inc., 1978.

Foreman, D. I., & Mitchell, R. *Scoring high in language* (Teacher's edition). (Books A, B, C, & D). New York: Random House, Inc., 1980.

Forhertz, J. E. *An investigation of test anxiety as measured by the TASC in content areas ranked difficult and easy with fourth and sixth grade students*. Doctoral dissertation, Southern Illinois University, 1970. (University Microfilms No. 71–09992)

Forsyth, R. A. *Describing what Johnny can do*. (Iowa Testing Program, Occasional Paper, No. 17) Iowa City: University of Iowa, March 1976.

Freeman, D. J., Kuhs, T. M., Knappen, L. B., & Porter, A. C. A closer look at standardized tests. *Arithmetic Teacher*, 1982, *29(7)*, 50–54.

French, W. J., et al. *Behavioral goals of general education in high school*. New York: Russell Sage Foundation, 1957.

Freyd, M. The graphic rating scale. *Journal of Educational Psychology*, 1923, *14*, 83–102.

Gaffney, R. F., & Maguire, T. O. Use of optically scored test answer sheets with young children. *Journal of Educational Measurement*, 1971, *8*, 103–106..

Gagné, R. M. Learning hierarchies. *Educational Psychologist*, 1968, *6*, 1–9.

Gagné, R. M. The acquisition of knowledge. *Psychological Review*, 1962, *69*, 355–365.

Gagné, R. M. *The conditions of learning* (2nd ed.). New York: Holt, Rinehart & Winston, 1970. (a)

Gagné, R. M. Instructional variables and learning outcomes. In M. C. Wittrock and D. Wiley (Eds.) *Evaluation of instruction*. New York: Holt, Rinehart, & Winston, 1970. (b)

Gagné, R. M. The implications of instructional objectives for learning. In C. M. Lindvall (Ed.), *Defining educational objectives: A report of the Regional Commission on*

Educational Coordination and the Learning Research and Development Center. Pittsburgh: University of Pittsburgh Press, 1964.

Gagné, R. M. *The conditions of learning* (3rd ed.). New York: Holt, Rinehart, and Winston, 1977.

Gagné, R. M., & Briggs, L. J. *Principles of instructional design* (2nd. ed.). New York: Holt, Rinehart and Winston, 1979.

Gagné, R. M., Major, J. R., Garstens, H. L., & Paradise, N. E. Factors in acquiring knowledge of a mathematical task. *Psychological Monographs*, 1962, *76*, (7, Whole No. 526).

Gagné, R. M., & Paradise, N. E. Abilities and learning sets in knowledge acquisition. *Psychological Monographs*, 1961, *75* (14, Whole No. 518).

Gaines, W. G., & Jongsma, E. A. *The effect of training in test-taking skills on the achievement scores of fifth grade pupils*. Paper presented at the annual meeting of the National Council on Measurement in Education, Chicago, Ill., April, 1974.

Gallagher, J. J. Measurement issues in programs for gifted students. In W. B. Schrader (Ed.), *Measurement and education policy: Proceedings of the 1978 ETS Invitational Conference. New Directions for Testing and Measurement* (No. 1), 1979.

Ganzer, V. J. Effects of audience presence and test anxiety on learning and retention in a serial learning situation. *Journal of Personality and Social Psychology*, 1968, *8*, 194–199.

Gardner, E. F. Value of norms based on a new type of scale unit. In *Proceedings of the 1948 ETS Invitational Conference on Testing Problems*. Princeton, N. J.: Educational Testing Service, 1949.

Gaudry, E., & Spielberger, C. D. *Anxiety and educational achievement*. New York: Wiley, 1971.

General Educational Development Testing Service. *Teacher's manual for use with official GED Practice Tests*. Washington, D. C.: Author, American Council on Education, 1979.

Gephart, W. J. Editor, take a test on taking a test on grading. *Phi Delta Kappan*, 1977, *59*, 266–267.

Gibb, B. G. *Test-wiseness as a secondary cue response*. Doctoral dissertation, Stanford University, 1964. (University Microfilms No. 64–7643).

Gladstone, R. Comment: Where is fashion leading us? *American Psychologist*, 1975, *30*, 604–605.

Glaser, R. Instructional technology and the measurement of learning outcomes. *American Psychologist*, 1963, *18*, 519–521.

Glaser, R. The processes of intelligence and education. In L. B. Resnick (Ed.), *The nature of intelligence*. Hillsdale, N.J.: Lawrence Erlbaum Associates, Publishers, 1976.

Glaser, R. *Adaptive education: Individual diversity and learning*. New York: Holt, Rinehart and Winston, 1977. (a)

Glaser, R. On intelligence and aptitudes. In A. J. Nitko (Ed.), *Exploring alternatives to current standardized tests: Proceedings of the 1976 National Testing Conference*. Pittsburgh: School of Education, University of Pittsburgh, 1977. (b)

Glaser, R. *The future of testing: A research agenda for cognitive psychology and psychometrics*. Division of Evaluation and Measurement presidential address presented at the Annual Meeting of the American Psychological Association, Montreal, Canada, September, 1980.

Glaser, R. Trends and research questions in psychological research on learning and schooling. *Educational Researcher*, 1979, *8* (10), 6–13.

Glaser, R., & Cox, R. C. Criterion-referenced testing for the measurement of educational outcomes. In R. Weisgerber (Ed.), *Instructional processes and media innovation*. Chicago: Rand McNally, 1968..

Glaser, R., Damrin, D. E., & Gardner, F. M. The tab item: A technique for the measurement of proficiency in diagnostic problem solving tasks. *Educational and Psychological Measurement*, 1954, *14*, 283–293.

Glaser, R., & Klaus, D. J. Proficiency measurement: Assessing human performance. In R. Gagné (Ed.), *Psychological principles in systems development*. New York: Holt, Rinehart, & Winston, 1962.

Glaser, R., & Nitko, A. J. Measurement in learning and instruction. In R. L. Thorndike (Ed.), *Educational measurement* (2nd ed.). Washington, D.C.: American Council on Education, 1971.

Glass, G. V Standards and criteria. *Journal of Educational Measurement*, 1978, *15*, 237–261.

Goddard, H. H. Four hundred feeble-minded children classified by the Binet method. *Pedagogical Seminary*, 1910, *17*, 387–397.

Goddard, H. H. Two thousand normal children measured by the Binet measuring scale of intelligence. *Pedagogical Seminary*, 1911, *18*, 232–259.

Goddard, H. H. Editor's introduction. In A. Binet & T. Simon, *The development of intelligence in children (the Binet-Simon Scale)*. H. H. Goddard (Ed.) & E. S. Kite (Trans.) Baltimore: Williams and Wilkins Co., 1916.

Godshalk, W. E., Swineford, R., & Coffman, W. E. *The measurement of writing ability*. New York: College Entrance Examination Board, 1966.

Goldberger, M. *A taxonomy of psychomotor forms*. (Occasional Paper No. 35) East Lansing, Mich.: The Institute for Research on Teaching, Michigan State University, 1980.

Goldman, R. D., & Hewitt, B. H. An investigation of test bias for Mexican-American college students. *Journal of Educational Measurement*, 1975, *12*, 187–196.

Good, T. L., & Brophy, J. E. *Educational psychology: A realistic approach*. New York: Holt, Rinehart and Winston, 1977.

Good, T. L., & Brophy, J. E. *Looking in classrooms* (2nd ed.). New York: Harper & Row, Publishers, 1978.

Good, T. L., & Power, C. N. Designing successful classroom environments for different types of students. *Journal of Curriculum Studies*, 1976, *8*, 45–60.

Goodman, B. *Scoring high in survival writing* (Teacher's edition). New York: Random House, Inc., 1979.

Gray, W. M. A comparison of Piagetian theory and criterion-referenced measurement. *Review of Educational Research*, 1978, *48*, 223–249.

Green, B. F. Comments on tailored testing. In W. Holtzman (Ed.), *Computer-assisted instruction, testing, and guidance.* New York: Harper and Row, 1969.

Green, B. F. In defense of measurement. *American Psychologist*, 1978, *33*, 664–670.

Green, D. R. (Ed.) *The aptitude-achievement distinction: Proceedings of the Second CTB/McGraw-Hill Conference on Issues in Educational Measurement.* Monterey, Calif.: CTB/McGraw-Hill, Inc., 1974.

Greenbaum, W., Garet, M. S., & Solomon, E. R. *Measuring educational progress: A study of the National Assessment.* New York: McGraw-Hill, 1977.

Greene, H. A., Jorgensen, A. N., & Gerberich, J. R. *Measurement and evaluation in the elementary school.* New York: Longmans, Green and Co., 1942.

Greene, H. A., Jorgensen, A. N., & Gerberich, J. R. *Measurement and evaluation in the secondary school.* New York: Longmans, Green and Co., 1943.

Gronlund, N. E. *Sociometry in the classroom.* New York: Harper and Row, 1959.

Gronlund, N. E. *Preparing criterion-referenced tests for classroom instruction.* New York: The Macmillan Co., 1973.

Gronlund, N. E. *Improving marking and reporting in classroom instruction.* New York: Macmillan Publishing Co., 1974.

Gronlund, N. E. *Measurement and evaluation in teaching* (3rd ed.). New York: Macmillan Publishing Co., Inc., 1976.

Gronlund, N. E. *Measurement and evaluation in teaching* (4th ed.). New York: Macmillan Publishing Co., 1981.

Gross, A. L., & Su, W. Defining a "fair" or "unbiased" selection model: A question of utilities. *Journal of Applied Psychology*, 1975, *60*, 345–351.

Gross, L. J. *The effects of three selected aspects of test-wiseness on the standardized test performance of eighth grade students.* Paper presented at the annual meeting of the National Council on Measurement in Education, San Francisco, April, 1976. (See also the doctoral dissertation, State University of New York at Buffalo, by the same title and date. University Microfilms, 1976, No. 76-9056)

Gross, L. J. Standards and criteria: A response to Glass' criticism of the Nedelsky technique. *Journal of Educational Measurement*, 1982, *19*, 159–162.

Guerin, R. O., & Smilansky, J. The accuracy of absolute minimum acceptable performance levels for multiple-choice examinations. *Journal of Medical Education*, 1976, *51*, 416–417.

Guilford, J. P. *Psychometric methods* (1st ed.). New York: McGraw-Hill Book Co., 1936.

Guilford, J. P. *Psychometric methods* (2nd ed.). New York: McGraw-Hill Book Co., 1954.

Guilford, J. P. *Personality.* New York: McGraw-Hill, 1959.

Guion, R. M. Open a new window: Validities and values in psychological measurement. *American Psychologist*, 1974, *29*, 287–296.

Guion, R. M. Content validity—the source of my discontent. *Applied Psychological Measurement*, 1977, *1*, 1–10.

Gulliksen, H. *Theory of mental tests.* New York: John Wiley and Sons, 1950.

Guttman, L. Relation of scalogram analysis to other techniques. In S. A. Stoffer, L. Guttman, E. A. Suchman, P. F. Lazarsfeld, S. A. Star, & J. A. Clausen (Eds.), *Studies in social psychology in World War II. Measurement and prediction* (Vol. 4). Princeton, N. J.: Princeton University Press, 1950.

Haan, N. Proposed model of ego functioning: Coping and defense mechanisms in relationship to IQ change. *Psychological Monographs*, 1963, *77*, (8, Whole No. 571).

Hakstain, A. R. *The effects of type of examination anticipated on student test preparation and performance.* Paper presented at the Annual Meeting of the American Educational Research Association, Washington, D. C., February, 1969.

Haladyna, T. M. Comment: On the psychmetric-edumetric dimensions of tests. *American Psychologist*, 1975, *30*, 603–604.

Hall, L. G. *Hall occupational orientation inventory.* Bensenville, Ill.: Scholastic Testing Service, 1971.

Hambleton, R. K. On the use of cut-off scores with criterion-referenced tests in instructional settings. *Journal of Educational Measurement*, 1978, *15*, 277–290.

Hambleton, R. K. Latent trait models and their applications. In R. E. Traub (Ed.), *New Directions for Testing and Measurement: Methodological Developments*, No. 4. San Francisco: Jossey-Bass, 1979.

Hambleton, R. K. Test score validity and standard-setting methods. In R. A. Berk (Ed.), *Criterion-referenced measurement: The state of the art.* Baltimore: The Johns Hopkins University Press, 1980.

Hambleton, R. K., & Eignor, D. R. Guideline for evaluating criterion-referenced tests and test manuals. *Journal of Educational Measurement*, 1978, *15*, 321–327.

Hambleton, R. K., & Novick, M. R. Toward an integration of theory and method for criterion-referenced tests. *Journal of Educational Measurement*, 1973, *10*, 159–170.

Hambleton, R. K., Swaminathan, H., Algina, J., & Coulson, D. B. Criterion-referenced testing and measurement: A review of technical issues and developments. *Review of Educational Research*, 1978, *48*, 1–47.

Hannah, L. S., & Michaels, J. U. *A comprehensive framework for instructional objectives: A guide to systematic planning and evaluation.* Reading, Mass.: Addison-Wesley Publishing Co., 1977.

Härnquist, K. Relative changes in intelligence from 13 to 81. I. Background and methodology. II. Results. *Scandinavian Journal of Psychology*, 1968, *9*, 50–82.

Harper, F. B. W. Specific anxiety theory and the Mandler-Sarason test anxiety questionnaire. *Educational and Psychological Measurement*, 1971, *31*, 1011–1014.

Harper F. B. W. The comparative validity of the Mandler-Sarason test anxiety questionnaire and achievement anxiety test. *Educational and Psychological Measurement*, 1974, *34*, 961–966.

Harris, C. W. Problems of objectives-biased measurement. In C. W. Harris, M. C. Alkin, & W. J. Popham (Eds.), *Problems in criterion-referenced measurement*. (CSE Monograph Series in Evaluation No. 3) Los Angeles: Center for the Study of Evaluation, University of California, 1974. (a)

Harris, C. W. Some technical characteristics of mastery tests. In C. W. Harris, M. C. Alkin, & W. J. Popham (Eds.), *Problems in criterion-referenced measurement*. (CSE Monograph Series in Evaluation No. 3) Los Angeles: Center for the Study of Evaluation, University of California, 1974. (b)

Harris, D. B. *Children's drawings as measures of intellectual maturity*. New York: Harcourt Brace Jovanovich, Inc., 1963.

Harris, M. L., & Stewart, D. M. Application of classical strategies to criterion-referenced test construction: An example. In M. R. Quilling (Chair.), *Criterion-referenced tests: Sense and nonsense*. Symposium presented at the Annual Meeting of the American Educational Research Association, New York City, 1971.

Harris, W. S. Agreement among NCME members on selected issues in educational measurement. *Journal of Educational Measurement*, 1973, *10*, 63–70.

Harrow, A. J. *A taxonomy of the psychomotor domain: A guide for developing behavioral objectives*. New York: David McKay Company, 1972.

Harvard Committee on Objectives of Education in a Free Society. *General education in a free society*. Cambridge, Mass.: Harvard University Press, 1945.

Heaton, J. B. *Writing English language tests: A practical guide for teachers of English as a second or foreign language*. London: Longman Group Limited, 1975.

Henrysson, S. Gathering, analyzing, and using data on test items. In R. L. Thorndike (Ed.). *Educational measurement* (2nd ed.). Washington, D. C.: American Council on Education, 1971.

Herndon, E. B. *Your child and testing*. Washington, D. C.: The National Institute of Education, U. S. Department of Education, October 1980.

Heston, J. C. *How to take a test*. Chicago: Science Research Associates, 1953.

Hieronymus, A. N. *Uses of Iowa tests of basic skills in evaluation*. Paper presented at the 61st Annual Education Conference, Iowa City, Iowa, December 1976.

Hieronymus, A. N., & Lindquist, E. F. *Iowa tests of basic skills* (Levels Edition, Form 6). Iowa City: Riverside Publishing Co., 1971. (a)

Hieronymus, A. N., & Lindquist, E. F. *Iowa tests of basic skills: Teacher's guide to administration, interpretation, and use*. Iowa City: Riverside Publishing Co., 1971. (b)

Hieronymus, A. N., & Lindquist, E. F. *Manual for administrators, supervisors, and counselors* (Levels edition, Forms 5 and 6): *Iowa tests of basic skills*. Iowa City: Riverside Publishing Co., 1974. (a)

Hieronymus, A. N., & Lindquist, E. F. *Teacher's guide for administration, interpretation, and use (Forms 5 and 6): Iowa tests of basic skills*. Iowa City: Riverside Publishing Co., 1974. (b)

Hieronymus, A. N., Lindquist, E. F., & Hoover, H. D. *Iowa tests of basic skills: Manual for school administrators*. Iowa City: Riverside Publishing Co., 1982.

Hieronymus, A. N., & Stroud, J. B. Comparability of IQ scores on five widely used intelligence tests. *Iowa Testing Programs Research Report*. (No. 2) Iowa City: Iowa Testing Programs, University of Iowa, 1969.

Highland, R. W. *A guide for use in performance testing in Air Force technical schools* (ASPRL-TM-55-1). Lowry Air Force Base, CO: Armament Systems Performance Personnel Research Laboratory, 1955. (Cited in Fitzpatrick & Morrison, 1971).

Hildreth, G. H., Griffiths, N. L., & McGavran, M. E. *Manual of directions: Metropolitan readiness tests*. New York: Harcourt, Brace and World, Inc., 1969.

Hilliard, A. G., III. Standardized testing and African-Americans: Building assessor competence in systematic assessment. In R. W. Tyler, & S. H. White (Chairmen), *Testing, teaching and learning: Report of a conference on research on testing*. Washington, D. C.: National Institute of Education, Department of Health, Education, and Welfare, 1979.

Hills, J. R. *Exercises in classroom measurement*. Columbus, Ohio: Charles E. Merrill Publishing Co., 1976.

Hirsch, E. D., Jr. *The philosophy of composition*. Chicago: The University of Chicago Press, 1977.

Hirsch, E. D., Jr. Measuring the communicative affectiveness of prose. Preprint of an unpublished chapter, 1978.

Hively, W. *Preparation of a programmed course in algebra for secondary school teachers: A report to the National Science Foundation*. Minnesota State Department of Education, Minnesota National Laboratory, 1966.

Hively, W. Domain-referenced achievement testing. In W. Hively (Chair.). *Domain-referenced achievement testing systems*. Symposium presented at the Annual Meeting of the American Educational Research Association, Minneapolis, 1970.

Hively, W., Maxwell, G., Rabehl, G., Sension, D., & Lundin, S. *Domain-referenced curriculum evaluation: A technical handbook and a case study from the MINNEMAST Project*. (CSE Monograph Series in Evaluation. No. 1) Los Angeles: Center for the Study of Evaluation, University of California, 1973.

Hively, W., Patterson, H. L., & Page, S. A. A "universe-defined" system of arithmetic achievement tests. *Journal of Educational Measurement*, 1968, *5*, 275–290.

Hoepfner, R., Stern, C., & Nummedal, S. G. *CSE-ECRC preschool/kindergarten test evaluations*. Los Angeles: Center for the Study of Evaluation, University of California, 1971.

Hoepfner, R., and others. *CSE-RBS test evaluations: Tests of higher-order cognitive, affective, and interpersonal skills*. Los Angeles: Center for the Study of Evaluation, University of California, 1972.

Hoepfner, R., and others. *CSE secondary school test evaluations: Grades 11 and 12*. Los Angeles: Center for the Study of Evaluation, University of California, 1974.

Hoepfner, R., and others. *CSE elementary school test evaluations* (1976 Revision). Los Angeles: Center for the Study of Evaluation, University of California, 1976.

Hoepfner, R., and others. *CSE secondary school test evaluations: Grades 7 and 8*. Los Angeles: Center for the Study of Evaluation, University of California, 1976. (b)

Hoffman, B. *The tyranny of testing*. New York: Crowell-Collier and Macmillan, Inc., 1967.

Hoffman, B. Psychometric scientism. *Phi Delta Kappan*, 1967, *48*, 381–386. (a)

Hoffman, B. Multiple-choice tests. *Physics Education*, 1967, *2*, 247–251. (b)

Hogan, T. P. *Survey of school attitudes* (Intermediate Level, Forms A and B). New York: Harcourt Brace Jovanovich, 1975. (a)

Hogan, T. P. *Survey of school attitudes* (Primary Level, Forms A and B). New York: Harcourt Brace Jovanovich, 1975. (b)

Hogan, T. P. *Survey of school attitudes (Primary Level, Forms A and B): Manual for administering and interpreting*. New York: Harcourt Brace Jovanovich, 1975. (c)

Hogan, T. P., Farr, R. C., Prescott, G. A., & Balow, I. H. *Teacher's manual for administering and interpreting: Metropolitan achievement tests (Elementary Level, Forms JI and KI)*. New York: The Psychological Corporation, 1978.

Holland, J. L. *Making vocational choices: A theory of careers*. Englewood Cliffs, N. J.: Prentice-Hall, 1973.

Holland, J. L. The use and evaluation of interest inventories. In E. E. Diamond (Ed.), *Issues of sex bias and sex fairness in career interest measurement*. Washington, D. C.: Career Education Program, National Institute of Education, Department of Health, Education, and Welfare, 1975.

Holroyd, T. A., Westbrook, T., Wolf, M., & Badhorn, E. Performance, cognition, and physiological responding in test anxiety. *Journal of Abnormal Psychology*, 1978, *87*, 442–451.

Hook, J. N. *How to take examinations in college*. New York: Barnes and Noble, Inc., 1958.

Horn, J. L., & Donaldson, G. On the myth of intellectual decline in adulthood. *American Psychologist*, 1976, *31*, 701–719.

Houghton Mifflin Co. *Preliminary technical manual for the Houghton Mifflin K–12 Basic Skills Assessment*. Boston: Author, 1978.

House, E. R. *The politics of educational innovation*. Berkeley, Calif.: McCutchan, 1974.

House, E. R., Glass, G. V., McLean, L. D., & Walker, D. F. No simple answer: Critique of the "Follow Through" evaluation. Mimeographed paper, Center for Instructional Research and Curriculum Evaluation, University of Illinois at Urbana, 1972.

Hsu, T. C., & Carlson, M. *Computer-assisted testing*. Unpublished report. Pittsburgh: Learning Research and Development Center, University of Pittsburgh, 1972.

Huck, S. W., & Jacko, E. J. Effect of varying the response format of the Alpert-Haber *Achievement Anxiety Test*. *Journal of Counseling Psychology*, 1974, *21*, 159–163.

Hunt, J. McV. Utility of ordinal scales derived from Piaget's observations. In I. C. Uzgiris (Organizer), *Infant development from a Piagetian approach*. Symposium presented at the meetings of the American Psychological Association, Montreal, Canada, August, 1973.

Hunt, J. McV. Implications of sequential order and hierarchy in early psychological development. In B. X. Friedlander, G. M. Sterritt, and G. E. Kirk (Eds.), *Exceptional infant* (Vol. 3). New York: Brunner/Mazel, 1975.

Hunt, J. McV., & Kirk, G. E. Criterion-referenced tests of school readiness: A paradigm with illustrations. *Genetic Psychology Monographs*, 1974, *90*, 143–182.

Hunt, K. W. Early blooming and late blooming syntactic structures. In C. R. Cooper & L. Odell, *Evaluating writing: Describing, measuring, and judging*. Urbana, Ill.: National Council of Teachers of English, 1977.

Hunt, K. W., & O'Donnell, R. *An elementary school curriculum to develop better writing skills*. (USOE Grant no. 4-9-08-903-0042-010) Tallahassee, Fla.: Florida State University, 1979. (ERIC Document Reproduction Service No. ED 050 108).

Husek, T. R., & Alexander, S. The effectiveness of the anxiety differential in examination stress situations. *Educational and Psychological Measurement*, 1963, *23*, 309–318.

Huynh, H. Statistical consideration of mastery scores. *Psychometrika*, 1976, *41*, 65–78.

Huynh, H. Reliability of decisions in domain-referenced testing. *Journal of Educational Measurement*, 1976, *13*, 253–264.

Huynh, H. Reliability of multiple classifications. *Psychometrika*, 1978, *43*, 317–325.

Huynh, H., & Perney, J. C. Determination of mastery scores when instructional units are hierarchially related. *Educational and Psychological Measurement*, 1979, *39*, 317–325.

Huynh, H., & Sanders, J. C. (Eds.) *Solutions for some technical problems in domain-referenced mastery testing*.

(Final Report) Columbia: Department of Educational Research and Psychology, College of Education, University of South Carolina, 1980.

Huynh, H., Saunders, J. C., & Garcia-Quintana, R. *Technical and practical considerations in setting standards.* Paper presented at the Annual meeting of the American Educational Research Association, Los Angeles, April 1981.

Iwanicki, E. F. A new generation of standardized achievement test batteries: A profile of their major features. *Journal of Educational Measurement*, 1980, *17*, 155–162.

Jacko, E. J., & Huck, S. W. *The effect of varying the response format of the Alpert-Haber Achievement Anxiety Test.* 1974. (ERIC Document Reproduction Service No. ED093992)

Jackson, D. N. Multimethod factor analysis in the evaluation of convergent and discriminant validity. *Psychological Bulletin*, 1969, *72*, 30–49.

Jackson, D. N. Multimethod factor analysis: A reformulation. *Multivariate Behavioral Research*, 1975, *10*, 259–275.

Jackson, D. N. Distinguishing trait and method variance in multitrait-multimethod matrices: A reply to Golding. *Multivariate Behavioral Research*, 1977, *12*, 99–110.

Jackson, P., Silberman, M., & Wolfson, B. Signs of personal involvement in teachers' descriptions of their students. *Journal of Educational Psychology*, 1969, *60*, 22–27.

Jaeger, R. M. The National Test-Equating Study in Reading: Pre-Anchor Test Study. *NCME Measurement in Education*, 1973, *4*, 1–8.

Jenkins, J. R., Bansell, R. B., & Jenkins, L. M. Comparisons of letter name and letter sound training as transfer variables. *American Educational Research Journal*, 1972, *9*, 75–86.

Jenkins, J. R., & Deno, S. J. Assessing knowledge of concepts and principles. *Journal of Educational Measurement*, 1971, *8*, 95–101.

Jensen, A. R. *Bias in mental testing.* New York: The Free Press, 1980.

Joffe, I. L. *Understanding maps, charts, graphs, and tables.* Belmont, Calif.: Wadsworth Publishing Co., Inc., 1971.

Johns, J. L., Garton, S., Schoenfelder, P., & Skriba, P. *Assessing reading behavior: Informal reading inventories (An annotated bibliography).* Newark, Del.: International Reading Association, 1977.

Johnson, A. P. Notes on a suggested index of item validity: The U-L index. *Journal of Educational Psychology*, 1951, *42*, 499–504.

Johnson, H. M. Some fallacies underlying the use of psychological tests. *Psychological Review*, 1928, *35*, 328–337. (Reprinted in T. Engen & N. Levy (Eds.), *Selected readings in the history of mental measurement.* Providence, R. I.: Brown University, 1955.)

Johnson, H. M. Pseudo-mathematics in the mental and social sciences. *American Journal of Psychology*, 1936, *48*, 342–351. (Reprinted in T. Engen, & N. Levy (Eds.), *Selected readings in the history of mental measurement.* Providence, R.I.: Brown University, 1955.)

Johnson, O. G. *Tests and measurements in child development: Handbook II.* San Francisco: Jossey-Bass, 1976.

Johnson, O. G., & Bommarito, J. W. *Tests and measurements in child development: A handbook.* San Francisco: Jossey-Bass, 1971.

Johnson, R. T., & Thomas, W. P. *User experiences in implementing the RMC Title I evaluation models.* Paper presented at the annual meeting of the American Educational Research Association, San Francisco, April, 1979.

Johnston, K. L. An English version of Binet's tests for the measurement of intelligence. *Training College Record*, November, 1910.

Jones, G. B., Trimble, M. M., & Altmann, H. A. Improving college students' performance through group counseling. *Journal of College Student Personnel*, 1970, *11*, 373–382.

Jones, L. V. The nature of measurement. In R. L. Thorndike (Ed.), *Educational and psychological measurement* (2nd ed.). Washington, D. C.: American Council in Education, 1971.

Kagen, J., & Freeman, M. Relation of childhood intelligence, maternal behaviors, and social class to behavior during adolescence. *Child Development*, 1963, *34*, 899–911.

Kagen, J., Sontag, L. W., Baker, C. T., & Nelson, V. L. Personality and IQ change. *Journal of Abnormal and Social Psychology*, 1958, *56*, 261–266.

Kamin, L. *The science and politics of IQ.* Potomac, Md.: Erlbaum Associates, 1977.

Kansas City, Kansas Public Schools. *Progress Report: Grades 4, 5, 6.* Kansas City, Kans.: Author, n.d.

Karier, C. J. Testing for order and control in the corporate liberal state. In C. J. Karier, P. Violas, & J. Spring. *Roots of crisis: American education in the twentieth century.* Chicago: Rand McNally College Publishing Co., 1973.

Karier, C. J., Violas, P., & Spring, J. Introduction. In C. J. Karier, P. Violas, & J. Spring, *Roots of crisis: American education in the twentieth century.* Chicago: Rand McNally, 1973.

Karlsen, B., Madden, R., & Gardner, E. F. *Stanford Diagnostic Reading Test, Red Level: Manual for administering and interpreting.* New York: Harcourt Brace Jovanovich, Inc., 1976.

Katz, L. G., & Ward, E. H. *Ethical behavior in early childhood education.* Washington, D. C.: National Association for the Education of Young Children, 1978.

Kaufman, A. S. *Intelligent testing with the WISC-R.* New York: John Wiley and Sons, 1979.

Kelly, T. L. *Interpretation of educational measurements.* New York: World Book Co., 1927.

Kelly, T. L. The selection of upper and lower groups for the validation of test items. *Journal of Educational Psychology*, 1939, *30*, 17–24.

Kibler, R. J., Cegala, D. J., Watson, K. W., Barker, L. L., & Miles, D. T. *Objectives for instruction and evaluation* (2nd ed.). Boston: Allyn and Bacon, Inc., 1981.

King, D. J. Comment: Control groups. *American Psychologist*, 1975, *30*, 602.

Kirkland, M. C. The effects of tests on students and schools. *Review of Educational Research*, 1971, *41*, 303–350.

Klaus, C. H., Lloyd-Jones, R., Brown, R., Littlefair, W., Mullis, I., Miller, D., & Verity, D. *Composing·childhood experience: An approach to writing and learning in the elementary grades* (Experimental version). St. Louis: CEMREL, Inc., 1979.

Kleinman, H. P., & Lukoff, F. I. Ethnic differences in factors related to drug use. *Journal of Health and Social Behavior*, 1978, *19*, 190–199.

Klopfer, L. E. *An operational definition of "understand."* Unpublished manuscript, Learning Research and Development Center, University of Pittsburgh, 1962.

Kohlberg, L. Stage and sequence: The cognitive-developmental approach to socialization. In D. A. Goslin (Ed.), *Handbook of socialization theory and research*. Chicago: Rand McNally, 1969.

Koslin, B. L., Koslin, S., Zeno, S., & Wainert, H. *The validity and reliability of the Degrees of Reading Power Test*. Elmsford, N. Y.: Touchstone Applied Science Associates, 1977.

Kowal, B. *Location in a curriculum hierarchy and performance on three standardized achievement tests*. Unpublished master's thesis, University of Pittsburgh, 1975.

Krathwohl, D. R. The *Taxonomy of Educational Objectives*—Its use in curriculum building. In C. M. Lindvall (Ed.), *Defining educational objectives: A report of the Regional Commission on Educational Coordination and the Learning Research and Development Center*. Pittsburgh, Pa.: The University of Pittsburgh Press, 1964.

Krathwohl, D. R., Bloom, B. S., & Masia, B. B. *Taxonomy of educational objectives: The classification of educational goals. Handbook II: Affective domain*. New York: David McKay Co., 1964.

Kravitz, A., & Dramer, D. *Scoring high in survival reading* (Teacher's edition). New York: Random House, Inc., 1977.

Kryspin, W. J., & Feldhusen, J. F. *Developing classroom tests*. Minneapolis: Burgess Publishing Co., 1974.

Kryspin, W. J., & Feldhusen, J. F. *Analyzing verbal classroom interaction*. Minneapolis: Burgess Publishing Co., 1974.

Kuder, G. F. *Kuder occupational interest survey* (Form DD). Chicago: Science Research Associates, 1976.

Kuder, G. F., & Richardson, M. W. The theory of the estimation of test reliability. *Psychometrika*, 1937, *2*, 151–160.

Kuhlman, F. A revision of the Binet-Simon system for measuring the intelligence of children. (Monograph Supplement) *Journal of Psycho-Asthenics*, 1912, *1*.

Kulhavy, R. W. Feedback in written instruction. *Review of Educational Research*, 1977, *47*, 211–232.

Kunder, L. H., & Porwoll, P. J. *Reporting pupil progress: Policies, procedures, and systems*. (ERS Report) Arlington Va.: Educational Research Services, Inc., 1977.

Kwansa, K. B. *Investigation of the relative content validity of norm-referenced and domain-referenced arithmetic tests*. Doctoral dissertation, University of Pittsburgh, 1972. (*Dissertation Abstracts International*, 1973, *33*, 3959–3960A).

Kwansa, K. B. Content validity and reliability of domain-referenced tests, *African Journal of Educational Research*, 1974, *1*, 73–79.

Landau, D., & Lazarsfeld, P. F. Quetelet, Adolphe. *International encyclopedia of the social sciences*, 1968, *13*, 247–257.

Langer, G., Wark, D., & Johnson, S. Test-wiseness in objective tests. In P. L. Nacke (Ed.), *Diversity in mature reading: Theory and research* (Vol. 1). *Twenty-second yearbook of the National Reading Conference*. Milwaukee: National Reading Conference, 1973.

Larsen, E. P. *Opening institutional ledger books—a challenge to educational leadership*. (TM Report 28) Princeton, N. J.: ERIC Clearinghouse on Tests, Measurements, and Evaluation, Educational Testing Service, 1974.

Lavit, R. J. A validation study of the test anxiety questionnaire with college students. *Psychology*, 1971, *8*, 2–3.

Lawshe, C. H., & Balma, M. J. *Principles of personnel testing* (2nd ed.). New York: McGraw Hill, 1966.

Lazarus, R. S. *Psychological stress and the coping process*. New York: McGraw-Hill, 1966.

Lazovik, G. F. *University of Pittsburgh Student Opinion of Teaching Questionnaire*. Pittsburgh: Office for the Evaluation of Teaching, University of Pittsburgh, 1978.

Learning Research and Development Center & Research for Better Schools, Inc. *IPI Mathematics continuum*. New York: Meredith Corporation, 1972.

Lennon, R. T. Assumptions underlying the use of content validity. *Educational and Psychological Measurement*, 1956, *16*, 294–304.

Leon County Public Schools. *Growth Report: Kindergarten*. Tallahassee, Fla.: Author, n. d.

Levine, M. The academic achievement test: Its historical context and social functions. *American Psychologist*, 1976, *31*, 228–238.

Liebert, R. M., & Morris, L. W. Cognitive and emotional components of test anxiety: A distinction and some initial data. *Psychological Reports*, 1967, *20*, 975–978.

Likert, R. A technique for the measurement of attitudes. *Archives of Psychology*, 1932, No. 140.

Lindquist, E. F. The theory of test construction. In H. E. Hawkes, E. F. Lindquist, & C. R. Mann (Eds.), *The construction and use of achievement examinations*. Boston: Houghton Mifflin Company, 1936. (a)

Lindquist, E. F. The construction of tests. In H. E. Hawkes, E. F. Lindquist, & C. R. Mann (Eds.), *The construction* and use of achievement examinations: A manual for secondary school teachers. Boston: Houghton-Mifflin Company, 1936. (b)

Lindquist, E. F. Preliminary considerations in objective test construction. In E. F. Lindquist (Ed.). *Educational measurement*. Washington, D. C.: American Council on Education, 1951.

Lindquist, E. F., Feldt, L. S., Forsyth, R. A., & Neckere, E. D. *Iowa tests of educational development grades 9–12, form X5*. Chicago: Science Research Associates, 1970.

Lindquist, E. F., & Hieronymus, A. N. *Teacher's manual: Iowa tests of basic skills*. Boston: Houghton Mifflin, 1964.

Lindvall, C. M. *Testing and evaluation: An introduction*. New York: Harcourt, Brace and World, Inc., 1961.

Lindvall, C. M. Introduction. In C. M. Lindvall (Ed.). *Defining educational objectives: A report of the Regional Commission on Educational Coordination and the Learning Research and Development Center*. Pittsburgh: University of Pittsburgh Press, 1964.

Lindvall, C. M. *Measuring pupil achievement and aptitude*. New York: Harcourt, Brace and World, 1967.

Lindvall, C. M. Criteria for stating IPI objectives. In D. T. Gow (Ed.), *Design and development of curricular materials: Instructional design articles*. (Vol. 2) Pittsburgh: University Center for International Studies, University of Pittsburgh, 1976.

Lindvall, C. M. *A perspective on the development of a specialization in educational evaluation within the Division of Educational Studies* (Working Paper No. 34). Pittsburgh: Programs in Educational Research Methodology, School of Education, University of Pittsburgh, 1977.

Lindvall, C. M., & Cox, R. C. *Evaluation as a tool in curriculum development: The IPI evaluation program*. (AERA Monograph Series on Curriculum Evaluation, No. 5) Chicago: Rand McNally, 1970.

Lindvall, C. M., & Nitko, A. J. *Measuring pupil achievement and aptitude* (2nd ed.). New York: Harcourt, Brace, Jovanovich, Inc., 1975.

Lindzey, G., & Byrne, D. Measurement of social choice and interpersonal attractiveness. In G. Lindzey & E. Aronson (Eds.). *Handbook of social psychology* (Vol. 2). Reading, Mass.: Addison-Wesley Publishing Co., Inc., 1968.

Linn, R. L. Fair test use in selection. *Review of Educational Research*, 1973, 43, 139–161.

Linn, R. L. Test design and analysis for measurements of educational achievement. In W. D. Schrader (Ed.), *Measuring achievement: Progress over a decade. Proceedings of the 1979 ETS Invitational Conference. New Directions for Testing and Measurement* (No. 5), 1980.

Lloyd-Jones, R. Primary trait scoring. In C. R. Cooper & L. Odell (Eds.), *Evaluating writing: Describing, measuring, and judging*. Urbana, IL: National Council of Teachers of English, 1977.

Loevinger, J. Construct validity of the Sentence Completion Test of Ego Development. *Applied Psychological Measurement*, 1979, 3, 281–311.

Loevinger, J., Wessler, R., & Redmore, C. *Measuring ego development. Vol. 1: Construction and use of a sentence completion test. Vol. 2: Scoring manual for women and girls*. San Francisco: Jossey-Bass, 1970.

Lohnes, P. R., & Cooley, W. W. *Introduction to statistical procedures: With computer exercises*. New York: John Wiley and Sons, 1968.

Lomax, R. G. *The multitrait-multimethod matrix: A comparison of alternative analytic procedures*. Unpublished master's thesis. Pittsburgh: University of Pittsburgh, 1978.

Lomax, R. G., & Algina, J. Comparison of two procedures for analyzing multitrait-multimethod matrices. *Journal of Educational Measurement*, 1979, 16, 177–186.

London, M., & Bray, D. W. Ethical issues in testing and evaluation for personnel decisions. *American Psychologist*, 1980, 35, 890–901.

Lord, F. M. The relationship of the reliability of multiple-choice tests to the distribution of item difficulties. *Psychometrika*, 1952, 17, 181–194.

Lord, F. M. The relation of test scores to the trait underlying the test. *Educational and Psychological Measurement*, 1953, 13, 517–549.

Lord, F. M. Formula scoring and number-right scoring. *Journal of Educational Measurement*, 1975, 12, 7–11.

Lord, F. M. A theory of test scores. *Psychometric Monographs*, 1952 (Number 7).

Lord, F. M. A study of item bias using item characteristic curve theory. In Y. H. Poortinga (Ed.), *Basic problems in cross-cultural psychology*. Amsterdam: Swets and Vitlinger, 1977.

Lord, F. M. *Applications of item response theory to practical testing problems*. Hillsdale, N. J.: Lawrence Earlbaum Associates, 1980.

Lord, F. M., & Novick, M. R. *Statistical theories of mental test scores*. Reading, Mass.: Addison-Wesley Publishing Co., 1968.

Loughlin, L. J., O'Connor, H. A., Powell, M., & Parsley, K. M., Jr. An investigation of sex differences by intelligence, subject-matter areas, grade, and achievement levels on three anxiety scales. *Journal of Genetic Psychology*, 1965, 106, 207–215.

Lyman, H. B. *Test scores and what they mean* (3rd ed.). Englewood Cliffs, N. J.: Prentice-Hall, Inc., 1978.

Madden, R., Gardner, E. F., Rudman, H. C., Karlsen, B., & Merwin, J. C. *Stanford achievement test: Intermediate level II complete battery test booklet* (Form A). New York: Harcourt Brace Jovanovich, Inc., 1972.

Madden, R., Gardner, E. F., Rudman, H. C., Karlsen, B., & Merwin, J. C. *Stanford achievement test, form A: Norms booklet* (Primary Level II through Advanced Level). New York: Harcourt Brace Jovanovich, 1973.

Mager, R. F. *Preparing instructional objectives*. Palo Alto, Calif.: Fearon Publishers, Inc., 1962.

Mager, R. F. *Measuring instructional intent: Or got a match?* Belmont, Calif.: Lear Siegler, Inc./Fearon Publishers, 1973.

Mager, R. F. *Preparing instructional objectives* (2nd ed.). Palo Alto, Calif.: Fearon, 1976.

Mandler, G., & Cowen, J. E. Test anxiety questionnaires. *Journal of Consulting Psychology*, 1958, *22*, 228–229.

Mandler, G., & Sarason, S. B. A study of anxiety and learning. *Journal of Abnormal and Social Psychology*, 1952, *47*, 166–173.

Mandler, G., & Watson, D. L. Anxiety and the interruption of behavior. In C. D. Spielberger (Ed.), *Anxiety and behavior*. New York: Academic Press, 1966.

Marland, S. P. *Education of the gifted and talented*. Report to the Subcommittee on Education, Committee on Labor and Public Welfare, U. S. Senate, Washington, D. C., 1972.

Marlett, N. J., & Watson, D. L. Test anxiety and immediate or delayed feedback in a test-like avoidance task. *Journal of Personality and Social Psychology*, 1968, *8*, 200–203.

Marshall, J. C. Composition errors and essay examinations grades reexamined. *American Educational Research Journal*, 1967, *4*, 375–385.

Marshall, J. C., & Powers, J. M. Writing neatness, composition errors, and essay grades. *Journal of Educational Measurement*, 1969, *6*, 97–101.

Masters, J. R. *Reliability as a function of the number of categories of a summated rating scale*. Doctoral dissertation, University of Pittsburgh, 1972.

Masters, J. R. The relationship between number of response categories and reliability of Likert-type questionnaires. *Journal of Educational Measurement*, 1974, *11*, 49–53.

Mayo, S. T. *Pre-service preparation of teachers in educational measurement: Final report*. (Project No. 5-0807, Contract No. 0E4-10-011) Chicago: Loyola University, December, 1967.

McCall, R. B., Appelbaum, M. I., & Hogarty, P. S. Developmental change in mental performance. *Monographs of the Society for Research in Child Development*, 1973, *38* (3, Serial No. 150).

McCall, W. A. *How to measure in education*. New York: Macmillan, 1922.

McCall, W. A., & Bixler, H. H. *How to classify pupils*. New York: Bureau of Publications, Teachers College, Columbia University, 1928.

McCormick, R. A. Proxy consent in the experimental situation. *Perspectives in Biology and Medicine*, 1974, *18*, 2–20.

McGregor, D. M. Scientific measurement and psychology. *Psychological Review*, 1935, *42*, 246–266. (Reprinted in T. Engen & N. Levy (Eds.), *Selected readings in the history of mental measurement*. Providence, R. I.: Brown University, 1955.)

McIver, I. Facing reality . . . racism and the psychological testing movement. *The Measuring Cup*, 1979, *1*(2), 6–7, 10.

McNemar, Q. *Psychological statistics* (4th ed.). New York: John Wiley and Sons, 1969.

Meehl. P. E. *Clinical versus statistical prediction*. Minneapolis: University of Minnesota Press, 1954.

Mehrens, W. A., & Lehmann, I. J. *Measurement and evaluation in education and psychology*. New York: Holt, Rinehart and Winston, Inc., 1973 and 1978.

Mercer, J. R. *Labeling the mentally retarded*. Berkeley, Calif.: University of California Press, 1973.

Mercer, J. R. *SOMPA technical manual*. New York: The Psychological Corporation, 1979.

Mercer, J. R., & Lewis, J. F. *Parent interview manual: System of multicultural pluralistic assessment*. New York: The Psychological Corporation, 1977.

Mercer, J. R., & Lewis, J. F. *Student assessment manual: System of multicultural pluralistic assessment*. New York: The Psychological Corporation, 1978.

Merwin, J. C., & Womer, F. B. Evaluation in assessing the progress of education to provide bases of public understanding and public policy. In R. W. Tyler (Ed.), *Sixty-eighth yearbook of the National Society for the Study of Education. PART II. Educational evaluation: New roles, new means*. Chicago: University of Chicago Press, 1969.

Meskauskas, J. A. Evaluation models for criterion-referenced testing: Views regarding mastery and standard-setting. *Review of Educational Research*, 1976, *46*, 133–158.

Messick, S. (Ed.). *Individuality in Learning: Implications of cognitive styles and creativity for human development*. San Francisco: Jossey-Bass, 1976.

Messick, S. Potential uses of noncognitive measurement in education. *Journal of Educational Psychology*, 1979, *71*, 281–289.

Messick, S. *Test validity and the ethics of assessment*. (RR-79-10) Princeton, N.J.: Educational Testing Service, 1979.

Messick, S. Constructs and their vicissitudes in educational and psychological measurement. *Psychological Bulletin*, 1981, *89*, 575–588. (b)

Messick, S. Evidence and ethics in the evaluation of tests. *Educational Researcher*, 1981, *10*(9), 9–20. (b)

Metfessel, N. S., & Sax, G. Systematic biases in the keying of correct responses on certain standard tests. *Educational and Psychological Measurement*, 1958, *18*, 787–790.

Meyer, G. The choice of questions on essay examinations. *Journal of Educational Psychology*, 1939, *30*, 161–171.

Michael, W. B., Hertzka, A. F., & Perry, N. C. Errors in estimates of item difficulty obtained from use of extreme groups on a criterion variable. *Educational and Psychological Measurement*, 1953, *13*, 601–606.

Milholland, J. E. Note on the further validation of the Alpert-Haber Achievement Anxiety Test. *Journal of Abnormal and Social Psychology*, 1964, *69*, 236.

Miller, R. I. The assessment of college performance: A

handbook of techniques and measures for institutional self-evaluation. San Francisco: Jossey-Bass, 1979.

Millman, J. Multiple-choice test item construction rules. Ithaca, N. Y.: Cornell University Press, 1961 (mimeographed). (Cited by J. C. Stanley & K. D. Hopkins, Educational and psychological measurement and evaluation (5th ed.). Englewood Cliffs, N. J.: Prentice-Hall, Inc., 1972.)

Millman, J. Test-wiseness in taking objective achievement and aptitude examinations: Final Report. Princeton, N. J.: College Entrance Examination Board, Educational Testing Service, 1966.

Millman, J. Reporting student progress: A case for a criterion-referenced marking system. Phi Delta Kappan, 1970, 52, 226–230.

Millman, J. Passing scores and test lengths of domain-referenced measures. Review of Educational Research, 1973, 43, 205–216.

Millman, J. Sampling plans for domain-referenced tests. In W. Hively (Ed.), Domain-referenced testing. Englewood Cliffs, N. J.: Educational Technology Publications, 1974.

Millman, J. Reliability and validity of criterion-referenced test scores. In R. E. Traub (Ed.), New Directions for Testing and Measurement: Methodological Developments, No. 4. San Francisco: Jossey-Bass, 1979.

Millman, J., Bishop, C. H., & Ebel, R. L. An analysis of test-wiseness. Educational and Psychological Measurement, 1965, 25, 707–726.

Millman, J., & Pauk, W. How to take tests. New York: McGraw-Hill Book Co., 1969.

"Mini-Survey": School district now has fast-poll system. The Mt. Lebanon View, 1975, November, 1, 2.

Mitchell, J. V., Jr., Reynolds, C. R., & Elliot, S. N. Test news from the Buros Institute. NCME Measurement News, 1980, 23–24, 6, 9, 16.

Monroe, W. S. An introduction to the theory of educational measurements. Boston: Houghton Mifflin Co., 1923.

Moore, J. C. Test-wiseness and analogy test performance. Measurement and Evaluation in Guidance, 1971, 3, 198–202.

Moore, J. C., Schutz, R. E., & Baker, R. L. The application of a self-instructional technique to develop a test-taking strategy. American Educational Research Journal, 1966, 3, 13–17.

Moore, M. R. A proposed taxonomy of the perceptual domain and some suggested applications. (TDR-67-3) Princeton, N. J.: Educational Testing Service, 1967. (ERIC Document Reproduction Service No. ED 016 266).

Monroe, W. S., & Carter, R. E. The use of different types of thought questions in secondary schools and their relative difficulty for students. University of Illinois Bulletin, 1923, 20 (34, Bulletin No. 14).

Morris, L. W., & Liebert, R. M. Effects of anxiety on timed and untimed intelligence tests: Another look. Journal of Consulting and Clinical Psychology, 1969, 33, 240–244.

Morris, L. W., & Liebert, R. M. Relationship of cognitive and emotional components of test anxiety to physiological arousal and academic performance. Journal of Consulting and Clinical Psychology, 1970, 35, 332–337.

Moss, P. A., Cole, N. S., & Trent, E. R. A comparison of multiple-choice answer formats in early elementary grades. A paper presented at the Annual Meeting of the Northeast Educational Research Association, October 24–26, 1979.

Moreno, J. L. Who shall survive? A new approach to the problem of human relations. Washington, D. C.: Nervous and Mental Disease Publishing Co., 1934.

Moreno, J. L. The three branches of sociometry. Sociometry Monographs (No. 21). New York: Beacon House, 1949.

Moyer, K. L. Observed school district errors in the Title I evaluation and reporting system. Harrisburg, Pa.: Division of Research, Pennsylvania Department of Education, April 1979.

Muller, D., Calhoun, E., & Orling, R. Test reliability as a function of answer sheet mode. Journal of Educational Measurement, 1972, 9, 321–324.

Murphy, L. B. Methods for the study of personality in young children. New York: Basic Books, 1956.

National Council on Measurement in Education. On Bias in selection. Journal of Educational Measurement, 1976, 13(1), whole.

Neale, J. M., & Katahn, M. Anxiety choice and stimulus uncertainty. Journal of Personality, 1968, 36, 235–245.

Nedelsky, L. Absolute grading standards for objective tests. Educational and Psychological Measurement, 1954, 14, 3–19.

Nesbit, M. Y. The CHILD Program: Computer help in learning diagnosis of arithmetic scores. (Curriculum Bulletin 7-E-B.) Miami, Fla.: Dade County Board of Public Instruction, 1966.

New graphs available to illustrate college management data. The College Board News, February 1979, p. 4.

Nighswander, J. K. A validity study of self-report and physiological measures of test anxiety, 1970. (ERIC Document Reproduction Service No. 039 564).

Nighswander, J. K., & Beggs, D. L. A study of the relationships between test order, physiological arousal, and intelligence and achievement test performance, 1971. (ERIC Document Reproduction Service No. 046983).

Nilsson, I. & Wedman, I. On test-wiseness and some related constructs. (Educational Reports Umea, No. 7) Sweden: Umea University and Umea School of Education, 1974.

Nitko, A. J. A description of the Individually Prescribed Instruction Project. In A. N. Hofstetter (Ed.), Leadership for curriculum development. Vol. 1 (1) (Seminar and Conference Reports and Proceedings Series). Nitro: West Virginia University, 1969.

Nitko, A. J. Criterion-referenced testing in the context of instruction. In Testing in Turmoil: A Conference on Problems and Issues in Educational Measurement. Greenwich, Conn.: Educational Records Bureau, 1970.

Nitko, A. J. Problems in the development of criterion-referenced tests: The IPI Pittsburgh experience. In C. W. Harris, M. C. Alkin, & W. J. Popham (Eds.), *Problems in criterion-referenced measurement.* (CSE Monograph Series in Evaluation No. 3) Los Angeles: Center for the Study of Evaluation, University of California, 1974.

Nitko, A. J. Criterion-referencing schemes. In S. T. Mayo (Ed.) *New Directions for Testing and Measurement: Interpreting Test Performance.* (No. 6) San Francisco: Jossey-Bass, 1980. (a)

Nitko, A. J. Distinguishing the many varieties of criterion-referenced tests. *Review of Educational Research*, 1980, *50*, 461–485.(b)

Nitko, A. J., & Hsu, T-C. Using domain referenced tests for student placement, diagnosis, and attainment in a system of adaptive, individualized instruction. In W. Hively (Ed.), *Domain-referenced testing.* Englewood Cliffs, N. J.: Educational Technology Publications, 1974.

Noll, V. H., Scannell, D. P., & Craig, R. C. *Introduction to educational measurement* (4th ed.). Boston: Houghton-Mifflin Co., 1979.

Northway, M. L. *A primer of sociometry* (2nd ed). Toronto: University of Toronto Press, 1967.

Novick, M. R., & Lewis, C. Prescribing test length for criterion-referenced measurement. In C. W. Harris, M. C. Alkin, & W. J. Popham (Eds.), *Problems in criterion-referenced measurement.* Los Angeles: Center for the Study of Evaluation, University of California, Los Angeles, 1974.

Novick, M. R., & Petersen, N. S. Towards equalizing educational and employment opportunity. *Journal of Educational Measurement*, 1976, *13*, 77–88.

Novick, M. R., & Thayer, D. T. *An investigation of the accuracy of the Pearson selection formulas* (ETS RM-69-22). Princeton, N. J.: Educational Testing Service, 1969.

Nunnally, J. C. *Psychometric theory.* New York: McGraw-Hill, 1967.

Nunnally, J. C. *Psychometric theory* (2nd ed.). New York: McGraw-Hill Book Co., 1978.

Nurss, J. R., & McGauvran, M. E. *Metropolitan readiness tests* (Levels I and II; Forms P and Q). New York: Harcourt Brace Jovanovich, Inc., 1976.

Oakland, T. The effects of test-wiseness materials on standardized test performance of preschool disadvantaged children. *Journal of School Psychology*, 1972, *10*, 355–360.

Oakland, T. *Pluralistic norms and estimated learning potential.* Paper presented at the annual meeting of the American Psychological Association, San Francisco: 1977.

Odell, C. W. *Traditional examinations and new-type tests.* New York: The Century Co., 1928.

Odell, C. W. *Educational measurements in high school.* New York: The Century Co., 1930.

O'Donnell, T. J. Informed consent. *Journal of the American Medical Association*, 1974, *227*, 73.

Office of Strategic Services Assessment Staff. *Assessment of men.* New York: Rinehart, 1948.

Ohnmacht, D. D. *The effects of letter-knowledge on achievement in reading in the first grade.* Paper presented at the American Educational Research Association, Los Angeles, 1969.

Oller, J. W. Jr. *Language tests at school: A pragmatic approach.* London: Longman Group Limited, 1979.

Omvig, C. P. Effects of guidance on the results of standardized achievement testing. *Measurement and Evaluation in Guidance*, 1971, *4*, 47–52.

Osburn, H. G. Item sampling for achievement testing. *Educational and Psychological Measurement*, 1968, *28*, 95–104.

Osgood, C. E., Suci, G. J., & Tannenbaum, P. H. *The measurement of meaning.* Urbana, Ill.: University of Illinois Press, 1957.

Osipow, S. H. & Kreinbring, I. Temporal stability of an inventory to measure test anxiety. *Journal of Counseling Psychology*, 1971, *18*, 152–154.

Osterhouse, R. A. *A comparison of desensitization and study skills training for the treatment of two kinds of test-anxious students.* Doctoral dissertation, Ohio State University. Columbus: 1969. (University microfilms No. 70-14081)

Osterhouse, R. A. Desensitization and study-skills training as treatment for two types of test-anxious students. *Journal of Counseling Psychology*, 1972, *19*, 301–307.

Otis, A. S., & Lennon, R. T. *Otis-Lennon mental ability test: Technical handbook.* New York: Harcourt, Brace and World, Inc., 1969.

Otis, A. S., & Lennon, R. T. *Otis-Lennon School Ability Test* (various forms). New York: The Psychological Corporation, 1977. (c)

Otis, A. S., & Lennon, R. T. *Otis-Lennon school ability test: Manual for administering and interpreting.* New York: Harcourt Brace Jovanovich, 1979.

Pearson, K. Historical note on the origin of the normal curve of errors. *Biometrika*, 1924, *16*, 402–404.

Perrone, V. *The abuses of standardized testing.* (Fastback 92) Bloomington, Ind.: The Phi Delta Kappa Educational Foundation, 1977.

Petersen, N. S. *An expected utility model for "optimal" selection.* (Iowa Testing Programs Occasional Paper No. 10), Iowa City: University of Iowa, 1975.

Petersen, N. S., & Novick, M. R. An evaluation of some models for a culture-fair selection. *Journal of Educational Measurement*, 1976, *13*, 3–29.

Pettit, L. *How to study and take exams.* New York: John F. Rider Publishers, Inc., 1960.

Petty, W. T., & Finn, P. J. Classroom teacher's reports on teaching written composition. In S. M. Haley-James (Ed.), *Perspectives on writing in grades 1–8.* Urbana, Ill.: National Council of Teachers of English, 1981.

Pfanzagl, J. *Theory of measurement.* New York: Wiley, 1968.

Phillips, B. N., & Weathers, G. Analysis of errors made in scoring standardized tests. *Educational and Psychological Measurement*, 1958, *18*, 563–567.

Pierce, W. D., & Gray, C. E. *Deciphering the learning*

domains: A second generation classification model for educational objectives. Washington, D. C.: University Press of America, 1979.

Pike, L. A. Short-term instruction, testwiseness, and the Scholastic Aptitude Test: A literature review with research recommendations. (College Entrance Examination Board Research and Development Report 77-78, No. 2 and Educational Testing Service Research Bulletin, No. 78-2) Princeton, N. J.: Educational Testing Service, 1978.

Pimsleur, P. Pimsleur language aptitude battery. New York: Harcourt Brace Jovanovich, 1966.

Poggio, J. P., Asmus, E. P., & Levy, J. An investigation of responses to omitted items under formula-scoring directions. Paper presented at the Annual Meeting of the American Educational Research Association, Toronto, 1978.

Pollack, R. H., & Brenner, M. W. The experimental psychology of Alfred Binet: Selected papers. New York: Springer Publishing Company, 1969.

Popham, W. J. Developing IOX Objectives-Based Tests: Procedure guidelines. (Technical Paper No. 8) Los Angeles: The Instructional Objectives Exchange, August, 1972.

Popham, W. J. An approaching peril: Cloud-referenced tests. Phi Delta Kappan, 1974, 56, 614–615.

Popham, W. J. Educational evaluation. Englewood Cliffs, N. J.: Prentice-Hall, Inc., 1975.

Popham, W. J. A lasso for runaway test items. A paper presented at the First Annual Johns Hopkins University National Symposium on Educational Research, Washington, D. C., October, 1978. (a)

Popham, W. J. The case for criterion-referenced measurements. Educational Researcher, 1978, 7 (11), 6–10. (b)

Popham, W. J. Criterion-referenced measurement. Englewood Cliffs, N. J.: Prentice-Hall, Inc., 1978. (c)

Popham, W. J., & Husek, T. R. Implications of criterion-referenced measurement. Journal of Educational Measurement, 1969, 6, 1–9.

Popham, W. J., & Lindheim, E. The practical side of criterion-referenced test development. NCME Measurement in Education, 1980, 10 (4), 1–8.

Power, C. A. A multivariate model for studying person-environment interactions in the classroom. (Technical Report No. 99) Columbia: Center for Research in Social Behavior, University of Missouri, 1974.

Plumlee, L. B. A short guide to the development of performance tests. (Professional Series 75–1). Washington, D.C.: Test Services Section, Personnel Research and Development Center, United States Civil Service Commission, January 1975.

Prediger, D. J., Roth, J. D., & Noeth, R. J. Nationwide study of career development: Summary of results. (ACT Research Report No. 61) Iowa City: Research and Development Division, American College Testing Program, November, 1973.

Prescott, G. A., Balow, I. H., Hogan, T. P., & Farr, R. C. Metropolitan achievement tests (Complete Survey Battery, Intermediate, Form JS). New York: Harcourt Brace Jovanovich, Inc., 1978.

Prescott, G. A., Balow, I. H., Hogan, T. P., & Farr, R. C. Metropolitan achievement tests: Teacher's manual for administering and interpreting (Complete Survey Battery, Primary 2, Forms JS and KS). New York: The Psychological Corporation, 1978.

Privacy Act of 1974, P. L. 93–579. United States Congress, 552 A as amended, December 31, 1974.

Prochaska, J. O. Symptom and dynamic cues in the implosive treatment of test anxiety. Doctoral dissertation, Wayne State University, 1969. (University Microfilms No. 71-29976)

Prochaska, J. O. Symptom and dynamic cues in the implosive treatment of test anxiety. Journal of Abnormal Psychology, 1971, 77, 133–142.

Pryczak, F. Use of similarities between stems and keyed choices in multiple-choice items. Paper presented at the Annual Meeting of the National Council on Measurement in Education, New Orleans: February 1973. (ERIC Document Reproduction No. ED 081 844)

The Psychological Corporation. Methods of expressing test scores. (Test Service Bulletin No. 48) New York: Author, 1955.

The Psychological Corporation. System of multicultural pluralistic assessment (SOMPA) for the meaningful assessment of culturally different children by Jane R. Mercer and June F. Lewis. New York: Author, 1977.

The Psychological Corporation. Metro: A norm-referenced and criterion-referenced system. (Advertising brochure for the 1978 Metropolitan Achievement Test) New York: Author, n.d. (b)

The Psychological Corporation. Resources for decision making 1980 (Catalogue) New York: Author, 1980.

The Psychological Corporation. Differential aptitude tests with career planning program: Sampler brochure. New York: Author, c. 1982.

Psychologists win long regulation battle on human subject research. Advance (Association for the Advancement of Psychology), March, 1981, Vol. 2, p. 5.

Public Law 94-142. Education for All Handicapped Children Act of 1975. U.S. Code, Vol. 28 (Section 1401 et seq.), 1975.

Purves, A. C. Evaluation of learning in literature. In B. S. Bloom, J. T. Hastings, & G. F. Madaus (Eds.), Handbook on formative and summative evaluation of student learning. New York: McGraw-Hill Book Company, 1971.

Ramseyer, G. C., & Cashen, V. M. The effects of practice sessions on the use of separate answer sheets by first and second graders. Journal of Educational Measurement, 1971, 8, 177–181.

Rankin, E. F., Jr. The cloze procedure—a survey of research. In E. L. Thurstone & L. E. Hafner (Eds.), The philosophical and sociological bases of reading. Fourteenth yearbook of the National Reading Conference. Milwaukee: National Reading Conference, 1965.

Random House School Division. *Sampler: Scoring High in Reading.* New York: Random House, Inc., n. d.

Rapaport, G. M., & Berg, I. A. Response sets in a multiple-choice test. *Educational and Psychological Measurement,* 1955, *15,* 58–62.

Rasch, G. P. *Probabilistic models for some intelligence and attainment tests.* Copenhagen: Danish Institute for Educational Research, 1960.

Remmers, H. H. Rating methods in research on teaching. In N. L. Gage (Ed.), *Handbook of research on teaching.* Chicago: Rand McNally & Co., 1963.

Reschly, D. *Comparisons of bias in assessment with conventional and pluralistic measures.* Paper presented at the annual meeting of the Council for Exceptional Children, Kansas City, Mo.: 1978.

Resnick, L. B. *The science and art of curriculum design.* A paper prepared for the Career Education Task Force, National Institute of Education, United States Department of Health, Education and Welfare, 1974. (Also, Pittsburgh, Pa.: Learning Research and Development Center, University of Pittsburgh, Publication No. 1975/9.)

Resnick, L. B., Wang, M. C., & Kaplan, J. Task analysis in curriculum design: A hierarchically sequenced introductory mathematics curriculum. *Journal of Applied Behavior Analysis,* 1973, *6,* 679–710.

Resnick, L. B., & Beck, I. L. Designing instruction in reading: interaction of theory and practice. In J. T. Guthrie (Ed.), *Aspects of reading acquisition.* Baltimore, Md.: Johns Hopkins University Press, 1976.

Rhine, W. R., & Spaner, S. D. A comparison of the factor structure of the test anxiety scale for children among lower- and middle-class children. *Developmental Psychology,* 1973, *9,* 421–423.

Richards, J. M., Jr., Holland, J. L., & Lutz, S. W. *The prediction of student accomplishment in college* (ACT Research Report No. 13). Iowa City: American College Testing Program, 1966.

The Riverside Publishing Co. *12 ways the Riverside Publishing Company Basic Skills Assessment Program can help you evaluate your Title I Project.* (Advertising brochure). Lombard, Ill.: author, n. d.

The Riverside Publishing Company. *Research that built the Iowa Tests of Basic Skills.* Iowa City: Author, 1982.

Robertson, G. J. Development of the first group mental ability test. *Normline,* 1 (2), New York: Harcourt Brace Jovanovich, n.d. (Reprinted in G. H. Bracht, K. D. Hopkins, & J. C. Stanley (Eds.) *Perspectives in educational and psychological measurement.* Englewood Cliffs, N. J.: Prentice-Hall, 1972)

Robertson, G. J. *Steps in test development* (Revised 7/78). Circle Pines, Minn.: American Guidance Service, 1978 (mimeographed).

Rokeach, M. *The nature of human values.* New York: The Free Press, 1973.

Rosenshine, B. V. Content, time, and direct instruction. In P. L. Peterson & H. J. Walberg (Eds.), *Research on teaching: Concepts, findings, and implications.* Berkeley, Calif.: McCutchan Publishing Corp., 1979.

Rosenshine, B., & Furst, N. The use of direct observation to study learning. In R. M. W. Travers (Ed.), *Second handbook of research on teaching.* Chicago: Rand McNally, 1973.

Rozeboom, W. W. Scaling theory and the nature of measurement. *Synthese,* 1966, *16,* 170–233.

Rulon, P. J. A simplified procedure for determining the reliability of a test by split halves. *Harvard Educational Review,* 1939, *9,* 99–103.

Russell Sage Foundation. *Guidelines for the collection, maintenance, and dissemination of pupil records.* New York: Author, 1970.

Sabers, D. L., & Klausmeir, R. D. Accuracy of short-cut estimates for standard deviation. *Journal of Educational Measurement,* 1971, *8,* 335–339.

Samuels, S. J. The effect of letter-name knowledge on learning to read. *American Educational Research Journal,* 1972, *9,* 65–74.

Sarason, I. G. Interrelationships among individual difference variables, behavior in psychotherapy, and verbal conditioning. *Journal of Abnormal and Social Psychology,* 1958, *56,* 339–344.

Sarason, I. G. Intellectual and personality correlates of test anxiety. *Journal of Abnormal and Social Psychology,* 1959, *59,* 272–275.

Sarason, I. G. Empirical findings and theoretical problems in the use of anxiety scales. *Psychological Bulletin,* 1960, *57,* 403–415.

Sarason, I. G. Characteristics of three measures of anxiety. *Journal of Clinical Psychology,* 1961, *17,* 196–197.

Sarason, I. G., & Ganzer, V. J. Anxiety, reinforcement, and experimental instructions in a free verbalization situation. *Journal of Abnormal and Social Psychology,* 1962, *65,* 300–307.

Sarason, I. G., Pederson, A. M., & Nyman, B. Test anxiety and the observation of models. *Journal of Personality,* 1968, *36,* 493–511.

Sarason, I. G. (Ed.) *Test anxiety: Theory, research, and application.* Hillsdale, N. J.: Lawrence Erlbaum, 1980.

Sarason, S. B., Davidson, K. S., Lighthall, F. F., & Waite, R. R. A test anxiety scale for children. *Child Development,* 1958, *29,* 105–113.

Sarason, S. B., Davidson, K. S., Lighthall, F. F., Waite, R. R., & Ruebush, B. K. *Anxiety in elementary school children: A report of research.* New York: Wiley, 1960.

Sarnacki, R. E. An examination of test-wiseness in the cognitive test domain. *Review of Educational Research,* 1979, *49,* 252–279.

Sarnacki, R. E. An examination of test-wiseness in the cognitive test domain. *Review of Educational Research*, 1979, *49*, 252–279.

Sax, G. *Principles of educational measurement and evaluation*. Belmont, Calif.: Wadsworth Publishing Co., Inc., 1974.

Sax, G. *Study guide for Principles of Educational Measurement and Evaluation*. Belmont, Calif.: Wadsworth Publishing Co., Inc., 1980.

Scannell, D. P., & Marshall, J. C. The effects of selected composition errors on the grades assigned to essay examinations. *American Educational Research Journal*, 1966, *3*, 125–130.

Schafer, R. *Psychoanalytic interpretation in Rorschach testing*. New York: Grune and Stratton, 1954.

Schaie, K. W., & Labouvie-Lief, G. Generational versus ontogenetic components of change in adult cognitive behavior: A fourteen-year cross-sequential study. *Developmental Psychology*, 1974, *10*, 105–320.

Schaie, K. W., Labouvie, G. F., & Buech, B. U. Generational and cohort-specific differences in adult cognitive functioning: A fourteen-year study of independent samples. *Developmental Psychology*, 1973, *9*, 151–166.

Scholastic Testing Service. *The High School Placement Test technical report*. Bensenville, Ill.: Author, 1976.

Schmitt, N., Coyle, B. W., & Saari, I. A review and critique of analyses of multitrait-multimethod matrices. *Multivariate Behavioral Research*, 1977, *12*, 447–478.

School Psychology Digest. SOMPA: A Symposium. 1979 *8* (1)

School Psychology Digest. SOMPA—A symposium continued: commentaries. 1979, *8* (2).

Schwarz, P. A. Prediction instruments for educational outcomes. In R. L. Thorndike (Ed.), *Educational measurement* (2nd ed.). Washington, D. C.: American Council on Education, 1971.

Scott, W. A. Attitude measurement. In G. Lindzey (Ed.), *Handbook of social psychology*. (Vol. 2) Reading, Mass.: Addison-Wesley, 1968.

Scriven, M. *The methodology of evaluation* (AERA Monograph Series on Curriculum Evaluation, No. 1). Chicago: Rand McNally, 1967.

Seiverling, R. F. *Educational Quality Assessment: A profile of Pennsylvania's program*. Harrisburg, Pa.: Office of Planning and Evaluation, Division of Educational Quality Assessment, Pennsylvania Department of Education, 1976. (a)

Seiverling, R. F. (Ed.) *Getting inside the EQA Inventory*. Harrisburg, Pa.: Office of Planning and Evaluation, Division of Educational Quality Assessment, Pennsylvania Department of Education, 1976. (b)

Seiverling, R. F. *Educational Quality Assessment in Pennsylvania: A decade of progress*. Harrisburg, Pa.: Division of Educational Quality Assessment, Bureau of Research and Evaluation, Pennsylvania Department of Education, 1979.

Shannon, G. A. *The construction of matching tests: An empirical statement* Master's thesis, University of Pittsburgh, 1973.

Sheriffs, A. C., & Boomer, D. S. Who is penalized by the penalty for guessing? *Journal of Educational Psychology*, 1954, *45*, 81–90.

Shriberg, L. D. Descriptive statistics for two children's social desirability scales, general and test anxiety, and locus of control on elementary school children. *Psychological Reports*, 1974, *34*, 863–870.

Silberman, M. Behavioral expression of teachers' attitudes toward elementary school children. *Journal of Educational Psychology*, 1969j, *60*, 403–407.

Simon, A., & Boyer, E. G. (Eds.) *Mirrors for behavior: An anthology of observation instruments*. Philadelphia: Research for Better Schools, 1970.

Simpson, E. J. The classification of educational objectives, psychomotor domain. *Illinois Teacher of Home Economics*, Winter 1966-67, *10*, 110–144.

Sirntnik, K. An investigation of the context effect in matrix sampling. *Journal of Educational Measurement*, 1970, *7*, 199–208.

Slakter, N. J., Juliano, D. B., & Sarnacki, R. E. *Is there a penalty for guessing?* Paper presented at the Annual Meeting of the American Educational Research Association, San Francisco, 1976.

Slakter, M. J., Koehler, R. A., & Hampton, S. H. Grade level, sex, and selected aspects of test-wiseness. *Journal of Educational Measurement*, 1970, *7*, 119–122. (a)

Slakter, M. J., Koehler, R. A., & Hampton, S. H. Learning test-wiseness by programmed texts. *Journal of Educational Measurement*, 1970, *7*, 247–254. (b)

Slakter, M. J., Koehler, R. A., & Hampton, S. H. Grade-level, sex, and selected aspects of test-wiseness. *Journal of Educational Measurement*, 1970, *7*, 119–122.

Slaughter, B. A. Improving student performance through teaching test-taking skills. In A. J. Nitko (Ed.), *Exploring alternatives to current standardized tests: Proceedings of the 1976 National Testing Conference*. Pittsburgh: School of Education, University of Pittsburgh, 1977.

Smith, C. A., & Morris, L. W. Effects of stimulative and sedative music on cognitive and emotional components of anxiety. *Psychological Reports*, 1976, *38*, 1187–1193.

Smith, R. F. *Grading the Advanced Placement English Examination*. Princeton, N. J.: Advanced Placement Program, College Entrance Examination Board, Educational Testing Service, 1976.

Smith,k R. J., & Barrett, T. C. *Teaching reading in the middle grades*. Reading, Mass.: Addison-Wesley Publishing Co., 1974.

Smith, W. L. Review of the cloze procedure as applied to reading. In O. K. Buros (Ed.), *The eighth mental measurements yearbook*. Highland Park, N. J.: The Gryphon Press, 1978.

Snider, J. G., & Osgood, C. E. (Eds.). *Semantic differential technique*. Chicago: Aldine, 1969.

Snow, R. E. Aptitudes and achievement. In W. B. Schrader

(Ed.), *Measuring achievement: Progress over a decade. Proceedings of the 1979 ETS Invitational Conference. New Directions for Testing and Measurement* (No. 5). San Francisco: Jossey-Bass, Inc., 1980.

Spearman, C. Correlation calculated from faulty data. *British Journal of Psychology*, 1910, *3*, 271–295.

Spiegler, M. D., Morris, L. W., & Liebert, R. M. Cognitive and emotional components of test anxiety: Temporal factors. *Psychological Reports*, 1968, *22*, 451–456.

Spielberger, C. D., Gonzalez, H. P., Taylor,k C. J., Algaze, B., & Anton, W. D. Examination stress and test anxiety. In C. D. Spielberger & I. G. Sarason (Eds.), *Stress and anxiety* (Vol. 5). New York: Hemisphere, 1978.

Stake, R. E. National Assessment. In *Proceedings of the 1970 ETS Invitational Conference on Testing Problems*. Princeton, N. J.: Educational Testing Service, 1970.

Stalnaker, J. M. The essay type of examination. In E. F. Lindquist (Ed.), *Educational measurement*. Washington, D. C.: American Council on Education, 1951.

Stalnaker, J. M. A study of optional questions in examinations. *School and Society*, 1936, *44*, 829–832.

Stanford, D. A children's form of the Alpert-Haber Achievement Scale. *Child Development*, 1963, *34*, 1027–1032.

Stanley, J. C. Rationale of the Study of Mathematically Precocious Youth (SMPY) during its first five years of promoting educational acceleration. In J. C. Stanley, W. E. George, & C. H. Solano (Eds.) *The gifted and the creative: A fifty-year perspective*. Baltimore: The Johns Hopkins University Press, 1977.

Stanley, J. C. Reliability. In R. L. Thorndike (Ed.), *Educational measurement*, (2nd ed.) Washington, D. C.: American Council on Education, 1971.

Stanley, J. C., & Hopkins, K. D. *Educational and psychological measurement* (5th ed.). Englewood Cliffs, N. J.: Prentice-Hall, Inc., 1972.

Stanley, J. C., & Hopkins, K. D. *Educational and psychological measurement* (6th ed.). Englewood Cliffs, N. J.: Prentice-Hall Inc., 1981.

Starch, D. *Educational measurements*. New York: The Macmillan Co., 1916.

Starch, D. The measurement of achievement in English grammar. *Journal of Educational Psychology*, 1915, *6*, 615–626. (Reprinted in Starch (1917, pp. 101-110).)

Stern, W. *The psychological methods of testing intelligence* (G. M. Whipple, Trans.) (Educational Psychology Monographs No. 13) Baltimore: Warwick and York, Inc., 1914.

Stevens, S. S. On the theory of scales of measurement. *Science*, 1946, *103*, 667–680.

Stevens, S. S. Mathematics, measurement and psychophysics. In S. S. Stevens (Ed.), *Handbook of experimental psychology*. New York: Wiley, 1951.

Stodola, Q. *Making the classroom test: A guide for teachers*. (No. 4, Evaluation and Advisory Service Series) Princeton, N. J.: Educational Testing Service, 1961.

Strang, H. R. The effects of technical and unfamiliar options upon guessing on multiple-choice test items. *Journal of Educational Measurement*, 1977, *14*, 253–260.

Strong, E. K., & Campbell, D. P. *Strong-Campbell interest inventory* (Form T 325). Stanford, Calif.: Stanford University Press, 1974.

Subkoviak, M. J. The reliability of mastery classification decisions. In *Criterion-referenced measurement: The state of the art*. First Annual Johns Hopkins University National Symposium on Educational Research, Washington, D. C., 1978.

Subkoviak, M. J. Decision-consistency approaches. In R. A. Berk (Ed.), *Criterion-referenced measurement: The state of the art*. Baltimore: The Johns Hopkins University Press, 1980.

Suinn, R. M. Psychometric characteristics of the test anxiety and general anxiety scales: Social desirability and reliability data. *Journal of Clinical Psychology*, 1969, *25*, 64–65. (a)

Suinn, R. M. The STABS, a measure of test anxiety for behavior therapy: Normative data. *Behavior Research and Therapy*, 1969, *7*, 335–339. (b)

Suinn, R. M. *Suinn test anxiety behavior scale (STABS): Information for users*. Fort Collins, Colo.: Rocky Mountain Behavioral Science Institute, Inc., 1971.

Suinn, R. M. *Suinn test anxiety behavior scale: Information brief*. Fort Collins, Colo.: Rocky Mountain Behavioral Science Institute, Inc., 1972.

Super, D. E. Vocational interest and vocational choice. *Educational and Psychological Measurement*, 1947, *7*, 375–384.

Super, D. E. *Appraising vocational fitness*. New York: Harper and Row, 1949.

Super, D. E. The dimensions and measurement of vocational maturity. *Teachers College Record*, 1955, *57*, 151–163.

Super, D. E., Crites, J. O., Hummel, R. C., Moser, H. P., Overstreet, P. L., & Warnath, C. F. *Vocational development: A framework for research*. New York: Teachers College Bureau of Publications, 1957.

Suppes, P. A survey of cognition in handicapped children. *Review of Educational Research*, 1974, *44*, 145–176.

Suppes, P., & Zinnes, J. L. Basic measurement theory. In R. D. Luce, R. R. Bush, & E. Galanter (Eds.), *Handbook of mathematical psychology* (Vol. 1). New York: Wiley, 1963.

Swaminathan, H., Hambleton, R. K., & Algina, J. Reliability of criterion-referenced tests: A decision-theoretic formulation. *Journal of Educational Measurement*, 1974, *11*, 263–267.

Swineford, F., & Fan, T. C. A method of score conversion through item statistics. *Psychometrika*, 1957, *22*, 185–188.

Tallmadge, G. K. *An analysis of the relationship between reading and mathematics achievement gains and perpupil expenditures in California Title I projects: Fiscal* year 1972 (AIR-35100-3/73-FR). Palo Alto, Calif.: American Institutes for Research, March 1973.

Tallmadge, G. K., & Horst, D. P. *A procedural guide for validating achievement gains in educational projects (Revised)* (RMC Report UR-240). Los Altos, Calif.: RMC Research Corporation, 1974.

Tallmadge, G. K., & Wood, C. T. *User's guide* (ESEA Title I Evaluation and Reporting System). Mountain View, Calif.: RMC Research Corporation, 1976.

Task Force on Assessment Center Standards. *Standards and ethical considerations for assessment center operations.* Unpublished manuscript, December 1978.

Taylor, D. D., & Redi, J. C. Criterion-referenced evaluation of student performance. *Journal of Medical Education*, 1972, *47*, 970–971.

Taylor, D. D., Reid, J. C., Senhauser, D. A., & Shively, J. A. Use of minimum pass levels on pathology examinations. *Journal of Medical Education*, 1971, *46*, 876–881.

Taylor, E. D., & Nutthall, D. L. Question choice in examinations: An experiment in geography and science. *Educational Research.* 1974, *16*, 143–150.

Taylor, H. C., & Russell, J. T. The relationship of validity coefficients to the practical effectiveness of tests in selection: Discussion and tables. *Journal of Applied Psychology*, 1939, *23*, 565–578.

Taylor, W. L. Cloze procedure: A new tool for measuring readability. *Journalism Quarterly*, 1953, *30*, 415–433.

Taylor, W. L. Recent developments in the use of "cloze procedure". *Journalism Quarterly*, 1956, *33*, 42–48.

Teachers face more tests to make the grade. *ETS Development*, 25(2), 1–3.

Terman, L. M. The Binet-Simon scale for measuring intelligence: Impressions gained by its application. *Psychological Clinic*, 1911, *5*, 199–206.

Terman, L. M. *Measurement of intelligence: An explanation of and a complete guide for the use of the Stanford Revision and Extension of the Binet-Simon Intelligence Scale.* Boston: Houghton-Mifflin, 1916.

Terman, L. M. The problem. In L. M. Terman (Ed.), *Intelligence tests and school reorganization.* Yonkers-on-Hudson, N. Y.: World Book Co., 1922.

Terman, L. M., & Childs, H. G. A tentative revision and extension of the Binet-Simon measuring scale of intelligence. *Journal of Educational Psychology*, 1912, *3*, 61–74, 133–143, 198–208, 277–289.

Terman, L. M., & Merrill, M. A. *Stanford-Binet intelligence scale: Manual for the third revision* (Form L-M). Iowa City: Riverside Publishing Co., 1973..

Terry, P. W. How students review for objective and essay tests. *Elementary School Journal*, 1933, *33*, 592–603.

Terwilliger, J. S. *Assigning grades to students.* Glenview, Ill.: Scott, Foresman, and Co., 1971.

Thomas, A., Chess, S., & Birch, H. G. *Temperament and behavior disorders in children.* New York: New York University Press, 1968.

Thomas, W. B. Guidance and testing: An illusion of reform in southern black schools and colleges. In R. K. Goodenow, & A. O. White (Eds.), *Education and the use of the New South.* Boston, G. K. Hall, 1981.

Thomas, W. B. Black intellectuals' critique of early mental testing: A little-known saga of the 1920s. *American Journal of Education*, 1982, *90*, 258–292.

Thorndike, E. L. Handwriting. *Teacher's College Record*, 1910, *11*, 1–93.

Thorndike, E. L. A scale for measuring achievement in drawing. *Teachers College Record*, 1913, *14*, 345–382.

Thorndike, E. L. The measurement of ability in reading. *Teachers College Record*, 1914, *15* (4), 1–71.

Thorndike, E. L. The nature, purposes and general methods of measurement of educational products. In G. M. Whipple (Ed.), *The seventeenth yearbook of the National Society for the Study of Education.* (Part II) *The measurement of educational products.* Bloomington, Ill.: Public School Publishing Co., 1918.

Thorndike, E. L. *Your city.* New York: Harcourt, Brace, 1939.

Thorndike, R. L. *Personnel selection: Test and measurement technique.* New York: John Wiley and Sons, Inc., 1949.

Thorndike, R. L. Reliability. In E. F. Lindquist (Ed.), *Educational measurement.* Washington, D. C.: American Council on Education, 1951.

Thorndike, R. L. Concepts of culture fairness. *Journal of Educational Measurement*, 1971, *8*, 63–70.

Thorndike, R. L. Editor's note: The problem of guessing. In R. L. Thorndike (Ed.), *Educational measurement* (2nd ed.). Washington, D. C.: American Council on Education, 1971.

Thorndike, R. L., & Hagen, E. P. *Measurement and evaluation in psychology and education* (4th ed.). New York: John Wiley and Sons, 1977.

Thorndike, R. L., & Hagen, E. P. *Cognitive abilities test (Form 3): Examiners manual.* Iowa City, Iowa: Riverside Publishing Co., 1978. (a)

Thorndike, R. L., & Hagen, E. P. *Cognitive abilities test (Form 3): Multi-level booklet for grades 3–12.* Iowa City, Iowa: Riverside Publishing Co., 1978. (b)

Thorpe, L. P., Clark, W. W., & Tiegs, E. W. *California test of personality: Manual.* Monterey, Calif.: CTB/McGraw-Hill, 1953.

Thurstone, L. L. A method of scaling psychological and educational tests. *Journal of Educational Psychology*, 1925, *16*, 433–451.

Thurstone, L. L. Attitudes can be measured. *American Journal of Sociology*, 1928, *33*, 529–554.

Thurstone, L. L., & Chave, E. J. *The measurement of attitudes.* Chicago: The University of Chicago Press, 1929.

Tinkelman, S. N. Planning the objective test. In R. L. Thorndike (Ed.), *Educational measurement* (2nd ed.). Washington, D. C.: American Council on Education, 1971.

Tittle, C. K., McCarthy, K., & Steckler, J. F. *Women and educational testing.* Princeton, N. J.: Educational Testing Service, 1974.

Torgerson, W. S. *Theory and methods of scaling*. New York: John Wiley & Sons, Inc., 1958.

Traub, R. E., & Rowley, G. L. Reliability of test scores and decisions. *Applied Psychological Measurement*, 1980, *4*, 517–545.

Treves, Z., & Saffiotti, U. *La 'scala metrica dell' intelligenza' de Binet e Simon: Nota preventiva*. Milan: Laboratorio civico de Psychologie, 1910.

Treves, Z., & Saffiotti, U. *La 'scala metrica dell' intelligenza' di Binet e Simon: Studiata nelle Scuole communali elementari de Milano. Esposizione e critica*. Milan: Laboratorio civico di Psychologie pura ed Applicata, 1911.

Tryon, G. S. The measurement and treatment of test anxiety. *Review of Educational Research*, 1980, *50*, 343–372.

Tucker, J. A. Operationalizing the diagnostic intervention process. In T. Oakland (Ed.), *Psychological and educational assessment of minority children*. New York: Brunner/Mazel Publishers, 1977.

Tuckman, B. W. *Measuring educational outcomes: Fundamentals of testing*. New York: Harcourt, Brace, and Jovanovich, Inc., 1975.

Tuinman, J. J., Farr, R., & Blanton, B. E. Increases in test scores as a function of material rewards. *Journal of Educational Measurement*, 1972, *9*, 215–223.

Tjyack, D. B. *The one best system: A history of American urban education*. Cambridge, Mass.: Harvard University Press, 1974.

Tyler, F. T., & Chalmers, T. M. The effect on scores of warning junior high school pupils of coming tests. *Journal of Educational Research*, 1943, *37*, 290–296.

Tyler, L. E. The intelligence we test—an evolving concept. In L. B. Resnick (Ed.), *The nature of intelligence*. Hillsdale, N. J.: Lawrence Erlbaum Associates, Publishers, 1976.

Tyler, R. W. A test of skill in using a microscope. *Educational Research Bulletin*, 1930, *9*, 493–496.

Tyler, R. W. The objectives and plans for a National Assessment of Educational Progress. *Journal of Educational Measurement*, 1966, *3*, 1–4.

Tyler, R. W. Using tests in grouping students for instructions. In R. W. Tyler & R. M. Wolf (Eds.), *Critical issues in testing*. Berkeley, Calif.: McCutchan Publishing Co., 1974.

Uhrbrock, R. S. Mental alertness tests as aids in selecting employees. *Personnel*, 1936, *12*, 229–237.

Ullery, J. W. *Development and evaluation of an experimental curriculum for the new Quincy (Mass.) vocational-technical school: Management and evaluation plan for instructional systems development for vocational-technical education*. (Fifteenth Technical Report, Project ABLE. Contract No. OE-5-85-019) Pittsburgh: American Institutes for Research and Quincy, Mass.: Quincy Public Schools, April 1970.

U. S. Bureau of Census. Money income and poverty status of families and persons in the United States: 1978. *Current Population Reports* (Advance Report), *Series P-60, No. 120*. Washington, D. C.: U. S. Government Printing Office, 1979.

U. S. Office of Education, Department of Health, Education, and Welfare. Education of handicapped children. *Federal Register*, August 23, 1977, *42* (No. 163), 42474–42518.

United States Office of Education, Department of Health, Education and Welfare. Education of handicapped children. *Federal Register*, 1977, Vol. 42 (No. 163 August, 23), 42474-42518.

United States Office of Education, Department of Health, Education and Welfare. Assistance to States for education of handicapped children. *Federal Register*, 1977, Vol. 42 (No. 250, December 29), 65082–65085.

United States Supreme Court. *Griggs et al., Petitioners vs. Duke Power Company*, No. 125, 401 U. S. 424, Decided March 8, 1971.

Uzgiris, I. C., & Hunt, J. McV. An instrument for assessing infant psychological development. Unpublished paper from the Psychological Development Laboratory, University of Illinois, 1966.

Uzgiris, I. C., & Hunt, J. McV. *Ordinal scales of infant psychological development: Information concerning six demonstration films*. Unpublished paper from the Psychological Development Laboratory, University of Illinois, 1968.

Vallance, T. R. Comparison of essay and objective examinations as learning experiences. *Journal of Educational Research*, 1947, *41*, 279–288.

Vernon, P. E. The determinants of reading comprehension. *Educational and Psychological Measurement*, 1962, *22*, 269–286.

Wagner, R. V. The study of attitude change: An introduction. In R. V. Wagner & J. J. Sherwood (Edjs.), *The study of attitude change*. Belmont, Calif.: Brooke/Cole Publishers, 1969.

Wahlstrom, M., & Boersman, F. J. The influence of test-wiseness upon achievement. *Educational and Psychological Measurement*, 1968, *28*, 413–420.

Walker, D. F., & Schaffarzick, J. Comparing curricula. *Review of Educational Research*, 1974, *44*, 83–111.

Walker, H. M. The contributions of Karl Pearson. *American Statistical Association Journal*, 1958, *53*, 11–22.

Walker, H. M. *Studies in the history of statistical method*. Baltimore: Williams and Wilkins, 1929.

Wallace, G., & Larsen, S. C. *Educational assessment of learning problems: Testing for teaching*. Boston: Allyn and Bacon, Inc., 1978.

Wallach, M. A., & Kogan, N. Modes of thinking in young children: *A study of the creativity-intelligence distinction*. New York: Holt, Rinehart, & Winston, 1965.

Walter, D., Denzler, L. S., & Sarason, I. G. Anxiety and the intellectual performance of high school students. *Child Development*, 1964, *35*, 917–926.

Watkins, R. W. Addenda to *report of recommendations to*

the *Testing Operations Board on the use of formula and rights scores*. Princeton, N. J.: Educational Testing Service, 1962. (Unpublished report cited in R. L. Ebel, *Essentials of educational measurement*. Englewood Cliffs, N. J.: Prentice Hall, 1972.)

Webb, E. J., Campbell, D. T., Schwarts, R. D., & Sechrest, L. *Unobtrusive measures: Nonreactive research in the social sciences*. Chicago: Rand McNally, 1966.

Wechsler, D. *The measurement of adult intelligence*. Baltimore: Williams and Wilkins, 1939.

Wechsler, D. *Wechsler intelligence scale for children: Manual*. New York: The Psychological Corporation, 1949.

Wechsler, D. *Manual for the Wechsler Preschool and Primary Scale of Intelligence*. New York: The Psychological Corporation, 1967.

Wechsler, D. *Manual for the Wechsler Intelligence Scale for Children—Revised*. New York: The Psychological Corporation, 1974.

Weidemann, C. C. How to construct the true-false examination. *Teachers College, Columbia University. Contributions to Education* (No. 225). New York: Bureau of Publications, Teachers College, Columbia University, 1926.

Weinstein, E. A. The development of interpersonal competence. In D. A. Goslin (Ed.), *Handbook of socialization theory and research*. Chicago: Rand McNally, 1969.

Weiss, T., Chisholm, S., & Miller, G. Tests without mystery. *Washington Post*, 1979 (October 27).

Werts, C. E., Jöreskog, K. G., & Linn, R. L. A multitrait-multimethod model for studying growth. *Educational and Psychological Measurement*, 1972, *32*, 655–678.

Wesley, E. B., & Wronski, S. P. *Teaching social studies in high schools* (4th ed.). Boston: D. C. Heath and Co., 1958.

Wesman, A. G. Intelligent testing. *American Psychologist*, 1968, *23*, 267–274.

Wesman, A. G. Writing the test item. In R. L. Thorndike (Ed.), *Educational measurement* (2nd ed.). Washington, D. C.: American Council on Education, 1971.

Whipple, G. M. *Manual of mental and physical tests*. Baltimore: Warwick & York, Inc., 1910.

Whipple, G. M. An annotated list of group intelligence tests. In G. M. Whipple (Ed.), *The twenty-first yearbook of the National Society for the Study of Education. Intelligence tests and their use*. Bloomington, Ill.: Public School Publishing Co., 1922.

White, E. M. *Comparison and contrast: The 1978 California State University and Colleges Freshman English Equivalency Examination*. San Bernardino, Calif.: Trustees of the California State University and Colleges, 1979.

Whitney, D. R. *Estimating the extent and effect of differences in guessing strategy*. (Research Report No. 70) Iowa City, Iowa: Evaluation and Examination Service, University of Iowa, 1974.

Whitney, D. R., & Sabers, D. L. *Improving essay examinations III: Use of item analysis*. (Technical Bulletin No. 11) Iowa City: University Evaluation and Examination Service, The University of Iowa, May, 1970.

Wick, J. W., Smith, J. K., Beggs, D. L., Braun, L. D., Nordstrom, C. D., Smith, M. R., Spiegel, D. L., & Stevens, J. A. *Comprehensive assessment program: Achievement series 12A*. Glenview, Ill.: Scott, Foresman and Co., 1980.

Wiggins, J. S. *Personality and prediction: Principles of personality assessment*. Reading, Mass.: Addison-Wesley Publishing Co., 1973.

Wilbur, P. H. Positional response set among high school students on multiple-choice tests. *Journal of Educational Measurement*, 1970, *7*, 161–163.

Wildemuth, B. M. *Test anxiety: An extensive bibliography*. (TM Report 65). Princeton, N. J.: ERIC Clearinghouse on Tests, Measurement, and Evaluation, Educational Testing Service, 1979.

Williams, R. L. The BITCH-100: A culture-specific test. *Journal of Afro-American Issues*, 1975, *3*, 103–116. (a)

Williams, R. L. Moderator variables as bias in testing black children. *Journal of Afro-American Issues*, 1975, *3*, 77–90. (b)

Wilson, J. A. Question choice in A-Level Physics. *Curriculum Studies*, 1976, *8*, 71–78.

Wine, J. Test anxiety and direction of attention. *Psychological Bulletin*, 1971, *76*, 92–104.

Wiseman, J. P., & Aron, M. S. *Field projects for sociology students*. Cambridge, Mass.: Schenkman Publishing Co., Ltd., 1970.

Witkin, H. A., Dyk, R. B., Faterson, H. F., Goodenough, D. R., & Karp, S. A. *Psychological differentiation*. Potomac, Md.: Erlbaum Associates, 1974. (Originally published by Wiley, 1962)

Witkins, H. A., & Goodenough, D. R. Field dependence and interpersonal behavior. *Psychological Bulletin*, 1977, *84*, 661–689.

Witkins, H. A., Moore, C. A., Goodenough, D. R., & Cox, P. W. Field-dependent and field-independent cognitive styles and their educational implications. *Review of Educational Research*, 1977, *47*, 1–64.

Wolf, T. H. *Alfred Binet*. Chicago: University of Chicago Press, 1973.

Wood, R. Multiple choice: A state of the art report. *Evaluation in Education: International Progress*, 1977, *1*, 191–280.

Woodley, K. K. *Test-wiseness program development and evaluation*. Paper presented at the annual meeting of the American Educational Research Association, New Orleans, 1973.

Woodley, K. K. *Test-wiseness: A cognitive function?* Paper presented at the annual meeting of the National Council on Measurement in Education, Washington, D. C., April, 1975.

Woodley, K. K. *Test-wiseness: Test-taking skills for adults* (2nd ed.). (The American College) New York: McGraw-Hill Book Co., 1978.

Yerkes, R. M. (Ed.). Psychological examining in the United

States Army. *Memoirs of the National Academy of Sciences* (Vol. 15). Washington, D. C.: Government Printing Office, 1921.

Yerkes, R. M., Bridges, J. W., & Hardwick, R. S. *A point scale for measuring mental ability.* Baltimore: Warwick and York, 1915.

Yoakum, C. S., & Yerkes, R. M. (Eds.) *Army mental tests.* New York: Henry Holt, 1920.

Young, P. B., & Ayrer, J. E. *The users: Who, what, where, when, and why? Benefits of an urban city-wide standardized testing program.* Paper presented at the annual meeting of the National Council on Measurement in Education, San Francisco, April, 1979.

Zieky, M. J., & Livingston, S. A. *Manual for setting standards on the Basic Skills Assessment Tests.* Princeton, N. J.: Educational Testing Service, 1977.

Zimbardo, P. & Ebbesen, E. B. *Influencing attitudes and changing behavior.* Reading, Mass.: Addison-Wesley, 1970.

Zoref, L., & Williams, P. A look at content bias in IQ tests. *Journal of Educational Measurement,* 1980, *17,* 313–322.

Zuckerman, M., & Spielberger, C. D. (Eds.) *Emotion and anxiety: New concepts, methods and applications.* New York: Lawrence Erlbaum Associates, 1976.

Copyrights and Acknowledgments

Bliss, L. B. "A Test of Lord's Assumption Regarding Examinee Guessing Behavior on Multiple-Choice Tests Using Elementary School Students." *Journal of Educational Measurement,* Vol. 17, pp. 147–153. Copyright 1980, National Council on Measurement in Education, Washington, D.C.

Diamond, J. J. and Evans, W. J. "An Investigation of the Cognitive Correlates of Test-wiseness." *Journal of Educational Measurement,* 1972, Vol. 9, pp. 145–150. Copyright 1972. National Council on Measurement in Education, Washington, D.C.

Crites, J. O. "Career Maturity, 1973." *Measurement in Education,* 1973, Vol. 4, No. 2, pp. 2-3. Copyright 1973, National Council on Measurement in Education, Washington, D.C.

Jenkins, J. R. and Deno, S. J. "Assessing Knowledge of Concepts and Principles." *Journal Council on Measurement in Education, Washington, D.C.*

PITMAN LEARNING, INC. *Preparing Instructional Objectives* by Robert F. Mager. Copyright © 1975 by Pitman Learning, Inc., Belmont, CA 94002.

PRENTICE-HALL, INC. Robert L. Ebel, *Essentials of Educational Measurement,* Third Edition, © 1979, pp. 111-112, 181, 248-249, 251. Reprinted by permission of Prentice-Hall, Inc., Englewood Cliffs, N.J.

Robert L. Ebel, *Measuring Educational Achievement,* © 1965, pp. 226–232. Adapted by permission of Prentice-Hall, Inc., Englewood Cliffs, N.J.

Robert L. Ebel, *Essentials of Educational Measurement,* © 1972, pp. 183-185. Adapted by permission of Prentice-Hall, Inc., Englewood Cliffs, N.J.

THE PSYCHOLOGICAL CORPORATION *Differential Aptitude Tests.* Copyright © 1982, 1972 by The Psychological Corporation. All rights reserved.

Modern Language Aptitude Test, Manual. Copyright © 1959 by The Psychological Corporation. Reproduced by permission. All rights reserved.

SCIENCE RESEARCH ASSOCIATES, INC. *Kuder Occupational Interest Survey, Form DD* by G. Frederic Kuder. © 1956, 1964, G. Frederic Kuder. Reprinted by permission of the publisher, Science Research Associates, Inc.

UNIVERSITY OF CHICAGO PRESS E. D. Hirsch, Jr. *The Philosophy of Composition,* © 1977 by The University of Chicago Press. Reprinted by permission.

Figures

1.1 "Education Commission of the States," *NAEP Newsletter* Vol. 10, No. 3, p. 67. Washington, D.C.: National Education Association Publishing, 1977.

1.3 Cooley, W. W. "Program Evaluation in Education." Address presented at American Psychological Association Annual Meeting, San Francisco, CA, 1977.

1.4 Bruininks, R. H. *Bruininks-Oseretsky Test of Motor Proficiency.* Circle Pines, MN: American Guidance Service, 1978. Reprinted with permission.

1.5 Cox, R. C., and Graham, G. T. "The Development of a Sequentially Scaled Achievement Test," *Journal of Educational Measurement,* Vol. 3 (1966): pp. 147-150. Nitko, A. J. "Distinguishing the Many Varieties of Criterion-Referenced Tests," © 1980, *Review of Educational Research,* Vol. 50, pp. 461-485.

1.6 Larsen, E. P. *Opening Institutional Ledger Books—A Challenge to Educational Leadership* (TM Report 28). Princeton, NJ: ERIC Clearinghouse on Tests, Measurements, and Evaluation, ETS, 1974. Reprinted with permission of ETS.

3.2 Blommers, P. J., and Forsyth, R. A. *Elementary Statistical Methods in Psychology and Education.* Boston, MA: Houghton Mifflin Company, 1977. Adapted by permission.

3.3 Based on data from "Money, Income and Poverty Status of Families and Persons in the U.S.: 1978," Current Population Reports (advance report) Series P 60, No. 120, U.S. Government Printing Office, 1979.

3.9 Based on data from Cole, N. S., and Hanson, S. R. *Assessing Students on the Way to College, Vol. 1: Technical Report for the ACT Assessment Program.* Iowa City, Iowa: American College Testing Program, 1973.

4.1 Hopkins, K. D., and Stanley, J. C. *Educational and Psychological Measurement and Evaluation,* 6th ed. Englewood Cliffs, N.J.: Prentice-Hall, Inc., 1972. Adapted by permission of Prentice-Hall, Inc.

4.3 Mager, R. F. *Measuring Instructional Intent, or Got a Match?.* Belmont, CA: Pitman Learning, Inc., 1973.

5.2 Kryspin, W., and Feldhusen, J. *Developing Classroom Tests.* Minneapolis, MN: Burgess Publishing Co., 1974.

5.3 Nitko, A. J. *Problems in the development of Criterion-Referenced Tests: the I.P.I. Pittsburgh Experience.* In Harris, C. W. et al (eds.), *Problems in Criterion-Referenced Measurement.* Los Angeles: Center for the Study Evaluation, University of California, 1974. Also adapted from Learning Research and Development Center and Research for Better Schools, *I.P.I. Mathematics Continuum.* New York: Meredith Corp., 1972.

5.4 Bloom et al. *Handbook on Formative and Summative Evaluation of Student Learning.* New York: McGraw-Hill Book Co., 1971. Used by permission of McGraw-Hill.

8.1 Feldt, L. S., Forsyth, R. A., Neckere, E. D., and Lindquist, E. F., *Iowa Tests of Educational Development: Manual for Teachers, Counselors, and Examiners.* Chicago: Science Research Associates, 1970. Reprinted by permission of the University of Iowa.

10.1 Cartwright, C. A., and Cartwright, C. P. *Developing Observational Skills.* New York: McGraw-Hill Book Co., 1974.

10.2, 10.3 Lindvall, C. M. *Testing and Evaluation: An Introduction.* New York: Harcourt, Brace and World, 1961.

10.3 Cartwright, C. A., and Cartwright, C. P. *Developing Observational Skills.* New York: McGraw-Hill, 1974.

10.4 Tyler, R. A. "A Test of Skill in Using a Microscope." *Educational Research Bulletin,* Vol 9, pp. 493-496. College of Education, Ohio State University, 1930.

10.5 Ullery, J. W. *Development and Evaluation of an Experimental Curriculum for the New Quincy (Mass.) Vocational-Technical School. Management and Evaluation Plan for Instructional Systems Development for Vocational-Technical Education.* Pittsburgh, PA: American Institutes for Research, 1970.

10.6 Berry, M. F. *Language Disorders of Children: The Basis and Diagnosis.* Englewood Cliffs, N.J.: Prentice-Hall, Inc., 1969. Adapted by permission of Prentice-Hall, Inc.

10.7 American College Testing Program, *Vocational Interest, Experience and Skill Assessment: Career Guidebook.* Boston: Houghton Mifflin Co., 1976. Reproduced with permission.

10.8 Lindvall, C. M. *Measuring Pupil Achievement and Aptitude.* New York: Harcourt, Brace and World, © 1967. All rights reserved.

10.10 Borich, G. D. and Madden, S. K. *Evaluating Classroom Instruction: A Sourcebook of Instruments.* Reading, MA: Addison-Wesley, © 1977. Reprinted with permission.
Lazovik, G. F. *University of Pittsburgh Student Opinion of Teaching Questionnaire.* Pittsburgh, PA: Office for the Evaluation of Teaching, University of Pittsburgh, 1978.

10.12, 10.13, 10.14 Cartwright, C. A., and Cartwright, C., P. *Developing Observational Skills.* New York: McGraw-Hill Book Co., 1974.

10.15 Evans, K. M. *Sociometry and Education.* London: Routledge & Kegan Paul, Ltd., 1962.

11.2 Ebel, R. L. *Essentials of Educational Measurement,* 3rd ed. Englewood Cliffs, N.J.: Prentice-Hall, Inc., 1979. Adapted by permission of Prentice-Hall, Inc.

11.4 Ebel, R. L. *Measuring Educational Achievement.* Englewood Cliffs, N.J.: Prentice-Hall, 1965. Also adapted from Kryspin, W., and Feldhusen, J. *Developing Classroom Tests.* Minneapolis, MN: Burgess Publishing Co., 1974.

12.3 Foreman, D. I., and Mitchell, R. *Scoring High in Language (Teacher's Edition).* New York: Random House, Inc., 1980. Also adapted from Random House School Division, *Sampler: Scoring High in Reading.* New York: Random House, Inc.

13.1 Kunder, L. H., and Porwell, P. J. *Reporting Pupil Progress: Policies, Procedures and Systems.* Arlington, VA: Educational Research Service, © 1977. Reprinted with permission.

13.2 Leon County Public Schools, *Growth Report: Kindergarten.* Tallahassee, FL. Reprinted courtesy of Leon County Public Schools.

13.3 Kansas City Public Schools, "Progress Report, Grades 4, 5, 6." Kansas City, Kansas. Reprinted courtesy of Kansas City, Kansas Public Schools.

14.1 Lyman, H. B., *Test scores and What They Mean,* 3rd ed. Englewood Cliffs, N.J.: Prentice-Hall, Inc., 1978. Adapted by permission of Prentice-Hall, Inc.

14.2, 14.3 Lindvall, C. M., and Nitko, A. J. *Measuring Pupil Achievement and Aptitude,* 2nd Ed. New York: Harcourt Brace Jovanovich, © 1975. All rights reserved.

14.3 Based on data from Lohnes and Cooley, *Introduction to Statistical Procedures with Computer Exercises.* New York: John Wiley and Sons, Inc., 1968.

14.4 Prescott, Balow, Hogan, and Farr. *Metropolitan Achievement Tests: Teacher's Manual for Administering and Interpreting.* New York: The Psychological Corporation, © 1978 by Harcourt Brace Jovanovich, Inc. Reproduced by permission. All rights reserved.

14.5 Karlsen, B., Madden, R., and Gardner, E. F. *Stanford Diagnostic Reading Test, Manual for Administering and Interpreting.* New York: Harcourt Brace Jovanovich, Inc. (The Psychological Corporation), © 1976. All rights reserved.

14.8 *Stanford Achievement Test: Individual Record.* New York: Harcourt Brace Jovanovich, Inc. © 1973. All Rights reserved.

15.1 Stanley, J. C., and Hopkins, K. D. *Educational and Psychological Measurement and Evaluation,* 6th ed. Englewood Cliffs, N.J.: Prentice-Hall, Inc., 1981. Reprinted by permission of Prentice-Hall, Inc.

16.2 Freeman, D. J., Kuhs, T. M., Knappen, L. B., and Porter, A. C. "A Closer Look at Standardized Tests," *Arithmetic Teacher,* Vol. 29, Issue 7, 1982, p. 52.

16.3 Blum, M. L., and Naylor, J. C. *Industrial Psychology: Its Theoretical and Social Foundations.* New York: Harper and Row, 1968. By permission of Harper and Row, Publishers, Inc.

17.1 Thorndike, E. L. "Handwriting." *Teachers College Record, Vol. II,* 1910, pp. 1-93.

17.2 Beck, I. L. *Comprehension During the Acquisition of Decoding Skills.* Pittsburgh, PA: Learning Research and Development Center, University of Pittsburgh, 1977. Also adapted from Beck, I. L., and Mitroff, D. D. *The Rationale and Design of a Primary Grades Reading System for an Individualized Classroom.* Pittsburgh, PA: Learning Research and Development Center, University of Pittsburgh, 1972.

19.1 Ayrer, J. E., and Young, P. B. "The users: Who, What, Where, When, and Why? Benefits of an Urban City-Wide Standardized Testing Program." *National Council on Measurement in Education,* 1979, p. 7. Reprinted by permission of the Office of Research and Evaluation, Philadelphia Public Schools.

19.2, 19.3 *Metropolitan Achievement Tests.* New York: Harcourt Brace Jovanovich, © 1978, 1980, 1982. Reproduced by permission. All rights reserved.

19.4 University of Iowa, *Profile Narrative Report.* Iowa City: Riverside Publishing Company, 1979.

19.5, 19.6 *California Achievement Tests, Class Management Guide.* Del Monte Research Park, Monterey, CA: CTB/McGraw-Hill, © 1978. Reproduced by permission of the publisher.

19.7 Dunn, L. M., and Markwardt, F. *Peabody Individual Achievement Test: Manual.* Circle Pines, MN: American Guidance Service, 1970. Reprinted with permission.

19.8 Hogan, Farr, Prescott, and Balow. *Metropolitan Mathematics Instructional Tests.* New York: Harcourt Brace Jovanovich, Inc., © 1978, 1979. Reproduced by permission. All rights reserved.

21.1 Otis, A. S., and Lennon, R. T. *Otis-Lennon School Ability Test.* New York: Harcourt Brace Jovanovich, Inc. © 1979, 1982. Reproduced with permission.

21.2 Thorndike, R. L., and Hagen, E. P. *The Cognitive Abilities Test (Form 3): Multilevel Booklet for Grades 3-12.* Boston: Houghton-Mifflin, 1978. All rights reserved.

21.3 Bennett, G. K., Seashore, H. G., and Wesman, A. G. *Differential Aptitude Test* (Form V). New York: The Psychological Corporation, © 1982, 1972. Reprinted with permission. All rights reserved.

21.4 The Psychological Corporation, sample of a *Career Planning Report for the Differential Aptitude Tests.* New York: Harcourt Brace Jovanovich, Inc. © 1982, 1972. Reprinted with permission. All rights reserved.

21.5 Cattell, R. B., and Cattell, M. D. *Culture Fair Intelli-*

gence Test, Scale 2, Form A. Champaign, IL: Institute for Personality and Ability Testing, © 1949, 1960. Reprinted by permission.

21.6 Bayley, N. "Development of Mental Abilities." In P. Mussen (ed.), *Carmichael's Manual of Child Psychology.* New York: John Wiley & Sons, 1970.

22.1 Crites, J. O. *Career Maturity Inventory: Theory and Research Handbook.* Del Monte Research Park, Monterey, CA:' CTB/McGraw-Hill, Inc., 1978. Reproduced by permission of the publisher.

22.2 Campbell, D. P., and Hansen, J. C. *Manual for the Strong-Campbell Interest Inventory,* Form T325 of the Strong Vocational Interest Blank, 3rd ed. Stanford, CA: Stanford University Press, 1981.

22.3 Hogan, T. P., *Survey of School Attitudes.* New York: Harcourt Brace Jovanovich, Inc. © 1973, 1975. Reproduced with permission. All rights reserved.

Examples

Ex. 3 Klaus et al. *Composing Childhood Experience: An Approach to Writing and Learning in the Elementary Grades, Experimental Version,* © 1979 by Cemrel, Inc. Reprinted by permission.

Ex.4 From *Handbook on Formative and Summative Evaluation of Student Learning,* Bloom et al. (eds.) Copyright © 1971 by McGraw-Hill. Used by permission of McGraw-Hill.

Exs. 70-71 Adapted from *The Construction and Use of Achievement Examinations,* (Hawkes, Lindquist, and Mann (eds.), pp. 145-146. Copyright © 1936 by American Council on Education. Used by permission of Houghton Mifflin Company.

Exs. 100-101 Hively et al. *Domain-Referenced Curriculum: A Technical Handbook and a Case Study from the Minnemast Project,* Center for the Study of Evaluation, University of California, Los Angeles, 1973.

Exs. 111-112 From *Principles of Instructional Design,* 2nd ed., by Robert Gagné and Leslie J. Briggs. Copyright © 1974, 1979 by Holt, Rinehart and Winston. Reprinted by permission of Holt, Rinehart and Winston, CBS College Publishing.

Exs. 113-116 Jenkins, J. R. and Deno, S. J. "Assessing Knowledge of Concepts and Principles." *Journal of Educational Measurement,* Vol. 8, 1971, pp. 95-101. Copyright 1971, National Council on Measurement in Education, Washington, D.C.

Exs. 120-121, 126-129 Hieronymus, A. N. and Lindquist, E. F. *Iowa Tests of Basic Skills,* Levels Edition, Form 6. Copyright © 1971 by the University of Iowa. Reprinted by permission of Riverside Publishing Company.

Exs. 122-123, 136-140 From *Comprehensive Tests of Basic Skills, Forms S and T.* Reproduced by permission of the publisher, CTB/McGraw-Hill, Del Monte Research Park, Monterey, CA 93940. Copyright © 1973, 1975 by McGraw-Hill, Inc. All rights reserved.

Exs. 124-125, 134-135 Prescott et al. *Metropolitan Achievement Tests,* © 1978 by Harcourt Brace Jovanovich, Inc. Reproduced by permission. All rights reserved.

Exs. 130-131 Stodola. Q. "Making the Classroom Test: A Guide for Teachers." Copyright © 1959 by Educational Testing Service, Princeton, NJ. Reprinted by permission. All rights reserved.

Ex. 133 Madden et al. *Stanford Achievement Test: Intermediate Level II Complete Battery Test Booklet, Form A.* Copyright © 1972 by Harcourt Brace Jovanovich, Inc. All rights reserved.

NAME INDEX

Aaronson, M., 484
Adams, J. A., 23
Adrian, R., 77n
Ahmann, J. S., 348, 559
Aiken, L. R., 566
Airasian, P. W., 495, 497, 498
Ajzen, J., 566
Alderson, J. G., 163
Aleamoni, L. R., 428, 430n
Alexander, S., 318
Aleyideino, S. C., 211
Algina, J., 422n, 458
Allen, G. J., 318, 319
Alpert, R., 318
Altman, F., 317, 318
Altman, H., 318
Anastasi, A., 26, 427n, 554, 554n, 555
Anderson, J. E., 554
Anderson, J. F., 580
Anderson, R. C., 222, 226, 226n, 227n, 229, 472
Anderson, T. W., 68
Andrew, B. J., 462
Angoff, W. H., 363, 371, 377, 461n, 550
Appelbaum, M. I., 555
Aron, M. S., 247, 276
Asmus, E. P., 323
Ayrer, J. E., 495
Ayres, L. P., 448, 496, 496n
Azuma, H., 396

Backer, T. E., 484
Baglin, R. F., 358, 473
Bajtelsmit, J. W., 314, 316
Baker, G. T., 555
Baker, R. L., 314
Balma, M. J., 423
Ballou, F. W., 448
Balow, I. H., 232, 369n, 380, 509, 510n, 512
Baltes, P. B., 557n
Barrett, T. C., 102
Barzun, J., 194
Bass, A. R., 46
Bausell, R. B., 83
Bayley, N., 556n
Beck, I. B., 83, 211, 455n
Beck, M. D., 624
Beckett, G. W., 323
Beckham, A. S., 523
Beere, C. A., 484
Beggs, D. L., 319, 375
Bella, D. A., 533
Bellak, L., 581
Bellanca, J. A., 344
Bellis, D., 361
Bennett, G. K., 428n, 545, 546n
Berdie, D. R., 580

Berg, I. A., 313
Bergan, J. R., 318
Berk, R. A., 300, 458
Berliner, D. C., 417
Berlyne, D. E., 567
Berry, M. F., 258n
Bianchini, J. C., 377
Binet, A., 372n, 520, 521, 534
Binstock, L., 452
Birch, H. G., 567
Birnbaum, A., 448
Bishop, C. H., 312, 313
Bixler, H. H., 372n
Bjerstidy, A., 270
Blalock, H. M., 422n
Blanton, B. E., 420, 421n
Bliss, L. B., 323
Blommers, P. J., 55n, 56, 58, 61, 62, 83, 345
Bloom, B. S., 99, 100, 102, 114, 129, 130n, 131, 142n, 143n, 144n, 148, 149n, 454, 606
Blum, M. L., 426n
Bobertag, O., 521
Boersman, F. J., 314
Bond, G. L., 83
Bond, H. M., 523
Bonmarito, J. W., 484
Boomer, D. S., 323
Borich, G. D., 260, 263n
Boring, E. G., 520
Bormuth, J. R., 163, 452, 453
Boruch, R. F., 36, 422, 422n
Boston, M. E., 452
Boucher, J. L., 23
Boyer, E. G., 261
Boykin, A., 349n
Bowles, S., 40
Bracht, G. H., 404
Bravais, A., 77n
Brenner, M. W., 521
Bridges, J. W., 521
Briggs, L. J., 96, 100, 101n, 216, 219, 221, 223
Brigham, C., 550
Brown, F. G., 38, 485
Brown, J. S., 512
Brown, N. J., 164n
Brown, R., 143, 156
Brown, W., 394, 601
Brozovich, W. R., 87
Bruininks, R. H., 23
Bryan, M. M., 557
Buckingham, B. R., 372n
Budoff, M., 553
Buech, B. U., 557
Bunda, M. A., 460
Buros, O. K., 163, 164, 416, 472, 482, 483, 484, 522

Burrill, L. E., 469, 473
Burton, R. R., 512

Cahen, L., 417
Calhoun, D., 521
Calhoun, E., 211
Callahan, R. E., 521
Callenbach, C., 314
Campbell, D. P., 573, 575n
Campbell, D. T., 246, 247, 422n
Campbell, R. N., 6
Canady, H. G., 523
Candor, C. A., 323
Carrier, N. A., 318
Carroll, J. B., 81, 84, 84n, 428n, 519, 551
Carlson, M., 452
Carter, R. E., 148
Cartwright, C. A., 244n, 251n, 252n, 253n, 255n, 257, 265n, 267n, 268n, 269n
Cartwright, G. P., 244n, 251n, 252n, 253n, 255n, 257, 265n, 267n, 268n, 269n
Carver, R. P., 300
Cashen, V. M., 211
Cattell, A. K. S., 552
Cattell, J. Mc., 74, 520, 534
Cattell, R. B., 552
Chadwick, E., 449
Chambers, A. C., 319
Chalmers, T. M., 310
Champagne, A. B., 123
Chane, E. J., 577
Chapman, J. C., 448
Chess, S., 567
Chi, M., 449
Childs, H. G., 521
Cicchetti, D. V., 533
Clark, W. W., 424
Cleary, T. A., 46
Clymer, T., 102
Coffman, W. E., 147, 148n, 151, 153n, 156
Cohen, D. K., 40
Cohen, J., 406, 407
Cohen, L. S., 417
Cohen, P. A., 87
Cohen, S. A., 316
Cole, N. S., 12, 37, 38, 44, 46, 86, 211, 325n, 551, 569, 570, 575, 576
Connolly, A. J., 448, 451, 512
Cook, W. W., 19
Cooley, W. W., 17, 18, 366n, 417
Cooper, C. R., 156
Coulson, D. B., 458
Cowan, J., 151
Cowdery, K. M., 573
Cowen, J. E., 318

SUBJECT INDEX

---

using with skewed distributions, 369–370
Starch English Vocabulary Test, 452
Stars in sociograms, 270
State Student Assessment Test, 42
Statistics, 50–89
Stem, 190
   see also Multiple-choice test items
Stereotypes of students, 277–278
Stress produced by tests, 47, 317–320
Strong-Campbell Interest Inventory, 567, 568, 569, 573–575, 584, 615
Structural pluralism model, 530
Structured personality measurement techniques, 581–582, 584
Students' rights, *see* Pupils' rights
Study questions for test preparation, 310
Study skills as a treatment for test-anxiety, 320
Subject Standardized Tests, 514
Subjectivity, 21, 28, 166
Subtest, 491
Success stereotype, 277
Suin Test Anxiety Behavior Scale, 319
Summated ratings, methods, 577
Summative evaluation, *see* Evaluation
"Sunshine" laws, 33
Supply items, 28
   see also Completion test items; Essay test items
Surprise-quiz, *see* Quiz
Survey battery, *see* Standardized achievement tests; Survey tests, multilevel
Survey of Problematic Situations, 27
Survey of School Attitudes, 578, 579
Survey tests, multilevel, 490, 491, 494, 499–507
   see also Standardized achievement tests
Symmetrical distributions, 55, 365
Synthesis as a *Taxonomy* level, 100, 606
System of Multicultural Pluralistic Assessment (SOMPA), 518, 529–533, 535, 614

Table of specifications, *see* Test plan
Task analysis, 425
Task-referenced grades, 314, 341*n*, 343, 348–350, 351
Taxonomy of Educational Objectives, Handbook I: Cognitive Domain, see Bloom's *Taxonomy*
Taxonomy of Educational Objectives, Handbook II: Affective Domain, see Krathwohl's *Taxonomy*
T-scores, Table BC.1, Figure BC.1
   see also Normalized *T*-scores
Teacher-made tests, 93–327
   compared with published tests, 494
   comprehensiveness needed, 134–135
   planning for, 117–136
   relation to curriculum, 122, 278–279
   Three Fundamental Principles of, 140–141, 165
   see also Administering tests; Completion test items; Essay test items; Matching test items; Multiple-choice test items; Observation methods; Rating scales
Teacher's editions, quality of tests in, 493
Teachers' rights to pupils' records, 34
Teacher's role in test validation, 422

Teacher time, efficient use of, 135, 147
"Teaching to the test," 325–326, 327
Temperaments as noncognitive variables, 567
Test anxiety, 140, 310, 317–320, 420
   and attention focusing, 317, 327
   components of, 317, 327
   measuring, 317–318, 327
   response patterns related to, 317, 327
   treatment of, 318–320
Test Anxiety Inventory, 319
Test Anxiety Questionnaire, 318
Test Anxiety Scale, 318, 319
Test Anxiety Scale for Children, 319
Test bias, in vocational interest measurement, 575–576, 584
   types of, 43–47, 48
   see also Item bias; Sex bias
Test booklet, design of, 306–308, 326
Test development, components of classroom, 119, 120
   curriculum organization and, 122
   importance of teachers' learning, 118–119
   instructional approach and, 121
   relation to teacher's values, 119
   standardized, 468–476, 486
   see also Teacher-made tests
Test items, basic function of, 191
   complexity of, 133
   item analysis for improving, 284–303
   limitations of verbal, 222
   for testing higher level skills, 217, 225–226
   types of, 20–21, 131
   see also Completion test items; Essay test items; Item analysis, Matching test items; Multiple-choice test items
Test manual, development of, 475, 486
   standards for, 37, 42, 47, 475
Test plan, constructing, 123–125, 135–136
   criteria for judging, 133–135, 136
   giving to student, 310
   relation to item analysis, 299
   relation to item selection, 301, 303
   of standardized tests, 469
Test publisher's catalogue, 484, 486
Test purchase, qualifications for, 485, 487
   see also Purchasing a test
Test security, 32, 42, 308
Test selection, *see* Selecting a published test
Test specifications, *see* IOX Test Specification; Test plan
Testing, facilitating learning by, 19
   as feedback to students, 19, 279
   individually versus in groups, 6
   integrating results from, 277–279
   legal aspects of, 11, 41–43
   as observation, 6
   relation to learning environment, 278
   relation to teaching/learning process, 119
   and quantification, 6
   social consequences of, 37
   see also Scholastic aptitude tests; Standardized achievement tests; Standardized tests; Teacher-made tests
Testing program, legal authority of, 43

Testing schedule, coordinating with other teachers, 309*n*
   for handicapped students, 310
Test-retest reliability, *see* Reliability coefficients
Tests, attributes measured by, 24–26, 29
   court challenges to, 42–43, 47
   labeling children with, 13, 14
   lists of published, 613–615
   meaning of, 6, 27
   as student motivators, 19, 28
   terms describing, 20
   types of, 6
   used for granting college credit, 514
   use in assigning grades, 17, 345–347, 350
   use in scientific investigations, 19
   using information from sources other than, 121
   as weapons, 19
   see also Testing
Tests of Achievement and Proficiency, 473, 499, 613
Test-taking skills needed by students, 311, 326, 327
Test-wiseness, 140, 177, 312–317, 325, 326, 327, 420
   individual differences in, 314
   as a learned skill, 314–316, 327
   meaning of, 312, 326
   measuring, 316–317
   relation to response sets and risk taking, 312–314
   taxonomy of principles, 313, 326–327
   teaching skills of, 315–316
Thematic Apperception Test, 581
Thorndike Dimensions of Temperament, 581
Thorndike Handwriting Scale, 266, 448, 449, 450
Three Fundamental Principles of Test Construction, 141,
   165, 186
3R's Test, The, 499, 613
Thurstone absolute scaled scores, 549
Thurstone method of attitude scale construction, 577, 584
Tracking, 557, 561
Transfer of learning, *see* Mastery
Transformed scores, 71, 361–381
True-false test items, advantages and criticisms of,
   170–174, 186
   anatomy of, 170
   constructing, 175–179
   guessing on, 174–175, 186
   propositions used for, 171–172, 173, 186
   recommended difficulty level of, 133, 300
   types of, 171, 186
   validity of, 172, 186
True scores, 389–390, 390–392
True score variance, 389, 390
"Truth-in-testing" legislation, 33, 42
Typical performance tests, 309

Uncertainty interval, 361, 402–403, 547, 548
   see also Standard error of measurement
Underachievers, 558–559, 561
Understanding, measurement of, 111, 115
Uniform distributions, 55, 365
Uniform Guidelines on Employee Selection Procedures, 11, 38,
   43, 48
Unimodal distributions, 55, 58
Unisex norms, 574–575

*University of Pittsburgh Student Assessment of Teaching
   Questionnaire*, 268

Validity, 412–440
   aspects of, 413, 438, 439
   as basis for legal action, 42
   of classroom tests, 113, 133, 413–414
   of criterion-referenced tests, 458–460, 462
   coefficient, 413, 427, 428, 429
   concurrent, 423, 438
   construct, 413, 417–422, 436–439, 440, 459
   content, 44, 95, 134, 146, 413–417, 437, 438, 439, **440**,
     459
   convergent, 413*n*
   criterion-oriented, 413, 422–435, 438, 439, 440, 455,
     459–460
   criterion-oriented versus criterion-referencing,
     454–455
   face, 413*n*
   factorial, 413*n*
   interrelationships among aspects of, 435–437, 439, **440**
   job-analytic, 413*n*
   meaning of, 412
   for placement decisions, 434–455, 438, 440, 460
   practical usefulness, 37
   predictive, 423, 438, 552
   procedures for judging standardized test, 481
   rational, 413*n*
   relation to base rate and selection ratio, 430–434
   relation to reliability, 413
   relation to test bias, 44, 46
   for selection decisions, 425, 434, 438, 440
   standard error of estimate: 427*n*
   steps for validating selection tests, 425–427, 438
   sufficient condition for content, 415
   summary of types of, 438, 440
   synthetic, 413*n*
   teachers' responsibility for, 36–37, 416, 422
   of true-false test items, 172
Valid negative and valid positive, 432, 433, 434
Values, influencing content of teacher-made tests, 119
   influencing teachers' grading, 343, 344, 350
   influencing test interpretation, 36, 278–279
   meaning of, 26, 567
Variability of scores, *see* Mean deviation; Range;
   Standard deviation; Variance
Variance, 67
Verbal mediation, in performance tests, 22
Verbal-performance discrepancy, 527, 529
Verbal tests, 22, 28
   see also Nonverbal tests
Verbs, action, *see* Instructional objectives
Vineland Adaptive Behavior Scales, 533–534, 614
Vineland Social Maturity Scale, 533
Vocational interest, definition of, 566
Vocational, Interest, Experience, and Skills Assessment, 258,
   615
Vocational interest measurement, methods of, 567–569,
   583
   purposes for using, 569–570, 584
   rationales for types of, 569

1901
College Entrance Examination Board
First CEEB entrance exam.

1905
Alfred Binet & Theophile Simon
First individually administered intelligence test.

1905
Manchu Dynasty
Ancient exam system abandoned.

1908
C. W. Stone
First professionally developed standardized achievement test.

1910
Edward L. Thorndike
Handwriting scale.

1911
P. H. Hanus
School survey movement begins and spurs standardized achievement tests.

1912
D. Starch & E. C. Elliot
Show that teachers' grades are unreliable.

1914
F. J. Kelly
Shows reliability of free response tests improved by using scoring key.

1914
World Book Company
First commercially available standardized achievement test: *Courtis Standardized Research Test in Arithmetic.*

1916
Lewis M. Terman
Houghton Mifflin Co. publishes his *Stanford Revision of the Binet-Simon Scale of Intelligence.*

1917
Committee on Psychological Examination of Recruits
Development of Army *Group Examinations Alpha* and *Beta.*

1917
Arthur Sinton Otis
First commercially available group intelligence test.

1920-1930
Certain American educationists and psychologists
Use intelligence test data to argue inferiority of certain ethnic and racial groups.

1920-1930
Certain black scholars from South
Research and critique genetic and social Darwinistic interpretation of intelligence tests.

1921
J. M. Cattell, E. L. Thorndike, R. S. Woodworth
The Psychological Corporation founded.

1923
T. L. Kelley, G. M. Ruch, L. M. Terman
Stanford Achievement Test developed.

1926
Ethel M. Clark
Founds California Test Bureau.

1927
E. K. Strong
Develops *Strong Vocational Interest Blank* at Stanford University.

1929
L. L. Thurstone
Develops attitude scales.

1929
E. F. Lindquist
Iowa Every Pupil Examination developed.

1935
Reynold B. Johnson
First test scoring machine.

1938
Oscar Krisen Buros
First *Mental Measurements Yearbook* published.

1931-1942
Ralph W. Tyler
Urges educators to test for developed educational abilities rather than facts and associations.

1938
Lyle Spencer
Founds Science Research Associates.

1940
Ben D. Wood
National Teachers Examination developed.

1943
E. F. Lindquist
Iowa Tests of Educational Development developed.

1945
E. F. Lindquist
Tests of General Educational Development (GED) and USAFI examinations developed.

1955
E. F. Lindquist
Design for high-speed, high-volume digital test scoring machine.

1956
Benjamin S. Bloom
Taxonomy of Educational Objectives.

1963
Robert Glaser
Calls for criterion-referenced testing instead of norm-referenced testing.

1968
E. F. Lindquist
Procedure for machine scoring test booklets directly.

1968-1976
Quantitative psychologists
Statistical procedures for detecting test bias.

1969
Arthur R. Jensen
Controversial articles on heritability of intelligence.

1970-1975
Educationists, psychologists, and lay public
Nationwide controversy on genetic interpretation of intelligence testing.

1974
U. S. Congress
P.L. 93-380 passes.

1975
U. S. Congress
P.L. 94-142 passes.

1979
N. Y. State Legislature
Passes truth-in-testing legislation.